SEAN O'CASEY

AUTOBIOGRAPHIES

VOLUME ONE

SEAN O'CASEY

AUTOBIOGRAPHIES

I

I Knock at the Door
Pictures in the Hallway
Drums under the Windows

CARROLL & GRAF PUBLISHERS, INC.
New York

CONTENTS

I KNOCK AT THE DOOR

PICTURES IN THE HALLWAY

v

I KNOCK AT THE DOOR

Knock, and it shall be opened unto you

To Breon and Niall

A CHILD IS BORN

In Dublin, sometime in the early 'eighties, on the last day of the month of March, a mother in child-pain clenched her teeth, dug her knees home into the bed, sweated and panted and grunted, became a tense living mass of agony and effort, groaned and pressed and groaned and pressed, and pressed a little boy out of her womb into a world where white horses and black horses and brown horses and white-and-black horses and brown-and-white horses trotted tap-tap-tap tap-tap-tappety-tap over cobble stones, conceitedly, in front of landau, brougham, or vis-à-vis; lumberingly in front of tramcar; pantingly and patiently in front of laden lorry, dray, or float; and gaily in front of the merry and irresponsible jaunting-car:

Where soldiers paraded, like figures taken out of a toy-box, wearing their red coats with yellow breastpieces; blue jackets with white breastpieces; and tight trousers with red stripes or white stripes or yellow stripes down the whole length of each leg; marching out on each royal birthday of the Queen to the Phoenix Park for a Review and Sham Battle, with guns and lances and swords and cannons; going by the Saluting Point at a quick march, or at a trot, and lastly, at a gallop, with a thunder of hoofs and a rattle of shaking cannon, that made all hearts quiver with hope for a new war; while the soldiers having got back to barracks when the fun was all over, rubbed down their sweating horses or cleaned their rifles, murmuring all the time against the birthdays of queens that gave them all so much mucking about for nothing:

Where a great poet named Tennyson, anticipating Hollywood, had built up in the Studio of his mind, his Come into the garden, Maud, the black bat night has flown; and had sent his cardboard kings and warriors and uncompromising virgins out into the highways and byways that sprinkled the lawns of the welltodo, men bowing low to the knights as they went galloping by like the wind in a hurry; and the maidens smiled and beckoned and sighed as the knights careered about among the roses and the hollyhocks, gathering on the points of their lances lovely little bunches of rosemary and rue:

Where energy was poured out in Bibles and tracts and hymns; and sweet little stories, swinging little boys and girls up to heaven or

3

down to hell; where the hosts of heaven, embattled, assembled for the fray on a croquet lawn; and all the passion, frightfulness, laughter, strife, tears, peace, defeat, victory, agony, and bloody sweat of heaven's war with hell sank into a delicately scented, gently moving, sweet conversing, pink and mauve and cream-coloured garden party:

Where it was believed that when children died of croup or consumption or fever, they were simply not, for God took them:

Where Ruskin, with his delicate mind and Christianly crafted hands, modelled his figures of speech with mud and tinsel; and Mr. Poynter, president of the Royal Academy, summoning up all his powers of imagination, and summing all that ever had been or would be in art, painted the *tour de force* and cul-de-sac of a visit to Æsculapius:

Where almost all found all in all in God on Sundays; and the rest of the week found all in all in bustles, Bibles, and bassinets; preaching, prisons, and puseyism; valentines, victoria crosses, and vaccination; tea fights, tennis, and transubstantiation; magic lanterns, minstrel shows, and mioramas; music-halls, melodramas, and melodeons; antimacassars, moonlighting, and midwives; fashions, fenians, and fancy-fairs; musk, money, and monarchy:

Where every shrubbery in every pet-of-heaven house held a monkey, stuck there by Darwin, a monkey that stretched out a sudden paw to rip a bit of fragrant lace from the petticoat of any lady stooping down to pull a sprig of lavender, sending the ladies flying with fear into the churches to pull and pull the bells, making all the clergy run like hell into the pulpits to yell Peace, be still, for there is nothing revealed that cannot be hidden away; and so queen and consort, peers, clergy, commons, and people buried deep this monkey bone of our bone and flesh of our flesh, thick edge of the wedge, whereby millions of years were thrust between themselves and other people and God, jerking away a sense of nearness so obliging that it put a latch-key into the pocket of every catholic and protestant for a private gateway into the kingdom of heaven.

And the woman in child-pain clenched her teeth, dug her knees home into the bed, became a tense living mass of agony and effort, sweated and panted, pressed and groaned, and pressed and pressed till a man-child dropped from her womb down into the world; down into a world that was filled up with the needs, ambitions, desires, and ignorances of others, to be shoved aside, pressed back, beaten down by privileges carrying godwarrants of superiority because they had dropped down into the world a couple of hours earlier. The privileges were angry and irritable; but the round-bellied, waggle-headed, lanky-legged newborn latecomer kicked against the ambitions, needs, and desires of the others, cleared a patch of room for itself from the trampling feet and snapping hands around it; was washed, napkined, and fed; added on three, four, or five ounces of weight every week, taking most of it from its mother and a little from the life around it; and so grew gradually, and gathered to itself the power, the ignorance, the desire, and the ambition of man.

Forty years of age the woman was when the boy was three, with hair still raven black, parted particularly down the middle of the head, gathered behind in a simple coil, and kept together by a couple of hairpins; a small nose spreading a little at the bottom; deeply set, softly gleaming brown eyes that sparkled when she laughed and hardened to a steady glow through any sorrow, deep and irremediable; eyes that, when steadily watched, seemed to hide in their deeps an intense glow of many dreams, veiled by the nearer vision of things that were husband and children and home. But it was the mouth that arrested attention most, for here was shown the chief characteristic of the woman: it quivered with fighting perseverance, firmness, human humour, and the gentle, lovable fullness of her nature. Small strong hands, hands that could slyly bathe a festered wound or scour a floor — wet cloth first, then the brush soap-foamed, tearing the dirt out, then wet cloth again and, finally, the dry cloth finishing the patch in back and forward strokes and twisting circles of rhythmic motions. A sturdy figure carried gracefully and with resolution; flexible, at peace in its simple gown of black serge, with its tiny white frill round the neck that was fair and unwrinkled still. A laugh that began in a ripple of humour, and ended in a musical torrent of full-toned mirth which shook those who listened into an irresistible companionship.

And all this was seen, not then, but after many years when the dancing charm and pulsing vigour of youthful life had passed her by, and left her moving a little stiffly, but still with charm and still with vigour, among those whose view of the light of life had dimmed and was mingling more and more with a spreading darkness; and vividly again, and with an agonised power, when she was calmly listening to the last few age-worn beats of her own dying heart.

This had been the shake of the bag, and she knew that she would never have another child. She had had seven before — three boys and one girl living, and one girl and two boys dead. Each of the two dead boys had been called John, and her husband said that this last boy's name was to be John, too. She thought for a long time. It seemed to be a challenge to God to do that, to give the name of John to this new child. He was undoubtedly her last child, and she wanted him to live. The two born before that had been called John, had died, died of the same thing, died of croup.

She remembered how the first had died, died before she knew he was dying, died of croup. Then after another two years, another boy had come, and they had called him John. Her husband had said we must have a boy called John. Her husband with doggedness and she with misgiving had called him John. He had been vigorous enough, and had sprawled and kicked a twelve-month way into the world, when suddenly he seemed to get a feverish cold, a little cough, and a watering from the eyes. Then one evening on her way to his bedside she stopped, frightened by the sound of a hard choking cough. Prompted, at first, by fear to go away and refuse to hear, she went slowly through the room to the bed, and found him struggling from under the clothes, his arms moving wildly, his eyes staring, his face bluish, and his breath coming in short and cluttering gulps. She remembered that, in a panic, she had slapped a bonnet on her head and a shawl round her shoulders, had gathered the little body into a blanket, rushed out of the house, down the street, climbed into a passing cab, calling on the driver for God's sake to drive fast, fast, fast to the Abercorn Hospital.

—He can do it, if He wants to, she murmured in the cab all the way to the hospital, He can save the child; the other died, but this won't, this won't, won't, won't die. With a thought, God can take this choking lump from the little child's throat, and give him back his healthy happy breathing.

And the child got it harder and harder to get its breath, and the choking effort of the child to breathe whistled agony into her brain. She tore up the steps of the hospital, rang and rang and rang the bell, pushed past into the hall when the door was opened.

—Get the doctor, she said, pantingly, to the porter, get the doctor, get him quick to look at this child of mine quick, to treat this little child of mine, quick please, for he's dying, but can easily be saved if the doctor comes quick, bring me quick to the doctor or let him come quick to me here, there's no time to be lost, for it's the croup he has, and he's dying fast and will be dead if the doctor doesn't come quick, go and get him, go and get him, go, go and get him quick.

And she had walked up and down, down and up the hall, waiting, waiting for the porter to bring the doctor, afraid to look at the convulsed little face hidden under the shawl, and trying to hear less clearly the choking cadences of the shivering cough shaking the little figure sheltering in her arms.

The porter came back and told her that the doctor was attending a patient, and would be with her in a brace of shakes.

—This child can't wait, she answered threateningly; and he must be treated at once, the other patient must wait, but this child is choking and may die any moment, man; where's the doctor, and I'll bring the child to him myself?

She ran over to a passing nurse, held the child firmly to her bosom with one hand, and caught the nurse's arm tightly with the other.

—A doctor for this child, nurse, before it's too late, she pleaded, for this child that's dying with the croup. See, his face is getting black with the choking; nurse, quick, please, for he's getting less and less able to breathe, and I'll hold the hospital responsible for anything that happens to him; for I've been left here waiting too long, too long, and the child choking, without any attention; for it's the croup he has, and I'm afraid he's dying.

The nurse led her gently over to a side of the hall, and pressed her gently down on a seat.

—Sit down, on the bench there, sit down, she said softly, and I'll get the doctor to see the child. She had shouted after the departing nurse, This'll be my second Johnny that'll have died of the croup, if you don't hurry.

And again she had asked God to help and hurry the doctor so that her child wouldn't die in her arms.

Suddenly she held her breath as she heard a curious rasping sigh, and her bosom shuddered as she felt the little body in her arms give a mighty straining stretch; then she knew that what she wanted to keep away had come to her; and she pressed to her breast a dear possession that had emptied itself of life. She had sat, stricken dumb, motionless for some moments, then she had laid the little form down on the bench, and looked at the rigid little face tinged with purple; she had closed the shades of the staring eyes, placed two pennies on the lids, and bound them there with her handkerchief.

Some time after, the doctor, followed by the nurse, came up the corridor, and she had called out to them, You came too slow, for God came quicker and took the child away. The doctor had come over to her, put his hand over the child's little heart, murmuring, Yes, he's gone; but no skill of ours could have saved him. And she had answered bitterly, None of you broke your heart trying.

She had taken up the dead form in her arms, and said to the nurse and to the doctor, Open the door, now, that I may pass out, and leave you all in peace.

The doctor had laid his hand on her arm to say, You can't carry the dead child home with you like that; better leave him in the deadhouse for the present.

She had answered hotly, I will bring him home, and lay him out at home, and bury him from the home where he lived and played out his little life, and let whosoever will try to stop me.

They had opened the door, and as she passed out the nurse whispered, Have you got your cab fare? but she passed out without giving the thanks of an answer.

She nodded to a cab on the rank opposite; when it came over, she got in carefully, hugged the body to her breast for a few moments, then laid it down on the seat opposite, stretched the little legs straight, placed the arms tightly down the body, instead of folding them over the breast in the form of a cross as the Roman Catholics were in the habit of doing. She kept her hand with a loving pressure on the breast of the child, for the jolting of the cab over the stones of the street made the body lie uneasy on the seat. She hadn't cried, but she pressed her lips tightly together, and with the fingers of one hand dressed the fair hair neatly back from the dead-cold forehead. This would be another painful halting-place in her own and her husband's life. All usual things would stand still till this was over. Had she come in a victoria, a brougham, or a landau, all the bells in the hospital would have been ringing attendance on her. Even the food eaten by her and her husband would taste of sorrow till his body had been buried, and they felt that their little boy's soul was getting accustomed to God.

In the agitated state of her mind she tried to think of a portion of the Bible that would soften a little the hardness of her trouble. She could think only of the widow, the widow's little son, and of Elijah. But there was no Elijah now to take this little son out of her arms, and stretch himself upon the boy, call three times upon the name of the Lord, and bring the living soul back again to the dead body — only a doctor who had delayed his coming, and a deadhouse.

Such a bright little youngster as he was too. Everybody admitted that he was far ahead of most children of his age. Peculiar look in his eyes that showed intelligence. Curious quick and alert manner he had. Not much movement in him now. In her heart she was glad that he had been baptised, though the Roman Catholic idea of original sin was ridiculous and laughable. Imagine that little child stretched there consigned to hell, or limbo, or whatever they called it, because he hadn't had a drop of water sprinkled over him. Terrible religion to believe in a thing like that.

She heard, subconsciously, the playing of a band and the sound of many voices, and the steady regular sound of many marching feet. Then the cab stood still. The sound of the band got louder, and the sound of the voices and the marching feet came close. The driver got down from his seat, and stood beside the window of the cab.

—We'll have to go a roundabout way, he said, or wait here till God knows when, for a fly couldn't get through a crowd like this, much less an animal like a horse. They're bringing Charlie Stewart Parnell to the Rotunda with bands and banners, where he's to speak on the furtherance of Home Rule for Ireland. That band knows how to rattle out The Green Above the Red, I'm telling you. They've the best belly-drummer in the whole bloody counthry. My God Almighty, looka the way that fella's twirlin' the sticks! He's nothin' short of a genius at it.

Then she heard a rolling roar of cheers breaking out that held on for many minutes, the cab-driver waving his hat, and yelling out a fierce and excited approbation.

—That's Parnell himself that's passed, he said, when the cheering had subsided, Ireland's greatest son. I'd sell me hat, I'd sell me horse an' cab, I'd sell meself for him, be Jasus, I'd nearly sell me soul, if he beckoned me to do it. He's the boyo'll make her ladyship, Victoria, sit up on her bloody throne, an' look round a little, an' wondher what's happenin'.

She shrank back into the shadow of the cab, and looked at her dead child lying stiff on the seat-cushions, stained with spots of tobacco and smeared with spilled beer. She waited dumbly for the crowds to pass, longing to get home so that she might bring her husband within the compass of her sorrow.

—The soldiers are all confined to barracks, went on the cab-driver; an' it's just as well, for we're in no humour to be lookin' calmly on at the red coats on their backs and the crowns an' roses in their caps, noddin' misrule and persecution to the whole of us. Parnell has taken from England's strength so that his name stands big in Ireland, an' that God'll keep him sthrong's a prayer that keeps on in an echo dying away to begin in a powerful prayer again.

—I happen to be a loyal woman, she had said, with all my hopes gathered round the person and the throne, though, she thought, it hasn't rendered me much, it hasn't rendered me much. God Almighty, heavenly Father, you might have spared this little son of mine.

She had been a good woman; she had done her daily round and common task, tainted with only a little grumbling; she had worshipped Him in spirit and in truth; she had held fast to the faith once delivered to the saints; her husband knew his Bible well, most of it in the letter and all of it in the spirit; always arguing and proving popery was dangerous and repugnant to the plain word of scripture; that the sinner could always go straight to God without passing round saints or angels, there being only one mediator between man and God, the man, Jesus Christ. After all, He might have let this occasion of the chastening of those whom He loveth slide aside from the smiting of her harmless innocent baby.

Or, even if He had taken the little boy when the boy was at home with his father and mother; or in the hospital with the doctor striving to help him, and the nurse watching the failure of the doctor's skill; it would have been more bearable and better than to have wriggled into death in her arms, and go off, with no-one she knew near enough to give her the pity of relationship or friendly company.

—Now, suddenly said the cab-driver, the procession's endin' an' we can follow on, crawlin' cautiously at the tail-end of it.

He jumped up on his seat again, said yep to the horse, and went on slowly, halting now and halting again whenever anything intervened to interfere with the progress of the crowd who marched with pride and defiance, carrying in their midst the Leader who symbolised the body, spirit, and soul of the marching people. On crept the cab following hundreds of flaming torches reddening the excited faces of the marchers, the glow forming a huge smoky golden halo above the heads of the crowd. On crept the cab after the mighty yellow and green banners that each section of the crowd carried, the bands playing with a reckless crash and blare that, for many, fashioned drab thoughts of risk into a vision of men gathering to the trumpet-call of God.

Slipping, at last, down a side turning, the cab passed through several streets, and then stopped outside her door. Stepping out of the cab, she bent down and in, lifted the little stiff shawled figure in her arms, and asked the driver the fare. One an' a tanner, he said, and added that he hoped there wasn't much wrong with the child, ma'am. Then as he caught sight of the little face as it slid from the fold of the shawl, he ejaculated, Jasus Christ, the kid's dead!

He took the one and sixpence silently, lifted his hat, mounted to his seat, gathered the reins in his hands, and quickly cantered away.

She brought the body in, laid it down on the bed, then went out to her husband. He had looked at her, and murmured, Oh, is he worse, then? They had gone into the room together; she had pulled off the handkerchief tied over the face of the little child, and the two of them had gazed at the rigid little face silently and long.

—He has stretched a lot, she said.

—When did he go? he asked.

—In the hospital, lying in my arms, before one came to look at him, she answered.

She felt his arm round her, pressing tenderly.

—Dear Sue, he said, my poor dear Sue.

She had quivered a little, and murmured brokenly, He is the second Johnny that has been taken from us. Perhaps we didn't do well, when the first died, to call the second one John.

The circling arm tightened round her. She looked up at him, and saw his face form into a fresh and firmer tightness.

—Sue, he answered, we may yet have another child; that other child may be a boy; if we should have another child, and that other child should be a boy, we shall call his name John.

FIRST THE GREEN BLADE

THE third Johnny, passing by the doggedness of his father and the superstitious anxiety of his mother, crawled a little further into life. Delicately and physically undecided, he crept along. He has a stout heart, said his mother, the first five years are the worst, and, if he can get over them, God is good. With ever-verdant care, she watched him. She gave him his full share in the attention she had to pay to others, and the little leisure she snapped now and again from her household work was crowded with thoughts for Johnny's fuller and firmer settlement in the world. She had nursed him viciously through an attack of bronchitis when he had made but a six months' journey into the world; but no cough had lingered, and he ran about and laughed like other children; so where there was life there was hope, and God was good. The others murmured, it's Johnny here and Johnny there; but she reminded them that they were well into the thick of the world, while Johnny had only started. But God had not forgotten, and the trial was sent at last.

When he was five, his mother noticed a look of torment in his eyes. They harboured a hot and torturing pain that made him rub them vigorously, and cry long and wonderingly in the sunny hours of the day and through the long dark hours of the night. Small, hardy, shiny, pearly specks appeared on the balls of his eyes. He began to dread the light; to keep his eyes closed; to sit and moan restlessly in the darkest places he could find. For many weeks life became a place of gloom, streaked with constant flashes of pain. They folded a big white heavy handkerchief into a bandage, and wound it round his head, like a turban, to guard his eyes from the touch of whatever sunlight tottered in through the little windows of the little house.

Johnny had no sense of danger, no fear of any possible loss, no idea that something was happening which would mean agony for many years, and be a persistent and inscrutable handicap to him throughout the rest of his life. He felt only a curious resentment that he wasn't as others of his age were, and as he himself had been, able to run, to shout, to rejoice when the sun shone; to go to bed tired and full of sleep when the sun went down, getting strength for another and another chance to run, to laugh, and to rejoice in the middle of the sun's encouragement towards merriment and play. It was a time when eye troubles were thought little about, nor any weakness of the body when the weakness didn't pin the body to the bed. Pennyworths of golden ointment, zinc ointment, zinc and rosewater were the eye remedies of the people, except when an eye was cut asunder by an accident.

Such things as smallpox, typhoid fever, diphtheria, and scarlet fever were the only blights that stimulated the doctors to rush about, hair-tossed and coatless, to blow, blow on the bugles of alarm, forcing the people to close up their houses, seal themselves away from the fresh air, and burn sulphur in their rooms, filling the place with fumes, like incense rising from an altar in hell.

It was a time when every infant on some day in each passing week had to be filled with castor-oil, and dosed with syrup of squills, first having their chafed buttocks rubbed with stuff that had the grittiness of powdered steel. A time when only a few brave men separated themselves from this dung-like heap of ignorance, and, in a few bare corners of the world, sought to learn more about the mysteries of life, disease, and death, rather than seek safety with the crowd that ambled and arsed its way easily and nicely about through the hours of life; life under cocked hats, red gowns, and black gowns, droning out the laws of men; life under snowy surplices droning out the laws of God; and life under silk-scented gowns droning out the laws of love.

So his eyes grew worse and the pain waxed sharper. His mother, from an eggcupful of zinc and rosewater, with a tiny piece of rag, bathed them three times a day, and at night smeared the lids heavily with golden ointment taken from a penny box; but no strength crept into the weakness and no softness into the pain. The others, irritated by his crying, warned his mother that the habit of crying would only make them worse, and told the boy that his eyes were beginning to look like two burnt holes in a blanket. His mother, recommended to it by a neighbour, applied a poultice of sodden tea-leaves, a remedy that had once cured the neighbour's child of a horrid redness of the lids; but no strength crept into the weakness, nor did any softness creep into the pain.

Then a friend of one of his brothers said that if the boy's head was plunged into a bucket of cold water and the eyes held open beneath the water for five minutes or so at a time, several times a day, this would bring hardiness to the most stubborn weakness any eye ever had. Johnny was seized and, screaming protests, his head was pushed down into a bucket of dead cold water till the eyes were underneath; and he was vehemently called upon to open his eyes, open his eyes, damn it, couldn't he open his eyes, and let the water get at them. When he struggled, cold and frightened, they pushed him further down till the water flowing through his nostrils gurgled down his throat, almost choking him, leaving him panting for breath, shivering and wet, in the centre of reproaches and abuse because he had kept his eyes fiercely closed underneath the water. Threats, thumps on the back, failed to make him promise that he would open his eyes under the water; and all round him despaired of the remedy, saying it was waste of time if he wasn't made to open his eyes under the water, not worth a curse so long as he keeps his eyes shut; if he goes blind, it'll be his own fault; while Johnny stood there obstinately, with his head bent down on his breast, shocked and shaken, the water from his saturated hair trickling, by way of his neck, steadily down his back, and by way of his cheeks, dripping down to his belly; crying over and over again, The bandage, the bandage, put the bandage over me eyes again, they're paining me terribly. And so no strength crept into the weakness, neither did softness creep into the pain.

Then they all forsook him, saying, Leave him to the pain, then, since he won't do the one thing that will do him good; he has been pampered too much for anyone to pity him. Only his mother harassed her mind for help; only she, with deep pity and unbreakable patience, stood between him and the chance that his sight might go, leaving him helpless in the hands of man and no nearer to God; only she raised the banner of fear for him in the face of everyone she met, and pried everywhere for assistance to save him from the evil of perpetual darkness.

One day his mother suddenly remembered that she had heard a sister make mention of a kid having sore eyes going to some place or another, getting treatment, and getting well again. So out she set with the bandaged Johnny to see her sister, going a third of the way by tram and the rest by foot, to a low-roofed white-washed cottage stuck in a place by the back o' beyond in the Tenters' Fields, where they used to bleach the linen, over by Dolphin's Barn. There she and Johnny had a nice tea with home-made scones well warmed in the oven, melting in your mouth before you'd time to sink your teeth in them.

—Johnny's a case for a doctor, said the sister. You cart him off to St. Mark's Ophthalmic Hospital for Treatment of Diseases of the Eye and Ear, that's in Lincoln Place, just beside the back enthrance of Trinity College. Everyone who isn't a pauper pays sixpence for a ticket, lasting for a month, with attendances three days in each week. Go on Monday, or Wednesday, or Friday, for on any one of these days you're sure to see Mr. Story, who's the greatest of living men, knowing how, when, and where to fiddle with the eyes. It's safer to go early at nine if you want to get away quick, for it's getting more and more crowded every day, an' everyone has to take his turn; an' sometimes the doctors take a long time over a case, especially if it is an ear; and you can do nothing better than to bring Johnny there to hear what they say and to see what they can do for him.

And Johnny's mother got up, and thanked her sister, and said she'd have to be goin', but she'd bring Johnny to the hospital the first thing on Monday morning. And Johnny's mother's sister kissed him, and put a new penny quietly into his pocket, and said God wouldn't let him lose the sight of his eyes.

Then they departed, and, going through The Liberties, came to where Meath Street meets Thomas Street. There Johnny and his mother took a tram which sailed along merrily as far as the top of Cork Hill, and was there stopped by a crowd.

—It's the Ball, said the conductor, the Vice-Regal Ball with all the gulls o' Dublin gawkin' at the notabenebilities flockin' in to a fine feed an' a gay night in Dublin Castle.

—An' we'll be stuck here for ages, said a woman in the corner.

—We might as well have a decko at the grandeur that's keeping the country going, before Mister Parnell and his poverty-stricken dupes reduce us all again to a state of nature, said a genteel-looking man, with a watery mouth and a drooping moustache, sitting in the centre of the car, as he got up from his seat, and climbed down nicely on to the street.

—The day isn't far distant, said the conductor, when that gent that's just gone out'll doff his hat to another tune, or hang as high as Gilderoy; and leaning against the entrance to the tram, he hummed:

Oh, black's your heart, Clan Oliver, and coulder than the clay!
Oh, high's your head, Clan Sassenach, since Sarsfield's gone away!
It's little love you bear us, for the sake of long ago,
But hould your hand, for Ireland still can strike a deadly blow.

Johnny's mother got up, climbed down, and helped Johnny off the tram.

—Little protestant boys should never listen to Fenian songs, she said to him; whenever you hear one, you must always murmur God Save the Queen to yourself.

Mingling with the crowd, they couldn't get out of it, and were carried along to a spot almost beside the entrance to the Castle where they found Ella and Archie gleefully watching the glory passing in to the fine feed and the gay-grand night of dancing.

—Come here, in front of me, said Ella, pulling Johnny beside her, and stay quiet and stand still and don't stir, till we see all the lovely lords and ladies tripping and trotting into the Castle.

—I'm bringing Johnny to a special hospital for the eyes and ears only, on Monday morning, said Johnny's mother to Archie.

—He ought to be brought somewhere, said Archie, for his crying by day and his crying by night is becoming more than most of us can stick.

—When I was on me way along, said Ella, the carriages stretched from the Castle Yard, down Dame Street, Westmoreland Street, through Sackville Street, and right into Cavendish Row. Oh, look at the oul' fogey in blazing blue, with a pile of gold braid on his chest, and a slip of a girl nearly on his knee, in that brougham just gone by us.

—Stuck fast in the arms of a pleasure he'll never feel, murmured Archie.

—I'll get Johnny up early on Monday, said the mother, and bring him to the hospital, whatever happens.

—Th' oul' fogey, said Ella, had a jewelled star hanging be a blue ribbon in the middle of the pile of gold braid—Order of the Garter, I suppose.

—Not the Garter, said Archie, for only a few, outside of princes of the Royal Blood, get the Garter. Mantles of purple velvet lined with silk the knights wear. Musta been the Order of St. Patrick you seen, for it has a blue ribbon an' the motto, *Quis Separabit*; but if they'd only known the right way to do things here they'd have gone the whole hog an' made the ribbon green.

—I wish I hada known about this hospital before, said the mother, for Johnny might have been saved a lot of pain by gettin' attention in time.

—Looka' the kids over there, ejaculated Ella, all in their bare feet an' without a flitther on them. Shame for their mothers to let them look on at a sight like this.

—The whole thing gives a great amount of employment, said Archie encouragingly. Even the photographers benefit, for the whole crowd get their photos taken after the ball is over, after the break of morn, after the dancers leaving, after the stars are gone, to be able to look back at themselves in their old age in their gala get-up.

—Sixpence a month, with three visits a week, isn't a lot to charge, if they can do anything at all for Johnny, murmured the mother.

—Some of the dresses of the duchesses cost hundreds an' hundreds of pounds, said Ella.

—And sweet goodbye to the kingdom, the power, and the glory, if we get Home Rule, added Archie.

—Well, we'll see what they can do for Johnny on Monday, said his mother, putting her hand protectingly on his head.

—Here's a crowd of them coming, said Ella excitedly, here's a great crowd of them coming quick and fast, thick and last, comin' thro' the rye, comin' thro' the streets, comin' to

The Castle Ball

As far as the eye could see or the mind wander, the Dublin streets were a running stream of landau, victoria, coupé, brougham, coach, and cab forcing a way to the Castle Yard, each vehicle heavy with the precious bodies and souls of earls, barons, bishops, ambassadors, judges, privy councillors, right honourables, most honourables, honourables, archdeacons, spiritual pastors, and masters and mistresses,

Sailor goo-goos in blue, white, and gold,
Soldier goo-goos in black, scarlet, and gold.
Top-heavy and stern in shakoo or busby, in helmet or bearskin,
finished off with a hackle or ball, a spike or a plume,
not a speck of the dust of the earth on their skin or their clothes,

all the others cock-hatted, knee-breeched, and sword-girded,
exhilarant all on their way to their master,
with their ladies in silks and their ladies in satins,
or swathed in poplin all finely brocaded,
and wearing rich lace from Valenciennes city,
made haughty by living through hundreds of years,
straight to the core of the Castle they streamed,
or they sauntered at ease talking lightly of things that had passed or
    were present,
while soldiers saluted or stood to attention,
stood stiff to attention,
busy blasting the lot though their lips never moved,
stood blasting the stir that kept them alert standing stiff to attention,
while heavy police in dull blue and bright silver
and glossy belts buckled too tight on their bellies,
moved hither and thither all puffing and sweating,
encircling the flurried showpieces of men,
escorted and sorted the highly-priced rabble across the courtyard,
safe into the arms of fine far-seeing footmen
all padded in plush, yellow, red, and plum-coloured,
satin coats of cerise and warm brown on their backs,
fatted calves swathed tight in the whitest of silks,
and their heads periwigged, merriwigged, and beribboned,
whose bowing shoved all the gay sheep to a shepherd,
a man made by God in a hurry and tired and eager to get the thing
    over and done with,
new-fashioned with orders by man and made mighty,
with his ugly shape tailored away in a suit of the best of black
    velvet,
knee-breeches he wore,
and his snowy-white shirt had a rainbow of ribbons,
a sword with rare gems in the hilt hanging cold by his side,
with his funny face pale with importance and pride,
he modelled a tentative waddle into a parade,
he toddled along with a fair rod in his hand,
like a message from God he came back and went forward,
and gestured and motioned and beckoned them on,
with O'Donnell then, fight the good fight again,
sons of Tirconnell, all valiant an' thrue,
make the false Saxon feel Erin's avengin' steel,
on for your counthry, O'Donnell aboo,

(someone was singing round a near corner),
went forward and backward and beckoned them on,
ambassadors bringing fair words from far lands,
and blue-hooded barons with hell-baiting bishops,
having after them tails of archdeacons and deans,
with everything honourable, hot with excitement,
trotting tense and refined neck and neck with the judges,
aligned with the elegant sailor geegaws and soldier gawgews,
with their ladies in poplins and satins and silks,
armed with flounces and fans, followed after the rod
held high in the hand of the figure dressed up
in the richly-made suit of the best of black velvet,
followed firm
on a fine and immaculate carpet of crimson,
on, Marmion, on, up the stairs, on again,
and on and on up to the room where the throne was,
where the man in the suit of the best of black velvet
litanied loud the great names of the land,
and the men bending low bent down to their bellies,
while the flounces and fans bent waist and bent knee,
slid back on a heel sinking into a curtsey as brave as you like,
in honour of kingship viceregally there,
and standing agley and agloom on the throne,
the well-pampered minds of the flounces and fans all fevered with
    fear,
for the slightest false movement in showing how well
they knew how to support and comport themselves there
in front of the blue-gartered leg of a goose,
would shatter and shame them,
in front of a blue-gartered leg of a goose,
whose little bow swallowed big bows and the bending.
Having learned fitly sless blessed to give than it is to receive,
the ambassadors wise and the archdeacons holy,
with all the great barons and judges most upright,
followed hard by all the right and left honourables,
tacked on to the soldier and sailor gewgaws,
hurried past hurried fast hurried on to the ballroom,
where the silks and the satins flourished flounces and fans,
in the chippendaled, palm-spotted, chandeliered ballroom,
there the couples were welting away on the floor in a giddy
    gavotte,

My wife and I lived all alone
in a little log hut we called our own,

legs lift and look from flying flounces and a bustle on each backside
bounces,

She loved gin and I loved rum,
I tell you what, we'd lots of fun,

while the right reverends, most reverends, and reverends sadly
mouched round the chippendaled, sheratoned banks of the room,
spiritually dead to the rollicking music of the red-coated, gold-braided,
heavy-epauletted, tight-trousered military band making things merry
and bright for the world,

Ha, ha, ha, you and me,
little brown jug don't I love thee,

while those known for their learned and godly conversation mean-
dered along by the margin of the river of jollity veiling a holy vision
against the sight of baroneted eyes peering and judicial eyes glancing
and right and left honourable eyes gleaming and soldier and sailor
eyes sparkling at the view of bare shoulders and sweet and white
breasts getting bigger and bigger as they popped in and popped out
from the bantering bodices worn by the right lovely damsels aglow
with delight at the shame of showing their partners nice things to be
remembered when the glee was over,

Oh I could ride a ride a ride a ladie,
a certain ladie,
in a lilac-scented room all warm and shadie,
hooks and eyes will come undone with little aidie,

Ha, ha, ha, you and me,
little brown jug don't I love thee,

On a sofa all but everything displaydie,
Venus showing off the sweet tricks of her tradie,
working hotly haydie, hotly hotly haydie,
we'd soon make something quick that wouldn't fadie,
yes I could ride a ride a ride a ride a certain ladie,

lifting legs from flying flounces all the time the spiritual pastors and
masters moped restlessly under the palm trees thinking dumb spiro
speriodically towards the tempered truth that the one way to keep
their flocks any distance from the danger of hellfire was to persistently

hold a red-hot poker tight to their arses, while outside under the Milky Way and the Pleiades, the landau, brougham, victoria, coupé, coach, and cab drove through the Castle gates into the yard paved with good and bad intentions, like the road to hell, defended with horse, foot, and artillery, courtyard of England's faithful garrison i neirinn of the saints and scholars and scuts and the glorious round towers and the dear little shamrock so green with the wolf-dog lying down and the harp without the crown and the sun-burst of Ireland between ourselves, be Jasus, the counthry is in a nice way between the two of them, while heavy policemen in dull blue and bright silver, and leather belts round their waists, buckled tight over their bellies, moved hither and thither, sweated and puffed, escorted and sorted the gorgeous highjinkers of Irish society carefully along to the narrow red way that led them safe into the arms of the figure, dressed up in a suit of the best of black velvet, who ushered them to the throne and to the one who sat upon the throne, like unto a jasper and sardine stone, having a rainbow round his feet like unto red rubies, white pearls, and blue sapphires, while from many elders having crowns on their heads, seated round the throne, proceeded the thundering of voices singing Hearts of oak are our ships, heads of oak are our men, who always are ready, and steady boys, steady, for we'll fight and we'll conquer again, and again, the soldiers saluted and stood to attention, stood stiff to attention, blasting by God, though their lips never moved, the ravishing stir that kept them alert, standing stiff to attention, Until the day break and the shadows flee away, we ought to go now for the last lone cab has gone in and the gates are shut and darkened, while the dances of them that make merry cannot be seen, neither can the voices of them that make merry be heard any longer, linger longer Louisiana Lou, and now we're back to where we started, said Archie, as they streeled home.

Two more nights of misery limped slowly by for Johnny, sitting up in bed, squirming his body and grinding his teeth; while his mother, with an old topcoat round her shoulders, stood over him in the shadowy light of a candle, holding old cloths saturated with cold water to his eyes, trying to mollify the pain, her face white with suppressed sympathy whenever he implored her to do something to take the pain away, murmuring that the hospital would do all that and more for him, and that he had only to stick it for two more short days; and when many hours had crept slowly and ashamed away, exhaustion lulled the pain, the saturated head of the boy sank more deeply into the drenched pillow, his mother put an arm around him, and hummed a hymn, There's a Friend for little children above the bright blue sky, a Friend who never changes, whose love will never die; our earthly friends may fail us, and change with changing years, this Friend is always worthy of that dear name he bears; and the two of them slumbered together.

THE HILL OF HEALING

AT half-past eight in the morning, washed and dressed, with a thick handkerchief over his eyes, Johnny, helped by his mother, ate sparingly of his bread and tea, for he was soon to be given over to a power that could do many things to hurt and frighten him, and force him to suffer a fuller measure of pain.

He went down the street, holding his mother's hand, as slowly as he could, so that what was going to come to pass might not come too quickly. Opposite the end of the street, he heard a tram stop, and felt his mother lifting him inside and helping him on to a seat, and saying, if he was good and gave the doctor no trouble, she'd buy him a sponge cake, and they'd take the tram home again. The tram, pulled by patient, muscle-wrenched horses, jingled along, stopping now and again to take passengers on and let passengers off, each pull, to get the tram restarted, giving the horses a terrible strain. The conductor came along, with his money-bag and gleaming silver punch, and gathered the fares, tuppence for his mother and a half fare of a penny for him. He heard the punch ring with a clear shrillness as the conductor holed the tickets which were given to Johnny by his mother to hold, a red one for her, she said, and a yellow one for him; an' maybe you'll be able to look at them when we're comin' back, for the doctors may do you so much good that you may be able to fling the bandage off when we leave the hospital.

They got out at Westland Row, and his mother led him down Lincoln Place till they came to the hospital, a timid shabby-looking place, having a concrete path, with a few beds dotted with geraniums, before the entrance which wasn't any bigger than the two windows that would form the front of a grocer's shop. Over the big shop-like windows, in big letters, were the words, St. Mark's Ophthalmic Hospital for Diseases of the Eye and Ear. Going inside, they found themselves in a long narrow hall, divided in two by a barrier of polished pine. At the upper end were two doors, one to let the patients in to the doctors, and the other to let them out when the doctors had finished with them for the time being. The hall was furnished with long, highly-polished, golden-coloured pitch-pine benches on which a number of men, women, and children were sitting, slowly moving up to the door leading to the room where the doctors were. Near the entrance was a huge stove, and near this stove was a table on which, like an offering on an altar, was a big book enshrining the details of the patients' names, homes, and occupations. At this table sat a big, heavy, stout man of sixty-five with a white beard, a short bulgy neck, an incessant cough, a huge head, the skull of which was bald and hard and pink and polished like the pine benches. He was called Francis.

Johnny's mother gave the details asked for—his age, where he lived, and that he suffered from a disease of the eyes; and when Francis was told that the boy's father was dead, he shoved the word orphan into the space required to denote the father's occupation. The sixpence was handed over, and they were given a ticket of admission which would also be used by the doctor to write down the prescribed remedies to be applied to the diseased eyes. These were made up and handed out to the patients at the dispensary, a little closed-in booth-like space with a sliding panel, stuck in a corner of the hall. They got, too, a large sheet fixed in a cardboard protector, having on it diagrams of the eye, so that the doctor could record the origin, nature, and progress of the ailment, to be filed and retained by the hospital for future reference. They sat down on the bench among the patients, and waited for their turn. The people were being admitted in batches of five or six at a time, the rest moving up nearer as the others went in. As they waited and moved up and waited, his mother read what was written on the ticket:

ST. MARK'S OPHTHALMIC HOSPITAL FOR ACCIDENTS
AND DISEASES OF THE EYE AND EAR

Out-patients attending this Institution, under the care of
MR. STORY
are to attend on
MONDAYS, WEDNESDAYS, and FRIDAYS
before ten o'clock
Each person (not a pauper) will pay sixpence for a ticket
which will last for one month from date of issue. This
Ticket must be kept clean, and presented open at each
visit, and preserved when the attendance ceases.

Johnny heard the people round him talking of their complaints, their pain, and their hopes of improvement.

—I have to go months yet, he heard a voice say, before there'll be any improvement. Steel chips in a foundry flew into me eye, an' they had to get them out with a magnet. They made me jump when they were doin' it, I can tell you.

—He had to cut the sthring, said a voice a little nearer, to separate the bad blind eye from the good one, an' now he's breakin' his arse to cut the blind one out altogether, sayin' that it's no use havin' a dead eye in your head; but I have me own opinion about that, for the dead one isn't so disfigurin', if you don't examine it too closely, so it 'tisn't.

—It's wonderful, murmured another voice, what a lot of things a man can do without, accordin' to the doctors.

—Some o' the buggers would give up the spendin' of the first night with a lovely woman he was after marryin' for a half-hour's hackin' at a man, said the first voice.

—The first real touch o' spring is comin' into the air at last, said a soft voice, a little lower down; in the people's park yesterday the main beds were a mass o' yellow daffodils. The whole time I was gettin' a mug o' tea an' a chunk o' bread down me, I was lookin' at them.

—Geraniums, red geraniums for me, said an answering voice, every time, every time.

—I don't know, I don't rightly know, answered the soft voice; to me, red geraniums or geraniums of any other colour seem to have a stand-offish look, always, while daffodils seem to welcome you to come in and walk about in the midst of them.

—There was a moment's silence, then Johnny heard the second voice saying, maybe you're right, but I still hold to the red geraniums.

—See that man sittin' opposite, said a woman to his mother, have a glance at his ticket, and you'll see it's printed in red—don't look over too sudden—see?

—Yes, he heard his mother say, I see it's printed in red, while ours is printed in black. Why is that, now?

—Because he's a pauper, and doesn't, as we do, pay for his treatment.

Johnny felt a glow of pride. He wasn't a pauper, and he held the card of admission out so that all could see it was printed in black.

Suddenly they found themselves in the doctor's room, and a nurse made them sit down on a special bench to wait for Mr. Story. It was a room full of a frightening light, for the whole north wall was a window from side to side, and from floor to ceiling. There was a ceaseless sound of instruments being taken from trays and being put back again. Tinkle, tinkle, tinkle, they went, and cold sweat formed on

Johnny's brow. All round the wall terrible pictures of diseases of the eye and ear were hanging. A nurse, in a blue calico dress, with narrow white stripes, was hurrying here and there, attending to the doctors; and everywhere there was a feeling of quiet, broken by a man's moan, or by a child's cry, that made Johnny tense his body with resentment and resistance.

At last, Mr. Story, a tall thin man, with a sharp face and an elegantly-pointed reddish beard, came over to them, and said shortly, bring the boy over to the window. Johnny was led over to the window, and the bandage taken from his eyes: the light, the light, the cursed, blasted, blinding light! He was seated on a chair; he was fixed between the doctor's legs; his head was bent back as far as a head can go; he could feel the doctor's fingers pressing into his cheek just below his eyes: the light, the light, the cursed, blasted, blinding light!

Open your eyes, said Story, and look out of the window; go on, open your eyes, like a good little boy.

—Open your eyes for the doctor, Johnny, said his mother.

—Open your eyes, said Story, sharply, open your eyes, at once, sir.

But the cursed, blasted, blinding light flooded pain in through the lids, and he kept them tightly closed. His mother nervously shook his arm.

—Open your eyes, you young rascal, she said.

But he sat, stiff, firm, and silent, and kept them closed.

—Story beckoned to two students. One of them held his head from behind the chair, the other held his arms, but still, firm, and silent, he kept them closed. His obstinacy forced them into fierceness; they took him out of the chair, while his mother, embarrassed, threatened him with all sorts of violence when she got him home. They stretched him, on his back, froglike, on the floor, students holding his legs, nurses holding his arms, while Story, kneeling beside him, pressed his fingers under his eyes firmly and gently, till with an exasperated yell, Johnny was forced to open them, and Story, from a tiny glass container, instantly injected into his eyes a tiny stream of what looked like cold water, which spread like a cooling balm over the burning ulcerated surface of his eyeballs.

Silently, then, he submitted to a fuller examination in a pitch-dark room, filled with little cubicles, in each of which a gas-jet flared; and from a mirror-like instrument strapped on the doctor's head, Story searched his inner eye for a fuller indication of the disease that took from his life the sense of sight in agony and sweat. After two hours of examination and treatment, Story returned to his desk, and beckoned

THE HILL OF HEALING

to Johnny's mother to come over to him. She came, slowly and anxiously, and listened to what the doctor had to say.

—The boy will not be blind, he said, writing rapidly on the case-sheet, but getting him well's going to be a long job. Bathe the eyes regularly in water as hot as he can bear it, afterwards with a lotion they will give you at the dispensary. Most important of all, some of the ointment, as much as will fit on the top of your finger, is to be inserted underneath the lids — not on, mind you, but underneath the lids — every night and every morning; and the boy will have to wear a bandage for a long time. He is to be given nourishing food, and he is to take a teaspoonful of Parrish's Food, after each meal.

—Can he go to school, doctor? asked the mother.

No, no school, he said snappily. His eyes must be given absolute rest. No school for a long, long time.

—If he doesn't go to school, sir, he'll grow up to be a dunce.

—Better to be a dunce than to be a blind man, said the doctor. The boy must be brought here on each Monday, Wednesday, and Friday till an improvement removes the necessity for attendance oftener than once a week. Get these remedies at the dispensary, he added, giving her the prescription, do all that I've told you, be patient, and don't let the boy go to school; and Mr. Story, with his elegant white hands, his red pointed beard and his morning coat, hurried away, followed by a flock of students, to attend to another patient.

—Me eyes must be pretty bad, said Johnny to his mother, as she was being fitted out with ointment, lotion, syrup, and bandage, at the dispensary, when he won't let me go to school.

Not to have to go to school — that was a thought full of a sweet savour. No schoolmaster, no lessons, no wear and tear of the mind with reading, writing, and arithmetic. He was saved from being one of the little slaves of the slate and satchel.

—It won't be nice, he murmured to his mother, if, when I grow up, I amn't able to read and write, will it ma?

—No, said she, it would be terrible; but, please God, you'll soon be well enough to go, for it might easily be as well to be blind as not to be able to read or write.

Then a nurse heavily bandaged his eyes, and his mother led him forth from the hospital, having finished his first day with an Institution that was to know him so well in the future that the doors nearly opened of their own accord when they saw him coming.

HIS DA, HIS POOR DA

AND all this time and for many months before, he who was called
Michael, the old man, his mother's husband, the father that begot
him, was lying in a big horsehair-covered armchair, shrinking from
something that everybody thought of, but nobody ever mentioned.

Out of Limerick he had come, walking the roads to find a job, and
settle down in Dublin. Down in Limerick, a catholic man had married
a protestant maid; all the children had been reared up in the thick of
the catholic religion; but the catholic father had died when Michael
was an infant, so his mother had taken the chance to bring up her
last-born in the true protestant faith once for all and once for ever
delivered to the saints. When Michael had grown up into a young
man, his mother had been taken up to heaven. Then his catholic
brothers and sisters began to quarrel bitterly with Michael over the
things that Jesus said and the things that Jesus did and the meanings
that were hidden in the things that Jesus did and Jesus said, and by all
accounts, Michael had a pretty tough time of it. So one fine day,
without as much as a goodbye or a kiss me arse to the rest of them, he
set his face towards Dublin, and turned his back on the city of
Limerick forever and ever, amen.

> Brandenburgh the ditch has crossed
> And gained our flank at little cost,
> The bastion's gone — the town is lost;
>
> Oh! poor city of Luimneach linn-ghlas.
> Out, with a roar, the Irish sprung,
> And back the beaten English flung,
> Till William fled, his lords among,
> From the city of Luimneach linn-ghlas.
>
> 'Twas thus was fought that glorious fight,
> By Irishmen, for Ireland's right—
> May all such days have such a night
> As the battle of Luimneach linn-ghlas.

Up he came to Dublin, and married Susanna, who became the
mother of his children, with Johnny as the shake of the bag. He was
known to the neighbours for many years in his simple suit, half-tall
hat, and blackthorn stick, bringing home his two pounds, weekly, to
his wife, like clockwork; liked by many, a little feared by all who knew

him, having a sometime gentle, sometime fierce habit of criticism; and famed by all as one who spat out his thoughts into the middle of a body's face. A scholar he was to all, who was for ever poring over deep books, with a fine knowledge of Latin, and a keen desire that others should love learning for its own sake, as he did.

And here he was now reclining in a big horsehair-covered armchair, shrinking from something that everyone thought of, but no-one ever mentioned.

A ladder on which he stood, it was said, had slipped from under him, and, in falling, his back had struck a chair, and his spine had been injured. Doctors came in by the door, examined him, asked him what was wrong; and he annoyed the doctors by replying that the doctor had been sent for to find out. The doctor ordered that the patient should be rubbed all over with fine lard, and then left, as wise as he was when he first came in. So the delicate sensitive face, fringed by a soft brown beard, grew paler and thinner day by day, the white shapely hands moved more restlessly over the rests on the chair, and the reading of his beloved books became a burden too heavy to bear. He wanted Ella to read Shakespeare to him, for Sue, his wife, wasn't much good at anything above Dickens (though she knew all about Falstaff); but Ella wouldn't, for Ella, studying to be a teacher, was too busy, and the dad, anyhow, had crept a little too close to the grave to be pleasant or interesting. And death was death and life was life and Ella was Ella.

There was a little more give and take in life, too, since his dominance had been confined to the armchair. The boys could stay out a little later; return, too, with a whiff of drink off their breath, and stand square-shouldered and proud-mannered in front of their mother, knowing that the probing eyes were dimming in the other room, and were trying to see through a darkness that buried in its silent blackness the coming call of God; and that lips that might have framed a message of scorn were now sadly forming messages claiming kinship with Jesus, son of man, and son of God, who came into the world to save sinners.

There was one comfort that, if he died, he would die in the midst of his books. There they were in the big bookcase, snug in a recess to the side of the fireplace. Marshalled tightly together, there they were, the books he used to read, pore, and ponder over: a regiment of theological controversial books, officered by d'Aubigné's *History of the Reformation*, Milner's *End of Controversy*, Chillingworth's *Protestantism*, holding forth that the Bible, and the Bible alone, is the religion of protestants, with an engraving of the fat face of the old cod stuck in the front of it; Foxe's *Book of Martyrs*, full of fire and blood and brimstone, *Popery Practical Paganism, Was St. Peter Ever in Rome?* having in it a picture of divines battering each other with books, and SS. Peter and Paul, in the clouds of heaven, looking down and laughing at the fighters, actually saying, if pictures could speak, Go it, boys, give each other socks. Like inspection officers, the English Bible, the Latin Vulgate, and the Douai Testament stood pompously together, and, to the right, *Cruden's Concordance* acting as orderly officer; a neatly uniformed company of Dickens', Scott's, George Eliot's, Meredith's, and Thackeray's novels; Shakespeare's Works; Burns', Keats', Milton's, Gray's, and Pope's poetry; on the top shelf, six or seven huge volumes, like podgy generals, of *The Decline and Fall of the Roman Empire*; and leaning idly by their side was Locke's *Essay on the Human Understanding*; and a whole crowd of school books that had been used by the boys and Ella, with a number of camp followers consisting of prizes they had won at Sunday school, such as *I and Jesus with the Zulus*; *Little Crowns and How to Win Them*; *Boys and Girls of the Bible*; *Gospel Garlands for Little Girls*; *The Sieges of Gibraltar*; *From Crécy to Tel-el Kebir*; while in the corner was a shy little book calling itself *Creation's Testimony to its God*; and locked away in a drawer, forbidden to be touched by anyone save the head of the house, lay a mysterious book which the father said confined the dangerous teaching of a Bishop Berkeley; and, mother added, was all about nothing being real, and that all things we saw were only images of our own ideas, and that such books were only to be read and thought of by minds big enough to understand that they were rubbish.

Her husband had spent most of his life among his books, and though it was nice to know that the whole neighbourhood respected your father as a great scholar, and at home with the Latin, said Ella, yet what use was it all when the time came for you to hand in your gun? Locke's *Essay on the Human Understanding* was all balls, said Mick, for the very look of the thing was enough to start you praying to God that the human mind would never become anything like what it was represented to be in the book.

Several times only, Johnny had come into touch with his father. When he was old enough to know about things, his father was ill, and he was bad with his eyes; and his father hated the thought that, because of his eyes, Johnny would grow up to be a dunce, a thing that was an abomination in the sight of the lord, his father, so the two seldom came together. Once when nobody was in the house, save his mother, and she busy in the sick room, he had been sent out to buy an ounce of Cavendish cut plug.

—The dunce will forget what he's been sent for before he's half-way there, his da had said, as his mother carefully fixed his cap on his head while his little body vibrated with anxiety and importance.

—No, he won't forget, said the mother, for he isn't quite the dunce you think he is, and bending down, she had whispered in his ear, now, remember, say it to yourself all the way to the shop, ounce of Cavendish cut plug, ounce of Cavendish cut plug.

And he had run swiftly and anxiously to the little shop three streets away, gripping closely the money in his little fist, murmuring rapidly, constantly, and breathlessly, ounce of Cavendish cut plug, ounce of Cavendish cut plug, ounce of Cavendish cut plug. Then he had run back as rapidly, anxiously, and breathlessly to his mother, who examined the little parcel carefully, and pronounced it to be good. She brought him in to his father so that he might deliver it himself, and his father took it from him silently and wearily, as he sat in his chair. Johnny stood with his head bent down, looking at the bony knees giving angles to the black trousers, and the small firm feet, thrust into slippers, nestling together on a small red and black rug stretched before the fire.

—Now, his mother said, expectantly, now you see, father, he didn't make any mistake after all.

Then the wasted sensitive hand left the arm of the chair, and Johnny felt it resting on his head, as his father said softly and sadly, No, he is a brave little fellow, and his father's son.

Shy, without the power to raise his head to look at his father, Johnny left the room, joyous and triumphant, murmuring, ounce of Cavendish cut plug, ounce of Cavendish cut plug.

Once again, when the parlour door had been left open, Johnny, passing by, had ventured to peep into the room. There he was sitting stilly in the large gorse-hair horse-hair armchair, rimmed with mahogany, the armchair that, after his father had died, had fallen asunder. All that Johnny could see was a thin white wasted hand resting grimly on the arm of the chair, and a patch of intensely black hair beneath a cricket-cap made of red, white, and blue segments. There was his poor da, or, his father, as Johnny's mother spoke of him to his brothers and sister, sitting facing the fire, with the little coloured mermaid in a glass bowl on a little table to his right, and a picture of Queen Victoria in her coronation robes on the wall to his left.

He must have sensed the boy peering in at him, for the head in the cricket-cap suddenly turned, and the boy caught a frightening glimpse of a white, wasted, agony-lined face, jewelled with deep-set eyes now gleaming with appealing anger at the boy who was looking in at him. Johnny saw the blue veins swell in the delicate hand that rested on the chair, and his ears were shocked by the sound of the low weak voice trying to shout at him, Go away, go away, you, and shut the door at once — this is no place for little boys.

Johnny had closed the door quick, had run for his life through the hall out into the street, full of the fear of something strange, leaving his da, his poor da, shrinking from something that everyone thought of, but nobody ever mentioned.

HIS FATHER'S WAKE

ONE very cold morning Johnny's mother wakened him up, saying, Get up, Johnny, get up, me poor boy; there are many things to be done, and you must be washed, and take your breakfast a little earlier than usual.

He rubbed away some of the matter that clung to his eyes, and shivered in his thin shirt.

—Ugh, he muttered, it's cold, it's very cold.

—There'll be many a cold morning to face from this out, said his mother, as she helped him on with his trousers, and rearranged the crumpled bandage on his forehead. Tell Ella, she went on, to give you a clean bandage.

—Not Ella, he said, you, mother: Ella's rough, and Ella doesn't care.

—Ella will have to do it this morning, she said, for I have to stay with your poor father.

He groped his way to the kitchen, and Ella caught him by the arm, saying, Come on here, till I bathe your eyes and wash your face. She sponged the caked matter from the lids of his eyes in water as hot as he could bear, grumbling most of the time she was doing it.

—It won't be long now till you'll have no servants to be dancing attendance on you. Cuddling's over, now, and you'll have to fend for yourself.

She washed his face and neck with particular vigour, combed his hair determinedly, twisted and bound a fresh bandage round his left eye, buttoned a collar round his neck, fixed his coat on, and brushed it briskly.

—Now, she said, sit down, take your breakfast, and give God thanks you have it.

He sat down by the deal kitchen table, the top worn thin by continual scouring, which had a white loaf in the centre, a drop of butter in the middle of a plate, seemingly miles from the rim, a cup and saucer, and, on the hob, a brown teapot that sparkled with the reflection of the flames that shot up every second from a warm coal fire. Tom was standing moodily by the fire, with one elbow leaning on the mantelpiece; Archie was drumming softly with his fingers on the window that looked out into the backyard; and there seemed to be a curious silence in the house; a silence that flooded in and flooded out whenever a door was opened; a silence that made the whole house feel silent and solemn.

—Four minutes past three, this morning, said Archie, just said to the mother, put your arms round me, Sue, and before she had time to call anyone, he was gone.

—I'm glad, murmured Ella, that mother has decided on having a closed-in hearse, for people that are anything at all always use a closed-in hearse.

—We've got the ground in perpetuity, said Archie, and no-one, bar ourselves, can ever be buried in it.

Something had run up against them, and had jolted them from one uncertainty into another. Not knowing exactly how to take it, they took it in silence; for the few words they said were invisible fingers pointing out the silence. They were harnessing, in ritual of word and manner, the disturbance and silence on to God, though His name was not mentioned. God would be present to help as long as they had to think of these things, for He was a very present help in time of trouble: Come in the evening, come in the morning, come when you're called, or come without warning.

The thing that had jolted them lay in the parlour, the little parlour, kept perpetually swept and garnished for visitors that demanded some ceremony, and were entitled to see all the best that the family had. The room with the horsehair-covered furniture, the polished mahogany cabinet, dainty little brackets, supported by little pillars, decorated with mirrors, that was called an overmantel; ecru lace curtains, girded in the middle with crimson knitted cords, on the windows. On a little table, by the window, a large glass bowl filled with clean water in which floated a coloured glass mermaid, with yellow hair, black spots for eyes, big breasts, with scarlet nipples on them, and a blue, yellow, and green tail, shaped like the tail of a fish. The mermaid had a golden comb in her hand, and she stared out of her glass bowl at all who came into the room and at all who went out of the room. Now her little black spots of eyes were staring at something that lay very still in a bed at the opposite side of the room. On the wall over the bed was a big picture of Lord Nelson Bound for Trafalgar's Bay, all his orders aglitter on his breast, and he stepping out like a whole man for his last scrap in this world. Beside him walked a man in a white beaver hat, green cutaway coat, and brown plush knee-breeches. He was looking up into Nelson's face with a look of worship for the great one who had inspired The boy stood on the burning deck whence all but he had fled, the flame that lit the battle's wreck shone round him o'er the dead; while with one hand the same man in the cutaway coat and the brown plush knee-breeches, in the same picture, pushed aside a stout enthusiastic fishwoman who was trying to get close to the sailor hero, wellaway and lack-a-day, on his last road to do battle for his England, home, and beauty. Facing Nelson on the opposite wall was a picture of Queen Victoria, all decked out in her coronation robes, with none of the fun and all of the pomp, power, wealth, and parade of her colonial and Indian empire peering out of her bulgy blue eyes.

Here in the same room, under the stare from the paper faces of Lord Nelson and Queen Victoria, protected by the rear-guard of his beloved books, lay Michael O'Casside from Limerick. Stretched out he lay, his firmly-closed eyes staring backwards, arms and hands lying straight down by his sides, his dark beard so neatly trimmed that there wasn't a hair astray, nicely folded up for heaven beneath a snowy sheet, a sharply-cut outline of stiffening flesh and bone: thought, education, toil, laughter, tears, sex, turned into dust and ashes.

Cold, stiff, and quiet the thing lay, while life outside hurried about settling everything for it, rushing to the registrar of deaths; going to leave an order for an open grave; selecting the coffin, heavy oak, with heavy brass plate and handles; hiring a four-horsed hearse; telling the clergyman the time of burial so that he would be on the spot to spread the rumour of the resurrection; letting people out who had seen the body and letting people in who hadn't; listening to and answering the murmur of questions.

—Hardly althered a bit although he was twelve and more months lying, but thank God that gave him a peaceful end to the end of it all, for he was a good man and quite happy now wherever he may be, sayin' that it was nothing short of hypocrisy to blame the romanists for veneratin' the relics of the saints when we ourselves snatched handkerchiefs an' tore them into shreds as sacred souvenirs because

Moody and Sankey had wiped their brows and their noses in them after gassy speeches and holy serenades in the Rotunda or Christian Union buildings filled with souls packed like sardines together busy beseechin' that their sins bein' red like crimson might be made as white as snow, an' now when I look at him the nose seems a little thinner, no, yes just a shade, though you'd hardly notice it if you didn't look close from where I'm standin'; he simply put his arms round Sue's neck she says, says Dear Sue, dear dear Sue, sighed and stretched and stretched and sighed again a little, and went away where the good niggers go a little pale an' haggard-lookin', but she's bearin' up wonderfully under it all, was a cruel blow but God will lessen the knock in it in His own good time an' in His own peculiar way, for I nearly dropped when I heard her sayin' such a thing to a woman still weak with the first impressions after losin' her husband only a few moments before holdin' Sue's hand in a vicey way, out of place an' terribly ignorant, underminin' the sympathy simmerin' in your soul for the sorrow starin' you in the face with her folds shall be full of sheep and the valleys shall stand so thick with corn that they shall laugh and sing, makin' a conundrum of the connection between what she was sayin' and the mystery of the stiffness that's stretched out undher the snowiness of the death linen, unheeding Sue telling her of the sore that spread over the butt of his spine and the doctors looking anxiously couldn't make it out having come quietly after he lay down on the bed he's dead in now, following the giving under him of his legs getting thinner an' thinner every day that passed by with Sue his wife never ending tending to him, larding his limbs every night regular in the hope of some movement coming into them out of a doctor saying that you couldn't tell what would happen if you tried hard enough, thinking of what she'd do if he died with an unreared child clinging to her, and the gameness of him refusing to have any clergyman near him in his last moments, holding on to the fact there's no mediator between God and man save only the man Jesus Christ, messing about trying to twist the thoughts of a man to things of no account, slipping soft and slow into the arms of Jesus like the winds that blow from the south sighing so soft and low, whisper their secrets sweet, whisper and I shall know that he never missed sending his children as regular as clockwork to church, Bible class, and Sunday school, keeping them from spoiling the sabbath by singing hymns in the twilight when the lights were low and the flickerin' shadows softly come and go whenever the weather stopped them from going to worship God in His holy temple, showing that he was in favour of worshipping in spirit and in truth wherever

two or three are gathered together in His name, hardening infancy
into the ways of the Lord who is the rock himself an' not Peter, at all,
who forgot himself whenever anything crossed the confidence and
quietness of his mind by a torrent of curses that must have made the
hair of the other apostles who weren't use to it stand on its end, listening to the crowing of the cock as he warmed himself at the fire and
hearkening to the little maid saying that his voice showed plainly he
must have come from Galilee, hiding himself frantically away from
what he was, which is as bad as shoving on to show yourself forth for
what you're not, like that Katie Johnston over there, trying to plunder
attention from everyone round her with her bustle so pronounced as
to form a swell altogether too lavishly extended over her behind, disturbing the gaunt and sober decency of the forms and signs gathered
together in a house that has a stiff dead man lying in one of the rooms
giving a species of serenity even to the pictures of Nelson and Queen
Victoria hanging on the walls, who came up from Ballina only a
couple of years ago wearing the airs and graces of having lived in
Dublin all her life, though a city-cut skirt on a pair of country hips
only helps to accentuate the difference between them, with the dry
cough and the red-glazed cheeks tellin' of a comin' dissolution that'll
happen vividly in the full knowledge of the present generation which
should recommend to her, if anything ought, the marrying of the
lunatic asylum attendant who's a bit queer himself, coming into constant contact with the mad people, and her mother making much of
him in season an' out of season an' Katie keeping him at arm's length
when she finds him thrilled and panting with the saucy delusion of
getting him to tie her shoe beneath a skirt lifted to show a leg fading
deliciously up under a cloud of white fancy flounces, or fastenin' a
brooch slyly sliding out of her breast, purposely done to let him fiddle
longingly with her diddies, an' after a little while when he was hot an'
full of a choky sensation, puttin' the pin back in its place herself an'
tellin' him an' thankin' him that would do nicely, gigglin' up in his face
when she saw that he had gone far enough to try an' tear off every
stitch she was wearing and fling her flat on the floor in front of the eyes
of all in the room, shy at the sight of fifty-four years of experience
gesturin' in frantic emotions that were only the resuscitation of a
withered imitation of youth's spring, and go for a woman young
enough to be a daughter as old as possible for the man to have,
though it's not easy to blame a supple-legged lassie of twenty-three
for thinking twice before takin' on the dhry, unlively, lack-pressure
embraces of an old cod controlled by his years from doing anything

desperate in the way of fanciful lovemaking which are unsuitable
considerations for the occasion here present with us, sitting as we
now are pressing the hard seats of chairs with tender bottoms burnin'
for something soft under them while we are waiting for the men to
come with the coffin so that the dead man may be made snug and
ready before he goeth to his long home far away from this one where
he'll nevermore have a portion, nor in anything that is done under the
sun we all hope'll be shining when the poor body's taking its last
tour through the streets, following the horses wearin' a resigned and
determined look on their faces of no turning back while they're pulling
their little cargo of what was once a man like meself, though I'm really
a woman an' different in every way after gettin' down me a dollop of
tea, I'll thry to forge to the front in the rush at the end of getting close
to the clergyman doing the needful at the rim of the grave makin' the
best of a bad bargain with God, tellin' Him of the words spoken by the
mouth of His own apostle that appearances didn't matter a damn and
that death had lost its sting and that the grave has been swallowed up
in victory.

HIS FATHER'S FUNERAL

JOHNNY watched the cabs coming into the street, eager to pick up
those who were going to his father's funeral: red cabs with black
linings, black cabs with yellow linings, green cabs with red linings, and
blue cabs with brown linings. The first stopped near the house where
his dead father lay, and the rest formed up behind, one after the other,
stretching like a string down the street, waiting for the rush to come
when the body would be carried out to be packed into the hearse
which hadn't arrived yet. The drivers of the cabs dismounted from
their seats and leaned against the walls of the houses in twos and threes,
forming a grotesque, shaggy, lurching frieze on the face of the sun-
mellowed, rain-stained bricks of the houses. A crowd of friends and
neighbours had gathered near the door of the house, and waited,
standing still and standing silent. There was a low murmur as the
hearse, like a huge, black, decorated gothic casket, drawn by four
black horses, each with a black plume on its head, came slowly
trotting up the street in state, and sidled with dignity into a space
right in front of the waiting cabs. The driver of the hearse and his
assistant, wearing big, black, tall hats, and long, heavy, blue silver-
buttoned coats, climbed quietly down from their high-up seats, and

hovered about near the door, waiting for the call to come in and nail the coffin down.

A cab suddenly swept round the corner, came at a rapid trot up the street, pulled up in a line parallel with the hearse; and the driver, jumping down, joined two other drivers, who stood smoking and leaning and talking together against the wall near the window of the house. The newcomer took off a hard bowler hat and wiped his forehead.

—The belly-band broke on the way, he said, an' be the time I put a stitch of twine in it, I thought he'd be planted, an' all the prayers said.

One of the other two drivers took a pipe from his mouth, spat on the path in front of him, and answered, Plenty of time, Jim — he hasn't been screwed down yet. Curious how long people take to say goodbye to a dead man.

—I'll give them another quarther of an hour, said the third driver, who wore a yellow muffler round his throat, if some good Jesuit 'ud come along an' give me a joram o' malt to lower down into me belly — didderay didderee didderum, he hummed.

—Me an' Jack, said the driver who had come in a hurry, had a great night yesterday. Afther dockin' t'animals, we opened with a couple o' pints in Dempsey's, then we had three more in the Bunch o' Grapes, slung another five into us in Henessey's, an' ended with the last o' three more in The Royal Oak as the shutthers were comin' down at the tick of eleven o'clock.

The man wearing the yellow muffler rubbed his hands together, and envy glistened in his eye.

—Not a bad sackful for a man to get down him in the latther end of a night, he murmured — didderay didderee didderum.

Johnny, standing by the heads of the hearse-horses, saw the boy Connor, who went to school with him, standing beside his mother, watching him, and leering whenever he caught Johnny's eye. Johnny moved nearer to him so that Connor could get a better view of him standing cockily near the hearse-horses, impatiently scraping the road with their feet and shaking the black plumes whenever they tossed their heads. Connor moved till he was just beside Johnny, though, sly enough, he held on to his mother's skirt, which he had stretched out as far as it could go. Johnny felt his head beside his shoulder, and heard him whisper in his ear, Go an' put your hand on a horse if you're as brave as you're thryin' to look.

Johnny stiffened with pride and stroked the band of crisp crêpe on his arm as he saw kids in the crowd watching him and Connor.

Stretching out a hand timorously, he stroked the haunch of the nearest horse. The animal gave a shuddering start, and kicked viciously, making the hearse shake and Johnny jump away from him in fright.

Gaaaa, you mischeevous little bastard, roared the driver wearing the yellow muffler, gaaaa, out o' that, an' leave th' animal alone, or I'll go over an' kick the little backside off you!

Johnny slunk away a little, and turned his back to Connor, so that his shamed and frightened face couldn't be seen.

—Fifteen pints between eight and eleven, said the driver wearing the bowler hat, I wouldn't ask anything betther, even on the night of me first daughter's weddin'. We got home, he went on, we got home, but it took two hours to do it, where it should ha' taken only twenty minutes: two solid hours o' mighty sthrivin', but we done it in the end.

—They ought to have the old man warmly folded up be this, said the man wearing the yellow muffler, didderay didderee didderum.

—The both of us were rotto, went on the driver wearing the bowler hat, the two of us strugglin' together, him helpin' me an' me helpin' him, whenever help was needed. We sung The Heart Bowed Down all the way home, fall an' up again, fall an' up again; I'd call it a red-letther night, even afther a day of thinkin'.

—Last week was a rotten one with me, said the third driver; a few roll-an'-tea-for-lunch laddies, who are always lookin' for the return of their fare in the change.

Johnny felt Connor beside him again, and whispering at him over his shoulder.

—Mother says, he whispered, that in a week or so you won't be so cocky.

—You're not comin', anyway, answered Johnny, for I heard me mother saying that she hoped the Connors wouldn't thry to shove their noses in at the funeral.

—Yah, sneered Connor, you're shapin'. Just because your father's dead you think you're big in your black suit, but me mother says it isn't new at all, but only dyed.

Johnny turned slantwise, looked at Connor in the eye, and murmured, If it wasn't for me father bein' dead, I'd go round the lane with you, an' break your snot.

—On the way home, said the man wearing the bowler hat, we met two lovely big-diddied rides, and they were all for us going home with them, but neither of us could let go his hold on the other, and so we had to keep everything buttoned up.

—Wonder they didn' thry to lift yous, said the third driver.

—We were so dhrunk, went on the man wearing the bowler hat, that we didn't know our own religion, but we weren't dhrunk enough for that.

—I'd ha' done something, said the man with the yellow muffler, even if I hadda lie down to do it, didderay didderee didderum.

A woman came running to the door of the house, looked about her, saw Johnny, beckoned excitedly to him, and shouted, You're to come in, Johnny, an' give your poor father a last kiss before he's screwed down.

Johnny stood still, shivered, and gaped at the woman standing in the doorway. He retreated a little, and caught hold of Mrs. Connor's skirt.

—I won't go, he said. I don't want to go in.

—Here, come in at once, sir, said the woman in the doorway, roughly, an' pay the last respects to your father, who's in heaven now, an' watchin' down on all your doin's, an' listenin' to all your bold sayin's.

—I'll not go in, he repeated plaintively. I'm afraid, an' I'll not go in.

—*I* wouldn't be afraid, Johnny heard Connor say, to kiss me father, if he was dead, would I, mother?

—Don't be afraid, son, said Mrs. Connor, patting Johnny's head, your father wouldn't do you any harm, an' when you're grown up, you'd be sorry you hadn't given him a last kiss.

—Come in, you little rut, when you're told, shouted the woman at the door, an' don't be keepin' every one waitin'.

She ran towards him, but he dodged her, and made off down the street, running full tilt into the man wearing the yellow muffler, trampling on his foot, and hitting his head into the man's belly.

—Jasus, me foot! yelled the man, you lightning-blooded little bastard, where the hell are you goin'!

—He's the dead man's little boy, said the woman, getting hold of Johnny's arm, an' he's wanted to give his dead father a last kiss before he's screwed down.

—An' he was makin' off, snarled the man, an' knockin' the puff out o' people. A nice way of showin' his love for his father.

—Let me go, let me go, screamed Johnny, kicking viciously at the woman's legs, as she dragged him towards the house. I won't go, I don't want to kiss him.

—Your mother'll have a handful in you when you grow up, me boy, she said, as she gathered him forcibly into the house in her arms.

She held him tightly in the midst of the crowd in the room waiting for the coffin to be screwed down. His mother turned round when he began to scream again, came over, and caught his hand in hers.

—Let him down, let him down, Mrs. Saunders, she said to the woman. Then she bent down over him, putting her arm round his trembling body and kissing and kissing him, she murmured, There, there, hush, nothing is going to happen to you.

He circled her with his arms, pressed his face into her skirts, and she felt his fingers cleaving through her skirt to the flesh of her thighs.

—I couldn't, I couldn't, he sobbed. Don't ask me, mother, don't ask me to kiss him, I'm frightened to kiss a dead man.

He felt a gentle, sympathetic pressure of an arm around him, and softened his sobbing.

—No one'll ask you to do it, she said. I'll kiss him goodbye for you myself. Just touch the side of the coffin with the tip of your finger.

She gently drew out his arm, and he shuddered deeply when he felt the tip of his finger touching the shiny cold side of the coffin.

—That's the brave little son, she murmured; and now I'll give your father a last kiss from his little boy.

She bent down and kissed the thing in the coffin, and he heard her say in a steady whisper, Goodbye, my Michael; my love goes with you, down to the grave, and up with you to God.

She stepped back, and he felt her body shaking. He looked up and saw her lips quivering in a curious way, as she said quietly to the waiting hearsemen, You may put the lid down on top of him now.

The hearsemen stepped forward and lifted the coffin lid from where it was resting behind the coffin against the wall, silently and quickly fitted it on, and, with things they took from their pockets, began to turn the screws, filling the tense quietness with the harsh grinding sound of the screws tearing their way down through the hard oak of the coffin. When the screws had been driven home, the hearsemen went out and stood beside the hearse. Six men, two at the head, two at the feet, and two in the middle, lifted the coffin up on their shoulders, and, in a curious body-bending way, carried the corpse, feet first, from his home to the hearse that waited outside to carry the body to the grave.

The man wearing the yellow muffler rubbed his hands gleefully together.

—We ought to be soon bowling along merrily to the boneyard, now, he murmured expectantly, didderee didderay didderum.

The three of them suddenly caught sight of the end of the coffin appearing in the doorway. They took their hands out of their pockets, and went with a hurried ambling run to the doors of their cabs, and sought their fares from the crowd that came pouring out after the coffin. There was a rapid noise of opening cab-doors, another rapid and sharper noise of the doors closing when the fares had climbed inside. The six men carrying the coffin, their arms locked over each other's shoulders, heads turned sideways to prevent the coffin edge from scraping their necks, walked slowly and rhythmically to the back of the hearse; the two leaders, stooping, rested their end of the coffin on rollers laid on the floor of the hearse, the middle couple bent down and slipped from under the coffin, the last couple pushed their end, and the revolving rollers carried the coffin into the hearse, and a hearseman closed the door.

Johnny was lifted into the mourning-coach by his mother, who followed after with his three brothers and sister, and they all settled themselves on the seat of the coach. The cab-drivers mounted to their seats, gathered their faded rugs of blue and green and red from the backs of the horses, folded them with a deft motion round their knees, sat down, took the reins in their hands, waited for the hearse and the mourning coach to pull out into the centre of the street, and then with a Yep, eh, yep, there, to the horses, followed, one after the other, and went with an easy, ambling trot down the street, wheeling round the first turning, wheeling again at the next turning till they were back in the street they had first left, slowing down to a walk as they passed the dead man's door, and then away at a trot again towards the cemetery miles and miles away.

Johnny, hedged in between his sister and brothers, edged towards the window, but his sister pulled him back as he was trying to let the window down.

—Sit easy, can't you? she said, you can't go looking at things out of the window at your father's funeral! Keep quiet with those feet of yours, or you'll pull the dress off me.

—Let him come over here, said his mother, and he can keep quiet and look out of the window at the same time.

His mother guided him beside her, so that with a little stretching of his neck he could see the world as it was passing by. They went slowly by the piece of waste ground at the end of the street where a huge Gospel tent was standing. He caught a glimpse of the long red scroll stretched over the entrance with the word Welcome in big letters on it. He thought of the night that he had timidly crept down and lifted the flap of the tent to have a squint at the crowd of faint figures filling the place, dimly shadowed out by the smoky light from many oil lamps.

He remembered how he had struggled and shouted out, Let me go, let me go, or I'll tell me mother, when a dark-bearded little man, with a pale face and cloudy eyes, had grasped him by the arm and had tried to pull him inside, saying in a curious, sneaky way, Another loved and little lamb for Jesus.

Hearse, mourning-coach, cabs, and cars, threaded their way through the tenement-hedged streets where swarms of boys and girls played and fought in front of the gloomy houses that had once, his mother told him, sheltered all the great lords and ladies of the land. Round into Cavendish Row where the houses were high and still mighty, with stately doors and flashing windows. Outside of some of them maids, with black or blue dresses and white aprons and caps with floating streamers, were polishing brass plates, letter-box flaps, and heavy knockers of bronze or brass.

—Dublin houses of the gentry when they come to town, said his mother.

—They have to die the same as all of us, said Ella, his sister. Dust they were and dust they shall become.

—It would hardly be fair for God to let them live for ever, said his mother. We're passing through Aungier Street, now, she added, glancing out of the window.

—Haven't we a long way to go still? Johnny asked her anxiously.

—No, she said, not a very long way now.

—But it'll take a long time to get there, won't it; a long, long time, really?

—We'll get there all too quickly, she said softly.

—There'll be quite a crowd at the graveside, said Ella.

—The full up of three carriages, twenty-six cabs, and six side-cars, said Michael.

—The number that's attendin' the funeral show the respect every one had for him, said Ella.

—An' yet he rarely spoke, and never mixed with any one, murmured the mother.

—It won't be very long till we begin to feel his loss, said Archie.

—We'll all only have to pull together, an' things'll be easy enough, said the sister.

—I'm the only one that'll miss him, said the mother, me an' Johnny.

—We'll look after you both, never fear, said Ella, so keep your pecker up.

—Steadily, shoulder to shoulder, steadily, blade by blade, added Tom.

The coach stopped opposite the cemetery, they climbed out, and, in a moment, the pathway swarmed with the crowd that had emptied itself out of the cabs and off the side-cars. From a carriage that had immediately followed the mourning-coach a tall, thin, black-bearded clergyman stepped, and hastened on in front to the vestry, provided for the robing of the clergy by the cemetery authorities.

The hearse pulled in through the central gates on to the main path, which cut the cemetery into two huge sections. One of Johnny's brothers took some documents from his pocket and handed them to a fat, pompous-looking, little man, wearing a big tall hat and black gloves, and who had a face like a frozen image. The little man took the documents, examined the brass plate on the coffin to see that the body therein was related to the person docketed and scheduled in the papers. He nodded assent, and the coffin was placed on a low car covered with flowing black draperies, and pulled by a well-groomed, gentle-looking black horse, enveloped in a black gown heavily embroidered with silver, so that only the eyes, the ears, and the feet of the animal were visible. A tall black plume rising from his forehead made him look like the nag that the Black Prince rode at the battle of Crécy. Overhead in a grey sky, spotted with timid-looking blue patches, dark heavy clouds were being tossed and pushed along by a northerly wind blowing steadily and reasonably, except that now and again it gathered strength and swept by fiercely, filling the cemetery with a mad rustle and a cold swish-swish from the bending branches of the trees as it went sweeping by. At intervals a sulky beam from a peevishly-hiding sun would dart out from a corner of the sky, flooding patches of the graveyard with a jeering, flippant brightness, rippling and dancing slowly over the headstones and the floral flotsam that Christians scatter about a cemetery to make the place look as jaunty, as merry, and as unconcerned as possible; then, after flushing the place with a timid brightness, the sun would glide away, slip back into itself behind the clouds, and the dismal gloom that was slinking round would press forward and cover up everything again. Elegant beeches, ivy-trunked oaks, dark, well-tailored cypresses, looking like guardians keeping things in their proper places, and fan-branched yews, looking like shy, saintly, Georgian ladies dancing a quiet, secret minuet to themselves, were ranged along the avenues and paths. Tombstones, tall and squat, square and round, old, middle-aged, and new, spread themselves everywhere, with an occasional lanky obelisk, like a tall boy peering over the shoulders of the others, seemed to gather closer together, stiffen, stretch, and stare and stare at the newcomer that had come to be planted, wondering who he was, whence he came, and whether what was coming would add to the dignity and ease of the dust that lay buried there.

Off the contingent started, the little fat man, with the tall hat and the face like a frozen image, leading in front of the bier, with the documents in his hand, directing the way to Section F, Plot B, Grave OX5432/2345, where the cargo of decaying flesh was to be stored against the day of the resurrection of the dead; after the black-palled bier, pulled by the black-palled horse, came the mother and Ella, with Johnny walking between them, then, close up, the various relatives of the dead man; and spreading out in a long procession behind, the friends of the family, silent and solemn-faced, marched up the main avenue towards the vestry where the clergyman stood, robed and ready to receive the body of his brother for committal to the clay. The silence was broken only by the soft fall to the ground of the horse's padded feet, the coo-cooo of a pigeon, the rustling of the leaves on the trees, or the cold swish-swish of the bending branches as a stronger wind went sweeping by.

The clergyman, with the big black beard, wearing a white surplice and a black stole, holding a prayer-book in his hand, open at the Service for the Burial of the Dead, waited till the bier came close, then turned and marched by the side of the little fat man with the face like a frozen image, and recited in a loud and serious voice:

I am the resurrection and the life, saith the Lord: he that believeth in me, though he were dead, yet shall he live: and whosoever believeth in me shall never die.

We brought nothing into this world, and it is certain we can carry nothing out. The Lord gave, and the Lord hath taken away; blessed be the Name of the Lord.

Coming to Section F, the cortège wheeled to the right, off the main avenue, and midway in a narrow path, a little to the left, they came to a heap of newly dug earth piled up beside an open grave. The coffin was lifted from the low black-palled car by four heavy-featured grave-diggers, who put ropes round it, and set it down by the side of the open grave. The black-bearded clergyman, walking carefully between the other graves so as not to step on one, slipped on a damp sod of grass, and was pitching into the grave, when one of the grave-diggers caught him, pulled him back, and set him on his feet again.

—A narrow shave, sir, he said, as the clergyman tried, with a hasty brush of his hand, to remove a hand-pattern of clay which the grave-digger's grip had left on his white surplice.

Johnny saw the sudden look of fright that had crossed the face of the clergyman when he was slipping, and thought how funny it would have been had the clergyman fallen into the grave, and the fun they'd have had pulling him out again by his white surplice and his black stole. He giggled. His mother roughly pulled him by one arm and his sister by the other, and he was pushed behind them, red-faced with fear and shame. The looks on their faces told him that there would be nothing funny in a clergyman with a white surplice and a black stole falling into an open grave. The clergyman straightened himself up, opened the book again at the proper place, and began to read, as a pigeon coo-cooed, and the branches of the trees, bending, gave a cold swish-swish as a stronger breeze came sweeping by.

Man that is born of a woman hath but a short time to live, and is full of misery. He cometh up, and is cut down, like a flower; he fleeth as it were a shadow, and never continueth in one stay.

The grave-diggers lowered and lowered the coffin into the grave, and took the ropes from under it. One stood back a little distance, and the other stood near the edge of the grave, hatless, with a fistful of earth in his hand, waiting. The clergyman went on:

Forasmuch as it hath pleased Almighty God of his great mercy to take unto himself the soul of our dear brother here departed, we therefore commit his body to the ground; earth to earth [the grave-digger threw some of the clay from his fist down on the coffin], ashes to ashes [more of the clay fell on to the coffin], dust to dust.

The grave-digger threw what remained of the clay in his fist down on the coffin; then he left the side of the grave and joined his comrade, the two of them throwing their eyes round, Johnny heard afterwards, to try to pick out the one that would be likely to give them a tip. The clergyman went on:

I heard a voice from heaven, saying unto me, Write, From henceforth blessed are the dead which die in the Lord: even so saith the Spirit; for they rest from their labours.

                    Lord have mercy upon us.
                    Christ have mercy upon us.

The grave-diggers hurried forward and rapidly began to shovel the pile of clay into the open grave in a strict and tense silence, again broken only by the pigeon's coo-cooo, and the cold swish-swish from the bending branches of the trees as a stronger breeze went sweeping by. Johnny looked up at his mother standing stiffly watching the grave-diggers filling the grave, and he saw that tears were streaming down her cheeks. He crept closer and closer to her, wrapped his right arm round her left one, squeezed and squeezed it, caught her hand in his and pressed and pressed and pressed it.

The clergyman lingered looking down at the clay falling on the coffin, his hands entwined in front of him, eager, possibly, for the thing to come to an end, sick of the dampness of the grass oozing through the thin soles of his boots, making his feet feel dead, dreading a cold to come, shivering a little whenever the trees gave a swish-swish as a stronger breeze went sweeping by; thinking of the bright fire in his study at home, with life and warmth filling every corner, and tea, hot and richly brewed, poured into dainty cups, with his wife dividing life into two parts by talking of the things that belonged unto her home, and the things that belonged unto her husband's parish.

The grave was filling up now—the men were working rapidly—and in another few minutes they would be topping it, and he could quietly slip off, remembering the sudden rise in shares this morning that meant a gain of one hundred and thirty-five pounds and a few odd shillings, which wasn't too dusty when you came to think of it—at the evening service on Thursday he must remember to speak finally to the church charwoman about pawning the two hassocks that had been newly covered only a few days before — she might lay her hands on other things — only a few feet from the top now, feet numb and hands raw and nipped with the damp of the whole place, shivering and sodden with desire of decay and death and darkness and drooping — the shovels are tapping the top of it now — so goodbye for the present, dear sorrowful sister in Christ, and comfort remember is His to bestow, for your husband's in heaven and happier far than we can be here, who are seeking a city that's hidden away, and Sion's its name, shining forever with light everlasting, out-ageing the sun and the moon and the stars that gleam through the day and glitter at night, and never forget when God's city's in bloom, the sun and the stars and the moon will only be dust in the streets, frail dust in the streets of the city of God — so hurry your thoughts through your grief to the day when Christ on the clouds shall come sweeping again through the sky from His Father, and the dead that were bless'd by a union with Him shall come out of their graves and stand to attention, saluting their Lord, this when they have done, they'll seek out the loved one they've lost and the ones they have left sporting on in the flesh, and remember, unbroken unbent in the faith, you will gather your loved one yourself to your breast, to enjoy him forever fresh-robed in a glorified body, unsickened by thoughts of the past or thought for the future, for these shall be merged and forgot in the sun and the moon and the stars which shall only be dust in the streets in the city of God, and His mercy shall keep you till then; so farewell for the present, dear sister in Christ, for the tea is at hand and the crumpets are ready and I must be vanishing now.

Heavily, for his feet felt puffed and softly numb with the damp that had oozed through the thin soles of his boots; stiffly, because his joints had tightened with the cold, the clergyman picked his path through the graves, crossed the main avenue, and dived into the vestry. As his mother lingered by the grave arranging the flowers that had been hastily placed there, Johnny saw him come out of the vestry, swinging a little leather case in his right hand, and hurry away till the trees hid him from view.

Ella touched her mother's arm, and said, You just come along now, Ma, and try to keep your pecker up; but her mother went on silently arranging the flowers on the grave, so Ella stole away to join her brothers strolling slowly along towards the main avenue.

For a long time Johnny waited and waited, till his mother turned away from the grave, and he saw that tears were streaming down her face. He crept up closer and closer to her as they slowly moved away, caught her hand in his and pressed and pressed and pressed it in a dead silence broken only by a pigeon's coo-cooo and the cold swish-swish of branches bending as a stronger breeze went sweeping by.

WE ALL GO THE SAME WAY HOME

THEY sauntered down the main avenue, uneasy, and fearful of the change that the leaving of an intimate thing behind them forever would bring into the thought, life, and action of the family. Death had dunted into the family life, and had stunned its functions for the time being. Nothing would be exactly the same again. There would have to be a new grouping and a new laying out of all things.

Suddenly Johnny saw the red coat of a soldier in the midst of the crowd who wore their dark-toned suits as if they were vestments.

—Look at the soldier, Ma, look at the soldier with a drum and crossed gold guns on his arm! he cried.

Johnny saw Ella's face go red, and his brothers grinning, as his mother hushed him, and said no-one must raise a voice in a cemetery.

Johnny stared at the red-coated soldier who had a lovely epaulette, like a sickle moon, on each shoulder, covered with white braid, sprinkled with little red crowns, and white braid all over his breast and down his arms, all dotted with the little red crowns. And over his back and shoulder there ran a cord which met just above his left breast and then fell down in two big lovely tassels of blue, yellow, and green plaited cords.

He's a bugler, thought Johnny, a bugler that blows the reveille every morning to rouse all the other soldiers out of their deep sleep, as one day the angel Gabriel will blow his own trumpet to wake up all the dead who lie around us here in thousands: Little Boy Blue, come blow your horn, the cow's in the meadow, the sheep's in the corn.

He saw his brother Tom go over and shake hands with the soldier; he saw Ella's face redden again as the soldier's eyes stared over to where she was walking along with her mother.

—He should never have come to the funeral, Johnny heard his mother say to Ella; you know the state your poor father'd have been in had he known you knew him — he would never sanction a soldier. For goodness' sake, don't speak to him here.

Johnny saw Ella tossing her head, but she said nothing.

Tom came to their side again, and, looking back, Johnny saw the soldier following them afar off.

—It's wonderful, the long sap-swollen grass that grows in a graveyard, said Tom.

—The best grass that grows anywhere, grows in a graveyard, said Archie. They must make a tidy bit out of the hay they get from it. Everything is money here, and nothing goes to waste. No-one ever yet saw a balance-sheet from a cemetery.

When they had passed through the big gate, and had come to the mourning-coach, Tom held back while the others climbed into it.

—I think I'll jog along back with Bugler Benson, he said, when the others had settled themselves in the coach; we'd be a bit crowded, if I came in.

—Oh no, Tom, said his mother complainingly; do come in, and for this one day, at least, let us all go the same way home.

Johnny hummed silently to himself as Tom, with a disappointed scowl on his face, climbed into the coach, and squeezed himself into a corner.

> We all go the same way home,
> All the whole collection, in the same direction,
> All go the same way home, so there's no need to part at all,
> And we'll cling together like the ivy on the old garden wall.

The coach delayed while the driver mounted and settled himself in his seat. Johnny, glancing towards the window of the coach, saw it curtained with a sparkling blue sky, cut clean in two by a deep black poplar, like a dark angel standing taut in a tight suit of blackest velvet, guarding 'gainst disturbance of the sleep of the dead.

The coach moved on, and then he watched the others sitting for a while silent, thinking of the upset and scattering that death had given to the even ordering of things. He seemed to feel that the sorrow that filled the coach was all in his mother's heart. This death was a curious business. Who killed cock robin? I, said the sparrow, with my little arrow, I killed cock robin. He could see the picture in the book, with the robin stretched out on his back, his knees tightly gathered into his red breast from which an arrow stuck out wickedly, and his little beak stiff and gaping open. And in a corner in a tree, on a bough, an evil-looking sparrow with an eye and a leg saucily cocked as if he had just done something grand. There he perched and stared and jeered in a tree, on a bough, with a little bow held wickedly under a wing.

—The grave looked to be one of the deepest I have ever seen, said Ella.

—It must be dug deep enough to hold four, said Michael, for that's the number allowed to go in when the plot's bought outright.

—It's our family property, altogether, now, isn't it? asked Tom.

—Absolutely, responded Archie; we hold the plot in perpetuity.

—Mother, said Johnny suddenly, if a bird wanted to shoot a boy with an arrow, how hard would he have to pull?

—Oh, I couldn't say, she said.

—Why don't you try to think of what you're going to say, said Archie to Johnny; for you mean how hard would a boy have to pull if he wanted to shoot a bird with an arrow?

—No, said Johnny to Archie, no, I don't. How hard would a bird have to pull if he wanted to shoot a boy with an arrow? For a boy to shoot a bird with an arrow, he wouldn't have to pull hard at all.

—Silly kid, said Tom, a bird couldn't hold a bow to shoot an arrow.

—How do you know he couldn't? questioned Johnny.

—Oh, do be quiet, said Ella.

—But how does he know a bird couldn't shoot an arrow?

Tom glared at him, and said, because we know he couldn't.

—But supposing, only supposing a bird could, went on Johnny, how hard would he have to pull?

—That, laughed Archie, would depend on whether the bird was a cock or a hen.

—Nice kind of talk, this, and father only a few minutes in the grave.

—This comes of letting him go to the funeral, complained Michael. He's getting twice too old-fashioned for his years.

—You'll have to keep very quiet for a few days, said his mother, till your father's been a little while with God.

—But why a little while, Mother, Johnny asked, when Sunday school teacher says that a moment and a million years is all the same to God?

—Oh, try to keep your little gob shut for a second or two! said Ella irritably.

Johnny fell silent. He hated, hated all these people, all, except his mother, with their big heads, big faces, big hands, and big feet. He was angry with them; but they were too big to fight, for one of them could easily stamp him under his big feet. He wanted to spit at them, to answer them back, but he shut his little mouth tight, and answered them never a word. But in his mind he sang, and sang loudly: And the birds of the air went a-sighing and a-sobbing when they heard of the death of poor cock robin, when they heard of the death of poor cock robin. If his da was as happy as they were eager to make out, getting warmed up again in Abraham's bosom, and sure of everything going where he was gone, why did they all sit so still and stiff and stony? How they all loved to cheat a kid out of anything he had a thought to do. And, anyhow, if they only knew, Who killed cock robin was a funeral song, wasn't it? Of course it was, of course it was.

Johnny, from the window, watched the jingling horse-drawn trams going up or down the street, the drivers holding the reins with one hand, and resting the other on the hand-brake. The coach was travelling twice as quick home as it had travelled to the cemetery, and soon they were passing between Trinity College and the Royal Bank of Ireland.

—I wonder will the Home Rulers ever be able to turn the Royal Bank of Ireland into an Irish House of Parliament? murmured the mother, as she glanced out of the window.

—God forbid they'd ever be able to turn such a beautiful building into a rendezvous of rowdyism, said Ella fervently.

—Parnell's the only gentleman in the whole gang, said Tom. They were watching their chance for years, and Kitty O'Shea is only an excuse for downing him. If they throw him over, clowns and pantaloons in a pantomime parliament are all that they can hope to be.

—He should have more respect for himself than to go and carry on with a married woman, said Ella.

—If all that's said about him is true, he should do the decent thing, and resign at once, said Archie.

—Ay, said Tom, and give the guttermen the power.

—They're not all guttermen, said Archie, and even if they were, they deserve all the more credit for lifting themselves out of it.

—There's no credit going to them, said Tom, for it's Parnell, the man they're hounding, that lifted them out of the gutter, and planted them on their feet.

—Why doesn't he get hold of some single woman, inquired Ella, and leave the married women alone?

—The people are showing what they think of Parnell, anyway, said Michael.

—Ay, the ignorant superstitious country gulls who walk in daily dread of their parish priests, said Tom scornfully.

—How do you know they're in dread of their parish priests? asked Michael.

—What about the priest who threatened to turn into a goat anyone that dared to say a word in favour of Parnell? Read the papers, man. And Tom spat out of the window.

—What about the men that are standing by him — are they in dread of the parish priests?

—Read the papers, read the papers, man.

—He has no right to make a fool of himself over a married woman, persisted Ella.

—Oh, we all know, said Michael, turning fiercely on Ella, that he has no right to make a fool of himself over a woman, married or single, so pocket that stuff and button it up, and let him answer the question of whether or no those who are standing up for Parnell are in dread of their parish priests?

—What about the priests preaching against Parnell from off the althars? asked Tom.

—Name the priests, name them! said Michael loudly; what althars, which althars, whose althars?

—Read the papers, repeated Tom; you wouldn't be so ignorant if you read the papers.

—I suppose you think you are the only one who was brought up to be able to read the papers?

—Read the papers, read the papers, man, chanted Tom.

—Oh, said the mother pleadingly, don't let us have any argument on our way home from your father's burial.

They sank into silence again, and sat moody till the coach pulled up at the door of their home, and silent and stiff and stony they went into the house. Tom gave a shilling to the driver who said Thank you, sir, and sorry for your trouble, before he drove away.

Johnny lingered outside, but his sister came out, caught him by the arm, and brought him inside, saying, Come in, come in; you can't be seen knocking about outside on the day your poor father was buried, and you'll have to behave like a different boy for a week or two. They went into the room where his mother and father had slept together, and where he had lain sick for over a year, and where he, at last, had died. The blind on the one window was still down, and the room was dark and solemn. His mother pulled a cord which sent the blind rattling up, and the light leaped in, touching with a curious brightness the dreariness that sickness and death had gathered, and that still loitered around the things sickness and death had left behind them.

—This room'll have to be well aired for a day or two, said Ella, as she and her brothers sat round a fire that the neighbours had kept going while they were away at the funeral.

Johnny wandered over to the window, and watched the redness of the sun in the sky over the house opposite.

—The damp and cold of the cemetery has gone right through me, said Ella, as she lifted her skirt to warm her legs.

—Look at the sun, look at the sun, Mother, cried Johnny, how red he is. Why is he so red?

—Oh, said his mother, glancing out of the window, I suppose he was feeling a little cold, and God wrapped a scarlet cloak around him.

—Does God like red, Mother?

—Oh, yes, yes, He likes red; there are quite a lot of flowers and things in the world that are coloured red.

—Does God like the colour red the best, Mother?

—Oh, I couldn't rightly say, Johnny; I think He likes all colours, really.

—And yellow, too; for look at the buttercups, the primroses, the cowslips, the daffodils, and, and the dandelions; He must be very fond of yellow, too, mustn't he, Mother?

—Yes, He must be very fond of yellow, too, Johnny.

—But I don't think He cares a lot for blue, Mother, for there's only the violets and the bluebells — but I forgot about the sky, the blue of the sky that's everywhere on a fine day. He must be specially fond of blue, mustn't IIe, Mother?

—What about a cup of tea, or something, said Archie, and never mind the colour choice of God?

—Lay the table, Ella, said the mother, and we'll have some tea, an egg each, and some cold meat that's left over.

—He seems to cotton on a good deal, too, to white, went on Johnny; for look at the daisies, the hawthorn, and the clouds. Curious that God likes white. Why does He like white — it's not much of a colour, is it, Mother? And black, too, for look at the dark night; but then He always softens that a little with a golden moon or the silver stars.

—Oh, chuck it, Johnny, chuck it, boy, broke in Michael, who felt uncomfortable, as they all did, with the name of God dangling around; half an hour's enough with God for one day.

—You mind your own business, said Johnny, fiercely turning on him; you're always trying to stop me when I say anything, but I'm not asking you, anyhow.

—Just you chuck it when you're told, said Michael angrily, and give me none of your lip.

—What would you do if I didn't chuck it? asked Johnny defiantly.

—Chuck it, chuck it, shouted Michael. You're getting just a little bit too crabby for Michael.

His mother went over to Johnny, and, bending down, whispered to him, Keep quiet, Johnny, and some other time when no-one but ourselves is here, we'll talk of all those things.

Johnny turned away from her, full up of a feeling to cry, but he shut his teeth together tight, and looked out of the window at the redness of the sun in the sky over the house opposite, making the roofs of the houses look like polished bronze. Big heads, big hands, big feet, big voices, bitter snap and bitter snarl. If he was only up to their size, or they down to his, he'd give them snarl for snap and snap for snarl. He drummed softly, then sharply, with his fingers on the window-pane, murmuring to himself, There was a little man, and he had a little gun, and up the chimney he did run, his belly full of fat, and his old cocked hat, and pancakes in his bum, bum, bum.

—Oh, stop that drumming, drumming, for God's sake, screamed Ella. We've had enough to bear today without having that kind of noise dashing through our brains.

—Oh, don't be always nagging at the child, remonstrated the mother, suddenly and angrily. You're all at him, if he only stirs. He can't be expected to sit or stand all days with his hands folded and his tongue still.

—You shouldn't take his part when you know he's in the wrong, retorted Ella.

—It's dangerous to open your mouth about him, grumbled Michael.

They all sat round the table, Ella cutting the bread and butter, while the mother poured out the tea. She gave an egg to each, keeping the smallest for herself. She filled out a cup of tea, which, with several slices of bread and butter, she placed on a little table beside the window, saying to Johnny, Take.this quietly here, now, where you won't be in anybody's way.

—Mother, he whispered, am I not going to get any egg?

—I'm going to give you half of mine, she said.

And right enough, when she'd broken and peeled the top of the egg, she spooned out the most of it, and spread it over several slices of the bread she had given to him. This was a treat, for it was nearly a year since he had enjoyed the taste of an egg, and he guessed that such a joy would not come near him again till Easter morning came. Eating his egg and drinking his tea, he watched the big heads and big hands guzzling down their eggs and tea and meat.

—Not much to be got out of an egg, muttered Archie; a dozen of them wouldn't make a fair meal for a man.

When they had finished, they grouped themselves round the fire, the men smoking, and Ella reading *The London Story Paper*. The mother brought in a basin of hot water, and began to wash up the things. Johnny climbed on to a chair, and helped her, handing her the cups to be rinsed, and then taking them from her and arranging them on the table when they had been rinsed and dried. He helped her to carry them out to be placed in neat rows on the dresser shelves in the other room. Johnny was feeling more comfortable. Life was resuming its old way. His father's death hadn't changed things a whole lot, after all.

When everything had reached its proper place, and they returned to the other room, Ella had her coat on, and was fixing her hat on her head before a tiny mirror hanging on the wall.

—You're not going out, are you? asked her mother.

—I am, for an hour or so, replied Ella, and Johnny saw her face go red; I'm going for a walk, I want a walk, I feel the need of a little air and exercise.

—The one thought in my head is the man I want to wed, that's my little, little drummer boy in red, grinned Michael from the corner of the fireplace.

—I think it would be better, remarked the mother; if you stayed at home for this evening.

—I'm going out, said Ella; and turning to Michael she snapped, You cock your thoughts on yourself, and never mind me.

She left the room, and they heard her close the door noisily as she went out into the street. There was silence for some minutes afterwards; then the mother took the cloth from the table, shook the crumbs into the fireplace, rolled the cloth up, and carrying it with her, went away into the other room.

Michael took his pipe from his mouth, and mixing a leer with a grin on his face, said, Ella'll have to keep her eyes skinned, or the wind'll blow her clothes up. Then he tapped his pipe on the hob, and hummed:

> The Drummer-boy in red to his little girl said,
> Come.
> When I've had a little fiddle
> With your little diddle middle,
> Then I'll play a tarradiddle
> On your middle liddle diddle
> White bum.
> When I'm fed up with the fiddle,
> This red-coat'd drummer kid'll
> Start a rapid tarradiddle
> On your liddle diddle middle
> White bum!

Tom tittered knowingly, and said, Now, Mick, now that's enough. Halt, the Buffs! What about going down to Nagle's for a few quiet pints?

—No sooner said than done, answered Michael; what have you got on you?

—Enough for tonight, said Tom.

Then they rose up from sitting before the fire, the three of them, and began to put their heavy coats on.

—I wonder, said Michael, how you'd get to know whether God Almighty likes blue, green, yellow, or red the best?

—Oh, shut up, Mick, said Tom, and let the kid alone.

—Red, I think, went on Michael, red like the red on a monkey's arse.

—No more talk like that in front of the kid, said Tom, tittering.

—Oh, shag the kid! said Michael, he'll have to learn about these things some day.

They planked their hats on their heads, called out to the mother that they were going out for a spell, Tom lingering to put his hand shyly on Johnny's head as he passed, and to say, Don't mind Mick, Johnny; you're all right, boy.

Johnny watched them going by the window, eager, talking with a strut in the tone of their voices; off to take their quiet pints of porter at Nagle's counter in Earl Street, well in sight of Nelson's Pillar.

Johnny watched the little lamplighter running, with his little beard wagging, carrying his pole, with a light like a sick little star at the top of it, hurrying from lamp to lamp, prodding each time a little yellow light into the darkness, till they formed a chain looking like a string of worn-out jewels that the darkness had slung round the neck of night. His mother returned to the room as he was stretching to see how far he could see down the street, and how many of the lights he could count. Going over to the fire, she sat down, and gazed steadily into the blaze.

—I was just thinking, Mother, he said, that green must be a great favourite of God's, for look at the green grass, and the leaves of bushes and trees; and teacher said that green stands for life, and God loves life.

He waited, but his mother did not answer him. He turned, and saw her gazing steadily into the blaze of the fire. He stole over and sat down beside her, and took her hand in his. And there they sat and stared and stared and stared at the flame that gushed out of the burning coal. Suddenly he looked up and saw the flame from the fire shining on tears that were streaming down her cheeks.

R.I.P.

AT the age of forty-six the father had died. The old man was dead, the old man was buried, buried deep in a quiet corner close to a cypress tree, a tree that faded away into the darkness of the night and came again to life with the sun in the morning. And the shadow of the cypress tree, on a sunny day, kindly covered the place where the dead man's face lay, veiling from the closed eyes the new things that were being done by those whom the dead man had brought up in the nurture and admonition of the protestant Lord, and in the strength of the best education the means of the fearless and honest dead man could give them.

—My children, he would say, raising himself up stiff and defiant in his chair, will get the best education my means, and the most careful use of those means, will allow. It isn't the best that's going, but it is the best that can be got by me for them. They will be, at least, fit for jobs that will give them a decent and fair living as things go with such as we are; and on themselves will then rest the chance of making a good position better, with the knowledge they have gained from a few men and a lot of books; and, later on, by the wisely-used experience gathered from things said and done by those with whom they'll move, and live, and have their being, they will be fit to fight in the fight of life when it comes to face them. Shield and spear shall they have when the day comes for them to go forward.

And so Michael and Tom had gone without a lagging step to Number 1 school, under Professor J. L. Ryan, principal of the five schools that formed the Central Model Schools of Dublin, where small fees were paid by parents; where teachers stood higher than teachers who taught elsewhere; where the books were dearer and superior to most of the others used in the ordinary National Schools. There they all were, schools, teachers, books, and pupils busy as hell, hunting out of their systems the danger of learning a single thing about their own country and their own people, save that the seventeenth of March was called St. Patrick's Day, and that it was morally permissible, all things considered, to sing The Harp that once thro' Tara's Halls the soul of music shed, provided the song was sung as if you were an' you weren't singing it, and that you were a little surprised to be hearing it sung at all, and especially surprised if you heard it gettin' sung be yourself, seeing that the harp was hangin' on the wall with all its music mute and its soul fled and its glory gone and its day over; so that you somehow felt it hardly decent to mention its name even at a late hour when the sun had long since gone down, and sleep was heavy even on the eyes of the young and hardy; an' if it was to be sung at all be protestant people, then it certainly should be sung *sotto voce* in the spirit prescribed by the articles, canons, and catechism of the church, and the laws and regulations of the viceroy and the officers and non-commissioned officers of the Royal Irish Constabulary.

Archie went to Number 2 school, under Mr. Boyd, presbyterian principal, and red-bearded Mr. Galleher, catholic assistant, who used to say, when he had a few jars in him, that presbyterians were decent men, but damned bigots. Mr. Boyd, on the other hand, when he was quite sober, as he always was, used to choose as often as he decently could when he held religious instructions, the text as a password to higher things, Ephraim — meaning Mr. Galleher — is joined to idols, let him alone.

So, after many days, the two eldest had to face the facts of life built up by the canons, articles, and creeds of the church, the traditions carried on by his excellency the viceroy — hard put to live on twenty-five thousand pounds a year — and the rules of the officers and non-commissioned officers of the Royal Irish Constabulary. Michael, at the age of fourteen, was a rare hand with the pencil. Pictures of a dog lying down by the lock of a canal, and one of a girl with a bird on her head, called The Kestrel, had been so admired by the dead man that he had had them framed and hung on the wall for all to see; and all who came saw, till one day Michael took them out to show them off, and never brought them back again — selling them for a bob or two, as the story went round a long time afterwards. If I only had had the money, the dead man had murmured one day when he was showing the pictures to a friend, I'd have made an architect of him, but the fees were too heavy; so he'll have to be satisfied to do his duty in that state of life unto which it shall please God to call him. So Michael took second place in an examination, and became a telegraph clerk; and Tom took first place in an examination, and became a sorter in the General Post Office of Dublin. There they had been working for some time before their father's death, orderly, peaceable, and respectable, wearing their trim little bowler hats, the badge of all their tribe; nicely-cut ready-to-wear suits; Michael, something of a dandy at the time, adding a curl to the quiff in his hair, a pin in his tie, and a slim cane under his arm, each, after contributing to home expenses, furnished out of his princely pound a week, as being poor, yet possessing all things.

Strange faces began to be seen in the Casside household, faces that stared for a few moments at Queen Victoria who stared back with her thinly blue eyes, and at Nelson, forever bound for Trafalgar Bay; strange faces that peered for a moment or two at the lonely little glass mermaid floating in her little sea gathered into a glass bowl; faces that eyed the array of books left behind by the poor dead man, looking wan and out-of-place where thoughts were fashioned into quick words about things that were born, lived, and died in the passing hours of a day; and when they had looked, they turned away to sit by the fire for a smoke, a drink, a chat, or a sing-song on a Sunday evening to the tune of the church bells that called and cried for all to come and worship, and fall down, and kneel before the Lord their Maker, seeing that they were the people of His pasture, and the sheep of His hand; called and cried to all to come and acknowledge and confess their manifold sins and wickedness, to the end that they might obtain forgiveness of the same, by God's infinite goodness and mercy; and

win the approval of the canons and catechism of the church, the
viceroy, and the officers and non-commissioned officers of the Royal
Irish Constabulary, and the Dublin Metropolitan Police.

But the crying and the calling of the bells went in through one ear
and out through the other, as sounds unasked for, and sounds unanswered. The altar now was the kitchen table, and in the midst of the
candlesticks, a huge gallon can filled with porter, with Michael and
Tom as swaggering altar-boys, and the red-coated drummer, with the
blue, yellow, and green tassels dangling on his breast, pouring the
beer skilfully into any empty tumbler that wanted to be filled; while
Johnny sat in a corner drinking ginger-beer, never noticing his mother
sitting in the opposite corner, silently knitting, looking up with a wan
smile on her face on hearing the red-coated drummer giving a pretended yelp when Ella pinched his thigh, or Ella giving a real scream
when he pinched hers; her peaceful and firm face dimmed by the
tobacco smoke that curled from the pipes of the smoking men. Silent
she sat, knitting, and thinking, maybe, of a silent man lying in a quiet
corner out under the cold stars, and the last hopes of her life but a few
dying blooms on a lonely grave; while Tom was singing, in a harsh
and staggering voice, a song of bustling battle:

> Side by side, in the crimson tide,
> In the days not long ago,
> On we dashed, and our bayonets flashed,
> As we conquered every foe.
> One by one, as the fight was won,
> I saw my comrades fall,
> An' I was the only one left to answer the last roll call!

With all the others joining in, and the voice of the red-coated
drummer loudest of all, to sing the sad brave words a second time,
their hearts swelling with desire to fight, to fight, aye to fall under the
Union Jack for any cause that a single thought could say was worth a
fight; Ella looking fondly at her drummer, as she dangled on her lap
a fine white hand having on one finger a slender ring decorated with a
circle of what was called seed pearls, and in the midst of the white seed
pearls, a tiny red speck that was called a ruby, bought in a pawn-
broker's with money won as a prize in a shooting competition; for
Ella's drummer was best shot in his regiment, and wore crossed gold
guns on his sleeve, and a little, blue-and-white drum with yellow
heads on the arm of his coat above his elbow, causing Ella to feel that
nothing was too good to be kept from her drummer, as she dangled
her ring about on her lap while Tom's staggering voice was singing his

song of bustling battle; and the mother sat in her corner silent, knitting and thinking, maybe, of a man whom God had taken from her and put to lie in a quiet corner out under the cold stars, her thoughts mixing with the tune of the church bells crying and calling on all people to come and worship, and fall down, and kneel before the Lord their Maker.

Her Michael was in heaven, anyway, resting in sure and certain and undivided peace; maybe looking down on her, and telling her, silently, to be brave. Things, too, might easily be a lot worse. As long as her two boys were working, even though Ella would lose her job when she married, her little Johnny wouldn't want; and that was something to go on with and remember, please to remember the fifth of November, of gunpowder, treason, and plot; but God stepped in, and saved the nation from a terrible calamity, and God would step in, and save her, and would never let her be confounded.

She cocked her ear, for that mouth of a drummer was saying something. His eyes were hazy, for they had lowered a second gallon of beer between them.

—The army's the greatest life goin', he said; if a man wants to see life, let him take the Queen's shillin'.

—The life here, said Michael, isn't even worth spittin' on, so we're well out of it, Tom, me boy — I one of the Queen's Sappers and Miners, an' you one of the Queen's Old Toughs.

—Can't help rememberin', broke in Tom, excited and glowing, the look on the kissers of the two superintendents when we told them to stick their jobs where the monkey put the nuts.

—Write to us, says I to them, said Michael, when we're lyin' under a foreign sky, an' the lads all pressin' round to bid us a long farewell.

—Here, at home, said the drummer, balancing his tumbler of beer in his hand, or afar in the wilds of India, Canada, Afghanistan, or Burma, what does it matter so long as we're faithful to the Queen, and honour the flag? A drink, boys, a drink to the soldiers of the Queen!

And the three of them, lifting their glasses, shouted, Soldiers of the Queen! and gulped down their beer.

Their mother's fingers ceased to move among the needles. That was why they had been so excited for the last few days; and so silent. They were leaving her, they were lost to her, they had 'listed. The gay, gaudy uniforms dished out to her soldiers by the Queen with the thinly blue eyes, had taken two sons from their mother. So she sat there staring at them drinking to the Queen's soldiers, while her hands ceased to move among the needles.

Tom noticed her staring at them, and, coming over, he put a hand gently on her shoulder.

—You've two sons soldiers, now, Mother, he said; but don't you worry, for neither of us, here at home, or far away in a foreign land, will ever forget the old woman. You'll be a proud woman when your son comes home in his red coat and his busby; ay, an' maybe with medals on his chest too.

They were leaving her, they were lost to her, they had 'listed. She tightened her sensitive mouth, nodded and smiled to the company, bent her head over her knitting, and the active fingers began again to move rapidly among the needles.

Leaving a parting pat on his mother's shoulder, Tom returned a little unsteadily to his place beside the drummer, took up his glass of beer, and gazed excitedly about him.

—The Royal Dublin Fusiliers, he said a little thickly, the Old Toughs, by the right, quick march for foreign lands where dusky faces grin and threaten, where spears are flung and shots are heard, where wounds are got and cheers are given, where swaddies fall and England conquers. But we are here to fill the vacant places; and huskily he sang a song, and huskily they sang it with him:

> On the banks of the Clyde stood a lad and his lassie
> The lad's name was Georgie, the lassie's was Jane.
> She flung her arms round him, and cried, Do not leave me,
> For Georgie was going to fight for his Queen.

—Raise it higher, said Michael; altogether, an' let the buggerin' chorus go; and so they did; Johnny, with a will, singing with the best of them:

> Over the burnin' plains of Egypt, under a scorchin' sun,
> He thought of the stories he'd have to tell to his love
>   when the war was won.
> He treasured with care her dear lock of hair,
> For his own darling Jennie he prayed;
> But his prayers were in vain, for she'll ne'er see again,
> Her lad in the Scotch Brigade!

—Michael, my Michael, murmured the mother to herself, as her fingers moved among the needles, it is good that you cannot hear your boys and girl singing in their hearts that there is no sorrow, but sorrow will come, though I have not your clear mind to tell them how. You will not know, for you are safe from knowledge where the weary cease from troubling, and the wicked are at rest; but the beginning of your dear peace has meant the end of mine.

And Tom went on huskily singing his song of love and war, and huskily all the rest of them sang it with him.

HAIL, SMILING MORN

ELLA found it hard to even doze during the night before the smiling morn that was to see her married to her man. The hilarious ecstasy in store for her tomorrow night was too much in her mind to let her close her eyes for long, for her beloved is white and ruddy, the chiefest among ten thousand. His locks are bushy, and black as a raven. His mouth is most sweet: yea, he is altogether lovely. So she longed for the night to end and the day to come, so that the day might end, too, and the night come again at last.

She had heard the bells of St. George's Church chime the hours, one after the other, one after the other, Jesu! she had heard the bells chime at midnight; and now she was listening to them chiming the hour of six in the morning; six in the morning, an' all's well, so she'd soon have to be getting up in order to be ready an' in good time for everything.

It would never do to keep the holy clergyman waiting. He was also the manager of her school, and to be kept on her hands as long as possible, if she wasn't to be kicked out of her job as teacher the minute she was married; for even a few more weeks' work would pay something off the hired furniture, though, in a lot of ways, she'd be glad to be rid of the whole of them, and so be able to devote herself to her home and her husband.

Let her think, now. Yes, everything was ready — the gold half-sovereign for the fee; though what a well-off clergyman wanted with a shining half-sovereign that she needed so badly herself she couldn't guess and daren't argue about, for it was here, and there, and gone, like Hamlet's ghost; gone, but not forgotten, either, was the gold wedding-ring that she herself was minding, to be given to her love when she met him at the front door of the church; the new dress, with its leg-of-mutton sleeves, carefully laid out over the back of a chair; the new frilled white petticoat carefully laid out over the dress; the snowy drawers, with deep flounces sweeping out around the edges, carefully laid out over the petticoat; the garibaldi blouse prettily folded on the seat of the chair, and the pink stays nesting on the blouse; and her new high boots going half-way up the calves of her legs, under the chair, and vivid blue bustle hanging by its ribbons from a hook in the wall — all well conserved for weeks in layers of lavender to entice and make glad the heart of the leading side-drummer in the first battalion of the King's Liverpool Regiment, best shot in the regiment, and regimental haircutter to the men.

And fine the drummer'll look in his red coat with its white braid and crescent epaulettes, his spiked helmet on his dear dark head; and the blue, yellow, and green bugler's cord slung around his breast an' back, with the two gorgeous tassels cascading down from his left shoulder; and with his short cross-hilted sword hanging from his hip he'll look like the knight of the burning pestle, or a peacock turned into a moving man, with a heavy square face, dimly lighted by two deep-black eyes, a thick dark moustache, jet-black hair carefully parted in the dead centre, and on the left turned into a jauntily curled quiff. A broad-shouldered body, short, thick, and sturdy legs, and a jerky and conceited way of walking like a peacock turned into a moving man.

From tomorrow on — though she'd have to put in an appearance now and again till her job was gone — she'd no longer have to sing in the parish church of St. Mary's. She'd sing, now, only for her drummer-boy; and Johnny, maybe, when he came on a visit to them after the two of them had settled down. No longer the rector would have the right to hold her tight as a teacher in the infants' school of St. Mary's at twenty-five Lower Dominick Street, the biggest house in Dublin, with its five stories up and five windows across; teaching a hundred and ten score kids from three to seven years old in a huge hall at the other end of a big yard, a hall as big as hell and as high as heaven, heated in the winter be a big stove that got red-hot an' gave out stifling fumes; savin' ourselves from suffocatin' be puttin' a galvanised bucket, filled with water, on the flue, an' moidered trying to keep the children from burnin' themselves, the way they'd be runnin' to see the sulphur blobs dancin' on the surface when the water boiled; and the windows stuck up near the roof to deliver the kids from the temptation of leppin' out through them whenever the lessons got too hard; to be opened, you had to strain at a long rope, though if you once got it opened you'd never get it shut, an' if you once got it shut you'd never get it open, so there they stayed tight and taut the whole year through the time that Johnny learned his ABC here, an' how to read an' spell words of two letters, so me he we be my no go to up it is or of ox an at am as in if us on, is it an ox? it is an ox, is it my ox? if it is an

ox it is my ox, so go up to the ox as it is my ox, I am at the ox, with
a little song to cheer him up in the winter when the north wind doth
blow and we shall have snow an' what will the robin do then, poor
thing, oh he'll run to the barn to keep himself warm an' hide his head
under his wing, poor thing, to be runnin' round after a surplice for
forty pounds a year bursting me lungs with the dint of singin' O be
joyful in the Lord, all ye lands serve the Lord with gladness an' come
before His presence with a song of sixpence for it is He that hath made
us an' not we ourselves, an' we are His people an' the sheep of His
pasture, never failin' to hear the baa-baas of the white sheep or even
the baa-baas of a black sheep astray in the wilderness stumbling up an'
stumbling down the mountains wild and bare, far off from the gates
of gold opened for all with a wide welcome in the first of only two
sacraments, namely baptism by which infants even are grafted into the
church as is laid down in the twenty-seventh article, and are therein
made members of Christ and signed with the sign of the Cross in
token that they shall never be ashamed to confess Christ crucified but
continue His faithful soldiers and servants unto their lives' ending,
with a cough from the stout protestants present to show they realised
only too well that this business of the signing of the cross is but a fond
thing vainly imagined and partaking in its essence and application of
an echo of the profane and old wives' fables believed in and loved by
the unfortunate roman catholics downsunk deep in grievous and
deadly superstitions winked at by the pope and bishops, pretendin'
that they came straight out of the mouth of the holy apostles starin'
outa the stained-glass windows at us all singing' at the top of our
voices that the Lord hath done marvellous things an' callin' on the
round world an' all dwellin' therein to sit up an' take notice of me real
mind dwellin' on a scarlet coat decorated gay with white braid dotted
with little red crowns an' the green, blue, an' yellow woven tassels
hangin' on his breast, an' the bugle hangin' at his side'll make him
look like Let me like a soldier fall upon some open plain, his breast
expandin' for the ball to blot out every stain, as we go up the aisle
facin' the altar to be reverently an' discreetly an' advisedly buckled
together for ever an' ever till death do us part from that day forward
for better'n worse an' richer or poorer in sickness or health to love an'
to cherish, to hate an' to perish, me Ma says if I marry him, for he's
rough and uncouth, but the love of a good woman'll make him gentle
an' meek an' mild, an' even if all the gilt an' braid an' swingin' tassels
are hidin' ignorance, after we've been married a day or two, a lesson a
night for a year'll learn him more than a swift way of picking out the

coloured letters of the alphabet, and the taking of a lower number
from a higher one will be less of a strain, for him to give up the drink,
too, after a loving talk before we go to sleep for the night is far spent
an' the day is at hand when me Ma'll realise how wrong she was in
thinkin' he knew nothin' more than how to beat a roll on a drum an'
blow a few bugle-calls, after her goin' into ecstasies herself at the
concert when she heard Nicholas on the stage, an' another soldier in
the back of the gallery unseen be any, with a muted cornet playing the
Alpine Echoes with a tenderness overpowerin' to anyone having anything even approachin' a heart to feel that in love certificates for
French an' music an' freehand drawing are but little things that are
here today an' gone tomorrow, for love can give up a lot without
missin' anything as long as his heart beats true to me his love, ready
to follow after him saying Whither thou goest I will go, where thou
lodgest I will lodge, an' where thou diest will I die rather than turn an
ear to the old woman's croakin' about the risk, I'm takin' it all like the
gipsy's warning not to trust him gentle lady, though his voice be soft
an' sweet, heed him not who kneels beside thee softly pleading at thy
feet, now thy life is in its morning, cloud not this thy happy lot, to be
saying prayers an' chantin' psalms an' singin' hymns an' teaching a
crowd of chiselurs who can pick up the truth the whole truth and
nothing but the truth that the top of the map is called the north the
lower part the south the right-hand side the east and the left-hand side
the west only be having it stung into them with the constant encouragement of the cane, with a few sweet cuts added to give good measure
and to hurry them off the broad way that leadeth to destruction on to
the narrow way that leadeth to a sure an' certain way of gettin' on in
the world when they grow up into fair women and brave men whose
hearts beat happily when the music arises with its voluptuous swell an'
soft eyes speak love to eyes that speak again unto the children of Israel
that they go forward to do the thing I have to do once me mind is made
up, for with his strong arms he'll be well able to keep and protect me
from all evil and cares not like the dawny white-collared mickeys only
fit for perchin' on soft-cushioned office-stools from nine till four an'
comin' home at the end of the week with barely enough in their pockets
to help towards payin' the rent while they're lookin' forward the
whole year through towards the one decent meal they allow themselves
when the bells are ringin' in Christmas Day an' the herald angels are
singin' an' salutin' the happy morn whereon was born a Saviour who
is Christ the Lord bringin' peace on earth to every country save only
this unhappy land soaked in superstition an' ignorant of all things

belongin' to its peace, hard set in a mad race after Home Rule with Parnell at the head of the hunt hallooin' them on who ought to know better being as he is a protestant an' the only gentleman among the gang of guttersnipes he's gathered round him muckin' up the dignity an' grace of the House of Commons an' eager to undo all the fine work done durin' the past few centuries in civilisin' the wild Irish, showin' them how decent an' handsome life may be made when it gets to know the truth as it is in Christ Jesus an' protestant an' loyal activities in general, I'd say that if these Home Rule gentry got their way there wouldn't be a protestant cathedral left standing an' we'd go about all our days wallowin' in blasphemous fables an' dangerous deceits fully set forth in the Romish Mass by which the very words of our Saviour are twisted into a meaning they were never intended to have, any understandin' at all is to know that the Irish must be kept down for their own good, for if once they got the upper hand the people who matter would immediately be made unsafe in the positions they are entitled to hold under the Union Jack which is the only flag left that for a thousand years braved battle an' the breeze an' has brought joy an' security to all who live under it an' remain respectable, shown be the fact that Victoria is known as the Great White Mother by all the peoples under her sway, excludin' the Fenians cruelly callin' her the Famine Queen, but we'll never let the Fenians or the followers of Parnell be anything more than spouters at a meeting or two or singers of God Save Ireland at night in their cabins with the windows closed an' the doors shut tight, which is only fair seein' that this is a free country an' everyone has a right to his own opinions, an' trying to keep people down only makes matters worse, like the damned English with their No Irish Need Apply after the Park murders, even though it was well known that it wasn't the English protestant Cavendish the Invincibles were after but the Irish catholic Burke who was noted as a prime boyo for preventin' the people from budgin' an inch beyond a common prostration he himself thought proper be hints quietly placed in his ear from the judges an' generals of Dublin Castle puttin' mounted Constabulary on the main road of the Phoenix Park after the deed was done, an' Marwood the hangman dancin' gaily around the giant Joe Brady while his assistant was tying him up for the drop with the rope placed fair an' nice around Brady's neck an' he marchin' on, never listenin' to the priest sayin' the prayers for the dyin', but only murmurin' Poor ould Ireland, poor ould Ireland with only less than a minute left to prepare to meet his God, leavin' behind him the unfortunate Irish lookin' an' roarin' for what they know they can't

get an' traducin' themselves early an' late by their figaries on the floor
of the House of Commons, with the great Marquis of Salisbury, if it
wasn't for Parnell, well able to keep them under his thumb an' constantly laughin' at them an' shakin' his head when he heard of Fanny
Parnell wavin' a newspaper over her head an' rushin' in to her mother
to say with a cheer that Arabi, ara be jabers, Arabi Pasha had beaten
the British in Egypt, forgettin' that many of her own brave people
were sheddin' their blood to keep up England's glory in spite of all the
agents an' bailiffs an' landlords who were meetin' with a sharp an'
sudden end in followin' their lawful rights an' duties, which hardly
bears thinkin' about seein' that it might well have been my own
Nicholas who is to become one with me before tomorrow's sun sets
that had been cut clean in two by a double-handed dervish sword,
soakin' the hot sands of the desert with his blood an' his fadin' ears
full of the yells of the heathen tramplin' on his poor body, carryin' the
black flags of the Mahdi an' his hordes pourin' outa the Soudan after
puttin' the finishin' touch on General Gordon, with ould Gladstone
cuttin' down a tree under the eye of the mornin' an' warmin' his well-
slippered feet be the fire in the hush of the evenin', failin' to lift a
finger in organisin' a column to go to the relief of the men who were
fightin' their last fight for their Queen an' Country'll never forget them
and the memory of the great things done will be green for ever, from
now on I'll have to be settin' these things aside to concentrate on
things far more important than Gladstones an' Gordons who are here
today an' gone tomorrow where the good niggers go, so put up de
shovel an' de hoe for there's no more work for poor uncle Ned for he's
gone where de good niggers go, and the rest is silence as Shakespeare
says, so it behooves your humble servant to tamper only with the
change tomorrow's bound to bring about in the things I think an' the
things I do from that day forth so help me God, to measure how I'm
goin' to live on what I get an' what I give outa what I get while he's in
the army for the next year or more before his twelve years with the
colours are up an' he gets his deferred pay of twenty-one pounds to
give us a start off, with his regimental pay an' hair-cuttin' allowance
amountin' to not more than fifteen shillin's a week all told, it'll be a
tough job to keep goin' without even allowin' for common emergen-
cies that are sure to crop up while he's there an' I'm here waitin' for
tomorrow's darkness when a girl that never lifted her clothes an inch
above her ankles'll have to take them all off an' give everything she
holds dear to the man of her choice in spite of me mother for ever
pickin' at me because poor Nicholas isn't anything higher than a

drummer, as if rank mattered in any way to a true-hearted an' pure girl who truly loved a man, an' furthermore if you look at their pictures what real difference is there between Nicholas with his gay red coat on his back an' his bugle by his side an' his spiky helmet on his head an' the Prince of Wales in his grand-cut coat an' ponderous puggareed helmet, makin' him look for all the world like Achilles on the warpath standin' with a gun in his right hand an' his left foot planted firm on the dead body of a poor Bengal tiger that others shot while he was nice and snug in an embrasured howdyedo howdah high up on the back of an elephant tired of rajahin' about the jungle to give a couple of hours' excitement to men whose life's laid out for them like the way a table's laid out for high tea, an' it's high time for me now to be settin' myself to get shipshape to meet me fate for there's the bell of St. George's soundin' seven an' if I was in the country I'd hear the lark, the ploughman's clock, an' herald of the morn.

She jumped out of bed, spread the bed-clothes over the rails, and opened the window wide so that the air might flood the room, and she and her clothes might win the first freshness of the morning.

She dressed herself in an old skirt, blouse, and shoes, went into the kitchen, lighted the fire, planted a big oval pot filled with water on the fire; returned to the bedroom, and remade the bed. When the water in the big oval pot boiled, she brought from the little yard a galvanised bath, set it in the middle of the floor, poured the boiling water into it, cooled it, judging a suitable heat with the tips of her fingers. Then she stripped herself naked, stepped into the bath, and washed her body all over, pinching with pride the plumpness of her thighs and the firmness of her breasts, budding red at the tips. Her Nicholas was going to find a lot of stimulating charms in his Ella. Naked and dry, she hurried back to the bedroom, and dressed slowly, with constant self-admiration, putting on the white chemise, drawers, and petticoat, afterwards washing her teeth, rubbing them briskly with a brush sprinkled with camphorated chalk. The only one in the house who did it. She opened her mouth wide before a small looking-glass, and admired them, for they were even, white, strong, and really beautiful. Then returning to the kitchen, she emptied the soiled water from the bath, and placed the bath back on a nail in the wall beside the privy. She felt proud in her new clothes, and thought of the exciting time she'd have when Nicholas would be helping her to take them off, one be one, in readiness for the crowning of their connection after holy church had incorporated the two in one. She would give her Nicholas a good time, and, in an hour or two, all she had would be his for ever an' ever, amen.

She filled the kettle, placed it in the heart of the blazing fire, and called up her mother.

The breakfast was a chill and bitter one, Johnny alone exhilarated, spooning an egg into him in honour of the great thing that was to happen soon in God's holy temple; while Ella and her mother sat sad, busy avoiding each other's eyes, sat silent and sad at the table.

—When I'm a big man, said Johnny, I'll be a bugler, like Nicholas, so I will, and blow Reveille when the day begins an' the Last Post when the day ends.

—Tom an' Michael, in their letters, say I'm doin' well, murmured Ella.

—I hope you'll never be a soldier, said Johnny's mother; and Johnny's joy was dimmed.

When she had nibbled a little toast and drunk a little tea, Ella went to her bedroom, washed her hands and mouth to get rid of any lingering crumbs, put on her coat and hat carefully, sat down on the bed, and cried a little.

Everything would be stretchin' out in front of me fine, she thought, pitifully, if it wasn't for the mind of my mother.

She was ready for any emergency, so she was, having with her something old and something new, something borrowed and something blue, and a lucky sixpence in her shoe — everything in apple-pie order, if it wasn't for the mind of her mother.

—Here's the cab for you, she heard her mother's voice cry from the kitchen.

Ella got up quickly, came into the kitchen, and watched her mother putting back the things that had been used at their breakfast.

—Goodbye, mother, said Ella.

—Goodbye, said her mother shortly.

Something's up between them again, thought Johnny. One 'id imagine the mother 'id be proud her girl was goin' to marry a soldier. He saw Ella's lips quiver, and he felt a catch in his throat. He snatched up his cap from a chair, and went out into the street to watch the cab and to wave a fond farewell.

Ella stood watching her mother for a moment, her hand patting the hat on her head.

—Aren't you going to say something to me, before I go? she pleaded.

—You've made your bed, an' you'll have to lie on it, replied her mother.

Ella went swiftly out from her mother's presence, straight to the waiting cab. A side-glance showed her figures standing at every door intently staring at what was happening outside of O'Casside's house. Far down the street, a ragged man, with head bent and eyes fixed on the ground, was singing querulously, The Anchor's Weighed. The driver held the door of the cab open for her, and Ella, tightening her lips to show all onlookers what she was made of, climbed into the cab, telling the cabman to drive to St. Mary's Church, while Johnny waited to wave his cap in token of farewell whenever Ella waved a fond farewell to him from the window of the cab. The driver got on to his seat, caught up the reins, said Gee up, gee up, to the mare, and the cab began to move away to the sorrowful song of

> A tear fell gently from her eye,
> When last we parted on the shore;
> My bosom heav'd with many a sigh,
> To think I ne'er might see her more.

The song suddenly stopped, and the singer stooped to pick up a penny that had rattled on the pavement beside him. Then the singer started again, as the cab was passing by him, and Johnny waited, cap in hand, to wave a fond farewell to Ella.

> The anchor's weighed, the anchor's weighed,
> Farewell, farewell, remember me,

the singer sang, with his head bent and his eyes looking down at the ground.

But Ella's face did not appear at the window, nor did her well-kept hand wave a farewell to Johnny, though he watched, cap in hand, till the cab turned out of sight round the corner of the street.

And so the bride went forth to meet the bridegroom.

THE TIRED COW

JOHNNY stood in the deep of the doorway, pressing back as far as he could go, to shelter from the rain pelting from the heavens. He watched the slanting lines of rain falling on the hot street, turning the dust into a muddy confusion as rain and dust, forming a rapid stream, rushed along the gutters, gurgling over the bars of the gullies and disappearing, like a little waterfall, down into the sewers below.

It's too hot an' heavy to last, he thought, as he watched it hopping

off the pavement, and glanced at the people in the houses opposite
hurriedly closing their windows to prevent the rain from slipping into
their front rooms.

How 'ud it be, thought Johnny, if God opened the windows of
heaven, an' let it rain, rain like hell, for forty days an' forty nights, like
it did when the earth was filled with violence, an' it repented the Lord
that He hath made man, causin' a flood till the waters covered the
houses an' the highest tops of the highest mountains in the land?
There'd be a quare scatterin' an' headlong rushin' about to get a
perch on the highest places, to sit watchin' the water risin' an' risin'
till it lapped your legs, and there was nothin' left to do but to close
your eyes, say a hot prayer, slide in with a gentle slash splash, an' go
to God; though you'd hardly expect to find a word of welcome on the
mat in heaven, if God Himself had made up His mind you were better
dead. But that could never happen now, for God had promised Noah,
a just man and perfect in his generation, there'd never be anything like
a flood any more; and as proof positive, set His bow in the cloud as a
token of a covenant between Him and the earth, for Noah to see
when, sick an' sore, he crept out of the ark to start all over again with
what was left of himself an' family, with the beasts of the earth, all
creeping things, and all the fowls of the air, male an' female, that he
had carried with him all the time the flood remained over the surface
of the earth.

There was the very rainbow, now, sparklin' fine, one end restin' on
the roof of Mrs. Mullally's house, and the other end leanin' on the top
of one of the Dublin Mountains, with the centre touchin' the edge of
the firmament; an', if only our eyes were a little brighter, we'd see
millions an' millions of burnished angels standin' on it from one end
to the other, havin' a long gawk at all that was goin' on in the earth
that God made in the beginnin', an' that had to make a fresh start the
time that Noah an' his wife, an' his sons, an' his sons' wives came
outa the ark with the elephants, the lions, the horses, and the cows
that musta given Noah the milk he needed when he was shut off from
everything, till the dove came back with the olive branch stuck in her
gob.

Johnny suddenly remembered that the day was Thursday, and all
the cattle would be pouring down to the boats that carried them all to
England. He stooped down, foraged out the key from under the
weatherboard (where his mother had left it, in case he should want to
go in), opened the door, and went in. He ran through the rooms till he
found the ashplant that Archie had cut from a tree in Finglas when

he was coming back home after having had a few drinks at The Jolly Topers. With the stick held tight in his hand, Johnny locked the door, replaced the key under the weatherboard, and hurried off down the street.

The rain was softly falling now, and the shining sun had made it golden. As he turned into drowsy Dorset Street, he could hear the cries of the drovers, pitched high or pitched low, as he ran along till he came to the corner of the North Circular Road, the broad highway from the cattle-market to the boats where the cattle were shipped to England to feed the big bellies of the English, as Archie said, while the poor ignorant Irish got the leavin's. Here he loved to stand to watch the passing beasts, holding his stick ready, shooing back any one of them that tried to turn aside from the straight road, running forward, when the animal turned with a low circular move of its horned head and a frightened look in its big eyes, to give it a parting swipe on the rump as hard as he could with the ashplant.

Here they were, in their hundreds, streaming along, holding up the traffic as they slowly crossed the road, a mist of steam hanging over them as the hot sun dried the falling rain that glistened on their hides. The drovers followed behind, giving vent to occasional ritualistic cries of hi-yup hi-hee-yup, encouraging the beasts on their way to the steamier pens of the cattle-boats. The drovers had taken it that the day would be a fine one, so none wore a coat or even a sack slung around his shoulders. Their clothes were soaking wet; water trickled down their faces from dripping hats and hair, and a scowl of discomfort marred every rough and ready face as they hi-yup hi-hee-yupped after the animals. Sometimes a cow would suddenly separate itself from the drove, and stretch out its thick neck to cool its steaming nostrils and take a drink from the rain-water that gurgled along the gutters; but an angry drover would quickly pounce out, bring his stick with a bang on the cow's flank, making her jerk her head up and scurry back to the drove, boring her way forward through the other animals from the swiftly falling stick. Then a herd of pigs came moving slowly by, grunting continuously, carrying their snouts along close to the ground, the drovers prodding them viciously behind the ears, if they halted in the march onwards. The pigs were Johnny's favourites, for their backsides were more like backsides than the backsides of the cattle and sheep, and the thwack of a stick as it fell on a pig's flank, and the sharp squeal he gave when the blow fell, were far more exciting than the silent start a cow or a sheep gave whenever a blow fell on them.

Johnny was in his element, rushing here and rushing there, hi-hee-yupping the cattle on in his own way, and getting in an odd shrewd knock with his ashplant on a cow or a sheep, before the animal was quick enough to dodge out of the way of the blow.

A cow turned left to try to meander down Dorset Street, but the bold Johnny and his ashplant stood in the way. The cow tried dodging, but Johnny, side-stepping left and side-stepping right, was always in front, with left arm extended, and right waving the ashplant, while he hee-hi-hee-yupped, eh, he hee-yupped right in the animal's face. The cow lowered her head and lowed. Johnny took a few steps backward.

—Eh, there, kidger, shouted a drover from the end of the herd, don't let the bastard dodge yeh! Let him have it over the snout; go on — right over the snout. He won't puck yeh. Go on — fair over the snout!

Johnny balanced himself on his toes, and brought the ashplant down on the steaming nose of the cow. She backed hastily away, turned swiftly round and hurried back into the midst of the drove, shaking her snout.

—Good kidger, good kidger, called out the drover happily; that larrup put the fear of God into her, hi-hee hi-yup, he sang as he followed the herd, Johnny stepping into the road beside him, eager to make the pride of driving the cow back into the right way last as long as possible; while the rain, made golden by the shining sun, continued to fall softly.

Suddenly the drover let an oath out of him as a tired cow ambled over to the side-walk, folded herself up, and lay down, with her fore-legs tucked in under her, right on the path where everyone walked, carin' for nothin', an' just starin' straight in front of her, with her tightly-filled udders pressed hard against the wet pavement.

While a second drover held the rest of the herd bunched up close to the side-walk so that other cattle could pass, the drover nearer to Johnny ran over to the tired cow, and began to hammer her with his stick.

—Yeh whore's get, he shouted, slashin' away at her; get up on yer hind legs, an' waltz along to where you're goin' — he-hee-yup hi-hee-yup!

But his yellin' an' cursin' an' slashin' couldn't get a stir outa her that lay on the path where everyone walked, just starin' out in front of herself, lookin' as if she saw nothin', an' never movin', no matter how hard an' heavy the blows an' curses the drover gave.

—Eh, you there, he called to Johnny, come over here, an' give a fella a hand to get her movin'; for if she's once allowed to settle down, she'll stay well set for the night.

Johnny hurried over to where the cow was lying.

—Now, said the drover, when I twist her tail, let the bitch's ghost have it as hard as you can with the stick.

The drover gathered th' animal's tail in his hand, and twisted it round his arm, twisted it so tight that he seemed to be pullin' it outa the cow's body. A drover passing with another herd paused and ran over, and he and Johnny hammered the cow with their sticks, and the other twisted and twisted her tail till the sweat was runnin' down all their faces. The cow gave a quiver and raised herself jerkily on to her hind legs, still keeping her forelegs tucked under her.

A little crowd that had gathered, led by a gunner of the Royal Field Artillery, shooed and shouted to encourage the cow away from her need of a rest; the drover increased the tension of the twist in her tail, and Johnny and the other drover quickened the strokes of the sticks. Hee-hi heee-yuphi-hee-yup, they all cried together, but the cow slowly bent her hindquarters again, and sank down to the ground, never movin', starin' out in front of herself, an' lookin' as if she saw an' felt nothin', while the rain, made golden by the shinin' sun, still kept fallin' softly.

—All me efforts gone for nothin' — curse o' Jasus on it! said the drover, wiping the sweat from the tantalised look on his face.

His fellow-drover who was guarding the rest of the cattle waved his stick impatiently.

—Come on, for God's sake, he shouted. We can't stay here till she makes up her mind to get up an' walk. The kidger'll keep an eye on her for us.

—Keep an eye on her, sonny, said the other drover to Johnny, for fear she'd shift her quarters. We'll be back as soon as ever we've planted the others in the pens at the North Wall. And he went off to join his comrade, leaving Johnny to watch the cow starin' straight out in front of her as if she saw nothin', while the rain, made golden by the shinin' sun, still kept softly fallin'.

Johnny stood in the deep of a doorway, cautiously keeping his eye on the cow. Beyond an occasional twitch of her tail, she gave no sign of life. Every beast in the forest is God's, he thought, an' the cattle upon a thousand hills. But a sthray cow lyin' on a rain-wet street is not enough to make God bother His head to give a thought about it.

Time crept on, and soon he saw crowds of children coming home from school. Some stopped to look at the quiet cow, but Johnny warned them off, tellin' them to go on off home, an' not be disturbin' th' poor animal. The sun went down, the rain still kept fallin' softly, but it was no longer golden; and Johnny shivered. He waited an' waited for the drover, but the twilight came instead, and the vivid red colour of the cow darkened. He'd wait no longer. His mother'd be home, and she'd wondher where he was. He came out from the doorway, looked around to make sure that the drover was nowhere in sight; then he stole away towards home. At the end of the road he looked back, and, in the purple of the twilight, he saw the dark mass of the cow still lyin' on the path where everybody walked, starin' straight in front of her as if she saw nothin', while the rain still kept fallin' on her softly; but the sun had stopped her shinin', and the rain was no longer golden.

THE STREET SINGS

GOLDEN and joyous were the days for Johnny when he was free from pain; when he could lift the bandage from his eye, and find the light that hurt him hurt no longer; that the shining sun was as good today as it was when the Lord first made it; glorifying the dusty streets, and putting a new robe, like the wedding garment of the redeemed, on the dingy-fronted houses. Now he could jump into the sunlight, laugh, sing, shout, dance, and make merry in his heart, with no eye to see what he was doing, save only the eye of God, far away behind the blue sky in the daytime, and farther away still behind the golden stars of the night-time.

The pain was gone, and life was good and brave and honest and wholesome and true. No sitting down, cramped in every arm and leg at school. No whining out, now, of numbers and of words; no reading that gave no hope, or put no new thing in front for him to see; no maps that made the living world a thing of shreds an' patches; no longing for the day to hasten its slow march forward; no wearying talk of God and His davyjack, the giantkiller; — nothing but the blue sky with its white clouds by day, and the black sky with its silver stars by night; no thought but his own — and God's warning against joy a long way off from him.

Sitting on a window-sill, he could watch the women scouring their doorsteps; or, possibly, one with a little more money, painting it a bright red or a fair blue; or, in old skirts and blouses, cleaning their windows with rags and paraffin, sometimes exchanging gossip from opposite sides of the street, both busy at the windows, and never once turning to look at one another.

He loved to see the bakers' carts trotting into the street, Johnston, Mooney, and O'Brien's cart at one end, and Boland's at the other, one coloured green and the other coloured a reddish brown. The carts were big and box-like, filled with double rows of shallow trays on which rested row after row of steaming loaves, tuppence or tuppence-farthing each. Underneath a deep deep drawer, going the whole length of the cart, filled with lovely white an' brown squares, soda squares, currant squares, and crown loaves, covered with their shining golden crust, ruggedly tapering at the top, like the upper part of a king's crown. He loved, too, to watch the milk-carts come jingling into the street, filled with shining churns, having big brass taps sticking out through holes in the tailboard, all polished up to the nines; though, as Johnny's mother often said, if they were as particular with the insides as they were with the outsides, the milk'd be safer to dhrink. From these big churns the milkman filled a can with a long snout on which rattled the half-pint and pint measures used to dish out the milk as it was required to the women waiting at the doors with jugs and mugs in their hands, to buy just enough milk that would temper the bitterness of the tea they so often made for themselves, their husbands, and their children. Whenever he was fit, Johnny used to help the milkman, running around with the long-snouted can, filling half-pints and pints of milk into outstretched jugs; the women constantly grumbling that Mr. Divene always gave them a betther tilly, so he did; Johnny defending himself be saying that he had to be careful with other people's property, so he had; and then, when the work was done, with the milkman sitting on the seat, he'd stand up in the cart, gather the reins in his hands, sing out a gee-gee-up, suit his balance cutely to the jig-jog of the cart, and drive the jennet back to the dairy.

Sometimes with other kids he'd stand stiff staring hard and listening curiously to a German band, foreigners — fleecing their pennies from the poor, so Archie said — wearing their blue uniforms braided with red or green, blowing their best into their big brass bugles; while the big drummer kept time, one two, one one, one two, to the tune of a song about a German soldier on his way with his regiment to the war:

> They marched along down the village street,
> Their banners floating gay;
> The children cheered to the tramping feet,
> As they marched to the war away;

But one of them turned around
To look back once again,
Although his lips gave forth no sound,
His heart sang this refrain:

Oh, love, dear love, be true,
My heart is only thine;
When the war is o'er, we'll part no more
From Ehren on the Rhine.
Oh, love, dear love, be true,
My heart is only thine;
When the war is o'er, we'll part no more
From Ehren on the Rhine!

On special nights, Johnny would hurry off to the back gate of the grocery store; would watch and wait for his opportunity to run over to the boxes that were piled against the wall, and swiftly pilfer all the lovely coloured sheets and slips of paper that had lined or bordered the boxes, gathering, like lightning, the blue, black, crimson, yellow, and green treasures to make crimson chevrons for his sleeves or yellow epaulettes for his shoulders; a green sash to go across his breast; blue belt round his waist; and many coloured strips waving gaily from his cap. Then, armed with a home-made wooden sword, he turned himself into a warrior, a conqueror of many, bent on battle, free from terror, ready to strike at the first enemy that came near, as he strode along streaming with coloured orders presented to him by Her Majesty Queen Victoria. Whenever a chance came, he would share his treasures with a group of catholic boys, just home from school, decorating them with minor-coloured strips, changing them into soldiers, sergeants, with an ensign carrying a many-hued paper flag, and a drummer bearing on his hip a tin, veiled in strips of yellow and blue, rallying away for dear life, while the boys sang at the top of their voices,

We are ready for to fight,
We are the rovers;
We are all brave Parnell's men,
We are his gallant soldiers!

a song Johnny didn't like, for he was afraid that, in some way or another, it had a connection with the Fenians; though his mother had told him his father had said that Parnell was a great protestant, a great Irishman, and a grand man; and it was a good thing there was someone, anyway, fit to hinder the English from walking over the Irish people. When all the battles had been won; every country conquered;

the army safely home again; the decorations carefully removed, collected, and put away again, till the army was needed again, it was grand to stand in the sunny street to wonder and argue about what would be the next best thing to do.

—Let's have a go at Duck on the Grawnshee, Touhy would say, an' I'm first.

—That me neck! Kelly would cry. Let's have Fox in the Den — a far betther game.

—Ball in the Decker, would be O'Halloran's choice; the daddy of them all, he'd add, an' I'm first.

—Count me out, if it's goin' to be Ball in the Decker, said Touhy.

—An' me, if it's goin' to be Duck on the Grawnshee, grumbled Kelly.

—Let Casside choose, then, said O'Halloran; an' for the sake o' the game, we'll fall in with whatever he chooses. Hands over your hearts, an' promise yeh'll abide be whatever he says.

The catholic boys got a thrill in playing with a protestant. All the things promised by the Church to them were far away from him. They stared with interest at the look of fear and wonder that came into his face whenever he saw them crossing themselves, or heard them muttering a Hail Mary to the chime of the Angelus. And Johnny, though he liked them, thought them strange and to be pitied; for it is written, idolators shall not inherit the kingdom of God; and these comrades of his worshipped images, said prayers for the dead, which is contrary to the plain word of Scripture wherein it is written, God is not the God of the dead, but of the livin'; and again, Blessed are the dead who die in the Lord; showin' as plain as a pikestaff that if you are good, and die, you go straight up; and, if you're bad, and die, you go straight down; so that when you're once dead, prayers availeth nothin'. Then, too, they had a mortal dread of the protestant Bible, the plain word of God, easy understood, even be kidgers; if you only have faith, and don't forget to ask God to open your eyes, you'll see all you want to see, an' hear all you want to hear, and understand all you want to understand of the truth as it is in Christ Jesus. Then they thought it a great sin to miss what they called Mass on Sundays an' holy days of obligation; and they had a curious custom of sprinkling themselves with holy water to keep the devil at a safe distance. Still, they laughed the same way as he laughed; and played the same way as he played; and shared what could be bought for a penny, whenever they had a penny to spend. So here he was in the midst of his catholic comrades, singing and shouting and playing and making merry in his heart; with no eye to see, save only the eye of God that never closed, now far away behind the bright blue sky; and farther away at night, hidden behind the shine of the silver stars.

—Let's have Ball in the Decker, first, said Johnny, an' afterwards, Duck on the Grawnshee; an' I'll be last in both for the sake of the game.

Then they all laid their caps in a row at an angle against the wall of a house. They took turns, Touhy first and Johnny last, trying to roll a ball into one of the caps, the player doing his best to avoid rolling it into his own. When the ball rolled into a cap, the owner ran over to his cap, the rest scattering in flight, caught the ball up, and flung it at a boy nearest and easiest to hit. If he missed, a pebble was put in his cap, but if he hit a boy, then a pebble was put in the cap of the boy the ball had struck. The game went on till a boy had six pebbles or more (the number being decided at the beginning of the game). Then the boy with the six pebbles in his cap had to stand by the wall, and stretch out his arm, and press the back of his hand firm against the bricks. Then each boy, with a hard half-solid ball, had six shots at the outstretched hand; each aiming at hitting it as hard as he could, and enjoying the start of pain appearing on a boy's face whenever the hard ball crashed into the palm of his hand. Each boy had to go through the ordeal, the number of blows being the same as the number of pebbles in his cap. Johnny liked the ordeal; his hands were small and firm and hard, and the impact of the ball stung his hand far less than it stung the softer and larger hands of his comrades. So the game went on till they were tired, and many eyes were blinking back the tears from the smart of hands that were red, and stung fiercely.

Then followed Duck on the Grawnshee, in which a marble was placed in a slight depression, making it look like a squatting duck. Round the resting marble, a chalk circle was drawn. The boy who owned the duck on the grawnshee stood, with one foot within the chalk circle, watching the other boys who shot their marbles from the kerb, trying to knock the duck off the grawnshee. If a boy failed to knock it off, he had to gather up his marble again without letting himself be touched by the boy who was doing the duck on the grawn-shee; if he was touched by the duck, with a foot in the circle, after lifting or touching his marble, then the touched boy became the duck, and the other joined the rest who were trying to knock the duck from the grawnshee. When the marbles thrown had stopped so near the duck that the outstretched hand of the boy who guarded the grawn-shee could easily touch any who ventured to pick up a marble, the owners had to stand still, and depend on one who was a good shot to send the duck flying from the grawnshee, for when the duck was off the grawnshee the touch lost its magic, and the boys could seize their marbles and run off without danger, till the owner of the duck had replaced it on the grawnshee. So Johnny shot his marble at the duck on the grawnshee, or stood, watchful and alert, with one foot in the ring, ready to touch any boy within reach who made to get his marble lying motionless on the ground near the grawnshee; shouting, laughing as he did so, for hunger was forgotten, time had stopped, and his joy was full.

Often in the evening when the stars were still pale in the sky, the boys would see the girls skipping at the other end of the street, as many as ten or fifteen of them jumping gracefully over a regularly turning rope. The boys would slink up nearer and nearer to the skipping girls; the girls would occasionally glance disdainfully at the boys, but in their hearts they wished them to come closer. With a defiant shout, weakened with the tone of a shy shame in it, a boy, bolder than the rest, would jump in merrily; the rest would follow him, and joyous faces of boys and girls would shine out of thin dusty clouds raised out of the road by the beating of the skippers' feet dancing in the way of peace.

Tired of skipping, someone would suggest a ring; and boys and girls, their shyness gone, would join hands in a great ring, a girl, pretending to be weeping with her hands over her eyes, standing in the centre. Older people, the men smoking, the women knitting or gossiping, would stand at the doors, and watch the circling ring, singing as it circled,

Poor Jennie is aweeping, aweeping, aweeping,
Poor Jennie's aweeping on a bright Summer day.
Pray tell us what you're weeping for, aweeping for, aweeping for,
Pray tell us what you're weeping for on a bright Summer day.
I'm weeping for my lover, my lover, my lover,
I'm weeping for my lover on a bright Summer day,

the girl in the centre of the ring would answer.

Or the ring would stand still with arms held high while a player would dart in and out of the ring under the upraised arms as the circle of boys and girls sang in a metre livelier than the first tune,

In and out the window, in and out the window, in and
out the window,
As you have done before.

> Stand and face your lover, stand and face your lover,
>   stand and face your lover,
> As you have done before.

Shy, grey-eyed Jennie Clitheroe, with her curly head hanging, stood before Johnny. He wished she hadn't picked on him, for a lot in the ring knew he was gone on her, and had seen his uncovered eye often seeking her out as she sat on the seat opposite in the Sunday school; and his face went scarlet as he heard the titters of the ring.

> Chase him all round Dublin, chase him all round Dublin,
>   chase him all round Dublin,
> As you have done before.

Johnny made off round the circle of players, dodging in and out under the upraised arms, with Jennie hotfoot after him. For a while he kept well in front, then slowed down so that she could catch him, but dodging her at the last moment so that she had to fling an arm round him. Pretending to struggle, he managed to give her girlish body a sudden and affectionate pressure, releasing her at once when the ring shouted Oh, Johnny, fie for shame!

So, in a cute and gentle way, this play and these songs touched the time when the girl would long to let him kiss her with the kisses of his mouth and his banner over her would be love.

Or, best of all, when the boys had come back from school; when they had done their home lessons, and had come out into the street to get what fun they could: some of them, with suitable sticks, would start a game of hurley; others would rush away, to return with old legs of chairs, ashplants with crooked ends, walking-sticks, or a rib of a big box, pared at one end to give a grip. Opposing sides would be chosen, and the real game would start — one group striking the ball up, the other group striking the ball down the street — pushing and cursing when the game went against them; and shouting and cheering when a goal was scored. And Johnny, with his long hair growing into his eyes; his bandage thrust like a wad into his pocket; his face flushed and wet with sweat, rushed here, rushed there, swinging Archie's ashplant, cursing, shouting, cheering with the best of them, pucking the ball viciously when it came his way, slashing at any shin that came too near the ball, his own legs trickling with blood from blows received from others, feeling no pain; for alive with energy, hunger was forgotten, time had stopped, and his voice rang loud in the chorus of the song of the street.

THE PROTESTANT KID THINKS OF
THE REFORMATION

ONE fine day, when Johnny's eyes were feeling better, he waved a joyous goodbye to two youngsters who lived a few doors down, and who were now on their way to school, well braced in their little satchels carrying books and lunch.

When they had disappeared round the end of the street, he took some marbles and a butt of chalk from his pocket; with the chalk, he marked a ring near the wall of the house, right under the window, placing a row of three marbles in the centre. He then went on to the road, took a sharp step forward which brought him to the edge of the kerb, and shot a marble from his right hand, aiming at the three other marbles in the centre of the ring. The first effort failed; the second knocked two marbles out of the ring; and the third, carefully aimed, sent the last one flying.

—Gettin' surer in me shot, every day, so I am, he thought.

Suddenly, a shadow like the shadow of a monster crow fell on the space between him and the marbles in the ring, and Johnny knew that the Reverend Mr. Hunter was standing just beside him.

Johnny had checked himself from letting the marble in his hand fly at the three in the ring, and now stood, silent, at the edge of the kerb, waiting to hear the voice and the word that was in the beginning; and the word that was with God; and the word was God.

I'm very glad to see, said the voice and the word, that your eyes are very much better so that you can pass away the time pleasantly playing marbles. But playing marbles isn't everything we have to do, you know. Little boys have other things to do in the world besides playing marbles. Now and again, of course, now and again; well and good; but not always, oh, not always. A little soldier of Christ has to learn many things, besides the way to play marbles; and you are a little soldier of Christ, aren't you?

—Yessir.

—And can you tell me when you were made a little soldier of Christ, Johnny?

—At baptism, sir.

—Quite right, Johnny; quite right, my boy. Had you not attended Sunday school, you wouldn't have known that; and it's so nice to be able to answer questions asked by grown-up people, isn't it?

—Yessir, replied Johnny, feeling a little proud of himself. Hunter wasn't such a bad fella, after all.

Much nicer, very much nicer, went on the clergyman, than playing marbles, isn't it?

Johnny tensed himself. So that was it. Oul' Hunter was trying to catch him unawares. Trying to make out he was in the wrong. Oh, it wasn't fair, it wasn't fair.

—Much nicer than just playing marbles, isn't it, John?

—Don't know, sir, I'd rather be playing marbles.

—But marble-playing is just idleness, John; and hardness came into the voice of Hunter. Don't you remember what the Bible says about idleness?

—No, sir.

—It says, John, the idle soul shall suffer hunger. Think of that, suffer hunger! That's what God says through the mouth of the wisest man who ever lived. The idle soul shall suffer hunger. So you see, we all have to be very much on our guard against idleness. And the voice and the word and the man went into the house, all business.

Johnny gathered up his marbles, replaced them in his pocket, and stood leaning against the window-sill.

It was terrible the way you had to be careful of everything you said. Hunter the runter the rix stix stunter, hunter the runter the rix stix stunter, he kept on murmuring.

He peeped in at the window, and saw his mother rise to her feet from washing out the floor, to greet the rix stix stunter. Keeping close to the window, he heard what was said between them.

He heard Hunter opening the ball with, Really, Mrs. Casside, your boy must be sent to school. It is plain that his eyes are much better, and it is very distressing to think of him spending his time playing marbles, playing marbles, day after day. In a few years, he will have to take his place in life, and it is necessary that he should be made into a firm protestant young man in this dark and sorrowful roman land. You know that we are hemmed in on every side by popery; and so each of us must do all he can to preserve the privileges so hardly won by the protestant reformation.

—Black balls, hunter, murmured Johnny, hunter the runter the rix stix stunter.

—Yessir, he heard his mother say, I'll do my best to send him next week.

—Oh, not next week, said Hunter peevishly — today. Now is the accepted time, now is the day of salvation. Come, get him in, and bring him down. You can finish what you're doing when you return. Less than half an hour will do it all.

—Pig balls hunter, murmured Johnny viciously, hunter the runter the rix stix stunter.

So, with his hands and face washed and a clean collar round his neck, Johnny was lugged off to school beside his mother, with the Reverend Hunter walking a little in front.

What past-gone long-gone dog-done thing had bred this dragging of him along at the backside of this soft-hatted stiff-collared chancer to be fitted in to the life of a protestant day school? Maybe because Moses had stopped to have a gawk at the burning bush; or that the Israelites were able to make mincemeat of the Amalekites; or that the followers of Christ were first called Christians at Antioch; or, maybe, it was really because of

The Protestant Reformation

In the sixteenth century the simple and pure gospel handed down by the apostles was, without doubt, in its last gasp and ready to go bang at any minute, which, had it happened, would have deprived us of the great peace, security, and freedom that Christians enjoy at the present day. The pope, cardinals, bishops, and priests, far from following after goodness and orderly conversation, were rushing round everywhere on palfreys, jennets, mules, and chargers, looking for thrills, and jack-acting in festive season and sad season, as if they, and they only, had a special permit to shake a lot of merriment out of life. Black friars, white friars, purple-hooded monks, brown-caped priests, crimson-cassocked cardinals, and mitred abbots were eating the people out of house and home, and there wasn't a sign to be seen anywhere that heaven was any the better for the taxing and tithing that went on without let or hindrance everywhere. Rags, bones, and bottles, framed in precious stones, were carried about in holy processions, and were honoured and venerated by the mutt-massed people. The holy college of cardinals was turning out saints by steam, and there were so many of them that if a man wanted to say Pray for me to each one of them, he would have to keep going hard for ten hours a day, without a break for breakfast, dinner, or tea, and even then, according to an unquestionable ecclesiastical authority, it would take him three hundred and sixty-five thousand years to get near the end of the litany, so that there was small chance of God getting a look-in in the way of hearing Himself talked about, and praised by His people.

It was commonly reported by those who were close up to the inner circle, that, if a monk was to be kept from straddling a judy, he had to be shut up in a stone coffin, and let out only under the supervision of a hundred halberdiers while he was having a snack in the first, second, and third watches of the day, but as this guardianship of the ladies was too costly and too troublesome, the monks had it all their own way, and there wasn't a lassie in the whole wide world who didn't know a codpiece from the real thing, even when her eyes were shut and her mind wandering. And if any man made as much as a murmur, he was hit on the head with an excommunication that sent him falling headlong down to hell, without the slightest chance throughout all eternity of ever touching the bottom, with the tortures getting worse every foot he fell, and the power to feel them getting stronger every second it took to fall an inch further, while, all the time, the poor tumbling soul was flushed with the remembrance that some monk was working overtime in an enjoyment that should have been his alone.

So the poor people were worn out trying to think of a change that would bring them a little less of the next world and a little more of this, and they secretly cried to God, and their prayers must have been heard, for during this time, or thereabout, an Augustine monk stuck in the monastery of Wittenberg began to turn over the leaves of the Book of Books, the Bible, that was anchored to a big-bellied desk with a heavy chain so that the Book of Books couldn't be stolen by those unable to read or write. And this monk, who was called Luther, read and read by sunlight, moonlight, starlight, and candlelight, till he was nearly blind, and he was greatly astonished at what he read therein, for it wasn't a bit like anything he had read himself, or had heard read by anyone else, it was all so good, so bad, so reading on and reading ever, he prayed when he was puzzled, and reviewed in his mind all that had been written, and all that had been preached aforetime about the heavens and hell, the earth and all that was under the earth, the sea and all that in it is, till he got to know just where he was standing, and found out that there were differences here and differences there which wouldn't bear investigation, and had a dangerous tendency to deceive and corrupt innocent, simple, and stupid people who were anxious to serve God in spirit and in truth to the best of their ability, so long as they could get bread from heaven in a less laborious way and at a reasonable price.

So Luther thumped his breast, saying as he thumped it hard and heavy, am I right or am I wrong? And a voice so still and small, that Luther could hardly hear it, answered first out of the darkness, and then a voice answered out of the light, so loud and shrill that it nearly burst the drum of his ear, each voice sounding together though they spoke at different times, saying, Get busy, man, and teach the truth of the gospel, for out of the teaching and the truth will come swarms of fighting men, beating of drums and blowing of bugles, big guns and little guns, and great ships of war, so that red men, yellow men, and black men will become, in course of time, the white man's lawful god-fearing and most obedient batmen.

And Luther rose up like a giant refreshed, and after heart-searching and mind-searching and soul-searching, he saw clearly that the one thing the church thought of was the laying-up of a lot for a rainy day, which was repugnant to the plain words of holy scripture, thereby causing an undue delay to the great multitude of souls that waddled and squirmed and shuffled along on the road to Mandalay where the gates of heaven lay.

So Luther told the simple people that they'd simply got to give up obeying rules and regulations, and use their own judgment about whatsoever things were true, whatsoever things were honest, whatsoever things were just, whatsoever things were lovely, whatsoever things were of good report, and to decide themselves as to what things to believe, what things to say, and what things to do, using the Bible, and only the Bible, as the general store of knowledge of what was and is and is to come.

But the popes and priests opened into a full stride of opposition, and they argued with him and fought him and persecuted him and tried in every way to double-cross and crucify him, but Luther stood firm to the shock in his smock like a rock and mocked them with many words, and laughed in their raging faces, telling them that they'd have to get up early in the morning, if they wanted him to sit still and sing dumb. So Luther kept thundering out the truth as it came straight from God, and the princes and many rich merchants who lived only for the truth as it is in Christ Jesus and was in Luther, and who scorned to do a wrong thing to their neighbour, in business or out of business, rallied and tallied and dallied and sallied round the doughty reformer, and cheered him up, and told him that the Lord was a very present help in time of trouble, so that Luther believed and spit on his hands and said, Let them all come, and he was made strong and hefty in his going in and going out and in his arguments from that very hour.

Then Luther decided to let things rip, and went at it, hammer and tongs, and made short work of the traffic of indulgences, a gilt-edged superstition that let anyone do anything from pitch-and-toss to man-slaughter, so long as a suitable fee was dropped in the back pocket in the pants of a priest. And the big princes and little princes, margraves and meregraves, landgraves and landgrieves, and merchants in gold and silver and silks, and merchants in ebony and ivory and coffee and tea, drew their swords, and cheered Luther on, shouting, Go on, Martin, old boy, in the name o' God, and give them socks and cut the bowels out of them, and show them we know the Lord is our God who is gracious and merciful, and high above all nations, and prove to them that souls that are pure and simple have only to skim a few texts from the Bible to know all things, and to know how to deal justly with men present and men past and men to come, and your name will be a banner and a shout and a buckler to generations of popery-purged protestants as long as the sun shall move and the earth stand still.

Then Luther got excited, and showed, by miles and miles of documentary evidence, that the most secret sayings which puzzled archangels could be easily understood of the veriest babes and sucklings, so long as they really wanted to know what was the truth and what wasn't the truth, as it was written aforetime by the holy apostles and prophets.

But the Devil, getting anxious about his status, stirred up the hearts of the pope, cardinals, abbots, and abbesses to anger, and they made bloody war on all who were determined to follow the commandments of God in a pure and simple way, and many fierce battles were fought between the followers of God on the one hand, and the followers of Satan on the other, so that thousands on both sides were slain in an effort to keep the Christian church from perishing.

But Luther, at peace with God and himself, went on purifying and surifying and curifying and furifying the Christian faith so that the frightened red-hatted cardinals, looking out of high windows, saw the people happily going by, and saw the people looking up to see all heaven opened up to them, and the cardinals were sore afraid in their hearts. When they saw this busy traffic of true worship going on, night and day, without let or hindrance, and heard the people singing heart-to-heart honest-to-God hymns, they hastened to hide behind the curtains, and wist not what to do.

And the truth, the whole truth, and nothing but the truth, so help me God, spread like lightning, and came with a great flush and rush and gush to such as those who had nothing else to do but look for it, so that the people in millions queued up to read the Bible, with their kids, and while the parents read the Book of Books, the kids went swing-swong on the chains that bound the Bibles to the desks, so that the lives of the people began to bubble-bible up and bible-bubble over with beauty and a singular blessedness, for all their hearts were filled with peace.

And it came to pass that the anger of those who possessed not the truth was kindled against those who had it, and a great dispute arose about the word, whence it came and where it stayed and whither it went, so that each fell upon the other in a fierce fight that has lasted down to this very day. And such as were taken captive by those who had not the truth, had their right hands cut off and their noses sliced up, and were burned at the stake with their heads up; but those who had the truth showed mercy unto their captives, for they cut off their left hands only, sliced down their noses, and burned them at the stake with their heads down, so that they died more quickly.

So the reformation came wholly to England and partly to Ireland, bringing with it the Bible and a burning love of truth, love, peace, righteousness, joy, and fair dealing along straight paths and round corners. And England went from strength to strength and from power to power, having the finest army in the world, and the greatest navy in the world, and the biggest budgets in the world, and the wisest statesmen in the world, and she set out and conquered many races, taming the wild ones with love and great tact, so that red men and black men and yellow men came and ate quietly out of her hand and all these things were done that it might be fulfilled, which was spoken by the prophets about those wondrous ones who never lost their love for or steadfast faith in the Book of Books, the Bible.

A wave or two of the truth as it was in Luther splashed over Ireland, and so in process of time, The Reverend Hunter was born in protestant circumstances that made him a sky-pilot, and Johnny was born a protestant in circumstances that placed him in the position of being lugged along at the backside of this soft-hatted stiff-collared egg-headed oul' henchman of heaven, to be added to his swarm of urchins cowering and groping about in the rag-and-bone education provided by the church and state for the children of those who hadn't the wherewithal to do anything better.

Hunter, Johnny, and his mother came to the gate of the school.

—In you go, said Hunter, and, if you try hard enough to be a good boy, you'll succeed, and God will bless you.

Off the spiritual pirate toddled, and Johnny and his mother faced forward to the gloom of the doorway leading to the inner gloom of the school.

THE DREAM SCHOOL

IN the dark porch, Johnny pulled back as hard as he could from the clasping hand of his mother, and whimpered, Doctor said I must do nothing but eat well and stay in the open air.

—You might as well be here, said his mother, as to be at home, boring your eyes out looking at the pictures in the books your poor father left behind him. Besides your father would be unhappy in heaven, thinking of his little boy growing up to be nothing but a dunce.

She opened the heavy door that was like the heavy door of a prison, drew Johnny inside, and he found himself fast in the middle of fear. They went up to the desk where the Principal sat correcting the exercises of the seniors. He was a man of sixty years of age, with colourless eyes that looked furtively at everyone and everything. He had a pink bald head surrounded by a tufty halo of white hair, and his face was partly covered with mutton-chop whiskers a little less white than the pallor of his face, brought about, Johnny was told afterwards, by too much quiet whiskey drinking. He was a native Irish speaker from Connemara, and his name was Slogan. He looked up with a quick furtive glance at Johnny and his mother.

—Ah, he said, welcome to the bright little new scholar the rector told me about, as he touched the boy on the head with his thin, pale, bony, bubbly-veined hand. Don't be afraid, little boy, he went on, pulling Johnny nearer to him till his pale eyes stared into the timid eye of the boy. He snatched up a snaky-looking cane from the desk, and held it out in front of Johnny's one good eye. There now, he added, see it for yourself — it's not such a terrible thing, is it?

—Johnny's a delicate boy, murmured the mother, and must be treated gently on account of his poor eyes.

—We correct our boys only when it is necessary, said the master with a tight-lipped grin. He got up from the desk, and catching the mother's arm, he turned her towards the door. Off you go home, my good woman, and give God thanks that your boy is where he can share in what will be for his good.

The master led him over to a class that was droning out tables, and sat him down on a bench between two boys, telling him to be good, keep his eye on the teacher, and repeat with the boys what the teacher was saying.

Four 'n one are five, four 'n two are six, four 'n three are seven, four 'n four are eight, went on the singsong chorus, while Johnny's one

eye glanced dreamily at the green, brown, yellow, and purple countries
on a map of the world, with the British Possessions coloured a vivid
red, and all surrounded with the pale-blue waters of the world, as all
the children of the whole wide world murmured four 'n five are nine,
four 'n six are ten, four 'n seven are eleven in the purple, red, green,
and yellow lands that he saw all round him as he walked along murmuring four 'n eight are twelve, four 'n nine are thirteen — going along
a great white road — a road white as the driven snow — that was
banked on each side of him with daffodils as big as breakfast-cups
nodding and nodding at him as he went along the snow-white road,
and stretching their blooms to let in big black bees with crimson bands
around their bellies, and big red bees with big black bands around
their bellies, and purple butterflies with satiny black dots on the tips
of their front wings and golden-satiny dots on the tips of their back
wings, having crimson feelers sliding all over the bells of the yellow
daffodils, and green butterflies with zigzag shining deep blue decorations on their wings that were bigger than any man's hand, and had
their tips bordered with bronze, and bigger butterflies still, with front
wings white having green stars on them and hind wings green with
white stars on them, flew with all the others in and out and through the
lovely sway of the gay and golden daffodils.

The sky above was a far deeper blue than the blue on the wing of
the blue-dotted butterfly, while through the deep blue of the sky sailed
white clouds so low down that some of them shone with the reflected
gold from the blossoms of the daffodils. Many beautiful trees lined the
road that Johnny walked on, and from some came the smell of thyme
and from others the smell of cinnamon. Some of the trees bent down
with the weight of blossoms, and numbers were heavy with plums as
big as apples, and cherries bigger than the biggest of plums that hung
in hundreds on their branches, so that he ate his fill as he walked along
the white road.

Then after turning a bend he came upon a huge high gate of bronze,
and on one wing of the huge high gate of bronze were figures, in
beaten silver, of boys beating drums of gold, and on the other wing of
the huge high gate of bronze were figures, in beaten gold, of boys
blowing trumpets of silver, and over the heads of the figures of boys
blowing trumpets and beating drums was the word SCHOOL. Johnny
halted and wondered, and as he wondered, the gates slowly opened as
the figures in beaten silver beat on their drums of gold, and the figures
of beaten gold blew on their trumpets of silver.

When the gates were fully opened two boys like birds came running out with short-handled sharp-pointed spears in their hands; and they bowed down low before him, saying: Hail to the child of God and to the inheritor of the Kingdom of Heaven. Enter, that wisdom, who sitteth on the seat of the mighty, may prepare the way before thy little mind to understand all the majesty and mystery of life that now is, and of the life that is to come.

And the two boys that were like birds, with the spears in their hands, led him gently through the open gate. And when they felt that he was trembling they said to him, Let not your heart be troubled, little boy. Then they stretched out their spears in front of his eyes, and he saw that the points of the spears were made of a sweet chocolate covered cunningly with the thinnest of silver tissue. And they walked through a lovely avenue of laurestilillium covered with great trumpet-shaped flowers that were a delicate white in the morning, a ruddy gold at midday, and a deep dark crimson when the sun went down; then, through a narrower avenue of crocuaxenillium, to a tiny glade filled with the greenest of grass and newest and freshest of blossoms where, on a bank of primroses, sat a grey-bearded old josser, who asked Johnny his name and where he lived, then wrote it all down with a gold pen, having for its nib a gleaming emerald, on a great big white blackboard trimmed with jewels. Then Johnny was led away to a bath, hidden in blooming hawthorn, in which the water was lovely and hot and fully perfumed. When he had been bathed, he was rubbed smoothly with soft sweet-smelling oils till his flesh became as the flesh of a little child; and then dressed in silks as gentle as newly-risen, dewy-grown meadow grass. Then he was declared to be fit and free to wander about or play with the big or little kids who swarmed everywhere over hill, meadow, and dale.

On every little hill was a tower, and on the top of every tower was a watcher to see if any child had grown tired so that he could be made to sit down and rest in beds of moss; or if a kid was anyway hungry the watcher ordered him a slice of currant bread and jam, and each watcher had a needle ready threaded to act should a seam burst or a button fly among the frolicking children. The paths all about the place were paved with tiles of vivid colours — red, green, lemon, ultramarine, orange, and black — fashioned in divers ways. Johnny found, when he made friends with some of the kids, that very few spoke English because it was hard to learn; so they mostly spoke in Latin saying *quo vadis* when they were coming, and when they were going replying *veenie vaynay vicinity vo*. Away in the distance spreading out for miles and miles to the right and to the left were orange groves and lemon groves, and the oranges were as sweet as the sweetest sugar and the lemons had the taste of honey with a faraway sense of bitterness in them. Pear, apple, plum, and cherry trees abounded, and were so cleverly trained that the highest fruit was well within reach of the tiniest kid that was prowling about, and was steady enough to stand on the tips of his toes. Beech trees, from which swings swung, were everywhere, and, in beds of huge red strawberries, tiny babies were resting on moss in nests of bulrushes. All the kids who were running, jumping, swinging, playing tag, and those little ones lying in their bulrush-nests who happened to be awake, unified their voices as one man and sang the song, We're happy all the day long here. With canes in their hands, cheery-faced women wandered about keeping a wary eye on the kids. The guides told Johnny in Latin that these women were specially employed to lash out with the canes at any kid who missed for a single second the joy that was to be got out of the things the place provided, and so made it sure that no kid could forget for a moment that he was a member of Christ, a child of God, and an inheritor of the Kingdom of Heaven.

Hidden away in a forest of blossoms were rows of low tiny-seated privies, and between them strutted up and down hundreds of clucking, gorgeous-coloured peacocks, and over the privies were bending boughs of lovely-scented shrubs, and in the midst of these lovely-scented shrubs were multitudes of tiny birds — red, blue, purple, green, and yellow — which immediately commenced to sing in chorus and kept it up the whole time any of the kids happened to be seated on one of the privies doing his duty to himself and to mankind in general.

The sun shone for ever gently, and nothing fell from the blue sky, save little showers of pollen now and again falling from the legs of passing butterflies and bees. Rabbits with black bodies and white heads and rabbits with black heads and white bodies came out in the evening from thick clumps of purple and white heather, whose every bell was as big as a thimble, and played with the children till the moon came out.

A trumpet blew a soft call, and they all sat down to a meal of fruit and snow-white bread, cooked in china ovens, hid away in little hills, and covered with heaps of wild honey gathered the first thing in the fresh morning from the hives that the bees packed in the hollows of the bigger trees. And when the night really fell, and they were jaded enjoying themselves, they all gently lay down to sleep in beds of musk and mignonette, with an orange moon in a purple sky staring them in the face, and each corner of the heavens gay with young and jostling stars. And Johnny slept sound.

Suddenly something crawled through the musk and mignonette, and his hand was torn by a bitter pain. He shot himself up and gave vent to a loud cry. He heard the sound of laughter all around him. He shoved the bandage from his good eye, and saw the whitish eyes of the schoolmaster staring down at him. Is this the place for sleep? he asked, while Johnny stuck the burning hand into his mouth so that the moisture might lessen the sting. Is this the place for sleep? the master asked again. Yes or no, boy? No, sir, murmured Johnny.

—Hold out the left hand, said the master, and we'll put a sting into it that'll balance the pain in the right so that both together'll keep you awake for a couple of seconds.

Johnny held out his hand, and the cane came down like lightning across his palm, sending a rending pain through his brain that made him quiver. He thrust the left hand beneath the socket of his right arm, and pressed it tight to stem the pain. He bent his head in an effort to hide the tears that broke out of his eyes.

—That little flip of the palm has made tears come, said the master. He's not much of a hero, boys, is he? And the school answered the question with a titter.

Put your hands behind your back, boy, said the master. Put them behind your back, raise your head, and look at your teacher, he roared.

Johnny, with a quick glance at the reddening weals dividing both palms into two parts, put them behind his back, and gazed mournfully at the teacher.

Three-time-one are three, three-times-two are six, three-times-three are nine, three-times-four are twelve, hummed the class.

A big-limbed, broad-shouldered boy of nearly fourteen, with a bush of tawny red hair and a face like a bulldog well able to smile, who was named Georgie Middleton, had silently watched, with a snarl on his lips, everything that had passed, and was now glaring at Slogan. He was the one boy in the school whom Slogan was afraid to flog.

Slogan lingered for some minutes listening to the class droning out the lesson. Then he turned away and began to resume the teaching of his own class.

—It was a God-damned shame to hit a half-dead kid like that, said Middleton loudly as Slogan passed him by.

PAIN PARADES AGAIN

A HOT stinging pain, growing keener, then fading away, then growing keener again, flooding into an agonized throb of the brain, told Johnny that the old ulcer that had nearly healed had given place to a new one, and that he was, once again, in for many hours of agony.

This is the school, this is the result of going to school, he thought. When his eyes had got better, he couldn't resist the temptation of straining them to see what the teacher was writing on the blackboard, nor could he keep from peering into the books used in the class to see the pictures, or to try to follow what the teacher was talking about. And this was the result of it all — many nights of twisting about in bed and every minute of it streaked with pain.

The curse o' God on every school that was ever built and every teacher that was ever born! The way they maddened him, the way they talked about it. Hoity-toity haughty holy holy Hunter, with his God, is behind all pain, and He will help every brave and patient little one to bear it: and sly an' sleeky Slogan chimin' in after holy Hunter with his, It would be a very bad thing for children if they could go through their young years entirely free from pain; that if they could, there'd be no standin' them, and that, although they didn't quite know what it was, there was a purpose of some kind or another behind everything that anybody suffered: and oul' haughty hoity-toity holy Hunter goin' one better be sayin' that God sent sufferin's to try us and that if we bore them as we should bear them, uncomplainin', we'd come out of them like refined gold that had stood the test of fire, and would surely shine in the sight of all the angels of heaven, who wouldn't know how to feel pain even if they tried, and who'd have a fine laugh if they could only get a chance of seein' haughty hoity-toity holy Hunter and sly and sleeky Slogan squirmin' about on their bellies with the pain that's shootin' through me eyeballs now!

He called and called out to his mother as he tossed about in the bed, and when she heard the call, she came quickly to his side.

—It's at me again, it's at me again, Mother, he said; it's at me again, and turning on his belly, he tried to thrust his head down deep into the hard and lumpy bolster that gave his head a little lift from the level.

—Maybe you're only imaginin' it, she said softly.

—Imaginin' it, he echoed. I tell you I'm not imaginin' it, he shouted. Shows all you care about it, he added.

—We'll go to the hospital, and the drops will make you all right once more.

She soaked rags in cold water, and tied them round his temples, waited till they grew hot with the heat of the pain, took them off, and soaked them in cold water again, and bound them round his temples.

—You'll have to try to go to sleep, Johnny, she said, in a strained voice, for I have to be up at five to get Archie's breakfast before he goes to work.

—That's all you care, he moaned, that's all you care about the pain.

On she kept, removing, soaking, binding, till he lay quiet in a troubled sleep, then she sank down beside him, dozed off, ready to hear when a sleepy moan would tell her that he had wakened, and that the pain was sharp again.

The morning's light crept in through the window, shone into her barely-closed eyes; and she woke, stiff, anxious, and tired. She strained her eyes towards the old alarm clock, and saw that it was moving towards five in the morning. Stiff and tired, she got up from the bed where Johnny lay stretched, lighted the fire, put the kettle on, and sat down to wait for it to boil. When the kettle began to sing she woke up Archie, then when it boiled, she made the tea, poured out a cup for herself, and drank it in thoughtful sips.

It looked as if her last kid would go blind. Curious, the doctors wouldn't tell her what it was was wrong. If she'd a couple o' guineas to give them, they'd tell her quick enough. Hurry into the hospital, let the drops trickle into his eyes, and then hurry out again: that was the ritual. Though what good it would do her or him to know what was wrong, God only knew.

She looked at the picture of Queen Victoria, with the little crown on her grey head and the white veil falling over her neck and down her bare shoulders. Enough jewels in her little crown to keep them all for the rest of their lives, with a little left over for the poor. Crown o' jewels, crown o' thorns, an' her own boy with a crown of soakin'-wet rags to deaden the pain in his temples.

Give your boy the best of nourishment. Broth, porridge, milk, butter, an' eggs, and a few flowers, I suppose, if there was anything left over. Well, it was easy for the doctors to order things when they hadn't to pay for them.

She made Archie's breakfast, and he came out, full of sleep, quickly swallowed his tea and toast, and hurried off to the *Daily Express*, owned by a Mr. Maunsel, flourishing then as the paper of the well-to-do and all the clergy in Ireland, where he worked in the Publishing

Office from six till seven for ten shillings a week. At eight she got Johnny's breakfast ready, by cutting some slices of bread and by adding some hot water to the stewing tea. She laid two cups and saucers on the table, a sugar-bowl, half-filled with caster-sugar, a cream-jug containing a ha'porth of milk, which was very precious, for it had to sanctify all the cups of tea taken by the three of them for the day. When all this was done, she looked over at the tangled figure on the bed, at the thin worn face nearly hidden by the damp cloths round the head, sighed and murmured, well, it could have been worse — he might have been born blind, and then there would have been no hope.

She went over to the bed, and gently shook the sleeping boy's shoulder. He stretched and muttered, all right, get up in a minute.

—Hospital, Johnny, this morning, hospital, she said, shaking him a little less gently. If we're not there be half-past nine, we'll be there all day. The kettle's boilin' ready for your eyes. Come sit up at once, it's the best thing to do — makes it worse to linger.

She brought a basin half filled with steaming water to the bedside, and helped him to bathe his eyes till the lids were softened, and he could open the one that was called good. She bound the bandage over the bad one, then he dressed, sat down, and ate his breakfast. His mother heaped slack on the fire, and damped it down. She washed up the soiled breakfast things, and put Johnny's cap on his head. From a drawer she took out the ticket which admitted him as a patient to the hospital. She looked at the date, and found that the ticket had expired two days ago, and she knew that she had no sixpence just then to get it renewed. Perhaps they wouldn't notice it, though often enough the porter glanced at tickets to make sure that all paying patients were keeping their fees up to date. She'd have to chance it.

They hurried down to the end of the street, and caught a tram that brought them near to the hospital, for a penny, Johnny burying his head on his breast whenever the sun peeped out from behind grey clouds that piled themselves together in the sky. They soon found themselves sitting on the polished pitch-pine bench in the out-patients' waiting-room. Every five or ten minutes, a bell tinkled in the room where the surgeons worked, a patient near the door rose and entered for examination and treatment, while the others moved up to make room for those that had just arrived. At last, Johnny and his mother found themselves at the door waiting for the bell to tell them that the surgeon was ready to see them. She removed the bandage from his head so that he would be ready for immediate examination, for the doctors didn't like to have their time wasted. The little bell tinkled, and they went in, this time to a handsome-looking young man who had become the Resident Surgeon. The young surgeon got the nurse to bring him the details of the case, filed for reference in the hospital records. He looked at the details, then glanced at Johnny and his mother. Johnny gritted his teeth when the surgeon lifted his head to look at his eyes, for the light flowing in through the enormous windows stabbed its way into them.

—Um, murmured the young surgeon, another of them. The left eye's become a lot worse the last few days, hasn't it? he asked. And you haven't been here, now, for some weeks.

—His eyes seemed to be nearly all right, sir, and I thought he needn't come any more.

—It is for us to say whether he is to continue to come or not. For the future he is to attend the hospital till the doctor tells you that the visits may cease.

—He has to go to school, the mother murmured.

—Good God, woman, said the doctor, the boy can't go to school with his eyes in this condition. The doctor's eyes glanced at her worn-out clothes. The boy doesn't get a lot of food, does he?

—Not a lot, sir.

—Well, then, said the doctor emphatically, if he can't get the food he needs, he is to get all the air he can. Air, air, air, keep him out in the air from morning till night.

—He doesn't do anything at school, sir; just sits and listens. The rector wants him to go, and says it won't do him any harm.

—That's for me to say, and not the rector, snapped the doctor. What's your rector's name?

—The Reverend T. R. S. Hunter, sir.

The surgeon wrote rapidly on a sheet of hospital notepaper. Give this to your rector, he said, and he read out what he had written on the sheet of hospital notepaper. To the Reverend T. R. S. Hunter. I understand that you press my patient, John Casside, to go to school. The boy's eyes are too bad to be troubled with school. He must remain in the air as much as possible, in the park, in the streets — anywhere. These are my strict orders, and you must not interfere in any way with the carrying of them out by the boy's mother. R. Joyce: Surgeon. Give him that, said the doctor, holding out the letter to Johnny's mother.

She made no effort to take it from him, and murmured, Oh, I daren't give the rector that, sir.

—Why daren't you? he asked.

—He would be annoyed, and it might do harm to the boy, later on in life.

The doctor remained silent for a few moments, then he slowly tore up the letter, and dropped the pieces into a waste-paper basket beside his desk.

—I wonder what the rector will do for the boy if he goes blind — give him a letter of admission to the Blind Asylum, I suppose. He handed her the prescription, and added, Get these things at the dispensary, and bring the boy to me on Wednesday, school or no school; and he tinkled the bell to show that he was ready for another patient.

After getting the remedies prescribed, they left the hospital, got on a tram, and reached home again.

Neither had mentioned one word about school; but Johnny rejoiced silently in his heart that for a long time, maybe for ever, maybe for years and maybe for ever, there would be no more of the misery of sitting still and stiff and sleepy in the droning out of the song of the spelling and the sums.

So he swallowed his spoonful of Parrish's Food cheerily, though no kind of a dinner had gone before, and said jauntily that he believed that the new young doctor would grow up to be a very clever doctor indeed; then he stretched himself on the horsehair-covered sofa for a rest before he went out to the street; while his mother, armoured in sacking to keep the damp out, scrubbed out the floor of the room. She was singing as she scrubbed, and Johnny saw her big black eyes sparkle as she sang:

> She was lovely an' fair as a rose of the summer,
> But it was not her beauty, alone, that won me,
> Ah, no, it was truth in her eyes, ever beaming,
> That made me love Mary, the rose of Tralee!

This was a damn sight better than the song of the spelling and the sums. And Johnny lifted his voice, and sang with her:

> She was lovely an' fair as a rose of the summer,
> But it was not her beauty, alone, that won me,
> Ah, no, it was truth in her eyes, ever beaming,
> That made me love Mary, the rose of Tralee!

—Lift your voice, Ma, let it go, chanted Johnny, let the house hear.

The two of them suddenly stopped singing, and listened. A knock with the knuckles had come on the door. The knock came again. She swiftly removed the sacking, and flung it under the sofa, went to the door, opened it, and God Almighty, it was the rector.

—I've called about Johnny, he said. Mr. Slogan tells me he hasn't been at school for the last few days. That's a pity, Mrs. Casside, a great pity.

—His eyes got bad again, said the mother, nervously fiddling with the leaves of a geranium growing in a pot near the window. The doctor gave me strict injunctions that I wasn't to let him go to school.

—Doctors differ and patients die, said the rector sarcastically. If we all carried out the doctors' strict injunctions, none of us would hardly move from the fire. What will the doctor do for him in after years when he has to make his way in life, unable to read or write?

—He has to go to the hospital three days a week now, said his mother, and on those days we can never manage to get back before twelve.

—Well, he can come to school as soon as he returns from the hospital. I will get Mr. Slogan to mark him present on these mornings, on the understanding that he will attend later on, so that you have really no excuse for keeping him at home. Now, like a good woman, put his cap on, and I will leave him at the school.

Johnny's mother, after some hesitation, got the boy's cap, and silently fixed it on his head.

—You'll be very glad later on, Johnny, said the clergyman, that your pastor insisted that you should go to school, so come along, now. If your eyes pain you a lot, Mr. Slogan will let you home a little earlier than the other boys.

—They're painin' me now, grumbled Johnny, and me mother heard what the doctor said.

—You mustn't argue with your mother, said the clergyman reprovingly, for she knows much better what is good for you than you do.

Johnny went slowly out, holding Hunter's hand. At the school, Hunter raised the latch of the door, opened it, and gently pushed the boy into the school-room.

—In you go, now, he said, and be a good boy. Then he softly closed the door and went his way.

Johnny hesitated for a few moments, listening to the murmur of the boys droning over their lessons. Then he went quietly on to join in the song of the spelling and the sums.

A CHILD OF GOD

JOHNNY's left eye, ever the weaker, got better in a month or so, and he could go about the world again in a cockeyed way still wearing a heavy bandage over it.

—Now that he goes to day school, there is no real reason for keeping him from Sunday school or church, said the Reverend Mr. Hunter, stroking his long black beard that was piped here and there with silver. We mustn't let him grow up into a pagan. The sooner he gets to know something about the things that belong unto his peace, the better, Mrs. Casside. He can sit quietly, and listen to his teacher, or join in the singing of the hymns.

He put his pudgy hand on the boy's head, and patted the bandage.

—You must do what God wants you to do, John, he said, if you wish God to cure your sore eyes, or help you to bear the pain that He sends upon us all at times. Remember the little gold crown, John, that God is keeping safe for little boys who bear pain patiently, and readily do His will. You'd like to come to Sunday school and church, to be with the other boys praying to God and singing His praises, wouldn't you? And the pudgy hand patted the bandage again.

The bandaged head bent slowly down on the breast of the boy, but he did not answer.

—Of course he'd love to go, said his mother.

—Oh, let the boy speak for himself, Mrs. Casside. Wouldn't you like to come to Sunday school and church, John?

The three of them stood still waiting.

—Say yes to the Reverend Mr. Hunter, said his mother.

—Please, please, Mrs. Casside, let the boy answer for himself. Wouldn't you like to come to Sunday school and church? he asked for the third and last time.

—I don't want to go to Sunday school or church, murmured the boy.

—You shouldn't say that, Johnny, said his mother. You know you love church and Sunday school.

—Why don't you like to come to Sunday school and church? asked the man and minister. Come now, answer, John, and remember, God is listening to you.

The boy lifted his head, and looked with the unbandaged eye at the cold common face of the man, half-hidden by the black beard and the round, soft, broad-brimmed minister's hat the man was wearing.

—The doctor said I was to use me eyes as little as possible, and I don't like Sunday school or church.

—Now, now, said the man and minister, neither church nor Sunday school can hurt your eyes, and you can hardly expect God to help the doctor make your eyes well again, unless you use the Sabbath Day to keep it holy; to worship God and give Him thanks and put your whole trust in Him. My own boy and girls love the Lord's day to come so that they may go to Sunday school and church.

—Ay, said the boy suddenly, because their father's a clergyman, and they can't escape.

—He'll be at Sunday school and church on Sunday, said the woman quickly, for whatever happens, he must be kept up to his religion.

—It will help, at least, to keep him off the streets, said the man and the minister. Now let us kneel down together, before I go, and offer up a little prayer to our heavenly Father.

The woman knelt down, leaning her elbows on the seat of a chair; the boy knelt down beside her; and the minister kneeling down too, faced the opposite way, and said in a cold and common manner: Oh God, our heavenly Father, giver of all good things, give Thy blessing unto this woman and unto this boy, that she may bring him up in the knowledge and fear of the Lord; that he, in full fear of Thee, may learn in all humility to submit himself in lowly reverence to all his betters, governors, teachers, spiritual pastors, and masters, and so grow more worthy to call upon Thee for blessing and mercy. Through Jesus Christ, our Lord.

The woman murmured Amen, and the three of them got up from their knees to face the world once more.

—Good-night, Mrs. Casside, said the man and minister; I'm sure John'll be a good boy, and give no trouble to his mother. And off toddled this black-whiskered, snug-souled gollywog gospel-cook who brightened up the will of God with his own.

On the Sunday morning, dull with a heavy drizzle of rain, Johnny's grumble that the doctor said he wasn't to go to school was met by his mother telling him that in years to come, when he was looking for a job, he might be glad of the minister's recommendation — clergymen had such a pull everywhere these days. So the boy was made ready, with his bandage washed the night before, his shabby little sailor-suit well brushed to make it look braver; broken-soled boots made to gleam with the rubbing in and polishing up of Cooney's cake blacking,

his mother thrusting in cut-out cardboard soles, full of a faint faith
that these would serve to keep the wet out from his feet till he came
home again; and, finally, on his head was placed the faded velvet
sailor-cap with frayed floating ribbons, and the gold-lettered inscription, H.M.S. Condor, giving the cap a grandeur that was a little too
much for it.

—Now remember, said his mother, giving him the finishing touches,
that if the minister speaks to you, you are to be very polite and take
off your cap when he's talking to you.

—The doctor did say, Ma, that I wasn't to go to school.

—The doctor hasn't to keep you, and doesn't know that I have to
keep the minister on my hands, so whenever he asks you again do you
like to go to Sunday school and church, be sure to say, yessir.

Ma, said the boy suddenly, doesn't God know everything a boy's
thinking?

—Yes, Johnny, and even everything he thinks before he thinks it.

—And He hates boys who tell lies, doesn't he, Ma?

—He doesn't love boys who tell lies.

—Well, said the boy with resolution, if I'd 'a said I liked going to
Sunday school and church, when I didn', it 'ud been a lie, an' God 'ud
'a known it.

—You young scut, she said, giving him a slight shake, if you thry
to make fun of your mother, I'll give you a welt that you won't be the
better of for a week.

—I wasn' tryin' to make fun of you, he said.

—Hold your tongue, she answered testily; you'll have to be a lot
older before you can understand these things. And for the future,
every Sunday morning, rain or shine, off you go to Sunday school 'n
church, and the sooner you fit yourself into that fact, the better.

With Prayer Book in pocket and Bible in hand, he went off in the
drizzling rain down Dorset Street, full of a feeling he didn't know was
rage, soothing his way along with a murmur of all the curses he could
think of.

A hundred yards on his way, he felt the first soft plashing dampness
sending the message that his mother's cardboard soles had yielded to
the wet pavement, and soon at each step he took, his boots gave vent
to that sucking, plashing sound telling of cold and saturated feet, that
would go on teasing him throughout the time of hearing the Bible
read and of the singing of praises to God. Keep him out in the air as
much as possible, and keep his feet warm and dry, said the doctor;
dry 'n warm, keep his feet dry 'n warm, said the doctor. Oh God, give

me a new pair of boots, a new pair of boots. Oh God, give me a new pair of boots, he murmured as he hurried along.

—Oh God, give me a new pair of boots, jeered a voice beside him, and there was Harry Tait saunthering beside him, havin' heard, too, everything he'd been mutterin'.

—Why don't you get your ma to buy you a new pair of boots? asked Harry. I wouldn't go to Sunday school with boots like them on me, so I wouldn't, not for nuts.

—Me others is gettin' soled an' heeled, lied Johnny, for he wasn't goin' to let Tait know that what he'd on was all he had; and they haven't been sent back yet, he added, as they turned into a narrow lane that led to the chapel yard of St. Saviour's Catholic Church. They lingered to look at a number of people filling bottles from a huge butt on a stand at the southern site of the chapel.

—Fillin' their bottles with holy wather, that the priests tell them'll keep them from harm 'n broken legs 'n bein' run over, 'n dhrives away the devil squealin', who has horns out of his head 'n flames shootin' out of his mouth that's biggern the Gap o' Dunloe, 'n nails on his fingers able to tear a man's belly open at one rip.

—Us protestants don't believe in holy wather, said Johnny proudly.

—Me mother always tells me to run whenever I'm passin' a roman catholic chapel, said Tait, in case anyone of them 'ud put an eye on a protestant boy with a Bible in his hand, or a Jesuit 'ud dangle an image in front of his face.

—I'm not a bit afraid of them, said Johnny, standing deliberately to look through the arched entrances at the people hurrying into chapel, dipping their fingers into stone fonts at the entrance of the porch, and blessing themselves as they went in or came out.

—I'm not afraid neither, said Tait, only me ma says that if ever they get the power again, they'll light big big fires in the middle of all the wide streets, 'n burn, bones 'n all, all the protestants they can lay hands on, till there isn't sign or light of one of them left.

—I know a roman catholic woman, said Johnny, when she meets me always asks me how is me eyes, and one day when it was rainin' she gave me a fistful of licorice balls.

—Me ma wouldn't let me take licorice balls from a roman catholic, so she wouldn't; 'n I wouldn't play with them, for they worship images 'n pray to people no bettern ourselves; 'n they hate the Bible, 'n are always goin' about watchin' to snap it out of the hands of little protestant boys 'n girls, to tear it into ribbons as soon as they get safe round a corner.

Johnny felt the damp from the drizzling rain seeping through his threadbare trousers, and he began to walk as quick as he could towards the street where his school lay, murmuring silently to himself, Oh God, let the rain stop; please, God, let the rain stop.

—See, Tait said, as they moved on, the Bible-marker me sister made for me; scarlet, with grand gold letters on it spellin', Immanuel, that me ma says means God with us. You've none, only th' oul' text-cards the teacher gives out, 'n I give away.

—Mother's nearly finished one for me, if you want to know, replied Johnny, that'll be as good as yours, bet you.

—Copier, copier, sneered Tait.

—No, I'm not a copier, for it's green, see now.

Tait lurched viciously against him, causing one of Johnny's feet to splash into the gurgling waters of the kennel.

—You're a liar, he said, for your mother's makin' none, for cause I heard me ma sayin' you were gettin' poorer 'n poorer since your oul' fella died, 'n soon yous 'ud not get goin' to Sunday school or church, the way you'd be without boots on your feet or a stitch on your back. You're afraid to put out your tongue for fear there'd be a black mark on it, so I knew you were a liar, see now.

Tait's a head over me, thought Johnny, 'n I have a bad eye 'n the other's too sore to look long at anything, so it's the best o' me play to keep quiet 'n say nothin'.

—You're a liar, an' that's a big big sin, specially about anything that has something to do with the Bible, and again Tait lurched violently against him.

—I want to go to Sunday school, so let me alone, an' don't be pushin' me.

—I'll push you if I like, said Tait savagely, so I will. Yah, if I had your scabby eyes, I wouldn't go out at all.

Red with shame, Johnny suddenly dodged round Tait and rushed furiously down Lower Dominick Street towards the house where Sunday school was held, and as he raced along, he could hear the mocking shouts of Tait following him. Scabby eyes, scabby eyes, scabby eyes!

Panting, he pushed open the heavy door at Number Twenty-five, across which was screwed a heavy brass plate telling everyone that this house was St. Mary's National School for Boys and Girls. Crossing the wide hall, mounting the wide front staircase to the first floor, he went into the front drawing-room where the junior members of the school gathered, and sat down, with his heart beating, near the window on one of the benches forming three sides of a square. On the end uncovered by a bench, on a chair sat, full and heavy, the teacher, Miss Valentine. While waiting for others in her class to come and for the school to open, she talked to various boys and girls, asking them questions about their fathers and mothers, their sisters and brothers, but she took no notice of Johnny; oh, she never noticed Johnny, no, she never noticed Johnny.

The walls of the room were a pinkish buff splashed with inkstains (for on weekdays the room was a secular school). On the walls were many maps and a chart that told you all the things, and showed you all the things a Cow gave to Man.

Then three other boys came in, Miss Valentine shaking hands with each as he passed her; but she never noticed Johnny, oh no, she never noticed Johnny.

On the floor where his feet rested, a little pool gathered from the water that oozed out of his saturated boots. His damp trousers began to feel cold and uncomfortable where he sat on them, and he fidgeted about so that the wet part of his pants might be lifted from his legs to keep the wet from soaking into his skin. He looked long and long at the fire at the other end of the room, and longed to be nearer to it, nearer my God to thee, nearer to thee.

Tait came in, and moved airily towards the class, shaping, as the boys often said he was, because his oul' fella had a shop, with his warm topcoat, polished boots, nicely parted hair, and a face like the face of a well-fed goose. He tried to slip into his place in the class, but Miss Valentine quick as lightning beamed on him, put her arm round his neck, and kissed him on the cheek; kiss me, kiss me mother, kiss me quick. Red in the gills, Tait sat down and glared at us, 'cause we grinned at her havin' kissed him. Two or three minutes more, and in came the Reverend Mr. Hunter who went up to a little table near the fire, warmed his hands for a few moments, and then turning to us all, said, Let us pray. There was a hurried sound of many moving as all knelt down on the floor to listen to the wary hairy airy fairy dairy prayery of the bearded shepherd the leopard the rix stix steppard. He prayed that all our eyes might open to see wonderful things coming out of God's law; that we might increase in that true religion only to be found in the Bible; and that these children here present might ask only for those things which it would please God to give them. Lots of things I liked, lots of things I wanted, lots of things I longed for, little drops of water, little grains of sand made the mighty ocean and the mighty land.

When me eyes are well again I'll land one on Tait that he won't forget in a hurry. I'll crooken his jaw for him; they'll have to shut up the shop while they're plasterin' up the crack in his kisser, a crack that'll be big enough to climb in and look out again, thrust 'n parry like the South Wales Borderers in the battle of Isandlwana at the towerin' Zulus teemin' in on top of them, fightin' till the last man fell, with Melville an' Coghill cuttin' their way through the blacks, thick as bees around them, gallopin', gallopin', gallopin' away with the colours tied round their middles, sweatin' with the ceaseless slash-slash of their swords, reddenin' the black back 'n breasts of the Zulus, with their blood fallin', fallin' 'n slidin' down dead under the gallopin' horses, mad with fright, 'n furious to save the colours tied round the middles of the men fightin' for England's honour, through Jesus Christ our Lord, amen.

Oul' whiskers finishes his prayers 'n we all get up from our knees 'n slump our bottoms down on the seats again facin' our teacher 'n waitin' for her to begin.

Over Hunter comes to our class, 'n lookin' at me, says, Glad to see, John, that your mother sent you to us, 'n hurries off to his own class held in a room below.

Then the band played 'n Miss Valentine commenced to make us chew chunks outa the Bible 'n the Prayer Book. The seventh, eighth, ninth, an' tenth verses of the sixth chapter of the second epistle of St. Paul to the Corinthians. You say the seventh verse, Sammy Good. The eighth verse, Benjamin, go on, By honour and dishonour, by evil report and good report. Go on, you now, Ecret, please. As poor, yet making many rich; having nothing, yet possessing all things. Good boy; now, you, Casside, say this after me, By the word of truth, by the power of God, by the armour of righteousness on the right hand and on the left, as deceivers, and yet true; as unknown, and yet well known; as dying, and, behold, we live; as chastened, and not killed; as sorrow-ful, yet always rejoicing; as having nothing, yet possessing all things, as — when you're speaking, Casside, don't keep your teeth so close together, but open your mouth a little more. Massey you, as poor, yet making away as fast as he can goes Melville to save Queen's 'n regimental colours, gallopin', gallopin' for all he's worth, lettin' fly with his revolver till the last round's gone, with assegais flyin' over him like swallows sailin' south, an' Casside, what are you moonin' for there, you're not payin' the slightest attention, or mindin' to keep your hands still, and look at your teacher, 'n listen to what Benjamin's saying, as there are also not three incomprehensibles nor three uncreated, but one incomprehensible, and one uncreated; for you, Casside, tell us where's that taken from; the psalms, no, not the psalms, not near the psalms, nothing to do with the psalms; if you were listening you'd know the Athanasian Creed, as also there are not three incomprehensibles nor three uncreated, but one uncreated and one incomprehensible; going on to the catechism tells us that we are to keep the sabbath day holy, for in six days the Lord made heaven and earth, the sea and all that in them is, and rested on the seventh day; we mustn't play marbles or spin tops or fly kites or anything, but lying on the grass in the Phoenix Park, me an' me ma came on her, with a fella in a green corner, kissin' 'n kissin' her, while me ma was whippin' me by as fast as she could, tellin' me not to drag me feet, for Miss Valentine's legs were outstandin' again' the green of the grass 'n the black dress driven up be the gaiety of the commotion of his hand comin' closer 'n closer to closin' the school.

Johnny slid off the seat on to his feet, bent his head and clasped his hands together, while the Reverend Mr. Hunter closed the mornin's work with the blessing of God the Father, God the Son, and God the Holy Ghost, evermore, world without end, amen. Then he came over to Johnny's class and sent a smile soaring around.

—Would you mind bringing little Casside to church, he said to Miss Valentine, for fear he'd meet with any accident on his way there?

—Oh no, I don't mind in the very least, responded Miss Valentine, not in the very least, for he's a dear little boy, sir, and a dimple twinkled in her cheek.

—Hurry along as quick as you can, said Hunter, for it's pouring out of the heavens, and off he went, leaving the sign of a good growl on Miss Valentine's kisser.

—Pouring outa the heavens, she muttered, and I'm left to pull this half-blind kidger after my heels. Look here, she said, gripping Johnny's arm, you'll have to step it out, or I'll be soaked through before we get half-way there, and I've no intention to be laid up on your beautiful account.

She buttoned her ulster tightly round her body, as she looked sourly out at the rain that was pelting down heavens hard, filling Johnny with fright as he thought how wet he'd be before he reached the shelter of the church-porch in Mary Street. Miss Valentine opened her umbrella with a hasty snap, caught the boy's hand in hers, and hurried him out, saying, C'm along, now, and no nonsense.

He was pulled along at a half-gallop his spine jolting whenever he stepped from pavement to street or from street to pavement, for he couldn't see when he came to the edge of a path, and sometimes nearly fell on his face when he struck his toe against a kerb, usually followed by an angry comment from Miss Valentine to keep, at least, his good eye open, and not pull her down flat on the mucky pavement.

—The ends of my skirt'll be ruined, she grumbled, for I can't hold it up, keep my umbrella straight, and attend to you all at the same time. It's a positive shame that your mother insists on sending you to school and church, and your eyes the way they are!

The wind blew against their backs as they scuttled along, and Johnny, hot and panting with the haste, felt cool trickles of water running down his legs where the beating rain had entered through the arse of his trousers.

They ran in by the gate, trotted over a narrow concrete path between grass beds, dived into the porch where members of the congregation were taking off wet coats, gabardine ulsters, and folding up streaming umbrellas, till the floor of the poor porch was a pool and the mat at the entrance to the nave a sodden mass of fibre; while the sexton in the middle of the porch was pulling a long rope, sinking his body when he pulled and rising when he let the rope go slack, shaking the bell in the belfry into a monotonous ding-dong ding-dong ding-ding-ding-dong, as the men, women, and children passed from the dim porch into the dimmer body of the church.

—Give your feet a good wipe on the mat, warned Miss Valentine, so that you won't soil the carpet in the aisle, as she went off to her place in the choir, to help in singing loud praises to God.

Johnny rubbed and rubbed his feet on the sodden mat, trying to get some of the water from his boots that were more sodden than the mat under them; and taking off his saturated cap, with drops of rain from his hair trickling down his cheeks, he went into the church and crept quietly into a pew on the north aisle, sitting down on the edge of the seat so that his rain-soaked trousers would press the less on his legs.

Then the bell gave a last little tinkle, and late-comers hurried in, and, after bending their heads down for a second or two in silent prayer to show everybody they had made no mistake and were in the right place, settled themselves in their seats and waited for the service to begin. Massey, passing by, caught sight of Johnny, and at once turned aside, sidled into the pew, and perched himself on the seat beside him.

Oul' Hunter, and his curate, a tall thin man, came out of the vestry and moved slowly over to their places in the chancel, one to the right, the other to the left, to the piping of a tune on the organ. Both knelt in silent prayer a little longer than any member of the congregation, because, of course, they were parsons. Then the tall thin curate began murmuring in a thin tired voice, while all the congregation stood up on their hind legs, O Lord correct me, but with judgment, not in Thine anger, lest Thou bring me to nothing. Dearly beloved brethren, the scriptures moveth us in sundry places to acknowledge and confess our manifold sins and wickedness.

—How would you like to have a swing outa Hunter's whiskers? asked Massey.

Johnny said hush, and giggled, screwed up his face seriously, for he was afraid that he would laugh out loud at the picture rushing into his mind of Hunter yellin' 'n yellin' while he was swingin' outa his whiskers, swing-swong swing-swong, now we're off to London Town, safe 'n sound in Hunter's whiskers, take your seats, take your seats, please, for I wish Massey hadn' come into my pew, 'cause he'll do somethin' to make me laugh, 'n Hunter'll tell me ma about it 'n turn her against me for days, 'n I hate the hard 'n cold look comin' into her eyes when Hunter howls a complaint against me; for even when I try to make up to her she'll shake her head 'n say No, Johnny, I'm black out with you for what you done in church; now we're kneelin' down to say the general confession, all together boys, one, two, three, 'n away, I beseech you, as many as are here present, to accompany me with a pure heart 'n humble voice to the throne of His heavenly grace, saying after me, that if it hadn' been rainin' we'd ha' gone to the zoo today, but, next Sunday, me 'n me da 'n ma are goin' first thing while you are streelin' off to Sunday school to cod with the monkeys that the rest of our life hereafter may be pure and holy so that at the last you have to be snappy on accounta if you weren't quick the buggers 'ud snap a bit outa your fingers 'n you have to be careful for the keeper's always knockin' about pryin' to see what you're up to, for me da says he knew a fella was pulled for squirtin' a chew of tobacco into a monkey's eye so that he squealed out, let us worship 'n fall down 'n kneel before the Lord our maker, an' the elephant's dangerous to thrick with, always eatin' spuds 'n carrots 'n cakes just like us to sit down while oul' Hunter's readin' the lessons in his white surplice an' the tall thin curate listenin' in his white surplice with a solemn puss on him waitin' his turn to read the second lesson, for the day I grow up to be a man I'll go to sea as a skipper of a three-masted schooner with mainsail 'n foresail 'n jibsail 'n topgallants 'n I'll run up 'n run down the ratlines same as you'd run up an' down stairs standin' steady in the crow's nest when she pitches fore 'n when she pitches aft, an' I believe in the holy catholic church, the communion of saints, the forgiveness of sins and the life ever sailin' an' sailin' thousands 'n thousands of miles over blue seas 'n green seas and black seas 'n red seas, an' I'll live on islands where honey's flowin' down the trees with none to eat it 'n none to share it but meself an' there'll be birds like thrushes only red 'n bigger, 'n birds like gulls only blue 'n bigger, 'n there'll be no goin' to Sunday school or church in the mornin' or in the evenin' 'cause everyone'll be happy, for there's Hunter goin' to preach, settlin' his glasses on his nose 'n coughin' a little before startin' on his sermon, sayin' somethin' about becoming followers of the Lord having heard the word in much affliction he rambled on an' rumbled on an' gambled on an' ambled on an' scrambled on an' mummy-mummy-mumbled on an' yambled on an' yumbled on an' scrambled on an' scumbled on an' humbled on an' grumbled on an' stummy-stummy-stumbled on an' tumbled on an' fumbled on an' jumbled on an' drumbled on an' numbled on an' bummy-bummy-bumbled on, while here 'm I sittin' in the pew shiverin' cold as cold can be with me wet clothes clingin' to me back 'n stickin' to me legs.

At last the sermon ends, an' up we get on our pins to sing a hymn, fortified forth in Thy name, oh Lord, I go, my daily labour to pursue; Thee, only Thee, resolved to know, in all I think, or speak, or do, well, so I will, so help me God, to stand in me trousers without lettin' me legs touch them. Kneelin' down we get the blessin' an' then stream out down the aisles towards the door into the porch to see the rain pouring outa the heavens and peltin' off the pavement.

The congregation grumbling graciously, havin' received a blessing, button themselves into their macintoshes 'n coats before they dash out into the rain on their way home at tip-top speed. Johnny shivered, hesitated, and lingered in the porch watching the rain pourin' out of the heavens an' peltin' off the pavement, hopin' that it 'ud ease off a bit before he started to toddle home, toddling home, boys, toddling home. We give the pretty girls the wink, we drink an' laugh an' flirt an' drink, an' when the morn has dawned we think of toddling home, boys.

Tensed with the dread of the drenching the rain would give him, he closed his eyes and prayed silently, his heart full of faith in his heavenly Father: Please, O God, let the rain stop quick so that I won't get any wetter on me way home.

Again he murmured the words as slow as slow could be: Please, God Almighty, let the rain be stopped that I may go home without gettin' any wetter than I am now, amen.

He kept his eyes shut, even the one sheltered under the bandage, as tight as tight, for a long long time, then opened them again, and saw the rain pouring out of the heavens and pelting off the pavement.

The sexton came out of the church, took off his black gown and hung it on a hook in the porch, put on a heavy topcoat, pressed a bowler hat down on his head, took a bunch of keys out of his pocket with a large one hanging from the middle, looked at Johnny and at the rain pouring out of the heavens and pelting off the pavement.

—Why haven't you set off home? Why are you lingerin' here? he asked.

—I was shelterin' from the rain till it stopped a little.

—Well, Johnny, me lad, you can't stay here. I have to lock up the church, and the rain won't ease off today, so you'd better dart off and get home as quick as you can. Besides, aren't you too much of a man to be afraid of a little drop of rain? If I was a young fella like you, I'd ask nothin' better than the excitement of dashin' home through the wind an' the rain.

Then he shut one half of the heavy oaken door, and opened up his umbrella. So Johnny looked brave, smiled at the sexton, hunched his shoulders, and ran out of the porch into the rain that was pouring out of the heavens and pelting off the pavement.

Then he ran and ran till he panted and panted; ran slower and slower; ran quicker and quicker, flushed and faint and frightened; feeling the rain slashing and slashing him, seeping and soaking through his thin clothes, flowing down his back and bottom, while his bandage hung heavy round his head; water mixed with sweat ran down into his good eye, smarting it, and making him blink so that he ran into a man hurrying home out of the rain, who struck at him and cursed, and stood and cursed after him, till the running boy was out of sight, as he ran on swiftly, sobbing softly, till he at last came into his own street, came up to his own house, and kicked desperately at his own door.

His mother opened the door to him. He slid in saying, I'm all wet, Mother, drenched through 'n through with the heavy rain.

She hustled him up to the fire, changed the soaked bandage for a dry handkerchief, stripped the steaming clothes from his fevered body, rubbed his shivering legs vigorously with an old bit of sheet, till life came to him again, and warm security took the sorrow out of his sobbing.

—A nice state for you to be in after bein' gathered into the arms o' God, she said, as she dried his dreeping hair. A church that 'ud send a delicate half-starved child home to his mother in your state is round a corner 'n well outa the sight o' God; while Johnny stood naked before the fire, shivering and crying more merrily now that heat was here, and comfort and sympathy and safety.

—Every stitch on him sappin' wet, she went on, 'n here now I'll have to be wastin' the little coal I have left tryin' to get your clothes dry before the mornin' for you to wear goin' to the hospital to get your eyes looked after. Ah then, if oul' Hunter comes here before I forget the wettin' you got, I'll give him a piece of me mind about the thrue 'n everlastin' gospel of man mind thyself, for if you don't no-one else will; 'n every one of them blind to the dhrenched condition of the kid stuck in the church there helpless, forgin' colds 'n coughs in his little chest; with his tiny ears trying to take in brassbound opinions issuin' out of a mouth stanced up high in a pulpit, pittin' the laws o' God against a child lowly sittin' in a big pew, fairly frozen with the cold 'n wet, an' he frightened facin' ununderstandable things shrouded in the veil 'n value of a white surplice, that, sold second-hand, would bring in enough to keep a woman 'n her kid for the length 'n breadth of a week, without the need of a thought for the want of whatever coin 'ud buy sufficient candle to light up the idea of a prayer in the last gleam of her mind to God before she plunged away into a night's sleep.

She put him to bed and gave him hot tea to drink, and covered him up, and tucked him in. He shivered and felt cold, and coughed and fell asleep and dreamed of a green ship with red sails and a yellow flag flying from a white mast sailing on a blue sea. He woke in the night, and felt cold and shivered and coughed, and couldn't, and gasped out, and found his breath gone. He got frightened and called his mother, and called and called till she got up in her shift, and rubbed his chest, gave him hot tea, and coaxed him to try to go to sleep again; but he shivered and coughed and cried.

In the freshness of the morning he was hot and dry-skinned, hoarse as hell, with a whistling breath that came with pain and went with pain and tightness. His eyelids were stuck together with the stuff that had oozed from his eyes during the night and piled up in a crust over his lids. His mother hurried up with her other son's breakfast, and got him off to his work. Then she hurried to the publican, J. P. Farrelly, J.P., a poor-law guardian, who gave her a red ticket for the doctor; then she hurried to the dispensary where the porter told her that her sick boy alone in his bed 'ud have to take his chance, and hurry or no hurry, she'd have to take her turn with the rest of the people; and that neither he nor the doctor was at the hasty beck and call of those entitled to Poor-Law Dispensary relief.

So she waited, and moved and moved up after those in front of her, till at last she left the red ticket with the doctor demanding his attendance on one John Casside, aged eight years; then she hurried home to wait and wait for the doctor, who came in the evening, said the boy had a bad dose of bronchitis, gave her a prescription, and said if she hurried she'd just be in time to get it made up before the dispensary closed.

Fixing a bonnet on her head and throwing a shawl round her shoulders, she sallied out and ran steadfastly to the dispensary, reaching it in time to get the medicine; then she started back again, walking swift when her breath gave out, and racing when her breath came again, till she reached home with tired legs and an aching mind, to give her boy his medicine, bathe the sweat from his face and breast, settle his bed, and sit beside him till he slowly sank into a cough-disturbed slumber.

One evening some weeks later he sat by the fire, better, with an old blanket round him, and his teacher, Miss Valentine, bringing a bag of oranges, came to see him. She said how sorry they all were that Johnny hadn't been able to come to Sunday school or church; but they all hoped he would soon be back with them again; and that the Reverend Mr. Hunter sent Johnny his love, and they were all very fond of Johnny, he was such a good boy, and and they knew it wasn't his fault that he missed Sunday school and church for the last few weeks, and and and she brought Johnny a lovely scripture picture-card that was given to those who attended, and and and and she hoped it would bring Johnny's thoughts nearer to God.

So Johnny's mother said Miss Valentine was very kind, and made Johnny say Thank you; and Miss Valentine shook Johnny's hand as she went away, with Johnny's mother showing her down the stairs and opening the hall door for her.

When Johnny was alone, he moved the bandage higher up on his head, put the scripture picture-card against his good eye, peered a long time at it, and saw a big bunch of daffodils and a verse from the Bible. Spelling the words out slowly, he could not make them out, but they were these:

And the light shineth in darkness; and the darkness comprehended it not.

BATTLE ROYAL

IT all began again when Johnny got over the attack of bronchitis — the wakening in the morning, feeling the hand of his mother shaking his shoulder, and calling on him to get up, get up; the washing of his eyes, heavily caked with discharge, bathing, bathing them in water as hot as he could bear it; then the careful insertion under the lids of his bad eye of a pellet of ointment called dominus by the hospital, because it was to be used at home, home, home, sweet home, and the fire out, full of atropine to distend the pupil, and so distend and weaken the ulcer on the cornea. Then the hot and hasty swallowing of tea and dry bread, the fixing of a sixpenny satchel over his shoulder, containing a lunch of two cuts of dry bread; and his mother's last warning to him to hasten himself a little, so as not to be late for roll-call, and have Slogan complaining to Hunter, and Hunter complaining to her; the slinking into school; the opening prayer; and then the song of the spelling and the song of the sums; the play hour arriving, the rush into the muddy yard, with its few patches, near the church, of grass and clover; the sitting down on one of the grass patches to eat the two cuts of bread as it was written, He gave them bread from heaven to eat; the watching of the others playing marbles, playing cards, smoking, flogging tops, or wondering what a group of bigger boys sometimes did between two distant buttresses of the church, catching some boy and knocking him down with a lot of loud laughter, while the boy on the ground cried out when the others fiddled with his trousers; then back to the school again when Slogan's bell rang a return to the song of the spelling and the sums.

One day at play hour, Johnny wandered over to a mangy patch of grass, sat down, and began to eat his lunch. For awhile he watched the thick smoke belching from the towering chimneys of the bottle-blowing factory, watched it spread and spread till all the sky in view was hidden by its yellow murk.

The golden gleam on an angel's wing, he thought, 'ud be well tarnished, if it passed even quick through smoke as heavy as that — he'd return to heaven looking like a chimney sweep.

Then he dimly watched a group of boys with pegging-tops, tops with long, sharp steel spikes in them. They wound cords round grooves in the tops, then slung the tops with a quick jerk to the ground, holding one end of the cord in their hand so that the top spun rapidly as the cord unwound, which, with a clever thrower, made the top spin on its spike with a pleasant humming noise. The boys had made a ring with chalk on the ground, and in this ring a boy's top lay quiet on its side. Each thrower aimed at hitting the top of the ring with the spike of his own top, and, if he did, he got three blows at the boy's top with the spike of his own top; and, if he managed to split it, then his top was a conqueror of one. One boy had a top that was a conqueror of twenty others. As he looked and munched his lunch, a passing boy stopped beside him.

—What'r you doin'? he asked.

—Just sittin' here, an' eating lunch.

—You're in Foster's class, went on the boy. What's your name?

—Johnny Casside's me name.

—I've jam on me bread, said the boy. Have you any?

—No, Johnny replied, I'm tired of jam.

—Shapin', jeered the boy, tryin' to do the big. You're sayin' that because you've none.

He suddenly gave Johnny's hand a sharp slap, knocking the bread out of it on to the ground.

—See, he said, turning the bread over with the toe of his foot, it's dry, not even a scrape o' drippin' on it.

A boy, older than either, came up, glanced at Johnny, and caught the other boy by the arm.

—Come on, he said, dragging his friend away by the arm, come on, and don't talk to scabby eyes.

Johnny's eye strayed over to where a few big boys were smoking between two buttresses of the church, and he thought he saw the big-boned, tawny-headed Middleton beckoning to him. Not feeling sure, he puckered his brows together, narrowing his good eye so that he could see better and make sure that Middleton wanted him. Then he saw Middleton beckoning again, and heard him call out decisively, Eh, you there, come over here a minute, you with the bandage over your eye.

With his heart beating, Johnny got up from the grass patch, and ran over to Middleton, and stood nervously before him, while the group of boys nearby stood and stared curiously and scornfully at him. Johnny looked up at the big-mouthed, red-headed boy, who looked down at him with a wondering, but not unkindly, light in his grey eyes; while the rest stood around, big-fisted, cruel, rowdy, and cute, waiting for the big Middleton to question him.

—What's the matter with your eyes, sonny? he asked.

—Ulcers, Johnny answered.

—What's ulcers?

—Things that grow on your eyes, an' give you lots of pain.

—What sort of an old bitch must your mother be to let you come to school and your eyes the way they are?

—It's not me mother's fault, said Johnny defensively. Oul' Hunter makes her send me.

—Hunter'd dock the supply of parish coal they get, if he didn't go, sneered a stocky boy named Massey, who had yellow buck teeth and big patches on the knees of his trousers.

Georgie Middleton looked savagely at Massey, and said, I'm speakin' to him, and not you, so shut your damned mouth. There's more'n him gets parish coal.

—Massey gets it himself — I seen it goin' in, said another boy, eager to please Middleton.

—Any brothers an' sisters? asked Middleton of Johnny.

—Three, two away in the soldiers, an' one sister, said Johnny.

Massey giggled and murmured, Wonder if she's good-lookin' enough for a ride.

—He doesn't know the difference between a girl an' a boy, said a dirty-faced fellow named Ecret.

—Yes I do, answered Johnny stoutly, one wears trousers and the other doesn't.

Doesn't she? went on Ecret; just you lift up a girl's clothes, an' you'll see she wears them all right — white, with frills on the edges, an' wide at the ends so's a fella can get his hand well up.

—Ever had a look at your sister in her skin? asked Massey, grinning.

—Let's take down his trousers, an' see whether he's a boy or girl, called out bullet-headed, thick-armed Ecret, whose boots were laced with twine, badly blackened over, as he laid a threatening hand on Johnny's shoulder.

Johnny struggled to free himself, but Ecret twisted his hand in the shoulder of Johnny's coat, and held him tight. Johnny lashed out with his foot, and just scraped Ecret's shin.

—You raspy little juicy-eyed sparrow, roared Ecret savagely, for one pin I'd lay me hand hard across your snot!

—Let's see you doin' it then, said Middleton suddenly. You who're so bloody quick with your hands, let's see you doin' it, an' we'll see what'll happen.

There was a tense silence. Ecret grinned foolishly and gradually loosened his hold of Johnny. It wouldn't be worth while dirtyin' a fella's hand on him, he murmured.

—Go on, go on; don't draw back now, persisted Georgie Middleton, while the others, scenting a row, gathered closer, and listened with glistening eyes to hear what would be said between the two big boys. One of them nudged Ecret, and whispered to him, Go on, Fred, give the cheeky chiselur a crack across the snot.

Ecret sniffed, and muttered uncomfortably, Oh, I don't want to disfigure anything that Middleton chooses to make his pet.

—You're a liar, shouted Middleton savagely, he's no pet of mine! I simply called him over to answer a few questions, and you couldn't keep from butting in with your spitty prate.

Ecret moved nearer to Middleton, and glared at him resentfully.

—Who's a liar? he asked threateningly.

—You're a liar, insisted Middleton.

—How am I a liar?

—In saying he was a pet of mine.

—I didn' say he was a pet of yours.

—Yes, you did.

—I didn't; I said if he was a pet of yours — didn't I, boys? he asked, turning towards those gathered round; didn't I use the word if in what I said?

Massey moved forward with steps that dragged a little, stood beside Ecret, stiffening his lurching shoulders, and glaring at Middleton.

—I heard Ecret distinctly putting the if into what he said, an' that's two agen one, he half-shouted triumphantly.

Middleton looked fixedly at Massey for a moment, then he went close up to him, and thrusting his face close up to the other's, said warningly, If you take my advice, Massey, you'll get your interference to crawl away while I amn't lookin'.

—I'll not crawl away, nor run away neither, said Massey, with fear-tinged doggedness.

Middleton brought his head closer to the head of Massey, till their noses almost touched, his face flushed, his eyes gleaming, and his hand tremblingly clenched.

—Don't be tryin' to thrick yourself into a mighty mood, he said loudly, for when I say Ecret didn' use the word if, he didn't, see!

—An' I say I heard him usin' it, said Massey, as doggedly as before.

—You're a liar, he didn't! shouted Middleton, and with a sudden thrust forward he bumped his head sharply against the head of Massey, making him stagger back a few paces.

Johnny was hemmed in to the front by the circle of boys who had gathered to watch the dispute, and though cold and frightened, a glow of joy warmed him as he saw the head of Middleton bumping the head of Massey.

As Massey staggered back, Middleton followed him up, swiftly, and again bumped the head of Massey with his own, shouting as he did so,

You're a liar an' a double liar, for he didn' use the word *if* from start to finish!

—Eh, there, eh, whose head are you bumpin? protested Massey, pale, tense, and quivering.

—Whose head am I bumpin'? mocked Middleton, knocking Massey's head harder than ever with his own; maybe you know, now, whose head I'm bumpin'!

Suddenly Ecret shoved Massey a little to one side, and stood, surly and snarling, before the excited Middleton.

—If the whole school's afraid of you, Middleton, we're not, he said, with bitterness; an' I say, with Massey, that I did put an *if* into what I said, and the head that bumps Massey's bumps mine!

Middleton hesitated to reply to this challenge, and glared redly at the two boys before him, weighing them up, their combined strength, power, courage, and skill in a rough-and-tumble fight. His eyes wandered from one to the other as they stood defiantly there, breathing heavily, and waiting to see what he would do.

Middleton tried to quickly measure the amount of resolution behind their stand. Should he go on and frighten them, and, if they stood firm, would he be able to maul the two of them together? It was risky, and his hesitation became apparent to those gathered around. Johnny's heart had gone as cold as the water bubbling from a spring in the dead of the night.

—I can't bump two heads together at the same time, he muttered lamely.

—No difficulty in it at all, if you want to do it, said Massey, a little more boldly: bump one, and you bump the two.

Middleton knew now that if he didn't go on, he would move back from his place as the big fellow of the school. He couldn't in his heart let himself lose his grip on this sense of power that stuffed his pride with sweetness. He saw that both of the boys who were glaring at him had noticed his hesitation, and were growing bolder. He knew that they thought he was beginning to be afraid.

—Bump Massey, and you bump me, said Ecret.

—Bump Ecret, and you bump me, said Massey.

Middleton clenched his hands and bared his teeth.

—If I wanted, he said, I'd bump the two of your heads together, and I wouldn't want to take a week's holiday to get ready for it; but there was an undecided ring in the tone of his growling voice.

—Well, only let us know when you're ready to start, sneered Massey.

—An' we'll not let an'thin' get in your way, added Ecret.

A big boy chucked Middleton by the sleeve of his coat. One down, the other come on, he whispered. Take them that way, an' you'll knock the stuffin' outa them.

—I'll punch the two of you, said Middleton, taking the hint, one down, the other come on.

—You're lookin' for something soft, said Ecret, for the two of us together's hardly a right match for you, so take us together, or cry off; an' there's the coward's blow, and he gave Middleton a slight tap on the shoulder with his closed fist, as the bell carried by Slogan tinkled a warning that playtime had ended, and all were to return to the song of the spelling and the sums.

—I'll fight you both, one down, the other come on, said Middleton fiercely, baring his hard, stained teeth. That's fair, with the odds against me — isn't it, boys? he asked, turning generally to the crowd around.

—One down and the other come on, chorused a number of the boys. That's fair, an' gives the odds to them.

—There's the coward's blow back again, said Middleton, lightly striking with his closed fist, first the shoulder of Massey, and then the shoulder of Ecret.

—After school, then, on the way home, in Brady's Lane, said Ecret.

The bell was now tinkling impatiently, and all hurried back to school in a buzz of talk and a cloud of exciting wonder as to what would happen on the way home in Brady's Lane. Slogan several times glanced curiously at the boys as they hummed over their work, sensing that something was on the mat, but deliberately taking no notice of the hidden excitement shown in the tenseness of the boys. Johnny, for the first time, hoped that the hour ending school would take a long time to come. He could slip away on the way home, but he knew that he must stand by the boy who had stood up for him. There was no escape from having to watch these three fellows pounding each other's faces. He hoped that someone would come forward and make peace; or, that somehow, Slogan would hear of it, and prevent the fight. Too soon he saw the head boy of each class collecting the books, and knew that the school for that day was nearly done. The boys brought the books up to an assistant teacher who piled them back in the press, and shut and locked the door. He saw the boys returning to their places to sit down or stand up, waiting tensely for the word of dismissal. He saw the sun shining on the bald part of Slogan's head as he bent over a book, made a mark, shut it with a sharp movement, and put it aside. He saw him stand up, and give the signal for the parting prayer. There was a shuffling noise as the boys went down on their knees. Johnny heard Slogan tell some boy to fold his hands and close his eyes, and then the prayer came booming over the quiet school, asking that all done that day might sink deeply into the young innocent hearts gathered together, and bring forth fruit to the boys' good and the glory of God's holy name, Amen.

There was a loud shuffle of feet as the boys hurriedly rose from their knees, and streamed impatiently out of the school. As Johnny moved out in the crowd, he felt a hand catching his arm, and looking up, saw the flushed and anxious face of Middleton looking down at him.

—You'll hold my coat for me, sonny, he said, and watch me turning the faces of two bowseys into chunks of bleeding beef.

Johnny smiled wanly up at him and murmured, You knock hell outa the two of them, Georgie.

—You wait, he answered, you just wait.

A group of boys walked round Massey and Ecret, telling them how best Middleton was to be bayed, harried, and, finally, tired out, so that when it was plain that he had weakened enough, they could sail in and finish him off in their own good time.

—For Jasus' sake, don't let him get one home on either of you, or else you're done; fence him off, and fight cute; dodge round him just outa reach till he puffs, then dart in under his guard and give it to him fair on the solar plexus.

In Brady's Lane, a narrow gutway running between the backs of a row of little houses and a railway bank, all halted and got ready. The backyards of the houses, with the group favouring Massey and Ecret, stretched across the north end; and the railway bank, with the group favouring Middleton, stretched across the south end of the gutway, forming an oblong in which the fight was to take place. Middleton slowly and firmly removed his coat and handed it to Johnny, who slung it over his shoulder. Then Middleton unbuttoned his braces at the front, and tied them as a belt round his middle, rolled up the sleeves of his shirt, showing his grimy and knotty arms, and waited, venomous and nervous, for the fight to begin. Two big boys, one from Massey's group and one from Middleton's, took charge of the affair, to see that everything was done on the square, and to watch for fouls. Middleton's second took a step forward, and announced to the other group that Middleton was ready. Massey and Ecret were trying to settle with their second as to which of them should first tackle Middleton.

—Best for Ecret to go in first, argued Massey, 'cause he's lighter than me, an' can dodge round an' take the puff outa him.

—I say you're the best, retorted Ecret. You're heavier than me, an' if you can only manage to give him a few homers in the higher bit of his belly, I'll dance in then and put the tin hat on him.

—Eh, you there, said Middleton's second, settle who's to go in first, will you, and don't keep Middleton waitin' here till he's groggy with age.

—Here, if you can't agree, said the other second impatiently, toss for the one that's to go in first; tails for Ecret, heads for Massey; and he deftly spun a well-worn halfpenny in the air. The coin fell and showed a head. First turn for you, Massey, said the second. Massey peeled off his coat deliberately, rolled up his shirt sleeves, and rubbed his arms briskly, while Johnny prayed that the battle would go against the two boys, and that Georgie would prevail.

—Ready? asked the second.

Massey nodded.

—Ready? again asked the second, turning towards Middleton.

—Long ago, answered Middleton, with assumed carelessness.

—Go, then, shouted the second, and Johnny added softly, The arm of the Lord and of Middleton be strong in the battle today!

Middleton stood still, his right arm hanging slantwise over breast and belly, his left held crookedly out from the shoulder, watching, with gleaming eyes, the crouching movements of Massey, taking a step forward and quickly stepping back again, waiting for a good chance to spring in and strike, while Middleton stood still, watching, with gleaming eyes, every movement of Massey's.

A window in one of the houses opened, and a woman thrust out a head, covered with tousled withering hair, and looked down threateningly on the fighters.

—What are yous all up to down there? she bawled. Goin' to tear an' rip each other up, are yous? Get outa that lane, yez gang o' blaguards, and do your fightin' somewhere else!

But Middleton never took those gleaming eyes of his off the crouching movements of Massey.

—G'on, get outa that lane, roared the woman again, or I'll send a polisman down on top o' yous in double quick time! Amusin' yourselves manglin' each other. Is that the sort of gentle God-fearin' conduct yous are learnin' at school!

Massey suddenly jumped towards Middleton who made a swinging blow at the head of the jumping figure, but Massey sprang back in time, and Middleton swung around on his toes to face towards Massey again and stand still; watching, with his gleaming eyes, every stir made by the crouching, creeping Massey, while Ecret, too, stood still, and watched and gnawed his knuckles nervously.

—Looka that, looka that, said the woman from the window; if the poor boy hadda got that knock, he'd 'a had his head opened. Aha, here he is, here's the polisman comin' round the corner, now!

Middleton turned to give a swift apprehensive glance behind him, and, like lightning, Massey sprang in as his fist shot forward, and as Middleton turned his face to the front again, Massey's fist crashed on to his mouth. Then Massey sprang back out of reach, and all saw rich blood welling fast from Middleton's split lip as he grinned viciously, and silently and steadfastly watched once more.

—I'm goin' down to the street this very minute, shouted the woman at the window, to send the bobby at a gallop up to yous, an' I hope the jail'll house the whole o' yous be tomorrow mornin'! and she pulled in her head, and banged the window down.

Massey suddenly dodged nearer to Middleton, dodged back, and shot forward again, and the heavy, hard, soiled fist of Middleton went whirling over his head as he sprang back to safety.

—Careful, Massey, careful, me son, said a friend in the watching group; he very nearly got home an' heavy on you that time.

—Is this the policeman comin' round the corner? suddenly asked a boy from the group of Massey's backers.

Again Middleton turned a swift look behind him, and again Massey sprang forward; but Middleton, anticipating by instinct or cunning, swung round like a flash, shot out his fist with all the venom and power that was in him as Massey sprang forward, and all heard an agonised grunt and squeal as it cracked on Massey's jaw, who staggered back, frightened and sick, while Middleton, following him up, swung his left fist under Massey's ear, sending him crumpled up to the ground to crawl away into the crowd on his hands and knees, making a quiet moan.

Ecret, pale-faced and lip quivering, stood at the edge of his group of friends, hesitating, but they kept pushing him out towards Middleton, saying, Go on, in with you; don't leave him a second for a breather, make a dash for it, man!

But he had waited too long, for as he made a few reluctant steps forward, Middleton came towards him with a savage rush. Ecret put out his hands blindly to stem the rush; they were swept aside, and, in a flash, there appeared on Ecret's face a horrible bloody blob; agony shot into his eyes, and he reeled round; Middleton's clenched fist splashing into the blob and spreading it over the whole face till one of the blows tipped him headlong over the huddled body of his friend, Massey.

The group that had favoured Massey and Ecret shrank back against the wall of the houses, and watched Middleton standing in his shirt and trousers, with a snarling grin on his blood-dripping lips, looking down on the fallen boys.

—You're not goin' to give in as quick as all that, he said mockingly. Maybe now yous'll believe that when I say Ecret didn't use the word *if* in what he said, he didn't, see!

Two boys came over to Middleton, and took him gently and proudly by the arm, beckoning Johnny to come over with the coat he was holding.

—Put on your coat, Georgie, one of them said. It's all over, an' all the two o' them want, now, is a chance to get well — a couple of girls' spits is all they were.

A glow of joy warmed Johnny as he ran over holding out the coat which Middleton put on slowly, with silent and sure pride, gloating as long as possible over the two kneeling boys, soaking their soiled handkerchiefs in the blood that flowed from their gashed faces.

Then Johnny and his friends gathered round Middleton, one of them putting a woodbine in his mouth, lighting it while Middleton puffed slowly, holding it carelessly between his split lips, now staining the cigarette with red streaks. Then they all turned and walked high-headedly away, talking and laughing over all that had happened, leaving the two boys kneeling in the lane, soaking their handkerchiefs in the blood that flowed from their gashed faces.

VANDHERING VINDY VENDHOR

JOHNNY, Georgie Middleton, O'Halloran, Kelly, and a few others were hard at it playing hole and taw with marbles when the Jew passed by. A gadabout glazier, his back was deeply bent by the weight of a huge frame filled with sheet glass slung over his back, and kept in place by wide straps crossing his shoulders, helped by a wider one circling his waist. The Jew was short and stocky; bushy-headed, and a tiny black beard, tinged with grey, blossomed meagrely on his chin. A pair of deep black eyes stared out from a fat white face. Long locks of jet-black hair straggled down his forehead. The trousers of a shabby black suit were well frayed at the bottoms; his boots were well down at the heels; a new black bowler tightly clasped his head; his neck was rasped with a high and hard and shining white collar, set off by a gallant red, green, and yellow patterned tie. The Jew's arms were held out in front of his body to strengthen the resistance to the heavy weight on his back. His body was so much bent that the back of his head was sunk into the back of his neck to enable him to look to his front and to see any possible need for his services. The sweat was trickling down his cheeks, and glistening patches showed where it had soaked through his clothes near his armpits and the inner parts of his thighs. He walked with short steps because of the heavy pressure of the burden on his back. As he trudged along, he kept twisting his head as well as he could, now to the right, now to the left, ever on the alert for a possible job, chanting tirelessly as he marched along, Vindys to mend, to mend; vindys to mend! He kept his eyes well skinned for any window that might have been broken by a marble, a stone, a ball, or a drunken husband, as he went on chanting his Vindys to mend, to mend; vindys to mend!

The sun was shining so brilliantly on the glass in the frame that O'Halloran said the Jew seemed to be carrying on his back the remnants of the pillar of fire that led his forefathers in the journey through the wilderness.

Every ten steps, he'd give the glass-filled frame a steady hoosh up on his back, never halting in his slow strut and never breaking the lilt of his Vindys to mend, to mend; any vindys to mend!

Suddenly the Jew hopped like a bird towards a broken window in a house fifty yards down on the other side of the street; and the boys, after gathering up their marbles, hurried down to see if Mrs. Muldoon would give him the job of putting in a new one.

The Jew lingered a little before the broken window that had been replaced by a sheet of brown paper. He gradually came nearer, then with a finger poked a round hole in the paper, and, bending forward, peered into the room. Leaving the window, he came to the hall door, knocked gently, and stood patiently waiting for the door to open.

—I wouldn't care to have that weight o' glass pressin' on the top o' me arse for the length of a day, said O'Halloran, as the boys stood watching the antics of the Jew.

—One o' the lost sheep of the House of Israel, laughed Johnny.

—I never remember seein' a Jew as shabby-lookin' as that fella, murmured Middleton.

—Looka the sun shinin' on the glass, said Kelly, the shirt must be stickin' to his back.

—I betcha he hasn't got such a thing as a shirt, jeered O'Halloran; betcha again that the collar he has is only a dicky.

—An' I betcha, rejoined Kelly, that in less than a year he'll be rollin' about in a carriage an' pair.

—Damn cheek of them comin' here, said another boy, thinkin' we're not well able to mend our own bloody windows.

—Doesn't look as if we could, does it? questioned Middleton tersely. That one has been like that for the last six months.

—More, added Kelly.

—I wondher where does he come from? murmured Johnny.

—Jericho or Jerusalem, o' course, said Middleton. Where the hell d'ye think he come from? They're pourin' into every country outa Palestine in sthreams.

The Jew again knocked gently at the hall door, and stood patiently waiting for the door to open.

—He'll hardly find Mrs. Muldoon ready to hand him out a welcome, said Kelly.

—Let's go over an' give him a hand with the knockin', said O'Halloran.   .

They went over to where the Jew was patiently waiting for the door to be opened, while his gentle and deep black eyes watched them suspiciously.

—Y'ought to knock a little harder, Mr. Abraham, said Kelly; the woman of the house is a little hard o' hearin'.

—A lot harder, oh, a lot harder y'll have to knock, Mr. Isaac, echoed Johnny gleefully.

—She'll hear it only if you knock the right way, Mr. Jacob, said Georgie Middleton; like this — and catching up the knocker, he gave several terrific bangs that shook the door, and could be heard a mile away. Then he stepped back, and left the door to the Jew. The Jew stepped back too, as if he were afraid of something suddenly happening after the thundering knock at the door.

Before he had quite caught his balance, the door was whipped open and a lean, grey-haired, angry-faced woman, with a kid of two in her arms, stood glaring at him.

—Who th' hell's tryin' to knock down the door on the top of us! she yelled. What d'ye mean, she asked of the Jew, be shakin' the house down? That's no civilised way to knock at any decent person's door. The Lord-Lieutenant himself couldn't dare give a loudher knock than that.

—They'll be goin' round shortly hittin' our doors with hammers, said Middleton.

—The vindy, said the Jew mildly, the vroken vindy; I put it een for negs to nodings.

—The vroken vindy, mimicked the angry woman, hoisting the child from one arm to the other; well, if you knock again as you knocked before, you'll have a vroken door to put in as well as a vroken vindy!

—I put it een for negs to nodings, pleaded the gentle Jew, the vindy.

—Ah, for God's sake, go to hell outa that, exclaimed the indignant woman. I've something betther to do than to be spendin' time an' money ornamentin' the house for the landlord. Carry the glory of your negs to nodings somewhere else, for the hand that put the vindy out can put the vindy in again. So saying, she hoisted the child on to the other arm, turned on her heel, and shut the door, leaving the Jew gawking at the closed door, and the boys gawking at the undecided Jew.

O'Halloran went over, and touched him on the shoulder.

—You put the vindy in, mate, he said confidentially. When the lady of the house sees it shining in its proper place, she'll pay. I know Mrs. Muldoon to be a decent woman. Isn't she, boys? he asked, turning to the others.

—She's the heart of the roll! chorused the rest.

The Jew hesitated; looked at the window, at the boys, and back at the window again. His right hand hopefully fingered the buckles binding the straps holding the frame to his back.

—So help mine Godt, he said, I put the vindy in for negs to nodings, I svear.

—You go ahead, oul' son, said Middleton, and put in the vindy. Mrs. Muldoon's a woman of her word, and won't see you sthranded, once the vindy's in — will she, boys? he asked of the others.

With one voice they all repeated that Mrs. Muldoon was the heart of the roll.

—Come on, then, he added, an' give Jacob a hand to get rid of his weight.

They all crowded around the Jew, unbuckling the straps, and helping to lift the heavy frame from his back, carefully leaning it against the wall of the house. The Jew took off his shabby black coat, and began the job of putting in the window.

He took from a drawer in the lower end of the frame a hammer, chisel, pincers, and putty-knife. The boys watched him knocking out the jagged pieces of glass that still remained in the frame of the broken window. The clever white hands, a little too plump, worked swiftly, chiselling out the hard putty, and taking out the little nails that had held the old pane of glass in its place. When all had been cleaned and made ready for the new pane, the Jew took a diamond from a hip pocket, measured a sheet of glass with a square, and brought the diamond, in line with the square, along the surface of the glass with a swift, shrill, scratching sound. Replacing the diamond carefully in his hip pocket, he broke the measured piece of glass from the sheet with a clever pressing twist of his supple fingers. This pane he placed in the cleaned-out groove in the section of the window-frame, skilfully and carefully driving in the little nails to keep it steady in its place. Then rolling some putty between the palms of his hands, he deftly dabbed it along the margin of the new pane of glass, pressing it home with his fingers, and smoothing it off with his putty-knife.

A tired smile came into his tired face as he worked away.

—Ireesh boys, he said, as he pushed the putty home, are so clevair andt so kindt, better than all oder boys, I svear. I do a goot shob, he murmured, giving the finishing touches to the putty border, a goot shob for negs to nodings, negs to nodings. When the lady see de new vindy, she say goot shob, goot shob; danks.

He wiped the sweat from his face into the sleeve of his soiled shirt, replaced the tools and remains of the putty in the drawer of the frame, put on his coat, gathered the straps of the frame in his hands, bent down and gave a mighty hoist that carried the frame on to his back, buckled the straps once more, and, going over, knocked gently at the door.

—A goot shob for a goot kindt lady, he said, as he gently knocked at the door.

He heard a loud titter from the boys; and the tired smile fell away from his tired face as the door stayed shut, and no-one came in answer to his gentle knock. He went on waiting patiently, the hot sun sparkling on the glass, heavily pressing on his bent back.

The boys slunk slowly away, tittering, and stood at the corner of a street higher up, watching the Jew waiting patiently at the door that never opened. The street was lonely. The curtains in all the houses had been pulled close together, or the blinds had been pulled down to keep the burning heat of the sun from the front rooms of the houses. No-one was in the street; it was dead silent; nothing but the Jew standing pensively at the door, and the group of boys laughing and jeering at the quiet knocking, knocking at the door that never opened.

—Eh, you there, the Jew heard a voice crying out from the midst of the laughter and jeering, here's another vroken vindy, Abraham, so you may as well make a goot shob of it while your hand's in, and the lady of the house's sure to geev you negs to nodings for it!

A little flock of sparrows fluttered down from the roofs of the houses, and gathered around the feet of the waiting Jew. They had caught sight of the dried bits of putty lying on the ground, and hoped that some kindly power would turn them into crumbs of bread; so they hopped here and there, cocking an odd eye at the figure of the Jew, waiting and wondering before the tightly closed door. Suddenly they all flew off again to the roofs of the houses as a stone bounded off the pavement, striking the Jew on the calf, tearing the shabby trousers and making a little gash in the flesh of his leg. His head, sunk down in the back of the neck, turned quickly to look at the group of boys standing at the corner; but they were all innocently looking away in the opposite direction, and the sunken head turned back again to see if the door had opened.

Another stone shot off the pavement close to where the Jew was standing. He turned slowly to give a wistful look at the boys; turned his head back to look at the door, gave a long look at the mended window, started to walk away, hesitated, and half turned to go back to the door, hesitated again; then slowly set off down the deserted street, his body bent far down by the weight of the huge frame, filled with glass, that he carried on his back; his arms stretched out in front of him to stiffen the resistance to the weight; the back of his head sunk deep into the back of his neck so that he could see where he was going, still chanting peacefully as he trudged along, Vindys to mend, to mend; any vindys to mend!

A loud cheer broke from the group of boys gathered at the corner, as they saw the Jew go.

CRIME AND PUNISHMENT

WITHOUT his usual cut of bread for lunch that day Johnny sat on a mangy clump of grass watching, with his good eye, Georgie Middleton and a group of cronies sitting between two church buttresses, playing cards, smoking fags, and arguing vigorously. He looked, came nearer; and Middleton lifted his head, and smiled.

—Come over here, and stand near me for luck, he said to Johnny.

Johnny came nearer, a little shyly, leaned a hand on Georgie's shoulder, and watched the play. They were playing twenty-fives for a penny a game and a ha'penny for the best trump out each deal. After every sixth game a boy took his turn for the following six games to stand aside and keep watch in case they should be suddenly surprised by oul' Slogan coming upon them unawares. Massey was now watching, and impatiently waiting for the six games to pass so that he could get back to the sport again. The cards were dealt, the tricks played and gathered, and Middleton won. Again the cards were dealt, given out, the tricks played and gathered, and again Middleton won.

—That's the third game for me, hand-runnin', said Middleton delightedly. Look alive, Ecret, and deal while the luck's my way.

—I'll deal, ejaculated Massey. That's the sixth game, now, and it's Ecret's turn to stand and keep nix.

—It's only the fifth, responded Ecret, there's another game to go yet.

—Sixth, I tell you, persisted Massey; didn't I count them carefully? So up with you off your hunkers, and take my place here.

—I tell you it's only the fifth game, growled Ecret, as he shuffled the cards.

—Sixth, sixth, sixth, repeated Massey impatiently, and he stretched over to take the pack of cards from Ecret's hands.

—No blasted bickerin', now, while I'm winnin', said Middleton testily.

—But fair's fair, grumbled Massey. I've watched here through the six games; and, accordin' to rules, it's Ecret's turn to take my place and keep nix for the crowd.

—Sit down then, snapped Middleton, eager to get another penny in the pool while he was winning; sit down, if you want a hand so badly, and Johnny, here, will keep nix for us all. He looked up at Johnny, and added, Make yourself useful, Johnny, be keepin' your good eye well peeled, an' if you see oul' balls Slogan turning the corner, give us the tip so that we'll all be talkin' about David watchin' Bathsheba havin' her bath, before he comes close.

Johnny became almost ill with fear that he wouldn't see Slogan quick enough, if he came round the corner. He hadn't the courage to say that his eye wasn't good enough; so he strained this one eye open, and stared fixedly at the corner round which Slogan would probably come, if he came at all. He prayed that he would not come, and that the bell would shortly be heard proclaiming that the time for cards was past, and that all must return to the song of the spelling and the sums.

—Somebody shy in the pool, said Middleton; only ninepence in it, so there's a wing missin' — who's shy?

—I am, said Massey, who was dealing the cards. When he had given them out, he added a penny to the pool. Ecret's lead, and spades is trumps, he added, peering expectantly into his hand.

They led and trumped and took their tricks; shuffled and cut and led and trumped and took their tricks, while Johnny stared and stared at the corner round which danger might come, and longed and longed for the warning bell to ring.

Suddenly there shot into his eyes a pain like the piercing of many needles, flooding into an agony that shocked his brain and flashed a glare of crimson light before him that made him clench his teeth and press his lids tight together till a stream of scalding evil tears forced their way between them, and ran hotly down his cheeks. Then he felt himself jerked back by the shoulders, and heard the sound of scrambling feet. When the pain subsided, he opened the good eye, and saw Slogan taking up the money in the pool, and gathering the cards, with a scowl on his face; while the group of boys looked on, embarrassed and silent. When Slogan had gathered up all the money and the cards, without speaking a word, he left them standing there, awkward and resentful.

Middleton turned savagely on Johnny.

—How the hell did you manage to let him sail down on the top of us like that? he snarled, but Johnny, burning with shame and shaking with sensitive fear, gave out no answer.

—Caught us all, like a lot of shaggy sheep, muttered Massey.

Middleton turned and struck Johnny sharply across the mouth with the back of his hand, making the boy's lip bleed, as he shouted, You half-blind, sappy-lidded, dead-in-the-head dummy, you couldn't keep your eyes skinned for a minute or two an' save the few bob we were bettin' from buyin' Bibles for the heathen buggers of Bengal!

—Caught us all, like a lot of shaggy sheep, muttered Massey.

Middleton gave Johnny a vicious shove that sent him reeling.

—Away, for Christ's sake outa me sight, you hand-gropin' pig's-eye-in-a-bottle, you!

The others laughed loud, crowded round Johnny, pushed and pinched him, as he turned and walked slowly away from them.

Turning the corner, he heard Slogan belling the end of the play-hour; and, passing the master, he entered the schoolroom, sat down in his place, and screwed his good eye into a lesson book, while his heart thumped in his breast. The boys poured into the school, and his classmates sat down beside him, whispering excitedly about all that had happened.

Suddenly the hum of the school was hushed, for Slogan, standing at his desk at the upper end of the room, was ringing his bell, and all the boys, save Johnny, knew that when the bell was rung from that place some very important thing was about to be said by the master. All that were in the school heard the master's voice coming out of the stillness, with a dull tone of joy in it, like the quavering notes of a sickening bird.

—As I was walking about the playground today — prowling about, I think you all call it—I caught a number of our more respectable boys deep in a very sinful pastime, a pastime that we can safely associate only with papist corner-boys; to wit too-whoo videlicet, card-playing, and gambling like good ones in this game with the devil's prayer book, forgetful that they were protestant boys baptised in the brine of the Boyne water giving them a great responsibility to behave blameless before God and man and roman catholics, who are always on the alert to exaggerate any little indiscretion that respectable protestant boys may commit. In the first feeling of righteous indignation that came over me, I was going to make an example of every boy connected with this sin by giving each a sound and thorough whaling; but instead of that, I will leave it to their conscience to punish them more than a firm application of the cane could. But there is a certain boy mixed up with it whom no-one would think, at the first go, could be connected with the card-gambling, and this boy must be punished; and I am going to punish this boy now, and punish him well. I am going to punish him in such a way that he will think twice before he indulges in the vice again. This brave little fellow, on whom I'm going to test the valour of my cane, was on the *qui vive* so that the card-school wouldn't be disturbed by the bold bad teacher, but this brave little boy didn't watch well enough. He fell asleep at his post, and in a few minutes he is going to feel very sorry that he didn't keep a better Spartan watch and ward. That little boy's mother is a widow, so he has no father to take care of him; and it is meet, right, and my bounden duty to do everything possible to make sure that no bad tendencies are allowed to creep into the nature of the widow's little son. And when I have reddened his backside with this cane, I'm sure he'll be a better and more careful little boy for a long time to come, and run a mile away from a card whenever he sees one. He swished the cane through the air, and grinningly asked the school, Who was he who said, spare the rod and spoil the child, boys?

—Solomon, sir, Solomon, sir, shouted a dozen of the boys.

—And in what part of the Bible do we read that counsel?

—Proverbs, chapter thirteen, verse twenty-four, shouted a dozen of the boys.

—And what are the exact words, boys?

There was a dead silence, and only one boy held up his hand.

—Well, Ecret, my boy, tell the dunces the exact words used by the wise man, Solomon, when he advises us to deal in a bright way with bold boys.

—He that spareth his rod hateth his son, sang out Ecret, with his head up.

—And wasn't Solomon inspired of God? asked Slogan.

—Yessir, responded the school.

—How do we prove that? questioned the master.

The school was silent.

—All Holy Scripture is inspired of God, said Slogan, and the Book of Proverbs is part of Holy Scripture, and chapter thirteen and verse twenty-four is part of the Book of Proverbs; ergo, the counsel in the verse, he that spareth his rod hateth his son, is holy and inspired of God without a possible doubt. So, boys, wouldn't it be very sinful of me to neglect or despise the teaching inspired of God, seeing that I stand in loco parentis to you all, and particularly to the widow's little son, brave little Johnny Casside?

—Yessir, Yessir, responded the whole school, all save only Georgie Middleton, for Johnny saw that his head hung down, and that he took no part in what was going on between the boys and their master.

—The ayes have it, said Slogan, nodding brightly towards the boys; so come along, Johnny, come along up here to me, my son, till I pay you the attention counselled of God, which will be painful, but which will, ultimately, add a lot to your moral and, I hope, spiritual progress.

—Slogan's callin' y'up, whispered a boy on Johnny's right; wants to biff you for playin' cards durin' playhour, so he does. But Johnny cowered his head down to the desk, and made no offer to stir.

—Eh, there, said a boy to his left, nudging him in the side, d'ye hear? He's callin' you. Y'are to g'up to him — d'ye hear?

—Come along, boy, said Slogan, down to Johnny; come along, and get it over. But Johnny hung his head towards the desk, and made no offer to stir.

—He hesitates, said Slogan. Thus conscience doth make cowards of us all; and thus the native hue of resolution is sicklied o'er with the pale cast of thought. Come on, come up here.

—He's not makin' a single move to stir, sir, said the boy on Johnny's left.

—Come on, come up, come up, come on, chirruped the master. Remember what your godfathers and godmothers promised for you — to submit yourself lowly and reverently to all your governors, teachers, spiritual pastors, and masters; so up you come; and in later years you'll rejoice when you remember the caning a good master gave you. Then he looked down at Johnny, and went on in a voice of quiet and steady sternness: Are you going to come up quietly, boy, to take your medicine, or must I go down, and wallop you up to me?

Johnny slowly and fearfully climbed out of the desk, and taking as many steps as possible, came towards Slogan, his heart thumping hard, and the sweat breaking out all over his forehead. He felt that Slogan wanted to beat away on him the fear that made him afraid to lay a hand on the other and bigger boys; for he had heard Middleton, Massey, and Ecret say that if Slogan ever tried any thrick of caning them, they'd open his bald skull with a slate. He halted a little distance away from the master, just out of reach of the cane.

—A little nearer, a little nearer, boy, purred Slogan; you've got to get it, so make up your mind to take it like a little Spartan. Tell me, boy, what's a Spartan? He doesn't know what a Spartan is, grinned Slogan, turning towards the school. Well, Spartans lived a long time ago in Greece, and were famous for bearing pain without a murmur. In Sparta every little boy, whether good or bad, was continually caned to make him hardy. So just shut your mouth, close your eyes, take your caning calmly, and all the school will look upon you as a little Spartan. I see your britches are a little threadbare, but that will make it all the more exciting for you. Now all we want are two strong and willing boys to come up here and stand ready to hold you down, if you squirm too much, so that you can get the full benefit of a kindly, if stern, Christian castigation. Whom shall I choose for the honour? And Slogan looked slowly and lovingly at the tense figures sitting in bunched-up lines in the yellow wooden desks.

—Will I do, sir? called out Massey, popping up his hand to attract the master's attention.

—You, Massey, said the master, will do nicely for one. You're pretty strong; and, if the need arises, I'm sure you will do your duty. Now, just one more. The biggest boy in the school ought to have the honour of holding the bold boy down — you, Georgie, come along here, and help.

Middleton's face reddened as he bent his head down to the desk and muttered, I'd rather not, sir.

Slogan put a hand behind a less-deaf ear, bent forward sideways, and said, Eh?

Middleton, keeping his head bent, raised his voice and said doggedly, I'd rather not, sir. I want no hand in any boy's batterin'; an' besides, the kid's too delicate to touch.

Slogan went white to the gills.

—Middleton, he said, with quiet bitterness, you had better learn to give an opinion only when your master asks for one.

Middleton suddenly stood up, and a dirty, dog-like scowl lined his harsh face as he pressed his soiled hands on the top of the desk so hard that the knuckles whitened.

—The kid had nothing to do with it, he rasped out; it was me and the others. He didn' play, an' doesn't know how, an' he kep' nix because we made him.

A deep silence spread over the whole school.

—Georgie Middleton, said Slogan, in a dead level voice, glancing over the whole school with his shallow eyes, will be leaving us all in a month or two to go out and fight his way in the world, and I'm sure we all wish him the best of luck. He is to try for a job in a big store where the manager wishes to give a start to a boy who has just left school. Mr. Middleton has asked our rector to give Georgie a character, and the rector has asked me for a general report of his conduct here. If Georgie wants to get on in the world with the help of a good start, I'd advise him to be careful to make his master think well of him. Am I right, Georgie Middleton? asked Slogan, now fixing his eyes on the head-bent boy.

Middleton fought his fear for a moment, then the whole school heard him murmur, Yessir, as he sank into his seat, shocked into the feeling that dangers flooded the way of an open courage.

—And don't you think, Georgie, that this boy here should be punished for his own sake? went on the master. There was a pause, and then the whole school heard the murmur of Yessir from the mouth of Middleton.

—Come along up here, then, said Slogan, and stand ready to help as soon as I need you. And Middleton, pale, and a little sick with shame, slouched up; and, sullen and bitterminded, stood near the radiant, iron-bowelled, ratty-hearted master, who put his hand out and patted Georgie's shoulder.

—You're a good boy, Georgie, he said, for you have had the manliness to acknowledge an error which many of us might very well hesitate to do; and there is more joy in heaven over one sinner that repenteth than over ninety and nine that need no repentance. And now, he went on, gripping Johnny by the collar of his coat, we start to cane a little conscience and a lot of caution into the soul of a wilful little boy.

Johnny shook when he felt the grip on his shoulder, and his stomach went a little sick with the foreknowledge of the pain that was to come upon him.

—Me mother said I wasn't to be touched because me eyes are bad, he said hurriedly and imploringly. Don't beat me, and I'll promise I'll never do the like again. Then he felt the searing sting of the cane across his thighs, and he screamed and tore at the master with his little hands, twisted his body and lashed out with his feet at the master's shins. Some of the kicks got home, the master gave a dog's yelp, and a burning glare of cruelty shot into his paly eyes.

—Here, Massey, and you, Middleton, he yelled, hold his arms stretched out over the desk till I knock the devil of resistance out of him!

The two boys caught hold of Johnny's arms and pulled him over the desk, leaving him at the mercy of the smiter, while the panting boy pleaded please, sir, don't. I didn't mean to watch for the card-playin', really I didn' — oh, you're cuttin' the skin off me!

But the bastard, sweating and puffing, with rigid snarling face and shining eyes, panted and sliced and cut and cut again and again. Johnny felt Massey twisting his arm, pretending that he was hard to hold. Slogan, at last easing off, gave a few more vicious strokes, then stopped to wipe his face in his handkerchief.

—Up on the chair with you, now, beside the desk, he said to the quivering boy, and let the school have a good look at you. A slice across the legs sent Johnny, with a suppressed cry, to leap quick on to the chair, chorused by a titter from the school at his haste to get there. Ashamed to rub the maddening sting in his backside and legs before the school, he balanced himself on the chair, with the eye-bandage that had loosened in the struggle, hanging round his neck, his eyes torturing him with the ache of the disease and the tears that had poured out of them, and his whole nature shaken with the confused wonder at what people were doing to him and what people were thinking of him; there he stood balancing on the chair, doing his best to check the sobs that tossed about the very beating of his heart.

Slogan looked at him for a minute, and then shook his head, and there was contempt in the shake.

—He wasn't much of a Spartan, after all, he said, turning to the school, with a grin, and the opinion I have of him now is less than the one I had before. Well, we'll have to be careful of him, for one sickly sheep infects the flock, and poisons all the rest. He glanced again at Johnny. We'll give him a minute or two to pull himself together and try to be a man, but if he goes on annoying the school with his baby blubbering, we'll have to cane him quiet — isn't that so?

—Yessir, chorused the school.

A bell rang for change of positions; those who had been seated in desks, formed into standing classes, and those who had been standing, sat themselves down in the desks. Johnny still shook a little with gentle crying till Slogan stood before him, angry, threatening, cane in hand.

—Finish the whinging, finish the whinging, boy, quick, or — and he shook the arm of Johnny. The boy tried to check the sobbing, tried to look calm, and sobbed again.

—Stop it at once. D'ye hear? Are you finished?

—Yessir, murmured Johnny.

—Finished, quite, quite finished, are you?

—Yessir.

—Well, let's hear no more of it. Not a squeak out of you, or the cane'll be twisting round your legs again.

With a steady effort of will, Johnny kept quiet, stood sullen on the chair, and waited and watched Slogan return to his desk, and bend over it to correct exercises. He looked at the thin stream of sunlight flowing in by the door, left open to give air to a room hot with the breath of children and teacher.

Then the bell rang again, and all that were standing filed into the desks. The Regulations of the Board of Education were turned with their face to the wall, and an oblong strip of millboard having written on it, Religious Education, was turned to face the school. Rapping on his desk with a heavy, glossy ebony ruler, Slogan silenced the murmur of the school. He put down the ruler on the desk beside him, and bent his hoary oul' head, saying softly, Let us pray.

There was a clatter of moving bodies as all got down on to their knees. Slogan knelt down, too, resting his hoary oul' head on his arms that rested on the seat of the chair from which he had risen to pray.

The ebony ruler lay motionless on the desk beside him. O Lord, open Thou our eyes that we may behold wonderful things out of Thy law. The ebony ruler lay quiet on the desk beside him. Our Father which art in heaven. Hallowed be Thy Name. Johnny could see the pink baldy head of him, with its hoary edging, as Slogan bent down over the seat of the chair on which his arms rested.

Johnny suddenly slipped down from the chair he stood on, a flood of mighty rage swept through him; he whipped up the heavy ebony ruler, and with all the hate in all his heart, in all his mind, in all his soul, and in all his strength, and a swift upward swing of his arm, he brought the ebony ruler down on the pink, baldy, hoary oul' head of hoary oul' Slogan, feeling a desperate throb of joy when he heard the agonising yell that Slogan let out of him when the ebony ruler fell.

Still gripping the ebony ruler, he made for the open door and the sun. He saw Georgie Middleton grip Ecret's shoulder as Ecret made a movement to rise and stop his flight. He saw, as he flew past, the hand of Massey stretched out to hinder, and he heard the blasting curse of Massey in his ears as the ebony ruler came down on the outstretched hand. Away out through the door he dashed, across the road, down the narrow mucky Brady's Lane, shinned speedily up the rough-cut stone wall of the railway embankment, dropping the ruler as he climbed, heard in a clitter-clatter way the rush of an oncoming train, cleft by a sudden frightened, piercing whistle, plunged over the rails, checked for a second or two by the rush of the wind carried by the train, as it went thundering by, saw dimly as in a mist a white-faced driver's mouth opening and shutting frantically; but pulling violently out of the intaking wind of the passing train, he sliddered down the other side of the embankment, ripping his trousers and tearing a rent in his leg with the jagged end of a jutting stone; rushed up the street opposite, turned down the next on the left, pushed open the hall-door of the house, burst into the room, and fell, exhausted and fainting, at his frightened mother's feet.

When he came to himself, his mother was bathing his body with water soothing and warm. The sting in his legs had ceased, for his mother had softened them with vaseline. He stretched his hand out, and gripped his mother's bodice.

—Don't let oul' Hunter or oul' Slogan come near me, Ma, he pleaded.

—They won't be let within an ace of you, she answered; but why did you come dashing in, and why did they beat you till your poor legs were covered with bunches of weals?

—Oul' Slogan bet an' bet me because he said I watched an' kep' nix for boys playin' cards behind the buttresses of the church at playtime. I couldn't get out of it for they were biggern me; an' besides, me eyes 'ud be in the way of me seein' how to use me mits in a fight; 'n I didn't want to, but they made me, 'n oul' Slogan came on top of us; 'n because all the boys were biggern me, he bet 'n bet me till he was tired.

His mother softly fixed the bandage round his bad eye, snuggled him gently under the bed-clothes, bent down and kissed him.

—Rest and sleep sound, she said, and forget all about it till the morning.

And he lay down safe with her who would watch over him, and wended his way into a deep sleep.

THE LORD LOVETH JUDGMENT

M RS. C ASSIDE sat down near the fire on a butter-box that had been covered with a strip of old red cloth. As she sat by the fire on the butter-box that had been covered with an old red cloth, she saw with a sigh that the straw in the mattress on Johnny's bed was coming loose quick and fast. The stitching of a hundred and one nights was failing to keep it together, and so she sighed. She saw the kettle, tarred from the smoke of the fire, tottering on the hob, its leaking bottom patched with little discs of cork and tin, sold in the hardware shops for six a penny on a cardboard sheet; the frying-pan and saucepans that were, thank God, still holding out; the cupboard standing big-bellied in the corner, safely guarding the little stock of delft. She saw, and shivered, that a number of the springs were beginning to show through the covering on the horse-hair sofa, now leaning a little faintly against the wall of the room under the window; the narrow strip of cotton twill that was doing all it could in its service as a sheet to keep Johnny's bare legs from the pricks of the straws sticking out of the mattress; the lean blanket and the coats struggling to keep him warm; the kitchen chairs, still sturdy; the steel fender, polished with emery paper till it shone like silver, battling the ashes back to their proper place; the pictures of Nelson Bound for Trafalgar Bay and Queen Victoria gradually growing old amid the fading roses on the wallpaper; the two-leaved mahogany table, bought by her husband from a Fenian forced to fly the country; the big box, coaxed from the grocer for sixpence, where the coal was kept, crossed by a plank carrying the bucket holding the fresh water, a bucket that had to be used, too, for the carrying down of the water spoiled by use; and on the window ledge the two geraniums, one white, the other red, and the purple-cloaked fuchsia blossoming blithely amid the wrack of the common things around them. She saw and shivered as she sat on the butter-box that had been covered with the strip of old red cloth.

The hours went by, and the boy slept sound. Archie came home from his work, took his tea, read the paper; asked why Johnny was in bed, was told that he wasn't well, and said that the kid was always sick; and then went out to have his fling in his own way after his day's work.

Then the darkness came, and the stars stared out of the darkness as she sat by the fire on the butter-box covered by the old red cloth.

If God be with us, she thought to herself, who can be against us? A great many can be against us, came in an added thought, and some of them are strong. She got up and lighted a duplex kerosene lamp that stood on the two-leaved mahogany table. If God be for us, who can be against us? Below in the hall she heard a commotion out of which her name was called. She went out to the lobby, and peered over the banisters into the gloom below.

—Who wants me; who's callin' me? she called down.

—It's the protestan' minister; he wants to see you; been lookin' for you; somethin' about Johnny; the protestan' minister, said lively and sad, young and old voices up to her out of the gloom. The regular beat of her heart changed to a troubled throb. She wished she hadn't spoken. She wished she hadn't shown herself. Wished she hadn't come out of the room. She wished she hadn't lighted the lamp. Wished she had stayed sitting still by the fire on the butter-box covered with the old red cloth, leaving whatever trouble had come to her alone in the gloom of the hall. Johnny must have done something very bad for them to flog him the way they did.

—Is that Mrs. Casside up there? The voice of the minister came up, like the voice of a harpy, up from the gloom of the hall.

—Yessir, this is Mrs. Casside talkin' down to you from the lobby. Won't you come up, sir, please?

—Please bring out a light of some kind, my good woman, that I may be able to see my way.

She returned to the room to fetch a lamp and a light to his path, the rough path that led the minister in the way to her room, so that he might bring forth light to the thing in her son's heart, quiet now in a dear deep sleep making darkness and light alike to him; unaware of the enemy at the gates about to enter where light is as darkness; seeking to set sorrow where joy should stand up, stand up for Jesus shall reign where'er the sun doth his successive journeys run, His kingdom stretch from shore to shore, till moons shall wax and wane no more, cursed be he that perverteth the judgment of the stranger, the fatherless, and widow.

With the lamp in her hand, she went out to the lobby, and held it as low as she could over the banisters, to light the minister's way up the narrow stairs to the room. She saw the faces of those who lived in the house and the house next door watching the protestant minister carefully climb the stairs to the lobby where the mother waited for him; watching him till he passed out of their sight into the home of the widow and her sons. The minister stood blinking in the semi-darkness as Mrs. Casside tremulously put the lamp back carefully in its place on the little mahogany table. She placed one of the sturdy kitchen chairs beside the minister, and he sat down stiffly. She sat down straight-backed on another, waiting for him to speak, with her hands clasped tightly together in her lap.

—I have left very important work, very important, to come here, he said, as he gave a glance around the smoky room, to have a talk to you about John. He paused for a moment, then went on. He ran away from school today, Mrs. Casside — do you know why?

—Yessir. He told me all about it. The big boys made him keep watch while they gambled with cards, and Mr. Slogan came up and caught them. Though he didn' lay a hand on any of the others, he laid heavy hands on Johnny; and then the poor boy ran away.

Just like these hopeless people, thought the minister, always making excuses for their children. Severity is the only possible kindness.

John didn't tell you, he said, out loud, that his master, Mr. Slogan, is, at the moment, ill in bed; that he had to be helped home after John had given him a savage and violent blow on the top of his poor head with an ebony ruler. Did he tell you all about that, Mrs. Casside? Then there is a bad, a very bad bruise on one of Mr. Slogan's shins from a vicious, a very vicious kick given by your son, John. Did he tell you all about that, too, Mrs. Casside?

Facing him, the woman sat silent and stiff and still.

—Now, went on the minister, we don't want your little boy to grow up to be a criminal; but if he is to grow up to be readily able to do his duty in that state of life unto which it has pleased God to call him, these dangerous inclinations must be checked, and checked, if necessary, with a very rough hand. Now, don't you agree with me, Mrs. Casside?

Facing him, the woman sat silent and stiff and still.

—If your boy won't willingly do it, then he must be made, must be made, Mrs. Casside, to order himself lowly and reverently to all his betters, went on the smooth, soft, cold voice. If this sort of conduct goes on unregarded in the way of suitable punishment, he will be encouraged to do again and again the things that will utterly unfit him to be a sober and decent member of society. The attack upon poor Mr. Slogan was the act of a right young blaguard. The boy has richly earned a severe caning, and he is going to get it; and then go down on his knees to his master, and humbly beg his pardon before the whole school.

Facing him, the woman, sitting silent and stiff and still, shivered.

—When Johnny wakes in the morning, I'll speak to him about what he did to Mr. Slogan, the woman said.

—The morning, the morning, said the minister testily; wake the little rascal up now, and tell him that I will meet him at the school the first thing in the morning; and that immediately after prayers, a severe caning will make an example of him before the whole school; and, that when he has been suitably punished, he will go down on his knees, and beg his master's pardon for his blaguardly conduct; so that, in future, he will never dare to raise a hand against anyone whom God has set in authority over him.

Facing him, the mouth of the woman sitting stiff and still quivered and spoke softly, very softly.

—The boy may be awake tonight with his eyes, sir, the quivering mouth said, and to do what you ask would be to torture him above what he might be able to bear.

—I tell you, said the minister impatiently, that you will ruin your little boy, if you go on coddling him in this way.

The mouth of the stiff still woman quivered again, and the mouth spoke softly.

—He has had dry bread and tea for a good many meals, since his father died, said the quivering mouth; clothes that shiver when a breeze blows; boots that just about hide the bareness of his feet; and hours of eye pain rock him restlessly at night — neither I nor God, sir, coddle the boy.

The minister stood up from the chair.

—Each of us must learn to bear with the tribulations which God may see fit to inflict upon us, and which may work out an exceeding weight of glory. But what you have to remember at the moment, Mrs. Casside, is that God is angry, very angry, with your boy. If he isn't punished one way, he'll be punished in another, and, very possibly, in a more severe way. He must be made to take his just punishment, lest worse befall him. I beg of you to be firm, Mrs. Casside.

He moved softly towards the door while the woman rose from the chair, crossed the room, and sat stiff, still, and silent, with her hands clasped in her lap, on the butter-box covered with the old red cloth, facing the minister, facing him fair, as she sat on the butter-box covered with the old red cloth.

—So, the minister went on, please be at the school with John the first thing in the morning. I will be there to take charge of the boy, and I can assure you that the punishment will be given under my own personal supervision; and, after it is all over, I feel sure we shall have a better pupil, and you will have a better son.

The soft mouth of the stiff and still figure, sitting on the butter-box covered with the old red cloth, hardened.

—Tomorrow, the soft mouth that had hardened said, tomorrow, sir, is one of the days when I bring the boy to the hospital.

The hard mouth of the minister twitched with irritation.

—There is to be no putting-off of the punishment, Mrs. Casside, the hard mouth said; remember that. The caning must be given while the blaguardly act is fresh in the mind of the boy.

The soft quivering mouth of the woman sitting on the butter-box covered with the old red cloth hardened to the hardness round the mouth of the minister.

—Tomorrow morning, the soft mouth that had hardened said, the boy will be where God, through the doctors, may give ease to his eyes. The harsh hand that fell on him today shall not fall on him tomorrow, or the next day, and its dark shadow shall he never see again. Tell that to Slogan from the boy's mother.

—Mrs. Casside, Mrs. Casside, said the hard mouth of the minister, tightening.

—Good-night, said the soft voice that had hardened. As you go, leave the door open so that the light from the lamp may show you some of the way down.

And the minister slowly put his soft hat on his head, and went his way.

Then the stiff and still and silent woman went over to the bed where the boy lay, and his sleep was sound; and she bent over and kissed him.

THE DREAM REVIEW

JOHNNY woke and tried to open his eyes but the thick red lids were tightly stuck together with the matter that had oozed from them during all the still hours of the night. Rubbing hard and roughly, he tried to force some of the yellow crust away, but the inflamed lids held together fast. He tore at the crust with his fingernails till the hardened matter burst and he could open his eyes a little. He peered out in front of him, but the room was full of darkness and he couldn't see. He closed them again, and slid his hand over the top of the bed feeling for his trousers. In its movement his hand touched the bandage that had fallen from his head during the night. He tied it loosely round his forehead, covering the left eye completely, and the right eye partly, with its folds. Again he slid his hand over the top of the bed in search of his trousers, but failed to find them. Sitting up and bending sideways, while the framework of the bed creaked and the old rusty laths rattled, he stretched out of the bed and ran his hand cunningly along the splintery floor. Touching a garment, he lifted it, and feeling the seat and fork and buttons, knew it was his trousers, and laid it beside him on the bed.

The morning must be well into the day now, for a long time ago, when he was only half awake, he had heard the postman bawling out the names on the letters that he had brought to the people of the house. He moved over to a warmer spot in the bed. Suddenly he heard the sound of children cheering, and putting the bandage away from his ears, he sat up, leaning on his elbow, and listened.

He heard the voice of his mother talking to some oul' wan at the door below. He slid out of bed, felt his way over to the door of the room, and opened it a little so that he might hear what the two women were saying.

—I couldn't think of lettin' him go, said the voice of his mother, 'n his eyes the way they are.

—Poor little chiselur, said the voice of the other oul' wan, poor little chiselur.

—I put a bit of cloth over the window, went on his mother, to keep th' light of the mornin' from wakin' him before they'd gone to the review, for Queen's birthday 'n all as it is, I couldn't let him go with Archie, 'n his eyes the way they are.

—Poor little chiselur, murmured the other voice, poor little chiselur.

—Looka the kids o' the school collectin' to march to Nelson's Pillar to take the thram to the Park Gate, where they'll get off an' walk to where the Royal Standard's flyin' square-quarthered with the Irish Harp, the Scottish Lion, 'n the English Leopards, waitin' for the gallopin' arrival of the Lord Lieutenant to start things goin', with hats off, attention, 'n presented arms to the playin' of the National Anthem. Johnny was lookin' forward to seein' the stiff consequential step of the grenadiers in the march-past, 'n the gorgeous sthrut of the kiltcd highlandcrs, 'n thc common 'n dignified go-by of the infanthry o' the line, the proud throt of the artillery horses, right o' the line 'n pride of the army, pullin' the guns, an' the gallant cavalry glintin' as they go by in a dancin' walk to the crisp tappin' of the kettle-drums: — but I couldn't think of lettin' him go an' his eyes the way they are.

—Poor little chiselur, said the voice of the other oul' wan, poor little chiselur.

Johnny closed the door softly, groped his way over to the window, touched the cloth that covered it, gripped it, tore it down, and flung it on the floor. The light from a May sky flooded the room. Pushing the bandage from his eye, he looked out through the window at the gathering of children headed by Slogan the schoolmaster and Hunter the minister, moving off on their way to witness the review. Each child wore a red-white-and-blue rosette and oul' Slogan carried a small Union Jack.

The light streaming into the long-darkened eye of the boy shot pain down to the roots of the socket; but he clenched his teeth and stared down on the street, saw Hunter lift a hand, and the gathering moved off in line, three abreast, cheering strongly as they strutted along, and singing joyously,

'The Twenty-Fourth of May, the Queen's birthday,
We'll let it rain tomorrow, but it mustn't rain today!'

Then Johnny darted a look at the sky, and saw that the sky was a bright grey, but not blue, and that the sun shone faintly.

He went over to the bed again, cautiously turned down the rotting clothes, crept in, drew the clothes up over him, and lay still for many minutes. Then he clasped his hands, intermingling his fingers tightly together, and lifted them higher over his head, stretching till the sockets of his arms cracked; murmuring in mild madness, O God, let the rain come, let the rain come quick, heavy 'n quick, comin' down on the streets, in the fields, 'n in the parks on the people 'n the children goin' anywhere, the whole day through, without ceasin' a second, to fall on everything, right out to a long way off from where I'm lyin' now. Let the faint clouds that are in the sky grow strong, deepen, and sthretch till they cover the spaces where there's none; 'n God, let the wind come too, a sharp wind 'n a bitther, to make the rain fall worse 'n harder, till it thrickles over the skin so that the joy sought afther be people 'n children may be hidden from them, bringin' a fear 'n a shiverin' 'n a heavy longin' to all that they were not where they may be, because of the bitther wind 'n the sharp rain fallin', right out to a long way off from where I'm lyin' now!

He thickened the folds of his bandage and covered his eyes again so that the light in the room became a deep darkness. He stayed still, breathing softly, creeping close to sleep, connecting his thoughts with a world of marching troops; the clatter of guns rollin' over the stony sthreet; the jingle of cavalry swords hangin' by the hips of the riders, breastplated, or braided 'n belted; 'n the infanthry heavy 'n the infanthry light thrudgin' along, less gloriously covered, but spick 'n span as the best of the others; cross-belted an' pouched; knapsacks hoisted high to the tops of their backs; rifles at the slope, 'n helmets 'n busbies sthrapped tight to the chin; steppin' out with a left-right, left-right, I had a good job but I left it; left-right, left-right; never missin' a beat, risin' up, swingin' back, comin' down all together: the feet of the young men poundin' out of the pavin'-setts a song of the nation's pride 'n power.

He could see the tightenin' up of the bodies of onlookers watchin' from the paths 'n windows as the regiment swung past with the officers' band playin'

> First we mopped the floor with him,
> Dhragged him up an' down the stairs;
> Then we had another go, undher tables, over chairs,
> Such a sight you never saw; before he'd time to say his prayers,
> Rags an' bones were all we left of the man who sthruck O'Hara!

folleyin' the regimental band of fifes an' dhrums, waitin' for their chance to play when the other band stopped, the fifes an' dhrums marchin' hard on the heels of the bearded pioneers, with axe an' pick an' shovel on their shouldhers.

It was a grand thing for the Colonel on horseback, an' he leadin' nine hundhred an' ninety-nine men, each armed with rifle, bayonet, 'n a hundred rounds of blank, the whole crush folleyin' him as one man, so that if he only gave the word, a left-turn at the double over the wall into the river, boys, they'd all turn left as one man, rest a hand on the parapet 'n vault plump into the river without askin' why, on accounta they daren't disobey any ordher of the officer commandin'; for theirs to do 'n die without to want a reason why is the beginnin' an' end of a soldier's life.

Johnny heard the onlookers murmurin' that he was the youngest colonel goin', with the Afghan 'n Burman medals lyin' snug on his crimson sash, on accounta havin' ridden with the troops from Kabul to Kandahar, 'n had followed in the wake of Colonel Burnaby, givin' the first welt to Theebaw afther a hot, heavy, 'n forced march of fifteen hours through a tree-darkened 'n thropical jungle.

They had come right up to a fortified stockade of the rebellious Burmans; had been given the ordher for the bugles to sound the charge; 'n in the middle o' yells, squeals, flyin' spears, glitther o' knives an' yataghans, beatin' o' gongs, bangin' o' bells, 'n blowin' o' bugles, the bayonets worked their way forward 'n slashed with red the bronzed breasts of the Burmans.

Johnny shot his hand down under the clothes on to his belly, and his first finger fell firmly on a nipping flea, 'n he rolled it tightly over his flesh, crushing it till it cracked, 'n then flicked it with his finger 'n thumb till it fell mangled on to the palliasse of the bed, formin' another little bitin' bastard gone where the good niggers go.

When what was left of the panic-stricken lepped over the stockade, flyin' hell for leather, to get away into the jungle, the Lancers in white dhrill and big sun helmets came floodin' out into the clearin' round the stockade, an' shoved their lances into the bellies 'n backs of the screamin' Burmans, yellin' Dew ay mong draw, British muscle behind British steel, diggin' the bowels outa them, 'n dungin' the jungle with them; showin' what they get for mockin' 'n jeerin' at British rule 'n British justice; seconded be a British cheer that made the animals wandherin' in the jungle cock their ears to listen 'n wondher at the few dark figures left to crawl away 'n hide in the thick 'n hot grass, mutterin' to their terrible 'n merciless gods of wood an' stone for help, before they stiffened out in the great stretch that was to last them for ever 'n ever.

Johnny suddenly tensed his whole body 'n tightened his mouth fiercely as a spasm of pain shooting through his eyes set his brain on fire for several minutes. Relaxing as the pain passed slowly away, he shifted the bandage so that the part dampened by the gush of water from his eyes lay off his forehead. Then he began to doze and dream again.

He saw the Colonel feeling the glossy neck of his charger, carryin' him proudly at the head of the Fermanaghs, marchin' left-right, left-right, I had a good job but I left it.

Suddenly, on the other side of the river he heard the skirl of the bagpipes, with the dark bass dhrone never ceasin' to nurse the tune of the tenors; an' the flow of the shawls, the wag of the bonnets, and the swing of the yellow-sthriped kilts showed the gay Grahams footin' it out to la-la-la, hielan' laddie, hielan' laddie, busy blowin' the guts outa themselves, an' thryin' to get all the notice that was knockin' about on the earth. Lettin' themselves go to get to the gate of the park before his regiment, they were; but he'd soon show them to the differ, if the motto of the Fermanaghs, *Sinneraria est magnificat sancteeorum*, Latin for great sinners are as great as great saints, meant anything off the common.

But the kilts let the hielan' laddies lash out with their legs in a walk that couldn't be betthered, so the Colonel gee-geed up his horse, gave the ordher of At the double; but the Grahams broke into a throt at the same time that sent them a little ahead of the Fermanaghs.

The Colonel raised himself in his stirrups and dhrew his sword.

—Come on, men, he shouted, an' show these hielan' bousies that the Fermanagh Fusiliers'll not enther any park arsin' afther any crush greedy for glory. So come on, me boys of Ormond Quay an' Stoney-batther. For your counthry an' your Colonel, gather to the gate of the park with a speed that'll make the others appear to be goin' backwards!

All the people cheered an' cheered, as the Fermanaghs surged forward at a gallop, heads sthrainin' to the front, shouldhers gathered together, breath comin' in heavy pants, grippin' their rifles tight at the thrail, sweatin' fast an' furious as they ran full-tilt for the park gate, with the Grahams dhroppin' their playin' of hielan' laddie to dash headlong for the gate, too, with the people on the paths shoutin' an' hissin' an' booin', an' runnin' out in front of the hielan' laddies to bar their way, gettin' a grip of the swingin' kilts, an' holdin' on like grim death so that the hielan' laddies had to halt in their stride 'n thry to prevent the excited crowd from tearing the kilts offa them; but many failed to hold on, 'n, except for bonnets 'n cross-belied cartridge pouches, were left runnin' about lookin' as they looked when they first came into the world, only a bit bigger.

Many made a beeline for the shops on the side-walks to cover their nakedness, settin' the women, who were lowerin' lemonade, screamin' in high ordher, an' sendin' them flyin' out to the sthreet, in fear, to see the whole crush o' the Grahams mucked up an' messed about 'n put to confusion, made worse be the officers soarin' in their saddles an' roarin' to their men to fall in, an' form fours, an' number off, an' get into column o' companies, to march on in the way they were goin'; their shouts shockin' into obedience those who had raced into the shops on the side-walks, causin' them to rush out again, thryin' to cover themselves suitably with their bonnets an' pouches; an' lookin' wildly at their officers for information and advice; scandalisin' the world-wide decency of the English army before the rovin' eyes of the Dublin people; while the policemen that were knockin' about called out for all to behave like sensible men 'n women, an' act like ladies an' gentlemen who have the knack of lookin' at only what they're told to see; while the Fermanagh Fusiliers were pourin' into the park in a lather of sweat, an' smilin' that the race had been won, without fear or favour from anyone, leavin' the Grahams in such a state of disability, on accounta the loss of their kilts, that hundhreds of them had to be rushed back to barracks in closed-up cabs to keep tongues from talkin' about the strange things suddenly seen in the city of Dublin.

When ordher was restored, 'n the Grahams seen that nothin' further was to be gained, they came marchin' into the park playin' the Cock o' the North, and sidled up alongside the Fermanagh boys rattlin' out the Rocky Road to Dublin in rare style.

Suddenly an aid-dee-cong dhressed up in green buckskin breeches, blue coat, blossomin' with gold braid, an' wearin' a cocked hat with a red-'n-black plume stretchin' out of it, like a sthream o' smoke 'n flame, came gallopin' up on a white horse, an' stuck himself between the two colonels, demandin' to know, without any shilly-shallyin', why all the commotion had been caused, an' remindin' them that they wore the uniform of Her Majesty the Queen, which ought to weigh with them towards keepin' away from anything that 'ud show up Her Majesty's throops in front of the Irish people, who were always on the keeveev to ferret out anything likely to cast a slur on the great thradition of the English army that stood for so much that was necessary to keep the world safe an' clean; an' if there was any more of this buggerin' about with the good name of the throops he'd let the Lord Lieutenant know all the details, an' have the officers responsible up on the carpet to show the reason why the Irish were allowed to sthrip important units of the armed forces, leavin' them ignorant as to what course to take under the circumstances of them bein' naked nearly from the waist down.

Then up spoke the Colonel of the Grahams, tellin' the red-an'-black-plumed get that we lived undher a constitutional monarchy, an' were all free to think our own thoughts an' carry on accordin' to the dictates of our conscience cryin' out against showin' reverence to a tandragee elegant-speakin', cock-hatted, aid-dee-cong bowsey, hot an' half-baked from a military nursing-home.

Here the Fermanagh Colonel gave his horse a jab o' the spur, an' got between the bargin' boyos; stickin' his bake in undher the cocked hat of the aid-dee-cong, looking him straight in the eye an' sayin', sotto-voice, Here, let's have this matther out with resthraint; for we would all be betther employed in attendin' to our duties than to be arguin' the toss with a fella who runs home the minute he gets the chance to tell his oul' wan everything; who's ready at the wind o' the word to come bargin' into the barracks to make a show of the whole regiment; so take a friend's advice an' buzz off before a puck in the royal snot unsettles you for the rest of the day, an' don't be shovin' your conk in where it isn't needed or wanted or valued; so push off while the sun's shinin', with your little arse nestin' safe in the saddle, on your horse back to where you came from, snug undher the flappin' of the royal banner; an', with that, the drum-major of the Fermanaghs suddenly let fly with his staff an' gave a larrup to the hind-quarters of the horse, sendin' the cock-hatted spitabout careerin' out of sight.

Then the Fermanagh boys an' the Grahams wheeled to the left, an' marched shouldher to shouldher down narrow leafy lanes, the blue sky over them diapered with great, spreading, gently-waving masses of red an' white hawthorn, makin' the soldiers bend low to save their busbies an' bonnets from bein' swept off by the thorn-sprinkled blossoms. On, then, an' out of the narrow, shady, leafy lanes to the fifteen acres, green an' level, an' slowly risin' into little mounds high enough to let regiments disappear when they'd done all they had to do for the moment; an' low enough to let them come into sight again suddenly when the time came for to show themselves to the civilians, ravenous for the march-past and the sham battle; big enough to easy hold the army of cavalry an' infanthry an' Medical Corps, with their white canvas-covered wagons havin' a big red cross on each side, so that any enemy would recognise at once that they were only there to splice up and tinker up the wounded; an' artillery, field an' horse, and the Army Service Corps, with their wagons, mostly pulled be mules, facin' towards the spot where the Viceroy 'ud first show himself.

Now he comes glidin' out in his victoria, dhrawn be four nutbrown horses, at a quiet an' respectable throt, with his lady puffed an' prim an' parasolled beside him; an' all the massed bands at the same identical tick o' the clock burst into God save the Queen; while the artillery, horse an' field, fired a royal salute o' twenty-one guns, half hidden be a thick shrubbery of hazel an' blackthorn bushes; big globes of thick white smoke, a little thin at the edges, rose from behind the bushes like balls o' wool, folleyed be big bangs that made the civilians thrill as they felt the ground shake an' quiver undher their feet, feelin' how safe they were in havin' such a multitude of armed men to frighten all foreigners; while the soldiers standin' in line gave a foo-dee-joy, be firing away, one afther another, so that the rattle o' musketry roamed from one end of the line to the other an' back again three times; the soldiers at the command of their officers wavin' their shakos an' helmets an' busbies an' bonnets an' bearskins on the points of their bayonets; at the same time givin' a three-times-three cheer for Her Majesty the Queen an' her heirs an' successors for ever an' ever.

Then the Viceroy, dressed in a black clawhammer coat, white waistcoat, cream buckskin breeches, brown topboots, an' a little black bowler hat, with a rosebud in his buttonhole, swung himself on to the back of a white horse sprinkled with black spots, an' set off, afther sayin' fare-ye-well for awhile to the grand ladies, folleyed be a sub-sovereign's escort of blue-tuniced, gold-breast-plated, silver-helmeted, red-plumed horse guards, an' a covey of equerries in green coats with silver-braided epaulettes, an' red coats with gold-braided epaulettes, an' green coats with bronze-braided epaulettes; with red stripes down green trousers, an' white stripes down blue trousers, an' green stripes down black trousers; trottin' quick between the ranks of the avenued soldiers, eyes front, standin' stock-still like wooden soldiers set down on a table be a boy; with the officers rooted in their proper places to the right or to the left or in front of their particular companies, as if all were undher a spell; while the inspection went on, passin' by field artillery in their blue uniforms, piped with yellow; an' horse artillery in uniforms of blue, with their coat so heavy with yellow braid that the men had to bend back to keep themselves from fallin' forward, with red flaps hangin' from their busbies, an' a yellow cord hangin' from the red flap down to the thick yellow cord on their shoulders, then coilin' undher the arm to be looped over the chest, an' at last danglin' down in two knot-like tassels on their chests. Flowin' round, the Viceroy went on to pass through the lines of the red-coated infanthry, with their blue facin's, an' buff facin's, an' white facin's, an' green facin's; the Viceroy throwin' an eye here an' an eye there to make sure that every chin-sthrap went undher the chin in the right place, an' that the belts holdin' haversack an' knapsack an' pouches crossed in the dead centre of the breast; an' the water-bottle hung fair an' square on the left hip; an' the pipeclayed belts showed no detrimental stains; an' that all the brass buttons an' badges sparkled with the dint o' polishin', reflectin' the upright cleanliness of the British soldiers standin' with their rifles at the slope, rememberin' that it wasn't theirs to reason why but only just to do an' die; with the colonel of each regiment meetin' the boyo at the right o' the line an' throttin' beside him till the last man of the regiment was reached, an' the Viceroy jogged on to inspect another regiment; folleyed by his equerries sittin' stiff on their saddles, their eyes fixed on the Viceroy's arse in front of them, movin' on to see that everything was in apple-pie ordher for their Queen an' counthry.

A few Fenian faces in the crowd among the Irish, gathered where the less respectable people were lookin' at the goin's-on, done a little booin'; but were soon collared be the police, an' cuffed out of the vicinity; though, of course, there was no real objection to the poor so long as they conducted themselves decently an' in ordher.

The Viceroy throtted through the line of the blue-tuniced, yellow-braided, white-plumed Prince Albert's Own Hussars, right in front o' the Queen's Lancers, lovely in their black-breasted red coats, long black plumes fallin' down over their square-topped helmets; through heavy dhragoons with red-plumed brass helmets; an' light dhragoons with black-plumed silver helmets; then cantherin' by the highlan' regiments, proud of their bagpipes, goin' strong, with their yellow an' green tartan; an' green an' white an' black tartan; an' red an' yellow an' blue tartan; lookin' as brave in their finery as any contingent in the whole British army; havin' their officers standin' like pillars before them, with their glitterin' jewelled dirks stuck in their stockin's.

At last he came to cock an eye over the Fermanagh Fusiliers, stickin' out their chests like good ones, meetin' the Colonel with a lazy lift o' the hand who came to a swift salute with the back edge o' his sword touchin' the tip of his nose; an', fallin' in, folleyed half a length behind His Excellency, noddin' his approval of the splendid shape the Fermanaghs were busy puttin' up, silent an' stiff as standin' dead men; till, nearin' the end of the rear line, he stood up in his stirrups an' clapped the Colonel on the back, sayin', It's thrillin' to see such a fine body of Irishmen waitin' the chance to lay down their lives for their Queen an' counthry; an' be God, the tattle that goes on about Irish disloyalty is nothin' but effan lies if you ask me. So keep this goin', Colonel, an' I'll put in a good word for you to oul' Vicky, an' depend on it, you'll have the Ordher o' St. Patrick bloomin' on your breast before the year's out, or me name's not Jack Robinson.

With that, he galloped off to the grand stand, smothered in scarlet an' gold, to take the salute of the march-past of the cavalry goin' by at a walk an' a throt an' a gallop; the horse artillery folleyin' fast at their heels; an' then the infanthry swingin' along at a quick-march of thousands on thousands of legs shootin' forward an' backward at the same moment, showin' the civilians the way to walk, with the rifle regiments carryin' their rifles at the thrail; but none of them comin' within a mile of the steppin' out as one man of the Fermanagh Fusiliers, with the well-dhressed Irish on one side an' the ragamuffin Irish on the other, cheerin' like hell as they sailed by to the strains of Farewell But Whene'er You Remember The Hour.

The sham battle came on, and off the Army went into hidlins; with the cavalry, artillery an' mosta the infanthry goin' one way, an' the Fermanagh Fusiliers an' Grahams goin' another, to meet in combat as soon as the artillery paved the way for it be limberin' up an' openin' fire on a scrawl of both regiments left where they were sure to be seen, so as to goad the artillery to concentrate to their hearts' content on them; the rest of the Grahams and Fermanaghs manœuvred round on their bellies an' caught the artillery in the rear, cheerin' in on them with a rush at the point of the bayonet an' a shout of Faug a balagh, takin' all their guns an' spikin' them before they could realise what was afther happenin'; dhrivin' them helther-skelther among the opposin' infanthry, causin' a panic an' a quick rethreat. But the cavalry, formin' up, came on at a gallopin' charge, leavin' the Fermanaghs and Grahams only a second to jump into a square an' meet them at the bayonet's point; while the inner ranks fired volley afther volley into the cursin' cavalry, pokin' with their lances an' slashin' with their sabres, but failin' to make any little laneway in the square formed be the volley-firin' fusiliers an' highlanders; till the frightened horses couldn't stand it any longer, an' turned tail, to rush off back on the poor devils comin' on, so that there was a terrible muck-up, an' in a minute they were all makin' full speed from where the volleys never stopped for a single second, mowin' down horses an' men in a shockin' rout.

The Colonel o' the Grahams, seein' the ways things were goin', jumped on top of his horse, drew his sword, an' shoutin', Now or never, now an' for ever, led them in a cheerin' charge afther the flyin' cavalry, seekin' shelther wherever they thought they could find it, fleein' hotfoot among the civilians; an' leavin' the whole fifteen acres litthered with sabres an' rifles an' busbies an' helmets an' colours an' guidons an' lances, while the bould Fermanaghs spread themselves out like a fan an' chased the flyin' enemy well beyond the bordhers of the civilian onlookers. The Prince Albert's Own Hussars, called the Cherry-pickers, because of their crimson trousers, flew panic-stricken, as fast as their horses could go, straight to where the Viceroy an' his butties were standin', gapin', on their grand-stand, an' there was a wild screamin' an' scattherin' of the silken an' satin clad ladies as the red-trousered hussars tore by; hundhreds fainted with fright an' thousands burst their stays an' split their drawers asundher, trying to get out o' the bed quick, when you get a backyard call, for fear of accidents; waitin' only to slip on your pants, handy on the floor beside the bed, an' out an' down the two flights o' stairs of ten steps each; holdin' fast bə the banisters, if you don't want to be listenin' anxious for the bell of 'n ambulance; goin' down the hall with the hands well out to keep any collision away; then out into the yard, straight on over the flags, like ice undher your bare feet, feelin' with your fingers yourself safe at last into the harbour, with the oul' mit searchin' out the right place to sit down on; your throne soggin' wet as usual, for the other lowsers in the house never give a thought to anybody else who may have a likin' for a dhry 'n decent method of meetin' nature; bravely hummin' their way through life, up to their ankles in their own slush; unfit to feel the need of anything outside of what they have to do themselves; an' always forgettin' the inlook an' outlook of others who are strivin' to do unto others as others should do unto them, which is only fair if you think it out.

A dash'll have to be made for the house as soon as me trouser's buttoned, for there's the rain slashin' off the roof; an' I can't stop here till it eases. Off I go now up the path into the house again, 'n up the stairs, into the room outa the cold an' the rain; with a swift wipe of the feet in the trousers an' a plunge into the warm bed, to listen to the rain fallin' on the flags, an' dullin' with rust all the glitter 'n pride 'n glare of plume 'n pennon 'n bugle 'n breastplate saggin' under the fallin' rain, fallin' swift on everyone right out to a long way off from where I'm lyin' now.

LIFE IS MORE THAN MEAT

JOHNNY didn't bother much about food or raiment. There wasn't much of either to be had, so he took what was given, and forgot to thank God.

Looking back, he could remember two suits that had come fresh to his body: one, a blue sailor suit, with gold anchor and gold stripes on the sleeve, topped with a blue velvet cap, having H.M.S. Condor in gold letters round the band; and a soft tweed suit, fitted after many trials, and finally accepted from a Jew for two shillings down, and a shilling a week after, till the full price was paid. He had it on now, patched and stitched till it was tired; coaxed with care to stay together a little longer. Each touch a warning that a tear was near, with his mother nightly nursing tweedy wounds, closing them up with deft and crinkled and patient fingers. Although all its early simple pomp was gone, it hung on hard to life, a shade from the sun in the summer, a shivering shelter from the seeping rain, the biting frost, and the cold blowing blasts of the winter.

Food was rare, though there was almost always a hunk of bread to be had, but it often tasted like dust and ashes in his mouth: dust to dust and ashes to ashes. After a few years of meagre fare, anyway, his belly ceased to put up a fight, and took patiently the bread and tea and Parrish's Syrup that trickled into it; getting a start of surprise when a potato came along; and battling hastily to create a welcome whenever meat or fish came tumbling in.

How good it was for John the Baptist always to have within his reach loads of locusts and wild honey. Going about his business, and never having to bother as to where the night would fall on him. When his hat was on, his house was thatched. And the Israelites, too — look at them! Quails flutthering outa the sky, croaking out, Catch me, catch me, so that nothing had to be done but wring their necks and roast them. (Though in all fairness, and to give God His due, He sometimes flooded the bay with fish, causing poor Dublin streets to ring with the cry of, Dublin Bay herrin's, tuppence a dozen; tuppence a dozen, the Dublin Bay herrin's; which meant a daily feast of hot or cold baked herrings for a week or more for all.) And the manna, too, dropped down from heaven for their special benefit, though it didn't keep them from grousing. Well, there was no manna dropping down on the streets of Dublin for poor boys to gather; only dung and dirt that the traffic pulverised into dust, choking the throats and cutting the eyes outa the passers-by whenever the stronger breezes blew.

Once a week, after Archie had given to the house what he had put aside to give it, Johnny and his mother set out to buy in the week's supply of tea and sugar. This meant a long journey to Lipton's in Dame Street. Before, they used to get these things in the London and Newcastle Tea Company who gave brass and bronze checks to their customers, according to the amount of tea bought, which were used, when enough had been gathered together, to buy chinaware and ironmongery. But Lipton had come, and other stores had to take a back seat.

So Johnny, furnished with a sailor's kit-bag, having large eyelet holes through which a cord ran so that the mouth could be closed, set out with his mother on a far journey for the corn and wine in Lipton's, on a cold and rainy evening.

How he hated the journey, and how tired the walking made him, for there was nothing stirring, nothing in the walk to make his feet light or lift them in a dancing step; often his mother had to tell him not to drag his feet, but to walk like an ordinary human being. Then, without knowing, he'd hang on his mother's arm till she'd cry out, oh, don't be dhraggin' outa me like that; can't you walk on the legs that God has given you? He'd take his arm away, and journey on through the wilderness of streets, shuffling his feet, and lagging a little behind.

What wouldn't he give, now, for a good topcoat, an' he goin' along Dorset Street, facin' the spittin' rain an' the penethratin' wind, whippin' in his face an' stabbin' him right through his coat an' trousers, an' tatthered shirt, making him feel numb an' sick as he dragged himself along afther his mother, protectin' himself as well as he could be holdin' the kit-bag spread out like a buckler in front of his breast.

He kept his eye on his mother ploddin' along in front of him, carryin' a basket an' an oilcan, dhressed in her faded an' thin black skirt an' cape, her shabby little bonnet tied firmly undher her chin, the jet beads in it gleamin' out of it as bright as ever; an' she steppin' it out, hell-bent for Lipton's, ignorin' all the shops that lined the way, stuffed out with all sorts of fine an' fat goods that God never meant her to have.

There were fruiterers who had piled out on the path heaps of apples an' pears from England, dates from Tunis an' Thripoli, figs from Turkey, and oranges from Spain, transported outa the sun by bullock or mule, in thrain an' boat to the wind-swept streets o' Dublin; all callin' out to be eaten; but Johnny and his mother passed heedlessly by, on their way to Samarcand and Lipton's.

Further on, they'd pass through an avenue formed be tiers on tiers of cabbages an' cauliflowers, bushels of turnips, bins of spuds, hanks of onions, an' bunches of carrots, ready to be plucked, weighed, scooped out, or handed over to anyone who needed them; but Johnny and his mother passed heedless by, turning neither to right nor left to view the kindly fruits of the earth.

Then they'd pass through an alley of butchers' benches piled high with cutlets, chops, beef for boiling, and beef for roasting; with the butchers in their blue and white overalls, bawling, buy away, buy away, new shop open; but Johnny and his mother went by unheeding, heading straight to where they had set themselves to go.

On from Dorset Street into Bolton Street, where his mother popped into a chandler's shop, and filled the can with half a gallon of oil, and her basket with quarter a stone of washing-soda, a bar of yellow soap, two candles, a penny box of Colman's starch, and some bundles of firewood, bought to fulfil what was spoken by the prophet, saying, Wash ye, make ye clean; to keep the hearth aglow; and to be a light to them that sit in darkness.

As they passed through the gauntlet of shelves and shelves of cheese, bacon, eggs, and piles of bread, made fresh from the sweet-smelling wheat, grand and golden, enough to feed five thousand, hallowed bread, bread to comfort the heart of man, bread from the earth, bread from God, on sale by the bakers, Johnny suddenly saw his mother step to the left, and hurry on, as a drunken man came staggering along the path. The man lurched in towards the shop, knocked against a tray of pigs' feet, and sent them flying all over the place.

Good God, man, what are you afther doin'! shouted the shop-boy, as he rushed over to gather them up, a crowd gathering to laugh at what had happened. Like lightning, Johnny slid a lump of bacon into the folds of his kit-bag, and snatched up an egg as he passed by, running like hell to catch up with his mother who was a little ahead. Catching his mother's arm, he cried that he was cold, and ran her trotting along till they turned down into the dark and gloomy King's Inn Street, and he was safe and thrilled, but trembling.

Through Liffey Street they went, a street of old furniture shops, all shuttered close now, the street deserted, save for an odd straggler trudging over the straw and sodden paper that littered path and road; up the quay, across Essex Bridge, both of them bending to battle the breeze that swept up the Liffey, down Capel Street, into Dame Street, and, at last, into the warm, brightly-lighted, busy, big shop of Lipton's.

Johnny paused for a moment to look at himself in the huge mirrors panelling the walls, just inside the great door, showing him and his mother as lean, skinny-looking gazebos entering the shop.

—They'll show us up as fat as fools, goin' out, said his mother, laughing.

The shop was crowded, full of white-coated counter-jumpers handin' out tea an' sugar an' margarine as swift as hands could lay hold on them; with men in brown overalls trotting along pushing mountains of tea an' sugar in packages on little throlleys, moving silently and cunningly through the crowded shop, to fill up the vacancies on the shelves.

They waited their turn to get their seven pounds of sugar, a pound of tea for one an' six, an' a two-pound pot of Lipton's special plum an' apple jam; Johnny packing them in the kit-bag, while his mother slowly and feelingly put back sixpence change into the pocket of her skirt, strengthened with added lining to keep such treasures safe.

—Well, that'll have to provide us with whatever else we may need for the rest of the week, she murmured, lettin' the sixpence go at last when she felt it settle in the bottom of her pocket.

Johnny swung the kit-bag over his shoulder, an' he an' his ma manœuvred to the door through the people thronging the shop; pausing to see themselves in the mirrors, looking like fat pigs, bulging cheeks, great round bellies, an' enormous bodies, showing how great the stuff was that Lipton's sold; then the pair of them plunged once more into the dark night, the spitting rain, and the biting breeze; Johnny feeling all these trials less when he remembered the egg in his pocket and the bacon in the bag.

Out in the street, moving slowly forward in the kennel, was an old grey-bearded man, with a creaking voice, singing dolefully to the busy street. The collar of his coat was pulled up, as high as it could go, and his neck and chin were sunk down in it as low as they could go to shelther them from the wind and the rain; but when high notes came, the head had to be lifted to get anywhere near them, so the thin neck rose out of its cosy nest, to sink back again when the high notes were over, and the low notes came back. Quite a number of people paused in their hurry, searched in purse or pocket to hand out a penny; and Johnny felt envious that money could be so easy earned be the cracked singin' of

> Let us pause in life's pleasures, an' count its many fears,
> While we all sup sorrow with the poor;
> Here's a song that shall linger forever in our ears,
> Oh, hard times, come again no more.
>
> 'Tis the song, the sigh of the weary,
> Hard times, hard times, come again no more;
> Many days have you lingered around my cabin door,
> Oh, hard times, come again no more!

—Since we haven't anything to give him, it isn't fair to listen, said his mother, pulling the arm of the pausing Johnny.

When they got home again, Johnny spilled the sugar, tea, and jam out on the table. Then he put the lump of bacon and the egg right where his mother could see them when she turned round after taking off her wet things.

When she turned, she stared.

—How, in the name o' God, did those things ever creep into the kit-bag? she asked.

—I fecked them, said Johnny gleefully. When the dhrunken man fell an' scatthered things, I fecked them as I passed.

—A nice thing if you'd been caught feckin' them, she said, in a frightened voice. Never, never do the like again. D'ye know, had you been nabbed, it 'ud have meant five years or more in a reformatory for you? Never do it again, Johnny. Remember what you've been taught: Take no thought for your life, what ye shall eat; nor yet for your body, what ye shall put on; for the life is more than meat, an' the body than raiment; and your heavenly Father knoweth that ye have need of all these things; so keep your hands from pickin' an' stealin', for the future; and she carefully placed the bacon and the egg in the press.

Johnny sat silent by the fire, drying his damp trousers. After a few minutes he saw his mother putting on her bonnet and cape.

—Where'r you goin' now, Ma? he asked.

—I'm goin' out to get a couple o' nice heads of cabbage, with the sixpence I've left, to go with the bacon tomorrow, she said.

THE RED ABOVE THE GREEN

JOHNNY had been confined to the house all day, save when he had been sent for a message; looking right and left down the street before he started; and then darting to the shop to get what was wanted, and back again to the safety of his home, as fast as his legs could carry him, for there was war between him and his catholic comrades. For the last few days whenever they had clapped eyes on him they had booed him, called him a swadler, or sent stones flying at his heels. They lay around corners to pounce on him, shake him up, push him about, knock anything he had in his hand out of it, and tried to land a kick

on his arse when he broke from them and ran. Only in the company of
Middleton or Ecret, when he was in the street, did he feel safe. Today,
coming home with a glass of beer (after his mother had said We'll be
extravagant for once in our lives, and had kept back a shilling out of
the rent), he had met Kelly coming along, picking and eating bits out
of a loaf he held under his arm. Kelly kept his eyes fixed in front of
him, pretending not to see Johnny; but just when Johnny was passing,
he suddenly shot out a foot, tripping him; but Johnny managed to
save himself from a bad fall, and only a little of the beer was spilled
on the path.

Johnny ran over in a rage, and smote Kelly hard in the snot,
sending him flying home with blood flowing out of his nose.

—Keep away from them for a few days, Johnny, advised his
mother, when he told her what had happened, till the whole thing's
over. They just all go daft when we show the slightest sign of doin' a
devoir to the throne. They'll soon forget all about it; and, anyhow,
you shouldn't be flauntin' your loyal rosette in front of their faces.

—It's jealous they all are, said Johnny, looking down at the red,
white, and blue badge shining in the lapel of his coat. They're boy-
cottin' me because their ma's won't bring them to see the illuminations
I'm goin' to see with you, tonight.

For all parts of the city of Dublin where the real respectable people
lived, and where the real respectable people worked, were celebrating
in honour of something to do with the Majesty of Victoria, Queen of
Great Britain and Ireland and Empress of India; to show their love and
manifest their loyalty to her in millions of lights and multitudes of
flags, banners, bannerettes, pennons, guidons, standards, gonfalons,
and divers other symbols displayed on decorated posts linked together
by lovely coloured festoons; pictures of the Queen and Members of
the Royal Family, placed cunningly in suitable spots where all could
see them without inconvenience or discomfort.

All this was done that her subjects might be reminded and stimulated to offer deep prayers quietly in their hearts, as they promenaded
round looking at these gay diversions, to the Lord our heavenly
Father, high and mighty, King of kings, Lord of lords, and only
Ruler of princes, beseeching Him to behold with His favour our most
gracious Sovereign Lady, Queen Victoria, so that she might always
incline to His will, and walk in His way; and be strengthened so that
she might vanquish and overcome all her enemies; shoving as quick as
they could into the middle of the prayer a petition that it might please
God, too, to endue the Lords of the Council and all the Nobility with

grace, wisdom, and understanding; and to give the Magistrates grace to execute judgment and to maintain truth.

And it was the bounden duty of the wealthy and respectable who had security and comfort in the sufferance of the Lords and the Nobility, to rejoice and be glad over the happy and prosperous life lived in the Realm of England and in her dominions; showing the Realm's glory and their own jubilation by hanging out all things they could lay their hands on, of a comely shape and a happy hue, from windows, walls, towers, turrets, battlements, steeples, spires, balconies, balustrades, pinnacles, belfries, gables, and all other prominent places fit to be adorned, as outward and visible signs of their certain faith of a happy life and a holy death under the rule and during the reign of Her Most Gracious Majesty.

The Sunday-school scholars were having a tea-party and a magic-lantern, but the door to these joys was closed to Johnny. Johnny had stayed away from Sunday school, and so wasn't legally, morally, or spiritually entitled to join in the merry-making. If boys didn't go to church or Sunday school, then God would see that they didn't go to parties.

So Johnny's mother had patted him on the shoulder, and said, Never mind, son; we'll go together on the top of a thram all round the town, and see th' illuminations and the flowers and the flags; better than any oul' magic-lantern or tea-fight, with its stale buns and wathery tea.

They had to try to fight their way into the tram, for it looked as if the whole district had poured out to see the sights. Mrs. Casside put Johnny in front of her, and shoved him steadily forward, crying out to the crowd that surged around her, Give a breathin' space, there, to a poor delicate child whose eyes are fit to look at things only durin' the first few weeks of the year. It'll be a sorry day for Dublin when no-one has a thought for a poor boy sufferin' the terrible handicap of ill-health.

The conductor leaned forward from the porch of the tram, stretched out a sudden hand, and pulled Johnny and his mother on, pushing them up the narrow stairs to the top, as he planked himself in front of the others, perspiring and pushing their way on to the platform.

—A man 'ud want St. Pathrick's crozier to knock a little decency into yous, he said viciously as he tried to turn the pushing into an orderly parade. A nice way the whole of yous musta been reared, with your pushin' an' shovin', like a horde of uncivilised savages that has never seen anything beyond the rim o' their own land! I don't know th' hell why Parnell's wastin' his time thryin' to shape yous into something recognisable as men an' women. Honest to Jasus, I'm gettin' ashamed of me life to mention I'm Irish in front of anyone showin' the meanest sign or vestige of dickorum. And all of yous riskin' the breakage of your bodies to see a few twinklin' lights set over your heads to do honour to a famine queen rollin' about in a vis-a-vis at a time the Irish were gettin' shovelled, ten at a time, into deep an' desperate graves.

—You mind your own business be pullin' the bell for decent people to get on the thram, an' decent people to get off the thram, said a man, having a wide watery mouth with a moustache hanging over it like a weeping willow; an' don't be so sure that the personalities thravellin' are set on givin' a delicate or delirious show of loyalty to anyone or anything thryin' to devastate the efforts of our brave Irish Party fightin' for us on the floor of the House of Commons!

Johnny turned and pulled his mother's sleeve.

That oul' fella, he whispered, is Georgie Middleton's da. Whenever he appears in the street, the boys shout afther him, Georgie Middleton's ma wears the pants of Middleton's da.

—Thrue for you, mister, said a fat woman with a big bustle on her big behind, puffing her way as well as she could on to the tram; for a man who starts fluttherin' idle thoughts in front o' people's faces, accusin' them of hidin' the harp behind a gaudy crown, is just takin' advantage of a special time; an' ought, if things were in a settled state, to be walkin' close to the danger of a sensible castigation.

—Speakin' for meself only, said the man carrying the wide watery mouth with a drooping moustache hanging over it like a weeping willow, I've serious business to deal with in the heart of the town; an' if th' illuminations were brighter than even all the comets terrifyin' the sky, an' blazin' along at the same time, I'd sit with me face fast in front of me, seein' only the need for Home Rule, an' the green flag with the sunburst in the centre, wavin' everywhere the thram brings me.

—A prime lot of pathriots yous all are, to be sure, said the conductor sarcastically as he pulled the bellstrap for the tram to start; but I notice once yous get safe in, none of yous get out till the cruise is over. It's waitin' a long time I'll be to see yous busy bandagin' your eyes to keep at a distance the signs an' shows of revelry when the thram pencthrates into the sthreets, alive with the flags of all nations, save our own.

—That conductor's a very sensible man, and shrewd, said Johnny's mother, as they settled themselves into a seat on the top of the tram, giving them a grand view of everything before, behind, and around them.

—The conductor didn't seem to be feelin' very gay over what's takin' place in the city, remarked Johnny, even though he manœuvred us safely up to a good place on the top of the thram. I don't suppose he understood what he was sayin'. It's ignorance, only just ignorance, isn't it, Ma?

—Just ignorance, Johnny. He was really kind, though; and we must always remember that kind people are to be met everywhere; for though people often think wrong things, they can often be quite good.

—Even among the catholic Fenians, Ma? questioned Johnny.

—Specially among the Fenians. Your poor father often said that Fenians were all honest, outspoken men. One of them lived in our house before he had to fly the country, ere you were born; an' he an' your father were great friends. The little table with the drawer, at home, was bought be us when he was sellin' the few things him an' his wife had, just as they were hurryin' off to America. Besides, some of the Fenians were protestants too.

—But we're not really Irish, Ma; not really, you know, are we?

—Not Irish? echoed his mother. Of course, we're Irish. What on earth put it into your head that we weren't Irish?

—One day, an' us playin', Kelly told me that only catholics were really Irish; an' as we were protestants, we couldn't be anyway near to the Irish.

His mother's face reddened and her breath came in little pants.

—Th' ignorant, cheeky, little roman catholic scut! she ejaculated venomously. I could tell the whole seed, breed, and generation of the Kellys that the O'Casside Clan couldn't be more Irish than they are; and that when the Irish ruled in Ireland, the Clan Casside was just as important an' princely as the Clan Kelly. If your poor father was alive, he'd show from documented histhory that the Cassides stretched back farther than the year of one. And protestants are catholics, too; not roman catholics, but catholics, pure an' simple; real Irish, without a foreign title like Roman stuck on to it. If your poor father was alive, he'd show you in books solid arguments, never to be gainsaid, that St. Patrick was really as protestant as a protestant could be; and that the early Irish didn't hold with many things roman catholics now make a part of their creed; but preached and taught only the pure an' unadulterated gospel that we protestants believe today.

The tram circled into North Frederick Street, and Johnny forgot

about St. Patrick and the protestants. The paths were packed with
people, and many who couldn't find room on the paths walked along
in streams beside the slow-moving tram, forging ahead like a lighted
barge in the centre of a living river. Johnny saw gleaming lights and
waving flags stretching out before him as far as his eyes could reach.
Proud he felt, and full of delight that he could feel himself a living part
of this great display given to show the Irish people's fond attachment
to mighty England's Queen.

—Looka the Orange Lodge, Ma, exclaimed Johnny enthusiastically; oh, looka the Grand Orange Lodge!

From every second window floated a Royal Standard or a Union
Jack. Lights gleamed behind the window blinds, coloured with the
Orange and Blue of Nassau. In one window, with the blinds up, several
radiant orangemen-faces could be seen staring down at the teeming
crowds below. Right across the face of the building stretched, in
gleaming gas-lights, the flaming cry of *God Save the Queen*; and above
this, surrounded by a bronze laurel wreath, the steadily-gleaming
gas-light date of 1690. Over opposite was the stately church built for
the presbyterians by Alexander Findlater, Gentleman Grocer and
Wine Merchant of the city of Dublin, with its great flag flying from its
spire, and its heavy railings, coloured a vivid blue with golden spear
tops, shining gloriously in the gleam of the illuminations all around it.
Every head in the tram leaned forward and every neck was stretched
to gaze at the brilliant and wonderful sight.

—Isn't it all lovely, murmured Mrs. Casside, her face aglow,
showin', if ever anything can show, that the best people in the land an'
the poorest people in the land are hand in glove with the respect an'
loyalty that has diapered the city in light an' colour in honour of our
Queen.

—Y'Orange gets! shouted a voice below, and Johnny saw two
policemen seize a shouting man who was shaking his fist at a window
in the Orange Lodge.

—There's goin' to be a row in a minute, said Johnny excitedly;
looka the man gettin' taken be the police.

—He's only a dhrunken rowdy, said his mother. You'll always get
some fool ready to complain of the silence of peace. But one among so
many can't count for much.

The conductor came up the stairs with a scowl on his face, and
moved along between the rows of passengers, collecting the fares. The
passengers, gazing on the gleaming lights, the fluttering flags, and
waving festoons, offered their fares in outstretched hands to the

conductor without taking their ravished eyes from the garnished streets. He took the money from the outstretched hands, punched the tickets, and dropped them into the hands rigidly held out to receive them; the passengers never turning a head so that the vision of colour and light and jubilation wouldn't be lost, even for a moment. The conductor kept shaking his head scornfully as he went from one outstretched hand to another.

—Poor Wolfe Tone, poor Wolfe Tone, he kept murmuring, as he mouched along, poor Wolfe Tone.

Johnny watched the conductor going over to the top of the stairs after he had collected the fares. He stood there, with a hand on the stair-rail, staring at the passengers gaping at the decorations; then he sang in a low voice, half to himself and half to those who were in the tram:

Once I lay on the sod that lies over Wolfe Tone,
And thought how he perished in prison alone
His friends unavenged, and his counthry unfreed—
Oh, bitter, I said, is the pathriot's meed.

I was woke from my dream by the voices an' thread
Of a band who came into the home of the dead;
They carried no corpse, and they carried no stone,
And they stopped when they came to the grave of Wolfe Tone.

My heart overflowed, and I clasped every hand,
And I blessed and I blessed every one of the band;
Sweet, sweet! 'tis to find that such faith can remain
To the cause and the man so long vanquished and slain.

—Who was Wolfe Tone, Ma? whispered Johnny, moved strangely by seeing tears trickling down the cheeks of the conductor as he sang.

—A protestant rebel who went over to France nearly a hundhred years ago, an' brought back a great fleet to help the Irish drive the English outa the counthry. But God was guarding us, and He sent a mighty storm that scatthered the ships from Banthry Bay.

—What happened to poor Wolfe Tone, Ma?

—He fought on a French warship till it was captured by the British; and then he was put into prison, an' executed there by the English government.

—Why didn' the Irish save him?

—Oh, I don't know. It all happened long ago, an' everyone's forgotten all about it.

—But the conductor hasn't forgotten all about it, Ma.

—Let's look at the lights and the banners, said his mother, an' not bother our heads about things that don't matter now.

The conductor continued to sing, with one hand resting on the stair-rail, half to himself and half to the others:

> In Bodenstown Churchyard there is a green grave,
> And wildly around it the winter winds rave—
> Far betther they suit him—the ruin an' the gloom—
> Till Ireland, a Nation, can build him a tomb.

A seething crowd, making for Sackville Street, got wedged together opposite the Rotunda, whose dome was a mass of vivid lights topped by an imperial crown, mixed in the motto of Honi Soit Qui Mal Y Pense. The tram, caught fair in the middle of the crowd, came to a dead stop, and waited patiently for the throng to loosen a little, so that it might go on its way.

—Be God, said the man with the wide watery mouth and the moustache drooping over it like a weeping willow, as he turned his head to speak to all in general, be God, they haven't spared any expense to turn Dublin into a glittherin' an' a shinin' show!

—It's a shinin' sight to the eye that wants to see it so, said the conductor, with a bite in his voice; but to the Irish eye that sees thrue, it's but a grand gatherin' o' candles, lit to look sthrong, an' make merry over the corpse of our countbry.

—If it is, aself, said the man who had spoken before, it's a grand wake, surely. The whole city's out admirin', an' if we could only get the whole counthry to join in, there'd be peace; aye, an' lashin's an' leavin's in the land as well. But it's comin', it's comin', right enough. It's close to us already, for what Dublin thinks today, Ireland says tomorrow.

Mrs. Casside leant over towards the man who had spoken, her face bright with agreement.

—You say the solemn thruth, she said. You've only to take a look at the streets to see that everyone's eager to settle down into a government of law an' ordher, with the crown to be at the head of all the people. Only let them alone, an' the people are frantic for quietness. It only needs a sight an' a time like this to bring us to our senses.

—An', said the man, with a flash of anger, what we're all longin' for 'ud be here before we expected it, if it wasn't for the ruffian, Parnell, thrippin' up the counthry into a dismal turmoil.

—Oh, said Mrs. Casside reprovingly, whatever Parnell may be, he's far from bein' a ruffian. I'd say he's a son of a grand stock, an' a thorough gentleman.

—Thorough gentleman! sneered the man. The dirty dhrop's in him, or he wouldn't be rallyin' all the gobeens of the counthry against the intherests an' comfort of the few decent people left livin' here. What's he aimin' at, if it's not at becomin' the uncrowned king of Ireland?

Mrs. Casside stiffened, and leaned back to get as far as she could from the man with the wide watery mouth, and the moustache hanging over it like a weeping willow.

—If the thruth must be told, said she, after a pause, an' things allowed it, the counthry couldn't have a betther king!

—Hear, hear, said several people in different parts of the tram.

—Well, responded the man, yous'll find him out when you've well forgotten the wise warnin' given be a man who'll hie himself outa the counthry the first chance he gets.

—It's a pity, murmured a soft voice from the upper end of the tram, that a certain person can't hie himself outa the thram as well as outa the counthry.

—I can pass a remark, can't I? asked the man with the wide watery mouth. There's no law agin the passin' of a remark, is there? Bedammit, it's hard lines, if a man can't pass a simple remark in a simple way on a simple subject.

—When a simple remark lengthens out to a pageant of lies, said the soft voice from the upper end of the tram, it's time for someone or another to signal once for silence.

The man with the wide watery mouth stood up from his seat, his face flushed, and his eyes sparkling.

—I say, he shouted, that an unbelievin' protestant's no kind of a man to be the leadher of the Irish Race! I'm not goin' to let meself be limited. What the people want 's a fair an' quiet way of differin' from each other, without heat or haughtiness, an' a decent regard for everybody else's opinion; an' fists shaken in me face won't frighten me! I say that Parnell's moonlightin', police-stonin' gang's ruinin' the counthry!

The conductor's head appeared above the top of the stairway. The scowl on his face had settled. He glared at the rows of people sitting on the top of the tram. He shook the satchel slung round his shoulder, rattling the money in it to attract attention.

—Look here, he said loudly, I can't have these goin's on on the top of me thram, disturbin' the passengers in the inside of the vehicle! If yous are so loyal as yous are anxious to show yourselves, yous ought to be able to keep the Queen's peace.

Down the conductor went again, as the crowd suddenly moved on, and the tram, finding room to go forward, glided slowly past the Rotunda over the crossing of Great Britain Street, giving all just time for a swift glance at Mooney's pub, with its well-known clock circled with lights, right into the glowing heart of the decorations and illuminations of the glorious thoroughfare of Sackville Street, the widest street in the whole of civilised Europe. There they were, the lights in their millions, the flags in their thousands, flaunting, flying, and fluttering from windows low down and windows high up; from roofs flat and roofs steep; blue, red, yellow, green, white, and purple flags; with Dublin's blue banner, endorsed with three flaming castles, holding many a place of honour.

Ay, and in many a place, too, swung the flag of Germany, with its black cross stretched over the field, or its savagely-beaked eagle ready to peck the eye of the world out; for Germany had conquered France only a few years ago, and she and England were going along, arm in arm; with the House of Saxe-Coburg-Gotha, and the House of Mecklenburg-Schwerin, and all the other Houses in Germany held in great esteem by all the rich and poor respectable protestants, Johnny's mother told him. And Johnny remembered once, when a German ambassador had visited his school, all the children, after months of preparation, and countless slaps, had sung, in his honour:

> Dear Fatherland,
> Each child of thine,
> Faithful and true, will guard, will guard the Rhine!

There, too, was the flag of Denmark, for since the Prince of Wales had married Alexandra, the Danish flag and England's henceforth flew side be side.

Every shop, warehouse, bank, and building fluttered with flags; and walls flamed with rose, shamrock, and thistle, harps here and crowns there, with lions and unicorns in special places. It was a gorgeous sight as the tram moved slowly through the street, walled with fire; with copings, pillars, pediments, balconies, and balustrades swathed in purple and crimson cloths, edged with the finest gold; and garlands of red, white, and blue joining them all lovingly together; fair and fine linen, taffeta, and tabinet of gentle weave, brought out and displayed with great cunning in honour of England's valiant Queen.

On the tram crawled between the people crowding the street, the driver constantly blowing his whistle as a reminder to the people to keep a way clear; over Carlisle Bridge, into, and up, Westmoreland

Street, Johnny pointing to the brightly-lit clock, surmounted by a sparkling crown, slung out of the office of the *Irish Times*.

—It's a great thing, said Johnny's mother, to see such enormous crowds so ordherly, beset only with the one thought of enjoyin' themselves. If the government 'ud establish a Royal Residence here, there'd be no more loyal and law-abidin' people in the whole livin' world than the Irish people. We're comin' now to the heart of it all, she added — Thrinity College an' the Bank of Ireland.

The tram slowly glided, with the crowd around it, into a wide well of gleaming, glittering, rippling lights, turning the night into a laughing day. Through the first few streets, Johnny had seen the jewels hanging from Dublin's ear and a shimmering circle of gems around her neck; but here he stared at the beautiful crown set lovingly on her head. Trinity College and the Royal Bank of Ireland were dripping in jewels of light, and the countless banners fluttered like broad blossoms flowering in the midst of flames. The great mass of people stood silent and still, gazing spellbound in the midst of the wonder. The silence was fraught with a quiet passion of esteem and fealty. It was the adorning of the rock of their salvation, and Johnny and his mother pressed each other's hands.

Out in the middle distance, Johnny caught sight of sparkling spots of silver shining out in the darker patches close to less brilliantly lighted buildings. They were the silver-mounted helmets of the police standing in batches, here and there, under the doorways and gateways of the buildings.

Suddenly a crowd of well-dressed young men, arranged in ranks like soldiers, one of them carrying a big Union Jack, began to sing with all the vigour of their voices and all the fervour of their young hearts:

> God save our gracious Queen,
> Long live our noble Queen,
> God save the Queen!

—The College Boys are out, the College Boys are out! shouted the man of the wide watery mouth, jumping to his feet, and hanging half out over the top of the tram. Now we'll see a snatch of the thruth at last!

But the vigour of the lusty singing voices was pushed down to a murmur by a low humming boo from the crowd, growing louder and deeper till it silenced the song and shook itself into a menacing roar of anger. A crash of splintered glass was heard, and pieces of a broken college window fell tinkling on to the pavement below. The menacing roar mellowed into a chanting challenge, low at first, but gradually growing to the tumbling booming of a great river in flood, as the huge crowd sang and pressed against the police in an effort to come closer to the College Boys:

> The jealous English tyrant, now, has banned our Irish green,
> And forced us to conceal it, like a something foul and mean;
> But yet, by heavens! he'll sooner raise his victims from the dead,
> Than force our hearts to leave the green and cotton to the red!

Someone raised a great green flag; there was a great cheer; the crowd pressed forward, and the police were hard put to keep them back; and broken glass from the college windows continued to fall tinkling on to the pavement below, as the song went on:

> We'll trust ourselves, for God is good, and blesses those who lean
> On their brave hearts, and not upon an earthly king or queen;
> And freely as we lift our hands, we vow our blood to shed,
> Once and forever more to raise the green above the red!

Johnny saw the singing crowd suddenly surge forward, break the line of policemen barring their way, and attack the College Boys with fists and sticks, driving them back, back, back towards the college gates. He heard a bell tolling inside the college; saw the heavy entrance doors open, and a crowd of other College Boys pouring out, armed with heavy sticks, all cheering and yelling as they hurried on to join their comrades attacked by the people. He saw the police struggling with the crowd, trying hard to keep together, and smiting as hard as they could every head that came within reach of a baton; but one by one they were falling, to be savagely kicked and trampled on by the angry members of the dense crowd. And there in it all stood the tram, like a motionless ship in a raging sea, while the gentle horses stood still together in the midst of the tumult.

Some of the crowd had got a rope, had flung it over the pole carrying a great Royal Standard, flying from a big bank building. Hundreds of hands tugged and tugged till the pole snapped, and the great flag came fluttering down among the delighted crowd who struggled with each other to be the first to tear it to pieces.

—Looka them pulling down the Royal Standard, moaned the man of the wide watery mouth. His mouth slavered with rage, and he could hardly speak. Where's the polish! Why don't the polish do somethin' — the gang of well-clad, well-fed, lazy, useless bastards! If I was betther dhressed than I am, I be down in a jiffy to show them how to jue their job.

—Betther if we hadn't come out at all, Mrs. Casside kept murmuring, keeping a tight grip of Johnny's hand. I wish we hadn't come out at all.

A frightened cry rang out as the crowd and the College Boys were fighting, The horse police, the horse police, here's the horse police! Far away up Dame Street, Johnny saw the silvered helmets of the horse police bobbing up and down, becoming brighter and drawing nearer second be second. A great wedge of the crowd pressed back into Grafton Street, pushing, shoving, and fisting its way on to get clear of the oncoming mounted police. Women screamed as they were shoved headlong back, and some men tried to lift terrified children on to their shoulders. In one place Johnny saw a yelling woman savagely trying to fight her way back to the thick of the crowd, screaming out:

Me Tommie's lost; he was pushed out o' me hands; let me back, God damn yous, till I find me Tommie! Oh, please, please, make way for me!

But the crowd was helpless, and she was pushed back and back, till Johnny lost sight of her, still screaming to be let back to find her Tommie.

The mounted constables were followed by a great crowd, booing and yelling, throwing stones, bottles, and even bits of iron; coming as close as they dared to the heels of the horses. Occasionally some of the police would wheel, charge back, and the crowd following would scatter; to come back again as soon as the mounted police had turned to their comrades. Once, Johnny saw a mounted constable stiffen in his saddle, give a little yelp, letting go his hold on the long truncheon so that it hung by the thong on his wrist, turn his face backwards, showing that his right cheek had been cut open by the jagged end of half a bottle, flung by a hating hand in the crowd. Other constables ran to help the wounded man from his horse; and one of them tied up the gaping cheek with a large handkerchief borrowed from a comrade.

Some of those fighting the College Boys shouted a warning as the mounted men came curvetting into College Street; the fighters broke conflict, and the enemies of the loyal College Boys retreated down Westmoreland and College Streets, some running with a limp and others with bent heads, and hands clasped over them. The man carrying the long green banner ran with them, but the weight of the pole and the folds of the flag fluttering round his legs hampered his running. The police, angry at the fall of their comrade, came forward at a hard gallop in pursuit of the fleeing crowd. One of them, galloping by the man with the flag, leaned over his horse, swung his long baton, and brought it down on the man's head, tumbling him over to lay him stretched out near the centre of the street, almost hidden in the folds of his green banner.

Johnny shrank back and pressed close to his mother, feeling her body shudder deep as she saw.

A mounted police officer came trotting over to the tram, leaned over his horse, and touched the driver on the shoulder with a slender whip.

—Take your tram to hell out of this, back to where it came — quick! he ordered.

The driver lepped down off his platform, unhooked the tracing-pole with one hand, turned the horses to the opposite end of the tram by the reins with the other, hooked the tracing-pole again, and climbed on to the platform. The conductor pulled his bell, and the tram moved slowly back the way it had come; out of the gas-glittering homage to a Queen; out of the purple and crimson and gold; out of the pomp on the walls and the bloodshed in the street; out of sight of the gleaming crowns and beaming blessings, back to the dimness of Dorset Street and home.

The last sight that Johnny saw, as the tram moved slowly away, was the mounted police making a galloping charge towards Dame Street, in the middle of a storm of boos and stones and bottles; and a lone huddled figure lying still in the street, midway between the bank and the college, almost hidden in the folds of a gay green banner.

I KNOCK AT THE DOOR

JOHNNY'S mother was very concerned about his education. So was Archie in a hazy and bullying kind of way; and so was Ella, who was nursing her first baby and whose husband was soon to bid goodbye to the army forever. Ella's education of her own husband was a failure, as Johnny said grumblingly, and now she wanted to fix her teeth in him. Many and mighty were the collogin' that went on between her an' her mother about poor Johnny's ignorance of all things.

One day Ella came, bringing a bundle of clothes for her mother to wash; when the washing was over, they sat down to a cup of tea and a crumpet, to start the talk all over again.

—I know he can't be let go on as he's goin', said Mrs. Casside, or, when he's a man, he won't even know the number on his own hall-door. He must be taught something, even though he can't go to school. The last thing throublin' your poor father's mind, before he died, was that Johnny was bound to grow up a dunce.

Ella sipped her tea, and thought for a moment.

—I can't help thinking that he should have been kept to school, in spite of his eyes, she said. Oh, I know the doctors said he mustn't, she went on swiftly, to forestall her mother who was opening her mouth to speak; but the doctors haven't to rear him. A common labourer is all he'll be able to be when the time comes for him to take his place in life.

Your own husband won't be much more, thought her mother; but she held her tongue.

—A common labourer, went on Ella, if he's sthrong enough even for that. It was a sad mistake not to have let him go to the Blue-coat School, afther all the trouble the rector and Mr. Purefoy took to get him admitted.

Her mother's mouth hardened.

—That's all over an' done with, she said. As long as I live, the boy'll never set foot in an institution.

—He'd be well fed an' clad, anyway, retorted Ella.

—They're a lot, but they're not everything. The boy hasn't much here, but he has a home.

There had been a great how-do-you-do about this Blue-coat School for Johnny. Ella and Archie had fed him with the grandeur of the boys' lovely blue uniform, with its deep collar and cuffs of chrome yellow, long trousers, glengarry cap, blucher boots that were fastened with buckle and strap, and, lastly, a natty cane to be carried under the arm. The brothers in the army had written home to say the idea was a grand one; and Johnny, himself, had pressed his mother to agree. But his mother had stood out against them all; and every time Johnny pleaded all the good things about the school, she put him off with, You're far betther off as you are, here.

—They'd teach him his religion, went on Ella.

—They'd hammer it into him, Ella. Every turn he'd take would be chronicled; and if one wasn't done as they had planned, the boy'd be broken into their way of doin' it; an' Johnny's my boy, an' not theirs. If they're anxious to feed him, let them feed him here; if they're anxious to clothe him, let them clothe him here. I'm not goin' to have the life in him cowed out of him, as long as I can prevent it. There's no use of harpin' on the Blue-coat School, for me mind's made up — the boy won't go into it.

—I'm arguin' only for the boy's own good, said Ella righteously.

—Everyone advisin' me about the boy says he's arguin' only for the boy's own good.

—You've only to look at him, said Ella, to see what's happening — he has hardly any forehead at all.

—I'm doin' all I can about that, an' it's certainly a little betther than it was, said the mother. Three times a day I brush it off his forehead as hard as I can for more'n quarter of an hour; an' the hair growin' close to his eyes is bound to wear away in time. An', afther brushin' it at night, I put a tight bandage to keep a pull up on the hair while he's asleep. Even if his eyes prevent him from learnin' much, aself, I'll not let him go through life with a low forehead. I'd like to do something for his teeth, but they'll have to take their chance.

Ella went over to rummage among the books left behind as unsaleable out of her father's fine store. She brought back a Superseded Spelling-book, by Sullivan, who held that by learning affixes and suffixes, Latin and Greek roots, you could net words in hundreds, as against the old method of fishing one word up at a time; a Reading Lesson Book; a Primer of Grammar; and simple Lessons in Geography.

—Here, she said, is all he'll need for the present. Make him learn the parts I've marked in each book, an', if he learns a like lot every day for a year, he'll know a little at the end of it.

Johnny was brought in from the street, and told what he had to do.

—I'm not goin' to do it, he said viciously; I won't do it. I'm good enough as I am.

—Very well, said his mother firmly, at the end of the week, no penny for your *Boys of London and New York*. Remember, no lessons, no penny for your paper.

Johnny was beaten. He'd as lief lose his life as lose the stories of Old King Brady, the Wonder Detective, Red Eagle, the Friend of the Palefaces, or From Bootblack to Broker, the story of business life in New York, all of which his mother helped him to read when he brought the paper home.

After Ella had read the big words for him, he put on his cap, and sauntered gloomily off to where there was a strip of waste ground near the railway, covered with coarse grass, dandelions, daisies, dead-nettles, plantains, rag-worts, an odd scarlet pimpernel, and patches of scarlet poppies. Choosing a fair spot of grass, bordered with poppies and daisies, he sat down, opened his books, watched, for a moment, bees busy in a clump of clover; and then began his studies.

Grammar, he tried to read, is the art of speaking, reading, and writing the English language correctly. It is divided into four parts, namely, Orthography, Etymology, Syntax, and Prosody. Orthography deals with the art of spelling; Etymology with the origin and derivation of words; Syntax with the proper construction of sentences; and Prosody with the laws and rules of poethry.

—Curse o' God on it! he muttered, isn't it terrible!

He opened the Reading Book, and found that Ella had marked the first few verses of *The Brook*, by Tennyson.

—Who the hell's Tennyson? he asked himself, as he slowly recited:

I come from haunts of coot and hern,
I make a sudden sally
And sparkle out among the fern,
To bicker down a valley.

—Coot an' hern, he murmured; I wondher what they are? Must be some kinda birds, ma says; but what kinda birds? He knew well the kinda birds sparrows were; not worth a tuppenny damn, for even Jesus said that two of them were sold in Jerusalem for a farthing; indeed, you wouldn't get even that for a dozen of them in Dublin. He had seen a redpole, a green linnet, a thrush, a blackbird, and a goldfinch, all in cages; they were all the birds he had seen so far; but he had never even heard of a coot or a hern. But this kinda mopin'll never get on with the work; and he started to recite again:

By thirty hills I hurry down,
Or slip between the ridges,
By twenty thorps, a little town,
And half a hundred bridges.

Till last by Philip's farm I flow
To join the brimming river,
For men may come and men may go,
But I go on for ever.

—Only one more verse, murmured Johnny, only one more river to cross.

I chatter over stony ways,
In little sharps and trebles,
I bubble into eddying bays,
I babble on the pebbles.

Sharps an' threbles — what did they mean? He knew that to be sharp meant to have an edge on anything that would cut, if you weren't careful; but what had sharp to do with the running water of a brook? And what was a threble? He sighed. The useless and puzzlin' things they made him learn. He knew what the sea was, because he had seen it at Sandymount. And a river, too, for one flowed through the city. What was the use of askin' him to learn what things were when he knew what they were already? But what about their own river, the Liffey? Where did it make its start? No-one could tell him. His mother didn't know; Ella didn't know; Archie didn't know. Somewhere or another, was all they could say. Didn't he know that himself! An' they're cross with you over something you don't know, an' just as cross when you ask them something they don't know themselves. Take the Tolka. That was called a river, yet it was only the size of a brook, for he had paddled in it, and had filled a jar with minnows out of it. Yet it was the river Tolka. Puzzle, puzzle, puzzle. Of course he remembered the time it flooded the rotting little white-washed cottages on its bank, and swept away swift the statue of the Blessed Virgin standing in the muddy space beside the river. The statue had floated back again against the flow, like bread cast upon the waters, returning after many days, and stayed floating beside the houses, till it was taken up, cleaned, painted blue and white, and put back on its pedestal again. Yes, when it was in flood, the Tolka was a river; but every other time, it was only a brook.

A slender shadow fell across the poppies and the daisies. Johnny looked up, and saw Jennie Clitheroe standing beside him. Each eyed the other for a few moments, shyly, in silence.

—Just comin' from school? he asked.

—Yes, she answered, just back from school. What are you doin' with the school books?

—Just havin' a little look at them.

She made a place beside the poppies, passed a hand along her skirt to tuck it in, sat down beside him, and fingered the books.

—Oh, I'm in the fifth standard, now, she said, and I passed out of these years ago. I'm learnin' Euclid an' everything.

Johnny gathered the books up and stuffed them into his pocket.

—Y'know the river Liffey? he asked.

—'Course I do.

—Well, where does it start from?

—How where does it start from? she asked vaguely.

—Where does it begin; where can you find it a thrickle before it swells into a river?

—It's not mentioned in any of my books, said Jennie, so it

mustn't much matter. D'ye know yourself?

—'Course I do.

—Where does it start, then?

—Ah, said Johnny mockingly, let the great scholar go an' find out.

Jennie picked a daisy, and began to pluck the petals off, one by one, murmuring, this year, next year, sometime, never; this year, next year, sometime, never; this year — and she let the last petal fall on the grass.

—This year, what? he asked.

—I'm goin' to be married, she said roguishly.

—Who'r you goin' to marry?

—Ah, she said mockingly, let the great scholar go an' guess.

He caught her by the shoulders, and pulled her back towards him.

—Tell me who'r you goin' to marry, or I'll hold you like this forever.

—You couldn't hold me a second longer, if I thried to break away, she said defiantly.

He pulled her back till her brown curls were pressed against his chest, and her deep brown eyes were looking up into his.

—You just thry to get away, he mocked.

She moved, but put no big effort into it, and then lay quiet, looking up into his face, smiling. Suddenly he bent down and kissed her twice hard on the mouth. Then he shoved her away in sudden shame, his face flushing. He jumped up and made off through the poppies and dead-nettles, frightened at what he had done.

—I'll tell me mother, she cried out after him.

—Tell her, then, he said defiantly, looking back at her, still sitting among the poppies, with a white butterfly fluttering near her. I don't care whether you do or no.

Girls tell their mothers everything, he thought, resentfully, as he walked away. Why did she let him kiss her, anyway? She could easily have broken away, if she wanted. She was more to blame, really, than I was. Oh, let her tell, if she likes.

He took the Reading Lesson-book out of his pocket, opened it, and recited:

> I chatther, chatther as I flow
> To join the brimming river,
> For men may come and men may go,
> But I go on for ever.

Well, he'd learned poethry and had kissed a girl. If he hadn' gone to school, he'd met the scholars; if he hadn' gone into the house, he had knocked at the door.

PICTURES IN THE HALLWAY

Time flies over us, but leaves its shadow behind

To the memory of the Rev. E. M. Griffin, B.D., M.A.,
one-time Rector of St. Barnabas, Dublin.
A fine scholar; a man of a many-branched kindness,
whose sensitive hand was the first to give
the clasp of friendship to the author

A COFFIN COMES TO IRELAND

An October sky was black over the whole of Dublin; not a single star had travelled into the darkness: and a bitter rain was pelting down on the silent streets. The rain had the still and unresisting city to itself. No one was out to feel it, and it seemed to pelt down harder in rage because there wasn't a soul out to shiver under its coldness and its sting. Even the heavy-coated and oil-caped police were hidden back in the shelter of the deepest doorways, uneasily dozing the night hours away, lulled into drowsiness by the slashing rain's pelting murmur falling on the spray-swept pavements. Everyone else was fast asleep in bed. Safe and sound oul' Dublin swept itself to sleep, well watched over by God and His Blessed Mother, assisted by the glorious company of the apostles, the goodly fellowship of the prophets, and the noble army of martyrs; each man, woman, and child having as well a guardian angel leaning over the bed, watching, with a well-cocked eye, the charge left in his care; so safe and sound and well oul' Dublin slept. Sound she was in sleep, and safe she felt, for God was there, and they were here, and the night was passing silently away, and soberly, except for the rain dancing a savage dance all over the city on the patient pavements. Behind heavy silken curtains, in happy-looking beds, slept the nicely night-gowned; behind tattered and tumbled curtains, on muddled mattresses, gowned in paltry calico or faded flannelette, slept the sisters and brothers of the nicely night-gowned. But the poor protestants turned up their noses at the guardian angels, for they didn't believe in them, and felt sure and safer stuck in the arms of Jesus, their rock of ages and their morning star.

Between two narrow sheets, thickly ribbed with patches, under the eyes of God, among the prophets, apostles, and martyrs, in the midst of the valley of sleep, slept Johnny in his skin, for he had neither calico nor flannelette to decorate his rest. Under a few old coats and several big squares of buff felt, showing the inky imprint of the *Daily Express*, pinched by Archie from the stereotypers' room, Johnny lay snug, for the fire of the day lay half awake still in the grate and the room was still warm; while his mother slept in the little room opposite, in a fast sleep, too tired to feel cold, finding in sleep the one glamour of a hard day.

The fire was the one thing that Mrs. Casside kept going without fail.

179

It was the one thing, she said, that made a house a home. Without a mother, she'd say, a home isn't much; without a fire, it's less. The poor must walk in the light of God and in the light of their fire. A full belly in a fireless room felt frosty; an empty belly beside a fine fire felt fuller. A bright fire, she said, in a poor home is the shadow of God's smile.

Johnny opened his sleepy eyes with difficulty, and saw over opposite the dull glow of the fading embers in the dusty grate. The fire was slowly dying, and the room was growing a little chillier, so Johnny's hand groped around the bed and pulled the *Daily Express* blanket closer round his naked shoulders; pulled it nice and tight around him, and closed his heavy eyes, while he dimly heard the rain pouring down outside and beating on the window-pane.

—Pity, he murmured, that a fire had to die down, to grow cold, to pass away, to change from dancing flame to throublesome dust an' ashes: like us, he thought, like ourselves, like every man; in everyone, the Sunday school says, sooner or later, the flame dies down to dust an' ashes. But me Ma says, he went on thinking slower and slower, me Ma says th' oul' Sunday school says a lot it shouldn't think, an', an' it's time, time enough to think o' dyin' down to dust an' ashes when you're old an' blind an' deaf an' dumb an' bothered.

As he tried to slide back into a warm and steady sleep, he heard a stir out in the rain-soaked, shivery streets, coming nearer and nearer till the stir was heard in the house, and nearer, till the stir was heard in his own room. Through his heavy-hanging lids, the shadowy glimpse of a dark form, like his mother, and another, like his brother, Archie, moving stealthily about the room, slid like a sly dream into his sleepy mind, and low, far-away murmurs told him they were talking together. He saw the tiny glow that still lingered in the fire suddenly darken down and disappear, and he felt faintly that his mother had flung a shovel of coal on to the fire. He waited in a drowsy stillness, watching and listening, till he saw bright flames rising steadily from the fire that had darkened down, and, in the midst of the rising flames, the dark form of his mother fixing the kettle firmly down on the top of the flaming coal.

—Tea, thought Johnny; she's going to make tea, so something must be up.

He raised himself up on his elbow, rubbed his eyes, looked over at his mother who was now putting some cups and saucers on the table; while Archie was tugging on his trousers standing by the old horsehair sofa which was a stately seat by day and Archie's narrow and nettlesome bed by night.

Now Johnny heard the patter of feet in the street mingling with the patter of the rain upon the pavements, and the sound of voices crossing and recrossing each other, crying Stop Press, Stop Press! He could hear the hasty Archie cursing querulously that a fella could never get his trousers on quick when he wanted to, and his mother muttering, half to herself, We'll get to know all about it soon enough; and the noise of windows and doors opening, and the murmur of the kettle singing her song, panting it out, panting it out, and she sitting in the midst of the flames rising from the red glow of the fire.

—What's wrong, mother? asked Johnny, his sleep falling from him, his eyes opening wider, his ears hearing heartily the sounds in the room and the sounds outside in the street.

—You lie down, you lie down, replied his mother, an' go asleep again.

—Why've you lit th' fire, an' why've you made tea? inquired Johnny.

—Poor Parnell's dead, said Archie, busy with his boots.

—It may be only a rumour, murmured his mother.

—We'll soon know for certain when we get a paper, muttered Archie.

Parnell! What had this man done that all the people were so upset about him, one way or another? The mention of his name always gave rise to a boo or a cheer. The roman catholics who wouldn't let a word be said against him a while ago, now couldn't pick out words villainous enough to describe him; while the protestants who were always ashamed of him, now found grace and dignity in the man the roman catholics had put beyond the pale.

Well, they could all breathe in peace now that he was dead. His Ma said his Da often said that the first chance the priests ever got, they'd down Parnell. And here he was now, down among the dead men.

The pattering of the feet went on in the streets outside, mingling with the patter of the rain on the pavements. Archie, safe now with his breeches and his boots on, whipped up his cap, and hurried out to try to get a copy of the Stop Press telling that a golden bowl was broken, a silver cord loosened, and a wheel broken at a mighty cistern.

For fiddling with a woman or something, the catholics had turned away from him. Kitty O'Shea it was who had brought the anger of the righteous overmuch upon him. Johnny, once day, had hadda row with Kelly over him, sticking up for Parnell when Kelly shouted Parnell was a bad bugger, an' no right-minded Irish kid 'id mention his name. He had answered Kelly, saying that Parnell was a mighty man of valour, and acquainted with thruth; and Kelly had chanted,

We'll hang oul' Parnell on a sour apple three,
We'll hang oul' Parnell on a sour apple three,
We'll hang oul' Parnell on a sour apple three,
     As we go marchin' along!

And he had chanted back,

We'll hang oul' Tim Healy on a sour apple three,
We'll hang oul' Tim Healy on a sour apple three,
We'll hang oul' Tim Healy on a sour apple three,
     As we go marchin' along!

Then Kelly had spat on him, and he had made for Kelly with eyes flaming, teeth bared, fists clenched, to diminish him, down him, and utterly destroy him outa th' land o' Canaan; but Kelly ran for his life, stopping a safe distance off to throw a stone; and they had fought a great battle, with stones, each aiming at the other's head, till a policeman appearing round the corner, they hooked it off to get outa reach of the horney's hand.

Now Parnell was dead, and they were crying it in the streets; and fear came upon them that the one man they had was gone. A great thing had been taken, and a lot of little things had been left. They'd have to go now through the valley of the shadow of life alone; face their enemies alone; fight their enemies alone; and they divided, and moved by every wind, unstable as water. The pillar of fire that had led them so long and so bravely and so brightly had died out; and they were all in the dark, like the protestant bishops.

Johnny's mother had wet the tea, and was sitting thoughtfully by the fire, waiting for Archie to come back with the Stop Press. Johnny was well awake now, and could fully hear the patter of the feet on the street outside and the more musical patter of the rain falling on the pavement. Something exciting had happened, and he wasn't going to be left out of it. Besides, getting up gave him a further chance of reading the grand adventures of Frank Reade, Junr., the Professor, Barney and Pompey, with their electric car in the unknown jungles of Central Africa. So he slid from the bed and began to put on his trousers. When he was dressed, he sat down by the fire on the opposite side to his mother, flung himself into the middle of the jungle, and waited, with his mother, for Archie to come back with the Stop Press.

His mother looked at him for a moment or two, then she got

silently up and put another cup and saucer on the table.

—You might as well have a cup with us, she murmured. It won't do you much harm to lose a little sleep on a night like this.

Johnny's mind was in the midst of the jungle, and his heart was gladdened by the warmth of the fire, when the door opened and in came Archie, wearing a solemn face, the glistening rain-drops gathered thick on the hair his cap hadn't covered, and with a paper snugly sheltered under the breast of his coat.

He went over, sat down by the fire, and opened the paper slowly.

—It's thrue, he said, it's too thrue — Parnell's gone from us for ever.

Johnny could hardly help tittering. He knew in his heart that Archie was forcing sorrow into his face; that he didn't care if Parnells died every day of the week; for often and often Johnny had heard him run Parnell down, for no one who didn't do that could stay very long working for the *Daily Express* and *The Warder*, whose weekly cartoons for years had been a generous denial of anything good, or semigood, or damnmy-semi-good in Parnell or his policy; for the owners of the papers were begotten of the whorus of England, through MacMourrough of the curses, the time the Normans came over the sea to set up a new civilisation where none was; blessed by the holy Pope, they came, with horse and sword and lance and shield and a sthrong desire for thrue religion to be fostered among the holy heathen Irish.

—In Brighton, when the clock was sthrikin' twelve, said Archie, he passed away. Give me love to me colleagues an' to th' Irish race, were th' last words he utthered in this world. He said he'd be with us on Saturday an' he's keepin' his word: he's comin' back to us on that very day — in a coffin. Archie crumbled up the paper viciously. The dastards have done it to him: in room 15, they slew th' man that made them. That's where it was done; that's where Parnell was sacrificed by Healy an' his pack o' conceited catholic curs. In room 15, they sthruck him down undher ordhers from that spidery-minded, Bible-basted bastard, Gladstone!

There, thought Johnny, th' pack gathered to down their Leader. They sat up all night so that they might be there first thing when the door opened. Their hearts were warm for the work. A pig grunted, a dog snarled, a fox barked, a wolf howled, and a rat squealed, waiting for the door to be opened. They were in a state of grace; Parnell wasn't. They were the ten or twenty righteous men who would deliver the Nation from God's and the catholic bishops' wrath. Parnell had forfeited the right to lead the holy men of the holy island of scuts and schemers. Besides giving an untidy look to Kitty O'Shea, the man had gone too far in other ways. Didn't he say in America that, None of us, whether we be in Ireland or America, or wherever we may be, will be satisfied till we have destroyed the last link which keeps Ireland bound to England; and didn't the large towns and small towns and great cities vie with each other to show him honour? Didn't Governors of States knock each other down going to receive him, in the dint of their hurry to get there first? Didn't armed soldiers line the streets he passed through, firing salvoes of artillery when his carriage came in sight; and didn't Congress make him come to speak to its members, and let them hear the message his heart had for Ireland and the world? Was there e'er an Englishman ever got that in the Land of the Stars and Stripes? Salvoes of artillery they got, right enough, and musket-fire at Bunker's Hill, Yorktown, and Saratoga; but that was a welcome that they didn't want.

But the O'Briens, the Dillons, and the Healys, mudmen, madmen, badmen, bedmen, deadmen, spedmen, spudmen, dudmen, poked on by the bishops, were dead set on making an end of him, so that they might keep a tight hold on the people they were grooming down for an insect seculorum life; for it was plain that Parnell was turning the people aside from the bishops that maketh them poor, and were striving to make their homes their own, and to plant and to mow and to reap and to sow in safety; forgetting that the real seeds to be sown were eternal seeds, and not just those that sprang up this season and died down the next; seeds that were likely to be trampled down, dug up, and scattered abroad in the medley of the plan of campaign; while in the distance, the Right Honourable Ewart Gladstone, with his big ear on his big head, cocked to hear what was going on, sat with his most honourable, most respectable, and most moral bum glued to the impregnable rock of Holy Scripture; sat on, and waited for the Irish swine-hearts to do unto Parnell as they wouldn't that others should do unto them, so that he could satisfy the Nonconformist conscience after the impudence of Parnell shoving his white and slender finger into the solid, cold, glittering eye of plump biblical piety fashioned in the new annunciation of the Westminster Confession. Then there was the scandal the good catholics felt had been given to the multitude of saints who had made her what she was and is and is to be; and in the heat of it all, whom did they hear calling over the banisters of the top story of heaven but St. Patrick himself, and he yelling at them out of a

Exordium Purgatorius Patricius

to stir themselves, and dhrain out this bad dhrop which had fallen into Ireland's pool of perfect virtue, so that I may have a little ayse where I now am, afther toilin' an' moilin' for yous, day in an' day out, for years, prayin' on the cowld top o' Croagh Pathrick for yous till I was near black in th' face; for, if yous don't do the needful, it's all up with me labour of huntin' yous into a state o' grace, unequalled in any other so-an'-so land th' wide world over; an' yous ought to know, since I didn't let it go with Oisin, son o' Finn, son o' Coole, I'm not going to let it go with Parnell, an' so make a show of meself before all the grinnin' foreign canonised bowseys gathered round me, here, waitin' for a chance to laugh outright an' inright, all of them glaumin' to see something that'll put a sthrain on perpetual piety for me Irish flock; an' a guffaw from them 'id be a poor thing for me to hear an' have to bear, considerin' th' pains an' penances o' Mount Slemish, an' then, afther I had slipped home, comin' back, sailin' over the sea, over th' boundin' wave, to bring th' thruth to Ireland, that was full o' Dhruids bendin' their knees to th' sun, thinkin' it to be somethin' above the ordinary because it went down every mornin' an' rose up every night; seekin' weary an' wasteful knowledge outa th' movement of stars an' comets, the nature of all earthly things, instead of confinin' their seekin' an' searchin' to the undherstandin' of things unseen, not made with hands, eternal in th' heavens; with me landin' first in Wicklow, an' dhriven out again be th' ignorant thicks; an' afther bearin' divers hard things pleasantly for your sakes, didn't I light the Paschal fire on th' hill o' Slane, right undher th' eyes o' Leary, King o' Taraxum, which when the king saw, he swore a mighty oath be the elements, an' sent for his high Arch-dhruids, sayin' to them, looka here, me fine fellas, yous 'ud betther find out who it is is after kindlin' a fire on the hill o' Slane, goin' again' the law of none to be lit for the time while th' fire on Tara flames; an' th' high Dhruids answerin' him, sayin', O great king o' th' Leinster-men, none of us know from Adam who has done this thing, but we warn you, if the fire on Slane isn't put out before the people have a chance o' seein' it, you an' your kingdom'll be *non est* an' done in for ever.

An' th' king, in a fit o' fury, hastened off at high speed in his chariot o' gold, followed be his chiefs in their chariots of silver, followed be their warriors in their chariots of bronze, right up to where I was and me companions were; the king, in a rage, jumpin' down from his chariot before it had stopped, near breakin' his neck with the sudden jolt he got, an' hard put to it he was to keep a look of dignity on him, an' he staggerin'; but when they came up, all they could see was a little

herd o' deer singin' a psalm round th' fire; so when I saw that his heat
had cooled a thrifle, I changed meself an' me comrades back into our
own fair forms again; but no sooner was I lookin' as per usual, when
the threacherous oul' varmint flung back his philibustherin' arm to
fling his fella-damnable spear to let the daylight through a holy saint;
but lo and behold, when the spear was tossed, it stopped short in its
flight, came to the ground upright on its butt, fornent me, an' started
to execute a Kerry dance round the fire, bowin' low to your humble
every time it passed, murmurin' to me, *laus* to youo, *laus* to youo, an'
then the king, the chieftains, and the warriors fell flat on their faces,
sayin' this is a great doing, and it is marvellous in our eyes; an' when I
thought they had been long enough on their faces, I told them, sayin'
yous can get up, now, an' thry to behave like decent people; an' with
that, they got up, hangin' their heads for shame, so that I took pity on
them, an' said to the spear buckin' about in th' Kerry dance, off with
you now, an' get back to where you came from. The spear stopped
dancin', and afther givin' me a low bow, throtted back to where the
king was, an' settled itself neatly in his hand again. Didn't I pluck the
shamrock, shovin' it undher their poor ignorant noses so that they
could get a good idea of the Holy Thrinity afther a short discourse.
Didn't I go fairin' east an' fairin' west, an' fairin' south, endurin'
many thrials an' various vexations, shapin' yous for th' joys o' heaven,
regardless o' cost, thrimmin' yous into a state of grace that won an
everlastin' ordher o' merit from G.H.Q. up here; givin' cause for
jealousy to the English cowled an' mitred boyos roamin' round here
who scraped into canonisation by the skin of their teeth, let in outa
pity that any counthry 'ud be left out of representation in th' city o'
Zion, which wouldn't be good democracy, an' might give rise to a
misunderstandin'; rememberin', too, all the sthrange an' wondherful
miracles that were done be me of changin' bees into butther an'
butther back again into bees; hookin' a cloud with me crozier outa the
sky, an' turnin' it into wolsey blankets for th' deservin' poor; turnin'
a corn-cub into a curate, a bell-wether into a bee-sheep, a chosen
chance into a chesty church, a porbeagle into a prayer, a penance into
a pokerface, a pagan into a pursebearer, the rights of man into the
benefit of clergy, an act of attrition into an *auto-da-fé*, a hell-incised
poverty into a *gloria in excelsis* destitution, the lure o' life into a set o'
rosemary beads, gatherin' th' joy o' the world round a cross; an' now
yous want to spoil it all, an' to bring these glories to a timely end, to
mar the merit of a creeping host descending down to heaven, makin'
what is bitther sweet, an' what is heavy light an' easy to bear. Ye

backsliders! seekin' security o' tenure when yous ought to be savin' your souls, followin' Parnell when yous ought to be followin' me, rushin' with money for the plan o' campaign, while your fathers in God sweat in an effort to collect their dues. There's no use in yous shoutin' at me that if yous as much as put a coat of whitewash on your walls th' rent goes up; let it; yous have heaven. I'm not listenin'; I want yous to listen to me, an' whisht about th' fear of wearin' decent clothes in case th' landlord 'ud see yous; let him; for the Lord is no respecter of persons, an' has a mitt outsthretched out for him in rags as well as for him in plushy broadcloth; so listen, an' keep quiet an' be still, an' ordher yourselves rightly to what I'm sayin', before the sanctified English bowseys here get to know I'm growin' hoarse sthrivin' to keep the members of me flock from throwin' off th' thraces of godly conthrol, an' sing silent about your livin' an' sleepin' an' dyin' undher one coverin', an' th' quarter acre's clause killin' thousands, an' that women are dyin' o' starvation with babies at their dhried-up breasts; for yous should be well used to these things be now, and, mind yous, while yous are watchin' your little homes gettin' levelled be th' crowbar brigade, or lyin' with your childher on the hard frosty road undher a red-berried rowan three, be night or be day, dyin' of hunger or perishin' o' cold, your last breath blessing' God for everything, yous'll all be slowly floatin' up here to me, unbeknown to yourselves, till yous are near enough for me to haul yous in be th' hand, the scruff o' th' neck, or th' sate of your throusers; only, when yous do come up, thry to act like civilised beings; don't shove, don't push, don't all thry to get in front, an' sweep, like rowdies into the New Jerusalem, but, number off, form fours, an' march in tidily, as if yous were all used to these things, an' that it was no novelty for yous to be in high-grade quarters, an' so show th' English saints up here, th' lowest o' them, esquires, that St. Patrick's children can enther into eternal bliss without gettin' excited about it.

An', once for all, let me hear no more o' someone diggin' a grave outside of a poor landlord's door; or of some decent catholic rent-agent havin' to walk well bent forward to keep himself from suddenly sittin' down be the weight o' buckshot poured into his innocent backside; or of hapless men stealin' about in th' moonlight, bent on business, with a mean musket stickin' its nose through the brambles an' briars of a hedge, waitin' for something to turn up, sendin' me flyin' for a dark corner to hide in, till th' explosion was over; an' don't have me comin' to this windy nook again, for it's not a warnin' yous'll get next time, but a blast that'll send yous all sluicin' down to th' lowest channels o' hell, where yous'll have all eternity an' a day or two longer to regret that ye ever laid a hand on another person's property; rollin' round like porpoises, yous'll be, in a sea o' fire, surgin', singein', scourgin', scorchin', scarifyin', skinnin', waves o' fire gorgin' themselves on every part of your bodies so that every ear, every eye, every mouth, every nose, an' every arse'll be penethrated be flames, each as sharp as a loony surgeon's knife, red hot, an' plungin' deep wherever its point turns; an' then it'll be no use bawlin' out to St. Patrick, Oh, St. Patrick, jewel o' th' Gaels, lift me up outa this, for th' love o' God; for there'll be no liftin' up or out, but only a deeper shovin' down each time a minute of a second passes, if yous don't listen to the counsel of your pastors an' th' witherin' advice of the grand oul' man, Gladstone, kissin' th' hand o' Mariar Curehelli for luck, when he was shocked by hearin' Parnell sayin' in his icy way, afther bein' asked what he thought of the great William, I think of Mr. Gladstone and of the English people what I always thought of them; they will do what we can make them do; an' the English awkward squad up here with their ears cocked, listenin' to every word, thinkin' themselves God's own household guards, an' never tired o' whisperin' that their form o' government might be inthroduced here with some advantage to keep things goin' straight; so on yous go, now, holdin' on to th' grand name yous have outa all th' glories of our past spare life, seen in th' lovely ruins scattered about from one end o' th' counthry to th' other, showin' your disconcern for anything in th' nature of a worldly vantage; an' don't let a few goboys sthruttin' round spoil it all be thryin' to keep a mad an' miserable sinner as a leader of the holy Irish people. So arise today through th' sthrength of th' love o' cherubim, in obedience to angels, an' down Parnell; in th' service of archangels, in th' hope o' resurrection to meet with a good greetin', an' down Parnell; in th' prayers o' pathriachs in predictions of prophets, in preachings of apostles, rise up today, an' down Parnell; in faiths of confessors, in innocence of holy virgins, an' in deeds o' righteous men, rise up today, an' down Parnell! Get a holt of that oul' balls, Tim Healy, who's as good as yous can get at th' moment, an' lift him into th' place of honour; take him, an' yous'll be safe in takin' heed of what I'm sayin' here over the cowld banisthers of heaven, in imminent danger of catchin' a chill, for the gauzy clothes supplied by th' commissariat department here's nice enough for ceremonial occasions, but a bit of a delusion when you leave the cosy corners.

We're just closin' down here, now; th' time be th' heavenly clock is exactly one-thousandth part of a second past the first hour of eternity, an' we're closin' down. God night, everybody, God night.

Johnny roused himself from his book, and saw Archie take down from the wall a fine crayon drawing done by Michael some years before, which had won him a bob from his Da, a fine crayon drawing of Charles Stewart Parnell, his bold, black-bearded, cold, Irish, menacing face that hid a wild, unwearying, tumultuous love for Ireland.

Archie reverently placed the picture on the table beside his cup of tea, while Johnny drank his, sitting close to the fire, feeling the presence of a calamity he couldn't fully understand. A large lot of crape, remaining safely in the big box after his Da's death, was brought forth by their mother, who cut some of it into strips, hemming the edges, and these sombre scarves were wound round and round the picture of Parnell. Then, on a white piece of cardboard, Archie, in beautifully-formed letters, wrote down, Give My Love To My Colleagues And To The Irish Race, afterwards fixing it firmly to the bottom of the frame. Pulling over the little table as close to the window as it could go, he placed the picture on it, safely propped up by several volumes of Merle d'Aubigné's *History of the Reformation*; and there stood Parnell, gazing out over the dim street, as bravely and defiantly as he would ever look out upon anything again.

—There he is now, said Archie, with defiant sorrow in his voice, lookin' out on the people who first denied, an' then betrayed him.

—It's sore they'll miss him, before many days are over, said his mother; an' we may be sure, if there's such things as rewards goin', there's one for him, wherever he is.

—What did he die of? asked Johnny.

—Sorra one knows, said Archie. All we know is that he's lyin' face down in a coffin, unlike any coffin ever seen be anyone.

—It's half-past three, Archie, said Mrs. Casside, glancing at the alarm clock, an' you've just time to get to your work, without puttin' yourself to a gallop.

Archie wound a brown muffler round his neck; put on a thick old ulster-coat; donned again his peaked hat with its two ear-flaps, kept up by being tied over the top; looked at the picture again for a second; saluted smartly, and murmured, Ireland's uncrowned King comes back in a coffin, an' half-dead Ireland now lies close beside him.

Then Archie went out into the darkness and the rain to do his work for the *Daily Express* and *The Warder*, in their despatch and publishing office, where he toiled from four o'clock in the morning till six in the evening, for fifteen bob a week and a free copy of the *Express*, daily, and another free copy of *The Warder* when the week was nearing its end.

After Johnny had finished his tea, his mother got him to bed again, while she sat staring into the fire, her chin cupped in her hand, and a puzzled, weary look in her black eyes.

Johnny closed his eyes and dozed, opened them again slowly; saw the wet grey dawn creeping in through the window, closed them once more, to open them on what he would see when the coffin came to Ireland.

The brown coffin came along, the box that held all Ireland had, sailing, like a drab boat, over a tossing sea of heads, falling, rising, and sinking again, polished by the falling rain; flanked on the one hand by the dirty dribbling railway station, and by the fat and heavy-pillared front of St. Andrew's Church on the other; but few were going in to bow before the altar, or mutter a prayer for the repose of a pining soul in purgatory; for all were here, all were here, gazing at the brown coffin sailing along, like a drab boat, over a sea of tossing heads, falling, rising, and sinking again, polished by the falling rain, silent, the coffin went on, in the midst of the rolling drumbeat of the Dead March.

Ireland's uncrowned King is gone.

And a wail came from a voice in the crowd, keening, We shall lie down in sorrow, and arise sorrowing in the face of the morning; there is none left to guide us in the midst of our sorrow; sorrow shall follow us in all our ways; and our face shall never wear the veil of gladness. We shall never rejoice again as a strong man rejoiceth; for our Leader has vanished out of our sight.

No damask, silk, or brocade threw beauty into the moving, silent throng; no rich banners, heavy with heraldry hatched a thousand years ago; not a single jewelled order flashed from a single breast, rising and falling with the dark rolling drumbeat of the Dead March; no bishops, posing as sorrow and salvation, in purple and gold vestments, marched with the mourning people; many green banners, shrouded with crape, flapped clumsily in the wet wind, touched tenderly, here and there, with the flag of the United States and the flag of France, floated over the heads of the stricken host, retreating with its dead to the place that would now be his home for ever.

An Ireland came into view, an Ireland shaped like a hearse, with a jet-black sky overhead, like a pall, tinged with a broad border of violet and purple where the sun had set for ever, silvered gently by the light of many cold and silent stars; and, in the midst of the jet-black sky, the pure white, set face of the dead chief rested, his ears shut dead to the wailing valour. Our uncrowned King of Ireland's gone.

A moving mass of lone white faces strained with anger, tight with fear, loose with grief, great grief, wandered round and round where the whiter face lay, set like a dimming pearl in the jet-black sky, violet-rimmed where the sun had set for ever, silvered softly by the dozing stars, sinking deeper into the darkness soon to for ever hide the wan hope of Ireland waning.

Out of the east came a sound of cheering.

Joy is theirs, cried a voice from the wailing; overflowing joy, for they feel safe now, and their sun is rising; their table is spread and their wine is circling; lift your heads and you'll hear them cheering:

The English!

SHAKESPEARE TAPS AT THE WINDOW

THERE they were all on the bed, nicely folded and smoothed out, laid ready for Archie. Johnny counted them again: the black tights, red satin slippers ornamented with gilt buckles, white silk shirt heavy with gold embroidery, round fluffy velvet cap with a feather encircling for the character of King Richard the Third.
it, and the long, gorgeous crimson velvet cloak, to furnish him out

Johnny, himself, looked gay and glorious in black tights, crinkled a lot, for they were a little too big for him; black silk shoes, stuffed with paper to make them stay on his feet, each shoe bossed with a pretty red rose, the rose of Lancaster; and a lovely black velvet coat, dazzled with silver, lined with blue silk and slashed in the wide sleeves with fluffy diamond shapes of white silk to give him a look of the imprisoned King Henry the Sixth, mortal foe of the hunchbacked Duke of Gloster. It had all been arranged that Archie and Johnny should give the prison scene where the poor King is murdered by the Duke determined to let nothing stand between him and the crown.

The scene, with one or two from *Conn the Shaughraun*, and a Minstrel Show, in which Archie was to sit in the right-hand corner making jokes and rattling the bones, was to be given at a charity concert to be held in the Coffee Palace, Townshend Street, a few nights later on. His mother had gone against it, giving out that that sort of thing was altogether too much for a boy of Johnny's age. She would have conquered, too, if Archie hadn't been the only one bringing in the wherewithal to keep the little home together. Johnny, too, had to be kind to Archie, and careful not to say anything that would offend, for, as well as keeping him, he gave Johnny tuppence a week, a treasure that gave him the power to buy *The Boys of London and New York* and a further volume of *Deadwood Dick* or *Frank Reade, Junr., and His Electric Airship*. So Johnny cleaned Archie's boots with a cake of Cooney's Paste Blacking taken out of its oiled green paper, and pressed into an old tin to keep it soft; ran errands for him; and generally laboured to please and serve his brother in every possible way. All the same, Johnny didn't like him, and did these things because there was no way out of it. When he was old enough to go to work, it would all come to a sudden end. Then, when he was told to go there or come here, or do this or do that, he'd say I'm goin' to be your servant no longer; you're big an' able enough to do all these things yourself. Just now he had to wear the handcuffs. So Johnny waited for time to bring him out of the land of Egypt and out of the house of bondage, to march straight into the land of Canaan,

> Caanan, sweet Canaan, I'm bound for the land of Caanan,
> Caanan is a happy place, so I'm bound for the land of Caanan.

Oh, it wasn't Canaan that should be beating into his mind, but all that Henry had to say to Gloster:

> Ay, my good lord: My lord, I should say rather;
> 'Tis sin to flatther, 'good' was little better:
> 'Good Gloster' and 'good devil' were alike,
> And both preposthevous; therefore, not 'good lord'.

He wished Archie would put in an appearance, to go over in costume the parts they had to play. He was more than minutes behind time already. He hoped nothing had gone wrong with the scheme. He had toiled and toiled over his part, saying it to his mother a hundred times, getting her to tell him, as well as she could, what the hard words meant; seeking out Ella when his mother failed, and getting her to give him the right sound and way of speaking them. He had learned the part from one of three volumes of the *Works of Shakespeare* won as a prize by Ella when she was a student in Marlborough House Teachers' Training College. Big and stately books they were, packed with pictures of battles, castles, and marching armies; kings, queens, knights, and esquires in robes today and in armour tomorrow, shouting their soldiers on to the attack, or saying a last lone word before poor life gave out; of mighty men of valour joining this king and reneging that one; of a king gaining a crown and of a king losing it; of kings and knights rushing on their foes and of kings and captains flying frantic from them; of a frightened man, with a naked sword in his hand, meeting a roaring lion in a city street; of men on a bare and bony heath sheltering each other from lashing rain, stormy wind, and noble lightning turning the jet-black sky into a deadly dawn of a day of wrath; of murderers slaying men, women, and children, with many other pictures of stirring and delectable things that happened before order, fair-play, and civility took root in the world.

Johnny moved about restlessly, sitting down and standing up, murmuring his part softly to himself,

> So flies the reckless shepherd from the wolf;
> So first the harmless sheep doth yield his fleece,
> And next his throat unto the butcher's knife.

Johnny wandered to the door, and looked anxiously up and down the street, watching and waiting for Archie.

—Oh, come in owre that an' don't be standin' at the door, he heard his mother call out sharply; what'll the people passin' think of you in that extraordinary get-up? Come in an' play with the things in the basket, an' keep quiet till Archie comes.

The basket his mother meant was a huge thing, quarter as big as a small room, brought to Johnny's place in an ass and cart driven by Archie and Tommie Talton, who wanted it out of the way for a few days to make room for a spread his family was giving in honour of his sister's wedding. Neither Mother nor Ella liked the idea of Archie getting too pally with these acting folk who were little betther than heathens and publicans, if you opened your eyes to the truth. And Ella had heard from a friend that Talton's sister had been married years and years ago; and what they really wanted was to get the stuff away safe from the bailiffs, who were expected to come down on them any minute for money they owed. Ella's friend said, too, that Tommie Talton and his brother Bill were just two mouldy down-at-heels mummers who snatched up a few frayed shillings a week by cod-acting in the Mechanics, a well-soiled, tumble-me-down theatre in Abbey Street, where no fairly respectable man or woman would dare to be seen.

Tommie Talton looked respectable enough. He was a long lanky young man of twenty-four, with a pale perky face, heavily pock-marked. His small head was covered with bunches of golden-brown curly hair. His eyes were pale grey, and so big that they seemed to take a long time to shut or open whenever he blinked. A tiny golden moustache lined his upper lip. He was gone in the knees, and though his feet were wide apart when he walked, his knees nearly knocked together. He wore a dark-blue suit, thin, and so bright with brushing that he shone in the sun like a knight in armour. A jerry hat was perched rakishly on the side of his head, pressing down on a golden curl that foamed out from under the rim of the hat and fell down over his ear. He walked with a saucy sway, like a knock-kneed sailor just beginning to get used to the roll of a ship. Johnny had liked him the moment he had seen him perched on top of the basket, with Archie carefully leading the little ass. Besides, he had brought in the basket treasures that the kings who rejoiced when they saw His Star in the east, and came to worship Him it shone over, might have carried in their caravan when they journeyed to the town of Bethlehem.

Only a day or so ago Johnny had nothing; now he had more than all the toys of all the boys in all the streets, even if they were gathered together into one big heap.

He thought of the toys he had had since he could remember: a little cart painted red and blue, a drum, a big bender kite of green an' yellow paper, with a blue tail, made by Archie when he was in a good humour, a Union Jack, a little bigger than his hand, got for answering Bible questions correctly, transfers, lots of regimental badges sent him by Tom and Michael. That was about all; oh, no, there was the half of the Noah's Ark he got the time he an' Archie were in the one bed sufferin' from scarlet fever, Archie gettin' the other half of the Ark. That same time, Michael an' Ella were down with it too, an' his mother put Tom in the same bed with Michael who had it the worst, so that Tom might get it too, an' she could nurse them all at the one time. An' she nursed them all without help from a single soul, though Tom escaped it, and had a gay time because he couldn't go to work, and got paid for doing nothing. When they were well, men had put them into the streets while they took away all the bedding and lighted sulphur in the rooms, pasting paper over the cracks in the doors to keep the cure from gettin' lost.

What's this comes after, bush an officer? bush an officer, bush an officer? Oh yes,

> The bird that hath been limed in a bush,
> With trembling wings misdoubteth every bush;
> And I, the hapless male to one sweet bird,
> Have now the fatal object in my eye,
> Where my poor young was lim'd, was caught, and kill'd.

Johnny fingered fondly the lovely things in the basket. It was filled with the costumes for *Macbeth, King Henry the Sixth, Richard the*

Third, The Shaughraun, The Colleen Bawn, The Octoroon, and other plays; with swords, shields, daggers, cutlasses, halberds, lances, armour, kepis, shakos, pistols, clergymen's robes and soldiers' uniforms, and silk, satin, sateen, dimity, and damask costumes in great an' wonderful variety.

Today he was a King, tomorrow he could be a Bishop, and the next day a Colonel. What other boy in the whole vicinity could come near him in all the glorious things that he possessed? If he was only a little older, or a little taller even, he could wear all these things well, without his mother havin' to put tucks in them to keep from thrippin' up an' makin' a holy show of himself before people ready to laugh from the crow of the cock to the last star's enthry into the night sky.

What a pity they hadn't chosen a bit outa *Conn the Shaughraun* insteada pouncin' on Shakespeare's stiff stuff. If they only knew, Boucicault was the boyo to choose. What did Tommie Talton say when they were takin' tea an' tinned salmon, the time the basket came, and Johnny's Ma had piped out of her that Johnny's Da always held by Shakespeare as the greatest writer of all time; an' Ella backed her up with a huh an' a sniff at the mention of Boucicault. This is what Tommie Talton said in the face of their fright an' their fury:

> *Shakespeare was a great choice: but Dion Boucicault was really quite as great a choice as Shakespeare. Shakespeare's good in bits; but for colour and stir, give me Boucicault!*

There they were stuck, an' couldn't say a single word in conthradiction; for Tommie Talton had known the theatre since he was a chiselur, an' neither Ma nor Ella had never as much as put a nose inside a theatre since they were born except to see a Shakespeare play. Ay, an' Archie capped it all be tellin' them that Tommie's brother, Bill, was the greatest Conn the Shaughraun that ever walked the boards. In a way, Johnny felt sorry over his Ma an' Ella makin' such sillies of themselves be displayin' their ignorance of things far beyond their understanding.

So wasn't it a sthrange pity that those in charge of the comin' event hadn't chose more o' Boucicault an' less o' Shakespeare? He'd be at home in the part of the priest in *Conn the Shaughraun*. Hadn't he done a good bit of it in front of Talton, with Archie as Corry Kinchella, the villain; an' hadn't Tommie Talton said, *Be God, that's wondherful for a chiselur like you!* How could anyone beat this:

FATHER DOLAN: *I'd rather see her tumble down in death an' hear the sods fallin' on her coffin, than speak the holy words that would make*

her your wife; for now I know, Corry Kinchella, that it was by your
means and to serve this end that my darling boy, her lover, was
denounced and convicted.

C. KINCHELLA: *'Tis false!*

FATHER DOLAN: *'Tis thrue. But the thruth is locked in my soul* (he
points finger at heaven), *an' heaven keeps the key!*

But that's not what I ought to be thinkin' of, but the part I have to
play. When the time comes, I won't know a word.

He pulled over two chairs, nailed together underneath by a baton,
with semicircular pieces to form arms, the whole covered with a
crimson cloth; and sat down in it, thinking.

Let me think, now. Yes, Archie says,

> Thy son I kill'd for his presumption

and I say

> Hadst thou been kill'd when first thou didst presume,
> Thou hadst not liv'd to kill a son of mine.
> Men for their sons', wives for their husbands' fate,
> An' orphans for their parents' timeless death,
> Shall rue the hour that ever thou wast born.
> The owl shrieked at thy birth, an evil sign;
> The night-crow cried, aboding luckless time;
> Dogs howl'd, an' hideous tempest shook down trees;
> The raven rook'd her on the chimney's top;
> An' chatthering pies in dismal discord sung.
> Teeth hadst thou in thy head when thou wast born,
> To signify thou cam'st to bite the world.

An' afther gettin' up from the chair before the last few lines, Archie
runs me through with

> I'll hear no more; die, prophet, in thy speech.

I'll have to tell him to be careful of that lunge, for he ripped me coat a
little, once before. An' I'll have to learn to fall betther. It's all very
well for Talton to say, just let yourself go. I did that once, an' nearly
broke me neck.

Oh, here's Archie, now, at last, thanks be to God!

Johnny heard Archie go into the other room where his tea was
waiting for him. Even if he took his tea first, Johnny knew Archie
wouldn't be long, for in anything new he was always bursting to be in
the middle of it. So he gave a last look-over and a last pat to the pompous garments, nicely folded and smoothed out and laid ready for
Archie to compose himself into the part of the hump-backed Duke of

Gloster. They were all there, waiting, beaming out their beauty through the gathering dusk. So Johnny sat down beside them, and waited, murmuring over the words of his part to himself, and listening to the cheers he imagined the audience would give when the scene had ended.

The gentle dusk crept away and dismal darkness sat in her place. But Archie did not come, and Johnny's heart was troubled. Let not your heart be troubled, neither let it be afraid. A ray from a street lamp sidled in through the window and laid a sad light on the pompous clothing, nicely folded and smoothed out, lying lonely on the bed. Everything was quiet; even silence lay sleepy in the room; and Johnny's bowels ached with disappointment.

—Johnny, Johnny, are you there? his mother called from the other room. Take your gay get-up off, and come an' take your tea.

He sat on for a moment; then he took off the black velvet, the blue silk, and the silver, and went on into the other room.

There was Archie, close to the fire, reading the pink-coloured *Evening Telegraph*, saying no word, taking notice of no-one.

Johnny sat silent, sipping his tea.

When he had read the paper, Archie got up, brushed his hair before a little glass hanging on the wall, lighted his pipe from a spill thrust into the fire, put on his hat and coat, and went out without a word.

—He's in one of his tanthrums, said his mother, as she sighed, because the whole thing's been put off on accounta the death of the Duke o' Clarence.

—It's a shame, she went on sighing again, as she sipped her tea, it's a shame that the young prince died, for they say he was the best beloved son of his sorrowin' mother, and a prime favourite with the poor old Queen.

ROYAL RISIDENCE

JOHNNY's mother had brushed and brushed his clothes, had darned some holes in his stockings, had bought him a cheap pair of yellow shoes; had fixed a new white collar round his neck, had spit a lot on his hair, calling the spit gob-oil, and brushed his hair till the skin on his skull stung; had put a tiny square of well-washed rag, carefully hemmed, into his pocket, warning him to use it whenever he felt the need to snuffle; planted his sailor's cap tastefully on his head, had slipped a dee into his pockct, telling him not to buy anything foolish with it; adding that pennies weren't easily come by; and, standing a little distance away from him, had said, I think you'll do all right now. The night before she had made him wash himself all over from hot water in a basin, so that he would be clean and presentable when his Uncle Tom came to bring him to see Kilmainham Jail.

—Your Uncle Tom's Crimean comrade has said that he may bring you with him, an' it's a chance that you won't get again in a lifetime to see the jail.

His Uncle Tom had come to time, and after promising Johnny's mother that he wouldn't let the boy see anything that might keep him awake at night, had taken the boy's hand and led him forth to see the sight of a jail where men who did wickedly were kept safe away from the temptation of doing anything worse than they had done before.

Johnny was proud of his uncle because he had fought in the Crimean War where a sabre-cut had sliced an arm from the shoulder to the elbow, where often, after a night's sleep beside his horse, his uncle's hair had been frozen to the ground; and Nurse Nightingale had bandaged the wound up with her own hand in the hospital at Scutari. Ay, an' his uncle, too, was a member of the Purple Lodge of the Orange Ordher, a great thing to be; though his Ma said his Da said that it was just as foolish to duck your head before a picture of King Billy as to duck it before the picture of a saint.

Johnny thrust his chest out, and walked swift beside the lanky figure of his uncle, glancing now and again at the soft dark-brown eyes, the wide mouth sthretchin' nearly from ear to ear, and the snow-white hair tumbling over his ears and falling over his forehead.

Away in a tram from Nelson's Pillar they went for miles an' miles, having first managed Cork Hill where the two tram horses were helped by another, called a pulley-up, that waited there to link itself in front of any tram wanting to mount the Hill; along Thomas Street, Uncle Tom pointing out St. Catherine's Church, where, he said, Robert Emmet had been hung, drawn, and quartered for rebellion against England.

—Is it a roman catholic church? asked Johnny.

—No, no, said Uncle Tom; it's a protestant one.

—You'd think they'd hang a roman catholic rebel outside a roman catholic church, said Johnny.

—But poor Emmet was a protestant, Johnny.

—Now, that's funny, said Johnny, for I remember the night of the illuminations, the conductor of the thram we were in, singing about someone called Wolfe Tone, an' me Ma told me he was a protestant too.

—Ay was he, said Uncle Tom, an' Parnell an' Grattan an' Napper Tandy too.

—They all seemed to have been protestants, murmured Johnny, relapsing into thoughtful silence for some moments. What's dhrawn an' quarthered? he asked suddenly.

—Oh, said his uncle, when a man's hanged, they cut off his head and divide him up into four parts.

—An' was that what was done to poor Robert Emmet?

— It musta been when he was sentenced to it.

—Why was Robert Emmet a rebel, Uncle?

—Oh, I suppose he didn't like to have the English here.

—What English, Uncle? I've never seen any English knockin' about.

—The soldiers, Johnny, the English soldiers.

—What, is it Tom an' Mick you mean?

—No, no; not Tom or Mick; they're not English — they're Irish.

—But they're soldiers, aren't they?

—Yes, yes; I know they're soldiers.

—They're Irish soldiers, then, Uncle, that's what they are. Aren't they, Uncle? Same as you were when you fought in the Crimea.

—No, no, no; not Irish soldiers.

—Well, what sort of soldiers are they?

—English, English soldiers, really.

—Then Emmet musta wanted to get them outa the counthry, as well as the others, if they're English soldiers. But Mick an' Tom' an' you are Irish, so how could you be English soldiers?

—We're Irish, but we join the army to fight for England, see?

—But, why fight for England, Uncle?

—Simply because England's our counthry, that's all.

—Me Ma says me Da said it isn't, but that Ireland's our counthry; an' he was a scholar, an' knew nearly, nearly everything, almost; so it isn't, you see.

Uncle Tom stroked his chin, glanced at Johnny with his big soft eyes, and looked puzzled.

—Isn't what, what isn't what? he asked.

—That England's not our counthry at all, and that everyone here's Irish.

—Well, so they are, said Uncle Tom.

—Well, went on Johnny, if Mick an' Tom are Irish, how can they be English soldiers?

—Because they fight for England; can't you understand?

—But why do they, an' why did you fight for England, Uncle?

—I had to, hadn't I?

—How had you?

—Because I was in the English army, amn't I afther tellin' you! said his uncle, a little impatiently.

—Yes, but who made you, Uncle?

—Who made me what?

—Fight for England?

—Good God, boy, don't you know your Bible? And Uncle Tom took a fat-headed pipe from his pocket, and was about to stick it in his mouth when he remembered he couldn't smoke in a tram, so he put it back again. Johnny felt that his uncle was puzzled, and a little cross because he was puzzled. So he sat silent, and for a few moments looked out of the tram window, thinking how hard it was to get anything out of the grown-ups unless they had a book in their hand. He wanted to know these things; he felt he must know. He glanced at his uncle's kind face. He had heard that long ago, and Tom a young man, that he had been a policeman, wearing comical clothes, sky-blue cut-away coat, top-hat, and white duck trousers; that he hated pulling anyone; that when he did, and they came near the station, his uncle would push the prisoner from him and say, For God's sake go home, and have a rest, and come out again when you've had a sound sleep; and that all the oul' fellas an' oul' ones called out after him when he passed, God bless you, God bless Mr. Hall who wouldn't harm anybody, so that, in the end, he had to leave the police.

—Where in the Bible does it say, Uncle, that the Irish must fight for the English?

—In the seventeenth verse o' the second chapter o' the first o' Pether, it says, Fear God, honour the king, so there you are, Johnny; we can't get out of it. Me father before me learned it; I learned it; and you're learning it now.

—An' whoever doesn't is a very wicked person, and is bound to go to hell, isn't he?

—Very wicked and bound to go to hell, echoed Uncle Tom.

Johnny thought for a moment, watching the horses' heads nodding as they strained forward to pull the heavy tram along.

—Me Ma says me Da said that Parnell was anything but a wicked man, Uncle.

—Parnell a wicked man? 'course he wasn't. Who said he was?

—Why didn't he fight for England, Uncle, then?

The fat-headed pipe came again out of Uncle Tom's pocket, who looked at it longingly, then put it back again.

—What are you goin' to buy with the penny your mother gave you, when we get outa the thram? he asked Johnny.

—Oh, just jawsticker or a sponge-cake or something — why didn't he, Uncle?

—Why didn't he who?

—Why didn't Parnell fight for England an' not go again' the Queen?

—I wouldn't say that Parnell went again' her.

—Oh yes, he did, said Johnny deliberately; for me Ma heard me Da sayin' once that Parnell paid no regard to the Queen; and would sooner rot in jail than obey any law made be her, an' that he worked, night an' day, to circumvent them because, he said, English law was robbery. An' Georgie Middleton told me he had a terrible row with his father because Georgie stuck up for Parnell, and his oul' fella was afraid of him, and slunk out to get dhrunk and came home cryin'.

—Georgie shouldn't go against his father be sticking up for Parnell.

—But why shouldn't he stick up for him, Uncle, when you say that Parnell wasn't a wicked man?

—Because Georgie Middleton's a protestant, that's the why, Johnny.

—Yes, but Parnell you said was a protestant too, so why shouldn't a protestant stick up for another protestant?

—Oh, you're too young yet to understand things, replied Uncle Tom with a little irritation. When you're older, you'll know what's right and what's wrong.

—Grown up, like you, Uncle?

—Grown up, like me, Johnny.

—When I'm like you, I'll understand everything, won't I?

—Yes, yes; then these things won't be a bother to you any more.

—But he was grown up, wasn't he?

—He, who?

—Parnell an' the Queen, and all them who went about arguing the toss; they didn't know, for when I was ever so little, I heard some of them shoutin' at me Da on accounta what he was sayin', an' he laughin' at them, an' makin' them more angry an' shout louder than ever.

Uncle Tom looked out of a side window to see rightly where they were. We're just there, he said; an' looka here, Johnny, while we're in the jail, say nothin' about Parnell, nor anything you think your poor Da used to say either.

—For why?

—Oh, there's no why about it — you've just got to do what you're told.

—Here we are, he added, as the tram slowed down amid a bright jingle of bells swinging from the horses' necks.

—The jail — right ahead, isn't it? he asked the conductor.

—Right ahead an' a little to the left, said the conductor; is the young fella's father one o' the boys?

—No, no, no; not anything like that, said Uncle Tom, as he swung off the tram and helped Johnny down, though Johnny didn't want his help, for he could spring off the tram a far sight sprightlier than stiff oul' Uncle Tom.

They hurried up Bow Lane into the heart of Kilmainham where everything made the place look as if it were doing a ragged and middle-aged minuet.

—There, said Johnny's uncle, pointing a thumb to the right, is Swift's Hospital that the Dean o' St. Pathrick's got built for the lunatics; and there to the right again, when they had got a little further on, is the Royal Hospital, where hundhreds of oul' men who fought for Queen an' counthry are kept safe in perfect peace; and, soon, we'll see the jail, so, when you're talkin' to your friends, you'll be able to boast about the wonderful things you've seen today.

There it was. A great, sombre, silent stone building, sitting like a toad watching the place doing its ragged middle-aged minuet. A city of cells. A place where silence is a piercing wail; where discipline is an urgent order from heaven; where a word of goodwill is as far away as the right hand of God; where the wildest wind never blows a withered leaf over the wall; where a black sky is as kind as a blue sky; where a hand-clasp would be low treason; where a warder's vanished frown creates a carnival; where there's a place for everything, and everything in its improper place; where a haphazard song can never be sung; where the bread of life is always stale; where God is worshipped warily; and where loneliness is a frightened, hunted thing.

His uncle pulled his coat open showing the Crimea medal shining on his waistcoat, with two bars striding across the coloured ribbon. They went through the iron gateway leading to the main door of the jail, the ready way in and the tardy way out, a heavy thick iron gate set deep, desperately deep, into solid stone, with a panel of five scorpions wriggling round each othcr carved out of the stone that formed the fanlight that gave no light to the poisoned city of Zion inside. As Johnny and his uncle came near, the heavy thing swung open, and a warder stood there, with the Crimea medal glittering on his breast, and a hand stretched out to greet Tom, who seized it and held it for a long time.

—Come along in, Tom, me son, and your young friend, said the warder. You're welcome, he's welcome, you're both as welcome as the rooty call blowing for dinner.

They went inside to the courtyard, the heavy thing swung back again, and Johnny was installed as a freeman among the prisoners and captives.

They went into the central hall, and, standing on the flagged floor, gazed at the three tiers of cells, with narrow railed lobbies on the first and second floors, and a narrow steel stairway leading to each of them.

—It's a great sight, said the warder, to see the prisoners coming in, in single file, step be step, hands straight be their sides, over a hundhred of them, quiet an' meek, marching right, left, right, left, each turning into his own little shanty when he comes to it; with half a dozen warders standing on the alert, and the sound of the steel doors clanging to, like the sound of waves on a frozen sea, all shut up safely for the night, to read their Bible or stretch themselves down and count the days to come before the Governor dismisses them and wishes them godspeed. Here, me lad, he said, opening a cell door, have a decko at the nice little home we provide for them who can't keep their hands from pickin' an' stealin'; or think by the gathering together of the froward, they can overcome the submission they owe to our Sovereign Lady; forgetting that they have to reckon with the goodness of God who will always weaken the hands, blast the designs, and defeat the entherprises of her enemies. Go on in, me lad — no fear o' the door closing on them who are the friends of those sent by the Queen for the punishment of evildoers.

Johnny went a little way into the cell, with his heart beating. It was spick and span, the little stool scrubbed till it was shining like a dull diamond, and the floor spotless. A slop-pail stood to attention in a corner; over it a tiny shelf holding a piece of yellow soap and a black-covered Bible, showing that cleanliness was next to godliness; and a tiny grating to the side of the door, letting the air through to keep the cell fresh and wholesome; all, in the night, lighted up by a baby-tongued flicker of gas in a corner, the light that lighteth every man that cometh into the jail, the captive's little pillar of fire, the prisoner's light of the world, a light to them that sit in darkness, with this light, needing no light from the sun, lead kindly light, amid the encircling gloom, lead thou me on till the day break and the shadows flee away.

Johnny stepped back out of the cell, for he could hardly breathe in it, and he felt a warm sweat dewing his forehead. Stone and steel surrounding loneliness, pressing loneliness in on itself, with a black-coated Bible to keep it company, and a jaundiced eye looking out of the darkness. They peeped into the chapel with its plain benches in the nave for the jailbirds and the seats on the side for the guards; and dimly, in the distance, shrinking into an archway, the althar, having on it two candles, one on each side of a crucifix that stood on the top of a little domed cabinet where, the warder said, the priest kept his God all the secular days of the week and took him out for exercise on Sunday.

—Here's something to see, said the warder, showing a fairly-sized room, lighted with two arched windows, for this is the room where Parnell was kept when we had him prisoner here. A man, he went on, if ever there was one, a sowl man. The least little thing you done for him, it was always thank-you, thank-you, from him even when you opened the door before you locked him up for the night. A sowl man, I'm tellin' you, Tomas, an honour to do anything for him, he was that mannerly, even to us, mind you, that you'd fall over yourself in thryin' to please him; and never the icy glint in his eye, unless the name of some big bug in the opposite camp was mentioned; oh, be Jasus, then the flame in his eye 'ud freeze you, ay, man, an' shook hands when he was leaving, too; imagine that, Tom, shook hands with us that was busy holdin' him down, though no-one in this world, ay, or in the next either, could really hold Parnell down; for even in here he was more dangerous than he was roamin' about outside, a deal more dangerous, for, with Parnell a prisoner, the Irish 'ud stop at nothin', ay, an' well he knew it — an' one of us, too, Tom, me boy.

—How one of us? asked Uncle Tom.

—Why, a protestant, man, makin' him fair an' equally one of ourselves. Not fit to do anything for themselves, the roman catholics must have a protestant to lead them. Looka at them now, an' Parnell gone! Gulpin' down the sacrament while they're tryin' to get at each other's throats; furiously tetherin' themselves to the roar o' ruin; twistin' into a tangle everything that poor Parnell had straightened out, with the hope of ever standing up against a single law that England likes to make gone for ever!

Johnny edged over to a window and looked out: there they were, a big gang of them, some with hand barrows, carrying stones, some with wheelbarrows, wheeling them away; and others, with great hammers, smiting huge stones into little pieces, each hammerer gruntin' as he brought his sledge down with a welt on the obstinate stone, while two warders, with carbines, watched well from a corner.

Earnest-lookin', evil-lookin', ugly-lookin' dials on the whole o' them, thought Johnny to himself.

—There, said their guide, pointing to a steel door opposite to Parnell's room, is the cell that Carey, the informer, lived in, afther he had turned Queen's evidence till he was taken down to Kingstown be three different journeys in three different cabs, an' put on board the liner, only to be shot dead when he came in sight of Port Elizabeth. But come on, now, an' see the best sight of all.

Tom's warder friend stopped by a cell door away by itself in a quiet part of the prison. He opened it, stepped back, stayed silent for a moment or two, then, bending over, said almost in a whisper, Gentlemen, the condemned cell.

Uncle Tom took off his hat, and when Johnny saw that, he took off his too; and they both tiptoed a little way into the condemned and silent cell: a little less like a cell, a little more like a room with its silent stool, silent table, little bigger than the stool, a cold fireplace, and a cold hearth.

—If only the walls could speak, murmured Uncle Tom, looking around and nodding his head wisely.

Johnny felt his heart tighten, and he wished he was well away out of it all; at play with Kelly or Burke or Shea; or tryin' to say something nice to Jennie Clitheroe. He'd look, an' wouldn't see; he'd listen, an' wouldn't hear; but would keep his mind fixed on pretty little Jennie Clitheroe. She had gone down to the counthry for a week. Wasn't it well for her! He had never been to the counthry yet. He had never been in a train — only watched them go by, leaning over the railway bridge in Dorset Street. Jennie was bringing back with her a bundle of yarrow stalks, and she'd give him some of them. He an' Jennie were to put nine of them under their pillows, and throw one over their left shoulders so that he'd dream of his future wife and she'd dream of her future husband. He knew who his future wife 'ud be, so he did, well: her name began with a J. And when he was throwin' the yarrow stalk over his shoulder, he'd say, sing-song like,

> Good-morrow, good-morrow, fair Yarrow,
> Thrice good-morrow to thee!
> I hope, before this time tomorrow,
> You'll show my thrue love to me.

—He sat there on that very stool, the warder was saying, sayin' nothin', only murmurin' here as he did on his way to the gallows, poor oul' Ireland, poor oul' Ireland. Brady, the best an' bravest of the Invincibles, never losin' an ounce o' weight the whole time, waitin' for the day, for the hour, for the last minute to come, for ever murmurin', Poor oul' Ireland, poor oul' Ireland. Underneath the flags outside, in one big grave lie the five of them, goin' to the grave without a word of who did it or how it was all done.

—A sinisther commination on any poor man's life, said Uncle Tom sadly.

—'Tis an' all, replied the warder, just as sadly; but fair in the square of a respectable life we've got to do, if we want to come to a faithful an' diminishin' end.

—Anywhere here, said Uncle Tom,' suddenly, in a loud whisper to his friend, where we could thrance the youngster, an' go for a dhrink?

The warder hurried them down a corridor, at the end of which was a door. He opened this, and they all went into a room where there was a fire, with a bareheaded warder sitting beside it, smoking, his feet inside the fender. In the centre was a dirty-looking table and some hard chairs; a frying-pan, saucepan, kettle, and teapot stood on the hobs. On a rack along the wall hung some warders' caps, two carbines, and some batons were hanging from hooks in the rack.

The warder, seated by the fire, turned and looked, then turned away again, and went on smoking.

—We're leafin' the kidger here for a few seconds, said Tom's friend; he'll just sit quiet an' be in nobody's way.

—He's welcome, said the warder seated by the fire, and went on smoking.

Tom's friend settled a chair by the fire for Johnny, and when he was seated, hurried away with Uncle Tom. The bareheaded warder sat still, never once glancing at the boy, but went on smoking, smoking, and gazing into the fire.

Johnny sat tight in his chair, wishing that his uncle would come to bring him home. He'd force himself to forget seeing the condemned cell, and think, only think of going home again, home, going home again, homeward bound —

> Homeward once more, homeward once more,
> The good ship is speeding for old Erin's shore;
> The exile's returning, no longer to roam,
> But to end his career in his own native home.

The bareheaded warder sat on silently, staring into the fire, smoking. Johnny began to lilt softly, very softly, to himself:

His counthry he loved, an' for Ireland he bled,
For which he was sentenced to hang until dead;
The sentence was not carried out, if you please,
Instead he was sentenced for years 'cross the seas.
For twenty long years, the prime of his life,
He was banish'd from children, his kindred, and wife.
Oh, how his heart yearns as he stands on the shore,
Awaiting the steamer bound homeward once more!

The bareheaded warder turned, suddenly, to stare at Johnny.

—If I was you, he said, I wouldn't sing a song like that here.

Johnny hushed his murmuring song, and gazed at the staring warder, puffing fiercely at his pipe, and staring straight at him.

—No, me boy, he went on, such a song doesn't sound decent in such a place as this.

Then he turned his head away, and stared again straight into the fire, as if he had been sentenced to staring for the rest of his life: I'm an old bird alone, he said, after a long pause, an' just waiting for what we all must meet. My own an' only son did three years, an' then had to fly the counthry. He was a Fenian, an' I never knew. Then the missus died. Three long years me own an' only son did in jail, an' then had to fly the counthry.

Johnny's heart went out to the old man. How bitther it musta been to have had a son who done three years in jail.

—Maybe, he said, your son, in the counthry he's gone to, 'ill do away with the disgrace he brought on yous all here.

The bareheaded warder sat and sat silent for a long time staring away into the fire, an' puffing his pipe.

—I'm proud of me son, he said slowly, proud of him, an' ashamed of me son's father. I'm tellin' that to you, young boy, because you haven't yet been fortified be the world against the things good men do. He took the pipe out of his mouth and jerked the stem over his shoulder towards the door. Say nothin' to them two dismissioners when they come back of what I said to you, young boy. He slapped the mouth of his pipe against the palm of his hand to loosen up the tobacco in it. I was in the Crimea meself, but I never wear me medal; never since the day me boy was sentenced to three years' penal servitude. Mind you, I'm only saying that there's a lot lyin' soft undher an althar no nearer heaven than a lot of others lyin' hard undher the flagstones of a prison yard.

Johnny sat still, thinking, for he didn't quite know what the oul' fella meant. The ould head had sunk down deep into the breast, and the pipe was shakin' in the oul' mouth. Johnny watched it tremblin', give an upward jerk as the lips tried to close upon it, then slide down the breast of the blue coat, and fall, scattering the silken ashes over the hearth, while the old warder slumbered on, and the fire began to sink down into a dull glow.

Johnny glanced over again at the batons hanging from the hooks in the wall, like dried-up little dead men, the batons that battered the bowseys. There must be a lot o' bowseys in Ireland, for his Ma told him his Da had said that the police were never tired of batonin' the people. It was the only way that God could bless Ireland, for God moves in a mysterious way His wondhers to perform. Yet the sleepin' warder looked a kindly oul' man. Maybe he was too ould to use a baton properly any longer. Maybe this was the very man who had brought food to the Invincibles while they were waitin' for to go to the gallows. Only a few steps away, five of them, Brady, Curley, Fagan, Caffrey, and the boy Kelly, were lyin' low, dead arms round each other, in one common grave, the warders an' convicts walkin' over them, day afther day. Johnny shuddered, and drew his chair a little nearer to the dying fire. The Invincibles, the Invincibles.

The dusk was falling, the fire was burning low, and the old warder slept on, sunk back in his hard chair, his hoary old head bent down deep in the hard breast of his trim blue coat.

Johnny remembered the cross cut deep in the path a long way up the road from the main gate of the park; an' the mounted Constabulary, a constant glint of silver an' black, goin' up, goin' down the road ever since the time of the killin', the shinin' steel of the harness tinklin' to the gentle throt o' the horses, watchin' an' waitin', with carbine and sabre, for the worst to happen. But the great We are the Invincibles had been there before them. The cab crawling about, holding men with revolvers itching their hands, A jaunting-car waiting, waiting some distance away, the driver flicking the mare with a whip to keep her warm and taut, the day Burke jumped off his car to join Lord Cavendish walking his way to the Vice-Regal Lodge, full of plans to circumvent Parnell; putting his foot down firmly on foreign soil, his fine head full of the fact that he would do unto Ireland as he would that Ireland should do unto him, fresh from England, with a fresh heart and a fresh mind eager to plant and to sow and to reap and to mow and to be a firmer boyoy-oy, to show how things could be done and should be done and must be done if the four parts of the United Kingdom were to go hand in hand through this vale of tears, strong and hopeful, firm and faithful, fond and free, bringing a new era to

Eire, a push afoot, a push ahead, and who will separate it? None. For ever. *Trio juncta in-aequalitas.*

There the two of them strolled along together, he and him, English and Irish, Lord and Commoner, boss temporary and servant permanent, protestant and catholic, warm-hearted Cavendish, cold-hearted Burke, open-faced Cavendish, dark-kissered Burke, the follower in front of the leader, follow me up to Carlow, listen to me, listen, me lord, a firm hand for Charlie, for Parnell is his name, me Lord, Ireland is his station, Wicklow is his dwellin'-place, an' the jail his destination — that's the plan, that's the plan of campaign, me lord.

The sun was setting redly while the cab crawled about, the jaunting-car waited, and the selected Invincibles were slowly nearing the man in grey; the butler who polished John Bull's silver in the back yard, who made a wheel from Ireland's harp to break her bones; the Irish catholic bodach was coming nearer so the Invincibles holding their knives hidden, untarnished by a tear of dew, nearer to the herculean Joe Brady and his companions, beside them; now, and their knives are deep in the man in grey who has suddenly left Ireland for ever. A second more, and Cavendish lay along him as sad and as still as the bonnie Earl o' Moray, his handsome head half hidden in the grass, lying quiet there till a coffin came to carry him home; beside the man in grey he lay, a memory now, covered soberly by a stately purple pall that the setting sun was slowly spreading over the sky, high above the rat and the lion as they lay in a desperate sleep together.

Johnny made a clatther by striking the fender with the toe of his boot, but the hoary-headed oul' fool slept on, his head bent down deep in the dark of his trim blue coat. He was sure that strange things strolled about in the dead of night in this queer place. The air was scorched with the thoughts of those who had suffered here. He knew that, for he couldn't keep Jennie in his mind for two solid seconds. Something was dragging his mind to dwell on things that had happened before he was born. Had he been a roman catholic, he'd ha' made the sign of the cross, but all he could say was, Jasus. Ay, Jasus help the Invincibles and the two men they slew. They were lying stretched out on the grass in the park and the cold night dew fallin'; while Skin-the-Goat was dhrivin' the cab as hard as the horse 'ud go out through the north circular road gate, and the car went gallopin', gallopin', gallopin' down the road through the fifteen acres, out through the Chapelizod gate, scattherin' the kids in wanton fear playin' on the road, out into the thick of the counthry, gallopin' out gallopin' on past hedges of hazel an' holly, past woodbines and bramble bushes, gallopin' still, goin' a long and roundabout way to the dark little torturin' room in Dublin Castle where they were bullied and borne about in bewilderment, first to the Inns of Quay Police Court, on to Kilmainham, then through the condemned cell to the last minute's walk before they were finished; an' Mr. Mallon, Justice o' the Peace an' Commissioner o' Police, just to show there was no ill-feelin', shook each one of them be the hand, an' wished them well on their way to the Land o' the Leal, feelin' fit from what he had done to preserve truth an' justice, religion an' piety in the land where the Queen's writ ran; while Marwood, the hangman, Ireland's only guardian angel, danced round Brady, crowing that it was the grandest execution of the nineteenth century, with the eye o' the world watchin'; while the big man stepped on, no flicker in his eye, no tremor in his limbs, no signal of fear in his face, no ear for the murmurin' of the prayers for the dyin', no crack in his voice as he went on through a gauntlet o' carbines, muttering the creed of the felon, poor oul' Ireland, poor oul' Ireland that was fadin' fast away from him; for it was time to be goin', goin' out of this sad place, goin' home before the heavy darkness came, an' he alone with the sleepin' warder who looked for all the world as if he, too, was sleepin' the sleep of the dead, seemin' to say in his stillness that this was the only sleep that had rest in a place like this is Tom's voice callin', in the corridor for me to come; and Johnny rose up and hurried out, leaving the hoary-headed oul' man asleep by the dying fire in the dusk, his head bent down deep in the dark of his trim blue coat.

THE HAWTHORN TREE

JOHNNY stood in the old waste field at the head of the street, looking at the hawthorn tree. It was a big tree, and its broad branches of rich white bloom were bending down so low that, if he sprang up into the air, he could easily catch one. The waste place was a tangle of weeds in a hurry to hide with their leaves and timorous flowers the rubbish that many careless hands had thrown about there. Scutch grass, docks and dandelions, daisies, small and big, and a few poppies did their best to hide the ugly things from the stately hawthorn tree who set off the weeds with her ladylike look and her queenly perfume. Her scented message of summer's arrival came pouring out of her blossoms, and went streaming down the little narrow street. A spicy smell, thought

Johnny, like all the spicy breezes that blow from Ceylon's isle, where every prospect pleases, and only man is vile. There were a few vile boys, all the samey, allee savee, in Dublin's fair city, if y'ask me, with wondherful chokers on them, too, like oul' Hunther holin' his head up as if he shook hands with God the very first thing in the mornin'.

There were other scents, too. There was another Big Tree at the corner of the north circular road, but that had a scent of whiskey an' beer flowin' out of it. This a scent from God, that a scent from the devil; for he had been told so once by a Leader of the Blue Ribbon Army, the Ballyhooley Blue Ribbon Army, the Band of Hope that lured innocent Protestant children into takin' a pledge against ever wettin' their little lips with any kind o' beer brewed from barley or rye or anything else that might show and shove them into rioting and drunkenness, separating them from their heavenly inheritance for ever. He had never worn the blue ribbon, nor had he ever been presented with a coloured testimonial in return for a pledge never to touch, taste, or handle it. He had a bad character. He had been seen with people who, if they got the chance, would simply dhrink Loch Erin dhry. He had, from time to time, and in one way or another, carried enough beer to float a good-sized ship. Anyone in the neighbourhood who wanted dhrink to be brought to them would look out for Johnny to go, get it, and carry it back to them. One thing he could do that was beyond the power of either Slogan or Hunter — tell with a single glance from his eye whether a jug or a can would hold half a gallon or only three pints of porther.

But he hated the smell of beer, and loved the smell of the hawthorn tree. The spice of Ireland, Ireland's hawthorn tree. And this grand tree was theirs. Right at the top of the little street it stood for everyone in the street to see it. The people of the street were always watching it, except in winter when it was bare and bony, cold and crooked. But the minute it budded, they took their eyes to it, and called it lovely.

Th' hawthorn tree's just beginnin' to bud, someone would say, just beginnin', and the news would go from one end of the street to the other. Th' hawthorn's buddin' at last. Did yeh hear? No; what? Why, the hawthorn's tree's burstin' with buds; I seen Mrs. Middleton a minute ago, and she says the hawthorn tree's thick with half-openin' leaves, so it is. And the first flower would send them into the centre of a new hope, for the praties were dug, the frost was all over, and the summer was comin' at last. And no cloud of foreboding came till autumn's dusky hand hung scarlet berries on the drowsy tree, and all the people, with their voices mingling, murmured, the long dreary nights, the reckless rain, the chilly sleet, the cowld winds, an' all the hathred in winther is comin' again.

Johnny turned his thoughts away from the thought of winter, and gazed again at the pearly-blossomed hawthorn tree. Here, some day, in the quietness of a summer evening, in a circle of peace, it would be good to sit here with curly-headed Jennie Clitheroe, nothing between them save the sweet scent from the blossoms above. It would be good, good, better, best, positive, comparative, superlative, an' God would see that it was good, and would no longer repent that He had made man in His own image.

If he wanted, now, he could easily climb up and break off a branch to bring the scent of the hawthorn tree right into his own home. But all the people round said it was unlucky to bring hawthorn into a house, all except his mother, who said that there was no difference between one tree and another; but, all the same, Johnny felt that his mother wouldn't like to see him landing in with a spray in his hand. It was all nonsense, she'd say, an' only a lively superstition; but you never can tell, and people catching sight of hawthorn in a house, felt uneasy, and were glad to get away out of it. So it was betther to humour them and leave the lovely branches where they were. Leave it there, leave it fair, and leave it lonely. Sacred to the good people, Kelly said; but he was only up a few years from the bog. They, the fairies, danced round it at night, he said, gay an' old an' careless, they danced round it the livelong night, and no matter how far away they were, they heard it moan whenever a branch was broken.

From under the shade of the hawthorn tree Johnny looked down the little street, and saw a stir in it. Down at the far end he saw what looked like little hills, one after the other, on each side of the narrow way. Women, opening doors and standing on the thresholds, were gazing about near where the little hills lay. I lift up mine eyes unto the hills.

Suddenly, he heard a call of Johnny Casside! Johnnie Casside! He turned his gaze to the right, and, a little way down the street, saw Ecret with hands cupped over his mouth to make his voice travel farther, calling, Johnnie Casside, your mother wants you!

Lower down still, he saw Kelly, with his hands cupped over his mouth, calling out louder than Ecret, Johnny Casside, Johnny Casside, your mother wants you quick! Th' dung-dodgers are here!

Johnny hated these dirt-hawks who came at stated times to empty out the petties and ashpits in the backyards of the people, filling the whole place with a stench that didn't disappear for a week. He sighed, and, leaving the shade of the hawthorn tree, hastened as slow as he could down the street to join his mother.

The whole street was full of vexation and annoyance. Women standing at their doors this side of the street were talking to women standing at their doors on the other side of the street, and murmuring against the confusion that had come upon them, upsetting all they had to do till this great fast of the purification had come to an end.

—Always comin' down on a body at an awkward time, was the king of the murmurs, managing to present themselves when the families were in the throes of doin' important things. If they didn't come on washin' day, they came when the clothes were flutterin' on the lines to dhry; an', if they didn't come then, they were knockin' at the door when the few white an' delicate coloured things a body had were bein' spread out to be carefully an' tenderly ironed.

—It 'ud vex th' heart of a saint, said Mrs. Casside, over to Mrs. Middleton, an' she standin' on the kerb in front of her hall door, comin' just when me two boys are home for a little leave. They'll come thrampin' in an' go thrampin' out, leaving the dirt of petty an' ashpit ground into the floor of the room an' the hall, an' the two boys expectin' everything to be spick an' span, an' a special ever-ready attention to them as a little compensation for the constant right turn an' quick march of the barrack square.

—It's a rare hard an' never-endin' fight we have, said Mrs. Middleton from her door on the opposite side of the street, again' the dust an' dirt we gather around us in the course of our daily effort to keep things in ordher. Here I am, with the youngsters all ready, bar the puttin' on of their caps, to take them over to me sisther's I haven't seen for months, living on a green patch be the side of the Tenters' Fields, who'll be waitin' for our arrival, an' sthrainin' her ear for a knock at the door, the time she's gettin' ready a pile o' pancakes for the gorgin' of the kidgers she sees so seldom.

—An' the dark row that'll shine over the whole place, went on Mrs. Casside, heedless of what Mrs. Middleton had told her, if as much as a speck violates the tender crimson of the boys' tunics, issued undher a governmental decree of a spotless appearance, so that no scoffer may be given a chance to pass a rude remark about the untidiness of the Queen's proper army.

—Now, looka the poor Mulligans, said Mrs. Middleton, meandering across the road to stand on the pavement a few feet from Mrs. Casside, watching her trying to pry up the tacks that held the faded oilcloth to the floor, shoving an old knife-blade under the tack heads, and gently forcing them out so as not to make the oilcloth any worse than it was, looka the poor Mulligans, with their four chiselurs down with the measles, two o' them lyin' in the room the dung-dodgers'll have to pass through, with the doctor shakin' his head over one of them, an' the mother's soul-case worn out runnin' from one to the other, thryin' to ward off any dangerous thing that may be hoverin' over their little heads, while the dung-dodgers are busy filthifyin' the whole place, an' she only havin' two hands on her to tend the children an' clean up the mess when the dung-dodgers are gone, before she dare sit down in the shade of a little less to do.

—Well, we'll only have to give her a hand when we're a little free ourselves, said Mrs. Casside, an' save the poor woman from suddenly dhroppin' outa her standin'.

—An', went on Mrs. Middleton, looka Mrs. Ecret, afther paintin' her hall door only yestherday, with a tin o' paint her boy providentially found — when no-one was lookin', I suppose — an' varnishin' it well to finish it off, all afther comin' to grief with them tearin' their baskets of dirt against it, comin' an' goin' out, refusin' to wait till the door was decently dhry, an' leavin' it lookin' for all the world like the poor little maiden all forlorn who married the man all tatthered an' torn. Though I'd say sorra mend her, goin' about like the cock of the south because her hall door was the only one on the sthreet that had had a lick o' paint on it since Noah first saw the rainbow. But there's always a downfall in front of them who sthrive to ape the airs of the quality.

Mrs. Casside gazed at the oilcloth she was lifting, and sighed resignedly.

—This is the last time I'll get this to stand the sthrain, she said. It's fare you well, me lady, the next time I thry to get it up. You're perfectly right, she added, turning towards Mrs. Middleton, for it's a bad thing to allow yourself to crow over worldly possessions, for we brought nothing into the world, an' it's certain we can take nothing away.

—Only a good character, murmured Mrs. Middleton, only a good character, an' God knows it's hard enough to take that away with us, either. Here's your Johnny, now, to help you, with a tiny sprig o' hawthorn in his hand. Don't let him bring it into the house, she said seriously, bending her head close to Mrs. Casside, for it's the same may bring with it the very things we thry to keep at a distance.

—An' what does it bring into the house with it? asked Johnny.

—Things that toss in a golden glory to a distant eye, said his mother, and, at the touch of a human hand, turn to withering leaves whirling about in a turbulent wind.

—And, said Mrs. Middleton, things that swing in a merry dance to a silver song that changes, quick as thought, to a dolorous sigh and a thing stretched out in a white-wide sheet in the midst of a keen an' the yellow flame from a single candle. So leave your little twig o' hawthorn on the window-sill outside, alanna.

—Ay, Johnny, said his mother, leave it there, for though it is only roman catholics who cherish such foolish fables, it's always safer to be on your guard.

Heaps of muck were appearing before the various houses in the street, growing bigger and bigger as the dung-dodgers added big basket after big basket of filth taken from the backsides of the houses. Each door would have a horrid hill outside of it till a cart came later on to carry them away. In and out, in and out of the houses went the dung-dodgers, carrying huge baskets on their backs filled with the slime and ashes of the families, their boots and clothes spattered with the mire that kept dropping from the baskets as they carried them out.

—Eh, you there, said one of the dung-dodgers who had stopped to light his pipe, over to the two talking women, Eh, you, quit your gostherin', and make ready for us, or we'll be with you before a thing's stirred.

Each of the women departed into her own house, and Johnny and his mother shifted their bits of furniture into safe corners, and tenderly rolled up their few precious yards of oilcloth and put it safely aside from the armoured feet of the dung-dodgers.

—Stay outside in the fresh air, said Mrs Casside to Johnny, till all the dirt is out, and then you can come in and help me to put the place to rights again.

Johnny went out to stand by the window-sill and fiddle with the spray of creamy hawthorn, all the while watching the dung-dodgers cleaning out his mother's place and Mrs. Middleton's opposite, watched them bendin' low under the heavy load in each basket, then dumping it with a grunt on the rising heap in front of the door. Sometimes they would pause to straighten their backs and pass a few remarks to each other, before they went back for another load. One of them, a stocky man, with a squint in his right eye, paused, sucked at his dirty pipe, and glanced over crookedly at a comrade helping to empty out the house opposite.

—Did yeh take me advice an' go to the Queen's yestherday night? he called out.

—No, I didn', replied the other, a burly fella with a voice like a croakin' corncrake. I'm follyin' me own bent, an' I'm goin' tonight to *Th' Bohemian Girl*.

—You can have your *Bohemian Girl* for me, said the other scornfully, and he hoisted the empty basket on his back again. Give your humble servant *The Lily o' Killarney*, an' th' tenor warblin' I Come, I Come, Me Heart's Delight, with Danny Mann, the divil's darlin', hurlin' the Colleen Bawn off the rock into the wather, an' me boul' Myles na Coppaleen leppin' into th' night-dark lake to pull her out again. And he marched off to add another load to the heap of muck outside of Johnny's hall door.

Johnny waited there, fiddling with the spray of hawthorn, till ashpit and petty had been emptied, and the dung-dodgers had moved on to the next house; then he went back to give a hand to his mother to coax cleanliness back again to the soiled flooring of their home. With the aid of a neighbour's broom, they swept the crushed cinders and ashes and some of the slime from the flooring. Then Johnny poured hot water from a kettle into a bucket, while his mother used a blue-mottled soap that made her hands shrivel and sting, washed and rubbed, time and time again, to make the first cleanliness of the place come to life again.

So she toiled as all in the street did on the day of their purification, in the midst of a dense smell, shaken with tremors towards vomiting, hard and fast at it, all together, boys, cleansing the sanctuary of her home, breathing the breath of death into her nostrils, scrubbing the floor, knees bent, worshipping dirt, washing away the venom of poverty, persuaded that this was all in the day's work; Johnny emptying out the sullied water and bringing in the clean for her, then watching her working without the sign of a song from her, breathing hard, conjuring away the turmoil of dirt with the aid of fair water and the blue-mottled soap that made her quick-moving hands shrivel and sting.

The day was stretching close to the evening when the place felt fresh again, the oilcloth was laid, and the bits of furniture stood at ease in their old places. Johnny hurried off and came back with a glass of beer for his mother.

—Fine head it has, she said, as she sat and sipped it.

—G'on, you, she said to Johnny, giving him a chunk of bread and butter, an' get as much of the fresh air as you can.

Johnny hurried out, and away with him up the street, past all the mounds of mire, to eat his chunk of bread in peace beneath the scented shade of the hawthorn tree.

CAT 'N CAGE

TOM was home on leave, his number dry, a good-conduct badge on a sleeve; for he was no longer a rooky, but had passed through all drill with colours flying, and crossed gold guns shining a little way above a cuff told the tale that he was a first-class shot in his regiment. He and Archie and Johnny were on their way through the crisp air of an autumn day to the Cat 'n Cage for a drink — beer for Tom and Archie, and ginger cordial or claret for the boul' Johnny. Along Dorset Street the three of them went, Archie and Johnny chucking out the chests and keeping well in trim with the military step of Tom, looking brave and fine and proud in the get-up of the 1st Battalion of the Royal Dublin Fusiliers: tunic as crimson as a new-blown poppy, long streaming black ribbons stretching down his back from the natty, square-pushing silk-edged Scots cap set jauntily on the side of his head, white gloves stuck neatly into his pipe-clayed belt, and a dear little cane, knobbed with the arms of his regiment, under his arm, a cane to be presented to Johnny as soon as Tom found it convenient to get another.

He had overstepped his leave by a day, and laughingly drew the picture of Captain Bacon's moustache bristling when he'd be brought on the mat before his officer for absence without leave.

—You'll lose your good-conduct badge, won't you? asked Archie.

—Not unless I get a regimental enthry, and that isn't likely, for I've got a clean sheet so far, and I'm in request for work in th' orderly room and that counts a hell of a lot. But, if I do aself, what about it?

And he laughed defiantly, thinking it great fun, and Johnny thought so too, when he heard Tom humming:

> Around th' prison walls,
> There I've got a token;
> All around Victoria's walls, picking tarry oakum.
> The shot dhrill an' the shell —
> Mind, boys, what I say —
> It's a military prison for a soldier!

While he was humming the last line of the tune, Tom whipped off the golden head of a dandelion, shooting out from a slit in the side walk opposite a bright-red brick building with the words on a wall telling everyone that this was Father Gaffney's Catholic School, built, his Ma said, to keep the catholics as far away as possible from the protestants, and leave them free to flourish in their errors, for as the Church of Jerusalem, Alexandria, and Antioch have erred, so also the Church of Rome hath erred not only in their living and manner of ceremonies, but also in matters of faith.

They stopped for a moment looking up the narrow street that ran like a narrow stream into the wide river of Dorset Street where they had lived for so long, and where the two elder ones had left for their first job.

—There, said Tom, pointing at the street with his cane, is where we lived for a long time, where the old man died, and where you, Johnny, ran around in petticoat and pinafore. Remember?

Remember? Ay, did he. From nine Innisfallen Parade he had run for the ounce o' cut Cavendish. He remembered, too, going out often with a white delft jam-jar in his hand to get thruppence-worth of threacle from Dunphy's o' Dorset Street, an' watching a dark, little, yellow-faced man, for all the world like a Chinaman, holding the jam-jar to a tap in a green tin barrel, watching the deft little yellow hand turning the tap to let the black sticky stuff flow down into the white jar, and then, like lightning, cutting off the dark sthream when enough had flowed for the money offered, and swiftly cutting with his thumb the threacle blossoming from the tap, and licking it off, before he handed the jam-jar back to Johnny with one hand, while he swept the three pennies into the till with the other.

A big, black, tarry canal-boat, filled with a cargo covered by a huge tarpaulin, was lying idly against the lock-gates, waiting for the lock to fill so that it might glide in and sink to a lower level. The sluice-gates were open, and the green water, laced with foam, tumbled through into the vast pit of the lock, adding its energy to the water that had poured in before, whirling madly about, and rising slowly to the level where the canal-boat lay, waiting for the lock to fill. The old nag that had heavily pulled the boat to where it was, cropped a few clumps of grass growing thickly near the railway wall, while the man who led him idly watched a loaded goods train that went lumbering by far away below. A sturdy, brown-bearded, dirty-faced man stood on the poop of the boat, gazing at the waters tumbling through the sluices of the lock, occasionally taking a cutty clay pipe from his mouth, and jetting a flying spit right into the heart of the green and white tumbling waters, seeming surprised and disappointed that the spit was so rapidly lost in the whirling cascade. A man on the boat, with a boat-hook in his hand, watched the spit disappear the moment it struck the water.

—We all go like that poor spit, he said to his comrade, a gathering together, a second or so in the mouth, a sudden jet of life, an' we're out of sight of all.

—Ay, indeed, said the brown-bearded man; casual spit or special spit — all gone together an' lost in a whirlin' medley.

—Oh, none of us is lost altogether, replied his comrade with the boat-hook, no, not altogether; no, not quite.

—No-one's no more nor a dhrownded dhrop in a mill-sthream, went on the one with the beard, a dhrop there in th' dark, showin' no sign at all, an' a dhrop here with the sun on it shinin' for a second, an' then meeting' th' darkness of th' other one. I know you're here an' you know I'm here, an' that's about as far as it goes. But what th' hell are you to a Chinaman, or a Chinaman to me? He comes as I go, or I go as he comes, an' him nor me is no wiser of one another. You don't know even who may be havin' a pint in Leech's opposite while we're talkin' here.

—I don't, agreed the man with the boat-hook, but I know who's not havin' one, and that's more important to me.

The bearded man shoved the pipe into his pocket, hurried swiftly along the narrow gangway to the aft where he grasped the tiller, ready to guide the barge, for the lock was full; Tom, Archie, and Johnny leaned against the great arm of the lock gates, and pushed the arm open through a gurgle of rippling water, men on the opposite bank doing the same with the other arm. The man with the boat-hook fixed it in a part of the gate, and began to pull and shove the barge forward past the open gates. When the boat had passed through, these gates were pushed shut again, and sluices further down were opened to empty the lock and let the boat sink to a lower level. Down and down hes went, slowly; the men's legs disappearing first, then their waists, till only their heads could be seen peeping over the stone parapet of the lock, the bearded man jetting a last spit into a far-away clump of daisies before his head disappeared altogether.

—Eh, there, shouted Archie down to the bargemen when the boat was well down and safely caged between the dripping walls of the lock, where's your barque bound for? Is it to Yokohama you're settin' your course, or dim an' distant Valparaiso?

—Farther than ever you'll wandher, you pinched an' parched an' puckered worm, shouted the man with the boat-hook, while he shoved the barge along out of the lock into the further stretch of the canal ahead.

Archie whipped out a handkerchief and waved it to the departing boat, as he chanted:

> Oh, Shenandoah, I long to hear you,
> Away, you rolling river;
> Oh, Shenandoah, I long to hear you,
> Away I've got to go 'cross the wide Missouri!

They turned away from the lock when the canal boat had drifted away down to where the ships go down to the sea, and pass out, over the bar, to the rolling billows beyond; and so on to where there are cannibals, an' spicy smells that make the sailors faint, an' lilies on lakes big enough to hold a house up, an' palms so high that the highest tufts scratch the lower clouds, and where there are wild beasts wandering through the streets of towns at night, touching their snouts to windows shut tight and doors barred soundly; an' places, too, where men are as small as a three-year-old nipper, dangerous, for they can well hide in the long grasses and send a tiny arrow, touched with poison, into the guts of a passer-by so that he drops dead just as he feels the first faint prick of the barb entherin' his thin white skin, and is never found again and is lost for ever; maybe the only son of a poor woman waitin' for him to come back, an' puttin' a light in the window so that he won't miss his way,

> A light in the window shines brightly for me,
> Her bold sailor lad who has gone far away;
> His absence an' silence makes mother's heart yearn,
> As brightly the light in the window doth burn,

so sure an' senseless is she that the wanderer will come back again, an' he, all the time, lying stiff, a flower forcin' itself out of his mouth maybe, the grasses climbin' over him, the night dew fallin' fast on him, gone home, gone for ever, gone to earth, gone to rest, gone to glory, gone to be with Christ which is far betther.

Crossing over Tolka Bridge, they passed out of the town into a hedge-bordered road, the great northern road leading to Belfast and the Irish north where the loyal and trusty true-blue followers of King Billy lived and defended the Protestant Faith and all ceevil and releegious liberty.

The hedges were beaming with the scarlet clusters of haw and hip shining forth from the midst of the gold and brown leaves of the declining may and dog-rose. The hips were fat and luscious-looking, their scarlet more riotous-looking than the lesser and more modest red of the haws. Johnnie Magories, Johnny called the hips, and he pulled a rare big bunch of them, half of them a dazzling scarlet, and the rest that hadn't ripened yet, the colour of rich gold slashed with crimson, for his mother who liked to put them in a jug that had lost a handle, to brighten up the room a bit, she said, and make us feel a little less like what we are. The room was always a little different, she'd say, when it showed a sprig o' green or a bunch of berries. They brightened up a dull room as the stars, on a dark night, brightened up the sky. They carried their colours so quietly, she said, that they coaxed you to feel a little quieter yourself. And, if you thought of them at all, you knew they were as lovely as the richest roses the rich could buy. You never knew how often a linnet's wing had touched them, or how often they had held up a robin while he sang his share o' song when the sun was low and the other birds were sitting silent. In time, like the rest of us, she said, they'll lose their gay colour, will shrivel, and get tired, but they will have had their day, will have shone for an hour, and that is something.

A brisk breeze, spiced with the pungent smell of weeds afire in the fields, blew about them, gave speed to a lot of clouds drifting in a silky blue sky, swung the bunches of berries in a gentle dance, rustled the brown and yellow leaves strewn under their feet, and sent many others whirling and falling to join the others that fell before them. Several jaunting-cars went trotting by them, packed with young men wearing white-cuffed green jerseys and carrying hurleys. Most of them were singing as recklessly as they could,

> Oh, for a steed, a rushing steed,
> On the Curragh of Kildare,
> And Irish squadrons thrained to do what they are
>   willing to dare!
> A hundred yards, an' England's guards
> Dhrawn up to engage me there,
> Dhrawn up to engage me there!

A policeman halted, stiffened himself, and gazed fixedly at the cars trotting by. The hurlers gave a jeering cheer and waved their hurleys on high. The policeman watched them away into the distance, with a foolish grin on his gob.

—As long as they rest content with shouting, he said to Tom, we don't mind much.

But Tom, Archie, and Johnny, taking no notice, walked by, eyes front, for they didn't want to be seen talking to a policeman.

—The horney wanted us to take notice of him, said Johnny.

With a clever swish of his cane, Tom whipped off a bramble twig that was sticking itself out over the side walk.

—The less anyone has to do with harvey duffs an' horneys the better, he said: ready to swear a hole through an iron pot.

—Ambush their own mother into the arms of the hangman, added Archie, if it meant a pat on the back from a head constable.

The blue of the sky had given way to the dimmy purple of the gathering twilight; the bright berries were hiding in the dusk; the trees were dark and drooping figures sleeping, yielding a densely drowsy welcome to the birds thrusting a way to a rest in the branches; the breeze still blew, but everything and every stir in the dusk grew quieter as the three of them went on their way to the Cat 'n Cage.

—Here we are at our home 'n destination, said Tom, whose mouth was watering for a drink.

They stopped before what was no more than a country cottage, with a small window at each side of a narrow door. A heavy, weather-soaked thatch covered the low roof. A low hedge surrounded a grass plot, separated by a path leading from the gate straight into the doorway. Along the grass plot, nearest to the hedge, sprawled clumps of neglected dahlias, still trying to carry soiled crimson and yellow blossoms, looking as if they, too, had been into the pub, had lowered a lot of drinks, and were just able to crawl out and lie around the border, or lean tipsily against the hedges. From two squat chimneys, one at each end of the roof, thin streams of delicate blue smoke rose unsteadily, stood straight for a moment, then staggered away into the higher air as if they, too, had had a merry time, and didn't quite know which way to go. The door had once been a bright green, but was now well faded and smeared with many dirty patches made by the rain, snow, and sun of many seasons. Swinging over the door was the sign of the house: a large square board, with a picture on it of a huge wicker cage holding a blackbird stiffly standing on a perch, while outside, with her nose close to the bars, and a thoughtful look in her eyes, sat a big black cat.

As the three of them walked up to the door, they saw shining through the dusty windows the gleam of blazing fires, singing out that there was a welcome and a fair snugness and a fine warmth to be found inside for all who came. Tom pushed the door open, and in he and Archie and Johnny passed into the warm beer 'n whiskey cosiness of the Cat 'n Cage.

The place was a bit dim from the smoke of several pipes and the smoke that was too tipsy to climb up the chimney, and, to Johnny, everything seemed to be floating about in a warm-smelling mist. Along the whole length of the room stretched the bar-counter of thick deal, once white, but now grimly stained with many porter stains and dirt carried in on the clothes of them who came in to take a rest and slake their thirst. At one end of the bar stood the three glorious beer-pulls, shaped like the spokes of a ship's wheel, made of glowing crimson porcelain and polished brass, having on the thicker parts of them lovely oval panels of gaily coloured shepherds and shepherdesses surrounded by their baaing sheep.

Four of the hurlers who had passed them on the cars were drinking by the counter near the beer-pulls, and a carman sat in a corner with a pint before him. The barman, a thick-necked man with bushy eyebrows and a partly-bald head, his big eyes, sleepy-looking, bent over the counter, listening to what the hurlers were saying.

When he saw Tom and his companions, he pulled himself slowly apart from the talking group and came over to them, sending a questioning look towards Tom as he came near, while the brisk gab of the hurlers suddenly ceased.

—Pint, said Tom to the questioning glance, glass o' plain, an' a small claret, warm for the boy, sweet.

The gay shepherds and shepherdesses tugged up the beer cheerfully, with a long, long pull an' a strong, strong pull, gaily, boys, make her go, and the pint and glass o' plain were handed to Tom and Archie, while a dandy-glass, half full of ruby liquor, was put into Johnny's eager hand.

Tom was a handsome fellow, and was swanking it a bit now before the hurlers. Five-foot-eleven in his socks, broad-chested, lithe of limb, ruddy-haired, a handsome ginger moustache sweeping his upper lip, grey eyes that sparkled when he was excited, genial, especially when he was drinking his beloved porter, a hater of quarrels, but a lover of an argument.

—Bet Mick has a sackful in him be now from the Jesuit he was to meet in the Cross Guns, he murmured, balancing the pint in his steady hand.

The hurlers were sending over quick, cross-grained glances at the redcoat, poising themselves in a little silent bunch beside the beer-pulls, while the barman, pretending to take no notice, wiped some dirty glasses and hummed half-softly to himself:

The fountain mingles with the river,
And the river with the ocean;
The winds of heaven mix for ever
With a sweet emotion.
Nothin' in th' worrld is single,
All things, be a law divine,
In one another's being mingle —
Why not I with thine?

Archie saw the black looks that the hurlers were bending on them, looks quickly given and quickly withdrawn, and he was nervous. Johnny, too, saw the looks, and saw Archie was nervous and that the hand holding the glass of plain trembled a little, saw him bending his head over towards Tom's.

—They're havin' a good gawk at us, he whispered.

—Eh? Who? asked Tom, for he was too full of himself to take notice of half-hidden scowls.

—Boyos, with the hurleys.

—Oh, said Tom, sending a swift glance to where the hurlers were, them? Gawks. Bog-trotters. Never seen anything higher than a haystack. Hayfoot, strawfoot fusiliers. Let them look their fill at one o' the old toughs. He lifted his glass level with his chin. Where it goes, he said, and gurgled down more than the half of his pint, leaving his fine moustache gleaming with a frothy dew. He pulled a handkerchief from his sleeve, and as he was wiping the frothy dew from his moustache, the door of the pub opened and in walked the boul' Mick, his pill-box cap set rakishly on the side of his small, tight head, looking like one o' God's guards in his superb crimson tunic, with its velvet blue-purple cuffs and collar, piped with yellow cord, skin-tight trousers, slashed with a wide scarlet stripe down each leg, and caught under his square-pushing boots with leathern straps to make them tighter still.

Tom looked at him as if he had seen an apparition.

—Jaysus, he ejaculated, I thought you were to meet a Jesuit in the Cross Guns!

The Cross Guns: Johnny knew it well, near to the bridge of the same name, called Westmoreland Bridge by the loyal Irish and the more respectable protestants, one of his brother's favourite pubs. He knew them all well, outside and in: Cross Guns; The Bleeding Horse, up behind the northern quays; The Big Tree in Dorset Street; Royal Oak in Parkgate Street, where the Invincibles had a last drink before going on to do in Cavendish and Burke; The Jolly Topers in Finglas, a well-known bona-fide house; Leech's beside Binn's Bridge; Galvin's in Capel Street; Bergin's in Amiens Street; The Brian Boru nicely stuck in the way to or from a burial in Glasnevin; Meredith's in Derrynane Parade could hardly be counted, for it was only a shebeen where drink had to be taken off the premises, unless someone stood at the door to keep nix for fear a horney hove in sight round a corner, though here they could always be sure of a few because Cissy, daughter of Meredith, was sweet on Tom, in spite of the oul' fella grumblin' that there was more goin' out than was comin' in, an' Cissy havin' to help the family be workin' from eight till six for half a dollar a week, in Williams & Woods cleanin' the fruit that came to the place to make the jam; and last, but not least, Nagle's in Earl Street, a rendezvous for all the post-office boys who had worked with Tom and Mick before they joined the Army. Johnny knew them all, had drunk ginger beer or claret in each of them; had listened to the rare manly talk beatin' round the house like the stirring wind or a bustling sea. And now he was in the Cat 'n Cage. He was getting on and filling out his young life with wondhers. Here he was in a pub miles from home, between two oul' swaddies, havin' his share o' dhrink with the best of them. Few more years an' he'd be workin', able to go his own way, swagger about the streets, an' show Jennie Clitheroe the sort he was.

—Go on, boys, dhrink up an' have another, Mick was saying; and, turning to the barman, added, same again here, mate.

The room wasn't large and the counter wasn't long; there was little more than a hair's-breadth between the red-coated elbow of Tom and the green-covered elbow of a hurler.

Red an' green, thought Johnny, red an green are the colours of oul' Ireland, an' an oul' ballad, sung be a one-eyed man mouchin' along Dorset Street, came into his mind,

> Green is the flag an' green are the fields of our sireland,
> While the blood our sons have shed has tinged the green with red,
> That's why red an' green are the colours of oul' Ireland.

Whenever a movement brought the red-coated elbow of the soldier into touch with the green-covered one of the hurler, the green-covered one would give the red-coated one a vicious shove away, but, beyond a wondering backward glance, Tom took no notice.

—Here's to the time, said a hurler suddenly, in a loud voice, raising his glass above his head, when there won't be an English soldier seen in our land from one end of it to the other!

The other hurlers clinked their glasses against his, and they all chanted,

Clink your glasses, clink,
Here's a toast for all to drink:
By every Irish Chief beneath a cairn,
Some day, without a doubt, we'll dhrive th' English soldier out
From every field an' glen an' town in Erin!

The door opened in the silence that followed the song, showing two tall Irish Constabulary men standing on the threshold, with their martial coats around them, the dusky bronze harp, with the crown over it, sleepy-looking on its oval bed of red cloth stuck in front of their round black caps, set to the side of their heads, a chin-strap keeping the cap in its perky angle, and their glossy black belts, with batons hanging from them, fencing their heavy coats into two long neat folds down the backs.

After dawdling at the door for a few moments, the two of them sidled up to the counter, Tom and his party moving up to their end of the counter, the hurlers moving closer up to theirs, so that the policemen had a little space at the counter between the backs of the soldiers on the left hand and the hurlers on the right one.

—Two Guinnesses, said one of them in an apologetic voice, for he knew that the barman and the hurlers knew they were supposed to be out patrolling the roads, and far away from the sight or even the thought of a drink.

The barman, all attention to these gods o' the Irish countryside, hurried the bottles of stout to the policemen, who moved over nearer to Tom and his comrades, who moved farther away still when they felt the touch of the peelers.

Quarrelsome Mick couldn't let well enough alone; couldn't let the silence sing its song of peace.

—If y'ask Mick, he said, when the redcoats weren't dhriven out o' Ireland when Parnell was high an' mighty, they'll hardly do it now he's down among the dead men.

Then Tom had to go one better — he was always weak enough to follow on where Mick led.

—Who was it threw Parnell to the English wolves? he asked in a voice meant for the hard of hearing. Was it the English redcoats done it?

—A sowl man, he was, chimed in Archie, lifting the people from their knees by the scruff of their necks. An' what did he get for it?

—A home in a coffin, said Mick, and a roomy grave in the famine plot in Glasnevin.

—Ay, said Tom, taking great gulps out of the beer, an' in their mangy hearts the priests an' people sang a Te Deum when they found he was dead.

—An' I'll go bail, said Mick, there were a few hurlers' hands helpin' to pack him into his coffin.

A hurler whirled round on his heel, his face tense, his eyes blazing.

—No hand here helped him into his coffin, he shouted, his face flaming in the black gap between the two Constabulary men.

—The whole bang lot o' them, said Tom, taking no notice of the hurler, deserted their Leader in his time o' need.

—Th' Irish always down a great man, said Archie, while they cling to a clyura as they did to Sheamus the shit at the battle o' the Boyne.

—Here, here, now, said the barman, shoving his gob over the counter in Archie's direction, there's to be no bad language heard here, for this is a highly respectable house, fully approved of be the magisthrates an' the parish priest.

—Now, boys, now, murmured one of the policemen, talk it over easy. This is a free counthry where everyone has a right to his own opinion.

—Looka Swift MacNeill, said Tom, now more excited than ever, but still keeping his back to policemen and hurlers, when he shouted at the Dublin meetin' of the National League, God forbid that the man who led us through darkness an' difficulty should be deserted be us — an' he the first to vote for the betrayal of his Leader to the English.

—An' he a Dublin man, too, said Mick; Dublin went awhoring when she bred that bastard who betrayed Parnell!

—Easy, easy, murmured the other constable.

The barman again leaned his gob over the counter, gently shoving a constable a little aside with his head to get nearer to Mick.

—Isn't it afther sayin' I am, he said, that no other language, other than that in common uttherance, is to be used in this respectable house?

— No bad language, no bad language, murmured a constable.

All, except the police, were getting very excited. The police were uneasy, and couldn't, rightly, without loss of dignity, slink out of the discussion now. So there the two of them lounged over the counter, trying to look undisturbed, stuck in the middle of the hubbub like a pair of crows among a group of coloured jays.

—An' what about Healy, said Mick, bitther an' brave with envy, swearin' at the same meetin' that he'd never, never desert the chief who had led Ireland so far forward; an' all the time, the Banthry bowsey, itchin' to make an end o' Parnell, even if he had to make an end of Ireland at the same time! Tim Healy, the biggest snake Pathrick left behind him! Healy's your hero now: muck that Parnell made into a man; the guck in the silken gown; England's fosther-brother! An' where's Ireland now? In Glasnevin. An' what's Ireland now? A mingy plot of grass in Glasnevin with th' name o' Parnell fadin' away on it out undher the frost an' the rain!

—Let the poor man rest, said a constable; he's dead, isn't he? So let the poor man rest.

—Who's dead, who's dead? asked a hurler fiercely, turning to face the constable.

—Parnell, replied the constable, softly and slyly, so let the poor man rest in peace.

—You an' your like 'ud like him to be dead, said the hurler, we all know that; but Parnell's more alive than ever he was! Rest in peace! That's what you and the political pathrols among the clergy'd like too. But Parnell'll never rest till the swarm of thraitors that hounded him to his death and flung Ireland's power into England's lap are sthretched out cold, unremembered be a single soul that's left to lift a hand for Ireland!

The carman, sitting in the corner, suddenly jumped up and slid over to where the talk was, wiping the drains of beer from his lips, his green-gone bowler hat balanced on the back of his head, a stained clay pipe waving in his left hand, like a conductor's wand, his dull eyes trying to force a gleam into them, and the corners of his big mouth twitching.

—It's sick I'm gettin', he said, listening to the whole of yous. If he'd ha' loved his counthry, he'd ha' known he wasn't fit to lead us when he committed himself with Kitty O'Shea!

—Who wasn't fit to lead us? cried a hurler, turning savagely on the car-driver.

—He wasn't.

—Who wasn't?

—Parnell, if you'd like to know.

—Is it Parnell who united the whole nation together, who coaxed the Fenians to follow him, who forced the Church to toe the line, is it him I hear you saying wasn't the man who was fit to lead us?

—Amn't I afther tellin' you, persisted the car-driver, that all that happened before Parnell committed himself with Kitty O'Shea.

—Jasus, said the hurler, with the sound of agony in his voice and the look of agony on his face, is it listenin' to an Irishman I am when I hear a thing like that!

—The holy clergy, said Tom mockingly, didn't open their mouths when O'Connell was goin' round the counthry scattherin' bastards everywhere. Gettin' them be steam, be God!

—I told yous twice before, an' I'm tellin' you for the third an' last time, said the barman furiously, that this double-meaning talk'll have to be heard only outa hearin' of the decent people who come into this decent house for entherthainment; and he again shoved his thick gob over the counter, thrusting it sideways and tilting it upwards at the angry hurler. An', furthermore, he went on, I'm not goin' to have any confusion here over Parnell either; for when all's said an' done, he's gone, an' a good riddance, bringin' disgrace on Ireland's fair name be committin' an immortal sin!

In a mighty rage, the hurler let fly and gave him one in the snot while it was well poked out over the counter, forcing a steady stream of blood to flow down his chin and over the white front of his dickey, and causing him to knock down a serene-looking row of newly-cleansed tumblers with a wave of his arm as he staggered back. He sliddered down to the floor, and sat, glancing now at the crowd outside the counter and then at the broken tumblers lying round him.

—Me nose's slit, he sighed loudly, an' me best glasses gone wallop, an' me only afther cleanin' them, too!

The two constables were afraid of the hurlers, for no-one could say, especially a policeman, what a hurler would do when he had a hurley in his hand. So they turned on the other party, very officious, and full of the law.

—Now, said one of them to Tom and Mick, you two members of Her Majesty's Forces betther be gettin' outa this, d'ye hear me? We can't have quarrelsomeness comin' into the quiet of the counthryside. So g'on, now, the pair of yous, before I have to inthervene to prevent any further tendency towards a breach of the peace!

—We'll finish the dhrinks we paid for, before we go, anyway, said Tom surlily.

—The minute they landed in here, said the barman thickly, through a handkerchief held to his nose, they started to row with these decent men here, and he pointed to the hurlers.

—They started no row with us, said the hurlers. What we said an' they said was said in quietness an' calm.

—Here, now, said a constable, touching Mick on the arm, swally up the remainder of what yeh have there, an' be off, like a good man.

—Oh, let the man finish his dhrink in a decent way, said one of the hurlers.

The policeman wheeled round to face the hurler.

—It's a dangerous thing for anyone to thry to obstruct a constable in the discharge of his duty, he said warningly.

—Didya ever hear the song that everyone's singin', now? asked Mick, with a wink at the hurlers.

—No, said Tom; what song is that, now?

—Goes like this, said Mick, and then he chanted, keeping his back turned to the policemen, knowing that this song was the song they hated and dreaded above all others,

> A Bansha peeler wint wan night,
> On duty an' pathrollin' O,
> An' met a goat upon the road,
> An' took her to be a sthroller O.
> Wid bay'net fixed, he sallied forth,
> An' caught her by the wizen O,
> An' then he swore a mighty oath,
> I'll send yeh off to prison O!

The hurlers tittered and the constables flushed.

—An' what did the oul' goat say? asked Tom.

—God, I've forgotten, said Mick.

—I know, I know, said Johnny eagerly, and he began to sing,

> Oh, mercy, sir, the goat replied,
> Pray let me tell me story O,
> I am no rogue, no ribbonman,
> No Croppy, Whig, or Tory O,
> I'm guilty not of any crime,
> Of petty or high threason O,
> I'm badly wanted at this time,
> For this is the milkin' season O!

One of the constables glared at Johnny and said viciously, What'r you doin' here in a place like this, me oul'-fashioned, cocky little kidger, with your ears open to catch any language that'll help to knock hell outa all decency in later life?

—I'm with me own two brothers, said Johnny sturdily.

—With your own two brothers, are you, now? Well, it's not in a place like this a lad o' your years ought to be, catchin' a glimpse of things not fit for you to see.

—I'm not goin' to ask your permission to come here, anyway, muttered Johnny defiantly.

—Oh, you're not, arent' you? Lappin' up your lessons well, eh? Guh, yeh cheeky little cur, bulky with impudence! Swinging an arm, the constable, in a rage, brought his hand to Johnny's ear with a box that sent him spinning towards the door, dazed and dumb and bothered.

Dazed with the blow as Johnny was, he saw the lovely sight of Mick sending a short jab to the constable's jaw that tilted up his head with a jerk, and, when the poor man's head was well up, a straight-left beauty to the poor man's chin that sent him in a curled-up heap to the floor. He saw the second constable putting a hand on his baton; he saw Tom taking a hurley from a hurler who gave it up with a wink as good as a nod to a blind horse; and he saw the second constable hesitate when he saw the hurley in Tom's hand and the look of battle in Mick's eyes. So he turned and went to kneel down beside his fallen comrade to give him comfort and bring him peace and make us all be just to him; while the barman hurried and scurried and worried to fetch a glass of brandy for the fallen bowsey, a red dribble dodging down his own nose; and the car-driver hastened to help the barman to help the constable who was helping his comrade; while the hurlers pressed to the door, beckoning Tom and his party to follow them, all hurrying out into the garden, making spacious steps for the gateway, Johnny in the midst of them, with a red ear and it tingling, praying the hand that struck him might be paralysed, that the eyes would have the power to see nothing but the paralysed hand, the ears hear nothing but the people talking about the paralysed hand, and the tongue have but the power to point it out to others.

—Come on, boys, said a hurler, let's scatther, an' get away as far as we can from here.

They heard a long shrill blast from a whistle, and, turning, they saw the dark figure of a constable standing, full-shaped, in the light streaming from the open doorway.

—Jasus, he's blowin' for the rest of them — we'll have to run for it!

—The car, the car, said Tom; let's take the car an' be off!

—We're city men, said a hurler, an' never held reins in our hands in our life.

—Nor have we, either, said Mick.

—I can, I can, said Johnny eagerly; I've often dhrove the milkman's jennet, an' he's often a hard thing to handle.

They heard an answering whistle from some distance away.

—Up with yous, up with us, said the hurlers.

They sprang up on the car, Mick and two hurlers on one side, Tom and two hurlers on the other, Archie in the rear, with his legs dangling down the back of the car, and Johnny climbed into the dicky-seat, gathered the reins in his hand, gave a sharp gee-up, gee-up, to the nag, and away they all went at a quiet trot down the road. Looking back, they saw a figure run out to the road to rush after the car — it was the car-driver coming after them for all he was worth.

—Eh, there, they heard him cry out, come back, yeh daylight robbers; halt there, with me mare an' car; eh, there, you, come back outa that, holy God, isn't this a good one! Eh, there, come back!

—Gee up, lass, gee up, me girl, said Johnny coaxingly, and the mare's trot became quick and brisk.

—Touch her up with the whip, said Archie anxiously.

—Y'ignoramus, replied Johnny sharply, an' you seein' she's cold from standin' so long! Wait till she warms up a bit, an' then we can make her go. Gee up, gee up, girl; yep, me lassie!

—Supposin' they search the city for us? ventured Tom anxiously.

—We're safe when we get away, said one of the hurlers. When the constables cool down, they'll find it hard to explain why they were dhrinkin' when they were on duty; the barman'll be anxious for the name of his house; and, whatever the jarvey may be, you'll find he's no informer.

The hedges were now passing them by with speed; away in the far distance they heard a few faint whistles; Johnny caught up the whip and gave the mare a flick or two on the flanks. Away she tore now, the hedges flying by like mad things, for the mare was tearing along at a swift gallop. Holding her with a loose rein, but keeping her well in for fear of a sudden need in front of them, Johnny felt hilarious, saving them all from the horneys.

—That was a gorgeous clip you gave the bastard on the chin, said a hurler, to Mick; it musta given him a new vision of hell open for sinners.

Along past numbers of little cottages, the little lights in their little windows flitting by them like falling golden stars; on over the bridge crossing the Tolka, giving a fleeting glimpse of the white-mantled Blessed Virgin standing alone among a clump of rain and river-soaked cottages; then a swift, winding turn up into Botanic Avenue, catching sight sometimes of the Tolka waters, singing her gentle song as she went slowly by the elders and willows, away on her short and simple journey to the Bay of Dublin O.

Along the Avenue, at a quick lolloping gallop, the tidy-limbed little mare goes on, a-pace, a-pace, a lady goes a-pace a-pace, a gentleman goes a trit-trot trit-trot, and a horseman goes a-gallop a-gallop a-gallop, couples in each other's arms, lying by the roadside or standing close against the walls, turning to look at the jaunting-car go racing by, with its redcoats and green jerseys arm in arm on the seats, glancing at the nipper driving, bent nicely over the mare, turning her round by the Botanic Gardens, the car swaying, the men holding on, stopping their chatter till the car levelled itself again to go swinging along the Glasnevin Road, several couples wandering slowly along, scurrying aside as close to the hedges as they could get, to let the car go fast past by them, along, along the road, Johnny flushed with pride, thinking he was the American Mail fleeing from the redskins, holding the reins as if he had never done anything but go at a gallop through all the days of his life, slowing down a little now going over Westmoreland Bridge, and pulling her gradually to a stop before the doorway of the Cross Guns.

—Where do we go, now? he asked.

They all leaped down from the car on to the side-walk.

—Tie her here to the lamp-post, said Mick, an' let us all scatther before they thrace us here, an' we end our ride with a night in chokey. The jarvey'll find her, never fear, an' not much harm done.

One of the hurlers patted Johnny on the back, saying, Well done, me young bucko; you're the one well able to handle a horse!

—He dhrove like Jehu, said Archie.

The hurlers raised their hands high over their heads and shook their hurleys.

—Parnell for ever! they shouted.

—An' Ireland, too! said Tom.

—An' Ireland, too! shouted the hurlers.

Johnny felt in his heart that he had done a good day's work for Ireland. Then he remembered he had left behind on the counter the lovely branch of crimson and golden berries, plucked for his mother; and his heart got a little sad again.

COMIN' OF AGE

JOHNNY was getting on in years now, growing old with the world and all who were in it. Lean and lanky he grew, with masses of hair growing low down in front, that his mother laboured to brush back from his forehead, saying he'd look as if he knew nothing if he hadn't a high brow. A few days before his fourteenth birthday, he could manage to read, skipping the biggest words, the stories in *The Boys of London and New York*, and the various coloured-cover penny adventure books, and *Ally Sloper*, a weekly comic, whenever he had the penny to spare for one of them. So, if you ask me, he knew nearly as much as there was to be known, and fit he was to take his place in the world, paddle his own canoe, and fill a job with the best boy going, as soon as he could get one. Every day Archie carefully scanned the 'Situations Vacant' columns of the *Daily Express*, on the lookout for a suitable chance for Johnny.

Early on one fair morning in April, Johnny was wakened by having his shoulder shaken by his mother.

—Get up, she said, get up, like a good boy, for Archie has just come across the very thing for you.

Johnny slowly opened his sleep-dim eyes and murmured, Let him speak, for I can hear as well lyin' down as I can sittin' up.

—Get up, get up, man, said Archie impatiently; and when you've washed your face you'll be betther able to take in what I've got to say to you.

Johnny got up, dressed, and washed his face, wondering how he could be able to understand better when all this had been done. Then he sat down by the fire to listen to what the one and only Archie had to say.

Archie opened out the *Daily Express* and looked earnestly into it. Then, in a stately and dignified voice, he read, A smart, respectable, and honest boy wanted. One just finished school preferred. Apply by letter to Hymdim, Leadem & Co., Henry Street, Dublin. There y'are, he added, the chance of a lifetime.

—Maybe a godsend, said his mother.

—A fine big Firm, said Archie, one o' th' biggest in th' whole city, an' protestant to the backbone.

—Johnny'll never know what he'll rise to, in a Firm like that, murmured the mother.

—Let him run down, now, to Ella, an' get her to write out a letther for him, applyin' for the job; an' another of her own as a school-misthress, sayin' Johnny was a good boy, an' most attentive to his studies, instructed Archie. Let her just sign it E. Benson, so as to show no sign that it was written by a woman.

—An' I'll ask Mrs. Middleton for the loan of her boy's new topcoat, said Mrs. Casside, for Johnny to have a betther chance of lookin' the boy the job was meant for; an', if he gets the job, we can get one for himself at a bob a week from oul' Greenberg. Hurry off, now, she said to Johnny, to your sisther, an' get her to write the two letthers; on your way there, buyin' a pennorth o' notepaper an' envelopes, a penny bottle of ink, an' a ha'penny pen, in case Ella 'ud be empty-handed. Then hurry back; I'll have th' coat waitin' for you, an' you can go at once and see if they'll give you th' job.

Johnny girded up his loins and set off at a quick walk to his sister's place in Summerhill, popping into a shop on the way and buying all he needed; quickening the walk to a quicker trot, then to the quickest gallop; sliding down, after a while, to a trot, then to a quick walk for a rest; then breaking into a gallop again, going on like Paul Revere to tell the town the enemy was on the way, till he came panting to his sister, showed her the news his mother had cut from the paper, and telling her what she had to do.

In a hurry, she washed her hands for fear of soiling the letter, and saying that when it was written he'd have to copy what she had written, for they'd know her neat hand was hardly the hand of a schoolboy. So when she had written, Johnny, with his face screwed up, and with much labour and care, wrote in a large-lettered hand, the following:

Dear Sirs,

    I have observed by an advertisement appearing in the *Daily Express* of this morning's issue, that your Firm is in need of an honest, smart, and respectable boy, and that you prefer to employ one who has just finished school. I venture to say that I have all the qualities required, and, as I have just left school, I beg to offer myself as a candidate for the position.

Very respectfully yours,

JOHN CASSIDE

Messrs. Hymdim & Leadem.

Ella then wrote on another sheet of notepaper:

St. Mary's National School,
Lr. Dominick Street.

The Bearer, JOHN CASSIDE, has been a pupil in the above school, during which period I have always found him a truthful, honest, and obedient boy, and, at all times, most attentive to his studies. I feel sure he will give perfect satisfaction to any employer good enough to use his services.

E. BENSON,
School Teacher

Johnny hurried home with the letters; dressed himself in all his faded finery, putting the almost new blue Melton coat, loaned to his mother by Mrs. Middleton, over the lot, and hastened off to join those who were busy battling with the world.

When he came to Sackville Street, he felt hot and a little out of breath. He felt the sweat oozing out between his thighs, making his trousers feel a little damp. He had gone too quick, he thought. His stomach felt as full as if he had just eaten a great meal, but he had had only a cup of tea and a cut of dry bread. Tight it felt as a tightly laced drum. If he could only pop into the job, without having to see anyone about it. Still, he was here, and in he'd have to go, and finish what he had begun. But better wait till he had cooled down a little; never do to show you were in a sweat to get it. Go in, cool and collected, and appear as if you didn't care whether you got it or not: and had just dropped in because you had nothing else to do, and the day was long. He'd sit here for a few seconds, till his heart got down to a quieter beat, and then go on: forward — the Buffs! He sat down on one of the pedestals of one of the General Post Office's great pillars, listening to the tram timekeeper, a brown-bearded man, wearing a half-tall hat, calling out for the trams to make a start: Sandymount, and away would go that tram; Palmerston Park, and away would go that tram too, with a tinkle from the bell the conductor pulled. All aboard for Palmerston Park, where the gentry lived. Most of them were moving to where the gentry lived, passing through the poorer quarters, out to where there were trees, air, and sunshine, where the gentry lived.

For the tenth time, Johnny took the letters from his pocket and read them, before he finally sealed them up for ever. Not so bad, he said, as he licked the flaps and closed them down, for if they want a genuinely honest, truthful, and willing boy, they needn't look over my shoulder for one.

He watched for a few more moments the soldiers streaming past him: Hussars, in their gorgeous crimson trousers; Army Service Corps, with their sober blue-and-white uniforms; Lancers, white-breasted, red-breasted, or yellow-breasted; Guards, in their tight little trousers, tight little white pea-jackets, tight little caps; Highlanders, with their kilts swinging — all on the hunt for girls; always strolling on the same side of the street, the west side, never on the other, where all the respectable people walked who didn't like to make a contact with a common soldier; from the corner of Great Britain Street, principally, to the Royal Bank of Ireland, back and forward, stopping when they made a catch, restlessly moving backwards and forwards, on the hunt for girls.

> While up the street, each girl they meet,
> Will look so shy, then cry, my eye!
> Och! Isn't he a darling,
> Me bould sodger boy!

He felt quite cool, now, so he licked three of his fingers, and smoothed his hair back from his forehead as far as it would go. He dusted the seat of his trousers, felt that his Eton collar sat still and safe, pulled the lapels of his blue Melton coat forward, and sallied up Henry Street, threading his way through the crowds of people coming out and going into the shops. Right into the big stores he dived, asking where he could deliver a letter that answered an advertisement wanting a truthful, honest, and willing boy. The far end of the great shop was pointed out to him, and he was told that when he passed through a door there, he would find a Mr. Anthony who would deal with the matter contained in the letter applying for the post. So Johnny went on a long journey by steep mountains of chandlery, terraces of lamps of every sort, table lamps, tiny lamps, bracket, hanging, hall, and reading lamps; small wick, wide wick, single wick, and double wick lamps; forests of brushes, hair, fibre, and twig; valleys of curtains, cloth, beads, and bamboo; huge rockeries of ironmongery; while overhead was a great gallery, circling the whole of the ground floor, filled with all kinds of delft and chinaware, beetling over all as if eager to look at all the other wonders piled in the valley below. Through all these he wended his way to a glass-panelled door leading to the packing and despatch departments. Pushing this open, he came into a long dark store, holding all the future supplies for the shop inside, and divided into heavy benches on which goods were piled, to be parcelled and packed and sent to various parts of the city and suburbs. On one side of this store, near the glass-panelled door, was a boxed-in office, full of windows, so that everything everywhere could be seen by a tiny lift of the head of anyone who might happen to be in it. In this office was a tall lean man, with a head like a fairly thin egg, whose hair began to sprout in the middle of his head, giving him the look of a waning scholar, who glanced up and looked at Johnny with a keen look in a pair of watery eyes that were thinly blue in colour.

Johnny, with his cap held respectfully under his arm, handed the two letters to this man, who was Anthony Dovergull, one of two brothers, owners of this big Firm of Messrs. Hymdim, Leadem & Company; the other brother (Johnny found out afterwards) was as jet-black as this one was fair, with a heavy moustache losing itself in a heavy coal-black beard (his brother was clean-shaven), with brilliant black eyes that never knew how to soften. He was as tall as his fair brother, but had thick legs, massive shoulders, like a bull's, that gathered together and bent, when he was angry, like a bull about to charge; and his only smile, seen when the House was doing good business, was like a wintry sunbeam finding a home in an icicle. The dark fellow watched over the front of the Firm, standing on a bridge stretching from one side of the chinaware gallery to the other, stood all the day like a skipper on the bridge of a ship.

Mr. Anthony Dovergull took the letters from Johnny, read them silently, and looked Johnny all over. Johnny was glad that he had Middleton's Melton overcoat on him. Then Mr. Anthony read the letters again, thought for a moment or two; then looked at Johnny again.

—You are a protestant, young man, are you not? he asked.

—Oh yes, of course, sir, answered Johnny, feeling that he had a close kinship with the mighty man in the boxed-in office.

—Well, we'll try you, said Mr. Anthony. You can start tomorrow morning. Hours, eight till six; wages, three shillings and sixpence a week; rising, of course, annually, if your services are found to be satisfactory. And he dismissed Johnny by turning to resume the work he had been doing when Johnny handed him the letters.

So here he was standing in the street again, a child of fortune, a member of Hymdim, Leadem & Company, and an inheritor of three shillings and sixpence a week. He had made a flying start. He would begin life at eight o'clock the following morning. In the morning his life would break into bud. Aaron's rod all over again; it would bud and blossom. He was a child no longer. He had put childish things far from him. He was a worker. Henceforth he would earn his bread in the sweat of his face. The earth was his, and the fulness thereof. Glory be to God. Out of the darkness had come a saving light.

And Johnny felt that it was good; and the morning and the evening were the fair'st day.

BRING FORTH THE BEST ROBE

JOHNNY was up betimes, gay and fussy, in the morning. He took no notice of his mother advising him to get down as much bread as he could, for he'd have a long fast; but hurried over his breakfast, and excited and nervous, got into the new array, brown coat, long trousers, grey cap, and new black boots, got from Mr. Greenberg the previous day.

Mr. Greenberg was a Jew; not an ordinary Jew, Johnny's mother said, but a most respectable one. He had never carried a pack, but had turned the front room of a little house in a terrace off the Drumcondra Road into a shop. There clients came quietly to be satisfied, after a bargain made in their own houses. He had come to Johnny's house the evening before, and had promised to fit out Johnny from top to toe for five shillings down, and the rest of two pounds ten to be paid at one shilling a week; the instalments to be paid on the first day of every month. Mrs. Casside had paid the five shillings deposit, and he had entered it in a little blue-covered pass-book below the articles bought: A brown suit, one pound; a navy-blue topcoat, one pound; pair of boots, ten shillings; and the grey cap, Mr. Greenberg said, because of the boy making a start in life, would be thrown in free. Thrown in free, he murmured again, with a sigh. He glanced round the room, saw its scanty furniture, and sighed again. Didn't look like a very promising customer. His eyes roved over the collection of books that remained out of all that Johnny's Da had loved. His eyes took on a look of surprise. He went over to where they were, and took one of them into his hand, a thick, heavy, purple-covered one. It was *The Wars of the Jews*, and he opened it, and began to read.

—One of my poor husband's books, murmured Mrs. Casside.

—Ah! said Mr. Greenberg, Josephus, Josephus; a great writer; a great man. Our people, our poor people. Have you rread it, Mrs. Casside?

—No, indeed, I'm sorry to say, she answered. But my poor husband knew it near by heart. Everyone regarded him as a great scholar. Nothing was beyond him.

—Ah! said Mr. Greenberg murmuringly, zee gruel, derreeble, veeked Romans! Ven they took Jerusalem and destroyed dee ceety, they crucified us in dousandts, dousandts, and dousandts. Zey could not get enough vood to make zee crosses they needed; dousandts and dousandts.

—What, the Holy Romans? asked Johnny.

Mr. Greenberg turned towards Johnny, with a puzzled look on his face.

—He means the roman catholics, explained Mrs. Casside.

—Not zee catolics, not zee roman catolics, said Mr. Greenberg. Zee old Romans, zee ancient vones, years and years ago, hunderts and hunderts of years before you or I vos born. But eet is all ofer now, he added; all ofer now. It ees lif, and — vot you say? he asked of Mrs. Casside.

—Live an' let live, she said.

—Live, and let live, he repeated. Ve are — vot you call it? — ceevilised now. He put the book back where he got it, and settled his half-tall hat on his head, and stroked his beard thoughtfully.

—Goodbye, he said, shaking hands with Johnny; you vill find zee goods vot you want: a vonderful bargain. And read zee vars of zee Jews, my boy, ven you half dime, ven you haf dime. It ees goot to read books; zey dell you zings, and it is goot to know zings; zee more zee better. Goodbye, my boy, and goot luck.

—Rather a nice old boy, for a Jew, said Johnny when he had gone.

—He's all right, replied his mother, but he knows how to charge, all the same. Had I had the ready money, I'd have got all he's given for half the cost, an' less.

Here he was now, dressed in the new garments, at a quarter-past seven in the morning, with his mother putting the last touches to them; pulling down his dark-blue topcoat behind him, fixing his cap straight on his carefully brushed hair; going to the door with him, advising him not to be nervous, and bidding him godspeed.

Johnny hurried along the almost empty streets and passed the closed-up shops, opening his topcoat wide so that the few who passed at this early hour could see that he was wearing long trousers. What a swell he looked, and what a man he felt as he trudged gaily and swiftly along. A few trams, with nobody in them, hung around Nelson's Pillar, looking higher and statelier for the want of a crowd. Only the pubs were beginning to open as he went by, grocers' porters slashing buckets of water in front of the brightly-painted fronts to take away the raucous smells and smudges of the night before. Johnny got to the

Firm nearly half an hour before the time of opening; and he leaned against the sombre revolving shutters, waiting for whomsoever came to open up the shop for the work of the day. There was nothing but a dog wandering up the street; and even the great General Post Office looked surly and sad. Opposite him loomed up the great drapery firm of Sir John Arnott & Co., another firm, he knew, stocked with good protestants as tightly as it was stocked with good goods. There wasn't a doubt about it; we were, in some way or other, a goodlier run of people than the poor roman catholics.

At five minutes to eight he noticed that men and boys began to gather, and lean against the sombre shutters, just as he was doing, some of them glancing at him, curiously, as they settled their backs into a comfortable position. Eight o'clock struck from the big clock outside Arnott's, and still no-one came to open the shop. He edged a little nearer to the waiting crowd so that he might catch a word or two of what was being said.

—Musta slept it out this morning, he heard one man say, when the clock showed it was five minutes past the hour.

—He's given us time for a longer smoke before dinner-time, responded another; but you'll soon see him come gallopin' round the corner. Didn't I tell you, he added, for here he comes fallin' over himself with the dint of hurry.

Johnny saw the long lank figure of him who had given him his job hurrying up the street, black suit, black bowler hat, black gloves, and black umbrella, like a thin black bat fluttering in a hurry along to get in out of the daylight. Anthony came up, and, without as much as a good-morning to a soul, opened the black wicket-gate in the centre of the shutters, and hurried in, the crowd of clerks and boy assistants pouring in, one by one, after him. And Johnny, last of all, went in too, and found himself in the lonely darkened shop full of the smell of soda, soap, candles, and beeswax.

They all streamed away to where they left their coats and hats, leaving Johnny standing alone, alone in a darkened world, with the hundreds of lamps hanging overhead looking like stars that had died down, had lost their light, and shone in the firmament no longer.

Presently, he saw a man at the far end of the shop beckoning to him. He went down and stood in front of a man with a pale, handsome, Jewish-like face, who looked him all over, smiled rather sarcastically, and said, Mr. Anthony tells me you're the new boy assistant, and you're to come with me so that I can show you what to do, and generally show you the way about the Firm. This man was Mr.

Prowle, an Orangeman, it was said, who was over the despatch of all things going away by rail or sea; a silent man, who spoke to no-one, and no-one spoke to him; always looking like a juvenile mariner, waiting on a painted ship upon a painted ocean.

He went before Johnny through the door leading to the despatch store, and, showing Johnny a huge pile of waste paper, said, Sort that, smooth the sheets out in their different sizes, put holes through them when the heaps are big enough, and string them up for use in parcelling up the goods we send away. When that's done, tie up all those clothes-pegs into dozens, and pile them neatly on the shelf behind you.

While he was working away at the waste paper, Johnny saw two messengers carry a small bench over into a corner of the stores, and cover it with a bright-green cloth, on which they placed a big white vase filled with red and yellow artificial flowers, making it look for all the world like a clumsy-looking altar. Then they carried two big parcels and placed them on the bench covered with a green cloth. Each parcel was backed by a big label, bearing on one the words, For Good Boy, Number One; and on the other, For Good Boy, Number Two. Stuck jauntily into the first parcel was a little paper Union Jack, with a bronze shaft as thick as a knitting needle, and a gilded paper point; on the other parcel, a little Royal Standard of the same kind. In front of each parcel stood a rather faded bowler hat, one lined with white silk and the other with crimson. And everyone who passed by wore a wide fat grin, holding tight to it, and not suffering it to depart when they had gone by. Johnny noticed, too, that Mr. Anthony, in his desk above at the top of the store, wore a grin too; a quieter and more subdued one, as if he had just done something good and pleasant and quietly noble.

Johnny was working like a good one, tying the pegs into dozens, when Prowle called him, handed him a slip, and told him to get the things mentioned on it and parcel them up for him.

Johnny stared at the pencilled slip, and couldn't make head or tail of it. Six lbs — that was clear enough, but what did *S sp* mean? Or *B w cls*, or *Bwx* mean? He looked and stared and looked again for a long time, till Prowle snatched the slip out of his hand.

—Can't you read? he asked sharply. What school did you go to?

—He went to college, said a packer at the other side of the bench, eager to fall in with Prowle; none o' your common schools for him.

—Six pounds of Sunlight soap, two of British wax candles, and a pound of beeswax — could anything be plainer. You'll have to brighten yourself, me boy, if you want to stay here. We don't want duffers. They're all on the shelves behind you; open your eyes and you'll find them, said Mr. Prowle.

Johnny strayed up and down the long avenue of shelves, looking for what was on the slip. Probing the spaces, he came near to the desk where Nearus, the head clerk of the stores, was writing. Nearus was a big fellow, over six foot, and broad-shouldered; good and kind of heart he was, as Johnny soon discovered; but he was rotten at the core, for, on the top of each cheek, he wore the rosy cross of consumption, and a cough told the tale of a tomb.

—What are you looking for, what are you looking for? he asked, in a rough-and-ready way, when Johnny came close to him; but there was a soft note in the bark of his voice. There you are, he added, pointing to some shelves; candles there; soap here; and the beeswax over your little head. He took down the things himself as he spoke, and laid them on the counter for Johnny. If you're in any fix at any time, come to me, and don't fret if I shout the answer at you.

So the long day wore on, with Johnny, under the firmament of heaven, tying up pegs into dozens, sorting out paper, running all sorts of errands, finding out how puzzling little words could be when they were written down on paper, discovering, like an explorer, the new regions of the big Firm, and learning where the multitude of differing stores were packed away in their various places; all the time glancing frequently at the bench covered with the green cloth, and wondering what was in the parcels, and why everyone smiled as they passed the parcels by.

Coming back five minutes before the time at lunch hour, he found Nearus alone, bending over his desk, busy with an army of figures. He glanced up when he saw Johnny signing on in the book that lay, like a warrior taking his rest, beside the big desk of Nearus.

—Eh, kid, he said, is that a new suit of clothes you've on you, or is it only an old one varnished?

—New one, sir, said Johnny; bought only yestherday.

—Well, it won't be worth a wax in a week here, man. No-one wears a new suit working. Bring an old coat with you tomorrow, and hide it under the bench to wear when you're working. It's enough to look a toff when you're coming in to start, or going out when you're finished.

—Thank you, said Johnny. I'll tell my Ma when I get home.

—Well, kid, he said, how do you think you'll like your job?

—I'm sure to like it well, said Johnny; all the people here seem so happy and smiling.

He beckoned to Johnny to come a little nearer, and bent over till his mouth was close to Johnny's ear.

—Keep your mouth shut and your ears open, and you won't see much, he said. They're all a gang of superior hangmen here. They're smiling today because they have to, for today is the great day of atonement. Know what atonement means?

—Being at one with someone who has had a row with you, said Johnny.

—If you din't knock it down, you staggered it, said Nearus. Well, we're all, for this one day of the year, at one with Mr. Anthony and Mr. Hewson, and that's why we're all smiling, my boy. The master is at one with the man, and the man is at one with the master. He stretched a big and thinning hand towards the bench covered with the green cloth. And that's the altar of friendship, he said.

—An' what's in th' parcels? asked Johnny.

—Goodly threasures for two goodly men, answered Nearus. An old suit that Anthony's tired wearing, and another that Hewson's tired wearing, for Enthrews, the packer here, and O'Reilly, the porter in the front shop.

—They must be two good men, murmured Johnny, for he wist not what to say rightly.

—Too good for God, said Nearus. He leaned over closer to Johnny, and whispered in his ear: Don't ever say anything to either of them; don't let them hear you saying anything to anyone else; don't even let them hear you saying your prayers.

Others began to come back from lunch. Nearus got close to his desk to fight the army of figures again, and Johnny went his way behind the great counter to his tying of pegs, sorting of paper, or any extra thing he might be called upon to do.

The long day wore on, and the quiet evening came, and the work slackened when it was but an half-hour before the time to quit.

And all the house was smiling, all except Nearus; for Johnny thought it would be a good thing to smile too.

Suddenly the big black Hewson came in from the front shop, and, joining the skinny, fair-eyed Anthony, both of them, smiling, sauntered down to where the bench, covered with the green cloth, was standing, looking like a clumsy altar bearing on it outward and visible signs of an inward and spiritual grace. Shortly afterwards O'Reilly came in from the front shop, and stood, smiling, at the north end of the store, while the packer Enthrews stood, smiling, at the other end, gently tapping straw into a case he was packing for the country. The vanmen, messengers, and other packers stood in a grinning group near the big gateway; and the clerks from the various despatch rooms, and the assistants from the front shop, came hurrying in and stood in a smiling row along the length of the warehouse, their eyes staring at the bench covered with the bright-green cloth. Then, after a fit pause, Mr. Hewson beckoned to Enthrews, and Mr. Anthony beckoned to O'Reilly; and the two came, each from the other end of the carth, trusting, not in thcir own rightcousncss, but in the manifold and great goodness of their two Masters, who were ready to bestow upon them some of the crumbs that would soon fall from the table covered with the green cloth.

And when they drew near, Hewson stretched out his hand and took a parcel, and handed it to Enthrews, at the same time that Anthony stretched out his hand and took a parcel, and handed it to O'Reilly. Then Hewson placed a bowler hat on the head of O'Reilly, and Anthony placed a bowler hat on the head of Enthrews, and lo! both were crowned, and a fine glory shone round about them; and a lowly murmur of praise went up from the clerks, assistants, vanmen, and messengers, as they saw this good thing done, and the murmur testified to the goodwill among men.

And Enthrews opened his mouth, saying unto Anthony, Thanks be unto thee, O sir; your kindness was unexpected, and your goodness endureth for ever.

And O'Reilly opened his mouth, saying unto Hewson, Thanks be unto thee, O sir; your goodness was unexpected, and your kindness endureth for ever.

Then the two men who had been so favoured went into a secret place to take off their old clothes and put on the new garments that had been given them; while Hewson and Anthony, smiling and chatting together in amity and peace, waited leaning against the bench that was covered with the bright-green cloth.

And Johnny, looking on, fancied he heard a voice from heaven saying, Let your light so shine before men that they may see your good works, and glorify your Father which is in heaven.

By and by the two came back rejoicing, clad in their new raiment, walking thc onc aftcr thc othcr, scllovish pride irrigating both thcir hearts, lifting their eyes to the hills, passing backwards through a lane-way of smiles; Enthrews with the little Union Jack sticking up from the band on his bowler hat, and O'Reilly with the little Royal Standard sticking up from the band in his.

And all hands were admonished by this display to behave better and to serve honestly the two men who, now and again, deigned to think of common men, and to look down from the ownership of might and mercy in the centre of Dublin City, hard by the protestant church on the one hand and the catholic church on the other.

A low, lorn murmur of satisfaction rose from the assembled clerks, assistants, vanmen, and messengers; and in the midst of the murmur Mr. Anthony and Mr. Hewson moved away from the bench that was covered with the bright-green cloth, and walked slowly towards the glass-panelled door leading to the front shop. Then Mr. Prowle lifted up his fine voice a little, in a respectable manner, and sang, and all except Nearus, who coughed and leant over his desk with his head bent down, joined in, singing softly, soberly and slyly, for very fear that God might hear them:

> An' here's a hand, my trusty fiere,
>   An' gie's a hand o' thine;
> An' we'll tak' a right guid-willie waught,
>   For auld lang syne!
> For auld lang syne, my dear,
>   For auld lang syne,
> We'll tak' a cup o' kindness yet,
>   For auld lang syne!

Then it was time to go; and all slunk their several ways home for the night, to eat, to whore, to sleep, perchance to dream. And Johnny went with them. Peace and fellowship were everywhere; but Johnny felt uneasy, and saw that it was not good; and the morning and the evening were the sicken'd day.

WORK MADE MANIFEST

So here he was, a start in life made, ploughing his first furrow in the workaday world of Dublin. Hould on now, an' let Johnny think of what he had to do in a day. It was he that had to do as much as any dry-land sailor. First he had to go to where the vanmen stabled their horses, in a lane off Cavendish Row, to gather the precious money collected by them on bills for goods bought in the shop, checking the amounts appearing in the vanmen's books, and signing for the sums received; throwing the notes and coins into a satchel, amounting to from fifteen to twenty-five quid; hurry back to the firm to deliver the money over to Mr. Anthony, always a little anxious that some day he'd be short of a shilling or two, for the vanmen wanted watching, and a bob would make a big hole in his week's wages. Then, when the money was at rest in the safe, he had to sweep the dirty straw and rubbish from behind the long bench that held the goods going by rail or sea, sweeping the rubbish out to the beginning of the passage leading to the cobbled lane outside the great wooden gate. As a protestant and a member of the staff, he swept no farther, but handed the heap of rubbish over to a roman catholic messenger, who carried it on to where it would be eventually taken away by the city scavengers. When loads of new stuff came up in lorries or in floats, he had to carry in the four- or six-stone boxes, open them with a steel ripper, and pack the goods, starch, soap, polish, or blacking in bins or on shelves behind the benches. Or, he would be sent to another store further down the lane, bordered on the other side by slaughterhouses, reeking of fresh and stale blood, into which cattle or sheep were continually pouring; to come out as skinned and bloody carcases, carried on the shoulders of sturdy men, with the purple of battle all over their clothes, who pitched the gaudy carcases into huge carts, which brought them to the butchers who cut them up into fancy shapes for the finer sustenance of man. Here in this further store came crates of chinaware; and Johnny helped to unpack them, and carry the chinaware in boxes, hard and heavy and biting into his shoulder, through the long despatch store, through the front shop, up seven flights of stairs — a holy number — to the special rooms where the chinaware was stored. When there were no more soap, matches, blacking, or chinaware to be carried in and packed away, Johnny kept from the deadly sin of sloth by helping to parcel up the goods that were to go away, putting them in order of delivery on the benches, in readiness for the vanmen to come and bring them out to the customers. Or, if he wasn't busy in this way, he'd go on errands, leaving an order for brushes in Varian's of Talbot Street; or hump a hip-bath, or a full-length one, over his head and shoulders to Phillipson's in Stafford Street, to have it scraped and japanned over again, so that its rusty nakedness might be hidden from sensitive eyes. It was a long day and a tiring day; but he had the assurance that for ever, now, he would be certain of his *Boys of London and New York* every week of his life, for ever and for evermore, amen.

Every worker in the front shop and every clerk, or the possible makings of a clerk, in the despatch department, was a protestant of one kind or another. The catholics drove the vans, took charge of the crates, muled in the stores, did the packing, and acted as messengers, pushing huge, deep, wicker three-wheeled prams filled with goods for customers throughout the day and half-way through the night for four, five, and six shillings a week. Each vanman, no matter how late he had arrived back at night — and none of them ever got home earlier from an ordinary delivery than ten o'clock — had to be at the stables by half-seven in the morning, to water and feed his horse, wash down his van, deliver what money he had to Johnny, harness up, and be at the shop for first delivery by half-past eight. On Fridays he was allowed to stretch out his hand for fourteen shillings in a little clean white envelope. All were married men with children, so they hadn't time to mind it. Had they been protestants, as Johnny was, they'd have known that the daily round and common task furnished all they need to ask; room to deny themselves — a road that daily led them nearer God. Stay quiet, an' you can hear the angels singin'.

Johnny had done all these things, and more; he had mingled with all these people, protestant goats and catholic sheep, for one long year; he had done well in his job; he had proved himself to be a truthful, willing, and honest boy; and had been rewarded with a rise, so that he went home, now, every Friday, with four shillings in his pocket instead of a meagre three and sixpence. Yet he wasn't satisfied. There was a sting of discontent in his heart. He had come to hate the shop and hate the men who owned it. Why, he couldn't say, rightly; but though the reasons were dim, the hate was bitter; ay, and he hated all, or almost all, who worked for the two Plymouth Brethren, Anthony and Hewson, who never mentioned God, but silently encouraged a number of desirables to go round and whisper in the others' ears that they would be pleased if any or all came to prayer, meditation, and the reading of the Bible in Merrion Hall on Thursday or Sunday nights at eight o'clock sharp, when Jesus Christ would be present on the platform.

There was one above all the others whom he hated. One there was above all others — oh, how he hated him! His was hate beyond a brother's — oh, how he hated him! This was O'Reilly, the porter, ex-R.I.C. man, opener and shutter-up of the shop, and custodian of the basement where the ironmongery was kept. A sweet boyo! A catholic that was the hidden eye and ear of the two Plummyth Breadiron. Everyone in the firm, front and rear, was afraid of O'Reilly, and everyone was sweet to him, with their Good-morning, Mr. O'Reilly, an' I hope you're well, as this leaves me at present. The four-leaved shamrock, Johnny called him, and left him gaping when he went by without sayin' Good-evening', an' how're you feelin' today, sir, with th' weather soft an' a hard wind blowin', an' winther touchin' our toes, an' all th' green things on th' earth shiverin'; an' you feelin' something must be wrong because you go to Mass, while your bosses go to meetin'-house, thinkin' it hard lines that things can't be done in heaven as they're done on earth so that you could live with them, world without end; an' they thinkin', on their side, that there must be something right with O'Reilly; for didn't the good man defend their faith, thcir hope, their charity with a baton and a musket in the good young days, an' now, in his oul' age, he was still wary in defending their feat, heap, and charyity by keeping a spy-eye on all those who earned their bread by the skin of their teeth; with his sleek, sliddery sludery sloppery gob going peek-a-boo, I see you idling there, skedulin' the time you took to draw your breath; with Hewson asking him today, an' a far-away smile on his kisser, how were his sons gettin' on at the Intermediate; an' Mr. Anthony sayin' to him, tomorrow, how right he was not to let himself or his wife or his children or his children's children resort with the kind o' neighbours circumstances obliged him to live among, addin' that O'Reilly ought to be well aware that O'Reilly wasn't an ordinary roman catholic, but really O'Reilly was gifted with the spirit of respectability of the Holy Ghost, given to very few people of really O'Reilly's class; for O'Reilly really breathed the breath of an honest devotion to persons and things most worthy to receive it, which was dispensationable according to the body and soul, life and teaching of their, and, in a minor sense, his, Lord and Saviour, Jesus Christ, amen, cross yourselves, and as you were before you 'listed.

So O'Reilly went on, and prospered, and stuck himself up to his neck in the bog of virtue, an' made holy affiance with the godliness of well-doing, never wearying of letting his bronze bosses know of anyone who swung the lead in the good ship we all toiled in; for everything was on the tongue and in the ear that met the eye that O'Reilly saw with; and a dhry thrio the three of them were, made be God Almighty when He hadn't much moisture to spare, for there wasn't the makin's of a tear among the three of them; an' it musta been a helluva shock to the best of them to have ever read that Jesus wept, feelin' that these tears, idle tears, were the one weakness shown by their Lord and Masstar.

A go-between and helper in the daily din was Sorrasaint, the Manager. Paler than Mr. Anthony, with white eyebrows, timidly tinged with yellow, a moustache the colour of straw that had been out in the rain overnight, shallow blue eyes he had, shallow as a puddle made shallower be a dhryin' wind, an' as tight as a tin flea he was, ever ready to pounce out and forswear anything in the way of an ankle undher a white petticoat; an' well Johnny remembered when he once found, in a crate of china, a lovely coloured picture of a dancing girl, showing a beaming face and a lingering leg flowin' about in a foamy sea of lace, Sorrasaint came up behind, like a thief in the day, snapped the picture out of Johnny's hand, whipped up a hammer, and smashed the dancing damsel into smidereens, throwing the hammer, in godly indignation, back into the straw again, an' walkin' away, like a gaudy Guardsman keen on his sentry-go.

These were the Four Feathers in the bowler hat of the Firm, who were, as well, deep in the web of God's confidence, an' high in the highlands of Erin's honour and Erin's pride, getting together all they could get, an' booking for themselves sunny places on the bonny banks an' braes of the Christal river, where a union of angels were busy furnishing Ellessdee-touched villas for them, ere ever their silver cords were loosened and their golden bowls were broken.

Johnny had been in the job now for a year and a half, and was busily waiting for promotion to the position of a clerk, if you please, over a sectional city delivery. Every day of the year and a half, bar Sundays, he had eaten his two cuts of bread, that the shop called lunch, sitting on the step of one of the pedestals of the General Post Office, looking out towards the bustling street when the sun gave courage to the spring and dreamy delight to the summer; looking in towards the portico, with shoulders bunched up, and the dry bread bitter in his mouth, when the cold winds blew, or the rain fell heavily; for only the girls of the shop were allowed to eat on the premises, no matter how the weather raved, or sputtered her cold venom on those who walked the Dublin streets, with thin blood in their veins, and thinner clothes to cuddle their skins from the blast.

But there was always the scarlet and gold, the blue and the white of the warriors going by him, with their pushers; or a Lancer officer trotting down the street on a fine bay on a fine day in a fine way, with his sword and sabretache jingling, and the plume in his Polish hat behaving well in the breeze; followed, at a respectable distance, by his faithful servant, maybe a Hussar or a Dragoon, looking only a little less stuck-up on his horse than his officer and gentleman master leading the way onward. Maybe, Johnny would watch the dust of the street, and he eating his daily bread that God sent him, dancing its cloudy dance along the cobbled way when winds blew swift and

sudden; or, better still, the skirts of the young girls blowing up when
the wind blew strong, sending a surge through him that he couldn't
say was wrong, and didn't know was right; but right or wrong, there
it was — a mighty feeling and a strange delight when a black-stockinged leg of a pretty girl came out of a drab skirt, like a sunbeam out
of a shadow. Then his thoughts would steal away to Jennie Clitheroe,
seeking to put a hand in hers, feeling a little rugged spot on a finger
where sewing had chafed her skin. He would dream of a green meadow
where they could lie together, deep in the green things growing on
the earth, the clover, the sorrel, the strong grass and the trembling,
with a cornfield in the distance, golden, and scarlet poppies, sleepy,
nodding at their feet.

But he was always too tired, when he came home at night, to go
after any of these things. After glimpsing the blue and white, the red
and gold of the soldiers; the helms and plumes of passing cavalry; the
sudden look of pretty legs sometimes shown by passing ladies; came
the labour of bearing piles of chinaware on his aching shoulders down
the shit-mottled lane, through the despatch department, along the
front shop, a-glitter no longer, and up the seven flights of holy, hilly,
helly stairs, thousands of thimes, hours and hours on end, till the shop
closed slowly, and Johnny wended his hot and heavy way home,
having helped to keep the great world moving.

And the morning and the evening were the tir'd day.

THE SHAME IS A THIEF AND A ROBBER

JOHNNY, working away, had grown in wisdom, if he hadn't grown
in grace. Although there was nothing against him, he knew the heads
of the house didn't like him. Many whispers had dribbled into his ear,
asking him to come to the meetings in Merrion Hall, but Johnny,
saying that he felt it was all very nice and comfortable and godly,
didn't ever go; and once, in a fit of recklessness, said to one of the
evangelical whisperers that he'd rather open a girl's bodice than open
a prayer-book, making the whisperer turn pale and turn tail and hurry
away in a hot quick trot. But, still an' all, he had learned a few things.
He could make out, without any bother, the differing handwriting of
assistants and vanmen; count money quick and correctly; balance
three hundredweight on a thruck nicely, and push it safely; lay out
orders swiftly, and parcel up goods; pack chinaware with any packer

in the shop; stand on a high ladder, and catch, with a cunning hand, packages thrown up to him for packing away on to high shelves; cleverly handle casks of oil; tip over heavy cases towards him, and edge them from where they were to where they ought to be; carry six-stone loads on his back through long distances for hours, without feeling faint at the end of the day; and fight his corner with the best or worst of those who worked around him.

The vanmen and messengers had fought shy of him for a long time, ever suspicious of a member of the staff; but one time, when a messenger happened to be in his way and delayed to get out of it, Johnny had given the fellow a hasty kick in the backside; and had suddenly found himself on his back in the straw from a puck in the snout the angry messenger had given him. He, thinking he had hit another messenger, got the fright of his life when his rage let him see it had been Johnny, one of the staff, hurrying to help Johnny up, and murmuring, for fear of losing his job, that he hadn't meant it, hadn't known it was Casside, thought it was only another messenger, and begging Johnny, with tears in his eyes, to say nothing about it. Johnny had shaken hands with him, saying, never fear, for a Casside was never known to be an informer; and, after that, Johnny was the heart of the rowl with vanmen and messengers, especially when they found out he could curse with the worst of them.

Johnny was feeling very cocky, and now marched about with a long-handled pen stuck behind his right ear. He had been promoted to the bright position of despatch clerk, over the Sandymount and Ringsend delivery, at a salary of six shillings a week. Every Friday he handed his mother four and six out of his wages, for he let on he'd only five, which was fair and square, for wasn't it him who earned the money, an' hadn't she only to sthretch out her hand to take it? An' looka all he gave her besides. He had now a free hand in getting goods for the customers his vanman served, so why couldn't he get a few goods for himself? No sooner asked than answered. Johnny in his heart decided that it was neither godly nor wise to muzzle the ox that treadeth out the corn. So, on principle, he never went home without bringing something with him; and, after a while, his mother, with a few frightened warnings to him to take care, made a few special pockets in his coat, deep and wide so that things could be spread out without bulging. So he carried home tiny cargoes of matches, soap, candles, borax, ink, blacking, ketchup, tins of enamel, Hudson's extract of soap and Monkey Brand that wouldn't wash clothes, an odd knife and fork now and again, a spoon occasionally, combs and hairbrushes, chamois leather, eggcups — though they were more ornamental than useful — salt-cellars, night-lights, knife polish, with a picture of Wellington on the tin, shoe-brushes, clothes-brushes, floor-cloths — particularly prized by his mother — small scrubbing-brushes, Goddard's Plate Powder that went to Tom and Mick to clean their buttons and badges, at tuppence a tin, little white-headed mops for cleaning lamp chimneys, among other things, with various little toys at Christmas for Ella's kids, and, any over, for the kids in the neighbourhood, Johnny getting the blessing of the mothers for his kind thought of bringing to the poor kids a real ray of Christmas kinsolation.

It was quite an innocent practice, thought Johnny; not like the heavy-handed foolishness of poor Botolph, the young clerk over the Rathmines delivery, who had landed himself in a raw plight with his picking and stealing; and was turned out of the Firm for ever one day as soon as he had come back from his lunch. Through a customer sending back goods paid for to the vanman at the door, Anthony found that no record existed of the payment in the vanman's book or in Botolph's ledger; and growing suspicious, they had watched for a week, and found that the bould Botolph entered up no bill that had to be paid, nor did any of them appear in the vanman's book. The vanman, pressed to explain, stammered that it must be a mistake; threatened with the police, he blurted out that this thing had been going on for some weeks; that the money received had been divided, two-thirds to Botolph and one-third to him; yessir, months, maybe, I can't well remember when I was led into it; it was Botolph who had enticed him to thievery, for he was naturally a very honest man, very, as all the world knew; Botolph had kept on appealing, persuading, nagging him, till he gave in for the sake of peace; he often an' often made up his mind to tell Mr. Anthony all 'bout it, but, somehow or other, it went out of his mind; an' wasn't it a poor thing that a decent, honest, sober, steady, and most respectable workman an' vanman should have been thrapped into thievery by a vicious, dangerous, eely gougher.

Botolph standing beside him, pale as the twin brother of death, moistening his cracking lips and biting his hot nails, backing, backing till his back felt the prop of a bench, for he was frightened and getting faint.

And Anthony, stern and stiff and tight-lipped, listened, and said, in a voice loud enough to be heard by the hard o' hearing, while all listened so as not to miss a word of it:

—You have been a vanman here in a Firm that any common man would be proud to work for; you have answered that honour by turning out to be a vagabond, a mean thief, a perverse reprobate, a ragged rogue. Leave my sight, you ruffian!

And the vanman, with tears trickling down his cheeks, departed from the sight of his master, Dyke giving him a vicious kick in the arse, followed by one from Enthrews, and one each from the messengers, while, finally, Johnny got one home on him as he passed out by the gate; but he suffered them all gladly, in return for the sad things he had done, and never putting a single sign of quickness into his steps as he went slowly down the passage.

They had brought down Botolph's sister to be in at the death. In she came between Hewson and Sorrasaint, a plump, reddish-haired youngster with grey eyes and a face full of freckles. Not a one to want to put yoor arms around, thought Johnny, unless your sight was failin'. She had been told of what had happened, and had been given her walking papers, everyone concurring in the impossibility of her staying in a Firm her brother had robbed.

She stood there, dressed in black, with a white frill on her neck, tight white-starched bands round her wrists, a black felt hat with a green bird's wing in the band, and a brooch of an ivory deer, running hard, in an oval brass-rimmed case, rising and falling on her bosom.

She stood there, a step away from her brother, two away from Anthony, a little handkerchief sheltering her face, crying softly into it, waiting to hear what Anthony had to say to her brother.

Anthony, when he had seen the stricken vanman fade away round the gateway, slowly turned his head, and gazed on Botolph slinking against the bench behind him, rigid, staring, and seemingly unable even to bend his head away from Anthony's snaky stare.

—Come nearer, sir, come a little nearer, said Anthony.

Botolph shoved himself away from the propping bench, and took a few paltry, shuffling steps nearer to Anthony.

—Were it not that we don't wish to make it known that our Firm could possibly graft a thief on to its staff, said Anthony, you'd be leaving my presence now tucked into the arms of two policemen. Though the sun may shine on the evil and the good, the sun will not be allowed to shine on the evil here. You have been given the privilege of working for a Firm with a reputation as high as any Firm could hold; you had a fine future in front of you; but you elected to become perverse and dishonest; and have brought shame upon your family and ruin to your sister. Had you not wickedly chosen a froward life, you would today have been receiving your wages instead of your dismissal. Instead of being a trusted servant, you are now but a low-minded rascal and a decently-clad thief. We are all very glad to be rid of you. Get out of my sight, you laundered vagabond!

And Botolph, moistening his stiff lips, trying to keep his twitching legs steady, stumbled away from the face of his master, Dyke giving him a vicious kick as he passed by, followed by one from Enthrews, and one each from the messengers who happened to be within range, Johnny finally getting one home on him as he shuffled out by the gateway into the lane. Botolph bore them all well, sighing for the sad things he had done, and feeling that these things were but a small penalty to suffer for his mischievous behaviour.

—Phew! said Dyke, with his nose in the air, and loud enough for Anthony, Hewson, and Sorrasaint to hear him, thank God that stink is gone! The air already feels a lot fresher without it.

Hewson and Sorrasaint turned and went back to their haunts in the front shop, and Anthony withdrew into his shell of an office, leaving the freckle-faced, red-haired girl, in black, standing against the desk of Nearus, with her face sheltered in her little handkerchief, and the brooch of an ivory deer, running hard, within the oval of the brass circle, rising and falling on her bosom.

After a few minutes of quiet crying, Nearus bent over his desk and touched her on the shoulder.

—Steal away home, girl, he said softly, and lie away as far as you can from everything that has happened to you today.

The touch startled her into movement. She moved away from the desk, keeping the little handkerchief pressed to her face; and the black figure, the felt hat, with the bird's green wing in it, and the ivory deer, running hard, went down the passage, out of the gateway, and passed out of the sight and scene of the shop for ever.

All this had happened yesterday, and Johnny was picturing it in his mind all over again as he walked along Sackville Street, glancing at the fireman sitting outside his sentry-box, smoking his pipe under the stars that filled the sky, and ready at a second's warning to unlock the fire-escape chained through the spokes of a wheel to a stone post, and hasten, with a crowd of eager civilians, to push it wherever the fire might be.

Johnny was hurrying on to meet his vanman, Dorin, at Dooney's pub in Great Britain Street, thinking all the time of the kicks, Botolph, and the ivory deer, running hard, on the bosom of a crying red-haired girl. Dorin, a day or two ago, had seen the heap of cracked delft and ironmongery that Anthony sold at a bargain price to Biddy, a street hawker who went round with a donkey and cart reselling the broken ware to the poorest people cast away into the slums. He had asked Johnny for a cracked teapot, and Johnny had given him a new one, adding that, if cautious arrangements could be made, he could give him many more things. Then had come the exposure of Botolph, and Johnny had arranged to hold a council meeting between himself and Dorin in Dooney's pub to arrange the business in a safe way.

Johnny glanced up at a sickle moon hanging in the sky among a throng of stars. What was it and what were they? He had looked in the pages of Ball's *Story of the Heavens* and at the pictures, but it was all too hard for him yet. But he would learn, he would learn. He wouldn't keep on being the ignoramus Archie had called him when he ventured to say a word in the argument that arose in Nagle's pub between Dalton and Archie over the battle of Aughrim and the Siege of Derry. If his father had made himself into a scholar by boring into books, his son could do the same. He was studying all words he didn't really know the meaning of, in an old dictionary his father had left behind him. More than that, he was busy learning something about physical, political, and commercial geography out of his father's old book, Sullivan's *Geography Generalised*. More than that, he was learning grammar, too; and history from his father's Merle d'Aubigné's *History of the Reformation*, and already knew a lot about Luther, Melanchthon, Erasmus; gentle Melanchthon, sturdy Luther, fiery Zwingli, scholarly Erasmus. God's own job they had, to overthrow the idea of the Pope's supremacy in the hearts of the people; and harder still to turn the church that had become the church of Babylon, back into the church of God again. But best of all the books that Johnny found useful was *The Comprehensive Summary*, an American book, holding a store of knowledge about many things, physiology, mineralogy, mythology, with a brief history of every country and nation that had ever existed, from the Babylonians straight through to the surrenders at Yorktown and Saratoga; winding up with the bugle-blast of the great American Constitution. Johnny got to know a great number of people, Cyrus, Zeus, Semiramis and Ninus, her husband, the builder of Nineveh, mentioned in the Bible; Xerxes, Leonidas, Alexander, who found the world too small to hold him; Hannibal, Caesar, Dathi, Agricola, Aurelius, Hector, Ulysses, Columbus — though he'd often heard of him before — Penn, the Quaker, converted in Cork; Washington, hardly ever heard of here, Franklin, his friend, who in odd moments when he had nothing else to do, fastened a key to a kite and discovered the electric current; and many another who, and a whisper was loud enough to say it in, were big men compared to poor little Hewson and Anthony among their pots and pans and soap and candles. He must remember to lift a few carriage candles tomorrow, for they gave a clearer light, and burned more steady when he was studying than the common ones that flickered and sputtered and hurt his eyes.

—Leon'idas, he murmured, the Leader of the Three Hundred at the Pass of Thermopylae, who knocked the lard outa th' Persians, accented, according to Walker's English Dictionary, on th' antepenultimate, and, once, when an old man came into a crowded theatre and sought a seat, the young Athenians pushed together to keep him out, which, seeing, made the old man hurry away to where th' Lace, Lace, Lace'daemonians were, who in a body rose to let the old one sit down. The Athenians, ashamed at themselves, burst into loud applause when they saw the kind act of th' Lace, Lace'daemonians; and the old man, rising from his seat, said, Th' Athenians know what good manners are, but the Lacedaemonians practise them! All very nice and proper, then, thought Johnny, but a hard thing to do these days.

He crossed over Sackville Street, turned down Great Britain Street, and came to Dooney's pub where Dorin was waiting for him, under the clock, with his eyes on the hands. They went inside, moved to a quiet corner, and Johnny took a small port on Dorin's invitation, while Dorin's eyes beamed over the creamy top of a pint of porter.

—Now, said Johnny, when he had taken half of the port, and Dorin had golloped down half of the beer, to business: After what happened to Botolph, we'll have to keep our weather-eye open.

—It was a lousy thing for him to go and dip his hand into the money, said Dorin; why couldn't he ha' played fair, an' stuck to simple goods, like us?

—An' then, added Johnny, to go scattherin' it around so that everyone knew he was diggin' up buried threasure somewhere.

—Th' white-collared get, said Dorin.

—You've got a boy nearly fourteen years old, have you?

—Ay, have I, said Dorin, an' though it's his father sayin' it, a well-up kidger for any fair dodge goin'.

—Well, said Johnny warningly, when I give you anything, you must never — never, mind you — dhrive up to your own hall-door to deliver it. It's soon the tongues of th' neighbours u'd get goin', blow on us, an' I'd begin and you'd end your further days in jail. So I'll never give you anything on any delivery, except your last one, so that you'll never be sure that I won't be dodgin' about the sthreet you live in, an', if I once see your van anywhere near it, you'll never get another thing outa me.

—Be Jasus! swore Dorin, I'd never do a thing like that. I'm not the one to frighten away th' goose layin' th' golden eggs. I'm no gaum. I'll work th' delivery in such a wise way that neither of the boyos'll fall into the suspicion they had lost as much as a burnt-out match.

—What we have to do is this, instructed Johnny. You get your eldest boy to meet you a good way from where you live. Give him whatever you have to give, an' dhrive on, so that he can carry th' things home as if they had been bought in a shop in th' usual way. D'ye understand?

—Entirely, said Dorin; but, Jack, wouldn't th' missus be betther than th' boy?

—Oh, no, no; not th' missus, said Johnny impatiently. On no account, or at any time, let th' missus come to collect th' goods. If a policeman happened to be knocking about, an' saw you givin' it to th' missus, he might be suspicious, an' start askin' questions. No, th' missus won't do. Th' boy'll look more innocent; he'll look as if he were your vanboy, an' a policeman passin' 'll take no notice.

—Be God, I never once thought o' that! ejaculated Dorin, draining a last drop from his tumbler of beer.

—Well, I did. We can't be too careful. He took a slip of paper and a pencil from his pocket. Now, he said, tell us what you're most in need of, for a start?

Dorin tightened his lips, and shut his eyes for a moment, taking a long swig from a new pint he had just ordered, opening his eyes for a second to put the tumbler back on the counter, and then closing them again, so that the darkness might be an aid to deeper thought.

—We need a helluva lot, he murmured, for all we had at th' start's bid us goodbye years ago. Th' missus washes a lot, always thryin' to keep things clean — soap, matches, starch, an' blue, f'rinstance.

—Righto, said Johnny, making some notes. I'll make up a fine parcel o' chandlery for you tomorrow evenin'. Now, anything else — saucepans, brushes, or things like that?

—Aw, Jasus, said Dorin, I wouldn't like t'ask you to get me things like that — we must be fair.

—Fair? queried Johnny.

—Well, I ought to give you something every time you make me a present.

—No, no; that won't do, said Johnny swiftly; none o' that for me.
It would make you careless, as if you were payin' for them, an' th'
money might make me careless, too. I mightn't watch to make sure
you were cautious, an' th' two of us would be landed. No; the minute
you don't do what we have arranged for you to do, the bargain ends,
an' it will never be begun again.

Dorin seized Johnny's hand and shook it again and again.

—I understand, he said heartily, an' your way's th' way it'll be
done. You're a decent lad, a real decent lad, heart o' th' rowl, he said;
th' real Annie Daly, he said, one in a thousand, a trusty mate, a lad
of a good breed, he said; not like th' rest o' them, nose-rags, toe-rags,
flittin' afther Mr. Anthony here, an' Mr. Hewson there, sucks who
would sell their mothers for a smile from a boss, he said; but you're a
change from all those, a dear change an' a genuine change; an' standin'
out as a sowl man, a solid man, hindherin' th' rich to give help to the
poor, sound an 'thrue in all your dealin's with your fellow-man.

Johnny's face flushed with pride, and he shook hands heartily with
Dorin. Then they left the pub, and parted at the corner of Sackville
Street.

—Safe home, Jack, said Dorin, again shaking hands with Johnny.
Rest assured, he went on, that th' missus'll never fail, come what may,
to inthercede for you whenever she goes to Mass, with an occasional
blessed candle for company before the shrine o' Saint Anthony
quietly beggin' help in our endayvours to knock a little reason outa
life.

The sickle moon fair followed Johnny home when he parted from
Dorin. He walked faster, and the moon moved quick in the heavens;
he walked slow, and the moon mended her pace to keep him company.
Slitting the heavens, she seemed like a sly shy face peeping through the
curtained stage to see how the house looked. Of all the brightness of
heaven, the moon was by far the nearest to him. Where was the sun,
now? Somewhere to the east; or, as the old story went, speeding along
the bitter waters of the north in Vulcan's golden goblet, on its way to
where the sun was to rise again, the first thing in the morning. Strange
belief. Ignorance of the early ages. Poor man.

What's this he was to get for Dorin? Dozen of matches, pound o'
soap, two packages of Hudson's Extract, one o' candles, some blue
an' blacking, a sweeping brush, and a three-pint saucepan. A fair
start, anyway.

The heaven and the earth. Look up, and they don't seem to be so far
away from each other. Anyhow, they were made together. In the

beginning, God created the heaven and the earth; pretty close, what? Yet, sometimes it seemed that they were a hell of a way asunder.

When he came to the door of his house, he looked up before he went in. The moon was right in front of his face. Reminding him of something. What? Oh, yes: the brassy circle enclosing the ivory deer, running hard, rising and falling on the sobbing breast of a red-headed girl.

Oh, well.

He went in; and the morning and evening were the froward day.

GATHER UP THE FRAGMENTS

JOHNNY was standing out in the lane at the back of the stores, looking up and down, and cursing Biddy.

All the breakages that came in the crates, provided they were able to stand on their feet, all the ironware and china and delft, injured in their transport from one place to another in the stores, were gathered together in a heap on a special bench and sold to a big-bodied, big-headed, and big-footed woman who had a face like an Aunt Sally, and was the dead spit of the manager's sister; so much so that this sister, who was the girls' overseer, was known privately to all the staff by the name of Biddy too. Johnny, by Anthony's orders, was waiting for her to come with her donkey and cart to take away the damaged goods, after a price had been arranged between her and Anthony, who battled for all he was worth to get the highest price possible for the desolate ironware and china, to be sold by Biddy afterwards to the poor swarming in the back streets of the city. It was drawing close to closing time, and, if she didn't come soon, by the time the bargain was made, and the things carried out, Johnny would be a long while behind his time of leaving for home; so here he stood in the lane, looking up and down, and cursing Biddy.

It was a happy evening, the sun shining hotly, and the sky overhead a deep, dear blue. The lane, stretching from Cole's Lane at one end, and Moore Street at the other, was half-filled with cattle, lowing in a frightened way; some of them trying to steal or run away from the murky entrances of the slaughter-houses, slipping madly, sometimes, in the slime of their own dung that pooled the cobble-stones. There was a heavy reek in the air of filth and decaying blood scattered over the yards, and heaps of offal lay about watched by a restless herd of ragged women and youngsters, taking their chance to dive in and snatch a piece of liver or green-slimed guts to carry home as a feast for the favoured. Johnny was well used to the discordant smell hanging in the air everywhere, for the yards where the cattle were killed were often used by his Firm for the storage of crates that couldn't find room in their own warehouses, an odd shilling being slipped into the hand of the butcher who happened to be making the sacrifices of the day.

Johnny had often slipped in the slime, had often fouled his hands in the filth clinging to the crates, as he pushed them over the blood-soaked cobbles, and he had often washed his guilty-looking hands in the great butt outside, used by the butchers for the same purpose, the greasy water in it always coloured with a bloody tint. The butchers were big bullocky men, greasy with the fat of dying and dead animals; kind under it all, for Johnny often noticed that they gave all they could of the bloody issues into the clutching hands of the tattered poor. They took with a sheepish grin the gracious nod Mr. Anthony gave them when he happened to meet any of them, as he sometimes did when he hurried into the outer stores to see that everything was safe and going on well, and no idling was knocking profits out of the Firm; for he had to be gracious to the men who provided him, free of charge, with cow-shit-covered storage space, where Johnny had so often seen the dying kicks of cattle, growing weaker, twitching in the last throes; then becoming, all of a sudden, stiffly still; where he had often heard the dying bleat of the throat-punctured sheep, entering their end on the cold cobble-stones, dying slowly in their own dung. He had seen the butchers suddenly hold back their knives, and the young and old watchers by the reddened gateway suddenly close their eyes to the bloodied treasures in the yard to bend their tousled heads, cross themselves, and murmur a Hail Mary when the Angelus tolled out its holiness from the bells of Pro-Cathedral.

The great blue sky, like a great blue flower, covered it all, with its golden centre sparkling back from the stones of the cobbled lane, marbled with the green slime and purple pools, some of them smoking faintly, like half-hearted burnt sacrifices to a half-forgotten god.

—This sort of thing, thought Johnny, should be done when the winter's harsh, when there'd be some reason for the poor animals to go out of the world from the stabbing frost and the driving rain and the bitter wind. Surely, it is a hard thing to be taken away in a shower of sun, and die under a blue sky's blessing!

Here was Anthony coming out of the back stores, hurrying back to his natural nest to poke his bake into the figures again, figures that had mounted up till they pierced heaven and threw a golden shower over the feet o' God.

Here he came, stooping, suddenly, like a hawk, to pick up a blackened cork that had fallen by the wayside, throwing it, with a true shot, into a box kept for oilcan corks that could be used again.

Here he came, picking his steps to keep his finely-polished boots, shining like his soul, from touching the slimy-shining green puddles, barred with blood; his watch-chain dangling, for his back was beginning to bend; the well-kept head was beginning to shrivel; his frosty eyes were beginning to drip when a breeze blew; sure he stepped, quick and careful, for he was of heaven, heavenly; he knew his lord, and was known of Him; and followed His voice into the glass-partitioned den for the steady lusty-fisted toll of the takings.

Ah! here was the boul' Biddy, at last, with her donkey and cart; and Johnny hurried in to tell Anthony that she was here, and viewing the desolate delft to decide how much value for the poor lay in the tired and tottering goods.

Along came the bent back; the shrivelled head, the dangling watch-chain; the frosty eyes, trying hard to send a gracious glance at Biddy; standing in front of her, rocking themselves ever so gently on their toes, and jingling keys and money in their pockets; the frosty eyes watching the seam-patterned face of Biddy staring at the woebegone crockery; the thinned-out mouth waiting for her to fire the first words at the shrivelling head, the bending back, and the dangling watch-chain.

—There's not much here today to make a poor woman's heart lep, she murmured. Sorra much you'll be asking for that pitiful heap of has-beens.

—Now, now, Biddy, be fair; be just. Have another look at it, said the figure, gently rocking on its toes. There's a fine heap of fair goods there, really. And you can have it all for twelve and six — not a farthing less.

—Arra, Mr. Anthony, your poor eyes must be seein' double this evenin', the hot sun havin' affected them, or somethin'. Twelve an' six, is it, you said? Is it a silver mine you think I have undher the stable where I keep th' animal? Fine heap d'ye call it? An' next to nothin' in it that's not more than ready to fall asundher, if you blew a cold breath on them. Won't I have all I can do to hand them over safe to any fool that comes to buy them? No, no, Mr. Anthony, fair is fair. Looka th' pots — you'll have to hold your hands undher them the whole time th' thing's cookin'

—Now, Biddy, Biddy, don't exaggerate. The cracks go barely halfway down the saucepans. With a little care in handling, they'll serve the poor people excellently, excellently. It looks the best, it is the best lot yet you've had before you. Come, now, be reasonable: say ten shillings, then? Look over them while you're carrying them out, and you'll see ten shillings is a reasonable, a most reasonable figure.

—I can see them fairly well from where I'm standin', answered Biddy, never turning her head a hair's breadth, but staring fixedly into the battered heap of goods; see them too well, I do, an' it must be jokin' y'are, sir, an' thryin' to take a rise out of a poor oul' woman. Ten shillin's! Is it deaf I'm gettin', thinkin' I heard someone say he wanted half a sovereign for a bewildered heap of incurable crockery?

—Ten shillings, and worth double, murmured the figure, tenderly rocking on its toes.

—Oh, then, it's not deaf I'm gettin', but only listenin' to a gentleman eager to make his joke to frighten a poor innocent woman. A gentleman who knows th' poor woman 'ud never redeem herself from lifelong poverty if she gave him what he's askin'. Ten shillin's! If th' moon was made o' gold, an' I had it on th' mantelshelf, I might be willin', if I was in a givin' mood, to part with th' half-sovereign. For goodness' sake, thry to think of th' job I'll have thrying to mesmerise th' shy buyers into imaginin' th' goods'll hold water, an' won't vanish into glassy dew if they hold them too tight.

Anthony stopped rocking himself tenderly on his toes, and stood stiff, a harder note creeping into the voice that had first been speaking in a velvety way.

—Well, he said, taking his hands from his pockets, and holding them by his sides, the last offer — seven shillings and sixpence.

Biddy turned suddenly to face Anthony, her figure, big and brawny, more supple than his, one hand lightly resting on a hip, her lively beady eyes staring into his so steadily that he bent his head lower than hers, and fingered the dangling watch-chain.

—Make it th' even seven shillin's, she said, an' I'll forget meself an' swing meself into foolishness for th' hundredth an' first time in me life.

—Seven shillings and threepence, then, said the bent head admiring the watch-chain, and say no more about it.

—Sorra a word more, she replied, barrin' a swift sigh over your anxiety not to look a little closer at what you're askin' seven an' thruppence for, for it's seldom I make a murmur against th' judgement of others, seein' that the Man above alone can alther another person's opinion, an', then, only afther an almighty effort, an' I can make bould to say that ever since I was a wee baby in arms, th' curse o' me life has been that I never could sthrive to make me own opinions go further than the margin of me own mind, for fear of imposin' anything in th' way of a notion on another, nosin' afther an aysey an' a righteous livin', an', out of a singular shyness that came natural to me, was never fit to beat down into a genuine bargain any one thing that was waitin' to pass from another's hand to mine, for a consideration, but well knowin' you to be a kind an' reasonable an' thorough gentleman, anchored to the way of fair dealin', it's no way backward I am in askin' you to let the poor lot go for th' first offer of seven shillin's sterlin' down.

—Oh, very well, said Anthony, mixing a sigh with a gracious grin, seven shillings, even money, then.

Biddy gave a mighty hitch to her heavy skirt, and fished out a dirty little linen sack from a hidden hip-pocket in an under petticoat, fished the money out of the little linen sack, counted it carefully, and placed it carefully into the slender, white, long, bony, well-shaped hand of Anthony, while the keys had ceased from rattling, and the money in his pocket was at rest; but the seven shillings were hurried off to the nest at the other end of the store, and placed in a safe, where a record was made of the sale in the accounts book, among the bigger figures, so that another little egg was laid in the nest behind the door.

All the hands had gone home, bar Johnny, who had to stay behind to see Biddy off the premises, and to help her carry the stricken goods out into the harshness of the waiting world. He was cursing Anthony for haggling so long over a blasted thruppence, and keeping him here in this damned den beyond his legal time.

Biddy began to carry out the badly-scarred goods, murmuring a constant stream of thoughts meant for Johnny and the wide wide world, and she handling with cunning every article she carried, watching each of them, as a mother would watch a dim and dying child, saying, Ah, another nearly gone beyond recall, an' too well paid for, God keep the air still, for, if a breeze blows, it's fallin' in coloured dust they'll be, an' th' best part of me half-sovereign buried deep in th' pocket of that grisly-faced perjured poacher — Jasus! that one nearly parted company in me hands — liftin' up his hand for silence when God is thryin' to speak a word for th' poor an' lowly. Ah then, their clawin' hands'll have to be watched an' waved away when they come to buy with their stormy handlin' o' delicate things like these, an their, oh, badly split, ma'am, this, an' looka th' crack here, ma'am, hardly worth liftin'. sure you'd spend the day takin' it from table to shelf or from shelf to table, in desperate fear it 'ud break its back in front of your eyes; then don't take any notice of it, ma'am, for I'm not pressin' you to buy, though, if you said th' thruth, it's particular good sight you'd need to have to see th' crack your thryin' to speak of, an', with a little use, it 'ud maybe close up an' go altogether — heart o' mercy! it was nearly goin' on me altogether, that time — but leave it there, if you don't like it, an' don't be combin' them with your fingers, if you please, for you can't expect newly-minted stuff to suddenly appear for your benefit, an' it's little the people round here 'ud understand th' way to use anything above something that had seen its best days; but th' next time I'm here, Mr. Anthony'll find a woman awake to what is due to her, an' can put a flush o' shame on his white sly kisser ever alert for the main chance, ever on th' make, ever head bent over on th' thrack of a lost coin, thryin' to make his Sunday-curtained gob look like a twinklin' star, an' it's oh, wouldn't I like to hammer me fist in it, an' muck it about a bit, an' dim its shinin'; but praise be to the Almighty God, it's little leisure he'll have to jingle his coins an' count his gains snibbed from an oul' innocent creature, when his shrinkin', shudderin' body goes woefully down the icy slope o' death, thin an' tottherin', naked as the day he was born on, with the cowld snow fallin' on th' oul' schemer's head, and the nippin frost askin' him how's he feelin'.

—There isn't one of them, she said, as she carried out the last few articles, there isn't one o' them any one whit betther than th' best o' th' petty scrawls that creep along to buy them, like to like, an' all chipped an' broken an' all cracked across, fit only for th' ashpit, but consigned to go on makin' themselves useful, an' makin' a holy show o' themselves be doin' everything badly.

She gave a malicious glance at Johnny, leaning against the gate, waiting to close it when she had carried all out, and listening to all the muttering mind of the dealer in dangerous delft.

—All some people's got to do, she said, in a loud voice, is to wait for a chance to pick up another Moses out of th' bulrushes. Blessed be God, it's a grand thing to have th' nice power o' standin' still while th' world works! Ay, an' after, cock an ear, an' then move round sayin' they heard something th' wind whispered into their imagination, steady an' prim to catch any innocent sayin', waftin' round like a thistle-seed plumed, an' turn it into a burnin' bush of a lie! A nice pass things have come to, when a body has to poke her way through a swarm of idlers!

She set the last woebegone article gently down in the straw, took the ass's bridle in her left hand, and gave the sleepy animal a poke with a stick she carried in her right one.

—You can safely shut the gate on me an' me seven shillin's, now, she said to Johnny, an' tell himself he'll not be a hell of a lot the richer for them. An' you, she said sharply, turning on the donkey, giving him another poke with the stick, making him blink into a sleepy stir, yep, now, rememberin' you're carryin' God's gifts to the poor, so go quietly with your clumsy feet, for me heart's in me mouth, in case it's a heap o' chanies I'll have left when we stagger into our destination.

—Farewell, called out Johnny, waving his hand carelessly, as the donkey started, Farewell, sweet Lady o' Shalott!

—Jasus! She jerked her donkey to a sudden standstill, splashed back fiercely through the slimy-puddled lane to where Johnny was about to close the gate, made a slash at him with her stick, that, had it got home, would have broken an ear in two!

—Yeh, yeh genteel, gaunty gutthersnipe! she yelled, out of a hoarse scream. I'll flatten your grinny bake, an' knock th' plume outa yer impudence, if you dare again to murmur, let alone to shout afther a decent female th' name of some evil woman of th' long ago!

—Go on, go on, about your business, said Johnny, a little frightened by the glare of fierceness in front of him, as he caught up a hammer from one of the benches to weaken the threat of the stick; go on, home, now, me woman, an' let me shut the gate.

—Oh! she shouted, you'd lift a hammer to a weak oul' wandherin' woman, you would, would you! Murdher you'd do, so you would, you collared an' tied tittherer, without a hem or haw of hesitation, regardless of the cost of reavin' the web o' life from a patient an' scarified Christian! And lifting her stick she made another skelp at Johnny's head; but he parried it with the hammer, and she barked her knuckles against the claw.

—Here, here, what's all this? said the voice of Anthony, who came scurrying down to stand between Johnny and the angry woman, now sucking her knuckle, and hissing with the pain of the wound.

—She made for me with the stick, for nothing at all, said Johnny.

—Oh, d'ye hear that! bawled Biddy. For nothin' at all, says he, an' th' place still hot with th' association of me solid decency with th' name of some unholy throllop of th' distant past!

Anthony clicked his tongue against his teeth, and a frosty look of rage fell on Johnny. Then a long bony finger on a long bony hand was stretched out to warningly tip the shoulder of the angry Biddy.

—Go home, good woman, he said; go home, and rest easy that, from this hour, my hands shall show you civility whenever you have occasion to come here on business.

—Thank you, sir, thank you, she answered with a curtsy. It's a wondher to me that th' makin's of such a fine young bowsey can find a snug niche in the business of a respectable firm. An' I warn him, she added, turning to go, that if he ever dares to call me outa me name again, the powers that be won't save him from a sudden awakenin' in another world!

Anthony turned his frosty eye to stare at Johnny; silently, he stared at him for a full twenty seconds.

—What did you say to anger the woman? he asked. Come, come, what low-minded gibe did you fling at the woman? he added, as Johnny, holding down his head, hesitated.

—I only said something about the Lady of Shalott, said Johnny surlily.

—Well, we don't want any reference to ladies of this or that place here, he said. Business and only business is to be attended to here. You are to keep yourself in hand, Casside, while you're here; when you're among your corner-boy friends, you can act the jackeen as much as you like. Shut the gate, now, and go home.

—I should be with my corner-boy friends now, said Johnny, in a surly mutter, if you hadn't kept me here an hour afther me right time of knocking off. If I went to Merrion Hall, I'd be well in here as a respectable boy.

A cloudy sneer rippled over the tight thin lips of Anthony, and his bony fingers twisted round each other, like the snakes on the head of Medusa. From a side squint, Johnny saw his pallid face redden, and his frosty eyes glitter with a cold glare. When he had closed the gate, shot the bolts, fixed and turned the keys in the padlocks, he heard the stinging voice, mottled with little shivers of anger, speaking to him.

—In Merrion Hall, Casside, there is a welcome only for decent persons, old or young. You would not be permitted to pass the door. The door is ever closed before rough-mouthed young roisterers. In our place of worship there is no room for an associate of coarse-minded ragamuffins; and, indeed, there ought to be no room for them here either; and, let me tell you, you're near the door, unless you show some sign of realising that it is a privilege to be employed by such a Firm as ours. Now, off you go home!

Johnny snapped the last key from the last padlock, turned on his heel, and lurched away down the stores, followed by Anthony with the dusky Hewson standing, like a sentry with a rod of steel for a spine, beside Anthony's desk-den, concentrating a cold, resentful, sneering stare at the lurching, rage-tortured Johnny, caught in the act of trying to stammer out a rebuke to his betters.

—It wasn't much of a job, thought Johnny, rapidly, as he lurched along. If he lost it, would he lose the world? Well, if this job was the world, the world was well lost. Was he going to go out from the presence of these two God-conceited bastards without a word? Without a sign, even, that he didn't care a snap of his fingers for them? An evil spirit took possession of him. He lurched no longer. He held up his head. He sang out in a voice that was half a shout,

> His broad clear brow in sunlight glow'd;
> On burnish'd hooves his warhorse trod;
> From underneath his helmet flow'd
> His coal-black curls as on he rode,
> As he rode down to Camelot.

Johnny felt that the two jaynusus were standing still, in wondherment an' fury at what he was doin'. Then he sang louder than ever,

> From the bank and from the river
> He flashed into the crystal mirror,
> 'Tirra lirra,' by the river
> Sang Sir Lancelot.

With a joyous gesture Johnny tossed the keys on to a bench, opened the glass-panelled door, passed out, and banged the door behind him. He heard it being pulled open again, swiftly; heard Anthony's voice calling loudly after him, Casside, Casside, come back here; heard Hewson's voice calling louder still, when Anthony's was silent, Casside, Casside, here; come here, sir!

—I'll come back at the usual time tomorrow morning, thought Johnny, in the usual way, an' with a brave face; an' see what they'll say; an' if they sack me, well, th' foxes have holes, an' th' birds of th' air have nests, an' I'll ferret out a place for meself, never fear.

On went Johnny through the darkened shop, swung the wicket in the shuttered entrance open, passed out, and let it bang back, turning homewards whistling, a gay march home in the midst of the glow and murmuring heat of the summer's shining sun.

And the morning and the evening were the fivid day.

ALICE, WHERE ART THOU?

JOHNNY didn't feel comfortable on his way to work the following morning. He was almost sure to get his docket. Well, if he did, aself, he'd stick it out like a man, and tell them they could go to hell for Johnny. That was the only way to meet the situation.

Still he felt uncomfortable and cold, and shivered a little. He hadn't said anything to his mother. Why should he, anyhow? She wouldn't say much, if he was sacked — that was the worst of it; if she'd only burst out an' bark at him, he'd find it easier to fight; but, no; she'd just sigh, an' that was hard to counter. Seven an' six a week wasn't a fortune, but it went a fair way to keep things from fallin' over; so, when it was lost, you couldn't really blame her for sighin' — when you thought of it. Ah, anyhow, another sigh or two won't take much out of a woman who has had a thousand an' two sighs in a lifetime.

An' he had to stick up for poor Dorin forcin' a man to walk, an' his thigh ripped open. Job or no job, he couldn't stand for that. Be God, there she was, walkin' right in front of him — Alice Boyd, the presbyterian. Yes, a pretty mot, right enough, with her mop o' curly red hair, her glittering green eyes, and her jib as jaunty as the jib o' Jenny.

He hastened till he fell shyly in beside the girl, setting his pace to keep time with the shorter and quicker steps of her little feet, while she carried her head high, for she had dropped into long skirts just a week ago, and felt all the world realised that she was a genuine woman, now.

—Why'r you goin' to work at this early hour o' the morning? he asked her.

—I have to make ready for the comin' of a special consignment of chinaware, she answered.

His tongue felt dry and his voice sounded husky as he said, I wish I was beside you all the time, givin' you a hand; but I'm a clerk, now; an' besides, I'm expectin' to get the push out of the job today.

—Oh! she ejaculated.

—Ay, indeed. I was kept over me time, yesterday, an' I gave oul' Anthony and Hewson what for, so I did. Just you watch, when he comes to open the shop, an' says anything to me; just you watch, an' see what I'll say about him an' his job.

She marched on, and was silent. He looked sideways at her, but his boasting hadn't prompted her to any admiration of him — he could see that; afraid to agree with anyone up against Hewson and Anthony; thinking of her own job. He was in the battle alone.

Passing by Nagle's pub, the porter, who was washing away from the front of the shop the filthy turmoil of the night before, suddenly slashed a bucket of water towards them, sending it streaming under their feet. Alice, with a little scream, caught up her skirt and jumped clear into the street, so as to save her dress from the slush that spread over the side walk. Johnny felt that he should have gone for the unruly porter, but his thoughts were all on the slim leg that Alice was showing in her search for any mark of the water or the slush. Still looking, and tucking her skirt towards the front in an effort to see the back of it, she showed her black-stockinged leg nearly up to the thigh, making Johnny's heart to beat and his face to flush.

—There's no actual damage done, is there? he asked, making over to her.

—I hope not, she answered. Can you see any?

He handled her skirt tenderly and lingeringly, tucking it up still higher, till a rim of white lace appeared, looking white and lovely against the black stocking that disappeared up under it. His hand moved along her stocking, feelingly, shaking a little as it felt the vibrant life running along the leg of the girl.

—You're all right, he said slowly, no damage done; only a tiny splash or two on the stocking. His hand began to sneak up under the rim of white lace, but she suddenly shoved it away and let her skirt fall down to her feet.

—That'll do, she said; I don't like that sort of thing.

They walked on, Johnny keeping as close to her as he could, occasionally giving her arm a saucy pressure with his fingers. About to cross Sackville Street, Alice stopped, looking undecided for a moment.

—You'd better walk one side o' the Pillar, she said, and me the other, to keep the shop from talking; and she stepped from the side walk to cross the street.

—Eh, wait a minute, will you? he said, catching her arm. I'll see you this evenin', comin' home.

—No you won't, for that would be as bad as them seein' us together now.

—After, then, he said huskily, pulling her towards him, and pressing his knee against her leg; sometime, somewhere, tonight?

—I don't know. Maybe I will, maybe I won't, she said.

—Tonight at Binn's Bridge at eight o'clock, certain, sure? We can saunter along the canal, and one arm was going around her, and a hand was trying to lift her skirt.

—Let me go! she cried, goin' on, and everyone looking. She jerked his arm away from her and hurried across the street.

—Don't forget, he called out after her; tonight, Binn's Bridge, eight o'clock — I'll be there!

But she went on, never heeding him. He, on his own side of the street, walked more slowly, passed the fireman guarding the fire-escape, and smoking his pipe at the door of his wooden hut; past the flower-sellers, piling up their old boxes into counters, laying out apples, oranges, and flowers of every hue in rising ranks for the coming day's sale; over into Henry Street, where troops of assistants were on their way to the several stores; and seeing the bony form of Anthony hurrying to open the shop with the speed of a man eager to marry the loveliest girl in the world, or to be at the funeral of his bitterest enemy.

Glancing over, he saw his little Alice hovering near Harrison's, the elegant pastrycooks, where Anthony took his lunch, waiting for the men to go in before her. He felt a tremor of fear when he came to the shop, just as Anthony was opening the little wicket-gate in the re-volving shutter. He'd wait till Anthony was well in, before he'd go; but, when the door was open, oul' Anthony stood back and waited for all the rest to go before him, a thing he never done before. So Johnny, making the best of it, had to go up, stoop down, with the cold eyes of Anthony staring down at him, and go in, with the cold eyes watching him behind, and the soft steps following his, follow, follow, I will follow Jesus; anywhere, everywhere, I will follow on; follow, follow, I will follow Jesus, everywhere He leads me, I will follow on, but the followed J. C. this time's Johnny Casside, for when he signed his name in the time-book, the cold eyes were staring down at the moving hand that wrote; and when he was at his desk, gathering together the postal orders that had come in from the customers in his district, there were the cold eyes of Anthony watching him, like a careless cat watching a mouse.

—Get them done quick, said Anthony, for you're wanted for another job this morning.

Setting out the goods required, making them into parcels, labelling them, entering names and addresses on the delivery sheet, were all watched over by Anthony. He was joined by Hewson before the delivery was half ready, and the two of them stood, side by side, watching the work of Johnny. Not a word was said to him of what had happened the evening before; but Johnny knew that they were taking it out of him for the affront he had given them the night previous.

—Want to make me nervous, thought Johnny, and so make a muddle to give a ripe cause for a growl; but Johnny was on his mettle, going about his work methodically, softly lilting Me Lodgins on the Cold, Cold Ground, doing all the parcelling and clerical work with deliberate ease and precision, while the boyos over the other deliveries in the store watched furtively, and wantonly wondhered; glad that a comrade was going through a tough time; all of them putting on an airy look of righteousness, as if to sing slow and soft, behold I am not as Casside is, but truly, ruly, schooly, pewly, fooly, dooly, humble servants, doggedly faithful in all things appertaining to their *simper feedielus*, and they praying all the while that Anthony or Hewson would blaze forth into a hunting reprimand at something that Johnny had done before, or that he was doing now; but, to their discomfort, everything was done fair and well, and Johnny stood beside the delivery, all packed, and waiting for the van to come.

—Now, said Anthony, out you go, and help carry up the new chinaware that the storeman is already unpacking.

So that was the game! Johnny was to be made go back to the menial work of long ago. He was to do what no clerk was, or ever had been, asked to do. He hesitated, whether to go, or fight it out. He saw the smiles on the kissers of the other clerks. They were enjoying the show, slow, slimy, slavish, sluddery buggers, the whole o' them!

—What about seeing the delivery safe off on its journey? questioned Johnny.

—Just do what you're told, said Anthony, with the withered pink line of his mouth thinner than ever.

—Without a murmur, added Hewson, with the vivid red pulpy mouth of him showing over his black beard, like a danger signal.

Johnny slouched out to the lane, ripe with rage, through the line of messengers and packers, all pretending to be busy, but all watching Johnny, first, then eyeing Anthony, following after him, with a smile on his face, a face like a skull with the eyes there still, and a thin film of sallow flesh tightly stretched over the bony frame, a death's head, with the tongue still wagging in it, looking over a high white collar, giving a graceless glance, now and again, at the gold watch-chain dangling in the hollow where a belly ought to be, with Johnny wishing that he was twisting a rope tight round the narrow bony neck.

When they reached the gate, Anthony suddenly turned south,

hurrying through a narrow passage of empty oilcans and tapped oil barrels, and shot into a water-closet, waiting for customers behind the cans and oil casks.

—A sudden thought musta sthruck him, that time, thought Johnny. Well, he has to sit down when the call comes, like the rest of us; though how a man of his means can use that horrible horse-trough of a closet, spattered and puddled with filth, I don't know; and Johnny shuddered as his mind's eye saw the terrible human midden, set to serve the whole of the outer stores staff. Prince and peasant, saint and sinner, slaundered lady and slut, each in his own way, and in his own good time, comes to that tremendous exercise. Clay, like th' rest of us, th' oul' sod. Formed out of clay. An' God made man outa th' dust of the earth. The natty suit, the collars an' cuffs, the gold watch an' chain — all dust. Himself is clay in a suit o' clay, hard clay, clay all!

—Eh, Jack, said Cary, the senior messenger, a lad of seventeen, with fiery red hair and a handsome foxy face, what's up? What's he got on yer taw?

—I gave the two o' them a lot o' lip yestherday for keepin' me over me time, said Johnny arrogantly, an' I'll give him a little more if he keeps flutterin' at me heels much longer!

—Me sweet yourself, said Cary encouragingly. Don't let your bone go with the dog. Stick up for yer rights. Th' boyo sourly needs a tellin' off from someone!

He hurried back to his oilcans, for fear Anthony would come out on top of his talking, and Johnny went on down the lane, turning into the stores, filled with crated and boxed goods that came by land, rail, and sea.

—Here y'are, said the head storekeeper jovially, pointing to a heavy box filled with chinaware, put that on your hump, and carry it to th' top room o' th' china warehouse, an', if you fall, don't wait to get up again, for the governor's not in a good mood today, and wants things done in a hurry!

Johnny gave a long look of malice at the face before him, brown-bearded, a narrow nose, with a top on it like a strawberry-coloured acorn; the face of a man who had been a sailor, with a waddle in his walk, and a habit of knuckling his forehead whenever he talked to the honourable Anthony.

Along came Anthony through the great gate to bend over the crate filled with chinaware, moving his white bony hand through the straw, as if he were looking for stray Spanish doubloons.

—How long will it take to empty this crate? he asked of the storeman.

—Not more'n a couple o' hours, sir; or less, the storeman added, with a meaning grin, with a boy waitin' to work with a will, as a young boy should.

Anthony took no notice of the remark or the grin, but stood there till Johnny had shouldered the box and moved off, following him then, and halting only when he reached his desk near the entrance to the front shop, leaving Johnny to sweat along and up the thousand and one stairs to the chinaware top store. Till dinner-time Johnny went on carrying his white man's burdens, Anthony's head darting forth, like the head of a bony snake, to watch him every time he passed till the half-hour after twelve sent him out for an hour's rest on a great heap of goods, covered with a tarpaulin, opposite the Custom House, there to munch his two cuts of dry bread and watch the steamship *Argo* unloading her cargo, wishing he was big enough to do that kind of work; lying back on the tarpaulin, sensing its happy red-hot heat from the rays of the sun, so different from where he worked, where there was no sun, and where the dim lights burned the livelong day; watching the ship, and wishing that he could go away with her, a great seaman, in a tall ship ribbed with brass, kissing the girls good-bye, an' ahoy for the seven seas!

But a clock in a pub opposite told him it was time to go back to his job as a landlubber, and crushing into a ball the paper that had carried his lunch, he flung it over the side of the quay to sail away with the ships, away, away, to th' Bay of Biscay O!

Back to the store, bending over the time-book, with Nearus leaning pensively over his desk, watching him, his gentle face pretty pale now, his cheeks hollow, the red spots on the bones of them burning brighter than ever, and a catching cough, every now and again, making him put his wasting hands apologetically over his pallid lips.

—You're in th' boss's black books, eh? he said, after a cough that seemed to shake him up a little.

—Black or white, said Johnny defiantly, it's all th' same to me.

Nearus bent over, after sending a swift glance to right and left, to make sure the coast was clear, and brought his wasting face close to Johnny's.

—Get outa this job, he murmured, before you're a day older. You'll never fit in here. They have their knife in you, so clear out while you're nimble enough to go further an' fare worse. I leave at the end of the week for Australia to get better air, so that this little cough of mine may go. Th' Jesus here's a money-changer in th' Temple. They'll dredge th' life outa you, if you stay long enough to let them do it.

He sidled safely back to the document on his desk as Dyke came striding up to sign himself in, pushing Johnny silently away from the book before he had firmly set down the last letters of his name.

—Mr. Anthony left word that you were to go to the top of the shop an' help th' girl there to clear a way for the new chinaware — th' only kind o' work you're fit for, y'ignorant louse!

—Not quite so ignorant as you think, said Johnny quietly; not even as ignorant as you may be yourself, he added, more quietly still.

—Scholar, be God, eh! sneered Dyke.

Johnny guessed that Dyke knew little — no more, surely, than any of his own brothers. He had often heard them talking, and their talk was always of the things they wore, the things they ate, the things they owned, a piano here, a tea-set there, the things they happened to see in the street, or a ride on a jaunting-car to the sea for an hour's holiday. Just enough to keep going, and to earn a pound a week. Dyke, he knew, lived with a childless wife in two rooms, in a three-story house, in a turning off Dorset Street, with a flower-box on the window-sill for a demesne. Every Sunday he marched to church with a jerry hat on his head, a walking-stick in a gloved hand, and a waxed moustache, keeping his head in the air, while his lordly wife walked by his side, dressed in solemn brown, her skirt, helped by a big bustle on her backside, waving scorn to her neighbours. This sort of people gave up learning, with a clapping of hands, as soon as they left school. He was learning because he loved to learn. A burden to them; a joy to him. They were called; but he had been chosen.

—Scholar or no, said Johnny defiantly, I'll bet you I know more'n you do! Come, are you game?

—Are you goin' to take the bet, Mr. Nearus? laughed Dyke.

—Never mind Mr. Nearus, said Johnny; leave him out of it; I'm challengin' you.

—Go 'way, go 'way, said Dyke — I've forgotten more'n you'll ever learn.

Out of the corner of his eye Johnny saw Alice setting some goods in a bin to be added to an order. He saw that she was listening with all her ears. Here was a chance to show what he was made of. It wouldn't do to let Dyke down him before the girl he fancied. She wouldn't think much of him if he did. O heavy lightness! O serious vanity! Here goes! He turned with a flushed face to Dyke.

—Before knowledge was, where was it thought the sun went to

when he set, and how was its diurnal rising explained to the ignorant people who lived on the earth then?

—Tell us, you, for God's sake, said Dyke.

—You don't know, said Johnny. I thought as much. Who was Leonidas, and what country was he king of, and what memorable battle did he fight? Who was Semiramis? Alcibiades? What are copal and indigo, and where do they come from? Jesus, we are told, was a carpenter's son; what was Muhammed? Who was th' headspring of th' Reformation, and on what door of what castle did he pin his ninety-five propositions against th' sale of Indulgences? Go on; answer!

—Oh, let's hear a few more first, said Dyke sarcastically.

—Well, then, said Johnny, warming up, yous have heard o' Shakespeare, I suppose?

—No, then, I haven't, answered Dyke mockingly, but maybe Mr. Nearus has. D'ye know anything about th' gentleman, Mr. Nearus?

—Oh, we've often heard of that, I think, said Nearus.

—Ay, you've heard of him; but how many of you know anything about him? Settin' aside the Chronicle Plays, name ten of the others. No answer? Yous couldn't. What's th' name o' th' play containin' the quarrel between th' two celebrated families, an' what was the city where they lived called? No answer? Verona, Verona, th' city; Montague an' Capulet, th' families. How does th' play start? Yous don't know even that much! A fight, a grand fight between the servants of the two houses; a fight that sped to th' people of th' city, givin' gashed breasts to some and bloodied heads to others!

—Yeh, get off with you! said Dyke viciously, lifting an arm to push Johnny away with a blow in the chest; but he saw sparks in Johnny's eyes, and his hand fell to his side.

—That's betther, said Johnny. I let no man bite his thumb at me, sir. I'll carry coals for no-one!

Dyke stared at him, and bent his brows, mystified. Johnny felt elated, for he knew that he had astonished Dyke, and that Dyke was bound to scorn his show of knowledge, because of the little he knew himself.

—G'way, little boy, said Dyke, for it's weak your mind's gettin'. Won't carry coals! Do I bite me thumb! Mad, be God!

—You do but show your ignorance, Dyke. I'm not one of your poor dismantled messengers. Fiery Tybalt's ne'er a match for Casside, when Casside's sword's prepared, and Casside stands to face him!

From the corner of an eye, Johnny saw that Alice was going.

—Good God! ejaculated Dyke, staring at Nearus, d'ye hear that? Gone cracked. Right enough — he's mad! And who's Tybalt? he asked Johnny, winking at Nearus.

—Ask me arse! said Johnny shortly.

—Nice kind o' language from a young boy, isn't it? Show's how you were reared. Tinker's talk from a clerk in Himdym & Leadem. Where'd you learn your language from — your mother?

—Leave me mother alone! cried Johnny furiously; leave her out of it, or it'll be th' worse for you!

—There, there, give it up, Casside, said Nearus. How's a man to do his work with this steady sthream of arguin' goin' on under his very nose. Go on to your work, an' don't flame up th' minute you're spoken to.

—That's all very well, Mr. Nearus, but I was only tellin' Dyke of what Shakespeare said, an' showin' him a fella with but seven an' sixpence a week may know more than one with a pound.

—Catch! cried Dyke, flinging a parcel, so suddenly, to a messenger, that he failed to catch it, making Dyke hurry over to pick it up and hand it to the messenger in the midst of a volley of abuse, followed by a sharp kick in the backside for his carelessness as he turned away, flushed and ashamed, to put the parcel into his barrow. Shakespeare! Dyke went on, with a dry contemptuous laugh, he'll do a lot for you; he'll bring you a rise at th' end o' th' year. Our duty here to our employers is the main thing we should all think about; so take pride in your work, an' leave Shakespeare alone.

Dyke was now bending earnestly over some parcels on the delivery bench, and Nearus was staring at documents on his desk, as if he were gazing, for the first time, at the face of a beautiful girl; for though they had, Johnny hadn't seen Anthony come softly in, and stand near, watching Johnny with a look of querulous complaint on his bony face.

For the moment Johnny existed only for himself, and in himself. They were foolishness; he was wisdom. He had the whip hand over them, for he knew more than they did; he knew that, now. His mind was a light that lighteth every man that cometh into his world. He was well over their heads, mounted on the white horse, the winged horse, called, called — what was it now? The one ridden by Theseus, or was it Perseus? He'd have to look that up again. But he was on the animal, anyhow, and the name didn't matter. Proud as he was of what he knew, nobody could deny that he was willing, eager to share with others. Not Dyke, though. Pearls before a swine; waste, sinful waste.

Nearus was different. Ignorant he was, but kind; ay, and manly. Tangled up in a cough, right enough; but a man for all that.

—Shakespeare's not for him, he said to Nearus, indicating Dyke; but for you, Mr. Nearus. Shakespeare's there — standing at your elbow. You'll find him worthy of you, I'm telling you.

—Be off, be off, said Nearus, without taking his eyes off the documents he was studying; too busy, too busy now.

—Some fools think he's dull, went on Johnny, heedless of the gentle warning given by Nearus that he should break off the talk, but I'm tellin' you he's not dull; he's all life 'n loveliness; ay, an' even brisk with battle, murder, an' sudden death! There's th' gentleness of the calm lake, if you want it; and there's th' crash o' th' tumblin' waves of a stormy sea if you——

—Look at the clock!

The hard cold voice of oul' Anthony, sounding right over his shoulder! A cold wind blasting the heat of his earnestness.

—Look at the clock, Casside, look at the clock!

Johnny stood where he was, silent. He was trying to think of what he would say, or of what he would do. At last he turned, with an untidy grin on his face, to look at Anthony.

—I was just havin' a little argument with Mr. Dyke and Mr. Nearus, he murmured.

—What does the clock say, Casside?

—A little argument about th' great Shakespeare, added Johnny.

—What does the clock say? insisted Anthony, the thin mouth disappearing into the contracted jaws of the bony skull.

—It says, said Johnny sulkily, that it is some time past the hour for resumption of work.

—And why are you standing gossiping here, idling your employer's time? Eh? You don't answer. You weren't so dumb a moment ago, were you? Were you?

—No, said Johnny, with a flash of anger in his voice, not quite so dumb.

—Far from dumb, in fact, sneeringly. Well, neither Mr. Nearus nor Mr. Dyke, I imagine, wish to carry on an argument with an impudent jackeen — at least, I hope not.

—Hardly likely, murmured Dyke with a tender glance at Anthony, who quietly smiled his approval; but Nearus held his peace.

—And Shakespeare, by all accounts, was an idle fellow, went on Anthony, full of vagabond songs, scarcely a good companion for anyone with a respectable outlook on life.

—A scurvy companion, in fact, said Johnny maliciously.

Dyke touched his forehead with a finger and looked significantly at Anthony.

—Be off to your work, said Anthony to Johnny, and let there be no more foolish talk or idleness, or we'll have just to get someone else more suitable to our needs.

—Out o' th' way! said Dyke, an' let them work who want to work, extending a fist towards Johnny's chest to push him away; but Johnny stepped quickly forward and brought a heavily-booted foot down on his toes, making Dyke give vent to a sharp squeal of pain, hearing it with joy as he turned and walked away to the work awaiting him.

Rage was quivering in him. He'd love to have Dyke an' Anthony be th' throat, squeezing even the terror of life outa them!

A thought came to him, like a full-blown rose: he'd read that somewhere, an' he'd thought it lovely. Where? He forgot. He'd go through the chinaware department, an' maybe see Alice in passin'. He'd fix his eyes on hers with a look that would say betther'n th' best words, ah, aha, me pretty little lady, you heard me talkin' Shakespeare to Dyke, an' know now I'm a fellow worthy of puttin' a hand on your delightful drawers, ay, an' undher them, too; ho-ho, I know me love be her way o' waw-aw-kin, I know me love be her way o' taw-aw-kin, an' when he'd get her out walkin' with him, he'd show her revelations.

Sure as anything, here was Suresaint hurrying down the stairs as if God was afther him! With a polished jerry hat on his head, an' his pallid face lookin' like th' face of a lively corpse. And his gleamin' walking-stick undher his arm. And a white-gloved hand half hidin' his horrible face. Here's his platter-faced sisther, Biddy, the girls' manageress, her big-arsed, lumpy body lumberin' up the stairs, never puttin' the slightest pass on him, or him on her, her face aflame, her eyes starin' right out in front of her as if she had seen a vision of hell open for sinners. There's th' crook of his walking-stick caught in the rails of the stairs, jerkin' it out from under his arm, an' he never stoppin' to pick it up, but rushin' down th' rest of th' stairs, an' shootin' outa th' shop like one possessed. And all the while, Hewson, at th' top o' th' stairs, with icy fire in his eyes, glarin' at th' figure tearin' outa sound an' sight o' th' shop an' all that therein was.

Suresaint had been caught! Oh, that was it! Th' ripe an' ruly villain had been caught. His hand had been where his hand shouldn't ha' been. Up th' leg of her drawers! Miss Vaughan's most likely. Must be it, else why should his ugly oul' sisther be in tears, an' he runnin' for his

life outa the shop? Th' whole transaction was written on the gob of
Hewson. What I have written, I have written. Must a' watched him.
Caught him rude-handed!

He passed by Hewson, now reinforced be Anthony, both of them
staring at where Hewson last saw Suresaint; hurried to be right behind
Biddy, noticin' all th' girls nudgin' each other, an' glancin' joyfully at
th' shame of the big-bodied oul' bitch; safe in th' thought that it was
her, an' not them, who were in th' way o' lamentation.

He climbed up to the very top of the house, stopped before a door,
opened it, and went in to a big attic kind of a room.

Such a sight you never saw, such a sight as he saw, when he opened
the door and went in:

There she was:

> Sweet and glowing, fair and sweet; flushed and fair, flushed
>   and comely,
> like a healthy hawthorn in a smoky street.

There she was, with her little hands moving about in a grimy bin;
sorting out the dusty china, there she was.

> Rise up, my fair one, and come away, my love,
> The time of singing of birds is come;
> The praties are dug, an' th' frost is all over!

There she was, with one little foot on the second highest step of a
ladder, and the other resting on the edge of a bin, her skirt so crinkled
by the stretched-out limb that an ankle and calf of one fine leg was
there for all to see, shining high over the hem of her white petticoat:

> There she was, like a lily squandered in a murky pool;
> Alice!

She turned her head, and her eyes lit up when she saw Johnny. He
stood there gaping.

—I was sent up, he said shyly, to give you a hand.

—Well, she said with a pout, you'll have to come a little nearer,
won't you, if you're to be of any use?

He went swiftly over to where she was, and stood there beside her
with a beating heart.

—You heard what happened to Suresaint? she asked.

—I saw him driven forth, an' I guessed the reason.

—Mr. Hewson caught him interferin' with Miss Vaughan an'
Miss Grice, she said. They let out on him in a note th' day before to

Mr. Hewson; couldn't stand it any longer. His sisther's gone with him too, thank God!

—Horrible thing for him to do, commented Johnny, No-one with a decent mind 'ud thry to do that sort of thing on a poor girl.

—Well, he done it, she said. It's not a nice thing to think of, much less to talk about.

There was silence between them for some time, while she handed down to him the china that remained in the bin.

—It was grand, she said, th' way you spoke up to that fellow Dyke, an' to that oul' Anthony!

—Didya hear me? he asked, swelling with pride. It's only th' beginnin', for Johnny Casside's not to be walked on — not even be th' lordly queen herself.

—I have to sthretch further in, now, she remarked, so don't forget to keep a steady hold o' th' ladder.

He drew closer in to the ladder, his eyes sparkling, his heart beating, and his hand timidly edging as near as it could get to the pretty, lace-fringed leg of the girl. She went on arranging the chinaware in the bin, but, stretching over a little more, the ladder wobbled a bit, and she let a quiet little squeal out of her.

—Steady, steady, Alice, dear!

—You're not holdin' it right, she said complainingly.

—Let me up there — I'm used to laddhers.

—You wouldn't know how to sort th' china, she answered, giving a graceful toss to her head that shook her wavy hair back from her forehead. No good, just holdin' th' ladder, however tight; hold me, instead, an' I'll feel safer. Oh, that's not any betther either, she said peevishly, when Johnny's right arm had firmly encircled her skirt; you're only making it now so's I can't move at all!

—Well, how'm I goin' to hold you so's you can move about th' way you want to?

—If you can't think of a betther way of holdin' than th' way you're holdin', then don't hold me at all!

He took his arm from around her skirt and again got a grip of the ladder, a tighter one this time.

—What d'ye think, Alice, he said, after a long pause, neither oul' Anthony nor Dyke knew nor wanted to know a single thing about th' plays of Shakespeare. Funny, isn't it?

—I see nothing funny in it, she responded snappily; for Alice Norris doesn't want to know anything about them either!

Johnny was puzzled. It was hard to know what to say to a girl. You never knew when you had them. No use of venturing to put a hand on her knee while she was in this cross mood. He'd chance a remark, anyhow.

—Nice stockings you're wearin', Alice; how far do they go up on your leg?

She glanced down at him with a mischievous light in her eyes, and gave her head a saucy toss.

—That's hardly part of your business, she said.

—I'm goin' to have a look, he threatened.

—You'll make me wriggle if you do, an' knock me off. I'm powerless up here. Help me to keep steady, or we'll never get finished. She smoothed her skirt with rapid, clever strokes of her hand, and pulled it a little higher on her leg. Just rest your hand on my ankle, an' then I'll feel safe.

He placed a hand on her neat little ankle, and slyly slid it up as high as her knee. Then something fierce and lovely shot through Johnny's blood. The rustiness of life fled from him, and a world of blossom circled him round about. The stir of Spring, the flush of Summer, the fruitful burden of Autumn, and the rushing of water in the Winter-time moved, flowed, and jostled together in his being; and God's love and care were here, full measure pressed down, and overflowing were here in the form of a pretty face and a quivering slim leg.

—Your skirt's a lot in th' way, he said, as he tucked it tighter behind her, up, up to the lacy halo of her drawers, half-way up her thigh.

—Fancy now, said Alice, beaming down at him, Anthony an' Dyke knowin' nothin' about Shakespeare! Hardly believable, is it? You'd imagine they'd be ashamed to show their ignorance, wouldn't you?

—Pretended to be proud of it, so they did, said Johnny; but I could easily see a shadow of shame in their eyes. Whoa, careful! he added as Alice seemed to give a little slip, and his hand slid over her garter, over the rim of her long black stocking, to hold and fondle her firm white thigh.

—Nearly down that time, she said laughingly, an' would have been if you hadn't been there to hold me. She took her foot off the rim of the bin, brought her leg back to the ladder beside the other one, and Johnny felt his hand being tightly pressed between her two thighs.

The ladder shook, and she half climbed, half slid down into his arms; he pressed her to him till she was panting for breath, he frantically searching to cover her mouth with his own, while she pantingly twisted her bonny head this way and that to avoid the contact.

—You mustn't, you mustn't, she cried; 'tisn't fair on me!

Suddenly the little head stopped twisting, the red mouth brushed his and rested there, her arms went round his neck, her luminous eyes closed happily, and her slim body answered back every venomous pressure given by Johnny.

He was clawing at her skirt when her eyes opened again, with a start; she tore his hands away, panting and pressing herself out of his grasp, till she stood, breathless and flushed, beside the little dusty window looking down to the distant street. Whimperingly she stood there, trying to smooth down her frightened dress and hanging stocking, patting back into order her rowdy locks of wavy hair, pressing her lips to keep them from quivering, and keeping her eyes well away from Johnny's hungry looks.

—You're a bad boy, she murmured cryingly, a bad boy to take me unawares, like that! To tumble me about as if I wasn't a good girl, such a sudden pounce that I couldn't even get breath to tell you to stop, fixin' on me before I knew where I was, seizin' on me like a savage, windin' me into a fear of a wicked thing impendin', ravellin' every stitch on me into an untidy tangle, plain to anyone careful enough to give a hasty glance at me! There, now, she went on, glancing out of the little window, there's Arnott's gettin' ready to put their shutters up, an' closin' time'll be here on top of us before I'll get anything like a quiet look into th' disturbance that's pictured all over me.

She made for the door with quick steps, keeping her face turned away from Johnny. He grabbed her by the arm as she passed, holding her at arm's length while she struggled to make him let her go.

—Oh, let me go! she said vehemently, let me go, you! I must tidy meself before I'm put to shame be wonderin' glances at the troubled look of my appearance.

—Give's a kiss before you go, Alice!

—Maybe it's a kiss you want, afther th' way you've surprised me with your disregard for a good girl's feelin's. Let me go, she added, whipping her arm from his loosening grip, and never again thry to hurt a young girl when she's helpless.

She turned round when she got to the door, hesitated, and looked a little tearfully at Johnny.

—If you thought a lot of a kiss, you'd take it, and be done with it; an', if you're genuine and want to, you can meet me tonight where you said, an' when we come to some grassy nook, you can tell me more about your Shakespeare; but you mustn't try to pull me asunder when you feel you'd like a little kiss. There, she said, coming back into the room, and looking brightly into his darkened face, I know you didn't mean to be so rough, an' we'll make it all up in th' quietness of th' night when we reach th' lanes o' Whitehall.

When she lifted her sweet face for a kiss, he hesitated, then he bent down and pressed his mouth to hers. She turned away and went swiftly from the room. He waited for some time, then went down the stairs into the shop, now darkened by the shuttered windows, where he saw Hewson and Anthony with their gobs together, and the assistants waiting for the signal to go. When he reached his desk, he took off his old coat and put on his good one, went with the rest out of the shop, and hurried home, thinking of the hour when he'd be close beside his Alice, fondling her, and pressing sturdy kisses on her mouth.

He lilted softly to himself as he went along, never minding a soul:

> The birds sleeping gently,
> Sweet Lyra gleaming bright;
> Her rays tinge the forest,
> And all seems glad tonight.
> The wind sighing by me,
> Cooling my fevered brow,
> The stream flows as ever,
> Yet, Alice, where art thou?

And the morning and evening were the sixth day.

TO HIM THAT HATH SHALL BE GIVEN

Oul' Anthony had got married; had been away for a week on a honeymoon; had come back with a comical smile cold on his kisser. He had left father and mother in Booterstown to cleave to his wife in Harold's Cross, as the Scripture hath commandeth. While he had been away, the staff had decided to make him a presentation. Johnny, hard-heartedly, had given a shilling — a tanner out of what he gave to his mother, and a tanner from what he kept for himself. Four suitable assistants had spent suitable nights going about from suitable shop to suitable shop, seeking a suitable present. At last they got one, and showed it secretly, by night, to the murmuring staff. It was a clock of black marble, speckled with grey, shaped like a temple, with two slender columns, one on each side. Over the top were gilt rays, spreading out, like the rays of the sun, and out of these rays sprang the delicate form of an angel, who was pointing to the face of the clock with one hand and up to the sky with the other. Around the upper semicircle of the dial were the holy words, *Tempus Fugit*.

They had set off on a jaunting-car, Dyke, Hyland, a Salvation Army sergeant-major, and head of the cutlery department, Woods, head of the chandlery — three of the oldest members of the staff — with Johnny, the youngest, to present the precious gift to Mr. Anthony. Johnny had jibbed at going, for it meant another ninepence, a fourth part of the car fare, missing from his treasure-store; but they had insisted that the most significant and the least significant of the staff should be there as a testimony of their loyalty and affection.

Up they drove to Anthony's place, and Johnny was in such a fluster at being about to enter his employer's house that he had but time and sense to catch a glimpse of a big house, surrounded by a hedge, with dark solemn cypresses looming out of the dusk, with a smell of lilac everywhere around him, before he found himself in a big, big room that he thought was the parlour, had not Dyke whispered that it was called the drawing-room. For the first time in his life, Johnny found his feet resting uneasily on a carpet. Real Persian, whispered Dyke. For the first time, Johnny found himself lost in a thicket of wonderful things, a huge glistening mahogany thing of doors and drawers, with plates and pitchers of gleaming glass on the top of it. A mighty mahogany sofa here, and stout mahogany chairs there and everywhere. In the centre, oh, a great mahogany table, with a top on it glossy enough for an angel to have a decko at himself and trim his wings by the gleaming of it; a narrow strip of white silk, edged with lace, and embroidered with flowers, ran down it from one end to the other; and in the centre of this, a great epergne of many branches, coloured a light green outside, and a deep pink within, stood, as proud as any seven-branched candlestick on the altar of the Church at Thyatira. Whatnots, sparkling with vases and silver-framed photos, were in every corner. Lovely wallpaper, splashed with deep yellow roses, showed off many pictures on the walls, while a shining piano leaned away by itself in a corner, with the name of Cramer on it in big gold lettering. There was a big fireplace, fenced by a big brass fender, full of big brass weapons, as heavy as those in the hand of Goliath. There were heavy blue curtains on the windows, with lacy ones nearer the glass, foaming with heavy tassels and fringe. A golden chiffonier, with many brackets, having on them knick-knacks of all shapes and sizes, hung over the mantelpiece, and on each side of it were lovely coloured photographs of the married couple, Anthony, to the right, pensive, leaning on a fluted pillar, with a book in his hand; and his missus sitting in a curved stone seat on a terrace, with a big harp beside her.

—A house of glory, thought Johnny, full of good things, lovely to look on and very fair to handle. No books about, thank God, for were they here, the desire to have them would make the envy in me bitther to bear.

He stood stiff and as calm as he could keep, well behind the other three, standing stiff, too, and close together, afraid to stir, facing the door, Dyke holding the clock in both hands before his belly.

The door opened and the two came into the room. Mrs. Anthony was dressed in light brown, with darker trimmings, and had ruches of stiffly-starched lace around her neck and wrists. Johnny saw that she was a little less plain than a pikestaff, but not much. The pair of them sat down in heavy chairs, right in front of the group carrying the clock, waiting for someone to say something.

—We've come, sir, and Mrs. Dovergull, said Dyke, with a little stammer, his face reddening, after he had been nudged by Woods who was nervously twisting a tiny well-waxed moustache, we've come, c-come to, in o-order to, or rather i-in appreciation of, for the purpose of, we thought it w-would be well to take, er this——

—Opportunity, whispered Johnny, behind him.

—Opportunity, went on Dyke, to show h-how we all felt towards the head of the Firm and his l-lady, an' how proud we all were to be let w-work undher such a fine gentleman.

—Hear, hear, murmured the Salvation Army sergeant-major.

—To you an' your lady, sir, said Woods, suddenly and rapidly, after having been nudged by Dyke, we beg to present this gift of a clock to mark the auspicious occasion of your sacred marriage, an' as a token of the affectionate connection existing between you, sir, an' all the members of your staff.

—Hear, hear, and amen, murmured the sergeant-major.

Anthony got to his feet, smiling, and Dyke, lifting the clock from his belly, gave the clock into the hands of Anthony, who then carefully placed it in the lap of his wife.

—Oh, dear, said Mrs. Dovergull, isn't it a lovely present!

Anthony, looking bonier than ever, passed a hand lightly over his tight lips, looked down at the clock, and turned towards the little group drawn closer than ever together, with Johnny half-hidden behind them.

—Gentlemen, he said, I and Mrs. Dovergull thank you all for the lovely and valuable gift you have presented to us. We gladly accept it, gladly, Mrs. Dovergull and I; and we thank you all!

He stopped, patted the clock gently, and nearly cracked his face trying to smile. Mrs. Dovergull went over to the big mahogany piece, poured out three glasses of dark-red wine, and handed them to the three seniors, taking no notice of Johnny. He watched the three gobs as they drank the wine that had been given to them: Dyke's carelessly, as if wine to him was but mellowed water; Woods', with his eyes half closed in ecstasy, as if his tongue had tasted the wine from God's vineyard, but this was better; and Hyland's, reverently and cautiously, as if the curious taste surprised him a little, but he didn't like to say so.

—*Tempus Fugit*, murmured Dyke solemnly, noticing that Anthony was looking at the gilded words *Tempus Fugit* — a reminder to us all!

—Time, like an ever-rolling stream, bears all her sons away, murmured the sergeant-major.

—Though Time can seem damned long, occasionally, said Johnny, feeling that he couldn't stand there all the time without saying something. A deep silence fell on the room, and Johnny felt that it would have been better to have kept his mouth shut.

—Tony, dear, said Mrs. Dovergull graciously, I think these three gentlemen wish to go now.

Johnny saw Anthony pull a tasselled cord hanging near the fireplace, and heard a bell tinkle in another room. Soon a maid appeared, and stood at the door, while the deputation stirred itself, moving in the maid's direction, guided by a cold grin on Anthony's face and a tight smile on the face of his wife.

—Goodnight Dyke, goodnight Woods, goodnight Hyland; we shall all meet again tomorrow morning, God willing.

Mrs. Dovergull's Goodnight, gentlemen, was almost smothered in the chorus of Goodnight, sir, from the three gentlemen, making for the door, which soon closed upon all the glory left behind as they passed out into the silent night, under the star-crowded sky, the majestic timepiece of the universe.

That was the Plough there, towards the north, and to the east, he thought, the Gemini, Castor and Pollux, children of Leda, the mother of Helen, who was the cause of all the uproar in Troy; and there was the Polar Star, the fixed star, the star that shone for Caesar, for he was constant as the Northern Star: poor Caesar, dead and turned to clay, stopping a hole to keep the wind away. Well, it'll be a small hole Anthony'll stop. A little Caesar, faintly present when he stands beneath a star.

They strolled down the residential turning, the three of them together, with Johnny walking close behind, on to the corner where they would get the tram going towards the city.

—He was delighted with the clock, said Dyke.

—Mrs. Dovergull's eyes were beaming, said Hyland.

—It'll add a lot to the room, said Woods.

—It would have been all right, if it wasn't for Casside, said Dyke; he shouldn't have been with us. I was against it, from the first. Nice thing to have a jackeen spoiling everything.

—Made a show of us, said Woods; Anthony saw it, an' Mrs. Dovergull, too.

Down at the end of the road, the three of them halted to wait for a tram, Johnny standing a little away from them. He suddenly remembered that he'd forgotten he had to get back, and that the car fare took him only to Anthony's house, so that if they didn't ask him to join them, or lend him tuppence, he'd have to trudge the whole way home. He edged nearer to them, trying to get enough courage to ask them for a loan. A minute or so passed, and then he heard the jingle of a tram coming along the main road.

—Here she comes! said Hyland.

—One o' yous give us a loan of tuppence to take th' thram back as far as th' Pillar? he asked shyly.

The tram stopped; the three of them climbed in without saying a word; the tram tinkled on again, and left Johnny standing alone, beneath the stars.

Dead tired, he'd been, after that long walk home. Not knowing the way properly, either, he'd wandered a bit before he'd found the right way to his own hall door. Well, if this wasn't pay day, he'd feel too full of the world. He could do with a rest, by God, he could! Still, today he'd buy the book, rest or no rest; rise or no rise! He had extracts of it from a book on Elocution, left behind by his father; and, since the bits of it were so good, what must the whole of it be like? Splendid as the unspoken word o' God was splendid! How was this some of it went? Ay, the bit afther Abdiel had given Satan a bloody coxcomb:

> Now storming furie rose,
> And clamour such as heard in heav'n till now
> Was never. Arms on armour clashing bray'd
> Horrible discord, and the madding wheeles
> Of brazen chariots rag'd; dire was the noise
> Of conflict; overhead the dismal hiss
> Of fiery darts in flaming volleys flew,
> And flying vaulted either host with fire.

So under fierie cope together rush'd
Both battels maine, with ruinous assault
And inextinguishable rage; all heav'n
Resounded, and hath earth bin then, all earth
Had to her center shook.

He had put by thruppence a week till he had one and six towards it, an' today, even if he didn't get the expected rise, he'd spare the other shillin', come weal or woe, and buy it! And when the day of rest came, he'd spend the whole of it with Johnny Milton.

Anyway, if things happened as they had happened so far, he was sure of a rise of a shilling today. So, then, he'd get the book without the actual loss of a make. For weeks he'd watched the lovely book in its blue and gilt binding in the little bookcase at the back of the open-air bookstall at Hanna's shop; for ever fearing that by the time he got the money, the book would be gone. Every evening, going home from work, he'd gone out of his way to make sure the book was still there. It was there yesterday, and it was bound to be there today. He hadn't done badly so far — he had three of Dickens' and four of Scott's; two of Balzac's and one of Hugo's; Ruskin's *Seven Lamps of Architecture, Sesame and Lilies, Ethics of the Dust, The Crown of Wild Olive,* and *Unto This Last*; Darwin's *Origin of Species* and *Descent of Man,* to be read when he knew more about things in general; two by Fenimore Cooper and three by Dumas; Tacitus' *Germania* and the *Life of Agricola* with Plutarch's *Lives* to keep them company; Reade's *Cloister and the Hearth*; Carlyle's *French Revolution* and Mignet's, too; Bunyan's *Pilgrim's Progress* and Sheridan's *Plays*; Taylor's translation of *The Aeneid* and a *Classical Geography*; Ball's *Story of the Heavens*; and, in poetry, the works of Byron, Shelley, Keats, Goldsmith, Crabbe, Tennyson, Eliza Cook — a terrible waste of sixpence — Gray, and the Golden Treasury, with the glorious Globe Edition of Shakespeare falling to bits; all backed up with Chambers's Dictionary, a stiff purchase, costing three shillings, bought after an old one, left behind by his father, had faded away in fragments. All these, with the old religious controversial works of his father, looked grand, and already made a fine show, above the delft, on the top shelf of the old dresser.

He'd add another fine volume to the stock today, Milton's *Works,* a blind man seeing more than a man with many eyes — that is, if he got the rise he expected. Well, it was next to certain, for everyone was talking about the rises that were due, and someone in the know had said that it was coming today for all who deserved it.

In passing to and fro about his work, Johnny had tried to search for a sign in the fixed look on the gob of Anthony, but there was only there the shuttered look that hid everything behind it.

Everyone was working with a will today. All smiles, too. Manna was expected to fall from heaven. Each looked as if he liked his job, and was in love with Anthony. Perhaps they were — for that one day, anyhow. It was an anxious time, waiting, especially for Johnny.

—D'ye know how much you're down for, Jack? asked Carey, a cunning look on his foxy face, and he caught Johnny by the arm as he was passing by.

—Is it th' rise you mean? No; a shillin', I expect.

—One an' six, me boy, said Carey knowingly.

Johnny thrilled, but doubted. Too good to be true. If he got a shillin', he'd be well satisfied. Another sixpence would be too much to look for, afther his row with Anthony too. Still one never knew: no use o' bein' a man of little faith.

—No, no, Carey, he replied, catch Anthony givin' too much. You can't lure me into that fancy. Who told you? Where'd you get that news?

—Ah! said Carey, with a cunning leer, that 'ud be tellin' you. Then as Johnny moved away, he came nearer, and whispered over Johnny's shoulder into his ear: Dyke it was; he knows — don't say I said anything about it.

Passing by Dyke, Johnny got a punch in the chest that staggered him and made him catch his breath. Dyke's face as he saw the pain he caused moved from a keenly pointed smile to a snarling laugh. Johnny, smiling eagerly, put a hand over his breast in mock defence.

—Huh! grumbled Dyke, following up the one blow with a rain of them, why you're picked for a favour, God knows! What Mr. Anthony sees in you it would be hard to say. Get away, you lost an' lumberin' looney! and Johnny thought he felt the force of good humour in the blows he ran from.

The rumour was right then — Dyke's manner showed it. He'd say nothing to his mother for a few weeks so that he could add some more books to his store. He had so few, and needed so many. His row with Anthony had left no ill-feeling. Maybe the reverse. You see, a fellow loses nothing by standing up for his rights: to thine own self be true, and it must follow as the night the day, you cannot then be false to any man. Good old Shakespeare — he knew more than most. Of course, he'd let Dyke thump him, without saying a word, but Dyke hadn't really meant to be rough. Just his way o' goin' on. At bottom, he was really a decent fellow. Dyke had told him of the rise in a rough way, but it was decent not to keep the knowledge to himself. Perhaps, even oul' Anthony wasn't quite so bad as he thought. Anyhow, he'd got to be a little stiff with those who worked for him, or he wouldn't get anything done.

He'd get another book next week. Ay, but what? Dickens? Carlyle? A new Shakespeare? No; th' old one would do grand for a little while longer. He'd not decide; betther prowl round th' stands an' see what was goin'; buyin' a book was a scrious thing.

Good God, didn't the time go slow! *Tempus Fugit* me arse! An hour dawdles into an age when you want it to hurry. There's oul' Anthony fillin' th' pay envelopes now, his long bony hands sortin' th' silver, slippin' th' coins into th' tiny envelopes, an' closin' th' flaps with a sly lick o' th' tongue an' a swift pressure of th' slender fingers.

While Johnny was writing a label for a parcel, Hyland halted beside him, his black eyes showing a good-humoured light.

—So Casside's down for a big rise, eh? Nine bob a week now, eh? Let's hope he deserves it. How'r you feelin' about it?

—Oh, all right, said Johnny, wearing an air of indifference; if it hadn't come, I'd have known what to do.

—What? asked Hyland.

—Fling th' job to hell! said Johnny carelessly.

—Really?

—Yea, verily, an' by my own help so I would.

—Talkin' big, jeered Hyland.

—Go to th' devil an' shake yourself! said Johnny.

He saw all the clerks, who had been paid, counting and recounting their gains, sorting the coins out, folding them together, and dropping them back again, gracefully, into their little envelopes, finally placing the envelope, with a kingdom of God look on their faces, into their favourite pockets. He hadn't been called in yet. He hoped he'd be sent for before he had to go to his dinner. He hoped to God he wouldn't have to go up and ask Anthony for what was coming to him. Like th' oul' bugger to make me, thought Johnny.

He heard a tapping on one of the windows of the counting-house, and, looking round, saw that Anthony was beckoning to him.

—There y'are, there's th' signal, Casside, said a number of the clerks.

Johnny, settling his hair on the way and giving a tug to his coat to make it sit straight, hurried to Anthony's little counting-house. The bony hand placed Johnny's little envelope on the ledge of the desk, without a word. Johnny took it with a Thank-you, sir, and hurried back to his own little desk, his heart beating and his joy full. He waited till he saw that the clerks were busy bending over their desks; then he opened the envelope and spilled the gleaming coins on to his desk that he might have the full feeling of handling the one and sixpence extra.

Good God, th' oul' fool had made a blunder! There was only five and six in the envelope — two two-shilling pieces, a shilling, and a sixpence. How well the blunder was made with his wages! Now he'd have to go back and argue it with Anthony, a hateful thing to have to do. He fancied he heard some titters over against him. With a flushed face and a disturbed heart-beat, Johnny hurried back to the counting-house.

—Excuse me, Mr. Anthony, he said, I'm afraid you've made a little mistake, and he smiled forgivingly; there's only five an' six in th' envelope, instead of seven an' six, sir.

Anthony looked up from a letter he was slowly typing, and fixed a cold grave gaze on Johnny's excited face.

—How much did you say? he asked.

—Only five an' six in it, sir.

—That is the correct amount for this week, said Anthony calmly, and went on with his typing.

—Oh, no, no, sir, said Johnny, seven an' six, sir — what I've been gettin' for a year.

—If you'd taken the trouble to look at your envelope, Casside, you'd have seen that we've fined you two shillings, making five and sixpence the amount due to you.

—Fined, echoed Johnny, fined for what, sir?

—For impudence and disobedience, Casside. Next week we hope we may be able to give you the seven and six as usual, and the bony hands went on uncertainly, clumsily, gropingly, at the typing.

Sick and stunned, Johnny was thinking, and not able to think; getting back to his desk, blindly; fullness of rage making him feel tight and breathless, his thoughts broken and confused, mixed up in a medley of anger that this thing had been done to him so slyly, so quietly, without a wind of the word reaching him, cool and calculated villainy — th' bony scoundrel, th' dead-fac'd whore's melt! Silently and steadily the money had been taken from him — may th' guts in his narrow belly corrode and swell and rise and burst out of the slit of his mouth! They all had known of it, and stayed their work to laugh at him, with Dyke leading them on, and cheerin' in their throats, in honour of Casside's hardship — may their ill-got lives be lost in a sludge of woe; may their hearts be cakes o' rust; and a tangle of rotting fibres burn in every twist and crook of their bodies, hieing them yelpin' to a bitther grave!

—How much of a rise did you get? whispered Hyland over his shoulder.

Without the power of answering, he was so stuffed with anger and dismay, Johnny crushed his cap on to his head, took his lunch from under his desk, and walked away out of the shop, down Henry Street, into Sackville Street, mechanically turning up Bachelor's Walk, the ringing of the hand-bells, announcing second-hand auctions all along the way, sounding as if they were coming from a far distance. He walked on, deep curses burning in his heart; walked on till he came to a stop before Hanna's benches filled with books of all kinds, many of which he would love to have, and bitter with the one thought that he had lost the power to buy even the poorest of them. For a while he managed to keep his eyes off the corner where Milton should be; but his eyes got there at last; and, sure enough, the book dazzled him, gleaming like a precious stone from a heap of rubbish, almost asking him, for God's sake, to come and take it.

Take it? For nix? Steal the damned thing? Good God, no; too dangerous. The youngster keeping an eye on the books outside wasn't there; strange, that. Must ha' gone to his dinner.

He peered through the dusty window: oul' Hanna was at the far end of the shop. Sorting out a new selection. Johnny's hand stretched towards the book; his fingers went round the upper end of the spine, and, gently and cleverly, he pulled the book out, handling it lovingly.

An old man came up and began rooting among the volumes, an old man with a hooky nose and a spreading beard, rooting with piercing eyes among the volumes. Johnny put the book under an arm and took up another, looking at it with eyes that didn't see, for there was a trembling mist before them. He dimly saw the man with the hooky nose, piercing eyes, and spreading beard take a book to his bosom, turn away from the stand, and enter the shop to pay for it.

Johnny then put down the book he was looking at, turned, and, with his heart beating like the heart of a bird caught in a squeezing hand, and his feet feeling as if they were trying to drag him back again, he sauntered away with Milton under an arm, expecting every second to hear a wolfish shout from Hanna calling for a policeman to come and catch a felon. He went on slowly, wheeling into Liffey Street, then tore along as fast as a rapid walk could take him. Excited, panting, and thoughtless, he turned into Upper Abbey Street, then into Jervis Street, not stopping even to glance at a casualty case getting taken into the hospital; into Britain Street, up Sackville Street, into Henry Street again, to bolt into the Henry Street Stores, flushed, covered with sweat, but with the sweet book cuddled under his arm.

He had risked a lot to gain a lot, and he had succeeded. He had a half-crown book in his hand and his week's pay in his pocket. God was good. No, not his week's pay, for two bob of it was snug in Anthony's pocket. A Robin Hood outa hell who robbed the poor to pay the rich. Was he goin' to let himself be robbed? Afther givin' a hard-earned shillin', too, to help buy him a clock? An' without a fight, either? He was in the right: no-one need tell him God would put a hand into the pocket of a poor man. He'd argue it out with Anthony. He'd get what was be right comin' to him, or go! Hyland, Dyke, an' th' rest weren't goin' to have it all their own way.

His file was packed with orders, but Johnny put no pass on them. And wouldn't, till he got what was rightly due to him. Then, he might; anyway, he'd see. There was Anthony, now, back from his haughty lunch, pegging away, in his clumsy manner, with his typewriter. Bony and slender as his hands were, they were slow and awkward at typing, Johnny could see that. All were back at their work, now, all busy, all but Johnny, who hung over his desk, trying to think of what to say to Anthony. He couldn't think, so he'd depend on God to put the right words into his mouth.

Several times he started for the counting-house, and several times he found himself back at the desk again, uncertain and afraid. Once he went as far as the entrance, but his heart failed him and he came back to his desk. He felt a little sick. He should have gone when he was roused, when the anger was on him.

Screw your courage to the sticking-place, said Shakespeare.

—Oh, to hell with it! he said, roughly to himself, here goes!

Straightening himself stiffly, he marched to the counting-house and stood near Anthony, waiting to be noticed. After a long interval, Anthony raised his head from his typewriter and looked at Johnny.

—Well, Casside, he said, what's the trouble?

Before he could answer, the dark form and dusky face of Hewson edged its way forward from the background, and Johnny found himself loosely hemmed in between the two God-bclauding brothers.

—Well, said Anthony again, what is it, Casside?

—I just came to say a word about the fine, sir.

—All that ought to have been said has already been said, said Anthony shortly.

Johnny conjured up all the new strength that had begun to come into his speech. He had written as many letters as he could to his brothers, trying to put into them all the things he had learned the week before, and choosing the most elegant words he could think of to describe what had happened in the locality. He had done it so well that Tom had praised him for the brightness and skill shown in the letters written to him. So with a little trembling in his mind, he settled himself down here to do what he could in his own defence.

—I don't think so, sir, he said; you, yourself have said but little, and I have said nothing at all.

—Oh! said Anthony in an astonished voice, and what have you to say about it?

Although, now and again, there was a slight quiver in it, Johnny's voice was firm and clear; and he felt that Dyke, Nearus, and the rest of them listened and were wondering.

—Well, sir, said Johnny, I'd like to know, first, what was the impudence and disobedience complained of, where it happened, for which I have been fined what is, to me, a very large sum of money?

—I see we have a lawyer amongst us! said Hewson, with a dark grin.

—It is recent enough for you to remember it well, said Anthony, and I've neither the time nor intention to go over it again with you. You have been fined, and there is nothing more to be said about it.

—That's all very well, sir, but I think I have the right to say something in my own defence. The occasion that brought about what you are pleased to call disobedience and impudence was really my own time; and it was you, sir, who were unjust in keeping me beyond the stipulated hour for leaving work.

Anthony had resumed his typing, pretending not to listen to Johnny, and there was a pause, broken by the jerky rattle of the keys clicking clumsily because of the unsteady movement of Anthony's fingers.

—Besides, sir, went on Johnny, had what you allege against me happened even in the rightful time of the Firm, the amount of the fine, if you weigh it with the weekly wage I get, is altogether too large ard unnecessarily severe.

Hewson roughly pushed in past Johnny, anchoring himself beside his brother; and the two of them bent over an invoice of goods, taking as much notice of Johnny as they would of a fly on a distant star.

—I have saved up hard to buy a book I want badly, said Johnny in a louder voice, and the fine had made my well-nourished plan go all agley.

—Book! snorted Hewson; maybe it's a book he wants!

—Casside, said Anthony, with a tinge of a smile on his bony face, attend to your work, and you'll have little need of books.

—I have attended to it well, responded Johnny vigorously, and for the past year not a single complaint has been made against me by a single customer. My need of books is my own need, an' that need's my own business, an' no-one else's.

—Casside, said Hewson viciously, it's plain that a fine is the one thing you can understand. Go back to your work or you may have a bigger fine to face this day week!

—I have no fear of a fine next week, for I refuse to be fined now; and what I am refusing today, I will refuse tomorrow.

—Go back to your work, Casside, said Anthony, a little more softly, in an effort to be kind, before you go too far.

—I'll go back when the two shillings taken from me are given to me again.

—Casside, said Anthony solemnly, you will have to submit to the fine imposed upon you, or — and he paused to make what he was about to say more impressive — or leave our employment. You must make your choice.

—I have already made it, said Johnny.

—What is it, then?

—To leave.

After a moment's hesitation, Anthony opened a drawer, rooted in it, took out some silver, and flung two shillings on the desk beside Johnny.

—It is plain, he said, that you are wholly unsuitable to us.

—That's possibly something to be unashamed of, said Johnny bitterly. And let me tell you there's another shilling of mine embedded in the clock you have at home! I could ill afford it. I gave it unwillingly. I thought joining in the gift would make things safer here. I need a book more'n you need a clock; but keep it; it will remind you of me when the clock strikes!

Anthony's face went a flaming red. He bent down over his desk and remained silent. But Johnny stood there, as pale as Anthony was flushed.

—Get out! said Hewson furiously. How dare you mention such a sacred thing? Get out, or get kicked out!

Johnny sensed that the whole staff was disturbed, and he glimpsed a worried look defiling Dyke's foxy face. He had made them sit up. Whenever Anthony looked at the clock, he'd remember what Johnny had said to him.

—No-one will kick me out, said Johnny. I'm going. God rest you merry, gentlemen. I'm due a rest, anyway. Farewell, a long farewell to all your greatness.

The fleshy hand of the dusky-faced Hewson sought his shoulder, giving him a push that sent Johnny colliding with the desk of Nearus.

—Get out! he said angrily; this Firm has no room for a vulgar corner-boy!

Dyke snatched the precious book from under Johnny's arm and flung it far down the passage-way into the dirty straw, a messenger meeting it with a kick that sent it away beyond into the dirtier lane.

—Follow your book, said Dyke, to your rightful place in the dirt of the street!

—There he'll find his happiness and his hope, said Hyland.

Nearus looked on and sighed and said nothing.

With his face pale as a lily lying in a dark corner, his mind a smarting hate, and rage rough in him, Johnny gathered himself together straight again, faced the two signalmen of God, saying savagely, in half a chant:

> I leave th' pair of you with your godliness and go;
> And when th' ending day comes, day of wrath, I hope
> You two may catch a glimpse of heaven's glory;
> Then sink down, sudden, down, deep down to hell,
> Amazed and sightless!

Half blind himself with rage, he left them, picked up his precious book out of the gutter, wiped with a handkerchief the specks of cow-shit from the cover, and wended his way homewards.

And the morning and evening were the seheaventh day.

TOUCHED BY THE THEATRE

ARCHIE was now completely gone on the stage, and Johnny was following close behind. Archie lived and fought and died and lived again in the toils of the great persons treading out their glorious lives,

gorgeous before the footlights. The Theatre housed the quick, the rest
of the world encased the dead. Some time before, they had formed the
Townshend Dramatic Society, had rented some unused stables in
Hill Street for a shilling a week. These they had gutted of all partitions,
had whitewashed the walls, putting a deep yellow border round the
top of them, with a harp in one corner, a wolf-dog in the second, a
round tower in the third, and a huge shamrock in the fourth so as to
show decidedly the true nature of the work. From old timber taken
from the loft they had made a stage at one end, and benches from what
was over. Ould lanterns, bought second-hand, shaded with cardboard, coloured yellow and black, did well as footlights; and a
turkey-red twill curtain went up or came down at the ringing of a
handbell. The stage was fitted with lovely parlour, hall, and landscape
sets, provided from the better parts of old canvas cut away from old
cloth thrown away by the Queen's Theatre. Here sketches were given
to audiences of forty or fifty, who paid tuppence a head to get in, to
see Archie playing the Duke of Gloucester to Johnny's Henry the
Sixth; or to see Johnny playing Brutus in the Forum scene, followed
by Archie as Mark Antony, friends in the audience shouting the
exclamations of the crowd for them; or the scene between Wolsey
and the nobles, sorted out to be one, played by Johnny in dark-blue
tights, yellow buskins, black trunks, brown velvet coat, and rich
green silk cape, lent by Tommie Talton for the bright occasion; while
Archie strutted as the Cardinal, in a red gown, topped with a low-
crowned, wide-brimmed jerry hat that had been soaked for days in
soda to remove the black colour, then dyed in crimson, with red
curtain cords laced round the crown, the heavy tassels hanging down
over his left shoulder. Johnny had to hurry out after the sly blow at
the Cardinal,

> An' so I'll leave you to your meditations
> How to live better. For your stubborn answer
> About the giving back the great seal to me,
> The king shall know it, and, no doubt, shall thank you.
> So fare you well, my little good Lord Cardinal,

to come back in a long black cloak and wide-brimmed black hat to
play the part of Cromwell to give Archie his chance in the cardinal's
great renunciation. As well, they played scenes from *The Octoroon*,
especially that between Jacob McClusky and Salem Scudder, Johnny
doing McClusky and Archie doing Scudder; and the scene between
Corry Kinsella and Harvey Duff in *The Shaughraun*, with lots of
others in Dick's little orange-coloured books of *Standard Plays*;

though Johnny didn't like the rowdy arguments that went on after-wards, for a lot didn't want to praise Archie, being main jealous of his natural gifts and acting vigour; doing all they could in cold water to disparage everything they'd seen him do, making Archie hot and irritable, threatening to tear down the curtain that his money had paid for, all the time asseverating that without him there wouldn't be much of a Dramatic Society left. Indeed, once during an interval in the performance given by the Anna Liffey Minstrel Troupe, playing in the Coffee Palace, Townshend Street, they had played the quarrel scene between Brutus and Cassius, Johnny doing Cassius, both of them crimson-cloaked, and wearing greaves and breastplates made from stereotype paper, silvered over, that Archie had pinched from the *Daily Express*. But the whole thing was taken silently by the audience, neither hiss nor clap was heard, and Archie got gloomy, and for long after he was content to play one of the corner-men, making a bigger noise with the bones than he did with Shakespeare.

Better times had come. Now Archie was a friend of Tommie Talton's brother-in-law, Charlie Sullivan, who did things of great magnitude when the theatre was the theatre, to an audience who knew what acting was; when he played the great Conn the Shaughraun, the great Shaun the Post, in *Arrah-na-Pogue*, and the greatest Miles-na-Coppaleen the world, or even Ireland, had ever, ever seen; filling the playhouses throughout the civilised world with laughter, softening it with sad and sympathetic tears, and making them thunderous with cheers, the way you'd like to shoulder him high, and carry him through the world's laudation.

But now, with the world's people fading into ignorance and low regards, he had to do the best he could for the drama by playing in the Mechanics' Theatre, in Abbey Street, strutting the stage there before a rough-and-randy crowd who came to while away the time, but who put great pass on the suffering and rollicking that shivered and shone on the stage; with the lights dim when the tears were falling, and the lights high when bravery took the branch, or when fun gambolled its way from the stage into the hearts of the laughing people watching from the darkness. Here Charlie played all the Irish plays, mixing them with *The Octoroon*, *The Corsican Brothers*, or *Saved From the Sea*, Johnny enjoying them on a free pass from a front bench in the pit, his brother Archie having a small part in each of them, training himself for a fuller future.

A kidger had brought a letter to Johnny from Tommie Talton, marked Urgent, asking to come to see him at once, without a minute's delay, on business; and here was Johnny, with his heart athrob, hurrying on to answer it. He turned swift into Temple Street, went past George's Church, dived into The Pocket, and knocked at a genteel door, a little parched for want of paint, with a white plaster horse, for ever on its hind legs, prancing, in the fanlight. This was a token that those who lived there, though a little down in the world, held fast to the fancy of living a select and lofty life among ordinary people. Every fanlight in the place exhibited a plaster horse, standing still, trotting neatly, or dancing sadly on its hind legs, like a tired animal rehearsing for a turn in a circus. These were carried about in baskets, by Italians, mixed with images of St. Francis, St. Patrick, and Madonnas with their children. Johnny had often watched them being sold; had often wished that his mother had had enough to be able to put one in the fanlight. Sometimes staring at the seller speaking to a housewife at her door, a look in the Italian's eyes motioning him to get away, he'd say, How much do they cost, sir? And the seller would ask, Weech — the holy ones, or the seemple horses? And Johnny, answering, the horses, would be told that the leetle ones were two sheelings, and the beeg ones four; the seller turning to the woman to say, once in zee vanlight, ladie, zay breeng a change, oh, so beeg, that no-one knows eet anymore vor zee same house; for zee leetle horse or zee beeg horse een zee vanlight leeft, leeft zee house up, up so high, ladie, zat zee house ees not zee same no more, oh, no, for eet has been leefted, leefted up, up; for zee horses geeves zee house, oh, deegneety, much, muchbeeg, waht you call a lot. Often the ladie would buy, Johnny envying her the horse, now taken so gently from the basket, though he knew well it was a sin to covet his neighbour's goods. But he'd go on coveting while there was anything left to covet.

These houses were let in floors to genteel persons; had oilcloth on the halls, a stand, where hats and coats were hanged, a big gilt-framed picture on a side-wall, variegated carpets with brass rods on the stairs, and an air that seemed to tell you to knock at the door softly. This was the first fine house he'd entered since he stood in Dovergull's, when they were presenting the clock; and though it wasn't as imposing as the other, it was grand enough to make him nervous; for patched boots and threadbare clothes didn't go well with the white horse in the fanlight or the cream curtains on the windows. He dared say they wanted him to earn a few pence by placing bills in some of the shops, telling all that *The Shaughraun* was in full swing at the Mechanics' Theatre.

He raised his hand to the knocker — a lily growing out of a bunch of grass — and knocked softly at the genteel door. Hardly had the sound died away in the nearness, when the door was opened by a little woman with a shawl over her shoulders whose hair was grey, who peered out at him through soft, dark eyes, fixed, sorrowful, in a pale troubled face.

—Is that Johnny Casside? she asked. Oh, come in, my son. I've been listening for your knock this hour or more.

She brought him into a room that was neither big nor small, with much furniture scattered about. There were big black-and-blue vases, swelling into wide bowls at the top, standing on the mantelpiece; from tiny brass hooks embedded in the wide bowls hung crystal glasses cut to catch the light, and a bright fire, burning lustily, threw dancing gleams of lovely colours into the glasses hanging from the vases. Right in the centre stood a large square mahogany clock, with a coloured pictured panel on it of two white swans swimming on a blue lake, fringed with dainty yellow and green palm trees. Over all was a huge coloured picture of Charlie Sullivan as Conn the Shaughraun, a roguish smile on his ruddy face, a fiddle strapped to his back, dressed in his tattered crimson hunting-coat, and the terrier, Tatters, at his heels. Dispersed round were pictures of him again as Miles na Coppaleen, with the keg of poteen on his shoulder; as Salem Scudder, paring a stick with a long yankee knife; and Shaun the Post, standing, well fettered, in a prison cell. Besides, there were smaller photographs of Tommie Talton as Corry Kinsella, as Captain Molyneux, and as the military O'Grady in *Arrah-na-Pogue*. A faded red carpet covered the floor, dotted with tiny fur rugs to hide the parts that had trembled into threads. In the middle of the room, a little nearer to the fire, stood a table covered with a white cloth, and having on it breakfast things for one.

—Give me your cap, she said, an' sit down be the fire. You'll have a cup of tea when Tom comes down. Isn't what you're looking at fine? Charlie himself, taken in his heyday, costing no end of money, just afther Charlie had shaken hands with kings an all kinds o' monarchs, elevated be the way he played his parts before them; an' God be with the old days, an' that's herself, she went on, pointing to a picture of an angelic-looking young girl that Johnny hadn't noticed before, me own daughter, me Mary, in the part o' Moya, who could hold a lily to one check an' a rose to the other without makin' either feel outa place, fitted be God with a smile that simply made an audience thrance itself into a feeling of kindliness for the world at large, before she gave a sigh an' took a soarin' lep to heaven outa the throes of thryin' to bring a new child into the world. I hear Tom's bed movin', the signal for me to put his egg on, for he's a changed boy, now, that used to have his breakfast sprawlin' in bed, and the first tint of the night comin' into the sky; now not lettin' me do a hand's-turn, dustin' and sweepin' his own room, makin' his own bed to save his old mother any exertion, lockin' the door, even, for fear I'd sneak up when he's gone, to lay a hand over things. Here he is, now, an' here's Johnny Casside waiting for your lordship, dying for a cup of tea before he harbours a thought of doing the thing you're going to set before him.

The long lanky figure of Tom came strutting into the room, dressed in faded black broadcloth trousers and a dazzling white shirt, spliced in many places, the cuffs frayed sharply, but still brave and challenging. His pale pitted face was merry with a grin; his hair a mass of golden curls, parted impudently by a curling-over quiff, cascading down elegantly over his pock-marked brow.

—Well, Johnny, me lad o' gold, he said intimately, as he slid into a chair beside the fire, and began on the egg, while Johnny munched a junk of buttered toast and sipped from a cup of tea, you know that tonight's Charlie's benefit performance? Well, Cleggett, who plays Father Dolan, 's gone and got ill; none o' the rest know the part, so we're in the devil of a hole. We want you to fill the part for us, me lad.

—An' well he'll fill it, too, murmured Mrs. Talton.

—Aw, no, no; indeed I couldn't, exclaimed Johnny excitedly; but the thrill of a cheering audience went through his beating heart.

—You're goin' to do it, said Tom emphatically. Haven't I seen you doin' the parlour scene to Archie's Conn, an' the one in Ballyragget House to Archie's Kinsella, to the manner born, too? Besides, you know the whole part, don't you?

—Yes, I know it all, said Johnny; the whole play, I know it nearly all.

Tommie jumped up, wiping bits of crumbs from his mouth, his eyes ashine, showing a problem solved.

—Me sowl man, he said heartily; now, Mother, turning to Mrs. Talton, measure him so that you can stitch enough tucks in Father Dolan's togs to fit him fair.

The breakfast things were swept from the table. The sombre garments of Father Dolan were spread out, Mrs. Talton measuring the length of Johnny's arms and legs and the width of his waist, making chalk lines on the black cloth as she measured, murmuring, Tucks won't be many, long legs, long arms, and fairly wide round the waist; but what about the hat? I can't put e'er a tuck in that.

—He wears it only a couple o' times, commented Tom; so he can carry it in his hand. Now for the theatre, me laddo, to run over the words, and give you the feel of the stage.

Johnny, all of a glow, hurried out with Tom, and they got a tram going to Nelson's Pillar.

—I heard th' oul' one muttering out of her, an' I tidyin' me room, said Tom. What was she blatherin' about? Tellin' you what a white-haired boy I'd become, eh?

—Yes, answered Johnny, how you did everything for yourself, makin' your bed an' all, even lockin' the door so as she wouldn't be able to tire herself doin' things.

—If she only knew, and he laughed loudly, pushing his jerry hat to a rakier angle on his curly head. I was at a low ebb a few weeks ago, and I pawned the blankets off the bed, so I do for myself, an' keep the door locked to prevent her finding out. It was all right then, for the nights were warm; but, Jasus, now I'm perished, an' have to bury myself undher old clothes from the baskets!

They got to the theatre, and found two men setting the first scene for the play. Part of a house appeared at the left corner, with steps going up to the door; and Johnny rehearsed the going and coming down of these steps, till Tom was satisfied that some of a priest's dignity appeared in his walk. Then they went over the more important scenes in the play, several times; then every part of the play where the priest appeared; and Tom's face was a beam of enthusiasm at the end of it all.

—Bravo! he shouted, running over and clasping Johnny's hand. Did yous see him, did yous hear him? he added, turning to the two men who had set the scene.

—Ay, did we, said one of them, an betther it 'ud be hard to get, if you et an' slept in Drury Lane, itself, for a month o' Sundays!

—Henry Irving's a great man, there's no denyin', said the other; but if some I know keeps goin' th' way he's shapin' now, Irving'll be devulged only as an I roved out kind of an acthor!

Tom plunged a hand into a pocket, took out some coppers, and tossed four of them to the two men.

—Out for a dhrink! he shouted.

Then there was great haste in hurrying over to a pub, for bread and cheese and a bottle of stout for Tom, and one of ginger beer with a ham sandwich for Johnny; then back to Tom's, where he fitted on Father

Dolan's clothes, more tucks being added here and there, till all was said to be well; then home, with his head spinning, Tom's advice to lie down and forget it all till the time came, ringing in his ears; with Johnny's mother, when she heard it, saying, that even were the stage what it should be, there wasn't much to be got out of it by any respectable person; everyone knew what the people there were like, livin' languidly a low life of gay an' coloured divilment; a lure of envy to them who had to stay in the straight road; wastin' away a boy's life, sightseein' the chamberin' of light men with fast women; when you should remember that neither your father nor mother was ever in a theatre, except to see the wondhers of Shakespeare's plays, done be God-fearin' men, full of honest laughter, dimmin' with tears whenever the occasion called for them; adding, as Johnny was going out, well, since you've committed yourself, do your best, and don't, for goodness' sake, make a show of the Cassides by givin' a bad performance.

Johnny raced all the way to the theatre, finding it dark and deserted, so that he had to edge away, come back, and edge away again for upwards of an hour, till he saw one of the men go in. Him he followed, and was told he'd come too soon, but could go to Mr. Talton's dressing-room and wait there till the time came for him to dress and be made up for his part.

A tiny room it was, made of thin board partitions, with a table scattered over with all kinds of face-paints and powder. The green coat and buckskin breeches of Kinsella were hanging from a hook, next to his own black ones; a little cracked looking-glass was on the table, propped up against a tin box; and on the walls a score or more of photographs and coloured pictures of lovely ladies in lovely dresses; dresses so disarranged by the pose of the girls, or the saucy pull of their dainty hands, that lovely legs were peeping at him from all sides and corners, and swelling white breasts all but out of the fair bodices the charming girls were wearing.

> My bodice, neat an' modest, oh, is slippin', sir —
> Be careful, sir, be careful, please;
> The silken thread that holds it up is rippin', sir —
> Oh, do be careful!
> There now! It's down about me waist,
> My pearly goods are all uncased,
> I hope they're temper'd to your taste —
> St. Patrick's Day in the morning!

My skirts are up above me knees, I'm dancin', sir —
Be careful, sir, be careful, please;
Your eyes are like twin stars o' fire, advancin', sir —
Oh, do be careful!
Good sir, you gave me quite a scare,
I hope you'll find your huntin' fair —
Yes, yes, you're bound to find it there —
St. Patrick's Day in the morning!

Tommie Talton came bustling in, and Johnny jumped away from the pictures. Tom's hat had a hastier rake on his head than ever; his face was flushed; and some of the smallpox holes in his cheeks seemed to fill up and empty again as he breathed.

—There's every sign of it, Johnny, every sign of it; we've done it, I think, at last.

—Yes? questioned Johnny.

—There's a queue forming already, me son. We're going to have a full house; and no paper, no paper, me laddie. Now sling yourself into your priestly duds, and I'll make you up. We've more'n half an hour, before the curtain rises.

Johnny got into the sober clothes of Father Dolan, and felt a bit astray in them. The tucks, ironed out, were still visible, and the trousers looked a bit wide, though the stiff white paper band, stitched to the coat, made a fine Roman collar. A yellowish-grey paint was thinly smeared over his face to take away the bloom of youth; thin streaks of brown across his forehead and under his eyes added a few wrinkles, and made him look thoughtful and serious. Flour scattered over his brown hair made it grey, and finally, a book, representing, Tom said, a Breviary, was put into his hand, and he was all ready for the fray.

—Don't forget not to take the book from your left hand, said Tom. Always keep the right one free for your gestures. He cocked his head to one side and stared at Johnny. You'll do. Look the part to the life. Perfect.

Tom was dressed for his part of Corry Kinsella, buckskin breeches, top-boots, green cutaway coat, white waistcoat, and grey tall hat. He dabbed some red paint on his cheeks, put short thick lines of black paint, to represent sideboards, before his ears, and a thick streak across his upper lip to represent a moustache. With his hunting-crop in his hand, he stood smiling, waiting the time to go on to the stage.

—We'd betther be goin' down, he said, for me bones tell me the time's gettin' short. Remember, he said warningly, to keep your head well up while you're speakin', so that the gallery can hear; never stand in front of anyone an' spoil the picture; and don't forget a priest always walks with dignity on the stage, an' speaks slow an' sure.

They went downstairs, Johnny's heart swelling so that his chest felt tight and his stomach felt queer. Passing through an iron door, splashed with the word SILENCE, they came on to the stage.

What with the lights and the curiously-dressed people standing about, silent and still, and the murmuring that floated up from the audience, the dirty stage and the dusty scenery turned into a golden world.

—Do like you done today, an' you'll do grand, whispered Tom, as he slid softly by to take his place where he was to make his first entrance.

Several people who passed patted Johnny gently on the shoulder; and he knew, if he failed, he'd for ever be undone; but he wouldn't fail, for he'd live the part for the time being.

There on the stage, behind the lights, in front of his eyes, stood the cottage of Arte O'Neill, in Suil-a-beg, with the ruins of Suil-a-more Castle a few feet away, and the Atlantic Ocean near enough to let the sound of its waves be heard; an' there was Captain Molyneux, of the 49th Foot, come to the place to capture the escaped Fenian, Robert Ffolliott, a convicted felon because he wasn't afraid to speak of Ninety-eight; and the green-coated Squireen Kinsella, striking his top-boots with his elegant whip, striding before the cottage, a villain, doing his friend, Ffolliott, out of his property, coming between the Fenian and his own beloved fiancée, pretending friendship all the time, but conniving with the grey-coated police spy Harvey Duff, to nail Ffolliott again, so's he'd be out of the way; with the black-coated Father Dolan, frantic, knowin' all, but darin' to say nothing conceived in the confessional.

Johnny stepped through the door into the glare, the white light, the dazzling place of play, sensing, though he didn't see, the vast gathering of watchers hidden in the gloom, waiting, wondering, pitching their tents of thought with the players in the pool of light that showed another world of good and bad, gay and glum; knowing and simple people, in silks and friezes, in crimson and green garments, and weather-worn grey, aligned together for good or evil, with God on the alert above to ensure that to the true, out of many tribulations, would come an exceeding weight of glory.

There he stood, now, outside the cottage door, his glance resting on the agitated Kinchella asking himself who was it had sent money to Ffolliott in Australia to keep him from starving; with Johnny's answer sounding loud and clear and strange, I am the man, Mr. Kinchella; the play flowing on with Johnny stressing the villainy of the Squireen, answering him when Kinchella pleads for Father Dolan's help in persuading Arte O'Neill to become his wife, I'd rather rade the burial service over her grave, an' hear the sods fallin' on her coffin, than say the holy words that would make her your wife; for now I know, Corry Kinchella, that it was by your means, and to serve this end, my darling boy — her lover — was denounced and convicted; and Kinchella's snarling denial, 'Tis false! cut be Johnny's 'Tis true; but the truth is locked in my soul, and heaven keeps the key! with the vindictive Kinchella threatening venomously, Then out of this house these girls shall go, homeless, ay, an' beggars, followed be Johnny's declaration with a force in it, like God's hidden thunder, rivin' a villain's last hope, Not homeless while I have a roof to shelter them; not beggars, I thank God who gives me a crust to share with them! going in slowly, leavin' Kinchella gnashin' his teeth in the midst of a storm of hand-clapping and cheers from the audience, incensing him with the feeling that his playing of the part was safe, while the main characters silently shook his hand, and the minor ones touched him respectfully on the shoulder; while the play went on to show the sisther of the Fenian fallin' madly in love with the English Captain; tellin' how Conn poached the Felon home out of Australia, and brought him safe to Father Dolan's house where, in the midst of their jollity, the redcoats come, informed of Ffolliott's whereabouts by Harvey Duff; the Fenian runnin' to hide in the kitchen clock, with Captain Molyneux questionin', an' Father Dolan stutterin' that he was, was here, but had, had—, an' Conn chimin' in with, Yissir, he wint away before he came here at all; then the Captain sayin' solemn, Have I your word as a priest, sir, that Robert Ffolliott is not under this roof? showin' Father Dolan strugglin' with his conscience, saved from a lie be the brave Fenian rushin' in to shout, No, sir; Robert Ffolliott is here; Conn consolin' the priest be sayin' that Robert would rather have the irons on his hand than the sin of a lie upon your soul; endin' with the grand tableau of the handcuffed prisoner embracin' his beloved, the poor priest, convulsed with grief, leaning his head on the table, the Captain pointin' the way out with his naked sword, an' Conn prevented be the claspin' arms of his Moya from flingin' a heavy bottle at the Captain's head, with a long, lone, sad sigh goin' up from the watchin' people. So it flowed on to the last scene where Kinchella, abductin' Arte and Moya, is shot be Conn, where Arte throws down the ladder from the cliff, preventin' any of the villains goin' to the waitin' lugger, on to Harvey Duff's flight from the furious people, beggin' mercy from Conn who flings aside the crouchin' Informer, sayin', Ay, as you spared me, as you spared the men at whose side you knelt before the althar, as you spared them whose salt you ate but whose blood you drank. There's death comin' down on you from the cliff above, there's death waitin' for you on the rocks below—Now, Informer, take your choice! And Robert, freely pardoned, no longer needin' to fly to America where Irishmen were held in honour and threated right, and made welcome, and given power, and shown favour, where no information was sworn against them, where no narrow walls were built to hold them tight, where no ropes were woven to hang them high, where no iron was forged to mar them manacled; but could stay at home, and marry his loved one, and Captain Molyneux, too, Englishmen and all, as he was; and Conn, happy at last, with his own Moya, and the priest's blessing at long last given.

And Johnny bowed his head with the rest, standing in the midst of a huge coloured bubble of applause, Johnny watching some of the people mooching out, wading through a drift of orange peel and crumpled programmes, with the curtain coming slowly, slowly down for the last time.

All of them, nearly, hurried away then, patting him on the back as they passed; but Johnny lingered a little, looking at the stage wistfully as the lights began to dim, and the fairy feelin' faded. Behind a wing he heard the voices of two men who played the minor parts of Kinchella's henchmen. He listened, for he had heard his name mentioned.

—Didja ever see the like before? said one voice. Whenever I met the cocky kid strollin' about, like a god who knew nothin', I'd ha' liked to have given him a wholesome paste in the snot!

—Father Dolan, how are you! I've a pain in me arse, lookin' at him. A sad sight I hope I'll never see again. Disasthrous, disasthrous! If you'd done it now—Oh, I'll say nothin'.

—Or you, Jem, but mum, though, not a word. The cocky kid done it; an', oh, Jasus, help the poor Theatre!

Johnny hurried up to the dressing-room, where he took off his stage clothes silently, only half listening to Tommie's praise, for a good deal of the glory was gone.

—You were really fine, said Archie, when they were on their way home. Even Sullivan said that only once before had he seen a better

Father Dolan — the time he once played it himself. Splendid he said you were.

—I heard him saying everyone was splendid, answered Johnny moodily.

—Ay, in an offhand way; but he didn't harp on anyone as he did on you. I got Harvey Duff over betther than ever before — they hissed like hell!

But the goodness was out of it, and the glory was gone for Johnny. To forget what he had heard the two bastards saying of him, he broke softly into a gay Dublin ditty:

> A sober black shawl hides her body, entirely
> Touch'd be the sun and the salt spray of the sea;
> And safe in the darkness her slim hand, so lovely,
> Carries a rich bunch of red roses for me!
>
> Her petticoat's simple, her feet are but bare,
> An' all that she has is but neat and scantie;
> But stars in the deeps of her eyes are exclaiming,
> She carries a rich bunch of red roses for me!
>
> No arrogant gem sits enthron'd on her forehead,
> Or swings from a white ear for all men to see;
> But jewell'd desire in her bosom most pearly,
> Carries a rich bunch of red roses for me!

—If I was you, said Archie, as they walked along Sherriff Street, I wouldn't go an get a swelled head.

DEATH ON THE DOORSTEP

TOM had finished his time with the colours, and had come home on the reserve with a fine character. His company officer, a Captain Bacon, had done what he could to persuade him to keep with the colours and go in for promotion. Tom had passed examinations in signalling, drill-instruction, map-making, and was skilled in all the then known books of infantry technique of attack and defence; and Bacon had got him the Lance Stripe as quick as he could. But Tom didn't wear it long. Nothing would make Tom put a comrade into the clink, or even report one. What they want, he'd say when the stripe had been ripped from his arm, is not a better soldier but a spying bully. Three different times the stripe went up; and three times it came down quicker still, for it wasn't in him to become a jailer or a judge's lackey. And so, though he loved a soldier's life, he left it, and came back to his own town-land.

On the other hand, Mick hated the life, and was always eager to get far away from the sound of a bugle. His life was a stormy one, and his records were packed with regimental entries. At the moment he was doing twelve calendar months, cells, for up-ending a company sergeant-major who had called him a good-for-nothing Irish bastard.

But Tom arrived home with a grand character from the records in the one hand, and a recommendation for work from Captain Bacon to the Superintendent of the Goods Department of the Meddleland Railway at the North Wall. He got a job as a goods porter at fifteen bob a week, and some months after, that of a shunter at eighteen shillings a week. So to be near to where he worked, the Cassides folded up their tent and rented two rooms in a four-roomed cottage near the North Wall, the other two rooms upstairs forming the home of a Mr. Sheelds, with a wife and eight children; noisy kids, half fed, their clothes things of shreds and patches; for ever quarrelling, rushing up or down the stairs; into the street, out of the street; doing quick and sudden jobs in the hall, fit to break a body's neck, if he happened to step on it, filling the house with the incense of poverty, playing uproariously with chaos till the deeper hours of the night shook them into showy slumber.

One morning, under the grey-blue cloak of an October sky, a morning that had, earlier on, wed itself to a bitter breeze, Johnny and his mother helped to load the few heavy things they had on to a little cart, drawn by a donkey, driven by a young fellow, like Johnny himself, with black tousled hair, and one eye missing; lost in a stand-up fight, he said, with a fella twice me size, who when he found he was gettin' bet, an' had me on the ground, under him, poked a bit o' pointed stick into me eye, and turned it round, so that the doctor had to take it out; but, all the same, when he done it, I nearly did for him for I ruptured him with a friendly kick in the balls. When all the things were piled on the cart, both of them had a good time welting the donkey till they got to the doorway of their new home. Sweating hard, Johnny helped One Eye to carry things in, while his mother went backwards and forwards, carrying the more fragile ware that was too precious to be trusted to the lumbering donkey.

They had been installed in their new home, now, for some time, with a little protestant church at their back, and a huge catholic church right in front of their face, the first called St. Burnupus, the second St. Damaman, Mrs. Casside passing the fact by with the remark of, The nearer the church, the farther from God. They hadn't been long in the house when they found it was alive with bugs. Tom and Johnny had been close to sickness several nights when the bugs came out, crawling over their shrinking bodies, spreading a bloody evil-smelling slime over them the times they were squelched savagely between angry groping finger and thumb. With boiling water, half filled with soda, Mrs. Casside had scrubbed every bit of wood in the rooms; day and night, for over a month, she fought the bugs, helped by Johnny raking their rotten holes out clean, pouring in poisons, mixed with paraffin, spluttering often, as if she was about to retch, getting some mortar from men working at the end of the street, plugging every hole up, and smoothing them over with a broken-bladed knife; till the time came when she could bring in neighbours to rejoice with her, saying, a silken skin can rest decent now, barring an odd nip or two from a sthray flea which could cause uneasiness to no-one.

Things prospered after the bugs had been banished. Johnny was getting an egg nearly every morning, instead of seeing one at Easter only; with meat for dinner often, and an odd pot of jam for tea. The kindly fruits of the earth were coming his way. His mother had a warm petticoat under a warm skirt, and a good pair of boots on her hardy feet. The big box on the lobby was always full of coal, for Tom added quite a lot to his few shillings a week. His wide, clumsy railway uniform of black corduroy was a wonder-sack; and often when he came home, he brought forth, like a conjuror, many a good thing for eating and for wear, such as eggs, butter, cheese, bacon, and tea; boots, caps, shirts, suspenders, and socks. Many of the surplus shirts and boots had been pawned, and with her share of the money Mrs. Casside had added a few luxuries to the home, cheap sheets, some cutlery, crockery, cheap blankets, and even a chair, bought from a neighbour whose home had been broken up by a sudden death.

When a crate or case looked promising, Tom, or some comrade, would crash the sharp lip of a heavy truck against it till it burst open; then he'd go to a foreman, reporting a damaged case, leaving it free for discreet and fruitful pillage when the coast was clear. A little from many rather than a lot from one was the motto of the men; and anyone who showed carelessness was left to do his work alone. Mrs. Casside for a long time was very nervous going into a pawnshop, expecting a policeman to jump out upon her from a shadowy corner in the shop, though she rarely forgot to offer up a prayer for the safety of Tom and the good name of the household. Johnny was too much afraid to pawn anything, though he ate the eggs, drank the tea, wore the boots, and, when the day was mild enough, opened his coat to show his bran-new shirt to the envious and gaping world.

But this happiness was too good to last long. God didn't want us to get things too easy, murmured his mother. For one day Tom came home to his dinner, cold and shivery, and Johnny noticed his eyes glazy. Dhrink, thought Johnny. He was irritable too, pushing aside his meal of steak and cabbage, grumbling that it was God's killing; and when his mother said it was good and fresh and tasty, he took it up and flung it, plate and all, under the fireplace. Then he sprang up, sending his chair flying, clapped his hat hard on his head and went out of the house, banging the street door after him. That night, late, he came staggering back, telling his mother he felt rotten, with a sharp pain in his chest, like a knife going through it, making him catch his breath badly. His mother handled him like a kid, took off his boots, helped him off with his clothes, smoothed out the bed for him, and covered him up warm. Then she ran out for oatmeal, making a bowl of gruel, forcing the unwilling Tom to swallow it down in hot sips, saying it would be like an inside poultice on his chest, and assuring him he'd be all right again, after a good night's sleep, Johnny sleeping on the floor so that his rest wouldn't be disturbed by anyone in the bed with him.

Throughout most of the night, Johnny heard Tom tossing about, heard his uneven breathing, mixed with the muttering of curses of God on the way these things attack a fellow; coughing, catching his breath; and cursing again; with the old bed he lay on creaking constantly, like a rusty signboard shaking on a windy night. Johnny felt a curious sensation, listening; felt as if something strange, something sinister might bring him pain, and carry confusion into the house, coming out of the hard irregular breathing of his brother Tom.

The next morning Tom was burning, and his breath was coming out of his mouth in coarse, frightened, stiff gasps, and his eyes were glittering in a queer way as he lay there, minding no-one, but moving from his back to his side, and from his side to his back again. When she saw him, Mrs. Casside sent Johnny off to get a red poor-law ticket, and to deliver it at once to the Dispensary for the attendance of a doctor. The next morning at midday the doctor, Shonelly, came, flat-footed, hard-headed, his cheeks a glossy red, ripening into purple on the tips of his cheek-bones. He had a shining bald head, like a huge island surrounded by a narrow fringy sea of wiry hair; and the backs of his hands were covered with dirty yellowish hairs as if furry gloves were being born to them. He had a thick collar round a bulging neck, so tight that he was hard set to bend his head. In he came, coughing up a lump of phlegm fiercely and spitting it into the fireplace.

—Where is he? he asked impatiently. In here? — Oh, I see — what's the matter with him? How long's he been like this? Get outa the way, for God's sake, woman, and let me see him. Huh! feverish; tongue bad; chest congested. Keep him quiet and warm, d'ye hear? Or better still, let him go to the Infirmary.

—No, no, said Mrs. Casside, not the Infirmary — we're not paupers.

—It's the best place for him. Come up to the Dispensary and I'll give you an opening medicine for him; and, putting on his hat, he made for the door.

—I'm anxious about him, murmured Mrs. Casside timidly, and I'd be glad if you could come tomorrow.

—Ay, and so would many another too, me fine woman, he said sarcastically; but I've more to do than to stand guard on your doorstep, ma'am. And off he hurried, telling his coachman to drive to the next patient, and breaking wind shockingly as he climbed into his oul' drab brougham.

Days went by, but no doctor came, leavin' poor Christians to die without movin' a finger to help them, Johnny's mother said, as she washed Tom all over to keep him cool, essaying to tempt him into a quieter mood than to be squirming about the bed from morning till night, and from night till morning.

Up she sat with him, till her face grew haggard and her eyes grew dim and her firm mouth twitched for want of sleep; while poor Tom grew worse; grew hotter; his quick breath coming and going with such a rasping whistle that you could almost hear it all over the house; his mouth agape, with his mother trying to trickle spoonfuls of beef tea down his throat, and Tom, near choking, spewing it out again, all over his bedclothes; his mother wiping his cracking lips and his sweaty forehead, looking wonderingly into his wide-open glassy eyes; he coughing till you'd think his lungs would break, and spitting up phlegm in a gasping gurgle, tinged with a darkish red colour that his mother wiped off with a gentle hand, while the other caressed his burning forehead.

One day Johnny, going in to see if there was any message for him to do, found her half lying on the floor, holding on to the bed with one hand, and to Tom with the other, and he with one leg pawing the floor, and she looking at him, a tear slidin' down a furrow in her face, all the time murmurin', Ah, Tom, Tom, Tom, I can do no more; I'm done in; I've failed you for once in me life.

Johnny, with fear in his heart, and it thumpin', helped her up, sat her down on the chair by the side of the bed, and be main force shoved Tom into the bed again, holding him down there, not rightly knowin' what to do; afraid to stay, and afraid to go for help, for fear of Tom gettin' up an' goin' out to do damage to himself before help could come; all the time keepin' his eyes shut so that he wouldn't see the horrid faces Tom was makin', an' thryin' to close his ears to the strained breathin' that forced itself out of Tom's gapin' mouth.

—I'm afraid for you, my son, his mother kept murmurin'; I'm afraid for you; I failed you this time; but I done me best.

—There's a knock at the other door, said Johnny. I betther go an' see who it is. Here, hold him down till I see.

But she sat on there, her hands fiddling with the quilt; her eyes closing; her breast panting, murmuring away, I failed me son this time, but I done me best.

—Eh, here, said Johnny roughly, shaking her shoulder, there's someone at th' other door — maybe th' docthor. Hold him till I go an' see who it is.

She slowly rose, slid over, falling across Tom's body so as to keep him where he was, an' he babblin' an' babblin' away a lot of mixed-up nonsense.

Johnny, opening the door and going out, saw a clergyman, as big as a big policeman, standing at the other one by the end of the hall, waiting for it to be opened. Johnny was about to turn swift to warn his mother to keep silent, and let the unwelcome visitor go unanswered; but the clergyman, hearing his movement, turned, and came towards him.

—Goodday, my lad, he said — and a handsome face he had — can you tell me if Mrs. Casside lives here?

—Yessir, said Johnny, before he could think of anything to say to ward him off.

—Oh, she's a protestant, isn't she? Can I see her? I'm the new minister, Harry Fletcher.

—I'm afraid not, said Johnny surlily; me brother's very ill, an' she's mindin' him.

Just then Mrs. Casside's voice sounded shrill and appealing, calling, Johnny, quick, come — he's risin', an' I can't hold him down!

Johnny dashed back into the sick-room, to see Tom half out of bed, his mouth agape, mumbling away, and his mother sliding down to the floor, exhausted, but still with a tight grip on the sick man's arm. The minister stood at the door staring, while Johnny rushed over and tried to push Tom back; but he was too far out of bed, and, push as he might, Johnny wasn't strong enough for the twisting and turning Tom.

Before he knew what was happening, the new minister was beside him, his arms were around the sick man, and Tom was safe in bed again, with the clothes neatly replaced around him, and the strong restraining hand of the minister pushing down on his chest. There he stood, staring down at the mumbling man for fully a minute.

—Mrs. Casside, he said, without taking his eyes off the sick man, your boy's in a bad way.

She never answered for some time; then murmured in a steady, dreamy way, Poor Tom! I've failed me poor son this time.

—You're worn out, woman, he said, turning his head to look at her, worn out completely. Why isn't he in hospital?

—There was only th' poorhouse one, she said, an' no son o' mine's goin' there.

—There's the Addlelaid, he murmured; what about the Addlelaid?

—You'd have to have some big nob behind you to push you in there, said Mrs. Casside.

He kept silent for a few moments, looking down at the uneasy man, his soft, elegant hand holding Tom safe under the clothes, Johnny at the window looking out at the shades of the Dublin Mountains, pale-blue heads above the houses, Tibbradden, Three Rock, Two Rock, Glendoo, and Kilmashogue, like a semicircle of lovely wonders stretched over the forehead of the city. And the tall clergyman still stood silently there, looking down on the twisting, hoarsely-gurgling figure stretched out beneath him.

—The Infirmary would be better than this, Mrs. Casside, he murmured.

—No, it wouldn't, she answered doggedly; they'd just sling him there, and leave him to rave alone. Here, at least, he'll have them who know and love him to touch, till he gets to the end of his journey.

—Run round as fast as your legs can carry you, and tell Georgie Middleton to come here at once, said the tall minister, suddenly, to Johnny.

Johnny, without waiting to put on his cap, ran for his life, sensing that the minister had hit on some idea of how to help them. When he got there, Georgie was reading a Deadwood Dick story; but after a little grumbling, he put his hat on and came back with Johnny.

—Georgie, said the minister, putting his hand on the lad's shoulder, I want you to stay here beside this poor sick man; to watch that he doesn't get out of bed; and to do whatever Mrs. Casside may want, till I come back. Will you do this for her and me?

—Yessir, he said at once; nothin' easier.

—Thank you, Georgie. Come along you, he added, gripping Johnny's arm, hurrying him out of the house, up Lower Sherriff Street, till they came to the rank of cabs and cars there.

—Climb up, he said to Johnny, while he got up on the other side; and to the jarvey, Addlelaid Hospital, my man — quick as your horse can go!

Away they went bowling along the roads, Johnny a little ashamed of his shabby get-up, and shy of this well-dressed, smooth, and gracefully-mannered minister. He kept silent, watching vaguely the many patterns of life moving swiftly past, trying to think and adapt himself to all that was happening.

—It's a pity, he heard the clergyman saying, and Johnny turned sideways to listen and show respect, a pity I didn't know of your brother's illness sooner.

That was all he said till they came to the hospital, and Johnny and the minister hurried into the hall. After mentioning his business to the porter, the minister went away with him, coming back after about ten minutes, talking earnestly to a white-robed doctor, who shook hands with the minister, saying, Anytime — the sooner the better. You're lucky to have been given a bed.

They hurried out to the car again, and were off, trotting back to Johnny's home.

—Well, said the clergyman, we've got him in as a patient. God send we haven't been too late.

Johnny murmured a shy amen, feeling that that much should be said in return for the minister's kindness.

When they got back, Johnny found Georgie Middleton humming a hymn (which instantly stopped when they entered), like a heathen priest mumbling an incantation; and Johnny could see well that he had been frightened of the sick man, deliriously raving, for a strained look of anxiety vanished clean off his face when they came in, and his hands got busy, pretending to straighten out the creases in the bedclothes. His mother, lying on the old sofa opposite, slumbered heavily, her black hair tossed, her hands twitching a little, and her breast regularly heaving with the happiness of sleep.

When the new minister saw she was asleep, he held up his hand warningly, and whispered, Let her sleep on, now, and take her rest; for the time may come when sleep will be far from her. We'll try to get him off without waking her, and I'll leave a note saying everything's all right. Let me see, now: we'll wrap him like a mummy in the blankets, and bind him with the sheets round the middle and under the knees to hamper his twisting. You, Georgie, help me to roll him in the blankets, and you, he added, turning to Johnny, help hold him when he's in them, while I bind them together with the sheets.

Georgie, with much panting, wrapped the thin blankets round Tom, while the new minister twisted the sheets to make them into long dirty-white scarves.

—Careful, sir, careful, murmured Johnny; don't test them too far; they're very far gone, and they're all we have.

The new minister went to work, binding Tom tightly into the blankets, so that only his arms could move, taking no notice of his ceaseless, raving, disconnected babble.

—Now, said the new minister, when Tom had been firmly trussed, Georgie, you'll have to go with this young man, here, to the hospital to help him on the way. I can't, for I've got to be at a Vestry Meeting in a short time. When I say the word, lift together. We'll leave the poor tired mother sleeping. Are you ready? Now!

They lifted him from the room, through the hall, out into the street, forced him into the cab, and stretched him down as well as he'd go on one of the seats, Johnny holding his head, and Georgie holding on to his legs to keep him from rolling off again.

—I'll pull the windows up, said the new minister, doing it as he spoke, and don't dare open one of them till he's safe in the hospital; and turning to the cabman, said smartly, Addlelaid, my man, quick as you can.

—Nothing terribly infectious? growled the driver.

—Nothing. Now off with you at full speed. Georgie has the fare, he added to Johnny.

Johnny tried to keep his eyes off the things that stuck out over the bulky, tossed-about bundle of clothes — a greenish feverish face, glaring eyes aglitter, and a drooling mouth sending out a stream of never-ending words that meant nothing. By and by the heat of the sick body began to fill the closed-up space of the cab with a warmth that distended Johnny's stomach, making him feel as if he were in the tropical glasshouse of a garden, tight shut, the heat mixing with the smell of palms slowly rotting away. So the heat here was tinged with an earthy smell, suffocating, sickening; the heat rising in vapour, covering the cab windows with a thick unhealthy mist, mirroring everything that passed by as vaporous, sinister shadows. Soon the sweat began to run down Johnny's brow and down his belly; and through the sweaty mist he could see that Middleton's face was turning yellow, and that his mouth had tightened, telling Johnny that he, too, was tightening his muscles to keep his belly from heaving. Sometimes Johnny's hand would steal out to open a window; but after what the new minister had said, he was afraid that a draught of air might bring death to Tom; and he prayed that the lack of it wouldn't bring death to him. Would they never reach the damned hospital? He bent over towards Georgie, and whispered, Where 'r' we now? But Georgie's mouth stayed tight, and his hands stayed clenched. Johnny, gasping, could imagine how the slaves felt, packed below-deck in the slave-ship; or how the poor sinner felt on his first arrival in hell; mistily seeing that Middleton had wrenched his shirt-collar open, and that his hair was wet and lank and lustreless; while Johnny bent himself as far as he could go to press his belly into a smaller space, and keep himself from puking. But the end came at last when they reached the hospital, the driver jumping down, running over to the big door, and ringing the deep bell.

—Go on, get out, quick, man, and bring them here with a stretcher, cried Georgie frantically, till we loose ourselves from this terrible burden!

Johnny climbed out, shutting the door behind him; but his stomach turned over, and running to the far side of the cab, he had to let himself be sick, scraping it with his foot, like a cat, in a vain effort to hide it a little, feeling a sharp shame, and wiping his slavered mouth in the sleeve of his coat as he hurried in to tell the porter all the details about his brother.

Two men came with a stretcher, pulled Tom from the cab, and carried him into the hospital, away down a long dark corridor; while Johnny sat down on a bench, pale and shaking, fearing every second that he was about to be sick again. After some time, Georgie Middleton came over and stood beside him.

—I have th' blankets an' sheets safe in th' cab, he said; I can do nothin' more here, so I'm goin'. Have you got your tram fare home?

—No, said Johnny, I haven't a make.

—I've only got th' six shillings Mr. Fletcher gave me for the fare;

and I daren't break in on that; and a solitary wing. Here, he said, after a pause, stretching out a penny towards Johnny, take it — it'll take you half-way home anyway.

—I don't want your wing, said Johnny proudly.

—Oh, aw right, he answered awkwardly. I hope the poor brother'll be awright, soon, Jack, he added; goodbye, old chap; and he left Johnny to his thoughts.

He sat there for a long time trying to think of something out of Milton, or Shakespeare, or Burns, to keep his mind off his uneasy stomach, till a smart young white-coated man with keen eyes came into the hall, looked around, and came over to where Johnny was sitting.

—You're the representative of Thomas Casside? Oh, you are. Why, in the name of God, didn't you bring your brother sooner?

—We thought the hospital couldn't find room for him, answered Johnny.

—Always the same, murmured the doctor testily; couldn't this and couldn't that — always an excuse. Did you try? he asked sharply.

—We thought it would be no use tryin', said Johnny.

—You thought! Oh, of course you did! What have you people got to do with thinking? Do you know your brother's dying?

Curious how they always blame us, thought Johnny resentfully. Had we kept him a little longer to die, there'd have been nothing about it. He would have died silently; would have been buried silently; and, bar a few tears from his mother, he would have been silently forgotten.

—We guessed he was dying, said Johnny out loud.

—Oh, you did, did you? Why did you bring him here, then?

—Our new minister made us.

—He did, did he? And you jumped at the chance to get rid of a nuisance, eh? And you expect us to cure him, eh? Well, you have great expectations! You fetch him here when his lungs are nothing but a crackling bunch of bloodied crêpe, and you expect us to cure him!

—We don't expect anything! cried Johnny hotly. Yous won't even let us die quiet. The new minister rushed in on us, ordered everything, did everything! Give us enough to pay for a cab back, an' I'll bring him home again! And Johnny lepped from the bench, flushed and stormy, to stare angrily at the astonished doctor.

—There, there, boy, said the Doctor, drawing in his horns a little. I daresay it can't be helped. You've given us a hard job without the ghost of a chance to do any good. Who minded him?

—His mother.

—Well, she kept his body quite clean, and made him decent to handle, anyway.

—Give us the cab fare, repeated Johnny doggedly, and I'll carry him home again.

—Oh, sit down, sit down, and don't get your rag out. Stay there till you hear the worst; or, if a miracle happens, till you're told you may go home. And he went away humming, I Hear You Calling Me.

Johnny sat down, with head bent, on the bench, trying to think of things that had happened to him long, long ago, seeing them in fleeting and patchy colours, of a red-and-black draughtboard tartan petticoat he had worn at five years of age, making him look like a kid of the Rob Roy Macgregor clan; of when he, Ella, Archie, and Mick were down with the scarlet fever at the one time; and of how their mother had safely nursed them through it all by herself; even making Tom lie with Mick, who had it the worst, so that he might get it too, and so enable her to get the damned thing over once for all; and of the terrible time they had had, when they were well, standing in the street, watching the men disinfect the little house, sealing up doors and windows, and lighting sulphur in the rooms, so that the place stank for months afterwards — but he mustn't be thinking of sickness; and of handling almost the first Lee-Metford rifle the English Army had, brought home for show by his brother-in-law because he was a first-class shot; and of watching him put in the clip of cartridges, and ejecting the bullet from the chamber by drawing the bolt; and seeing him fix the dagger-like bayonet on the muzzle of the new gun.

A middle-aged man, with a merry grin on his bearded face, came out of the corridor into the hall. He nodded pleasantly to Johnny, and kept brushing his jerry hat vigorously with the sleeve of his coat. Presently he came close to Johnny, sent a swift look down the corridors, bent down low to whisper.

—Yeh, phih, he whispered in a whistling way, there's more duffers nor doctors here. He opened his mouth, wide as it could go, in front of Johnny's face, and closed it again. See? A dark spot at the butt o' th' tongue. Want to make out it's cancer. I know different, see? Kep' me in till now to see a specialist. Wastin' me time. I'm afraid it is, says he. Pah! He bent down closer to Johnny's ear and whispered, when I was younger, I was too free with the ladies — that's what it is. But I'm not here to teach them; let them find out for themselves; and he went towards the door. Cancer, me neck! he exploded as he disappeared.

Good God! there was the gong-like clock striking eleven. How long were they going to keep him here?

He half closed his eyes, and again thought back through the years, remembering how often he'd gone along the dusty, weary road to the Pigeon House Fort, passing in through the gateway and through the courtyard, glancing at the old guns sticking their snouts through older portholes, like aged fools thinking themselves for ever young; of picking cockles on the brown strand; of lying on the silvery dunes, in the sun, careful of the speary grass that grew there, sharp as surgeons' knives; or of walking along the breakwater, mighty with well-laid, wide, and deep granite blocks, dark-brown nets spread all over it to dry, velvety emerald-green seaweed tangled in their meshes, like locks from the hair of a mermaid raped off in the bed of the sea; or, when the day danced swift with the wind and the tide came ahead in a hurry, sending shouting waves over the side, their tops breaking out into silver, shaking salty showers over his head, like a sharp, laughing chrism from God.

He shivered; he was getting cold, sitting here so long. He'd think of something warmer than the spray of the sea; or of going to Beggars Bush Barracks to see his brother-in-law at Christmas-time, and sitting in a big room, before a roaring fire, on a cold wet night, waiting for the Cloak Call to go so that his brother could leave, wearing his heavy coat; watching the men confined to barracks decorating the room; hanging dark-brown and grey blankets on the walls, fixing squares and ovals of silvered cardboard on them; and, here and there, splashing these squares and ovals of silver with lovely Merry Christmases and Happy New Years in holly berries threaded together, and cunningly fixed to the cardboard with pins. Other soldiers were making paper chains of divers patterns and many colours to cross and re-cross the room just under the ceiling; most of them radiating from a huge golden star in the centre, which was flanked by a smaller silver one at each corner of the room. From the ceiling, too, hung hundreds of thin threads, barely visible, carrying little tufts of the whitest wool, thousands and thousands of them, making it look for all the world as if it was snowing thick and fast; Johnny's brother-in-law standing restlessly at the door, waiting for the bugle-call, while Johnny was eager to stay and tire his eyes out with long and lasting looks at the beautiful things around him.

Then through the babble of the working soldiers came the sudden sound of the bugle-call, Benson's quick, last pull at his coat to make sure the folds were right, his impatient, Come on, me laddo, and the passing away from the glowing fire, the blood-red berries, the rustle of the gaily-coloured chains, the golden star and the silver, out into the wide, cold, bleak square, with the rain falling steadily, passing the sentry, standing stiff, like a drab mummy, in his box, out through the gaping gate, hurrying away to where the tram stopped so as to be in time at the market, before the geese were gone.

Twelve! There's the gong-like clock striking the hour of twelve! The poor oul' wan must be worn out, waiting for news. Well, if Tom hadn't passed out by now, there should be some hope. It was wrong, really, to keep the poor old woman in suspense. They should be able to say, one way or the other. He felt himself falling, and pulled up with a jerk. Jasus! He was falling asleep. He forced his eyes open. The whole place was dim. They'd darkened the hospital for the night. A little dull red glow starred the darkness at the end of each corridor; and a pale dusky jet in the hall barely gave him enough light to make out the walls. He hoped he wasn't going to be kept there till the dawn of day. A new day was here already. Night's candles are burnt out, and jocund day stands tiptoe on the misty mountain-tops. It would hardly be a jocund day for him. What's this the next line was? How the hell did it go? Oh, no use of trying to think out Shakespeare here. Where pain was host, there was no room for poethry.

Strange how the glimmer of little things reminded you of bigger things hid in the heavily-veiled mystery of the past! The tiny pale-blue glimmer dodging the deeper darkness of the hall reminded him of poor little Finnigan's wake, and all that went before it. How a group of them were playing madly on a slope bordering the canal, and Finnigan running down it, couldn't stop, and when he came to the canal's edge, took a frightened lep that landed him with a horrible splash into the middle of it! He could still see the pale bewildered agony of the boy's face, his arms wildly threshing the water, making it foam around; and the ripples circling over it when the little head sank down again, to be threshed into a wild agitation when the head broke through to the surface for the second time. He saw again one frantic boy madly pulling up some bulrushes growing by the side, and throwing them out to the drowning lad, thinking they might be of some use to him, unmindful of his bleeding hands where the fine edges of the bulrushes tore through his flesh. He had shouted to a group of men playing cards in a field near by, and Mick had come racing along, throwing off his hat and coat, and tearing off a collar and tie as he ran, never pausing, but jumping up from the edge and coming down in a dive with the skill of a kingfisher, right in the centre of the rippling centre where

Finnigan had gone down for the last time. He saw the boy again when Mick had ferried him out, standing, bent double, on the bank, water cascading from his wide-open, gasping mouth, his legs shaking, his teeth chattering, his eyes staring, a torrent of sobs tormenting his breast, and he spluttering out that he daren't go home; that they'd morgue him for fallin' in, an' he'd stay where he was till his clothes dhried, so that no-one would be th' wiser when he got home.

So all day, there he sat shivering, his friends sitting in a circle round him to hide his nakedness; and when his friends left him in the evening, he still sat on, waiting for a later hour to go home, and slip to bed without anyone knowing what had happened to him; sat there when the stars were out, with a damp shirt on him, and the rest of his clothes hanging from the arm of a lock; sat there shivering, with all the lonely company of night around him.

Some time after, Finnigan fell ill, and was dead in no time; and Johnny went to see him; going into the little room where he lay cosy in his coffin, its deep yellow sides richly polished, the brass handles, wherever the glow from the tall wax candles crept to them, gleaming like genuine gold.

—Come closer, alanna, said Finnigan's mother, an' see how little he's changed. Come closer, for he was fond of you; and it was your own brave brother saved his life.

The smell of the room, a blend of whiskey, tea, the polish on the coffin, and the wax of the virgin candles, filled his nostrils as he came closer to see the face of his young friend changing, slowly changing, to the silent, steady face, the face of his brother, his brother Tom; and as he was stirred with amazement, he thought he heard a sombre voice saying sharply, Get up, who are you, and what are you doing here? This isn't a night shelter for the homeless.

Dimly he saw a young-looking nurse staring down at him, her hand on his shoulder, shaking him.

—What do you do here? she asked. There, the clock is striking two!

—Waiting to hear about my brother, miss. He was brought here as a patient, and I was ordered to wait for fear he'd die.

—Well, she said, you can't wait any longer. They have forgotten all about you. It was stupid of you to wait so long. Here, hurry off, and get to bed.

—He may be dead, nurse, so I'd betther make certain before I go. By waiting so long, I've earned that little privilege.

—What's his name; what's the patient's name? she asked impatiently.

—Casside, Thomas Casside, nurse.

She hastened down the dark corridor, leaving him on his feet, swaying a little, his legs cramped and cold, his eyes heavy with sleep, in the dusky hall of the hospital. After a long, long time she came hurrying back.

—The patient is still the same, she said rapidly. Dangerously ill; but still the same. She drew back a heavy bolt, swung the door open; and he passed out to wander sleepily through the empty streets, with the forlorn message soaking his mind in uneasiness.

When he got home, he found his mother sitting by the fire, humming a tune; the kettle humming another on the hob. He sat down on a chair, and stretched out his cold, damp, stiff hands to the fire.

—They made me wait, he said, to see if he would die. He's holding out yet.

—I know, she said. You shouldn't have waited so long. Hours ago, an easy peace came on me, and I knew he wouldn't die. You take this cup of tea, now, and don't worry.

WORK WHILE IT IS NOT YET DAY

A LETTER from the new minister had got Johnny a job as vanboy in the great wholesale firm of Jason & Son, wholesale newspaper, magazine, stationery, fancy goods, books, and hymnbook merchants, that gave employment to hundreds. This was his first morning at his new work. He was to begin at a quarter to four, an' finish God knew when.

The alarm clock, lying on its face, gave a muffled r-r-ring, as if it was getting a cold, and his mother's voice called out, Johnny, it's three; there, it's ringing for you to get up.

Silently he got up and dressed himself quick by candlelight, for it was very cold. It had snowed heavily all the day before, and it was freezing now. Rapidly he slipped on his trousers, socks, boots, collar and tie, waistcoat and coat, and, finally, a muffler his mother had bought to keep his throat and chest warm. He'd have to get a good topcoat, if the job lasted. He slipped Part One of O'Growney's *Simple Lessons in Irish* into his breast pocket, hoping to get an odd squint at it in some quiet corner while he worked. The tram conductor he had heard singing about Wolfe Tone, the night of the illuminations, had given it to him during a theatrical night in the stable of Hill Street, saying, I couldn't make anything out of it; but you're young, and everyone should know the language of his country; ending be him singing with his head up, lookin' at th' sky, and Johnny's hand clasped in his, all because Johnny was a protestant,

> English deceit can rule us no more,
> Bigots and knaves are scattered like spray —
> Deep was the oath the Orangeman swore,
> Orange and Green must carry the day!
> Orange, Orange,
> Green an' Orange!
> Never to falter an' never bethray —
> With an amen, we swear it again,
> Orange an' Green will carry the day!

Johnny hunched himself together when he opened the street door, and stepped out into the lonely loveliness of the snowy-shy streets, bitterly gay in the throngs of frosty gems that had blossomed on the bosom of the snow. Each window-pane passed had within its narrow boundaries a silvery city with a host of delicate pinnacles, a wilderness of fragile ferns, or an interlaced forest of fairy trees. The houses looked like stout and steady dames, clad in jet-black velvet, with ample snowy wimples draped on their sturdy heads, and pools of gaslight gave a dusky yellow glow to some, like old gold bows fastened on them to set them off, and show there was a touch of gaiety in them still; while overhead hung a deep and densely purple-black sky shaking out fire from a swarm of glittering stars, as if God were shaking out the golden crumbs from the richly-woven cloth covering His holy table. A poor boy walking in a silver way, canopied by velvet, purple-black, and dizzily pendent with a weight of jewels that dared the wondering eye.

As he walked along, crushing the frosty gems beneath his feet, he thought of the Irish lessons he was learning: Atá bó in san gurth, there is a cow in the field; agus atá sí bán, And she is white. Quite easy, really, when you get goin'. Seán was his name in Irish; his right name, and not John at all. Atá Seán óg agus laidir, agus atá sé fuar. Sean is young and strong, and he is cold — that's thrue, anyway. I wondher what the new minister would say, if he caught him speaking Irish? A Fenian, he'd say, a Fenian! Ignorance, pure ignorance, laughed Johnny; a man speaking Irish can be as loyal to Queen and country as anyone else. A decent minister, though, that had made a great conquest of Johnny. He had won Johnny back to the faith of his baptism; to become once more Christ's faithful soldier and servant.

He was sanctifying his kinship with God through the Sacraments, through public worship, through prayer, and through the Scriptures. God would help him, and make this new job he had a stay to the home, now that Tom was idle, having been dismissed because of a strike; and Archie was away on a tour with a *Saved From the Sea* company on one-night stands in the smaller towns of the west and south.

Under the guidance of Harry Fletcher, he had passed through the rite of Confirmation; his head had been touched by the hand of a bishop in the Church of the Twelve Apostles; he had renewed his baptismal vows openly; had helped in the singing of *Veni Creator Spiritus*; and he had received a fuller grace from the Holy Ghost. The day had been a lovely sunny one, in early spring. The hedges and gardens of Clontarf were full of life; the birds were all excitement; the leaves of the trees kept up a whispering chatter with a gentle breeze that ran in and out among them, as Johnny and his companion, Nicholas Stitt, trudged to the church. He passed curly-headed Jenny Clitheroe, quite a young woman now, walking with several companions to the church too. He raised his cap timidly as he passed, and glanced shyly at her; but she closed her eyes, and gave a little disdainful toss to her head. A lady-girl cashier in Sir John Arnott's select drapery house, he was too poor for a nod from her, as she went her way to church, in her green dress, with the walk of a queen.

The church was packed with people, and the organ was singing soft music when they were guided to their seat by the tall, kind, and handsome Harry Fletcher, looking fine in his short white surplice and long, heavy black cassock sweeping gravely round his silken-slippered feet. The girls sat in rows on one side of the nave, becomingly dressed in blue, black, or dark green, with lacy veils on their heads, flowing over their shoulders and down their backs. The boys sat on the other side, trying to look solemn, unconcerned, or confident, all in their best, with tidied hair, white collars, and sternly-polished boots.

From the big east window ahead of him, there were the twelve apostles, baked in brightly-coloured glass, looking down on them, carnivalled in bellalluring robes of blue, yellow, red, green, black, brown, purple, orange, Hebrew umber, Chinese white, and Hindoo crimson, glowing like titan tulips in a Persian garden. The sunlight, now, came strolling through them, their eager faces shone with a thousand tints, their coloured cloaks rippled as if blown by a gentle breeze from heaven, their limbs quivered as if they were about to step forward in a sparkling procession over the heads of the congregation. Rays, like tongues of fire, from their coloured cloaks, flooded and swept away the demure modesty of the lacy girlish caps, joyously changing the sober little ladies into radiant lassies, waiting for the gong to go to dance. But the apostles came not forth, dallying till the sun suddenly slackened; then the sparkling hues faded, and they became again figments of coloured glass, jailed in a leaded window, gorgeous only when the sun was bright with a brotherly interest.

Then they began to go up in pairs, kneeling together at the altar rails to let the bishop lay a hand on each head, and dedicate them anew to God's service. When Johnny knelt there, and felt the soft, white, plump hand of the bishop, peering out from gently-scented lawn that had never smelled from the evil smear of a bed bug, he knew that he had got his first great share in the priesthood and kingship of Christ.

There was the dark form of Nelson looming up before him, now, thrusting his haughty head into the purple sky, looming like a rod of discipline over the people, out of the dark, in Dublin, Ireland's sailor boy, one arm missing and one eye gone; but watching with that one eye the slum kid rolling in the mud; the lady or gentleman rolling round in carriage and pair; the red-slippered bishop in flaunting canonicals on his way to say High Mass in his cathedral; the bobby bringing a drunk safe home to the police station; the bloated, blossom-faced whores waiting for randy men to go with them to the stews to see the sights: high he stands there, while Wolfe Tone's first memorial stone lies deep buried at the head of Grafton Street. And as Johnny goes by, he seems to sink as he sank down on the deck of the *Victory*, saying, Kiss me, Hardy, kiss me quick, me spine is spearsed; remember Emma, pip, pip, hurrah!

Johnny was soon beside the long outspread pile of Jason's wholesale department, with its rusty red-brown front, grated heavily on the side walk to admit the heavy bales of goods; and, sliding up, he mixed himself with about thirty lads and men, leaning sleepily against the front of the warehouse, waiting for the time to come to begin. The stars had gone now; the sky had lost its tinge of purple, having turned into a heavy sludge of thick darkness, and broad and wavering flakes of snow were falling fast.

—Who's th' boss here? he asked of a short man with brown bulgy eyes, now half closed, his head nodding as he leaned against the wall.

—Show-a-leg, he answered drowsily.

—Show-a-leg? Why's he called that?

—You'll see when you see him, he answered.

Presently, Johnny saw them push themselves away from the wall, and turn shivery faces towards the wide door. Out of the soaking darkness came a fat squat figure, hidden in a long thick coat, side by side with a smaller squat one, both moving in a rolling waddle to the door. The bigger figure put a big key into the keyhole, whistling lightly as he did so, swung the double doors back, and led the troop of sleepy men and boys, coughing the damp cold out of their lungs, into a vast cavern of inner darkness that pressed heavily down on Johnny's heart.

—Anyone's got a match, light the lights, said a thin hoarse voice that came from the dumpy figure, an' th' rest o' you stand by to take th' papers.

Johnny heard the scrunching of nailed boots on wood, the striking of matches; then several feebly flaming gas-jets crept out of the gloom, showing in the dimness a vast room traversed with many wide coarse benches. In the centre, high over the benches, ran a glass-panelled roomy corridor, reached by stairs that were first cousin to a ladder. Here, later in the day, the real Boss had his perch, with his clerks sitting in two rows, back to back, looking down through the windows on their more hard-working brothers in the vast and worried room below.

In the shadowy dimness Johnny saw the squat figures, as in a glass darkly, taking off their topcoats; but when they had waddled into a timid pool of yellow gaslight, he saw that the bigger one was short and stout, with a head as big as the globe of the world in a first-class school, and as beautifully bald, set on a neck that was no neck at all; he had tiny eyes that glittered like smoky sparks, and were half hidden by beetling brows, as if over each a portcullis was about to drop and close both of them up for ever; but most remarkable of all were the thick legs curving out from the hips in such a bandy way that, when his two clumsy feet met below, his legs formed a perfect circle, as good as any correct compass could draw. When he walked, he seemed to be a huge, badly-made ball rolling along over uneven ground. These circular legs leered horribly whenever they wobbled into a pool of light, for they were enshrined in a pair of highly-polished black leggings reaching to his crooked knees. The smaller figure of his son showed himself a thinner copy of the fat father, the big head, the smoky glitter of the eyes, the bitter brows, the splendidly circular legs, covered in knickerbockers and thin black cotton stockings. Both of them perpetually wore conceited grins, ever putting a jaunty air into their waddling, evidently finding a lot wrong with the straighter legs, normal heads, and natural necks of most other poor men.

A van drove up with a cargo of *Irish Times,* followed by others filled with *Irish Independents* and *Freemans' Journals,* men and boys hurrying out, and coming back staggering under loads of papers on their shoulders, and dumping them on the various benches. Here other men, holding invoices in their hands, called out rapidly the papers required by country agents; others counted out the papers with great speed from the heaps on the benches, throwing them on brown paper wrappings to be snatched up by others, and parcelled up for the vans to take them to the several railway stations. It was hurry here and hurry there, carrying, dumping down, calling out, selecting, wrapping up, tying, pasting of labels, and flinging the finished parcels of papers into their different bins; and in the midst of the stress waddled Show-a-leg and his son, both of them looking like what you'd surely sometimes see prowling about in the dim time of life, among the swishy reeds, the tangled ferns, and the seamy shade of slimy mosses.

The twisted father and the twisted son put a gayer stir into their movements than any of the others, working with a sinisterly merry energy that wasn't merry at all; aimed at showing that such an early hour should have no terrors for manly men; seeming to make of the dismal gaslight, full of hiding shadows, a port of call for sunny places, dancing girls, and the perfume of many blossoms. Many of the sleepy ones stiffened up straight, slyly borrowing some of Show-a-leg's twisted gaiety, coaxing quickness into their tired bodies; the *miserere meuses* trying to look like kids galloping about for the first time on the golden sands of the seashore; while outside in the darkness the snow fell swiftly in ribbonlike streamers, looking from where they worked like white painted bars stretching across the prison-faced entrance to the warehouse.

Johnny was quietly shoved about so's he'd look ridiculous before the twisted toads. Parcels to be made up were snatched away just as he stretched out a hand to get them; the twine was always in the hands of another when he wanted it; and the paste seemed a mile away when he had to fix a label. Grinning, they all watched Johnny testing his way to be one of them, with the bandy-legged one glowering at him curiously, giving a cue to the rest for a wider grin whenever he nodded his head doubtfully towards Johnny.

—Come along; look alive, boy; take the sleep outa your eyes; leering at Johnny's hesitation to push aside a hand snatching the twine, or a brush from the paste-pot. Pounce on it, pounce, boy, he roared, an' don't stand like a dead three on a lonely road! Is it a special bench you want with a staff to hand you out the work, or what? Here, gripping Johnny's arm, watch how it's done; see? Johnny watching the sagging, puffy cheeks, the tiny glittering eyes, wished for a red-hot iron to make jelly of them. Now, off you go — oh, you've missed that too! Here, you'd break my patience! Go out and carry in the news-papers, for I'm afraid you'll never be quicker nor an oul' aged coolie!

So midst the voices calling out ten *Independents*, twenty *Freemen*, five *Irish Times*, five *Freemen*, twenty *Independents*, ten *Times*, twenty *Times*, five *Independents*, ten *Freemen*; the crackling of brown paper as the papers were wrapped up in them; the swish of the brushes as the labels were pasted on; the scratching of tired feet over the rough boards; the thud of horses' hooves, timid of the frost under them; the inspiring hisss-hissss of Show-a-leg, as if he were currying a horse in a stable — Johnny joined the line of men and boys following each other, bearing burdens of newspapers on their shoulders, like blacks in a jungle so that the whole of distant Ireland might know the newest news.

—Here, said Show-a-leg, suddenly gripping his arm, there's our own vans, at last; load up your van for Kingsbridge, an' look smart. Get a barrow, get a barrow!

Johnny strolled over, struggling to walk with dignity, to a barrow by the side of the warehouse. He stooped down to pick up the pull of the four-wheeler, but a shove on the shoulder sent him to sit on the floor, tempting a loud titter out of the onlookers, and he heard a voice in his ear, saying, Away, wee mon; away to Hull! This is for the Northern — 'way ow'r thot!

Belfast bowsey, trying to please his boss, thought Johnny. He walked about for a bit, looking for another barrow; but they seemed to be all rattling about, some filled with parcels, taking them to the vans; some returning empty for another load. He came back to where the boss was busily loading a barrow.

—All the barrows are engaged, sir, he said.

—It's funny how I could get one, isn't it? Show-a-leg answered. Here, take this one I've filled for you, slow-worm.

He'd take things quietly, if only for the sake of the new minister. After all, they were all children of the same Heavenly Father. Johnny seized the pull-handle of the barrow, and dragged it vehemently out into the falling snow, and on to the frost-bitten pavement. Furiously, he flung parcels into the van till it could hold no more, even with a tarpaulin stretched over to keep them steady and tight.

—Up with you, now, said oul' bandy-legs, an' take your load to the station. Keep your eye on him, he added to the vanman, for God's sake, for he's so innocent he'd deliver the lot to the Mendicity Institution if he wasn't watched!

—I've got more'n enough to do to keep th' horse on his feet, grumbled the vanman, an' he with his legs ready to go every way at once on the icy roads.

They were off, going at a careful canter down the street, round on to the Northern quays, the driver sitting tense, the horse sweating with fear whenever his hooves slipped on the shining road. Several times he was nearly down, but some way or other the driver saved him, digging his teeth into his lower lip as he drove, and cursing the frost deeply when the horse was trotting safely again.

The snow had stopped falling; the black sky had brightened to a purple-bluish hue over their heads, and a silver road slid away under their feet. A darker line below them showed the river Liffey flowing slowly by, here and there a little brighter with dimly-shimmering patches of floating ice. Past the Four Courts, a big black building looking as if it budded out of the purple sky; or was stretching up to get the counsel of Heaven into its ass's ear; the blinded figure of Justice looking out over the whory hills of oul' Ireland; over the bridge, its icy covering sparkling in the lights from the passing van, making it a straight turning into a fairyland of snowy people living in ice-made houses; out quick again into the goods' yard of the Great Southern, pulling up, with a loud whoa, before the wide gate of the parcels office.

—I'll be glad when this cursed frost is over, said the vanman, pacing about, stamping his feet, clapping his red and swollen hands against his shoulders, while Johnny piled the parcels on the counter to be checked; me mitts is frozen; as cold as a kiss from a dead woman.

—You'd want gloves, murmured Johnny sympathetically.

—Where'd I get gloves on fourteen bob a week? queried the vanman peevishly. Gloves! Tell me that, will yeh?

—I don't know, said Johnny.

—Yeh don't know, eh? Well, neither do I. D'ye expect a man of fourteen shillin's a week to be rowled in rugs like Charlie Jason? Kid ones, maybe, you'd like to see me sportin'. Well, I haven't gone as low as that yet. Eh, he added, turning to the checker, didya hear what he's afther saying — that I should be wearin' gloves!

—Steel gauntlets up to the elbow, he'd like to see us wearin' maybe, said the checker mockingly.

—Heavy leather, lined with the softest chamois, an' thrimmed with fur 'ud give us freer movement, said the vanman.

—An' twenty tiny mother-o'-pearl buttons on the wrist, added the checker.

—An' tassels near the thumbs, laughed the vanman.

—An' sturdy muffs to pack the glovely hands in when the cold gets colder, said the checker.

—An' furry flounces round our necks as well, said the vanman, to keep our diddies warm.

—Will the young prophet tell how we wor' to work for our employers got up in a get-up like that? asked the checker, leaning over his counter to get a closer look at Johnny. No, he went on, going back to the sorting of the parcels, when it's cold, it's cold; and the burden's there to be borne.

—An' th' Man Above is always there to the fore, murmured the vanman.

—An' th' Man Above is always there to the fore, echoed the checker.

—Here, up with you again, said the vanman to Johnny, and let's get back. Th' Man Above never meant any of us to be one of the gloved brigade.

Out they were again, trotting with decent haste between the rows of sable buildings, on the sparkling silver road, and under the purple sky. On a night something like this, thought Johnny, the King of All, the Giver of Life, the Prince of Peace was born. Under a slantin' roof He was, sheltered from the snowy ground an' warmed by the heat of the animals who danced all the livelong night with the dancin' stars; the bare trees, shovin' aside the terrifying frost, blossomed, and hung out fruits for one night only, strikin' all frost-hardened thravellers with wonder an' fear; crowds of wild flowers sprang up through the snow, an' bent their coloured faces towards where the little Infant lay; the frozen brooks snapped their icy coverings, brimful of song as they tarried or hurried in their flowing; and many there were who stood still to listen, for they wist not what had happened when they heard a brook breaking into song:

> The Lord of all life from His heaven has come,
> Sing out, sing loud, sing merry, sing long;
> Without note from a fife or a beat from a drum,
> Sing out, sing merry, sing all;
> The Lord of all life in His mercy has come
> To save merry man from his murdherous fall,
> Sing out, sing all!

Th' winter-worn trees are all sprightly again,
Sing out, sing loud, sing merry, sing long;
Ripe apples hang there, with red cherries for men,
Sing out, sing merry, sing all;
Only death became lonely, and hurried off when
Jesus came to save man from his murdherous fall,
Sing out, sing all!

The rolling stars reel about, drunken with glee,
Sing out, sing loud, sing merry, sing long!
The slow-moving cattle dance jigs on the lea,
Sing out, sing merry, sing all!
And panting birds, coming from rooftop and tree,
Sing of man's rise from his murdherous fall,
Sing out, sing all!

Kings of great multitudes come from afar,
Sing out, sing loud, sing merry, sing long;
With gifts of three kinds in a fresh golden car,
Sing out, sing merry, sing all;
And rich-scented spice in a diamond-clad jar,
For Him who saves man from his murdherous fall,
Sing out, sing all!

Sprinkle His home with green laurels and yew,
Sing out, sing loud, sing merry, sing long;
With red berries of holly and mistletoe too,
Sing out, sing merry, sing all;
For there's nothing now missing from me or from you,
Since He came to save man from his murdherous fall,
Sing out, sing all!

Play on the dulcimer, harp, and the horn,
Sing out, sing loud, sing merry, sing long;
Th' poor Devil's looking both haggard and lorn,
Sing out, sing merry, sing all;
For Jesus lies happy asleep in the corn,
The Saviour of man from his murdherous fall,
Sing out, sing all!

Bring out the ould fiddle and play him a tune,
Sing out, sing loud, sing merry, sing long;
Cold December's at one with young hot-headed June,
Sing out, sing merry, sing all;

For th' curse of our birth has been chang'd to a boon,
Since He came to save man from his murdherous fall,
Sing out, sing all!

White linen we'll give to the Virgin so fair,
Sing out, sing loud, sing merry, sing long;
And a bonny bright comb for her radiant hair,
Sing out, sing merry, sing all;
For the Babe a red cross, with a rattle and ball,
To show how we're sav'd from our murdherous fall,
Sing out, sing all!

He brought the Kingdom of Heaven to the heart of man, thought Johnny, an' —

Suddenly, his thoughts were scattered violently out of his head as he was jerked out of the van, and went sprawling on to the road, thrusting out his hands to save his head so that the palms tore over the frost-covered cobbles, scraping the skin in ragged patches from them, the frost biting into the bleeding flesh, making him feel a little sick as he lay still where he had fallen.

—Eh, get up an' lend us a hand, an' don't lie dhreamin' there! he heard the voice of the vanman shouting.

He dragged himself up from the thorny frost and saw the horse on the ground, entangled in the harness, with a shaft pressing into his belly, plunging about with fright in his eyes; while the vanman was struggling to force the horse down flat, keeping back from the frightened and frantic movements of the horse's head and feet.

—Come over, man, the vanman cried to Johnny, an' help me shove him over, so's I can sit on his head, an' keep him from breakin' a — yeh, yeh bitch's get! he roared at the horse, when the animal's plunging head knocked his shoulder, yeh nearly got me that time!

Johnny ran over, seized the struggling horse's head, daubing it with blood from his lacerated hands, and pushed with the vanman; but the power in the animal's neck was too strong, and he plunged about as wild as ever.

The first tram of the morning came jingling up and stopped beside them. The driver and conductor lepped off and came running over to help their brothers. The four of them pushed together, and the horse's head was slowly forced down flat on the frosty stones.

—Kneel on his head, now, said the vanman to Johnny, till we disjoin th' harness an' shove the van back; but for your life don't stir till I yell at you to jump clear.

Hurriedly and cleverly the three men unbuckled the harness, gently forced the van back till the shaft was clear of the horse's belly, then ran it swiftly to a safe distance. The vanman brought some sacks from the van and spread them out on the ground beside the animal, tucking in some of the edges under his hooves, so that when he tried to rise, his feet might get some kind of a grip on the icy stones. Then standing away, and holding the reins loosely, he shouted to Johnny to stand clear.

When the horse no longer felt Johnny sitting on him, he lifted his head, looked around, then rose, half sitting on his haunches, and with a sprawling, sliding movement, he jumped up, snorting, and stood shivering with fear and the cold, waiting to be put back into the van again. Then Johnny had time to see that the conductor was his old friend of the illuminations and the Irish Lesson Book.

—If y'ass me, said the driver, I'd say if I had Charlie Jason's money, I'd see me horse's hooves were well cocked before I'd let him thravel on an icy road like this.

—A stiff mornin' to be out undher the sky in, the conductor said, coming over, and shaking hands with Johnny. Betther times when we have our own again — Is sinn féin, sinn féin, he said. He bent down his head towards Johnny's ear. Good news about Fashoda, eh? The tricolour in the Soudan, eh? The French are on the say, they'll be here without delay, says the Sean Bhean bhocht — God deliver the good news quick, he added, turning an urgent face up to the dark sky. Goodbye, me son. And away the tram jingled towards the Gateway of the Phoenix Park, the conductor whistling the Marseillaise for all he was worth, and waving a hand to Johnny.

On his way home to breakfast, oul' Show-a-leg gave Johnny the job of pushing a handcart full of parcels to Amiens Street Station, for carriage to Belfast and intermediate places. Johnny swore deeply as he answered, Right y're, sir; but stopped short when he remembered his recent visit to Communion, feeling he'd broken the third commandment. From henceforth he must limit his communications to yea and nay, for more then these cometh of evil.

—Go on, push it, boy, he heard Show-a-leg shouting from the entrance; don't be afraid of it — push it along.

Johnny started it with a straining push through the snow, now lying seven or eight inches deep on path and roadway, going off with a prayer mumbling from his mouth that Show-a-leg might somehow escape from the worm that dieth not and the fire that couldn't be quenched.

It was hard going for him. The damp snow clung to his eyelids, forming a moist veil over them so that he could hardly see; besides, he often had to bend to give greater force to his push, making the soft snow slip so that his feet went from under him, jerking the parcels about in the road. Opposite the police station, in Store Street, he sat down on the shafts for a rest, taking out his little Irish book, bending carefully over it, so that the snow couldn't damage it, and tried to learn a few more words. Atá an sneachta a tuitim síos, he murmured, coining little sentences from what he saw around him. Agus deir Sé leis an tsneachta, bise ar an dtalamh, is mar sin abhi sé: And he said of the snow, be on the ground, and it was so. When I earn enough in the week, I must join the Gaelic League.

He got up from the shafts, shivering a little, and pushed hard on to where he was going. When he came to the long, steep slope leading to the platform of the Great Northern, he began to pant, and had to bend double to make the handcart move. Slower and slower it went; more and more he panted, till the cart stopped altogether; and he sat down again on the shaft to get back his breath. Weak for want of his breakfast — that's what it was. Since three, and it was now past eight, without a bite wasn't good enough. Six hours of hard goin' and he was still waiting for a cup of tea. His torn hands troubled him, too, sticking to the shafts when he held them too tight. He'd go bail the two Jasons weren't far from a fire. Even in warm weather they'd come in on cars, deep in rugs, mummified in thick topcoats and comforters, looking, all the while, like silent, miserable, bundled-up complaints to God. Acting, too, as if they'd been born in Bethlehem; for he'd read in a paper that one of them had taken the chair at a revival meeting given by the great Gineral Booth, who thought when he was sousing people with words he was sprinkling them with the blood of Christ, Who, in honour of their distant salaam, had decorated them with a nice house, warm clothes to wear, and fair things to eat from a white table-cloth the first thing in the morning. Well, the way of the Salvation Army wasn't his way. He didn't like their rough-and-tumble tribute to God; their turgid rush to Heaven; their way of shouting into the ear of Jesus; their rowdy way of pulling Him about to make Him face their way; their raucous manner of praise, like a drunken man bawling his unsteady way home; their ponderous thought that the more miserable and rotten they were, the more God thought of them.

—Eh, sir, Johnny called to a passer-by, muffled up to the eyes, and carrying an open umbrella to keep off the snowflakes, could you give us a shove up to the top of the slope? A Pharisee, he thought, as the figure carrying an umbrella, and muffled up to the eyes, went on, turning neither to the right nor to the left.

Carriages and cars and cabs packed high with trunks, cases, and rugs passed by, bearing snugly-clad persons to catch the next train to the north.

—Eh, sir, said Johnny to another muffled-up figure slouching along on the snowy footpath, could you give us a hand to shove this up to the top of the slope?

The muffled figure turned towards him, a red nose rose out of the depths of a black muffler, looking like the beak of a bird poking over the edge of its nest, and a cold voice answered, You shouldn't take a job if you aren't fit to do the work the job entails; the nose sunk down again, the muffled figure turned aside and went on its way to the station.

Johnny seized the shafts again, pushing hard, pushing harder, pushing his hardest; but the cart never moved an inch ahead. He sat down again, holding up his hot face so that the cool snowflakes might fall on it and calm his temper. An outside car, now, came trotting down on its way back to the stand to wait for another fare. The driver was so muffled up that his thick scarf seemed to meet the rim of his jerry hat, making him look as if the horse and car were carrying off an empty, tied-up bundle of clothes. It stopped beside Johnny, and he heard a voice from between hat and scarf saying, Can yeh not get up?

—No, said Johnny, an' I don't know what to do. Out since three, and haven't had me breakfast yet.

The jarvey jumped down, swung his horse round to face the station, took some thick cord from under a cushion, and tied one end to the axle and the other to the tailboard of Johnny's cart.

—Keep a tight grip of your shafts, he said, an' we'll be where you're goin' in a second. He sprang on to his seat again, and away went the horse at a quick trot, making Johnny's arms crack with the effort he had to make to keep a firm grip on the shafts of the handcart that went ploughing through the snow. When they were safely under the huge roof of the station, Johnny untied the cord, and put it back under the car cushion.

—Thank you, he said fervently; you were a good Samaritan to me today. Then he saw that the jarvey was the same from whom they had taken the car in the mad drive from the Cat 'n Cage. He saw the jarvey looking at him curiously when he was replacing the cord under the cushion.

—Haven't I seen your gob somewhere before? he asked good-humouredly, rubbing his hands briskly.

—Did you? asked Johnny dubiously. Oh, I don't think so, unless you saw me passing by some day in the street.

—No, not just in the street, said the jarvey musingly; somewhere more important. Doesn't matther, anyway, he added. An' now, one good turn deserves another — a mulled pint 'ud go down well on a day like this.

Had he had anything, Johnny would have given it to him; but he hadn't a red. It was a bitter moment for Johnny. He'd have given a lot to have been able to give a little.

—I'm sorry, he said, but this's my first week afther being idle, I don't know how long; and I haven't had any pay yet.

—Ara, g'on ower that, said the jarvey, grinning, you've got a juice left, surely — deep down in th' oul' pocket, wha'?

—Honest to God — not as much as a make!

The jarvey's face crinkled into a rippling frown as he watched Johnny bending over the cart, pretending to be examining the parcels.

—An' was it for this th' poor oul' animal pulled a caravan o' parcels up a steep an' icy hill? he asked hotly. Is that the kinda reception she gets for doin' you a wide an' weighty kindness? D'ye think just because th' poor animal isn't a Christian, you can make her what return you like for gettin' you out of a hole? C'm on; let's have the juice, an' be done with it!

—I tell you, said Johnny, red and uncomfortable, I haven't got it to give.

—Y'aven't got it to give! echoed the Jarvey. I mighta known I was right, for your oul' gob shows well th' kind y'are! He wrapped the rug angrily round his legs and gathered the reins into his hand. Well, he added, giving the mare a vicious cut of the whip that made her jump, if I was that mean, I'd let the world alone, and the mare, the car, and the jarvey tore down the sloping drive at a furious trot.

Johnny packed the parcels into the van of the outgoing train, mad with his mother that he hadn't had enough to silence the jarvey's tongue. The snow still fell; the dawn couldn't stir from behind a dark and broody sky; all the sparkle of the frost had been hidden by the new snow; the purple glow had gone when Johnny, having packed the cart in a corner, went home to get his breakfast.

THE CAP IN THE COUNTING-HOUSE

HE was back in the dimly-dead warehouse again. He had been too tired and wet and cold to eat much, so he'd nibbled the bread and swallowed down a cup of tea. While he ate, his mother ran out and came back with a penny box of boracic ointment, anointing his rasped and aching hands with it as he sat by the fire. Every damned joint in his body ached. He had bathed his smarting eyes in hot water, while his mother, kneeling down beside him, tied some sheets of brown paper round his legs so as to keep his wet trousers from touching his skin. Then she took a clean sugar-sack from her bed, made two holes in one end of it, fixed the sack round his shoulders, passed some twine through the holes, tying the ends together so that his back and shoulders should be protected from the falling snow.

—You didn't eat much breakfast, she had said, anxiously.

—I'm too tired to eat, he had answered.

—You look it, she had answered, with a slight sigh. If the job's goin' to hurt you like this, you'd better give it up — we'll manage somehow.

She looked out of the window, watching the snow coming down softly, so softly, like a week-old mother crooning to her week-old baby; so gently, and yet making work harder than it ought to be. You want a topcoat badly, she had said, turning to Johnny again, when he was about to go; don't try to rush; take everything quietly and with caution; and if, in the end, it proves too much for you, we'll have to look out for something else. Jason's isn't the only place God made.

Here he was back in the dim dead-house again, parcelling papers and magazines; pasting labels; tying string endlessly; in the midst of floating dust, dim light, the passing to and fro of heavy, tired, dragging footsteps, and the murmur of voices saying nothing. The smell of snowy slush, mixed with the smell of damp leather, filled his nostrils, while the steam from human breath formed a heavy haze round the jaded light that the gas gave. Dusky figures, like sagging designs formed by apprentice potters, moved about, topped by motionless faces, moving in the web of gloom, slandering life in silence; while overhead the shadowy clerks crouched in the glassy boxes, like dingy crabs in a dusty aquarium. And all this dead movement and dying murmur went on in the breathy mist and dusky glimmer, before the fluttering white curtains of the falling snow, filling the wide entrance with its lacy flickering strands, dodging here and there, as if in play with each other, but ever, at last, falling to weave a thicker covering for the footway and the road.

A musical voice, a dark tenor, is calling out in the mist now, calling the papers to be placed together to form a parcel for some country newsagent; it is a gentle voice, but, here and there, a firmer tone dances into the pattern of the gentle sound. Whose was it? Johnny, lifting his head to see, moves his glance through the mist to find the owner of the voice so musically calling out the sordid names of *Ally Sloper, Answers, Tit-Bits, Pearson's Weekly, Sunday Companion, Scraps, Weekly Budget* and *Forget-me-not*. Nearer now, he sees a tall, slender young man standing beside a bench, with a wheen of orders in his hand, reading out the names of the papers written on them. He has a pale face, very gentle, very handsome, with firm lines round the delicately-formed mouth. He is gently but strongly built, with the signs of speed and energy in his taut and upright shoulders and straight back. He wore a blue suit, and his white neck was encircled by an unassuming but very neat collar and blue tie. In the lapel of the coat he wore a button badge, having on it a Celtic cross with the words The Gaelic League over it, and Country and Tongue beneath in the Irish language.

—God save you, said Johnny to him in Irish.

A pair of soft luminous eyes looked at him for a moment wonderingly, then the gently-firm voice responded with God and Mary save you, my friend.

—I see you go with the Gaelic League, Johnny said, indicating the button in the other's coat.

—A Gael I am, he answered, without shame to myself or threat to you.

Johnny hesitated; he saw that the fellow before him had more Irish than he; he himself knew some, but couldn't put it together readily; hardly enough for fair and ready speech, yet; but it was thrilling to be talking in a language others there couldn't understand.

—What's your name? he asked; mine's O'Casside, Sean O'Casside, a Gael too; born in Dublin, and proud of it.

—Mine's Sean O'Connolly, he answered back; and it matters not if Belfast, Cork, or Dublin be an Irishman's place of birth.

The darkness outside faded suddenly into sunlight; the snow fell timidly, and the few flakes dodged from side to side, as if to escape capture and injury from the sunny beams darting down to caress the shivering street flooding the entrance of the warehouse with a golden curtain, the twisting flakes of snow looking like shimmering jewels caught dancing in its golden mesh, giving the warehouse prison a golden door; chasing the cold and dreamy snow into a glittering restlessness like a Quaker virgin, warm with sunny wine, blending a deep meditation with a sprightly dance.

—Do you believe, asked Johnny, that Ireland ought to be free, and that the English are our enemies?

—I believe it, indeed, he answered.

—An' so do I! exclaimed Johnny heatedly. Is sinn féin sinn féin, he went on, echoing the tram conductor. He took Sean O'Connolly's hand, and shook it warmly, I'm one with you, he said; Ireland must be free, and the English Garrison must go!

The slim and firm youth leant over towards him and recited with quiet fierceness,

' Peannaidh is fiabhras dian i dteas na dteinteadh,
Gan charaid, gan liaigh, gan biadh, gan stad ar íota,
Gan leabaidh, gan rian, gan Dia, gan gean ag daoinibh,
Ar Ghallaibh i mbliadhna, o's iad do chreach ar muinntear.'

Johnny felt a curious and tingling admiration for this handsome young lad who spoke Irish so calmly and well; firmly, too, and with a faint note of defiance in its sounding. Johnny knew that every Gaelic Leaguer was up against the venomous opposition of England's Government, and up against even the scorn of not a few of their own countrymen. Indeed, while they were speaking, titters were heard round about them; and while Connolly remained cool, as if he heard them not, Johnny's face reddened, and he yearned to strike away the mocking curves from the mouths of the gigglers.

Happening to glance upwards, he saw the head of Fitzgerald, the boss, sticking out of a little watch-window in the glasshouse. He was craning his neck, and peering downwards to see who were wasting their time talking; Johnny saw, too, in the misty gloom, slow movements of pale faces looking up, while they tried to brighten their dim energy with quicker movements to show the boss that all was well with them.

Then the voice of Fitzgerald spoke from the upper house, and Johnny heard a voice from heaven saying Casside, Casside, no wasting of the firm's time. Go down to the basement, and get the covers ready for tomorrow morning's despatch; and Johnny saw that the entrance-way was a golden net no longer. The sunlight had crept quick from the cold street; the darkness came down swift from the sky; and the falling snow dropped into a level, steady quietness again.

A young fellow for a Fenian, thought Johnny, wandering from the murky warehouse to go down to the deeper cellars, there to sort out thousands of covers for tomorrow's labour; to paste thousands of labels on these covers, so many to an hour, as he who came before him had done; or get sour looks and hot words from the frock-coated demon in the glasshouse, busy seeing that the lesser divils didn't lose a second getting out the literature of hell: wrappers for the dailies here; wrappers for the weeklies there; and wrappers for the monthlies over yonder; slashing a broad blue mark on each that properly contained the list of papers required and their number, safely pinned to a corner of the wrapper; setting aside in a special place any wrapper in which the list was missing. Ay, a young fellow for a Fenian; young and handsome; young and firm; young and kindly; young, and maybe dangerous, for, like Robespierre, he believes everything he says.

—Fine fellow, that Connolly, he said to a big-footed man tying parcels at a bench, as he was passing to where he was to start his own work. What is he?

—Despatch clerk, said flatfoot shortly.

—Ardent Gaelic Leaguer, too, went on Johnny; are you one?

—Me? asked flatfoot, with surprise in his voice; is it me you mean?

—Yes, you, confirmed Johnny.

—I have me work to do, was the answer.

Over the paste-pot a lanky-faced lad was dipping a brush, and Johnny, poising his own for a moment, said, Fine young fellow, that Connolly chap — he who speaks the Irish.

——Does he? asked lanky-face; never heard him.

—Ay, does he, said Johnny; and well, too. I have a little myself. I wish I had more. Don't you?

—Move a little away, murmured lanky-face; move away, man; there's always someone watchin'.

—Yes, but wouldn't you? persisted Johnny.

—No, I wouldn't, he snarled. Maybe it's Irish we want! A full pot an' the fire to boil it is what I want.

—But, insisted Johnny, a full pot and a fire to boil it isn't the be-all and end-all of life.

—It is to me with a wife an' three kids, an' fifteen shillins a week, an' a house in Merrion Square to keep goin'. And he moved away from where Johnny was standing.

When he had been working away for an hour or so, and was bent over the rustling wrappers, Johnny saw a dirty hand slide into the blue-purplish patch of light tingeing the bench from the tiny gas-jet over his head, and a leaflet fluttered down before his face. He read it as it lay there before him:

Come And Be Born Again!
Grand Gospel Meeting in the Christian Union Buildings
Tomorrow Night at Eight.
Adjutant Thrimble of the Belfast Brigade of the Salvation Army will Give the Devil a Knock-Out Blow.
The ex-Boxer will tell what he was when the Devil had him; and what he is, now that Christ has a Grip of him.
Come, and receive the Gift of Salvation, without Money and Without Price!
Silver Collection.
Chairman Jason will ask a Blessing.

Johnny crumpled the little slip in his hand, and tossed it contemptuously on to the cold pavement beneath his feet. A Christian was born again at Baptism. Born of water and of the Spirit. The rest of a Christian's life is a confirmation of that Faith, embraced at the Fount; a sanctification of his nature by the salutary reception of the Sacraments, through which fallen man enters into the very nature and substance of eternally enjoyable Godhead; is confirmed co-heir with Christ Jesus; grows in the grace and wisdom of Sonship, till earth releases him to rise into the unfathomable glory and joy of God, the Father's welcome. God and the Gaelic League; not such a curious cross-road mingling as some protestants might think; for where in the protestant prayer-book is there a finer declaration of faith, or a finer spiritual petition, than in Holy Patrick's Cry of the Deer?

He went on pasting the labels on the wrappers. A small hand shot into the little patch of purple-bluish light forming a dim pool on the bench, and a second leaflet fluttered down before his face, saying,

Tomorrow at Eight o'clock.
Gigantic Rally of the Socialist Republican Party of Ireland.
Foster Place.
Come in your Thousands.
Tom Ling and Jim Connolly will speak.
Workers Arise!

Out in the street, snow on the ground, and the wind bitter, to hold a meeting — Johnny shivered. Socialist — what was that? Jim Connolly — same name as his friend above; but Johnny had never heard of him. He crumpled up the leaflet in his hand, and let it drop so that it got a lodging on the cold, cold ground. He peered about him, but couldn't make out which of the crouching figures had dropped the leaflets — one for God, the other for Man. He had no interest in either. He went on with his work of sorting out the wrappers. Again a stealthy hand moved into the bluish-grey light, and turning his head, he saw a form slinking off into the deeper gloom of the cellar. Creeping about like black-beetles, he murmured; all afraid, bar Sean Connolly. He bent his head nearer to the handbill lying before him, and read:

Rotunda, Tomorrow Night. Eight o'clock.
98 Great Commemoration Concert.
Address: Shelmalier, Bargy Man, and Kelly of Killan.
Harp; Fiddle; Flute.
Songs and Recitations.
Tickets: 2/6, 2/– & 1/–
Muscáil do Mhisneach, a Bhanba!

Three appeals to him, the humblest Roman of them all: for God, for Man, and for Country; three so different from each other, yet all alike in so far that each was made in the dimness, silently, and in fear. They were beetles here, with different badges on their backs: some with the cross of Christ; some with the harp of Ireland; and some with whatever the sign of Socialism happened to be. The call to freedom from sin, freedom from employers, freedom from national oppression, had each been delivered stealthily, in the murky darkness; afraid of the light because their deeds were good. He didn't like it; didn't like to be even distantly connected with this fear of being caught in the pleasuance of an idle moment. He was down among the dead men here. If he wasn't yet actually lying down, he was sitting up in his coffin here, with a murky mist for a shroud, and a bluish-grey gas-jet for the light of heaven.

If he stopped much longer here, too, his eyes would suffer from the dim light in the brown darkness. The muscles were stretched already, cockling up in his efforts to pierce through the dimness to see what he was doing. He'd leave. He'd leave with a flag of defiance in his hand, held high. But how?

A soft, slingy touch from a hand came to his shoulder, and a timid voice murmured, You're to go up for your pay. Mr. Fitzgerald tole me to tell you.

He climbed up the dismal stairs, passed through the warehouse, into the entrance to the stairs leading to the counting-house, where a number of men and boys, in single file, stretched along the stairs, waiting their turn to go in and draw their money. He saw that as each one entered by the brown and golden door, marked COUNTING-HOUSE, he hurriedly took cap or hat from his head.

Why are they doffing their caps as they pass in? asked Johnny of a wide skull near him in the midst of the cold fog at the foot of the stairs.

—Don't you know your manners? came from the wide skull. Aren't we goin' in where Mr. Charles is? An' isn't it a good thing to show suitable respect to those who provide for us? Isn't it a way of showin' Mr. Charles what we think of him?

I'll show him what I think of him, thought Johnny; for as he was leaving the job, anyhow, he might as well kindle a flare of defiance before he went for good. He'd doff no cap. Refuse before the others, too. He'd show some of them what he was made of. His body ached; his eyes were red and blurred; and his head was dizzy with the down-pour of toil that came on him here. Start from bed at three in the morning; going all the time, nearly, till six or seven in the evening, and getting something like a penny-farthing an hour for the work he did. No time left to read, or to learn by heart all the fine things in the books he had. They gave him Sunday to rest, and to pay his respects to God. Well, he'd take his chance to pay his respects to them, now.

He darted up the stairs, two at a time, and placed himself just out-side the golden-lettered door of the counting-house.

—I'll take no cap of mine off, he said, loudly, to be heard by all. I'll wear my cap like a bronze helmet, and pull the beaver down; and he pulled the peak of his cloth cap down over his forehead, far as it would go. The rest gazed at him, moving closer together, giving him plenty of space so as to show there was no bond between them and him.

—Open the door, and let the gallant boyo in, said the voice from the wide skull below.

With a rowdy swing Johnny opened the door and went in. A thick glossy, dark-red linoleum covered the floor; deeply-cushioned chairs were there for the comfort of customers; in front of him was a long, polished, brass-railed counter panelled with Tuscan glass, making all behind it invisible; in the centre of the glass panels was a small window with a purple plate of thick glass above it, having on it the word CASHIER in broad letters of black and gold. To the left stood a mahogany-partitioned office, its upper part panelled, too, with Tuscan glass; a narrow door stood in the centre, and on its pane of glass, purple-bordered, was the word PRIVATE in big gold letters. Johnny knew that behind the purple, the gold, and the mahogany Mr. Charles

Jason sat, not too far away from a sparkling fire, sweeping his office over with a glow of heat and comfort. Johnny went over to the cashier's window, and, peeping through it, saw a perfectly bald, stout-bodied man bending over a drawer half filled with tiny white envelopes.

—Name, name, sir! snapped out the bald-head as soon as he heard someone standing by the little window.

—Casside, Casside! snapped back Johnny.

The bald-head stiffened a little at the snappy tone of Johnny; hesitated; then the ringed hand took an envelope from the drawer and placed it on the little sill before the little window. Happening to glance up as he did so, the cashier saw that Johnny's cap covered his head; and the ringed hand snatched the little envelope back again.

—Take off your cap, he said disapprovingly; but Johnny stood staring into the face of the bald-head, raising no hand to do so.

—Do you hear me, boy? and the voice of the bald head was threatening; take off your cap.

—Give me what's comin' to me an' never mind me cap, said Johnny, conscious that the door behind him was open and the crowd was gaping in at them.

—No wages are given to those who know no manners, said the cashier, angrily and with decision.

The hero-heat that surged through Cuchullain in the core of a fight surged through Johnny now, and he swelled out with the dint of fury.

—Hand the money out, he said loudly, a leibide! Hand it out in the zone of a second, you fat, faltherin' caricature of creation, or woe'll find you, quick an' early!

The bald-head stepped back so swiftly that its spectacles hopped off its nose and dangled, from a ribbon, on its belly. The pasty face went purple and its voice panted indignantly, Mr. Charles, Mr. Charles!

Then, through the little window, Johnny saw the long face, pale eyes, greying golden beard, and bent shoulders of Mr. Charles coming into the cashier's office with short mincing steps, on his toes, like a creaking and cracked-up ballet dancer, to stare with wonder at the cashier and Johnny's head thrust through the little window.

—What is it? what's wrong? what's the matter? what has happened? lisped Charles nervously, trying to look fierce, but with a hand on his office door so that he could dart back quick if danger showed a sign.

—This, this blaguard — didn't you hear him, Mr. Charles? This, this, cor-corner-boy, here, the cashier stuttered, wouldn't remove his cap.

—That is the custom here, sir, Charles said to Johnny, and it must be honoured.

—Well, said Johnny, it's goin' to be honoured, now, more in th' breach than in the observance.

—He has used, sir, villainous, villainous language — didn't you hear him, Mr. Charles? A caricature, he said, and some terrible name I never heard before!

—Where'd he come from? Who is he? Who took him into the Firm? asked blond-beard.

—It was a ghastly mistake, whoever did it, sputtered the cashier.

—You go back to where you came from, said Johnny vehemently, thrusting an arm through the little window and pointing a finger at Jason; go back and count your gains behind the back o' Jesus; but before you go, tell this bald-headed boyo to hand over all that's comin' to me, quick!

—Give it to him, hand it to him, let him have it, let him have it, and go! ordered Jason. God bless us, how did such a person ever come to be employed here!

The cashier flung a little envelope on the sill of the little window. Johnny spilled the coins out, counted them, and dropped them carelessly into his pocket. Then he turned, pushed his way through the crowd at the door, hurried down the stairs, out into the darkness and the falling snow. A deep black sky it was, as if God was giving Dublin one of His black looks; unstirred by a star it was; as black as the streets were white, as if the city's face were paling under the black wrath of God.

—Well, thought Johnny, my mother will be glad I left it. Now I can find a little time to read the books I love; for I won't be going to bed, any longer, designed for death with the hard work here.

From a public-house, a little lower down the street, a stream of misty yellow light came from a wide window, forming a dusky golden patch on the side-walk outside. In the centre of the yellow glow, like a beetle in a daffodil, stood a dark form, his shoulders gathered up into his neck, a golden trumpet to his mouth, playing tenderly and well, straight to the door, and through the door, to the men and women drinking cosily inside:

> The light of other days is faded,
>   And all their glories past,
> For grief with heavy wing hath shaded
>   The hopes too bright to last.

Johnny jingled the nine shillings in his pocket, pulled up the collar of his coat as high as he could make it go, and turned his steps homewards.

THE SWORD OF LIGHT

JOHNNY wished that he had more light; more light to see by; and light in his eye to see with, for the light of the body is the eye. Well, he'd seen a lot more than some with perfect eyes. Strange that God, who had given so much mighty light to the world in sun, moon, and stars, gave so little to some people. The old and new testaments had a lot about light in them; and Christ Himself talked quite a lot about it, even saying that He was the light of the world. Then there was the light that lighteth every man that came into the world — whatever that light could be; Let your light so shine before men that they may see your good works; the light this and the light that, till everyone was dazzled by it. And yet in most places it was as scarce as rubies. Hardly a house that he had been in that wasn't dark in daylight. The sun, they said, shone on all; yet, really, if you looked round, many saw very little of it. He knew street after street in which there was no sun. Where was it in Hymdim & Leadems? Or in Jason's? Was it in oul' Anthony's smile that had as much heat in it as the singed wing of a moth. And as for Jason — he kept the sun locked up in the counting-house. The old sun was doing his best, but many blinds were pulled down to warn him away; or hide him from those who needed him most. Like the sunburst of Ireland for ever hidden behind the King of England's crown. A great shower of jewelled hands were veiling the sun's face, and hiding his light from many men.

It was a wintry night. The room was bitterly cold, and dismally dark, too, save where a yellowish trickle of timorous light crept through the window from a gas-lamp on the edge of the pavement outside, so long a swing-swong for the children that it now bent forward over the street, looking like an old man who had lighted a light in the hope of finding a lost piece of silver. On the little old table, now the colour of dull ebony, Johnny had been silently and insistently learning more of grammar, geography, and of history, by the smoky ray of a tiny oil-lamp, flickering every other second, making the words dance before his eyes, as if they were alive and wanted to escape from his boring stare. Whenever he got tired of these things, he read some bit from the *Deserted Village*, or from Ruskin's *Crown of Wild Olives* that lay wide open on the little table before him.

He guessed he must be cold; but his mind was warm, and the state of the rest of his body mattered little; though he did his best to keep it from the more biting cold by wearing an old coat over his good one; two poor pair of trousers; his muffler tied tightly round his neck; and his cap crammed down over his forehead. He had been hard at it since six o'clock in the morning — fifteen solid hours, and he wasn't tired yet.

Sometimes a sly longing stole over him for a hot cup of tea, a longing that he banished by a deeper look into the book before him; there was no fire to heat the water, for the coal had to be watched, and the little tea they had needed a strict jurisdiction to make it last out the usual meals for the rest of the week. The paraffin, too, was nearly out. With his last few coins he had bought half a gallon; had hidden it in a corner, and had warned his mother that it wasn't to be touched by a soul, save himself. Now its last few inches were giving a flickering salute to the glories of Goldsmith, Ruskin, and Marlowe.

He raised the little lamp between his hands, placed it close to his ear, and shook it cautiously. Enough for another night or two, he murmured. Well, so far he had never been shook for what he needed. God had always managed to furnish forth a candle or a drop of oil. Though the barrel of meal had often wasted, the cruse of oil had never failed; and so the light of the past gave a new gleam to the light of the present. He would never be now without the light that lighteth every man coming into the world; for surely this had something to do with that light; was that light which could never be quenched. The light of other days would light the days to come. Shakespeare in his way, Marlowe, Goldsmith, and Ruskin in theirs, were lights showing him where to plant his feet safely; kindly lights guiding him to a fuller light in the future.

He paced slowly and cautiously to and fro, murmuring passages from Shakespeare or Goldsmith, putting sense and feeling into them, quietly; for in the other room his mother slept, and he didn't wish to wake her. She had had a hard day, washing for his sister, Ella, for nothing; and for another woman for sixpence and a glass of porter, which, she said, put new life into her. He paused at the window, and looked out on the naked night. A thin, sour, sharp-faced sickle of a moon tried to peer out of a cloudy wind-tossed sky, looking like a maid peeved with a wind that sullied her neatness. Over beyond the canal towered the ugly bloated spire of the catholic church, a tapering finger on a fat hand beckoning to the ships that came sailing into the Bay of Dublin. The saint after whom the church was called had gone out alone to meet the clanging Normans when they came trotting on to take Dublin back to their hairy bosoms; the saint asking when his nose got the smell of the steel in the line of their glances, Is it peace, my dear Christian brothers, is it peace? And they had answered sweetly, saying, It's bloody wars unless you and your cross-brained viking Tooles give way, give wisely, give all. And the saint had bowed, saying, All that we have is thine. Then the iron-skinned warriors stroked their beards, murmuring, It is well. So in the midst of their lances, shields, and battle-axes, the saint rode back in triumph, the people cheering because of his valour in bringing peace and poverty to them.

Nearer than the thick-bellied steeple gleamed the rosy red lights of the railway signals, looking like fiery red buttons on the dark-blue coat of our lady of the night, with the sickle moon a dull gold curb in her night-blown hair.

Every other moment from the shunting yard came the clanging crash of heavy goods wagons striking each other as the shunters harried them from line to line; or, sometimes, a succession of clangs was heard when a running rake of wagons came into sharp collision with another rake so that the two might be made into one.

All round where Johnny was looking, ah, many, many years ago, the Danes and the Irish grappled together in their last fierce fight; the last long fight between darkness and light. Here the black-browed Thor went down before the gentle, golden-headed Jesus. Here the white and pearly dove pecked out the eyes and clawed out the guts of the vengeful and vindictive raven. Here the sign of the Hammer shrivelled up in the sign of the Cross; and darkness and fury fled before sweetness and light. Here the skirl of the Christian war-pipe shrilled at the bellowing of the heathen horns, helped by the lapping drone of the sea as his waves came curling in from Dublin Bay. The Danish Dubliners watched from their Woden walls the armies hacking and slashing and slaying and thrusting each other through till the number of heads floating on the waters and lying on the land seemed like a bloody fall of hailstones.

And all the purple laughter of the battle came bouncing out of a game of chess. Brian Boru requested Mailmurra, King of Leinster, to bring to Kincora, Brian's little grey home in the west, three of the longest, loveliest, whitest, most golden masts of timber that could be hewed out from the fair woods of Feegile. Poor Mailmurra couldn't refuse, for he was fief to Brian, whom he hated, seeking slyly to stir up the Danes against the High King. Before this, just for policy's sake, Brian Boru had given him a cloak of bright and precious silk, all edged with gold, with a bright shining silver brooch to keep it company. To ease his annoyance at having to bear the timber for Brian, the King of Leinster got the Chief of Offaly to bear one of the stately masts of golden timber; the Head of the O'Phelans to carry the second; and the Prince of the O'Murries to go with the third. All went well till at the foot of the mountains an argument arose over how to handle horses; the upshot being that O'Phelan called Mailmurra a suckhole, and Mailmurra called O'Phelan a bad dhrop in a good breed, when O'Phelan buttoned up his coat, turned on his heel, an' stalked off, saying, It's snaky-minded a man would want to be to go safe along a road with a Mailmurra; Mailmurra bawling afther him, Bah! back o' me hand to you, bowsey!

So Mailmurra had to set about doin' for himself what the O'Phelan had left lyin' in the road; toilin' so hard with the length of timber that the silver brooch burst away from his cloak, flew off, and disappeared from sight over the hip of the highest mountain. When he got to Kincora, he gave the cloak to his sister, Gormlaith, Brian Boru's wife, who made another brooch for him from a mould of bubbling silver handy on the fire beside her; an' she all the time naggin' him for bein' Brian's servant, dancin' attendance, a thing unseemly for a Mailmurra to do; a thing his father, or his father's father, or his father's father's father, wouldn't do for all the wealth an' valour owned be Greece an' Throy together; the tormented Mailmurra stealing away to look over a game of chess, when she was bent down biting a stitch of thread, hotly played between Brian's son and Kevin of Glendalough, the poor man thinking to do well by his host's son be advisin' him to make a move that lost him the game.

—That was the kind o' counsel that made Dublin's battle of Glen Mawma break on the Danes! snarled Brian Boru's son in the reddenin' face of the poor King of Leinster.

—If I gave counsel then that broke the battle on the Danes, answered Mailmurra, in tortured quietness, I'll give them counsel again that'll make th' battle break on you, yeh pup!

—Let's see you do it then! shouted Brian's son, leppin' up in rage an' scatterin' the chessmen: I dar' you!

With that, on fire with anger, Mailmurra left; and so that he couldn't drink in the great hall that night, went to bed at once, tearin' off at a flyin' gallop before the crack o' dawn, without as much as an

I'm off, or So long, or even a kiss me arse, or a ha'p'orth to Brian Boru awake on his canopied bed devisin' out schemes to double-cross the innocent King of Leinster; hearin' of which the white-haired, white-whiskered Brian bounds outa bed with barely a screed on, to send a favourite gillie of the Dal Cash, dressed up to kill, afther the flyin' King to deludher him back again, so's Brian could have a quiet serious chat with him. The gillie goin' all-out caught up with the King on the bank of the Shannon not far from Killaloe, bowin' low to him, and givin' him Brian's message of love an' consternation at him goin' without a word, when the King turned on him suddenly an' let the unsuspectin' man have three such skelps on the skull with a skudgel of yew he had in his hand as cracked the gillie's head in three different places, so that he had to be hurried back home to Kincora on a hurdle, raisin' the ire of the warriors there that a Dal Cash Munsterman should be cudgelled by a Cal Dash Leinsterman. Seizin' their spears an' mountin' their steeds, they prepared to ride off afther the King, Brian stoppin' the warlike traffic with an uplifted hand, ordherin' them to their beds again, sayin' that Mailmurra would come to no harm on Brian's land; ending with his hand on his heart an' a tear in his oul' eye that they'd demand an answer for what had been done at the King o' Leinster's own doorpost; while the wily Mailmurra, when he got home, summoned lesser kings, princes, big chiefs, and little chiefs be bell, book, trumpet, drum, cymbal, flag, beacon, fire, an' candlelight to let them know of the gust of slights an' slanders blown upon him while he sat a guest in the Halls of Kincora, sending messages to the vikings of Orkney, Shetland, Man, Norway, and Iceland, urging them to come sailing on the first waves that surged into Dublin Bay to join up with the Danes there to force Brian Boru to give battle on the plains of Moy Ealta an' the land stretchin' from the head of Howth to the walls of Dublin on the banks of the river Liffey. So that a game of chess gave rise to the holy slaughter of pagan and Christian the time horrid hairy Brodar, with the great black raven on his chest, runnin' for his life, came upon the tent of poor oul' Brian, an' he on his knees prayin' for all he was worth to the great white Christ, with Brodar shoutin' at him for an oul' crawthumper to get up an' meet his doom, to make Brian lep to his feet an' whip up his sword an' let Brodar have it, slicin' off his legs with a wonderful slanty sweep of hiss sweapon, one from the knee an' t'other from the ankle; though while he was topplin' down, Brodar, aflame in a yell of agony, in the name of Thor, let the good Christian King have the beneficial edge of his biting battle-axe on the white-haired head, splitting it in two to the two lips that were just shouting the holy name of Jesus. And the darkness of hell enveloped the soul of Brodar, and he shot down deep; but the light of God shone round about the soul of Brian, and he went up high; and peace came to Ireland, dancing, and had a most happy week-end.

He must stop his dusky dreaming, and go back to the glow of his work. But he still lingered at the window, looking out at a world of a few dark shapes, the pompous steeple, the red lights of the railway, the yellow pool of light given by the gas-lamp on the edge of the sidewalk, and the slender, ogling slip of a moon, peering slantwise from the gloomy clouds, like a sly wanton eyeing a timid man from behind a curtain.

A big striding figure flashed darkly into the dusky pool of light and went swiftly by the window. Mr. Harry, murmured Johnny, on his way to a Vestry Meeting, or something. The poor man was having a harrying time with the true-blue protestants because, they said, he was a ritualist, though he asserted he was only determined to carry out the rules of the rubric in decency and order. They had had their eye on him ever since he came to the parish, some of them hissing softly as he came in to lead the church service when they saw the black cassock, which they called a Roman garment, flowing decently from under his white surplice, down to his feet. The Orangemen loudly and defiantly spoke the creed when it was being intoned by the choir, shouting out Popery! when Mr. Harry and others turned towards the east as the creed was sung. They shouted at Parish Meetings that the yellow fringe on the communion table turned it into an altar; maintaining that the crimson and golden crosses on the confirmation certificates were busy corrupting the minds of the innocent young protestant people they were given to, ensnaring them into the woeful superstitions of the Romish church. Stones were flung at the church windows, and a brick once landed on the organ, putting the player out, and causing consternation to the kneeling congregation. It was current all over the parish that the bould Harry would have to give up his sacerdoting practices or go. A good many rallied round him; but they were, like Johnny, the poorer members of the flock, and were, of course, of little use to him. The others closed their purses, making Mr. Harry's job a very queer one, slowing down things, and he found it hard to fight against a sullen and resentful Select Vestry. If Johnny had had money or a fair job, he'd have sailed into the fight on Harry's side; but he had neither, so he had to be content to follow afar off. He hadn't had the courage to tell Mr. Harry he'd lost his job; he was hoping that he'd be asked about it soon, then he'd tell Mr. Harry everything, and Mr. Harry would certainly have a look-out for something new for him. Pity he hadn't dropped in as he was passing the house.

A knock came to the door. Harry Fletcher — it must be he. He screwed his face round by the corner of the window, but it was too dark to see who the figure could be. If it was anyone for his mother, he'd send them to hell! He'd let no-one wake her. But he was almost certain that the knocker was the boul' Harry. He went from the room, opened the street door, and there was his old friend, the tram conductor, with a grin on his face, and his hand stretched out.

—Just slipped down with th' song all written out for you, he said, taking the pipe out of his mouth, and spitting on the pathway; *Speeches from the Dock*, too; an' th' *Life of Wolfe Tone*; an', if you've time to listen, I'll sing the song for you, so's you'll get the air all right.

Johnny brought him into the dark room that was barely aware of the light from the smoky lamp. He was ashamed that he wouldn't be able to offer him a cup of tea. The brightness of Goldsmith and Ruskin faded before the black bitterness of having nothing to give. Not even a bit of a fire for a friend.

—Not nearly as cold as it was, said the conductor, as if he sensed the bitterness of Johnny's thought; not nearly.

—I wasn't feeling a bit cold, said Johnny, so I didn't bother to light a fire.

—Waste o' good coal, murmured his friend; but Johnny noticed with pain that he kept his topcoat on him. There's the *Life*, he went on, laying on the table, in the little pool of light the lamp gave, a paper-covered book. You'll like it — th' way he got round the French Government to send a fleet to Ireland, an' th' bitther curses he let out of him when the great fleet sent to save Ireland had to weigh anchor, hoist sail, an' go back to France. Aw, Jasus, it was cruel! Some day, he said, laying a hand on Johnny's shoulder, you'll come with us to Bodenstown, an' by his grave pray for more men like Wolfe Tone. Here's the speeches givin' what the Irish felons said standin' in th' prison dock, when they faced death or lifelong imprisonment. You've heard *The Felons of Our Land* sung, haven't you?

—No, said Johnny, never.

—No? Well, one verse goes like this.

—Sing soft, whispered Johnny, for mother's asleep in the next room.

—Righto; I'll sing as soft as a far-away echo. With an arm round
Johnny's shoulder, he sang soft and slow and simply:

> Let thraitors sneer and tyrants frown, oh, little do we care —
> A felon's cap's th' noblest crown an Irish head can wear;
> An' what care we, although it be trod by a ruffian band —
> God bless th' clay where rest today, th' felons of our land!

Johnny felt the arm round his shoulder quiver, and a strange thrill
stole through his own veins, stiffening his body, as he listened to the
sad and defiant song.

—You nearly know the air of *Who Fears to Speak of Ninety-eight*
already, the conductor went on in a husky voice after they had stood
dead silent for some seconds. I'll sing just two verses soft, an' you can
hum the air as I'm singin' to make sure you've got the air right.

> We dhrink th' memory of th' brave,
>   Th' faithful an' th' few;
> Some lie far off beyond th' wave,
>   Some sleep in Ireland, too.

> All, all are gone, but still lives on
>   Th' fame of those who died;
> An' thrue men, like you men,
>   Remember them with pride!

There was a long silence in the darkened room, pricked by the little
golden pool of light on the bronze-hued table, broken by the tense
breathing of Johnny and his friend.

> Th' dust of some is Irish earth,
>   Among their own they rest;
> And th' same land that gave them birth
>   Has caught them to her breast;
> And we will pray that from their clay
>   Full many a race may start,
> Of thrue men, like you men,
>   To act as brave a part!

—Are the Fenians to the fore yet? whispered Johnny, close to his
friend's ear.

—I'm afraid, I'm afraid not, lad, answered the conductor sadly,
close to Johnny's ear. Then his hand sought Johnny's, and he pressed
it. Maybe they are, though. You never can tell. Anyway, we're here,
aren't we? What are you readin' now? he asked, to relieve the sense of
tension.

—*Crown o' Wild Olives*, said Johnny, by John Ruskin.

—Ruskin? Curious name. Irish, was he?

—A Scotsman who wrote splendidly. Listen to what he says about war: War, the greatest of all games — the play of plays, the great gentleman's game, which ladies like them best to play at — the game of war. It is entrancingly pleasant to the imagination; we dress more finely for it than for any other sport; and we go out to it, not merely in scarlet, as to hunt, but in scarlet and gold, and all manner of fine colours; though, of course, we could fight better in grey, and without feathers. Then the bats and balls are very costly, costing now, I suppose, about fifteen millions of money annually to each nation; all of which you know is paid for by hard labourer's work in the furrow and furnace. A costly game! — not to speak of the consequences. The cost is all paid for, we know, in deadly work somewhere. The jewel-cutter, whose sight fails over the diamonds; the weaver, whose arm fails over the web; the ironworker, whose breath fails before the furnace.

—An' how, may I ask Mr. Ruskin, are we goin' to get th' English outa Ireland without it?

—Without what?

—Without war? Ruskin's only another oul' cod, with th' gift o' gab!

—He wrote about other things, said Johnny, a little indignantly, and he wasn't a cod. Listen to this, spoken before a gathering of business men who were about to build an Exchange in the Yorkshire town of Bradford.

—Aw, Sean, Exchange! interrupted the conductor. What have we got to do with an Exchange?

—Listen, listen for a second, man! Here's a word or two of what he said: Your ideal of life is a pleasant and undulating world, with iron and coal everywhere beneath it. On each pleasant bank of this world is to be a beautiful mansion; stable and coach-houses; a park and hothouses; carriage drives and shrubberies; and here are to live the votaries of the Goddess of Getting-on — the English gentleman with his gracious wife and lovely family——

—There, you see, Sean — the *English* gentleman!

—Wait a second: Irish or Englishman — a gentleman's all the same.

—It isn't, I'm tellin' you; it's different.

—Listen, listen a minute more: the gentleman was always able to have the boudoir and the jewels for the wife; beautiful ball dresses for the daughters; and hunters for the sons, and a shooting in the Highlands for himself. At the bottom of the bank is to be the mill, not less than a quarter of a mile long, with a chimney three hundred feet high. In this mill are to be in constant employment a thousand workers, who never drink, never strike, always go to church on Sundays, and always express themselves in respectful language. There, you see — there's something in all that, isn't there?

—An' what's in it but a lot o' blather? Right enough, maybe, for the gloomy English gropin' after little things; for the Saxon sireless squatters an' Clan London's loutish lords, ever rakin' cinder-heaps for specks o' gold; but th' Irish is different — we have th' light.

—The Catholic Faith, you mean? asked Johnny.

—No, no, no, he said impatiently. That's there, too; but I mean th' light o' freedom we're goin' to win from th' English — th' leprosy o' want desthroy them!

The tall figure of Mr. Harry Fletcher again flashed past the window, and a second later a knock was heard at the street door.

—It's our new minister coming to see me, said Johnny, with some embarrassment.

—Couldn't I slip out without him seein' me?

—There's only the one way out, said Johnny testily.

—Well, look, said the conductor, pointing behind him, I can half lie behind the sofa there in th' dense of th' darkness, an', unless he's th' eyes of an owl, he'll never notice me. He hurried over and got behind the sofa, sitting down on the floor, so that only the very top of his head could be seen by Johnny who knew he was there. Johnny went out, opened the door, and Mr. Fletcher and he came back into the room.

—Hard at work, I see, the minister said, glancing at the books on the table. Good lad; you'll soon know more than the best of us.

—Sit down, said Johnny, hastily shifting the books the conductor had brought him into the darkness; sit down, sir.

—I'm afraid I've disturbed you, the minister said, sitting down on Johnny's chair and putting his bare hands as close as he dared to the blackened chimney of the lamp, trying to get some heat into them; but I shan't keep you away from your glory long. I've just come, John, to bid you and your mother goodbye.

—Goodbye? echoed Johnny, with distress in his voice.

—Yes; I can't stay any longer — there are too many against me.

—Fight them, said Johnny vehemently; fight them, sir!

—I have done so. No, it's goodbye, John; I have to go. My bishop advised that it wasn't a good thing to provoke contention among Christian people.

—Christian people! But you have done nothing but obey the rubric.

—In the spirit, yes; but the deep-set emotions of an ignorant evangelism is still strong, preventing our poor people from seeing the truth in the Scriptures and the church's tradition.

—Some of them have been at me about you and your ways, said Johnny, trying to turn me against you. They were very bitther about Sanctus, Sanctus, Sanctus, written in gold on the wall above the communion table, turning it, they said, into a High Althar.

Johnny joined in with the musical laugh of Mr. Harry. They're saying, too, that you've a crucifix over your bed.

—The symbol of our salvation can hardly be an evil thing, murmured Mr. Harry.

—They complain, too, went on Johnny, that you encourage prayers for the dead.

—It has been the custom of the church for hundreds of years to pray for the dead, said Mr. Harry, rubbing his hands, and holding them out towards the little lamp again; and we have lost a lot of comfort and spiritual communion with our departed loved ones by giving it up. Before we go into the presence of God, the best of us need a purifying period in paradise. That was where Christ's soul went when we say He descended into hell; not the hell of the damned, Gehenna; but Hades, the blessed place of the spirits departed in the faith and fear of the Lord. Surely it is good to pray that God may give them eternal rest, and let perpetual light shine upon their suffering souls.

—We say in Irish, said Johnny, of one who is dead, Solus Dé dá anam — Light o' God to his soul!

—Eh? said Mr. Harry, puzzled; Irish what?

—Irish, Irish language, you know, murmured Johnny ashamedly.

—Oh yes, yes, quite, murmured Mr. Harry so indifferently that Johnny's face was reddened, and he wished he hadn't said it.

—A prayer for the departed, went on Mr. Harry, is plainly implied in the prayer for Christ's church militant here on earth, too.

—Quite, murmured Johnny, trying to get back his ease of manner after the thoughtless slip of mentioning the Irish language.

—And you remember that lovely collect, beginning Almighty God with whom do live the spirits of them that depart hence in the faith?———

—We humbly beseech thee, of thy gracious goodness, said Johnny, taking the words from Mr. Harry, so's to show he knew it, shortly to accomplish the number of thine elect, and to hasten thy kingdom; that we, with all those that are departed in the thrue faith of thy holy

name, may have our perfect consummation and bliss, both in body
and soul — what could be plainer? asked Johnny.

—The Fathers of the church are even plainer still, John. We must
ever strive to keep the fairest expressions of the Faith alive and fresh
in our hearts, till such time as the Irish church may cordially show
forth her eternal and beautiful brotherhood with the rest of the family
professing the one, holy, and apostolic faith. And now I must go. He
rose from his chair, and Johnny saw that he shivered a little with
the cold of the room. Is your mother in — can I say goodbye to
her?

—I'll waken her up, said Johnny, hesitating to leave the room for
fear his friend should be seen crouching down behind the sofa; she's
asleep; she's had a hard day, but I'll waken her up to say goodbye.

—No, no; you mustn't do that, said Mr. Harry earnestly. Let the
poor woman sleep on and take her rest. Give her my love, and say
goodbye for me. He pulled at the collar of his coat at the street door,
as if he wished to cover his ears. Well, goodbye, goodbye, John —
you're a good lad; goodbye, and God bless you. And the next moment
Johnny was watching him striding away into the darkness, never to
be seen again by him or his mother.

—What was th' pair o' yous thryin' to do? asked the conductor,
when Johnny had come back into the little room. Whew! I'm cramped.
Was it thryin' to copy our mode o' religion yous were, or what?

—No, no; not at all, said Johnny sharply. What we spoke about
was our own religion. We belong to the one, catholic, and apostolic
church.

—There's me for you, now! I always thought yous were protestants.

—So we are — in a way; but we're catholics, too.

—An' how in religion can you be two things at the one time?

—They aren't two things; St. Patrick founded our church as he
founded yours.

—That's the first time I ever heard tell St. Patrick was a protestant.
Anyway, yous don't respect the Pope.

—On the contrary, we have a great respect for him.

—Yous have? Well, that's th' first time I've heard protestants
respect the Pope.

—Not all protestants respect him, of course; the very ignorant ones
dislike and deride him.

—Well, that doesn't matther much, so long as they're Irish. How
does he stand in, regardin' her?

—He — her — who?

—Ireland; the minister who's just left?

—Oh, he? She never enters his head.

—A gay lot o' foreigners there's in this counthry!

—He isn't a foreigner — he's Irish.

—Irish — an' Ireland never enthers his head!

—There's a lot that way. Some of your catholics are just as bad.

—Worse! A scowl came on to the conductor's face, and his hands clenched. Sell her, be God, some of them would! Ay, an' did. Leonard McNally, Pether the Packer, an' th' bastards who bethrayed Parnell!

—What d'ye think of the Irish Socialist Republicans? asked Johnny.

—Connolly, Ling, an' that crowd? Not worth considerin'. What we have to do first is to desthroy th' festherin' weeds clingin' to Ireland's feet an' hindherin' her movements.

—And who are they? asked Johnny.

—The Irish Parliamentary Party! and the conductor's scowl got darker, and his hand clenched more tightly. Redmond an' his gang, paddlin' in the flow of England's brutal, bawdy, gaudy grandeur. They are the new English yeomen of the guard, all dhressed in their jackets green; golden English epaulettes are on their shoulders; the English King has given a timely tap to all their shouldhers, an' their knees are bendin'. I'm off now.

Johnny went with him to the door. There was the dull, heavy steeple of the church vaunting its faith even to the sky; there were the bawdy clouds, now hiding, now showing the nakedness of the slip of a moon; and there were the railway lights, staring like red eyes of animals from a jungle of darkness.

—I'm goin' to call you Sean from this out, said the conductor, as he held Johnny's hand at parting; mine's Ayamonn, Ayamonn O'Farrel, from the O'Farrels of Longford. Well, Slán agat, achara. He bent down and whispered tensely into Johnny's ear, Th' Sword of Light is flamin' still!

—What sword of light?

—Th' Fenians! And without another word, he hurried off, leaving Johnny standing by the door.

The Sword of Light! An Claidheamh Solis; the Christian Faith; the sword of the spirit; the freedom of Ireland; the good of the common people; the flaming sword which turned every way, to keep the way of the tree of life — which was it? where would he find it?

He went back into the darkened room, sat down, leaned his elbows on the table and his head in his hands. He glanced at the little smoky lamp and fancied that it had changed to a candle — a tall, white, holy candle, its flame taking the shape of a sword; and, in its flaming point, the lovely face of Cathleen, the daughter of Houlihan.

His head bent lower, heavy with thought. There, under his eyes, on the pages of Ruskin's book, lay a glittering silver shilling. Harry Fletcher's gift? Couldn't be; there was no shilling there when he took Harry to the door. It was Ayamonn's gift. Johnny felt his friend knew that, had it been offered, it would in pride have been refused; so he simply left it quietly on the pages of an open book. Johnny took it up and handled it and sighed; then a shudder went through him as he remembered that the minister had gone away for ever, and that he would have to ferret out a job for himself.

I STRIKE A BLOW FOR YOU, DEAR LAND

JOHNNY'S whole world was divided against itself. England was at war with the Boer Republics. His brother Tom, who had had a job of temporary postman at twelve shillings a week and was on the Reserve, had been called up; had been dressed in khaki, helmet and all; had marched, with a contingent of his regiment, the Dublin Fusiliers, through the city, Johnny by his side, carrying his rifle, and had gone long ago to the front, after promising Johnny he'd bring home a bunch of hair from Kruger's whiskers. He had gone up to Natal under General Sir Redvers Buller, and nothing had been heard of him for weeks. Johnny was troubled that he might have perished in the battle of Tugela; for Johnny and Tom had a real affection for each other. Thousands of Irishmen were out there on the veldt, risking all for England; for her honour, and, Johnny thought bitterly, for the gold and diamond mines of Johannesburg. She had been fortified in her attack on the Boers by testimonials from the Basutonians, Zululonians, Matabelians, Bechuanalandians, Bulawayonians, Mashonians, and the Kalomonians, who had all in a great chorus sung hail hallelujah to the great white queen mother, Victoria.

All civilisation, save alone the Irish. Ireland had become a place of stormy argument, with Dublin as its centre. Every man, woman, and child fought battles hour by hour, either for the British or the Boers. Transvaal flags were in everyone's house, in everyone's window, or in everyone's hand. At times spontaneous processions formed in the streets, marched through the city, booing every redcoat that passed, and often coming into collision with the irritated police. All fancy goods shops and newsagents were filled with Boer symbols; streams of ribbons flashing the colours of England's enemies flowed through every street and sparkled in every second window. Every patriot carried in the lapel of his coat a buttoned picture of Kruger, Steyn, Botha, Joubert, or De Wet; and a story went everywhere that De Wet was really Parnell come to life again, and up in arms against the English. Day and night the office of the *Irish Independent* flashed on a screen the latest news, a red light burning for a British victory and a green one for a Boer success, thousands gathering to cheer when the green light shone, and to groan and hiss when the red light was shown. A Transvaal Committee had been formed, with Arthur Griffith and some Irish Members of Parliament, to help the brave Boers to an Irish ambulance. A meeting had been called, but the Castle had proclaimed it; and Dublin tossed her head and clenched her teeth.

Today Johnny and Ayamonn were standing in the crowd watching the lights, when the news was flashed on the screen that the British had lost ten guns, and a great cheer, thundering defiance, made the street tremble in an agony of joy. Ayamonn, hoarse with mad emotion, whipped his hat from his heavily-haired head and waved it round in circles, as he shouted with the crowd.

—We should ha' gone to where th' meetin' was to be, he said, proclaimed or no.

—We're better here, said Johnny; for he didn't relish the chance of a tussle with the police; and here he knew that wasn't likely to happen.

In the crowd, right in front of Johnny, stood a lissome young woman dressed in a gay dark-green dress suit, the skirt barely reaching to her ankles; a black bolero jacket, trimmed with flounced epaulettes which were rimmed with a brighter green than the green of the suit, and flecked with scarlet. She wore high-laced boots that disappeared up under her skirt, which, whenever it was swung by a lively movement of the girl's, showed the fringe of a white lace petticoat. Perched daintily on a curly roll of reddish hair was a dark-green felt hat sporting a black-and-white wing of a bird in its side. Several times Johnny's knee had touched her thigh, timidly at first, then with steadier resolution; and now, with a beating heart, Johnny found that that the girl hadn't taken her leg away from his touch.

Ayamonn, full of himself, was gently swaying to and fro, as far as the crowd's pressure would permit, and singing, half to himself and half to the crowd, his eyes filled with a far-away look:

'My boyish ear still clung to hear
Of Ey–eyrin's pri–ide of yore,
Ere Norman foot did dare pollute
Her in–independent shore;
Of chiefs, long dead, who rose to head
Some gallant pathriot few;
Till all my aim on earth became
To strike one blow for you, dear land,
To strike one blow for you,
To stri–ike one blow for you, dear land,
To stri–ike one blo–ow for youooo!'

A woman striding towards middle age, wearing a disorganised straw hat on her tousled head, patched boots, one brown, one black, the brown one darkened with blacking to make it feel more at home with the other. She wore a black-and-white check skirt, the white square making up to the black ones by the grime gathered in street and house, the whole scalloped by wear and tear along the edges. She wore a large brown shawl flowing down to beyond her hips. Suddenly, she darted out from the crowd to a vacant place on the side-walk, flung her shawl open with a sweeping flip and tucked it more closely round her body, as if she were clothing herself in armour.

—I don't care who hears me, she shouted, for we're full of life today, an' — puff — we're gone tomorra. To every man an' woman their own opinion, square or round or crooked or cornered, which is only right an' proper, an' a fair division. Sayin' nothin' calculated to hurt a soul, I'll say yous are a lot o' starin' fools, watchin' an' waitin' for somethin' yous'll never be spared to see. I wondher, she went on, raising her voice to a screaming pitch, I wondher what all of yous, what any of yous 'ud do, if England went undher!

—Die with joy! a man's voice shouted from the crowd, and a great cheer added an amen to the declaration.

The protesting woman flapped her shawl like a bird flapping its wings, gave a clumsy little lep from the pathway into the air, flapping open her shawl again, and closing it tighter as she did a nervous defiant dance on the pathway.

—There's ne'er an element of surety in your shoutin', she yelled, or the pourin' out of your poor white ignorance an' coloured venom. It 'ud be fitther for yous to work to help yourselves than to set yourselves dhreamin' of help for the Boers; for listen to me — in about as much time as it 'ud take a clever hand an' a sharp knife to peel an apple, England'll put the sign o' death on Kruger an' his gang!

The lissome young lassie standing in front of Johnny, with her leg touching his knee, moved angrily, and turned her pretty head to stare at the yelling woman; and Johnny cursed the oul' one for an ignorant, meddling bitch. Then with a handsome wriggle of her young body, the girl slid from the crowd and stood, red-faced and defiant, before the ill-dressed, blustering woman yelling out for England.

—Will you go home, for God's sake, woman, she said fiercely, an' clap yourself in bed, since you can't help yourself to a suitable understanding! We're serious people here, in no way wishin' to confuse our decency with the dirty tournament of England's attack on inoffensive peoples.

—General Roberts, General French, an' General Kitchener, three Irishmen — remember that! shouted the blustering woman. They'll soon put the lonesome sign of death on Kruger an' his gang!

—Will they now? asked the young woman. You know all about it, don't you? Well, if I read the news right, Gatacre didn't do it at Colesberg, or your great Lord Methuen at Magersfontein, where he led thousands of th' poor bewildered Scots o' th' Highland Brigade to leave an everlastin' farewell to their wives, sisthers, an' sweethearts. And your Buller hasn't done it at Colenso, has he?

A policeman, big and brave, for he knew there were hundreds of his brothers less than half a street away, came up, and eyed the pretty lass with an evil look, his mouth, thought Johnny, wathering for an excuse to haul her to the station, so that he might handle her hidden loveliness while he was doing his duty.

—Eh, you, he said to the lissome lassie, draw it mild an' let the woman have her say. The law allows free expression of opinion to all.

—Come on back here, sweet lass, whispered Johnny, going over slyly, and timidly touching the girl's arm, and never mind that ignorant and insignificant woman; but she brushed his enticing hand away, and he went back to the crowd abashed.

—Irishmen all! yelled the older woman, flapping her shawl, doing her little lep up from the pavement after every sentence, Kitchener, Roberts, Kelly-Kenny, French, Mahon, fightin' for England. Five o' th' best, an' Irishmen all — remember that, now!

—Maybe you've forgotten how th' English went clattherin' down Nicholson's Nek, so's you couldn't see their heels for dust, went on the young lassie, an' thousands now of their best are floatin' fast dead an' down th' Tugela river, headin' out for the sea!

—Irishmen all — you can't get over that, now! screamed the oul' one. Whenever oul' England's in a quandary, up comes th' Irishman, tearin' up he comes, an' turbulent to pull her out of it — ah! me faithful, darlin' Dublin Fusiliers!

A surge of many people cheering came from some distance away, like the first rolling billows of a tidal wave. Ayamonn sniffed, tossed up his head, and listened.

—Something's goin' on below, he said; come on, me boy!

—We're all right here, said Johnny, pulling back, and it's safer to stay where we are.

—We don't want to be safe, cried Ayamonn, making off for the wider vista of Dame Street, followed by the pretty red-haired girl; and the crowd, turning from the lights, swept down, carrying Johnny with them close to the girl, knocking over the boisterous oul' one just as she was doing her little lep from the pathway, and flattening the burly constable against the wall of a building. When they streamed into Dame Street, they mingled with a tremendous crowd, cheering fiercely, and waving hundreds of Boer, Irish, French, and American flags. Some way after the head of the crowd was a brake, a long car, benched on both sides, drawn by two frightened hearse horses. A stout, short, stocky man, whose face was hidden by a wide-awake hat, was driving them. Several other men, pale-faced and tight-lipped, sat on the seats, facing each other; and with them was a young woman with long lovely yellow hair, smiling happily, like a child out on her first excursion.

—Look, Sean, me boy, look! shouted Ayamonn, didn't I tell you we wouldn't take things lying down much longer! That's James Connolly dhrivin', and that little man with the square jaw's Arthur Griffith; an' th' lovely lady's Maud Gonne — help us, Jasus! an' we'll win our freedom yet! Come on!

The horses were moving along at a steady trot, the crowd were keeping up a trot in unison, and after the brake a large mass of heavy-coated, helmeted policemen trotted sullenly, and as nimbly as their bulky bodies would allow. That part of the crowd nearest to the police were laughing animatedly and jeering into their red and sweaty faces, goading them with cries of Shake a leg, there, bring your knees up; take id aysey, me poor men; hay foot, straw foot; keep your chests in an' your bellies well out; it's a damned shame to have th' poor men runnin' their guts out — cruelty t' animals, so 'tis; at th' double, min — quick march; eh, keep back there, an' give th' min breathin' room.

—Keep as close to th' brake as you can, said Ayamonn, pulling at Johnny's arm, while Johnny kept fast hold of the girl's hand, who twined her dainty fingers round his. Pushing hard, they were soon but a few steps behind to one side of the brake, near the great persons who were sitting, tense and tight-lipped, there. In high good-humour they all were, with the police helpless, jammed in the crowd, looking ridiculous as they lumbered along stiffly in an unsteady trot.

Now brakes filled with police forced their way through part of the crowd and followed those trotting along on foot. Passing by the gates of the Castle, there, snug in that deep gash of the city's body, were drawn up all the squadrons of the Horse Police. There they sat their horses, darkly seen for a few moments by those marching by, in the shine of silver on helmet and tunic; gloomily they sat there, a frozen frieze on the façade of the Castle, motionless; not a jingle from stirrup, bridle, or bit, not a hair of a helmet-plume stirring. As they passed and saw, the murmuring, chattering people grew silent, and nothing was heard but the trotting fall of the feet of the crowd; nothing seen but the dark forms, silent, behind the shine of the silver· And Johnny remembered when he last saw such a sight he was safe on the top of a tram, warm and confident, close to his mighty mother's side.

The procession swung into Parliament Street, everyone tense, silent, expectant, waiting. Johnny heard the sound of a sharp order, saw the dark figures coming to life; heard another sharp order, and saw many flashes of light as swords were drawn; saw the plumes stirring as the horsemen moved; heard another shouted order, and the squadrons came galloping down on the crowd. Johnny tried to push a way towards a side street, holding on to the hand of the girl, but they were wedged fast in the crowd, and they were swept beyond it. He saw the people in the brake stand up to watch the charging police, and the driver checked the horses to half turn round and look back over the heads of the swaying crowd. The flashes of steel light were rising high and falling on the heads of the people. The air was deafened with shouts and screams and curses. Those nearest the edges began to seek safety in the side streets; the manly jog-trot of the procession was now but a medley of scuffling feet; the clack of iron hooves on the stone setts, mingled with the cries of those who hadn't yet felt the fall of a sword, and the sombre silence of the Horse Police, trotting here, trotting there, prancing their horses against the tumbling breasts of the people, lifting their heavy sabres as if drilling to the musical notes of a murderous tune, to let them fall on frantic heads trying swiftly to wag aside from each glittering blow.

The people were resisting now. Poles, sticks, bars of iron, and bare fists were contesting the fight with the police.

The horsemen had made a mistake by coming down on them too quickly, giving them no time to scatter, so that wedged together, cut off from a way of escape, the sabre-stormed people were forced to fight back. The Dubliners were angry, and, caught like this, they became a troublesome mass of fighters. Stones snapped asunder some of the chin-chains, and police were riding about bareheaded, with blood trickling down their faces. Some of them had been pulled from their horses, and were struggling on the ground beneath a mass of pummelling fists. Their batons were being used by men in the crowd, and a few had swords which they gripped tensely, but didn't like to use.

—We're caught in a thrap! said Ayamonn hoarsely, grinding his teeth, caught in a thrap!

Johnny put his arms across his chest, pushing out as strong as he could, to keep his ribs from cracking, the sweat rolling down his face and his breath coming out in bitter panting gasps. The girl, flattened beside him, had closed her eyes, and her little red mouth was gaping open. Many dark figures were writhing curiously on the road, dotted here and there with a helmeted body, crouching down on hands and knees, blood dripping on to the setts from some hidden wound. A horseman, well in advance of his comrades, was forcing a way towards Johnny and his two friends, kneeing his horse through the crowd, hacking away with a sabre gleaming sourly in the grey air. Johnny saw a gleam fall on the face of an elderly man, saw a bloody cheek suddenly separate itself from the face and fall away from it, to be frantically clapped back to its place, with a yell, by the stricken man, who suddenly sat down on the road, moaning, pressing his two twitching hands to the horribly gashed face with all his power. Still Johnny stood staring at the slashing horseman, coming closer; still Ayamonn crouched, his arms held high, sheltering head and face; still the pretty girl stood with her eyes closed and her little red mouth gaping. Back, inch by inch, came the crowd, melting before Johnny as the horseman advanced to where but a few yards separated them from the slash of his sabre. A man in front of them, carrying a gaudy Boer flag, screamed when he saw the gleam circle over him, and then sank down without a murmur when the flash fell, letting the flag go from his grip, and as it toppled backwards, the staff came to rest on Johnny's shoulder. Now the horseman curveted round to where they stood, and Johnny saw a pair of eyes, like flaming carbuncles, fixed on him from under the helmet's peak; saw the thick mouth of the half-mad man opening and shutting nervously, the heavy yellow teeth clashing together as he roughly swung his horse round to where they stood. In the madness of fear, Johnny gripped the pole of the flag with both hands and blindly thrust it forward at the rider with all his might as the horse came prancing round on his hind legs. The hard, sharp, wooden spearhead of the flagpole caught the rider on the side of the neck under an ear, and Johnny caught a glimpse of an angry red tear where the spear had struck, as he tumbled off his horse with a sliding crash on to the hard ground, letting a smothered grunt out of him before he lay stunned and still there. Johnny felt a horse's hoof grazing his leg, splitting a trouser-leg from knee to ankle; he saw Ayamonn running furiously over to the fallen rider; saw him stamp his heavy boot on the horseman's face, and though the hard rim of the helmet saved the face from being caved in, Johnny plainly saw that the iron heel had left a horrible bloody blob on the rider's chin; he felt Ayamonn pulling him madly by the arm, and shouting at him, This way; up this street, for Jasus' sake, or we're for it when the others come!

Then they ran; the three of them ran up a side street, ran through the streets before them till they had utterly lost the sound of the tumult in the place they'd left behind them.

Diving into a pub, Ayamonn called for three halves of malt, hot, to get them sober, he said, and to take away the chill that follows the brazen heat of a battle. Johnny smiled, tried to look indifferent, then hurried out to lean against a lamp-post and be sick on the road, Ayamonn watching him anxiously from the doorway.

—All right? he questioned. It's the terrible pressure of the crowd that's upset your stomach. Come in an' get th' ball o' malt down you, an' you'll be right as rain.

—Yes, said Johnny, the pressure of the crowd — that was it; but in his heart he knew that it was fright and the things he had seen. He was no soldier. Never would be — he felt it. There was no use trying; but he'd say nothing before the girl. He went back into the pub.

—That was a glorious prod you gave th' helmeted bowsey, said Ayamonn — right undher th' lug! Save us, you did. He'd ha' sliced us as you'd slice a salmon. God, I did laugh when I seen him hurtlin' off his horse! Well, we stood up to them today. Our dhreams are comin' thrue. Eh, he said suddenly to the barman who had put three whole balls of malt on the counter, I said halves; and Johnny knew that he hadn't enough to pay for the whole ones.

—That's all right, whispered the barman, leaning over the counter, th' dhrinks are on me, see? I guess what you've been doin' — standin' be th' Poor Oul' Woman, wha'?

They all shook hands with the barman, murmured good health, and lowered the steaming amber whiskey. Johnny felt the cold leaden pain in his belly change into a delightful glow of comfort, and his face flushed with a new contentment. He saw the colour creeping back into the girl's face, the sparkle leaping into her dulled eyes, and he saw, with a thrill, her two pointed breasts falling and rising deliciously behind the sweet shelter of her bodice. He caught her arm in his hand and squeezed it, pressing it tighter when she smiled happily back at him.

—Look at his leg, she said, indicating to the barman Johnny's torn trousers; a prancin' horse done it. A wondher he wasn't desthroyed! And the scared face of the falling horseman again came before Johnny's eyes.

—Now, we'd betther scatter, said Ayamonn, when they'd come out of the pub: I this way, yous that. Slan libh till we meet again; and off he went, while Johnny and the girl, in a roundabout way, walked to Ballybough, she with her arm in his, and he pressing it close to his side. He felt lovely thoughts singing her beauty straying through his head, but his heart beat so fast, and his chest felt so tight, that he could hardly say a word.

—You're limping a little, she said, when they were passing over the Tolka.

—The leg's hurting a little, he said.

—Here we are, she said, stopping before a cottage in a little avenue. You'll have to come in for a second an' let's have a look at it. I can put a stitch in your trousers at the same time.

—No, no; I couldn't, he said shyly; thanks all the same, though he longed to go in and seek out a chance to fondle her; I'd better leave you now, really.

—You're a shy fellow, she said, laughing. There'll only be th' two of us, so you needn't worry, and she opened the door with a latchkey. She gave him a pull towards her, saying sharply, Ah, go in, man, or you'll give the neighbours another chance for a fancy-born story.

They went into a little room to the right off a narrow hall, furnished with a table on which was a white cloth and the stuff for a meal, some ham, bread, and an egg in a cup waiting to be boiled, while a shining tin saucepan sat itself within the fender before a brightly-burning fire. Along the wall, under the window, ran a sofa with two big crimson and dark-green covered cushions on it; two rather stiff upright chairs, leather-bound; against the wall opposite, a mahogany cupboard, having on it a gilded vase and many photos of the girl in various positions, with a parasol on the seashore, sitting on a carved stone bench, with a book in her hand, leaning against a fat and fluted pillar; and one, that made Johnny's eyes linger there, of her in low bodice and tights, and a saucy smile on her wide and neatly-curved little mouth. A warm brown carpet, sprinkled with large blue blossoms, covered the floor, and yellow curtains prettily draped the window. The wallpaper was cream-coloured, with trellises of yellow and pink rosebuds everywhere your eye went. Pictures from the Christmas number of *Holly Leaves* covered some of them, and a few were hidden safely by a green-coated Robert Emmett waving a plumed hat over the mantelpiece. Johnny's eyes gave a swift glance at all those bright things, but came back to linger on the photo of her little ladyship wearing the low-cut bodice and the charming tights.

—That's a good one, she remarked, noticing where his eyes had strayed. I'm a good dancer, and whenever there's a panto or anything on with a chorus, I get a job in th' front rank. An uncle of mine lets me have a couple of quid a week, so I don't do too badly. An' how d'ye like me, she added roguishly, in a fie-for-shame costume?

—You look lovely, he said earnestly; you look lovely as you are; and you would blossom forth fair in anything.

—I see, she said, her face flushing pleasantly, you can put a silvery sound into your words when you want to deludher a poor girl. But sit down there till I see to your leg, an' we can talk afterwards.

She put a kettle on the fire, and fetched a basin and a towel from another room. When the water was hot, she poured some into the basin and gently bathed his leg with an old clean linen rag.

—There's a bruise there, she said, an' it has bled a little. When the wound was clean, she smeared some vaseline on a white handkerchief and tied it firmly round his leg.

—There, that should feel easier now, she said. When we've had some tea, I'll do your trousers. Me name's Daisy, she added, Daisy Battles. She went on chatting while she made tea and boiled two eggs. She cut some ham, and placed an egg before him. Eat, she said; you must be nearly starving.

He felt too full and excited and expectant to eat, but he swallowed the egg and drank a cup of tea, watching her making a tidy meal of it.

—Me skirt an' petticoat an' what I wouldn't like to mention are all creased an' twisted with the crush of the crowd. I'll have a job to get them into a proper shape again. Well, it's all for oul' Ireland anyway.

When they'd finished eating, she pulled the table back with a swift movement to the far end of the room, and placed the sofa lengthwise in front of the fire.

—That's much nicer, she said. Sit you down here, an' take off your trousers while I get a needle and thread. Go on, she added, laughing, seeing him hesitate, don't be so shy — I won't look at you, I promise; and she hurried out of the room. Flushed and agitated, he took them off, sat down on the sofa, took off his jacket and draped it over his bare legs. When she came back, he saw she had a dark-green shawl swung from her shoulders down to her hips, fastened over her bosom by a large oval brooch framed in dull gold, having on it a naked girl in ivory standing daringly out from a black velvet background. She sat down beside him, took up his trousers, and began to mend the rent in the leg. He guessed now that there was nothing beneath the dark-green shawl but a thin chemise or something. Frightened, he turned his gaze to the fire, and saw there a glance of agony on a twisted face, a blazing red mark under an ear, and a chin smashed into a bloody blob. He turned his face to watch her stitching.

—God, she said, looking down at his feet sticking out from under his jacket, what tiny feet you've got! An' hands, too! patting one of them; lady's hands an' lady's feet. But you've lost your tongue. Haven't you ever talked to a girl before?

—Of course I have — in Irish, too.

—In Irish, eh? You know Irish then?

—Of course I do.

—What's tabhair dham póg, then?

—Give me a kiss, of course.

—Well, give me one, can't you? Well, you take care not to hurt yourself when you're kind to a girl, she said, after he had bent shyly over and kissed her lightly on the cheek. What body would believe you bowled a policeman from his horse? There now, that looks a little better, and she held up the trousers with the long rent neatly sewed together. No one'll know you were in a fight, an' you goin' home; and she flung them over the back of a chair behind the sofa.

—That's a nice brooch you're wearing, he said, pressing closer to her now.

—Isn't it? A present from the oul' uncle, taking it out of the shawl, and handing it to him. Supposed to be Vaynus. Naughty girl in the altogether. She shook her shoulders, and the shawl fell from her, leaving her in chemise and stockings. You'll scorch your jacket, and she whipped it off his legs, and flung it on the chair behind. My goodness, I can hear your heart thumping from here!

—Isn't yours thumping too? he asked. Let me feel; and he pulled loose the bow-ends of the ribbons, opening her chemise halfway down so that her taut white breasts with their rosy nipples appeared bare before him; and he pressed his hot hands over them. Then he tugged at her chemise to raise it higher on her legs, and she half rose from the sofa to let him do it properly, before she stretched down on it to wait for his coming.

Some hours afterward she was lying on the sofa, the shawl around her, the brooch, with its dull gold rim framing the naked lady, fastening it together over her bosom; but the naked lady was naked no longer, nor did his hands ache to tear away the dark-green shawl hiding again her many buoyant beauties.

—You're in a great hurry, she said, looking at him through half-closed eyes. Can't you stay a little longer?

—I can't he said. I have a lot of work to do.

—Work! she echoed. Work on a day like this? What kinda work?

—I have a lot of things to learn, Daisy.

—Well, she said, giggling, you've learned a lot with me today, haven't you? You'll be a knowin' fellow from this out. Won't you come to see me soon again?

—Yes, of course I will. Goodbye for the present — I must be going.

—Well go, she said, sharply; no-one's keepin' you. You're a good boy, she said in a softer tone, holding out her hand. There, as he pressed it hard, don't break it. You have me half dead, she added roguishly, an' poor me thinkin' you too shy to do anything dangerous! Shut the door softly afther you; and closing her eyes, she lay back on the sofa with a happy long-drawn sigh as he left her.

ALL HEAVEN AND HARMSWORTH TOO

JOHNNY'S brother, Archie, had thrown up the stage as a bad and mad job. After serving as a property master in Dublin's Theatre Royal, he had gone on a crazy fit-up tour in the West with a company playing *Saved From the Sea*. One of the nights he had been put to take the money at the door; had found that when no more came, he had taken just enough to pay a third-class fare to Dublin on the midnight train. Leaving the rest of the company to do their best to keep the people happy, he hurried to the station, flung himself into a carriage corner, and arrived home, covered with white Connemara dust, wearing an old narrow-caped long coat, used for the part of Myles na Coppaleen, with three-ha'pence in one pocket and a hen egg in the other. One day, some time after, walking a country road, he had seen a big, long, well-dressed gentleman in trouble with a punctured bicycle. He came over to help, and being skilful with his hands, he soon sent the gentleman home on his way rejoicing. While mending the bicycle, the big gentleman had chatted to Archie, and mentioned that his firm, the Harmsworth Irish Agency, was in need of a clerk; and the bould Archie had ventured to offer himself for the job. One good turn deserving another, Archie got a month's trial, and proving satisfactory, the big, long man, Herbert Knox McKay, of His Majesty's Militia, and Dargaville Carr, the senior partner, had agreed to make Archie's job permanent at a pound a week. So here Archie was now, for over a year, confidential clerk of Messrs. Harmsworth's Agency, trading in the Irish distribution of *Answers, Forget-me-not, Home Circle, Golden Stories, Home Chat, Sunday Companion, Comic Cuts* and *Chips*, the pioneer ha'penny boys' papers, the *Marvel, Union Jack*, and *Pluck*, the *Wonder, Boy's Friend*, and the pioneer sixpenny monthly, the *Harmsworth Magazine*. Johnny had now got a sort of a temporary job there, too, of five hours' work on five days of the week for five shillings a week, which paid the rent, provided two dinners in the week of threepence-worth of liver, or of scraps of meat for a stew, and tuppence-worth of spuds, still leaving tuppence in hand for a possible emergency.

Archie, flying high, had married the daughter of a clergyman's son's son, but neither Johnny nor his mother had seen the lady; for Johnny's broken-down appearance didn't look nice, and their home was no fit place to bring the daughter of a clergyman's son's son. The poor man, so it was said, had been fond of the bottle; and his family, after his death, and before it, were left in the rough and rocky lap of poverty. But Josephine Fairbeeley still remained a lady. On a visit to the office to see Archie, she had passed Johnny by one day — a little, stumpy, plain, perky-faced lass, with an air that said to all she thought beneath her, I'm a lady born, a lady bred, an' when I die I'll be a lady dead. The one other assistant, a fellow named Drolly, gathered, it was said, cheaply out of a Foundling Hospital, in a muted whisper told Johnny that that was Archie's missus. She passed out again, with a disdainful nod to the foundling and a trivial glance at Johnny, unembarrassed, for she wist not who he was; but passed out with the pointed chin stuck out, a proud tilt to the snub nose, and a veiled glow of self-esteem shining from the dull grey eyes set deep in her perky, pawky, pucklike face. A sting of resentment shot through Johnny's emotions at being set aside for fear the knowledge of kinship should bring the wilt of shame into her walk and the frown of distant association on to her pawky face. But it lasted only for a brief while; for Johnny was building a house of his own in which there was no room for his brother or his brother's wife. And scornful thoughts of things outside of it were hardening his heart. He knew now that he was far and away his brother's superior, who never ventured to dispute an opinion of his, knowing, if the argument went far, he'd but show an ignorance he was eager to hide. At the moment, Johnny was trying his hand at German, but his funds allowed him to purchase only a second-hand tattered German grammar for threepence, that led him nowhere; and he was fain to wait a better time to bring a chance to get some better books to help him. Anyway, he was learning his own tongue gaily; and his already fine grasp of English gave him always a readiness, and sometimes put a sparkle into what he said to many who had been blessed with an everyday chance from the time they were born. Poor Archie was but small beer to him now.

He wasn't long in the job till he found that the foundling was a sneak, encouraging the enthusiastic Johnny to try to convince him of the rights denied to their country; listening attentively to his warm and eloquent arguments, and then running off hot-foot to pour all, and more, of what Johnny had said into the wide-open ear of militia McKay. And ever after in life Johnny found that all charity boys were dangerous; and here began a feeling of hatred to the Christian kindness that half-filled bellies with food, and stuffed the mind with fear and meanness. This bright specimen was a bouncing brave of the Young Men's Christian Association, and didn't stop there; oh, no, he must make himself a member of a clean Christian clique whose dirty duty it was to prowl round — after having had first a cold bath to keep their privates from rising in alarm — and give a godfly reprimand to any man seen speaking to a whore; or to go through the country lanes where courting couples lay close, threatening to inform the police of an act against public decency if a skirt went higher than a knee, or a manly finger dared to touch a trouser button. Johnny thought that if this discordant hound of heaven ever strayed towards him, and he with a girl, he'd make a daub of his ugly face; muck and mash and mangle about his ugly face, and make a daring daring daub of it; hoe the image of God out of it; and leave it lying lost and lorn in vacancy!

One day while Archie was at the bank, and Johnny was waiting for

Drolly to fill in parcel dockets before taking the packages to the transport agents, the boul' Herbert Knox McKay walked in, gigantic in the full-dress uniform of an officer in the King's Royal Rifles — sword, sabretache, an' all. He lingered in the delivery and packing room to show himself off to Johnny and the foundling. He was well over six foot, big-chested and broad-shouldered, but one of his knees was made of clay. A mile of a walk would send the leg sagging, in spite of it being bound up with all sorts of surgical tapes. Whenever he was in uniform, he took a car as often as possible so as to save the poor game-leg. When he had popped in, Johnny had been reading a book which he shoved into his pocket, but not before the warrior had noticed it. There he stood, facing Johnny, a gloomy figure in the foggy room, looking, in his uniform, like a smoky manual trickling from the nearest crack to hell.

—Reading, eh? What have you been reading? he asked.

—*The Life of Theobald Wolfe Tone*, sir.

—Good God! he nearly shouted, and stalked into his office. In a few moments he was at the door again, the yellow face, stuck into the sombrely-plumed busby, staring at Johnny. That sort of thing isn't read here; not here; not in a Harmsworth office. I'm surprised you haven't the decency to think of your respectable brother. The uniform I'm wearing is the sign of what all connected with Harmsworth's believes and honours, and represents what is to go on here.

—You mean belief in monarchy, sir, do you?

—In monarchy, yes; and in everything sacred to every decent man!

—Well, sir, insisted the foolish Johnny, if you can spare me some of your time, I shall be happy to argue the why and wherefore of Republicanism.

—Republicanism? With me? Argue with me! Goood God! And the uniformed figure disappeared behind a banged door.

A fear-God-and-honour-the-king fellow, thought Johnny, who neither honours his king nor fears his God; for if he honoured the king, he would honour all men, since the king is but an exalted symbol of the subject; and if he feared God, he would readily argue with his fellow-man, for is it not written, Come, let us reason together, saith the Lord of Hosts. Well, what I have said, I have said; but from the cold glint he saw in the Militia Captain's eye, he knew things would never be the same again here, and that the money for the rent, the liver, and the spuds was in danger.

He remembered, as he waited, how when McKay and McKay's wife had taken a new house and had shifted the furniture in, though not quite ready to live there that day, he had got Johnny to watch for two nights running in case of burglars. Johnny had gone to the tall, wide house, with its lovely bay windows and laurelled garden; had lighted a fire in the kitchen to keep him company; had sought for food and found none; had hurried back home for some tea and bread from his mother's small store; had watched faithfully the two long nights, a poker handy in case of invasion. On the third morning, and it pouring with rain, the boyo and the wife had come bustling in to take possession. She at once ran over, seized the tongs, and hastily began to take from the fire those lumps of coal that, though blazing, hadn't yet become red, piling them safely and prudently on the hob for future use. McKay went from room to room, followed by Johnny, to see that everything was there. He craned his neck from one of the windows, and said, Oh, he's there all right. Johnny saw that it was the gardener he meant; for, looking in the same direction, he saw the man digging, an old sack round his shoulders.

—I suppose he shouldn't be out in that rain, murmured McKay; with a bad cough, too; but he seems to like it.

—He's afraid, said Johnny; afraid to give up. Shall I run out and tell him?

—No, no, said McKay; don't disturb him. He probably wouldn't feel comfortable if he thought he wasn't earning his money fairly. You can go now, he added to Johnny; everything seems all right.

Johnny hesitated, expecting a fee, but none was offered; so he shrugged his shoulders resignedly, remembering he had told his mother the vigil would mean a few more bob for them, and that she'd scarcely credit the story that nothing had been given; yet he shrugged his shoulders, took his billy-can from the hob, saying to Mrs. McKay, There, you've more room now to store the coal; and turning on his heel, he left them salvaging as much of the coal as they could. Prudence, he thought, is one of the cardinal virtues.

Fairly common minds that consorted with the faith of the common newspapers, thought Johnny, watching the advance of the world through the mind of the baronet; Harmsworth, the Immanuhell of journalistic vulgarism, arraying the legitimate gets of King-Kong in the robes of glory once worn by the saints, sages, prophets, and poets of England.

The senior partner, Dargaville Carr, was an opposite to Mr. McKay. He was slender, handsome, with a boyish face, ever tinted with an indifferent smile. He was good-humoured, careless, with the charming manner of an Irishman who cared not how the world wagged so long as he had satisfaction waiting on his desires. Rarely he came to the office, and when he did, he came dressed fit to kill, with a fine geranium or a dainty rose fast fixed in his buttonhole. He came with a quick good-morning to everyone, a quicker run to the inner office, an opening of the big roll-top desk, a shutting of it again, and away he was with another hearty smiling good-morning to everyone. Johnny liked Dargaville Carr. Johnny had seen the original agreement between Carr on the one hand, and Harmsworth on the other: wherein was laid down in set terms, in fair handwriting, that for several hundreds of pounds, duly paid over by the said Carr to the said Harmsworth, the said Harmsworth, Journalist, would contribute his brains to the founding of a weekly journal to be called *Answers to Correspondents*, which, when founded, and in circulation, the aforesaid Dargaville Carr, Gentleman, would contribute a further sum in sterling, in return for which he would receive, without fail, the benefit of the profits flowing from the sale of the said paper in Ireland; and any Irish profits that might come from each and every and all subsequent and subsidiary publications that might spring off the foundation of the original weekly journal.

So it was that a Harmsworth, called forth by destiny and the needs of the English people, heard the English calling Come over and help us, as St. Patrick had heard the voice of the Irish calling centuries before; so he said to his lord, Carr, Lord, here am I; send me, that we may deliver the goods, sanctify the English, and lead them backward to the knowledge belonging to their pees and queues; that I having been desirous, above all other things, of pupularity, may, at the end, drink dupe of the peerian spring that flows sweet Afton beyond the common ken of man's a man for a' that, and brings hellarity to all who drink its waters. And his lord gave him a bag holding two hundred shekels of gold: Go in pride, my sin, make England thy wish-pot and cast thy shoe over shedom; for it is written: in Dublin shall one be born before whom all hads shall bow, and infonts and succkerlings shall give thee willcome, and the great ones there shall be akneeled and anulled for ever. And it shall come to pass that thou hast pitched thy tint in England, then shall I send thee a bag of shekels as big as the one thou now hast, forasmuch as thou wilt do as much and more, unto me when the shekels multiply their numbers. And he answered all that I have is mine.

It was Johnny's job to bring all the packages of papers, with which the firm dealt, to the stations, or newsagents who preferred to deal with them direct, rather than with Jason's; to hunt the goods out of the boat's hold at the North Wall whenever they were late; to help in the sorting and parcelling of the papers; and to pack away the unsold copies for transport as waste paper. He pushed the packages to their various places in a handcart that had long since seen its best days. One of its rests was broken, and swung about like the broken leg of a horse; two spokes were missing from one wheel; one of the iron tires was loose, and Johnny had to carry a hammer with him wherever he went to give it an odd knock back into its right place; and both linch-pins were broken, so that they had to be carefully tied in with twine to keep the wheels from falling off — a constant source of worry to Johnny, who had always to keep an eye fixed, now on this wheel, now on that, to make sure each was all right, and watch his way through the traffic at the same time. This old car, bought second-hand, was part of the firm's economy, as was the saving of old paper, old rope, and old twine.

Cursing and sweating, he pushed the haggard car along, on a lovely evening in the late spring. Packed high it was with the latest number of the *Harmsworth Magazine*. Rotten Dublin; lousy Dublin, what had it for anyone? What had it for him? Poverty and pain and penance. They were its three castles. The gates of Dublin: poverty, pain, and penance. And the *Harmsworth Magazine*, giving, with the aid of its kind, to Dublin the glory that was Greece and the grandeur that was Rome. Now he was a barrennut. Thank God, the Gaelic League was doing all it could to turn the Irish people from a descent into a vulgar and idiotic Tophet; but, so far, with little success. The Orange cover of *Answers* covered the whole country. The priest had it in the inner pocket of his soutane; the teacher had it on his desk; the student had it under his arm; the labourer had it round his lunch; the soldier had it in his sentry-box; the postman in his bag; and the policeman had it on his beat; for *Answers* stooped to conquer. Tomorrow would be the day for that joy journal; and he'd be carrying a heavy cargo again, for there was a new competition on, offering as first prize a thousand pounds down, or two pounds a week for life. An' everybody would be stretching out a hand for it. Lousy, rotten, tiring Dublin, an ignorant perjury of life.

He pushed on through Parliament Street, up Cork Hill, through Lord Edward Street, into Cornmarket, delivering here, delivering there, till he reached James Street where he emptied the ould hand-cart of its last parcel. Then he sailed down Watling Street to go home-wards by the quays, for he loved to see the river Liffey when the sun was setting, passing by many shops and houses looking like poor bewildered whores bullied with too long a life.

Harmsworth and his henchmen! He pictured them assembling round their master to hear the orders for the year: Bullcalf, Feeble, Snout, Mouldy, Shallow, Wart, Fang, and Snare. He heard him say unto them: Attention! We're here to follow, not to teach. Look out for likely whims, and cater to them. Who are we to look down on ignorance? No, look up to it, for it has great power. Get down to it; you won't have to go far. The less you know the better. What do you know? What can you know? What do you want to know? Nothing. Repeat that after me. Don't forget these essential points: One, the English girl has ne'er an equal. Two, marriage is a mainstay, with the baby, and, of course, Mother. Three, the prickle of a sprig of holly in everything you say about Christmas. Four, England will always weather the worst; and don't let either God or a good story be far from your elbows. Better learn all that off be heart. Salem. It's your life. We are the eyes of the world, the ears of the world, the voice of the world. We bring the second ark. Shiloh. Learn that off be heart too.

The twilight was getting close to the skirts of day when Johnny swung his chariot on to the quays confining the river like a pair of lusty arms round a pretty lass. Over to the sou'-west the sky was a vivid green mantle, bordered with gold, a crimson gold that flowered grandly against the green, darkening into a gentle magenta higher up and farther away in the sky; and farther away still, the faint glimmer of the first stars was peeping out from a purple glow of purple gloom. Numerous empty lorries, floats, vans, and drays were flowing quickly past him, each of them, under the magic sky, looking like flaming chariots making for a battle front. He saw golden arrows of the sun shooting up side streets, leading from the quay to God knows where. Here the hard, set, and leering faces of roughs leaning against a corner had changed into sturdy faces of bronze where the sun's shadow lingered, and became darkly golden where the sun's departing beams strayed towards them. The bridges looked like golden pathways, growing grey dauntlessly, turning from pride to get gentleness and peace. He left the crippled handcart by the side of the street, and went over to lean upon the river wall to gaze at Dublin in the grip of God. The old tattered warehouses and shops, bespangled with the dirt of ages, had turned to glory. Children, born into a maze of dirt, their vagrant garments clinging wildly to their spattered bodies, put on new raiment, satinised with the princely rays of the sun, as if she had winced at their ugliness and had thrown her own fair mantle over them all. The great dome of the Four Courts shone like a golden rose in a great bronze cup. The river flowing below was now a purple flood, marbled with gold and crimson ripples. Seagulls flew upward, or went gliding swooning down through thin amber air; white gems palpitating on the river's purple bosom. And far away in the deep blue the stars grew braver, and sat with dignity in their high places, bowing the sun away out of the silken heavens. Johnny bowed his head and closed his eyes, for it was very beautiful, and he felt that his city could catch an hour of loveliness and hold it tightly to her panting breast.

A rippling thrill of emotional ecstasy crept through him, looking at the sky above and at the river beneath; all this beauty and much more, everlasting, to be his and all men's through the life, passion, and death of the wonderful Jesus, when the glare of this poor life slowly darkened into death. He sang softly and fervently, watching the mauve and golden buildings, the crimsoned waters of the river beneath him, the sky like a mantle streaming from the shoulders of God, the Father. Softly and fervently he sang, sang softly to himself and the loveliness around him:

> When our brisk hands build strong where work is done,
> Where steel is forg'd, or gentle silk is spun,
> All work well finish'd, with work that's well begun,
>   Let it praise Thee, let it praise Thee!
>
> All th' white joy that shines in children's play,
> And th' rich laugh that rings when youth is gay,
> All th' still pleasure in life now turning grey,
>   Let them praise Thee, let them praise Thee!
>
> Even when horrid poverty and pain
> Darkens th' senses with their stinging stain,
> And human hearts are bow'd beneath the strain,
>   Give us strength, Lord, strength to praise Thee!
>
> In th' wide streets where th' rich are in full cry,
> In th' wide stores where workers serve and sigh,
> In th' dark crannies where th' poorer lie,
>   Give them grace, Lord, grace to seek Thee!
>
> Hearten our city's strife with manners mean;
> Blend with our bread the bread of life unseen,
> With a gay rose's beauty in between,
>   We beseech Thee, we beseech Thee!

He resolved to be strong; to stand out among many; to quit himself like a man; he wouldn't give even a backward look at the withering things that lived by currying favour with stronger things; no busy moving hand to the hat for him. He would enlarge on a spare life, never pausing to pick up a prize that perished as soon as the hand grasped it. His treasures would be simple things, like those gathered together by St. MacCua, who had a cock who served his owner by crying lustily at midnight to warn the saint it was time to greet the day with his first devotions; a mouse that saw the saint wasted no more than five hours a day in sleep, nibbling at his master's ear, should he sleep on, till the torment brought the saint to himself, and encouraged him to keep up his devoirs to Almighty God; and a fly that strolled along the lines of the psalter as it was being read aloud by MacCua, settling on the last word murmured when the weary saint rested, remaining there, still as death itself till the saint came back to resume the reading of a canticle declaring penitence or praise. And, O Lord, wasn't it the dark hour for the saint when, one day, his three treasures died, each within a minute of the other, compelling the heartbroken man to write to Colmkille complaining of the great loss these three pets meant to him; getting back a note from the Dove of Iona counselling him not to be cast down, not to wonder at the sudden taking-away of his flock, for their loss was but one more instance of the quick departure of the world's wealth, poor MacCua regarding the Dove's gentle joke as a tender reminder that he shouldn't have been so much attached to the treasures of this fleeting world. So, something like MacCua, he would seek the things that endured; his treasures would be books, bought by the careful gathering of widely, scattered pence. From life he had learned much; and from books he would learn more of the wisdom thought out, and the loveliness imagined, by the wiser and greater brethren of the human family.

He rose up out of his sturdy thinking and his soft singing, went over to the handcart, and began again to push it along the golden road, with the dome of the Four Courts on his left still looking like a great yellow rose in a great bronze cup. At a corner of a street, lower down, a hurdy-gurdy began to play a dance tune in a violet shadow. He stopped again by the river wall to listen. The player was robed with the sun as if for a religious festival. A young woman, dressed in a dark-red bodice and a black-and-white striped skirt, tapped her feet in the same violet pool and swung golden arms to the beat of the gay music. Then she began to dance. Johnny watched her. She laughingly beckoned to him with a golden hand. He flung off his coat, took a great red handkerchief from a pocket and bound it round his waist like a sash. He hurried over, caught in the golden glamour of the dancer's face, beat time for a moment to the tune, got the swing of it, and then jumped into the hilarious dance of the young woman. At a little distance, a group, more soberly clad, for they stood in the deep shade of a huge building, here and there flecked with the red rays of the sun, stood and watched and quietly clapped their hands. The young woman caught Johnny's hand in her own, and the two of them whirled round in the bonny madness of a sun-dance, separating then so that she whirled into a violet shadow, while he danced into a golden pool, dancing there for a little, then changing places, he to be garbed in the hue of a purple shadow, and she to be robed in a golden light.

—Grandchildren of kings! he shouted, in the midst of the dancing; sons and daughters of princes, we are one with the race of Milesius!

—The finest colours God has in His keeping are round us now, she panted.

—Th' sword of light is shining!

The violet shades grew darker, the golden light was tinged with scarlet, but still they danced, and still the player played, waving a dark hand against a green plane in the sky, and beating lustily to the time of the tune with an excited foot in a purple pool. Then they tired, their movements slackened, went slower, waned faster, and finally came to an end with their arms round each other, while the dusky figures in the watching group clapped their hands softly, murmuring that it was well done and was worth the doing. He gave the hurdy-gurdy man his last sixpence and kissed the girl goodbye.

—You're lovely staying still, he said, and brimming over with a wilder beauty in the sprightly dance; may you marry well, and bring up children fair as Emer was, and fine as Oscar's son; and may they be young when Ireland's free, when Spanish ale foams high on every table, and wine from the royal Pope's a common dhrink!

He shoved his handcart along again under the motley dome of the sky, tired, but joyous, praising God for His brightness and the will towards joy in the breasts of men, the swiftness of leg and foot in the heart of a dance, for the gift of song and laughter, for the sense of victory, and the dream that God's right hand held firm. The green, the scarlet, the gold, and the purple — what were they but the glow from the wings of the angels pathrolling the streets of the city.

But the glory of the angels was departing, for the jubilant colours dimmed into darkness, save where, in the distant horizon, a crimson streak showed where the curtains of night had not yet been pulled together. God's shadow was still there, for every church he passed had floods of people pouring into them. He lingered by one of them, and watched the flood going in by the main door, tributaries flowing more gently in by doors on the side, paying a minimum sixpence there, and, at the main gateway, anything above a penny to the Confraternity man standing in the porch, holding a long-handled box, with a wide slit cut in the top to receive the coins, hopping swiftly about, shaking the box encouragingly before those ready to give, and shaking it threateningly under the nose of those who tried to slip in without paying their due. A poster on a gothically-topped board told all that a Mission was being given by a Dominican who was to preach on 'Hell and the Many Roads that Lead There'; and Johnny felt a whiff of brimstone as he looked through the wide-open door. Thoughts of a frightful form and hue hurried through his mind, and harried him, for he saw himself fixed in, and frozen fast in fire eternal; fire keener in its thrust than tusks of steel, while whirlwinds of icy winds and smoky storms, suffocating the burning air, raged all around him, plunging his soul from the deepest misery to a misery deeper still; with senses tuned by immortality to their highest pitch, impaled by justice to endure them all; buried in a screaming pain, yet rushing pell-mell to a fiercer, biting woe; ever shrieking for a chance, that died ten thousand years ago, to come to life again; a shriek, once uttered, sunk to silence by the malice-mongering laughter of hardened devils tossed to hell in heaven's first battle with an evil power. O Lord most mighty, O holy and most merciful Saviour, he murmured, deliver me not into the bitter pains of eternal death. He looked through the wide-open door again and saw, up at the far end of the nave, the shining altar, surrounded with carpeted steps, gay with glittering lights, glowing on a great gilt crucifix, hanging behind, and in its centre some sacred vessel, covered by a pure white veil.

A holy city's our city of Dublin, thought Johnny; more ancient than Athens; more sacred than Rome; as holy as Zion. From every window, if one had only eyes to see, flew a banner that was a red, brown, white, or blue scapular, each with some holy words of the Lord, or one of His saints, embroidered across its field; and from every pillar and every wall hung festoons of rosary beads, the precious jewels of a poor people. Night and day the air was alive with an ever-lasting murmur of Pater Nosters and Hail Marys, Sé do bheatha, a Mhuire dhílis, he murmured, atá lán de grása; 'tá an Tighearna leat (God thy life, O sweet Mary, who art full of grace; the Lord is with thee). Other lands might boast of their lions and unicorns, their double-headed eagles, or the fleur-de-lys; but here we had the Sacred

Heart, sliced with the wound the lance made, and duplicates of the massive keys of St. Peter, hanging at the girdle of the Pope. There were more saints in Ireland to the square inch than in any other country or the globe. All the people, at a penny a week, were preparing for a good death; all were enlisted in the army of prayer, praying for the holy souls, prostrate in purgatory; snug on many a manly chest, and lying shyly between the breasts of many a fair potential bosom, lay a tiny miraculous medal, warming away the chill of the fear of disaster or death from the souls of them who wore it. St. Dominic knew the streets of Dublin as well as those of Calahorra; his hand, that fell hot and heavy on the Albigenses, lies gently on the heads here; for of his three great rules, poverty and fasting are kept by crowds of people, though the third of silence has yet a long way to come; and St. Francis has gathered more pale and scarlet roses from the wretched wrecked streets of this city than he ever gathered from the grove outside of Portincula.

It was dark now; each street-lamp hissed as he passed it; all the buildings were dark, grim, and lowering; the passer-by moved jerkily along, and his joints were creaking; all the sparkling dresses of an hour ago were folded up and put away; and Johnny was just pushing a crippled handcart down a sombre street. He came up with an old, heavily-grey-bearded, bent man chanting a hymn mournfully along the kerb-way. He wore a long, old, grey top-coat reaching to his heels. A section of the hem at the back had ripped away and trailed behind him on the cobblestones. His white head was reverentially bare, and he carried his dinged and faded bowler in a hand behind his back. He walked slowly along the kennel, his face turned sideways towards the footpath, watching the passers-by to see if any would show a sign of a search for a coin, ready to bring the hat with a gentle sweep in front of him to capture any coin that might be offered. On he moved, three slow steps at a time, then a pause, then another three slow steps forward. Moving with him, three steps, a pause, then three more steps, were a group of gaping children, a sad audience to a sadder song. They stared open-eyed whenever an emotional tear welled from his eye and trickled down a furrowed cheek. When he came near, Johnny saw that the old singer was irritated by the staring kids, saw a wicked light in his moist eye when he happened to glance at them, and a muttered complaint rippled roughly through the chanting flow of the hymn. Happily plaintive he made the hymn, and bitter the mutter meant for the children:

To Jesu's heart all burning with fervent love for men —

—G'way, little gapers, keepin' me from doin' justice to meself!
   My heart with fondest yearning shall raise the joyful strain —
—Hell an' hot wather to yous, for idle little ruts!
   While ages course along, blest be with loudest song,
   Th' Sacred Heart o' Jesus by every heart an' tongue!
Johnny pushed on, walking alongside two men, chatting together,
who were going in the same direction.

··—That oul' fella's hymn-singin's after givin' me a sudden idea about
the lone picture I have a doubt of, th' one showin' a kinda deer an' a
letther that's half an eff an' half a dee.

—Now isn't that curious, rejoined the other. What was it?

—Th' deer, a hart — see? and the letther a dee or an eff — Hartford
— see?

—Begod you've got it! Though I never hearda Hartford.

—Nor me, either; but it must be right. What the last ten'll be like,
God knows — stiff ones, I'll take me oath. He rubbed his hands
together, and crinkled his face with a smile; but the missus is doin' a
Novena for me, an' if that doesn't bring luck, I don't know what will.
A thousand down, Bill, or two pounds a week for life. Jasus, if I won!
I'd never see a poor day.

Heaven and Harmsworth close together. Goethe's last wish for
more light at last fulfilled. A roaring British Buddha. He comes, he
comes, he comes o'er the waters to me. Pieoneers, O Pieoneers. A silk
umbrella and the handle of a broom. Boomlay, Fumelay, Doomlay,
Zoom. The Congo Comes to Canterbury.

Johnny began to hurry home, for an earlier rising lay before him;
Answers, the Golden One, would be out tomorrow.

PICTURES IN THE HALLWAY

A NEW rector was expected to come soon to the parish of St. Burnupus. Strange ministers from different parishes came Sunday after
Sunday to conduct matins and evensong, to preach tired-out sermons,
and so hold the fort and keep the young flag flying. The few who came
to church regularly, whispered that the new rector was a fine preacher;
and that was most important, for the pulpit, not the Holy Table, was
the important point in a protestant church. There was waiting for him
a tiny world of faint religion, vague, timid of anything a step away
from a rare reading of a Bible verse; a happy or tearful belief that God

made a call and left a card at baptism, marriage, or the burial of the dead; a faith that felt easy when *Abide With Me* was sung at evening-tide, or, *Now that Daylight Fills the Sky, We Lift our Hearts to God on High*, by whomsoever happened to be in church at half-past eleven on a Sunday morning, and *Hark, the Herald Angels Sing*, while the big and small bells rang out on a brisk and bonny Christmas morning. Regular worshippers were few, for here there was small chance of making a good thing out of Christ. The children were kept busy, piling Bible story and Bible verse into their memories, fast and furious, making up for their parents' sang-freud, sleeping long and soberly Sundays, in the warmth of their beds; reading newspapers fattened on stories of battle, murder, and sudden death, or of jangling jingles in the bedrooms of the nicely rich; eating their fancy's fill in the early evening; yawning their way back to bed again when the moon began her gentle dance in the sky. The parish had raised a sleepy head on a reclining arm when Harry Fletcher came, to have a look at him who came in the name of the Lord, had opened its drooping eyes a little wider for a small moment, and had fallen back into a deeper sleep when Harry left. The people had an idea, in a dazed way, that somehow or other God had made a wonderful world, underfoot and overhead; though underfoot was rough, marred with dust, and stony. Their way to heaven was a lifelong journey through never-ending streets of dingy houses, some of the wayfarers stopping now and then for a drink in a gayer house, glass-framed, and painted a shining red or green, and gilded. In the daytime, making a brush at Varian's, pushing a truck in a railway store, handling a pick on the roads, dishing out tea and sugar in a tea store, carrying a hod up a shaking ladder, or filling in invoices stuck all day to a standing-steady desk: there we all were (or, as Johnny was himself, an inspector of public buildings — the name given to an out-of-work in Dublin), amaking atonement with God in the best way that they could for the fall of Adam, the sin of disobedience bringing death into the world and all our woe, the sin that gave room for the more sinister and desperate one of original sin; for as the psalmist hath said, I was born in iniquity, and in sin hath my mother conceived me; a hard lot to live down, thought Johnny, for every pretty girl that passed sent Johnny's heart singing,

> Under th' blossoming mulberry bush
> A girl's undone in a panting hush,
> When th' stars are bright, where th' grass is lush,
>   On a saintly summer evening.

Good-looking girlish faces and shapely legs apart, the hard, beam-
less, grey, sleety mist of the dourer protestantism chilled Johnny; and
he crept forward out of it into a brighter and more musical conception
of the Christian faith. Colour had come to him, had bowed, laughing,
and now ran dancing before him. He had saved some of what he got
for doing an occasional job, and had bought a tiny box of paints. He
had always loved sketching, and had, in younger days, covered every
scrap of fair paper coming into the house, as well as the back parts
of pictures in books, with his ideas of battles, and, later on, of men and
women; but now that colour had come to him, he longed to be a
painter, and his very bowels yearned for the power to buy tubes of
cobalt blue, red lake, chrome yellow, Chinese white, emerald green,
burnt sienna, and a deep black pigment. Long and prayerfully he had
looked in at the window of a big shop in Dawson Street that sold these
things, his eyes ravished with the water-colours displayed there; at the
brushes, thin and delicate; the piled-up boxes of paints of every sort
and size; the pyramids of tubes filled with glowing colours; all so near,
yet so far, so far away from the reach of his hand and the further reach
of his longing soul. He would sometimes curse his poverty, and finish
with a soft prayer that means would be provided to let him buy what
would give him a chance to put on paper the wonderful colours his
eyes saw and his heart loved. He was too ragged and too shy to venture
a visit to the portly, pompous, and awe-spreading National Gallery.
He did the next best thing: at second-hand book barrows he picked
up, for a few pence, two books enshrining pictures by a religious
painter called Fra Angelico, and one showing lovely things his eyes
had not yet seen, far away from Dublin, of wood, lake, pond, and
peasants thrown together, like a sudden burst of music; all by a
fellow named Constable. With all he had learned from the Bible and
the Prayer Book it was but an easy jump into the brightly-tinted
world of Angelico; and from the little church of St. Burnupus, in its
desolate seat among the dust of the dowdy streets, the cinders of the
bottle-making factory of North Lotts, for ever pouring out its murky
plumes of smoke, the scarred heaps of mouldering bark and timber
chips round Martin's timber yard, the dung of the cattle, passing in
droves down to the quays, the smell of the beer-soaked sawdust,
floating out from the wide-open doors of the pubs, blending its smell
with that of the foul rags of the festering, fawning poor, Johnny
ferried himself safely to the circle of delicate blue showing forth
Angelico's golden-haired Saviour clad in a robe of shimmering
creamy grey, a shining orb in a beautiful left hand, a halo of heavy

gold, transversed with a crimson cross, encircling His heavenly head; or, there He was, standing in a purple arch of the heavens, staff in hand, looking with love on two Dominican brothers, one of whose hands timidly touched the Saviour's, the two of them dressed in robes tenderly cream, covered with sombre black cloaks cunningly tinged with green, standing there gazing at Christ with a look that reverently called God their comrade. Again, with Angelico, he wandered through clouds of angels, a little stiff with innocence, thronging the skies like gaily-coloured Milky Ways, crimson or green or blue-gowned, powdered with stars or roses or golden fleurs-de-lys. Sometimes he chanted hymns softly to himself, strolling towards heaven through a field of pinks and roses, meeting often on his way more lovely angels, blowing with fattened cheeks through golden trumpets, or stringing delicate white fingers over graceful psalteries or zithers, sounding in honour of the Blessed Virgin, while her Son fixed another gem in her crown of glories.

Again, under the green, sunlit, or dewy trees, planted by Constable's imagination, giving shade and gracefulness to an eager sun, he wandered afield; or looking down where the ripening corn was striding upward to a golden grandeur, he wandered down quiet paths rimmed with vivid green, touched in with lavish blossoms, shyly forcing forward to kiss a greeting to the careless passer-by; while red-brown cattle, drowsing in the field beyond, stood knee-deep in the sappy grass, the honeyed smell of clover brooding delicately over the sleepy meadow, soothing the sweating brows of boatmen poling barges down the placid river full of sunny nooks making the green shades greener; gentle houses peering out from among the stately elms, the plumy poplars, and the proudly-nurtured ash with its sweeping foliage, moving in the wind, like a dancing Fragonard lady, coy with pride, and fancying herself the gem of the world around her; and over all the greying silver and the tender blue of a fresh and beaming sky.

So, through these two men, beauty of colour and form above and beside him came closer; came to his hand; and he began to build a house of vision with them, a house not made with hands, eternal in his imagination, so that the street he lived in was peopled with the sparkling saints and angels of Angelico, and jewelled with the serene loveliness Constable created out of the radiance of uncommon clay. Even when the rooms were bare of fire and scant of food, he sang and wondered that life had so much to give; and he tried to share all these sights with his mother; but he saw they had but a timid and feebly-whispered message for her, sending her more eagerly back to the motherly care of her crimson geranium, her golden musk, and her fuchsia, with its purple bells and white waxy sepals drooping royally over the sadness of the cracked and withering window.

Into this glowing dwelling-place of Johnny's came the new rector, to take up the pastorate of St. Burnupus. Quietly he came, introduced by the city's archbishop, who left the smoke, the cinders, the timber chips, the dung, and the hearty smell as quick as he decently could in his carriage and pair, when he had safely dumped down the new rector where he was to work for the salvation of souls. The archbishop left behind a man of middle height, some forty-five years of age, a sweet face, bearded brown, now firmly streaked with silver; eyes that sometimes glowed with a ripe autumnal friendship, and sometimes glittered with a wintry scorn; small, delicate, graceful, and sympathetic hands; a warm, sensitive, and humorous mouth; a fine presence, gracefully rugged, that endorsed the confidence of a broad and scholarly mind. A man among men; few there were that could stand beside him, and when the place was found where these few were, it would be hard to say the best of them was as good as he was.

A great stir came to the parish with Edward Morgan Griffin, son of a Methodist minister, and once one of the secretaries of the Hibernian Bible Society, so that here was one who was surely a hale protestant after the Orangeman's pattern, and a joy for ever to the simple soul believing that salvation came with the mumbling of a text of scripture. The choir began to sing well, and Johnny sat with them, singing lustily when he was in the mood, the rector telling him not to be afraid to let himself go. Bible classes flourished, and Foreign Mission work was strongly aided, Johnny acting as secretary to this activity. The vestry was enlarged and made warm and comfortable for smaller meetings. The school grew so that it had to have a new wing added; and the religious life of the parish became vigorous, homely, orderly, and genuine under the direction and with the encouragement of the new rector. Orangemen, purplemen, and knights of the grand black chapter, with civil and religious liberty stamped on their stony faces, hemmed him in, smiled at him, and patted him on the back. Cordons of orange and blue and purple were all around him; and, for a time, all new work was born in contentment and charm. The Orangemen were headed by the people's churchwarden, Frank Donaldson, secretary to the Grand Loyal Orange Lodge of Dublin, a man to whom any speck of colour on a church wall or in a window meant popery and *auto-da-fés* of burning protestants every morning in Rutland Square, and twice a day on Sundays. His pale, pitiless face for ever stared in front of him, seeing nothing but the evil and the danger of a fringe on a church cloth, and a devil's conjuring trick in the sign of the cross; Edward Doosard, Inspector of the Quay Police (doddering old men, in their childhood, watching the warehouses of the Port and Docks Board, showing gold and brass where the real police showed silver, the dockers cursing them, and the carters cutting at them with their whips whenever they got in the way), his ruby face, jowled like Dutch cheeses, his bull-neck forming a circle above a white collar, like a thick rubber hose, a rusty-fleshed fat hand almost always stroking a bristly moustache, and his piggy eyes trying to tell everyone that he was a pillar of protestantism; and John Glazier, foreman in the Great Western Railway Goods Store; a true-blue, if ever there was one; a man who would be ready to die for his faith, his rugged face carved like a stone creviced by centuries of frost and rain; his jagged teeth showing grimly when he mentioned some taint of ritualism in some protestant church; his hands twitching as if they were edging towards a pope's throat. His was the hand of the one in the three that Johnny could hold tight; and here, now, they stood on a high bank, a-swing with millions of moon-daisies, looking down over a fair valley, watching — an eye for the green, and an eye for the orange and blue.

THE BUTTLE OF THE BOYNE

Here on this side of the Jordan stretched out the forces of the great, glorious, pious, and immortal King Billy, Brandyburgers, French Hueforgetmenots, Swiss Swingillians, Dutch Blue Guards, Scandalnavians, the Dublin Quay Police, under Inspector Doosard, and the boys from Sandy Row, with orange banners, blue, purple, and black banners; and there on the other side of the river were the Irish, with one green banner bearing the rising sun; these moving to the left, and the others moving to the right so that they would, sooner or later, come with a clash against each other. Over there, on the opposite side, close to Dinmore Church, watching the Irish army, all dhressed in their jackets green, with spreading white cockhades in their hats, singing in mournful numbers, *Quick! We have not a Second*, King James sat on his horse, facing south, munching his fists in an agony of sufficient for the day is the evil thereof; his wide-brimmed hat, fairily plumed, pulled down over his black brambly brows, crossing himself from right to left and from left to right so as to make no mistake, in sheer bewilderment at the cannon-balls sailing, sailing over from fifty protestant guns, ever belching orange flame and blue smoke from their snarling muzzles, twitching himself nearly outa the saddle at every shot; green ribbons knotted on his shoulders, and green ribbons flying from his hair, with *Erin Go Brag* stamped on every inch of them to act as a charm; a harper on his right hand playing *Remember the Glories of Brian, the Brave*, for all he was worth, to get heard over the cannon-fire, be the main strength he used in plucking the strings; and a piper on his left hand blowing himself daft in the tune of *I'm Asleep and don't Waken Me* so as to dhrown the thunder of the thousand-and-one protestant dhrums of the stalwarts of Sandy Row and the Diamond, beatin' out the tune of *Lilly Bullero Bullen a Law*, facing forward in front of King Billy's army itching to go over and down the rabble that adored a god of bread, and signposts carved and coloured; egged on be cowled monks, with ropes round their bellies, that should, be right, be around their necks; carrying loads of lumber to be set up in their churches to give each corner its own miracle; the thought of it all causin' John Glazier to send a straight spit of disgust out an' over an' into the Boyne.

—If only Sarsfield would shake himself loose, said Johnny; if only Sarsfield could come to the front; if only Sarsfield would head his horsemen, we'd dhrive King Billy an' his bullyballs head-short back to their downlands an' dykes on the farther side of the Zideree Zee.

—He can't move, shouted Glazier joyously, for he's bound to the chain that binds the beast; an' looksee that bright one forbias us, with a dhrawn sword in his hand: Art thou for us, or for our adversaries? he called out, above the roaring roll of the drums; and the bright one said, Nay, but as captain of the Lord's host am I now come; and Glazier shouted, Hail! well met, brother; for if you stole a big pig, sure, I stole another. There's the Dutch Blue Blackguards makin' for the river through a broad vale of golden buttercups; plunge! in they go, up to their middles in water, holdin' their muskets over their head: keep your balls an' powder dhry, me boys, an' your hopes high, for there's no Finn McCool here now to toss a thousand men in a single second an' a double throw from where he was to the Isle o' Man in the Sea o' Moyle's seethin' centre; oh, an' look at them three bleatin' bastards, Redmond, Dillon, and wee Joey Devlin, dodgin' behint a round tower, with a wolf-dog lyin' down forbye them; an' up on the highest bough of an oak-three, the oily-faced

Gladstone, watchin' them, with his Home Rule Bill, that would be Rome rule, in his hip-pocket, nimble for any evil that would dislocate the onward march of the protestant cause of Erin.

—They're driven back, th' Irish are dhrivin' them back! shouted Johnny; for the green jackets had lepped into the water, had come on with their pikes outstandin', hurling the Blue Blackguards head-over-tip back to the bank they'd just jumped down from, on they came tearin' ahead, singin'

> Hurrah for the sons of the Shamrock,
> Who always victorious have been;
> And where is the nation can equal
> The boys of old Erin, the green!

while King Billy on his great white horse galloped along the margin of the river where masses of fragrant meadow-sweet were being flattened by the falling bodies of Blue Guard and Black papist, their white cluster cozened to crimson by the oozing away of the last few moments of life left livin', an' he yelling in a tantrum of fear; Where's me Hueforgetmenots, where's me Inniskilleners, where's me Boys from Sandy Row, an' Doosard with his Dublin Quay Police! Stir yourselves, there, or we're in for popery, brass money, and wooden shoes; throw back the rebels, an' save the laygal government, an' bring peace an' protestantism an' prosperity to the deluded people of Erin!

—Up, Sarsfield! yelled Johnny.

—Up, King Billy! roared Glazier.

And they turned aside and smote each other, so that their noses bled, and their teeth loosened; and they wrestled, the one with the other, on the grassy bank, among the moon-daisies, between the hedges that were a wild wondher of dog-rose and bramble-blossom.

Then the Inniskilleners, in their orange tunics and true-blue trews, headed be Johnston of Ballykilbeg, wavin' a purple flag with the picture of Randolph Churchill on it, holdin' th' torch of truth, all gallous boys, brethren of the Shepherd's Poy, each with the bumpy gallopin' journey on the back of a goat through a wilderness behind him; each had sat on his arse watching the burning bush, and had crossed the Jordan with Joshua; for they, the orangemen, purplemen, and blackmen, were even as the men of the tribes of Reuben, the men of the tribe of Gad, and half of the tribe of Manasseh, who went armed before their brethren till their brethren should find rest in the land given them be God; so that each man bore on his breast the sacred number of two and a half; close behind them came the Hueforgetmenots, in their black-and-white uniforms, a crimson plume in their heavy helmets, a silver Bible shining on their breasts, cheerin' for love an' learnin', with the young, apple-cheeked Duke o' Skumberg at their head, his pristine protestant conscience well locked up in steel; and, to the right of the line, the tut-tut-tuttering old Dublin Quay Police, all in shorts, Edward Doosard leading them off, with a hazel wand in his hand to divine where the water was when he came to the river.

—Oh! look at it — the white, young, romish-wrinkled face of that Harry Fletcher peerin' through the cannon smoke, an' a popish biretta on's head, spoutin' th' Athanasian Creed outa him, an' he turnin' towards the east an' prayin' for the pope's intentions! yelled out Glazier, above the rool of the thousand-an'-one drums, as he broke off from Johnny's attempt to give him a half-nelson; an' there in th' more distant smoke's th' dim face of St. Burnupus' rector, devoted to the formularies, an' shilly-shallyin' with the scarlet woman, the whore of Babylon, who's dhrunk with the blood of the saints, hard at it in the midst of the soaring an' falling bumballs, redhot from the cannons' mouths!

—If y'only knew, you poor pitiful ignorant man, the Pope's praying as hard as he can for the success of the protestant King Billy, an' the defeat of the catholic James! said Johnny, trying to get a grip on Glazier again.

—It's a lie, a red an' a roarin' lie! yelled Glazier; for the Pope couldn't pray for anything good an' wholesome, an' th' Vatican's kindled a thousand candles to be burnin' all night before a thousand images to bring about th' desthruction of the good King Billy an' the protestant cause! Till hell with th' Pope, an' God save King Billy! and Glazier caught hold of Johnny's throat.

—Yeh bloody bigot! yelled Johnny, catching hold of his, God save th' Pope, an' to hell with King Billy!

They struggled among the moon-daisies, their hands circling each other's throats, panting, and hot with envy and hatred; while the cannons blazed away with their venom, and the drums rolled out the glory of strife, till Johnny saw the Irish yielding their bodies to the musket-balls, and the points of the pikes, slowly reeling back, slowly giving way, slowly dying for a foreign king; saw King James turn his horse's head and begin a gallop fast and fearful on the rocky road to Dublin, with Sarsfield, head down, riding beside him, filling the air with and fooling the air with the shout of, Change kings, and we'll fight the battle over again!

Johnny flung Glazier aside and crossed the river by a shallow ford, for the tide was ebbing fast. Looking back, he saw Glazier standing in the midst of blue, orange, and purple banners keenin' over the bodies of Johnny Walker, the clergyman, and the apple-cheeked Duke o' Skumberg, now white as a fresh-blown water-lily, bleachin' in the sun. He shook his clenched fist at Glazier, then turned and dashed through the scattered yellow irises and flattened meadowsweet, leppin' over countless green-jacketed bodies, now part o' the ground they were sthretched on; dim now are all the hopes for the catholics in the silver Mass-bell; dying away fast is the thought of drinking the red wine and the yellow ale woven in gaudy dhreams of golden jollity; sighing they go, with the crowds of muddied white cockhades they go, forlornly floatin' down the tide.

—Come back, come back! he shouted after the fleeing king; come back, Seumas, a chaca; come back, Seumas, the shit!

But the king, lying forward on his horse's neck, flew on, forward to a narrower cell of life, to be sealed up for ever with tormenting delusion. All round were soldiers, enamelled in dust and sweat, worn out, their tired senses shrinking from sleep, streaming towards Duleek to get quick on the road to Dublin; and far off, in front of them, oreoled in a cloud of dust, ran Redmond, Dillon, and wee Joey Devlin to get away from the flying bumballs and the beat of the protestant drums. To his right the village of Oldbridge was a big ball of rolling black smoke from which shot scarlet plumes of flame wherever the thatch of the people's houses blazed. Over in the thick shelter of bushy brambles, half hidden there, heedless of the torturing thorns, frightened faces peered out, watching their simple houses turn to a smoky memory. Farther on to the right, where the struggle had been bitther, he thought he saw, as in a glass darkly, the bearded gentle face of Mr. Griffin stooping over faintly-stirring forms, here holding the hand of a bluecoat, there the hand of a green-jacket, a look of sorrowing wonder on his sweet face, for nowhere was there a herb to heal this wound, nowhere a prayer potent to absolve a sorrow like unto this sorrow.

Johnny turned and ran off with great speed, catching up with an old officer puffing his way along from capture or killing. His green coat was torn and muddy, his feet squelched in his sodden jackboots, one golden epaulette hung in tattered shreds from a shoulder, and his tired eyes, dull as a long-dead blue flower, stared in front of him as he ran. He had flung away belt and scabbard, but carried his sword, naked, in his hand.

—Why're you runnin' away? shouted Johnny at him. Are the Irish all turned cowards? Why don't you stand your ground?

—Who's running away? puffed the officer. We're not running away, I'd like you to know. This movement's only one with a prearranged plan to take up a betther position. We're tempting th' enemy on, boy, whose black soul's fresh from Satan's arms. They may win the battles, but we'll win the war. That bumball fell a little too close, eh? The world's with us. All God-fearing people are on our side. For God and humanity — those are the holy stakes we're playing for, and the battle we've just fought'll go down in history as an epic; for in it was really a defeat for th' dour and bestial, sullen monarch Billy and all his sooty-nurtured crew. He thought and planned to smash us in five minutes; but it took them five long and hotly-passing hours to break and batther through, giving us the vital time to prepare to meet him in a betther place.

—I know of no betther place than the one you're runnin' away from, said Johnny.

—If you don't, we do, but we don't tell everyone, and so aid the enemy. If you go on with undermining talk, me boy, you're just as well in an enemy column.

—Isn't me whole nature longin' to see you win? said Johnny.

—Act accordin', then, if it is, the officer panted. He gave his wrinkled face an ugly twist and pressed a hand to the small of his back; th' oul' kidneys are at me again, he moaned. I'm too far gone for this sort of thing.

The two of them were whirled into the little town of Duleek in the midst of a clay-soiled, swearing, sweating crowd of brown-clad foot-soldiers who had come pouring over the fields on to the white road. Swarming in and swarming out of the little cabins they were, and in and out of the few little shops, frantic for food and drink, prising up the floors, plunging their spiked staves into the thatch to see if any food had been hidden there; for the villagers had fled away and were hiding, waiting for the flood of hunger-mad men to ebb off outa their sight and hearing. Quarrels were breaking out between those who had found nothing and those who had found a little. Here on the threshold of a thatched cabin, two breathless men, one armed with an ugly staff shod with heavy iron on one end, the other with a thick-bladed sabre, were defending the place against an attacking group, armed in the same way, out to capture the bitten loaf of bread and the bit of meat they saw inside on a table; unmindful that they, too, when they had downed the two opposing men, would have to turn aside from their hunger and defend the bread and meat from others pressing on behind to seize the treasures. Farther down the narrow rutty street, a little war raged round a small keg of beer; already wounded men were trying to crawl away from the strife, while two forms lay before the keg, stretched out stiff to show that they were dead, and claimed to be left alone in peace. In a corner of a trampled field of corn, a shouting excited group were sticking a squealing, dodging pig with their pikes, and slashing at him with heavy cavalry swords as he ran this way and that, streaming with blood, to escape the death that was so surely coming to him; while in the distance an attentive ear could easily hear the rolling thunder of the protestant tom-toms beating a triumphal march forward. Many, having wrung the very last drop of movement out of their bodies, lay in a deep stupor on the dirty street, stirring no-way, even when heavy feet stamped careless down upon them. Some were holding a shattered arm to their breast with a sound one; many more wore bloodied clouts around their heads; and a few who had gone as far as life could take them, sprawled in the gutter, murmuring mercy out of Mary the Mother o' God for the last time in this world. From an upper window in a higher house, a young officer bellowed an appeal for a little order out of the seething crowd, but the jaded men, stampeding and roaring round for quietness and food, had no ear for him; and left him there, white-faced and agonising, with a shouting mouth making a dumb appeal for a rally that would face about to fight again for a sacred cause. A strong sun made the smell of blood and sweat seem horrible, while loud cries shot out on every hand, cries of resentment against the bitter thought of the depredations that would surely follow their defeat.

—Where's it goin' to go we are, now? and the questioner held up his staff shod with iron at the end: looka, that's what they gave us to meet the charge of a gallopin' horse; to shove aside a cannon-ball flyin' hot in the air; or th' fall of an invincible sword fashioned at a forge in Toledo, or, maybe, in Damascus itself!

—Th' bastards! cried another; it wouldn't penethrate through cow-shit! Only give us the waypons, an' we'll fight again, an' show them, with no food an' less dhrink to nourish us!

—Twelve cannons against their fifty, an' six taken away be th' flyin' king for company, and th' other six sent to where they warn't wanted, said a third. A reasonable an' a ravin' curse be ever on th' head o' th' dastard wherever he goes; an' if he was standin' before me now, it's a sharp an' sudden look at th' closin' door o' heaven I'd be givin' him; for it's th' shamblin' caution of this king in nothin' but in name that has brought to light the gapin' death wounds shown in many a poor riven body today!

Th' poor oul' Boyne, thought Johnny, stepping over a stiff figure that had a rugged little cross, made of hazel twigs, pressed close to a pair of blackened lips; the river that had on it the home of the Dagda, the earth-builder; the river hailed as a friend by Ptolemy; the river of a thousand kings; the river that in its frown of winter and its song of summer must have often flowed in fear, listening to the thundering gallop of the Grey of Macha and the Black Sainglain, once the battle-steeds of the terrible battle-goddess, Morrigu, the Battle-Crow; and the battle-creaking clang of Cuchullin's bronze-poled chariot tearing along its banks, shaking the whole valley as it shook when the waters of the magic well burst forth to chasten Boann, the beautiful daughter of Nechtan, for her contempt of it, bruising her madly, its foaming waves striking at her and chasing her quick to the sea; or the clang of shield on shield and the clash of steel against steel when the Fenians tossed their foes about in battle. No more are you, now, proud river than a poor fancy of your old form, reaching the low level of a charmless holy wather for th' protestants of Ulsther.

Shoving a slow way through the crowd of excited, swarming soldiers towards a lane at the west side of the town, the officer, pulling Johnny after him, slipped and planked a jackboot on a green-jacketed body squirming about at the end of the lane, turning it over to show a sloppy-red breast, with waxy fingers dabbling in it, and blue lips in a waxy face that murmured in a faint bitterness, Thinka what he's brought on me; God o' th' wondhers, thinka what he's brought on me! The cowardly kindled dastard, with his, Spare me poor English subjects, when he seen me land a larrup on a Sassenach's skull that scatthered his thimbleful o' brains an' sent them to feed th' minnows o' th' Boyne; checkin' me to a halt so that I got th' musket ball that would ha' passed by had I moved another half-foot forward!

—Look, said the officer agitatedly, pointing a hand to the north, there go the tips of their orange-and-blue banners rising over the slopes beyond! If we stop much longer, we're done. Let these curs become captives — they'll soon find that even th' little they have here'll be less still when the orange lily blossoms where the river Shannon flows. Oh! this ache in the kidneys! Like the stab from the beak of the Morrigu! I go for a fond sleep to a little grey house in the west, to a friend at Yellow Furze, for a fond sleep and a sad sleep.

—An' leave the flag, an' leave your men, and throw away the white cockhade! said Johnny, dismayed, for he could now plainly see the rugged face of Glazier, with its flapping ears, grinning at him and making a mock of him, thumb to nose, on the summit of a hill looking down on Duleek.

—I'm leaving nothing! answered the officer angrily. I still stand for the fight in defence of our Christian inheritance. This is going to be a fluid war; and I can give vital help where I'm going. Whoever holds out the longest'll win in the end; and we'll do that; but I must have sleep, and a long rest to let the kidneys settle themselves. You cut across the fields and get to the road further down, and hurry off to Dublin. I go to my little grey home in the west, little grey home in the west, under a spreading chestnut tree, and roses round the door, for a simple sleep for a few hundred years or so; and then we'll show them there's one more river to cross, and that our indominus indominant people are prepared to live or die for altar and throne. So goodbye, young friend; remember we're one at heart if you be Ireland's friend, there are but two great parties in the end; only two in the end, so goodbye for the present, and away he faded, faded into the smoke of the cannons; and Johnny turned and ran, too, away, away from the rabble of hungry and disconcerted soldiers making a merit of disorder and uproar in the narrow street of the town of Duleek; and just in time, for as he ran he was followed by a mocking shout from Glazier, and looking back, he saw coming over the smoky hill beyound the town, the boul' boy, followed be Inspector Doosard, leading on the tut-tut-tuttering fogeys of the Dublin Quay Police, stepping like deers prancing over the mountain heather, headed by their fife and dhrum band shrilling out the tune of *The South Down Militia* composed be Colonel Blacker of Sandy Row and Downing Street. On, on he ran, closing his eyes, and stopping his ears while passing by the siege of Athlone and Limerick and the desolation of Aughrim; opening his eyes for a second when he saw, in the core of a flash of lightning, Sarsfield galloping out of Limerick, in the wind and rain, at the head of half a thousand horsemen, fast galloping, faster still, a hard, fast, head-bent gallop to fall on the Williamites at Ballyneety; galloping through them, shouting when a senthry called out for the password, Sarsfield's the word, and Sarsfield's the man, through them, over them, past them, wheel, and a hard, fast, sword-slashing gallop back again, through them, and over them, Galloping O'Hogan, knee to knee with Sarsfield, his face alight with joy in the darkness; then down with a lep, to blow, as high as half-way up to heaven, the great siege guns gathered together to batther in the walls of Limerick, and the long mighty tin pontoons, built to span the Shannon, to blow them up with a bursting roar in a sheet of flame and a rending thunder of smashing steel flying far that was a shout from Ireland, and she on a hill, deafening the yellow-faced loons, and dazzling them, flying all ways to shake themselves free from the biting swords of Sarsfield's men, showing what Sarsfield could ha' done had Sarsfield had his way, giving the shock of hope to Ireland, and encouraging the people to call their sons, not Patrick, after the saint, but Patrick, after the soldier; till after the red lightning-flash and the long, long journey, Johnny stood now on the lawn in front of the church of St. Burnupus, engaged in a fight to see whether the Orangemen could be shifted by the votes of the Vestrymen from the Select Vestry of the parish. They, through the Select Vestry, where they had the majority, ruled the parish, and had harassed the rector for a long time, turning turk on him because they thought they saw a romish gleam in the white of his eye; because he had refused to admit that their institution had had a divine origin; and because he had refused to become a chaplain; because he had even opposed the loan of the church for an annual Orange Service, when the Orangemen came in orange, purple, and black sashes, heavy and hanging with silver regalias of King Billies crossing the Boyne, open Bibles, crowns and anchors, an' God knows god wot; with their dames hooked to their arms, wearing bunches of orange lilies in their bosoms. When they'd settled themselves, they sang suitable hymns, such as, *Tramp, Tramp, Tramp, th' Boys are Marchin'*, *Sound th' Loud Thrumpet an' Tickle th' Dhrum*; read suitable verses from the one and only; and had a suitable sermon preached by a suitable cleric from a suitable text; the rector holding that a church was the place for the worship of God, and not a place for the veneration of any King Billy, however noble, good, or wise a king or man he might have been; adding that they could hardly blame the catholics for their doulia veneration of the saints, their hyper-doulia veneration of the Blessed Virgin, when the Orange Brethren seemed to give a fuller and more gorgeous veneration to the Prince of Orange, to the Rev. Mr. Walker, and to the defenders of the Walls o' Durry; and because they thought, on account of the rector's reverence for the sixth chapter of the gospel according to St. John, he seemed to hint at the real presence of Jesus in the sacrament of the Lord's Supper. They disliked, too, the idea of him showing such favour to Johnny, poverty-stricken and ill-kept; asking him to his house, discussing all kinds of questions with him, welcoming him every Sunday to the vestry before the service began when the rector was to preach, to sing a hymn with him, or recite a prayer that the rector's words might be blessed and bear fruit in the minds of his hearers. All this, in spite of the warning that Johnny was a Fenian, a few of them saying that his mind was swelling with every sort of caustic comment on England's hold of Ireland; and that he had even tried, in their hearing and in front of their very eyes, to confound the plain warrant of Holy Scripture with the falsifying fables of the Fathers and the popery-drenched pamphlets of the Puseyites on the Invocation of Saints and Angels, Regeneration in Baptism, and Prayers for the Dead; for Johnny often opposed even his own beliefs to heighten an argument. Because of these things, the Orangemen had opposed most of the plans of the rector, making everything he tried to do unhappy and uncertain, so that those who liked him were constrained to interfere, and use their votes to banish this unruly and unreasonable opposition; and Johnny led them on, visiting their houses, and persuading them to come and take their part in the activities of the parish. A good few of the workers were working late, and the time for voting had been extended to eleven o'clock. Such a thing, and such intense diversity, had rarely been seen in any parish before, and all was silent and determined excitement. So here was Johnny standing on the lawn, near the schoolhouse door, doing the part of a sentry to see that no disentitled or unentitled person came to cast a vote. An April night it was, with a fine moon out in the sky, and the buzz of spring in the cool nippy air. There she was like a golden disk in the breast of a blue-mantled angel, showing herself off to everything coming within her silvery circle, making the bloated spire of St. Damnaman's look like a gleaming dagger held up in the huge hand of a blackman; and giving the few shabby shrubs on the lawn a mantle lovelier than the finest ever woven for the kingly back of Solomon. It was a quarter before eleven now; Johnny knew from his list that all his friends were present; that a few doubtful ones, and some who had shouted their devotion to true-blue protestantism, hadn't yet shown themselves, and he wished that the clock would go quicker. When the first chime of the hour was struck by the clock inside, Johnny saw that the door was made fast and tight against all newcomers, and then strolled into the crowded room where the scrutineers were already making ready to count the votes. Up at the top, beside them, sat the rector, close to his eldest son, a bright and genial youth of fifteen years. Dotted here and there were the Orangemen whom Johnny knew, and he saw the yellow head and genial pug-face of Georgie Middleton stuck between the bulbous one of Doosard and the lean and hungry-looking one of Donaldson: his old pal of the school had crossed the Jordan to come under the orange-and-blue banner of the House of Nassau; had become one of the half-tribe Manasseh, or a warrior of the tribe of Reuben or of Gad.

An hour of whispering passed while the votes were counted, selecting twelve good and true men to help the rector in the work of the parish. Then in a sudden silence, the result was handed to the rector's churchwarden to be read out to the vestrymen; and Johnny saw by the grim smile on Walmsley's face that the blue-and-orange banner was low in the dust. Again he saw the flowing river and the blue sky over the yellow irises; he again scented the presence of the river-banked mass of meadowsweet; heard the diminished sound of the protestant drum; saw from the midst of the moon-daisies the gathering of the Irish, with James, a chaca, left behind, and Sarsfield at their head.

Not a single name of the Orange party's choice appeared on the list of elected members, and a great clapping of hands sounded a *feu de joie* for the Orangemen, who stood up, and went out in silence and an angry shame. When Georgie Middleton was passing by, Johnny held out a hand to him, but Middleton struck it down and passed by and went out. Glazier halted for a moment before Johnny and stared him hard in the face.

—I never thought I'd live, he said bitterly, to see a Jesuitical manifestation in this parish! But, looksee, all of ye, we are prepared to fight to the last man, and die on our own doorsteps if need be, for a protestant althar and a protestant throne! And he and his friends passed out to walk under the wonders of the moon.

The vestrymen, their work done and battle won, filed out, murmuring good wishes into the rector's ear. Coming over to Johnny, he shook his hand warmly, saying, Thanks, John, for all you did. It's a pity it had to be done, he added with a sigh, for even minor disunity is far from desirable.

—It has, at least, placed you among friends, said Johnny.

—I deeply wish you were one of them, John.

—I can be one without being on the vestry, said Johnny, embarrassed, but pleased. Better men than I have been selected.

—They didn't think of you, said the rector; had I been of them, your name, John, would have been thrust forward. He placed a hand affectionately on Johnny's shoulder. You are a remarkable soul in many ways, and your presence would have been a great encouragement to me.

—The mother'll be glad you won; she sent her best wishes.

—Thank her for me, John. A dear and intelligent woman — she

always reminds me of my own mother, and a soft light shot into his keen eyes. I suppose we must call it a victory, John, though I had rather there had risen no need for a fight; and that we Christians were content to hold the faith in unity of spirit, and in the bond of peace. Good-night, dear friend, and God be with you. He shook John's hand again and went his way, with his son, to walk under the wonder of the moon.

When all were gone, and the lights out, and the door shut, Johnny went his way home, the midnight moon laying down a silvery carpet under his passing feet, slow to move towards sleep, and end the day. By his help, the orange banner had been replaced by the green flag, or the blue, with the sunburst awake in its centre. Whatever its colour or symbol might be, how well it would look flying from the turrets of the church, like a rare jewel entrusted to hold together the silvery mantle of the shining moon.

He shook himself. He was staying too long in the Hallway looking at the pictures. All done by others. Very beautiful and strong, but all done by others. He'd have to start now doing things for himself. Create things out of his own life. He'd begin to make pictures himself; ay, pictures, too, that would be worth hanging in the Hallway for other people to see.

DRUMS UNDER THE WINDOWS

Study that house.
I think about its jokes and stories.

To Dr. Michael O'Hickey
A Gael of Gaels, one-time Professor of Irish in Maynooth College. In a fight for Irish, he collided with arrogant Irish bishops, and was summarily dismissed without a chance of defending himself; taking the case to Rome, he was defeated there by the subtlety of the bishops, helped by a sly Roman Rota, ending his last proud years in poverty and loneliness.

Forgotten, unhonoured, unsung in Eire, here's a Gael left who continues to say Honour and Peace to your brave and honest soul, Michael O'Hickey, till a braver Ireland comes to lay a garland on your lonely grave.

AT THE SIGN OF THE PICK AND SHOVEL

PUG-FACED, pleasant-hearted Georgie Middleton had pulled him to the job, hearing he was idle; big gang at work on a railway siding, more wanted; make a man of you. He brought Sean straight to the Foreman, had whispered into his ear, One of ourselves, and the Foreman, a modified true-blue, had decided to give him a start. A big man was the Foreman, over six feet and broad-shouldered. A handsome face, spoiled by a big crooked clumsy chin, falling away from a large mouth, well shaped; deep clefts from each corner of a handsome nose furrowed the cheeks to the frame of the chin, looking like taut ropes keeping the heavy chin from falling away altogether; but he'd taken him on, and that was a decent thing to do.

The ganger, Christy Mahon, looked doubtfully at Sean when he came to the job with a navvy shovel on his shoulder. Mahon was another big and powerful man of fifty or so, wide-shouldered and deep-chested; lazy as sin, and as ignorant as a kish of brogues. Doesn't know the name of his own religion, couldn't recognise the number on his own hall-door, and hardly make out a bee from a bull's balls, one of the workmen whispered to Sean, a few days later. He had a rugged, rather distinguished face, a heavy grizzled moustache, a bush of the same sort of hair, tousled as if it had never come within sight of a comb, and his chin, hardy and strong, was covered with a week's growth of hair. There was one remarkable thing about him — he had a very small arse for such a big man, and the part of his trousers there looked like the drooping mainsail of a ship in a fitful wind when he walked. Too much beer, whispered another workman to Sean, a few days later. This ganger mostly remained torpid, but was under the habit of sudden fits of passion for an hour's occasional work to show the others how it was done; and would seize a shovel or a pick to work like a nigger for a spell, the effort gradually declining till the tool dropped from his hand, and he sank into torpidity again. He spoke through his nose in a querulous way, and got good-humoured only when he was half-seas-over by drinking the bullage from empty whiskey barrels, made by steeping the damper ones with boiling water till the whiskey still in the wood had soaked its way into the water. He lived in Yellow Walls, near Malahide, the stronghold of

405

the Talbots, where he had a whitewashed cottage with clay floors, a wife, two children, less than an acre of ground, and an animal that he said was a cow. He was the richest man in the hamlet. All life centred round the cow. Up every night he had to be when she was calving, squatting on the bare earthen floor of the byre, a huge, shaking, shadowy figure in a dim pool of light from a storm-lantern, watching every twist and turn of the cow, sensing her condition in every moaning bellow she gave, echoing each moan in his own aching, wondering heart; with his wife at home in bed on her back, ears cocked to hear a possible yell from her husband to come and give her fellow a hand with the suffering animal; while the few houses round hers sank into the night's silence, for they had not on them the care of a cow calving. There he sat in the darkness and dirt, cooped in with the cow, the heat from her body and the steam from her nostrils enfolding them both and making them one, a thick needle threaded with a thick cord near by, ready to stitch her belly up if it got torn during the delivery. His life, literature, art, and leisure were all embedded in the cow calving.

Every morning at four o'clock, this ganger forced himself from bed to catch the four-fifteen coming from the black north, nodding in the cold carriage with three comrades till it was five-to-six, and time to climb from the carriage resting in a Dublin siding, when they heard the bell calling them all to begin a day's work. He got home again, with his comrades, at eight o'clock, so doing sixteen hours a day at his everyday job with a few hours added to till his patch of ground and care for the cow; yet withal, he had plenty of leisure to go to Mass on all the Sundays.

This shaggy, lumbering, dim-minded man looked at Sean doubtfully, shrugged his shoulders, and grumbled to his gang, God in heaven! What kind of a scrawl am I gettin'? For Sean stood mute before him, a blink of fear in his eyes as if he expected to be set to move a mountain. Didja never ever have ne'er a shovel in your hand before in your life? he asked.

—Ay, said Sean; but not this sort of a one.

—An' which would you liefer start with — pick or shovel?

—Don't mind, said Sean carelessly; it's all the same to me.

—Ay, it's all th' same because you don't know how to use nather.

—Give him a shovel, said a stocky, red-bearded man anxiously, for he'll be penethratin' one of us if he thries to use a pick.

Sean thrust the shovel feverishly into the earth already hacked out of the little hill that was to make way for the new siding. It was a hard push to the broad-bladed shovel, with a short handle, and a crook like a crutch on the end of it, a push given by all the strength in his forearm only, unaided by the thrust of the knee the navvy gives whenever he forces the shovel home. He emptied what was on the shovel into a waiting cart, and thrust the blade into the hacked-out heap again. By the time a crawling half-hour had passed his hands were smarting; the veins in his forearm seemed to be knotting themselves together; salt sweat was trickling down his forehead and cheeks, oozing into his eyes, making them burn and veiling their vision with a salt smart. Now his chest was getting so tight that he could breathe only in short intermittent gasps. The first quarter of this work would do him in; he could never come back to this ordeal by sweat, pain, and breathlessness. He was flabby, soft, inalert, and useless. Through a reddish mist he saw the rest of the gang working away easily as if they were made of well-oiled steel. He sensed that they were enjoying themselves watching him, grimly glad to see his staring eyes, groggy legs, and hear his gasping breath.

—Not worth a damn to me, he heard the ganger mutter as he turned away to miss the new man's agony; lifts up as much on his shovel as a new-hatched hen 'ud lift up in her bake.

A low lot, thought Sean, a low lot to have to work with, and all rejoicing at the poor show I'm making. The less I'm able, the more hilarious and comfortable they'll feel. Oh, if Georgie was only here, but he's a tradesman, and above this crowd.

A tall, dark, raven-haired man edged closer to him, saying softly out of the corner of his mouth, Go easy, take your time, draw it mild; watch me. You'll kill yourself the way you're goin'. Lower the shovel, bend quietly, don't jerk; now, the knee against the crutch of the handle — shove! Lift gently, don't jerk, and fling with a slight swing of both arms — see? Don't be afraid to straighten your back when you feel a sthrain, so's to keep yourself from gettin' too stiff. It'll all come to you in a few weeks, and you'll be as good as the best.

Try as he would, it only grew worse in spite of Bob Harvey's attempt at tutoring, and through the mist Sean saw the ganger shaking his head with annoyance, though he had kept his back turned on Sean's agony. His arms had grown into things torturing his body, and his gasping breath seemed to cling to where it was in his lungs, stifling him, rather than to tear a way through his gaping mouth. Sweat was hiding the blue sky above him; the sky itself was damp with sweat, the whole earth was tired and aching, all save only those dim figures working by his side, laughing silently at him for thinking he could become a navvy; but it was for food, for security, for freedom from want, and stick it he must. Now things at a distance seemed to be swinging about, as if they had suddenly gone tipsy, and the earth shook like a thing infirm. Every shovelful now pulled a bigger strain out of his taut, rebelling muscles; put a sharper ache into his creaking back. He was going slower; he could barely get the heavy shovel from the ground. He got reckless, gave a might lift and a jerking throw, sending a shovelful of earth and stones clattering against the neck and over the head of the startled ganger, knocking a pipe from his big mouth so that it fell to the ground and smashed itself into many pieces.

—What th' hell! he roared. What d'ye think y're throwing' — thunderclaps, or wha'? Is it buryin' poor men alive yeh want to be? He looked down at the shattered pipe. A year's hard work seasonin' her gone for nothin'! Here, get a hold of a pick instead, th' way we won't have to be diggin' people outa what you've buried them in!

But the pick in Sean's lacerated hands was worse than the shovel, for he didn't know how to swing it neatly back over his shoulder within a small space, but swung it clumsily and widely so that those who worked next to him hurried away to give him room, and stood bunched together, watching in wonder the wild swing of the pick, effective in his hands as it would be in the hands of a child of twelve.

—Oh, Lord, what am I goin' to do with the boyo at all! burst out of Christy Mahon; keepin' three men from work to let him do a little. You're only ticklin' it, man. You'll kill somebody, so you will; that waypon's deadly in your dangerous hands; you'll drive it deep into the broad of somebody's back before you're done. You'll never do on this job. It's not fair to me. *Christy Mahon, is this all you've done for the day?* the Foreman'll say when he sthruts up; an' he after sendin' me a man that's burnin' to hamsthring half th' men workin' with him; an' afterwards their mothers or widows comin' in black blamin' me for permittin' murdher to be done in all innocence be a fella fortified be not knowin' what he was thryin' to do! Go on, an' get into it! he roared to the others, for it's a risk yous have to take, dependin' for safety on a smart lep outa th' way when yous see the point of the pick comin'.

So it was, too, carrying sleepers, slippy, hot, and pungent with the soak of creosote, he at one end, and a man at the other. They fought shy of joining him for fear he'd let his end go before the right moment, jabbing their end into their bodies, or nipping a finger by failing to give the heavy baulk of timber a tuneful swing before casting it from the permanent-way wagon. Bob Harvey, the tall, raven-haired ex-

Guardsman, was the only one ready to man the end opposite to him, giving him slow sage counsel, showing him how to keep a proper poise forward or backward, counting the swings quietly, one, two — go! and in a little more than no-time Sean swung sleepers out of a wagon, or on the ground and on to the ordered piles, in perfect tune with his partner's help. Carrying the twenty-five-foot rails, six or eight men at one end, and the same number at the other, he was always opposite the ex-Guardsman, and his and Sean's shoulders and hands were always interlocked; and though he went home, night after night, a clumsy-moving mass of aching stiffness, seeing when he got home an anxious look in his mother's eyes, and heard her murmur, when she saw the raw red on the palms of his hands, Maybe the job's too much for your strength, he stood up to it, silent, with no shadow of a song near his lips, and no sigh either, grim and grand; mouth-clenched resolution his armour, and the determination to become as good as the next his shield and buckler. His first fortnight's pay opened the heart of the dirty little grocer, purveyor of the workers' district, so that for the first time for a year and more he and his mother fed well. He went on wringing power and confidence from the passing hours, till the aches gradually left him, and the stiffness was gone. His body now became flexible, his arms strong, his legs firm in tackling shovel, pick, crowbar, rope, scaffolding-pole, wheelbarrow, hod, or sledge with the best of them, beating the ex-Guardsman who got pale and whimpered when asked to mount higher than the sixth rung of a ladder; and, at last, found himself the one man in the gang who could mount a ladder with a hod carrying near eight stone in it, balancing it with equal ease on right shoulder or on left.

God, he felt proud all right. Felt as proud as he did when he first fell into step with Shakespeare. His body now was in fine alignment with his mind. *Mens sana in corpore sano*, that's how it went, he thought; and, if the words were curious, the sense was sane. He often inflated his chest now, forty-four inches round normally; often felt the sturdy muscles in arm and thigh; and as he swung pick or sledge-hammer, thrust in shovel, hung on a rope, or swarmed up a ladder with a hod on his shoulder, song once more bubbled brightly from his lips. And to him, most of the songs were new; songs of an Ireland astir, awake, and eager; an Ireland forging fresh thought out of bygone history, and present hopes to create a glowing, passionate, and permanent chapter from which a great nation would be born. Oh, silver trumpets be ye lifted up, and call to the great race that is to come! cried Yeats, and Sean cried the call with him too. The sword was being polished, the rifle cleaned, and a new banner of green, white, and orange was being attached to the old staff, and was nearly ready to be broken out to fly in the four winds of Eirinn. Dr. Douglas de Hyde was rushing round, shouting in at the Dublin Castle Gates, It's a Gael I am without shame to meself or danger to you; in at the windows of Trinity College, A country without a language is a country without a tongue; on every hill in the country, Waken up your courage, O Ireland; and in at the doorway of Maynooth College, in rather a quiet way, Irish in the New University — or else . . . !

Gaelic Leaguers were pulling reluctant and timorous native speakers from the darkness of their little grey homes in the west, hardly waiting, when they laid hands on one, for him to get his coat on, shoving him where he didn't want to go, amid the clapping of white hands; mixing his tatters with the elegant array of tweed suits, high white collars, and poplin ties of civil servants, doctors, chemists, revenue officers, and teachers, hauling the frightened fellow into the midst of garrulous emotion, declaring that the native speaker was all in all to Ireland, was Ireland, all Ireland, the whole Ireland, and nothing else but Ireland, so help us God; the long-hidden Ireland, chidden Ireland, forbidden Ireland by the Ascendancy gang that ruled the land. The native Irish speaker was forced to walk upright through a fierce white light beating on him everywhere, and he seeking often in his heart a kindlier darkness so that he could slink into the friendliness of gloom again; but they placed him to the forefront of every meeting, applauded every word that came out of his mouth, assuring him that the day of shame for the native speaker had gone for ever; for now whenever two or three were gathered together in the name of Ireland, there was the native speaker in the midst of them.

And while all these respectable, white-collared, trim-suited Gaelic Leaguers, snug in their selected branches, living rosily in Whitehall, Drumcondra, Rathgar, Donnybrook, and all the other nicer habitations of the city, nuzzled round the bewildered native speaker, away went, without money, with often an empty belly, on rusty bicycles, under scorching suns or pelting rain, eyes gleaming, backs bent, hands blenched by the tight grip on the handlebars, unmindful of the hawthorn in June, changing the hedges into never-ending miles of nuns' veiling, or the sparkle of frost on the twisting roads, or of mountains towering up around them to threaten or protect, or of the gentle lap-lap of the waves on a summer sea, or of their battering on to the beach when the winds of winter blew, went the travelling teacher; backs bent, eyes gleaming, hands asweat or frozen on the handlebars, their feet going round endlessly on a glorious treadmill, went the travelling teacher, rushing here, dashing there, to teach a class, to help found a new branch, spreading the Irish as a tree sends forth its pollen, seeking neither to gain a reward nor to pay a penance, but for thee, only for thee, dear land, and for thy language that it may come back to us, be brought back to us by persuasion or by force; snatching time reluctantly to take a meal, spending a few restless hours in jaded sleep, exposed to sun and rain and wind and frost and snow and black sleet, hot and cold by turns, many of them sliding with a wan sigh into a grave by the wayside where they went, worn and worried, into a quiet end from the warm fight and the hope that flickered wanly in most hearts save their own fiery ones; others seizing their bicycles ere they had flattened in their fall, to bend their backs, evoke a gleam in their eyes, to grip the handlebars till the knuckles whitened, and dash off, too, through shower and shine and storm, wet with summer's dew, or soaked in wintry sleet; on, on endlessly, endlessly, reckless and frenzied, endlessly cycling on through country road, through village street, by hilly paths, lifting the heads of grazing mountain-sheep to glance and wonder, skirting mountains alive with their loneliness, a goat, browsing rapidly, lifting a bearded chin to cast a sudden look at the stir that marred his solitude, unawake to the need of the fevered man's hurry to keep a step ahead of time; to bring their lovely language back to the Gael, he hastened on, endlessly, hastening on, the muinteor taisdal, the travelling teacher; Caitlin ni Houlihan busy in the woods nearby searching for leaves to weave a garland, but finding naught but bramble and coarse gorse, thistledown and thorns, jagging her bare feet, but searching still, and silence everywhere.

Here and there, in one or another hole or corner, Tim Healy was mocking Dillon, while down south William O'Brien was trying to fight everyone in his All For Ireland League, unaware, the fools, that when they killed Parnell they killed themselves too; while their followers sauntered in and out of the House draping their souls with all the moods and manners of their masters, carrying in occasionally a stuffed wolf-dog to give a mechanical bark to show that Ireland still lived through joy and through tears, while Johnny Redmond smilingly waved a bright-green flag smelling sweetly of the fragrant English rose.

Far away from it all, a tiny group of men followed Jim Connolly through the streets to the cul-de-sac curving round the circular side of the Royal Bank of Ireland, a large slouch hat covering Connolly's head, a large round head, fronted by a rather commonplace face, its heaviness lightened by fine, soft, luminous eyes; the heavy jaws were

jewelled with a thick-lipped sensuous mouth, mobile, and a little
sarcastic, bannered peacefully by a thick and neatly-trimmed moustache. His ears were well set to the head, the nose was a little too thick,
and gave an obstinate cast to the bright eyes, and a firm fleshy neck
bulged out over a prefectly white hard collar. The head and neck
rested solidly on a broad sturdy trunk of a body, and all were carried
forward on two short pillar-like legs, slightly bowed, causing him to
waddle a little in his walk, as if his legs were, in the way of a joke,
trying faintly and fearfully to throw him off his balance. Silent, he
walked on, looking grim and a little surly, followed by the tiny dribble
of followers, one of them carrying a box so that, when Connolly spoke,
he might be lifted up before the people as he preached the gospel of
discontent smoking faintly in the hearts of most men. Up on the box,
the soft slouch hat came off, and the hard, sparsely-covered head
turned this way and that, the mobile mouth flickered with words, red
with the woe of the common people, words that circled noisily over
the heads of the forty or fifty persons hunched clumsily together to
oppose the chill of the wind that whipped around the corner of the
curving, graceful, classical hip of the Bank, murmuring in the mellowed, matronly, plump loveliness of its lines and curves, *Here in my
ample and elegant belly lies safe the golden life of Ireland, fractifying
warmly there, fulfilling the Jehovahian command to multiply and
replenish the earth.*

A step aside, within the counter-spoiled building, lay the dead
ashes of the last fire lit in the Assembly Room of the Irish House of
Lords; a fire that had warmed the backsides of the Lords in their
crimson-plush coats and black-satin breeches, or black-satin coats
and crimson-plush trousers; or of them that strutted in a bright-blue
Volunteer military coat, gleaming yellow trousers, all bedecked with
crimson braid and the richest of gold embroidery, that voted for the
Act of Union with England, side by side with the Maynooth catholic
bishops; or against the Act, side by side with the Orange Lodges of
Dublin and Belfast.

Here was Up Griffith's seed of life for Ireland, needing but her King,
Lords, and Commons to form a coloured trinity that would forge a
terrifying power in Ireland of the Wise Welcomes, darken the seven
seas with Irish shipping, deaden the song of birds with the hum and
whirr of machinery, and flood the quays, the streets, the homes of
the two gigantic Atlantic ports of Galway and Sligo and the one-way
street town of Blacksod Bay with corn and wine and wool, oil and
amber, mahogany, teak, and rosewood to build houses for the Irish

to live in; juniper gin and jars of spices; Indian muslin, cashmere shawls of crimson and white, or green and turquoise for every Irish snowy-breasted pearl, each colleen dyas, for every girl milking her cow, each dark rosaleen, every dark woman of the glen, and every red-haired man's wife; tobacco the rarest the sun could season, peculiar birds for all the parks, bales of shimmering silks from China, and snowy ivory, too, for beads; luscious figs and pomegranates in curious coloured wickerwork baskets, lying in down of the Tibetan ducks, all gums and perfumes of Arabia; and dainty leather for ladies' shoes, all tooled for style in a Persian garden; sherbet rich in crystal vases for a ploughman's drink through the pull of the harvest. Jasus Christ, the vision was lovely!

It was all written in the book of *Resurgamise Upsadaiseum Hungarius*, a huge tome five feet long, three feet wide, and two feet deep, containing in itself all the lore that is or ever was, all laws, licences, customs, pardons, punishments, perquisites, genealogies, constitutions, magna chartas, social contracts, books of rights, das kapitals, origins of species, tallboy talmuds, speeches from the dock, carried about everywhere on the back of Up Griffith Up Davis, as a pedlar carries his pack, compiled from the original sources by the sage himself, deep in a corner under a secret rowan-tree, in the dim cloisters of the old Abbey of St. Fownes, the Soggart Aroon acting as secretary, assisted by Kelly and Burke and Shea all in their jackets green, with the Bard of Armagh stringing the harp to *He's the Man You Don't See Every Day* to give their minds a lift.

Here Sean was now, free for the moment from the pick and shovel, for it was Sunday, of a January, on his way home after playing centre-field in a hurling match, and having had tea with a comrade hurler, stopping for a few seconds to listen to this man, Connolly, who was trying to destroy the fine work being done by Up Griffith, and make a medley of his cut-and-dried Hungarian Gospel. A thin, haggard, lugubrious young fellow, wearing a red tie, moved aimlessly through the little crowd, droning out the titles of a bunch of colour-covered pamphlets that he carried in his hand, a drone that was half a whisper and half a threat, *Socialism Made Easy*, a penny a copy, only a penny the copy; tuppence each, *Can a Catholic be a Socialist?* only tuppence each; the truth for tuppence; Hubert Bland's great work, *Can a Catholic be a Socialist?* The gaunt young man, whose name was Tom Egan, was the most cheerless sight ever seen by Sean. Everything about him had a downward drag; his jaws sagged down to the edge of his chin; his long nose seemed to be bent on pulling itself out of his face; his eyes were mirrors of energetic despondency; his lips were twisted into lines of deeply-cut complaints; but in the midst of all this misery his red tie blazed in his shallow bosom.

—Who's th' big-bodied man gettin' up to speak? asked a man of him as he passed displaying the pamphlets.

—That's James Connolly, our secretary, an' if you knew all you should know, you'd know without askin'.

—Secretary of what? asked Sean.

—Aw, God, th' ignorance here's devastatin'! said Egan, giving a wryer twist to his melancholy mouth; Secretary of the Irish Socialist Republican Party, an' if you knew all you should know, you wouldn't have t' ask. Penny each, *Socialism Made Easy*, be the renowned Socialist Leadher, James Connolly.

—It doesn't look to be a mighty force of a party, murmured Sean.

—Aw, you count be numbers, d'ye? and he looked with pitiful tolerance at Sean.

—There's certainly something in them, said Sean; God fights on the side of the big battalions, you know — or so Napoleon said.

—We aren't concerned with Napoleon, an' God has nothin' to say in this meetin'.

—Jasus, don't we know it! burst from the man who had asked the first question.

—An' if you were with us, comrade, said the gaunt one, laying a hand on Sean's shoulder, and ignoring the ignorant remark of the ignorant man, you'd make one more.

—I thought you said you didn't put any pass on numbers?

—With a hurley stick under your arm, a gay blue-and-green jersey on your chest, and, I suppose, a cushy job, you can well afford to mock the woe of th' world!

—I am a labourer, and that's not quite a cushy job; I have no desire to mock anything, and there's more things than woe in the world.

—What more is there, comrade?

—There's joy and a song or two: the people sang as they went their way to tear the Bastille down.

—You're too oul'-fashioned for me, mate, said the gaunt one. Look! there's your proper leadher there, and he gestured to the fringe of the crowd, a little way from where they stood; Arthur Griffith, who's stopped to have a little quiet silent laugh. Well, he'll wake one day before he knows the night is gone to find himself and his gang swept away by what he's scornin' now.

Right enough, there was Up Griffith Up Thomas a Davis, hunched close inside his thick dark Irish coat, a dark-green velour hat on his head, a thick slice of leather nailed to his heels to lift him a little nearer the stars, for he was somewhat sensitive about the lowness of his stature. His great protruding jaws were thrust forward like a bull's stretched-out muzzle; jaws that all his admirers spoke of, or wrote about, laying it down as an obvious law that in those magnificent jaws sat the God-given sign of a great man. And Arthur Up Griffith, to give him his due, did all he could to give the fiction substance and fact. As plain as a shut mouth could say, he said he was Erin's strong, silent man.

What was he thinking of as he stood there, grim and scornful? Tormenting himself with the fading vision of a most lovely lady whose golden hair was hanging down her back, so full of fire that a tress of it would give light to a group threshing corn in a black barn on a dark night. Maybe stroking the right hand, oh! worthy right hand, that had laid a whip on the back of a little tittle-tattle Dublin editor of a gossip journal when he whispered *spy* about the Helen of Eireann who had the loveliness to launch a battle and go through it with the walk of a queen. He hid his hatred of a rival in the wrapping of Erin's noble emblem, boys, the green flag, around him; he composed gnarled remarks in his weekly paper against him who embroidered lovely cloths to put beneath the feet of the fair one, to shelter their grace and whiteness from the dust of the street; and sang songs that made a flame of her fair ear and sent a swell into her bosom with the pride of what a singer can say out of a purple-and-white love. Art Up Griffith Up Thomas a Davis's cold eyes saw the black-maned head of Yeats in the clouds, saw it on the earth beneath, looking at him from the *Book of Kells,* and staring down from the ceiling of the simple room wherein he slept. So he began to mock at the phantoms, saying that the fashioner of the play *Caitlin ni Houlihan* had become a king's pensioner; that he had walked away from her four beautiful green fields into an English paved court; Ochone, widda Malone, d'ye hear me talkin? And widda Malone said she'd heard right enough, and th' name that was once a jewel in Erin's girdle had dwindled into a dull stone; and Willie Reilly and his dear colleen bawn said, He was never much; he is nothin' now; and the Rose of Tralee said that he was just a lonely gateway now, where no-one enthered; and Mary sitting on the stile murmured it was all very shocking; the minstrel boy went about saying that Yeats now was no more than the seams on the grass showing where a house once stood; while Nora Creena closed her eyes, nodded her pretty head sagely, and murmured the less said about it all the better. A pensioner of an English king — pooh! bah!

Instinctively Sean stood by Yeats, in spite of the little he could guess then, and the less he knew. We have too few, too few such men to spare a one like Yeats the poet, and the Gaelic Leaguers who heard him grew silent. Devil a much you fellows do to keep a few shillings jingling in the poet's pocket. What about the Israelites who took gold, silver, and jewels from the Egyptians before they left them? If England pays the man's rent, then let it be counted unto righteousness for her. None of you know a single poem by Yeats. Not even *The Ballad of Father Gilligan.* And the poor oul' gaum, Cardinal Logue, condemning *Countess Cathleen* though he hadn't read a line of it. We were paying a deep price for that sort of thing since Parnell went away from us. He himself had read the ballad only.

There the little squat figure of Griffith stood, no tremor stirring the spectacles on his nose. Probably thinking more of Yeats than of Connolly, thought Sean. It wasn't Connolly's face Griffith saw, but Yeats's, and the evening was full of the poet's verses. Well, the golden tresses would gleam no more for Yeats, at any rate. The small white feet would seek another pathway, one of thorns rather than of broidered cloths or dreams. Oh, Cathleen ni Houlihan, your way's a thorny way! And Ireland's rock of ages, Griffith, stiffened with elation, firm in his Irish woven tweed, armoured with the stamp of Deunta in Eirinn on its collar and on the seat of the pants. And wasn't Up Griffith a poet himself? You bet he was. What about the one written to give Major McBride a lift in the Mayo election?

> God bless you, John McBride, aroon,
> God bless your Irish corps!
> With courage of the Keltic race you've gone to help
>   the Boers.
> True friends by Bann and Liffey banks,
> By Suir and Shannon side,
> Send you their hearts' best sympathy —
> God bless you, John McBride!

Let Yeats arise now and go to Inisfree, and stay and hide himself well there in his strict cabin of clay and wattles made — though, if y' asked me, thought Griffith, he wouldn't know what wattles were — and let him sow and hoe and crow over his nine bean rows, and live on them, with honey from the hive of the honey bees, and his evening full of the linnet's wings, regardless of the fact that no-one in Eirinn wants an evening full of a linnet's wings. Far more profitable for them to go to hear me lecture on how Hungary hitch-hiked herself into independence; or to listen enthralled to the gallant deeds done by the wild swans of Coole—whatthehellamisaying—by the wild geese in far foreign fields from Dunkirk to Belgrade, the O'Haras, Maguires, Reillys, McGauleys, O'Briens and O'Bradys, with hosts of other leaders, and men of many clans, fighting for anyone that would furnish them with a sword, a good word to go on, and a glass of malt at the end of a battle.

Sean edged nearer to where the great man, Griffith, stood surrounded by the gaunt one, now behind, now to his left, to his right a moment later, and then circling in front of him, murmuring balefully in Griffith's direction, *Socialism Made Easy*, by the renowned James Connolly, only a penny each. But the great man with the brain of ice, in the greatcoat, underneath the green velour, never moved. The widely-lensed spectacles and the thick moustache and the thrust-out chin listened in cold silence to Connolly's words; and Sean remembered how, at meetings in the rooms of the Sinn Fein Central Branch, Up Griffith had often called on Sean to speak, and he had spoken eloquently in Irish and English, amused that Connolly, Pike, Ling, and a few other Irish Republican Socialists had to listen silent and respectful to the flow of the Gaedhilge, understanding not a word of what was being said; with Up Griffith sitting bolt-upright and grim in the chair, huge jaws forced forward, ears cocked, though he understood no more than he'd understand the sad songs sung by the Children of Lir tossed about on the foam of the Swanee river. So he edged nearer till his elbow gently touched the stiff frame standing in the greatcoat.

—It's cold it is the night that's in it, he said in Irish.

The widely-lensed spectacles, velour hat, and intrusive moustache turned towards him, the rocky road to Dublin jaws thrust themselves farther out over the turned-up collar of the greatcoat, but the clenched mouth remained shut; then all turned, and, without a word, went their way.

—Little bourgious bastard! growled the gaunt one, glaring after the little conceited figure. Not enough banks in the counthry but he must start another — him and his Sinn Fein Bank! The dumb yahoo! Curse o' God on the bit he is above an ordinary little bourgious bastard!

Thinking, most likely, of what Connolly has been saying, thought Sean as he followed the great man slowly. *Cheek of those fellows stating the English were brothers. Connolly should know better. But my icy brain can never be deceived.* A capitalist government would never destroy capitalist property. *Bah! As if an English government cared a damn about Irish property.* Dog won't eat dog, says Connolly. *Nonsense! Besides the Irish aren't dogs, even if the English are.*

Griffith doesn't understand Ireland, thought Sean; no, in no way. He is simply delighted to dream as he walks through Ireland's junk-shop of all the tawdry paraphernalia of 1882. He hasn't the slimmest connection with a Gaedhilge proverb or a Gaedhildge song. He has no inkling of what burns in the breast of him who looks back on, and lives with, the

> Outlawed man in a land forlorn,
> He scorned to turn and fly;
> But he kept the cause of freedom safe
> On the mountains of Pomeroy.

He never even walks with the shade of Swift, for if I brought him tomorrow to be with them who work with me; among Christy Mahon, Bob Harvey, Bob Jones who'd sell the King of Ireland's son for a pint, Ned Smith who'd steal a cross off an ass's back, and all the rest, he'd be lost. His highest vision is no higher than the counter in his Sinn Fein Bank. He strikes a match, and thinks it the torch of freedom. A lighter of little gas-lamps to show the Irish where to walk. The sword of light would turn him to ashes if ever he tried to hold it. Ah! he's thinking of Trinity College; for he saw the green velour turning to look at the austere facade if the memorable building, sighing, prob-ably, that the young man inside didn't hear ear to ear with him. More inclined to Yeats's poetic bombast than to me. One of England's strongest bastions. Here was a group of them coming along now, singing *Daisy, Daisy, Give Me Your Answer, Do,* shouting it out with vengeance and vim. Oh! the vulgarity of the anglicised Irish mind! To think that Thomas a Davis had once gone in and out of those gates. Hardly believable. They surged uncivilly around him, jostling him out into the gutter. Oh, Cathleen ni Houlihan, your way's a thorny way!

—God, it's Arthur Griffith! shouted one of them.

—*Alumna licentiae, quam stulti libertatem vocabunt,* bawled an-other, waving his cap over his head, shouldering Up Griffith with a sly sliding movement, making the man nearly lose his balance; but he recovered, walked slantwise back to the side-walk, bypassing the students, and marched on without either a word or a gesture.

Sean felt angry, for Griffith was something of a leader, deserving jail from the point of view of the conquerors, but deserving respect as well. Strange, he thought, swinging his hurley into a poise that could swiftly jab the ribs of anyone likely to try to jostle him from the pathway. Strange and curious, he thought, that one able to speak Latin, who got a golden education denied to Griffith or himself, having a fine home in the country or in Rathmines, son, maybe, of a clergyman, a doctor, or a judge, strange he didn't know what decent manners were. He could calmly understand them hotly cracking skulls in the emotional medley of a royal visit, when the Dubliners were out with the battle-cries and their green flags; but in the cold of a quiet wintry night when citizens moved about intent on business, recreation, or love, indifferent to their national submission for the moment, to spout abuse on a citizen without warrant even of English law, or the gallant provocation of opposing tirades, was, to Sean, a thing that couldn't be understood of common sense or tangible decency. Let them look to it if they pushed him a hairsbreadth away from where he was walking. But they didn't; they passed by and took not the slightest notice of him as he followed Arthur marching on sturdily ahead as if nothing had happened.

The next day of a dark cold morning, Sean in the forge blowing the bellows to make the fire roar so that the smith might repoint his pick blunted by the work of the day before, for the soil of the deep trench navvies dig, to sow great iron pipes to carry a main supply of water, is hard and stony, and the point of a pick is soon deprived of its eagerness to bite: here in the yellow-and-red gleam of the flame of the fire, watching the smith Dick Bagnal's lanky form waiting for the pick to redden, one sooty hand on the butt of the pick, its point in the heart of the fire, Sean saw again the meeting of the night before, the squat, swaying form of Connolly speaking from his box, and the cold staring lens-covered eyes of Griffith watching, the big mouth beneath the great moustache grim and clenched and silent. Both of them out for Ireland, all for Ireland, yet neither of them could understand her. Both were a wide way from the real Ireland, and it was not in either of them to come closer. One man alone, of that time, had in him all that prophesied of the Ireland yet to come; the Ireland that would blossom into herself many, many years from now. This man alone had the hand to hold the sword of light. He held it now, and its rays were sparkling all over the valley of the Boyne. There were visions of handicrafts, of furniture, of woven garments, new, yet full of the scent of the days gone by; of pottery decked with the coloured glory of Keltic spirals and intricate, waving, twisting patterns, new too, but touched with the grandeur of the *Book of Kells* and the gaiety of the *Book of*

MacDurnan; here, where of old time protestant men for King William
wrestled to the death with catholic men for King James, falling with
the arms of hatred round each other by the borders of the Boyne, was
seen again the sway of the scarlet, green, grey, or saffron kilt; here
was heard the musical scream of the war-pipes; here were heard the
countless stories of Eireann, long in thrall, with the scent of freedom
clinging round them still; and song burst out, and filled the valley
with hope; and the plough and the cross shone on the biggest of
banners; and *The Irish Peasant*, one of the finest papers Ireland ever
had, told all about them; while among all this gay-coloured energy
and excitement walked the dark-eyed, black-haired W. P. O'Ryan,
shy, sensitive, one with the peasant, the worker, and the scholar. All
aglow he was, and firm set to make the Pope's green island a busy
place and beautiful. Half a step behind came a Man, a bacon-curer,
the surety of the paper, and a helper with money for the things they
thought of doing, whose heart was warm with the coloured resolution
all around him. All was fine till the clergy came to murmur against it,
and Cardinal Log lashed out to yell that it was a shame to undermine
the Holy Faith! And the Man's wife said to her husband, You've got
to hearken to what these holy men witness against them and thee.
Have nothing thou to do with this bad bold man, O'Ryan, but cast
him off, and come thou into the house, lest an evil thing befall us here,
and lest worse befall us when we pass away to Purgatory. And he
hearkened unto his wife, and shut himself up in his own house, condemning certain things written by O'Ryan, already condemned by
the Cardinal, though never read by him; for the Cardinal had the
power to see a hole through an iron pot; and so O'Ryan was left alone
to fight a host of snarling clergy who silenced song and story, drove
away the marching, kilted men, hunted O'Ryan from the Boyne to
the Liffey, then to the Dublin Quay, and finally from the last spot
where his clinging feet still stood, away, away with you, from Ireland
altogether, away from her for ever and a day! And Sean wondered
that Hyde said nothing, that the Gaelic League made no moan, and
Griffith, indifferent to a greater man, shook no angry fist, but let him
go, and so he went for ever. And Sean was sad, for it was O'Ryan who
first gave his written words a value, and spaced his thoughts over a
fine column of *The Irish Nation*; words, under the name of *Sound the
Loud Trumpets*, that struck at the educational system Augustus Birrell
was hanging around Ireland's neck. Over the grave of this brave man,
this cultured man, a silent hurrah; a big, broad, and scornful spit on
the grave of the Cardinal.

Down in the deep trench, shored up with planks and cross-pieces, a long way from Ireland's four beautiful green fields, side by side with the huge glossy black cylinders, Sean watched the broad backs of the navvies bending, rising, and bending again, as they worked on, making way for another length of the monster black pipe, looking like a prehistoric ebony worm that men were uncovering now after a rest of a million years; while far above their heads a dim damp dawn crept slowly over the sky. Not one of these brawny boys had ever even heard of Griffith or of Yeats. They lived their hard and boisterous life without a wish to hear their names. A good many of them had done seven years' service in the British Army, and now served on the Reserve, for sixpence a day wasn't to be sneezed at. What to them were the three Gaelic candles that light up every darkness: truth, nature, and knowledge? Three pints of porter, one after the other, would light up the world for them. If he preached the Gaelic League to any one of them, the reply would probably be, Aw, Irish Ireland me arse, Jack, not makin' you an ill answer, oul' son. What would the nicely-suited, white-collared respectable members of the refined Gaelic League branches of Dublin do if they found themselves in the company of these men? Toiling, drinking, whoring, they lived everywhere and anywhere they could find a ready-made lodging or room. They didn't remember the glories of Brian the Brave. Beyond knowing him as an oul' king of Ireland in God's time, they knew nothing and cared less. Their upper life was a hurried farewell to the *News of the World* on Sunday morning, and a dash to what was called short twelve Mass in the Pro-Cathedral, the shortest Mass said in the land; and then a slow parade to the various pubs, and a wearisome wait till the pubs unveiled themselves by sliding the shutters down, and let the mass of men crowd in for refreshment. And yet Sean felt in his heart that these men were all-important in anything to be done for Ireland. Well, there was no sound of a linnet's wings here; nothing but the thud of the pick, the tearing sound of the shovel thrust into the gravel, the loud steady pulse of the pump sucking away the surface water, and the cries of the men handling the derrick from which the huge pipes swung, and the irritating squelch of the men's boots as they sunk into, and were pulled out of, the thick and sticky yellow clay. While he swung the sledgehammer down on the hardy head of the bright steel wedge imprisoned in a gad held by a comrade, to break through a harder crust the pick couldn't penetrate, he cursed himself that he couldn't afford to spend a month, a fortnight, or even a week in a summer school at peace in an Irish-speaking district. Three or four visits, and he would be as fluent a speaker of the Gaelic as any in Ireland. Even now, with all their chances, all their means providing them with the best of books, there were few of them could speak as well and as rapidly as he; and none of them with such a fire of eloquence. Few of them hadn't heard him speak at one time or another, yet never a one of them had even asked why he didn't go to Rinn or Tourmakeady when the summer sun shone, and share with them the joy of living with their very own. If he went up to a meeting of the Coiste Gnotha, the Head Executive of the Gaelic League, and, leaning over the table they sat around keeping time in their talk to the snores of Edward Martyn, asleep in an easy-chair, said, Look here, boys, I love the Irish; I've learned a lot; I want to spend a holiday in an Irish district, Connemara for preference, but I've no money; couldn't you people fork out enough to fix me there for a week or two, so that my Irish may be as the rain falling on the earth, or the lightning splitting the black clouds, what would happen? The tidy-minded, uninspirable secretary, Paddy O'Daly, would come over, grip his arm, lead him to the door, and say, Now, now, we're engaged in very important business. The like of them would hurry by Whitman spitting out of him as he leaned by a corner of the Bowery. And doing so, they'll die, for whoever walks a furlong without sympathy walks to his own funeral dressed in his shroud. Ah, to hell with them!

—Eh, there; look out, Jack! warned his mate: the sledge near missed the wedge that time!

POOR TOM'S ACOLD

SEAN stood silently in the room looking long at the fearful figure of his brother, Tom, crouched in the comfortable armchair before a sunnily-blazing fire, for the night was cold, and a white frost was calmly settling down on the paths and street outside. He felt a choking in his throat, and tears trickled down his cheeks, but Tom couldn't see them, for his eye-strings had broken, and he was blind.

Tom had done well and done ill since he had come home from the Boer War, jaunty in his khaki uniform, helmet and puggaree, the Queen's coloured box of chocolate in his kit-bag still full of the sweetmeat, for what soldier could eat chocolate given by a queen? And he had kept it just as it had been given to him during a parade on the brown veldt, in the shadow of high kopjes when many bugles had blown the cease-fire, and the ragged De Wet, with many a curse, had stabled his horse, and had flung his rifle and whip into a corner, easing his sweating body on a sofa till another chance came to strike again, galloping over the veldt or crouching behind a kopje.

War's wager won, Tom had gone back to his job as a postman, was shortly after promoted to his old job of a sorter, finally becoming head sorter in the morning mail running from Dublin to Belfast, this job bringing another and much higher one almost within his reach: he was getting on well and worthily. Then he married: married an ignorant catholic girl who in some way had influenced him towards a newer home, and a companionable bed. Agatha Cooley was a yellow-skinned, stout woman, badly built in body, and mind-sly in a lot of ways, as so many toweringly ignorant persons are; her best knowledge lay in guessing what a newspaper was trying to say. She could struggle through a short letter with pain and anxiety, her finest phrase always being that of hoping all were in the best of health as that left her at present. A lid that drooped half-way down over one eye gave one side of her face the appearance of falling into a jocular sleep, and, watch as he would, Sean had never seen it lift or fall; it stood still like a fading yellow blind whose worn-out spring refused to send it more than half-way up on a dark and dusty oval window. She dressed in a very dowdy, slovenly way, and spoke in a voice from which a rough life had mobbed even the dimmest tinkle of music. She was a cook-general when Tom met her, and how or where they met, or how the rather fastidious Tom had been gathered into her bosom, none of the family ever knew. Before they were married, Tom had brought her once or twice to see his mother; but do all we did to make things merry and offhand, the core of every effort was uneasiness, for poor Agatha could do nothing but sit straight on her chair, prim and fat, sipping her glass of beer, making herself look as unrefined as possible; giving a flat yes or a flatter no to every question, till one grew tired of asking, turning away to other thoughts, leaving her there to sit and sip her beer in peace. She had got Tom, and there she sat, thick and stout, like a queen cactus on a kitchen chair of state.

Mrs. Casside had an anxious time of it, for she had an old protestant dread of a mixed marriage, and all her time now was a silent prayer that, in some way or another, the marriage would drift into a happy unfulfilment. She told her trouble to but one outside the family — the Rev. Mr. Griffin, who agreed with her in a scholarly way, though Tom had only once ever put his foot inside his church, feeling very uncomfortable till he got out again. The Rector prayed in the little room, with Mrs. Casside, that God in His goodness would see the dear woman's son safe, and lead him from the tangible danger of marrying one alien in religion, and different in manner and outlook in life, his words mingling with the laughing shouts of children swinging from a rope tied to the lamp-post just outside the window. Sean wasn't bothering about her alienism in religion, even for Tom's sake, for he knew that Tom had slid away from all of them. The smell of a pub was incense to Tom, and its portals had the beauty of a Persian garden, with an everlasting fountain of sweet waters in the midst of it. The hold of the faith had weakened well on Sean himself. Though he hadn't said farewell, the anchor was getting weighed, and his ship of life was almost about to leave the harbour. He no longer thought that God's right hand, or His left one either, had handed the bible out of Heaven, all made up with chapter and verse and bound in a golden calfskin. Darwin's flame of thought had burned away a lot of the sacred straw and stubble, and following men had cleanly shown how incredible much of the bible was, contradicting itself so often and so early that no-one could argue with it, rearing up an imposition of fancy, myth, and miracle coloured by neither fact nor figure; depending on a crowd who, as Coleridge said, didn't believe, but only believed that they believed, ready to strike at, and drive away, any sincere and sorrowful heart daring to murmur, I can believe no longer.

No, it wasn't Agatha's religion that troubled Sean, for she had none save to eat and drink and sleep and be afeared of fancies; it was her slovenliness that tortured him, her drowsy ignorance and deep-set superstition that seared his imagination; for Tom was the one brother whom he liked, and, in his heart, he knew that this marriage would be the end of Tom, and that he would be separated even from the bawdy exhilaration of the pub.

God was no good, and the marriage took place, how, or where, no-one seemed to know. Tom just came to the home one day and, in a silent silence, took his box away. For some years after, he was rarely seen, and it was gossip that told us where he was living. Occasionally at the railway station, Sean, with his dinner in a handkerchief fixed to a billycan tied to his belt, hurrying to his train for a country job at the screek of dawn, met Tom who murmured a hurried hello, and Sean gave him the railwaymen's signal of greeting of a raised index-finger as he passed by to his train. All the same, three fine kids came out of the mating, Sam, Sylvester, and Sally; the little girl, a real handsome kid, the younger boy, handsome and sturdy, and the older one strong too, his boyish face an annoying blend of his father's good-nature and his mother's tireless querulousness. They rented a small house with three steps up to the door, a shining brass knocker, and a bow-window. This residence, with a few others, stood out grandly in the narrow terrace, for the rest on the opposite side had only iron knockers, no bow-windows, and no steps up to the doors. Here with a selection of fair furniture, especially what was in the room with the bow window, fine lace curtains on the window, with dark yellow blinds at night, and a plant on a round mahogany table, Tom made quite a splash, and for a time all went well as a marriage bell. Once in a blue moon Tom would pay a flying call to see the mother, send out for a jug of porter, and, with bread and butter, drink it with her, chatting rapidly about what had happened at work, but never a word about what had happened at home; and Sean gave a guess that these lunar visits were spell-snatched out of acrimony and thorny-worded leisure time. Once Sean caught a glimpse of what was happening. It was Tom's day off, and Sean had taken the day to help in a local election, and when he came to Tom's terrace he came on the bould boy polishing the brass knocker. Tom brought him in for a cup of tea, pointing a thumb warningly upwards, and murmuring, She's up in bed, not feeling too well. In the kitchen, Sean noticed a pile of delft draining on a shelf, the things of yesterday mixed with the things of today, and he knew that Tom had washed them.

—What's wrong with her? asked Sean, with a pointed gesture of a thumb upwards.

—Not feeling too well; just not feeling too well, he murmured.

Down the road, in one of the houses on the opposite side of the terrace, Sean was told that this was a common thing on Tom's day off; and that it was he who kept the children's hair combed, bathed them often, and tried to see that the boys got their meals in time to allow them to attend, without blame, the local Christian Brothers' schools.

The time came when Tom himself wasn't feeling too well, and came oftener to see his mother — not to complain, but, maybe, to look at the old, hardy, encouraging face that had weathered so much of the stormy world. At first Tom took his inability to work with pretended joy — a holiday on full pay, he called it. The Post Office doctor attended him, gave him remedies, but Tom got weaker and weaker, and nothing stayed on his stomach. One day, out with the pipers' band, Sean hurried home to get a letter about a festival they were to attend, found Tom there, sitting heavily on a chair, his breath coming in gasps, and when asked what was wrong, I came upstairs too quick — all right in a minute, came staggering out of his mouth. When he came to himself a little, he sent for a pint of porter, but this time his mother drank it alone. His face, once so ruddy and confident, had waned into the pallor of a half-dead man.

—What's wrong with you, old man? asked Sean.

—Dunno right; something; I'll be all right again soon.

—But what does the doctor say 'tis?

—Didn't say, Jack; can't be anything serious, or he'd say, wouldn't he?

—You'd think so, said Sean doubtedly.

—Well, I'll be getting back home to rest awhile, and a flash of meek panic at the journey before him flickered over the pale face; getting back now, I'd betther. He stood up slowly, and a shaking hand put a hat on his head. Well, so long, Jack; so long, old woman; and his shaky legs carried him out of the room.

—I don't like the look of him, said Mrs. Casside; I don't like the look of him at all. A man of his age, only, should be fortified with all but the full strength of one of twenty. Whisht! He's callin', Jack — run!

He ran down the stairs to find Tom sitting breathless and near fainting on the last step of the flight, a kid with a squint staring at his panting breast and gaping mouth. He stood for a moment beside Tom, a hand resting on his shoulder, afraid that he would have to help Tom home, and he in full piper's dress, and sorry for himself that he had come home, and so plunged into all this annoyance.

—What's wrong with you, man? he asked, a little harshly; but Tom went on panting his breath out through an open mouth, motioning with a death-nacred finger for Sean to keep silent. So silent he stayed till the fit passed, and the breath of his brother came more softly again.

—Ran down the stairs too quick, he said at last. Could you manage, Jack, to see me home a bit of the way? and a tense look of appeal shot into the gentle grey eyes of the sick man.

—I've got to join the band again, Tom, we're advertising a coming concert, and the work has to be done.

—Right, old man, I know, murmured Tom. Never mind; I'll manage; but he bent his head to hide his frightened disappointment, for he dreaded to be weak in the presence of strangers.

—I'll see you a little of the way, said Sean, softening. Cheer up, old sweat — you'll be all right yet.

—All right yet, echoed Tom; yes, all right yet; but Sean didn't like to look at the glassy film creeping over the eyes of his brother.

He helped him to his feet, putting an arm around his body, while Tom put one over his shoulder, and so they went down Church Road, slowly, slowly, gradually getting nearer to Tom's half-way home, the the sick man frequently stopping to get his breath, the passers-by stopping to stare back at a death-faced man whose legs were like loose bending wires trying to keep straight, kept going with the help of another in a green kilt, shining brooches in breast and at knee, jaunty balmoral cap, and flowing crimson shawl.

—Don't talk, don't even try to talk, advised Sean; just do your best to move, and lean well on me, for he was anxious to get his brother home, and flee to sunnier company, to march stiffly proud by the side of the pipers. Suddenly he heard the roll of the drums, and buried in the roll the opening and unruly skirl of the pipes being filled with air before the pipers got into the start of the tune at the end of the second roll.

—There they go now, he thought; at a distance, thank God, for he didn't want the band to come swinging past, and he carrying a half-dead man home. He felt the sweat running down his belly and along his legs, for the kilt was warm and heavy, seven yards of material swinging from a man's hips; and his arms were aching. Worse than a hard day's work, this!

On the two of them struggled up the quiet terrace; quiet no longer, for all the doors were opening to let the people see where the music was coming from, and what band was playing it. On and on, past all the little doors, little windows, little front gardens with little gates, each with different-shaped beds, but with the same flowers growing in them all: tansy with its hotly fragrant smell, its deeply fronded leaves, and its humble yellow button of a blossom; mignonette sending out its dainty, delicate perfume, a little disdainful of the vulgar scent of the tansy; purple rockets whose seed-pods turned to wonderful disks of nacred silver, fit to make tiny wings for tiny angels; blood-red dahlias, portly and pompous-looking, like eighteenth-century gentlemen ripened into a stout dignity with rich wine; orange marigolds with their ragged and crooky stems and dishevelled leaves looking like harridans of the Coombe wearing patched disordered skirts round their bodies and gorgeously gay orange bonnets on their heads. Variegated clumps of sweet-william prim and apart in their own private corners; brown, yellow, white, and blue-purpled pansies living for themselves, and taking notice of nothing; hurrying, gaudy-coloured nasturtiums, trying to climb everywhere, like upstarts at a sedate garden party; and bushes of violet and delicately mauve michaelmas daisies, their dark, sober green leaves and tall stems gathering together for company, silently sneering at the richer display of the other blossoms.

—Do you think you could go a little quicker, old son, asked Sean, before the band brings the crowd surging round us?

—Must try, must try, Jack, Tom panted back; and with a galvanic power of will he stiffened his poor wavering legs, and hastened on past the rest of the gardens, till they passed through his own little plot, asway with neglected blooms, Sean knocking impatiently at the door, while Tom lay almost lifeless against it, his waistcoat coming out and sinking in like a blown and pricked balloon, with the dint of palpitation, his glazing eyes bulging, and his mouth again agape in an effort to pacify the turbulent commotion of his frightened heart.

Sean's mind held only thoughts of the concert that was to raise funds to help Dr. O'Hickey with his fight in Rome against the bishops who were opposing essential Irish in the New University Ireland had wrenched from the hand of her enemy. Irish in the New University, or else! That was the one way to talk, to fling a challenge right into the teeth of the snarling Birrell and his hoary henchmen, the bishops! Dr. O'Hickey go brath! A lion's roar, a wolf-dog's bay beside the pigeon-cautious coo of Dr. Douglas Hyde, and the scholarly and elegantly brushed phrases of Eoin Mac Neill, an Aaron's rod that rarely bore a bud. Hyde would venture a boo to an English goose, but ne'er a boo to an Irish bishop. That would be asking too much. Oh, O'Hickey, me jewel of Ireland — there's one man left in Ireland yet! No priest, bishop, archbishop, cardinal, or pope is going to be let impede the onward march of Ireland. Such a scandal has never been seen here since the dastard who, having sold his country, successfully sought the votes of the citizens of Athlone, leaning on the arms of two bishops. Sadleir and Keogh, be God, and the Pope's brass band! But *ne plus ultra* O'Hickey — a Parnell with a Roman white choker round his neck, fighting the battle of Banba's language. I hear you speaking: If the New University is to be a West Briton one, it will be made so by an act of treachery to Ireland on the part of the University Senate, five of whom are distinguished clerics, two of whom are bishops. These Lords and Gentlemen of the Senate must be told that, wily as they are, they will not be suffered to cozen and delude the Irish people. Michael O'Hickey, you are my soul within me; our love and our strength in the day of strife, our rosc catha, a piercing eye of battle leading us on to a new and freer life!

Here they come, now, chests out, eyes proud, aswinging grandly round the corner, drummers and pipers in full play, mantling the narrow terrace with martial music; the rolling of the drums echoing through the little houses giving them a proud passion to find a sword somewhere; the shrill of the war-pipes sending a thrill through every ear that had been already half stuffed with the dust of death — like poor Tom's; the green kilts, crimson shawls, and gay ribbons draped on the drones fluttering winsomely whenever a breeze blew, fanning a new resolution and a strict courage into all who followed; here they come, here they come, the pipes and drums of war, to scatter away the quiet resignation of timorous people, their big crimson banner before them, the silver lion asparkle on its bloody field, roaring out, forward, forward! Forward for Ireland, like the Scots Wha Hae at Bannockburn; march on, march on, to liberty or death, like the French with bloodied fingers tearing down the stones of the Bastille; march like the marching of the men of Harlech, for of battle we'll not cheat them; on like the whirlwind riders on the desert sands of Abdel Kader, son of a slave, first of the brave, swift-riding Abdel Kader; farther, farther on, for the rifle brown and sabre bright can freely speak and nobly write, and prophets preached that truth right well, like Hofer, Brian, Bruce, and Tell — Christ, will the penduloous-lidded, yellow-faced bitch never open the door!

The door opened, and Tom's yellow-skinned wife glared at them sleepily from the half-lidded eye, and balefully from the wide-open one, like a lassie direct in descent from the one-eyed coon — no, like a woman Balor of the Blows. Sean caught up Tom in his arms and carried him into the little bow-windowed room, laying him down as gently as his hurry could, in the easy armchair by the empty fire-grate. Mercy on us! his bones were like flints against his breast, and pressed sharply into Sean's arms. Then he patted the sandy-haired head and turned to go.

—A nice state to bring the poor man back in! said Agatha bitterly. Dhrinkin' with his oul' wan I suppose he was, forgettin' all about his wife an' childher. Well, it looks as if he was bein' punished for it. Thryin' to get all she can outa th' poor man, that's what it is, so it is. I'll put a stop to it, so I will. I will, see now. Now run off in your gay get-up an' leave me here with all th' throuble.

A rich surge of rolling drums and valiant skirl of a defiant march came sweeping into the lonely room as the band swung by outside the window, and Sean caught a glimpse of crimson shawl, crimson banner, and the jaunty feathers rising out of the pipers' balmorals, set a little rakishly on their boyish heads.

—A nice noisy commotion to bring to th' ears of a poor sick man, she said. God forgive you! — that's all I can say.

Sean noticed that Tom's lips were moving. He bent down close so as to hear the pale words from the thronging sound of rolling drums and skirling pipes that filled the room with martial animation.

—Cold, Jack, he heard Tom whispering; feeling bad and cold, very cold.

—You'd better light a bit of a fire for him here, said Sean to Agatha — he says he's very cold.

—I'd betther, had I? I'm to take insthructions from you, am I? Your money'll pay for it, I suppose, will it? An' what has him cold, I'd like to know? If he'd ha' stayed in his own home, he wouldn't be cold now. His lawful wife's th' proper person to know whether he's cold or no, if y'ask me. Sorra mend him, if he is cold, aself, for his flighty way o' goin' on. Is it any wondher he's cold, an' has no luck th' way he regards his poor patient wife? Oh, ay, slink away now when th' harm's done, do. Guttherbred highlandher, guttherbred highlandher! she said loudly, following him to the door.

Through the harp blows the cold wind. Ah, Tom, if it had only been a comely face, a rustling petticoat, and a slender leg that had betrayed your poor life to a woman, enhanced by a shimmer of a little silk. But no! It was pendulous breasts, a ponderous belly, a clumsy foot, and a vacant yellow face that brought you close to this! A drab, hard cushion on which to stretch your life. But a small spark left now, all the rest on's body cold.

He was again amid the roll of the drums and the skirl of the pipes, forgetting Tom, and thinking only of Ireland. The drums of Ireland, of Inis Fail, the Isle of Destiny, beaten by tempestuous hands, were tossing the patriotic air into wildness, shaking every window in every city, town, and hamlet, and tapping a tocsin at every door, giving a quiver to the tidy walls and corbelled ceiling of the Viceregal Lodge, sending the cloth-covered butlers and plush-covered footmen to whisper in corners where they couldn't be seen, hurrying out to the wind-swept plains of Kildare to circle slowly round the lonely grave of Wolfe Tone to liven his dust-filled ears with the sound of the drums at the head of an Ireland marching!

Busy in the circle of drumming, Sean had a visit from Tom's eldest son, who said his Da felt bad, very bad, and wanted Sean to come to him. Catching up the latest issue of *Sinn Fein* to leave with his brother, he hurried along, warning the young boy that he hadn't time to stay long. He found Tom crouched in the armchair beside the fire, his

tawny head sunk on his shrunken breast, his white handsome hands
resting on the arms of the chair.

—Well, old man, how goes it?

He sat there silent for a long time, never stirring, making Sean feel
uneasy, for he had no time to think of these things. Then he lifted the
finely-formed head a little to murmur, I'm beginning to think, Jack,
I'm on the edge of the end.

—Aw, nonsense, man, you're only a little downcast. Not a condition of thought for an old Dublin Fusilier. I've brought a copy of *Sinn
Fein* for you to lift your mind away from depression. And he laid the
paper on his brother's knee, putting a gentle and encouraging hand
on his shoulder.

—No use, now, Jack; I'm afraid I'll never read again: my eyes have
gone; something burst — the strings, I think.

Jesus have mercy on us! Tom was going from them. Like their
father before them, he was trying to die on his feet. Well, Sean could
do nothing. He wasn't a Hercules to wrassle with Death and throw
him down with a half-nelson.

—Where's Agatha? he asked.

—Don't know. Shopping, I think. Kids outside playing. It's a hard
thing to keep alive, Jack; hardly worth the effort. Then he fell silent
again, his bony hands resting motionless on the arms of the chair. I
think I'll give in, and go, he said suddenly; help me up and into bed,
Jack, me oul' son.

—Ah, thought Sean, he's about to leave the view from the little
bow-window for ever. He took off his coat so that it wouldn't come
in his way, helped Tom up out of the chair, and saw that he couldn't
even try to walk. He edged him gently over to the wall, leant him
against it, and then turned his back to his brother.

—Now, me son o' gold, fall forward on to my back, put your arms
around my neck, hold tight as you can, and I'll carry you up the way
an Indian woman carries her papoose.

Tom fell gently forward, and clasped his thin arms around Sean's
neck. With a gentle hoist he had Tom up; up the ten stairs he bore him
as he'd often carried a sixteen-stone bag of cement, into the little
bedroom. There he laid him down against the wall, squirming round
with a hold still on him, lest he'd fall; lifted him up in his arms, and
carried him like an infant to the bed. Here he stripped him to his shirt,
got him in, and covered him up warm, standing still to look down on
the pallor-stricken mask of what was so short a while ago a lively,
laughing, proud, and buoyant face; a handsome one too, with its

straight nose, bold forehead, the blue-grey eyes full of the animation of taking things as they came — now unsightly cavities of decaying jelly — the fierce-looking tawny moustache veiling the kind mouth, and the poor neck, thin now as a pipe-shank, that had once bulged out the stiff stern collar of his soldier's crimson coat.

—Tom, oul' son, he asked in a gentle whisper, do you really feel very bad?

—Only for the three chiselurs, I'd be all right; I'm doing me best to live.

—He's game to the end, thought Sean. He's deliberately fighting it alone; no murmur against the dark dullness of the grave. He isn't asking me to stay; he doesn't seek a wife's sympathy, or a mother's comfort. Happier are the dead that are already dead, more than the living that are yet alive. Not a mother's son of a gun of us knows whence we came or whither we go. Some shout that they do, and carry banners of belief in their hands; but the banners, too, will soon be dust sprinkled on the dust of the bearers. Kindly Tom, poor kindly Tom. He rushed into the brightness of the pub, the one brightness within his reach. Well, God is as likely to be there as in the Viceroy's satin-walled residence, or the Guinness's mansion of high style and tabinet. Not a son of a gun of us knew who he'd meet, or what he'd see, or a ha'p'orth when the time came to go. A bird's flight from the ground to the roof-top, and then the same bird's flight from the roof-top to the ground, and life was over. He bent down towards the bed till his mouth was close to Tom's waxy ear. You know Mr. Griffin, don't you? A grand man. Would you like me to bring him to you for a minute's talk?

—Anything you like, Jack; only for the three chiselurs, I wouldn't care a lot.

—I'll go get him then; I just heard Agatha coming in, so you won't be by yourself. So long, oul' soldier!

He hurried out to where Agatha was taking off her hat in the hall, and touching her on the arm, said, I'm off to bring Mr. Griffin to him. Keep an eye on him, and stay with him, for he may slip off any minute now.

—Yous would all like him to go, wouldn't yous? Oh, I know well, but he'll stay in spite of yous all. An' don't throw any ordhers at me, if you please; I know quite well what a wife's duties to her husband is.

Sean left the house, and ran, and hurried, when running lost him his breath. What was he hurrying for? To bring the Rector to say a word in season to a fellow hurrying off in an opposite direction. What word? The word that was in the beginning? Possibly. The word that was with God; the Word that was God. He was hurrying to bring God to the dying Tom who was on his way to meet Him, as it were, half-way home. But Tom had never bothered his head about what the word might be. His holy grail was a pint tankard filled to the brim. Yet Sean could proclaim to all the angels of Heaven, to all the gilded prelates of the Church militant here on earth, that Tom was a decent fellow. He had done foolish things early and late and often, but who the hell hadn't? The pint tumbler in the midst of a pub's glow, or the half-gallon can at home were Tom's own true guiding star. But what about the boyos who made what filled them? The fellow who rebuilt St. Patrick's Cathedral out of some of the profits made out of the stuff that thousands of poor Toms swallowed? The National Church of Ireland balanced now and for evermore on barrels of beer and whiskey. The church where Ormond Butler's men and Kildarian Geraldine's men sliced each other to death right before the altar, like alto-relievos come to life there, making the Pope himself to force the Lords Mayor of Dublin City to bereave themselves of their flaunting red gowns and lengthy golden chain of office every single Corpus Christi Day, and go walking barefoot, weeping away, a yellow tip of flame on a lighted candle the one ornament in a sad token of humilia- tion for a sin cleverly and enthusiastically committed by others; the church where the Irish were told straight off and straight out that Henry the Eighth was their lawful, legitimate, legible, rightful king; and only an hour or two later the city was deluged with banners of orange and blue, and Dutch troopers wearing big-plumed, high- rimmed, three-cornered hats, and thigh boots, with spurs with rowels on them as big as circular saws, came clattering through the streets, led by King Billy with his long sword on one side of him, and a bible broad hanging by a silver chain from the other side of his saddle- girths, who led them into the church to get rid of their thanks to God for the vast victory of the Boyne, burying the Duke of Schomberg in a copper coffin under the tiled floor with his martial cloak around him; and here, too, Edward the Seventh, when he was but a prince, was made a knight of the illustrious blue-ribboned, quiz se berrabbit Order of St. Patrick, sitting near the chained shot that whipped off the head of General St. Ruth and he leading the French cavalry at the battle of Aughrim; and it was here, too, that poor Swift constantly kept tor- menting God to stir up the Irish into burning everything English except her coals.

It was this history-chequered church, so wittily and winsomely

built in the form of a Latin cross by placing a lot of absolutely equi-
lateral triangles together, showing the choir, nave and transepts to be
a perfect Latin cross according to its kind, and the aisles, nave, choir,
and transepts, surrounding this one, in the same accurate system
of trinified triangulation, presented another perfectly proportioned
Latin cross that must be seen to be believed: it was for this church
that Benjamin McGuinness forked out a quarter of a million of the
best to keep the walls from falling asunder, amid cheers and beers,
thanksgivings, blessings, songs of praise and appreciation, brandish-
ing of croziers, waving of embroidered copes, throwing-up of ornamented mitres, swinging of bells; the archbishops, bishops, deans
and deacons leading the vast multitude in the singing of He's a jolly
good fellow that nobody dare deny, while peers of the Order of the
Goose that laid the Golden Eggs and knights of the Coined Cross of
St. Croker Crispin led McGuinness up the long aisle by the hands, a
scene unequalled anywhere at any time on this terrestrial ball, though,
singular to remark, no mention at all was made of the thousands and
thousands of Toms who lowered millions and millions of pints of
porter fundamentally providing the wherewithal to allow this church
to stay standing for the certain shelter of God and His greater
glory.

But he mustn't forget Tom lying alone and dying alone and facing
a never-ending future alone. He must argue it out with himself. Never
a word of blame about his wife. Never a complaint about what had
ever happened to him: a kindly and a brave man. A shield that caught
the sneering shafts shot by Mick at Sean when he was a kid; his, Let
Jack alone — he's all right, was an ever-present help in time of trouble;
a knight or, at least, a man-at-arms of the illustrious Order of St.
Patrick.

There's always a dark feather among the coloured feathers in our
cap.

> The cleanest corn that e'er was dight
> May have some pyles o' caff in;
> So ne'er a fellow creature slight
> For random fits o' daffin.

Look at Bobbie Burns himself! A hard case, by all accounts, but
who, save a Catholic Young Man or a Young Men's Christian Associate, or an odd bishop, priest, or deacon, would say that Heaven was
too respectable a place for Bobbie Burns to find a corner in? What was
it Laertes said about the dead Ophelia when the cautious clergy were
affording her a maimed burial in Elsinore? I tell thee, churlish priest,

a minist'ring angel shall my sister be, when thou liest howling. And from her fair and unpolluted flesh may violets spring! Ay, Laertes, violets of the deepest blue for ever spring from poor Ophelia's gentle and bewildered dust. And maybe, from the tired and dried-up dust of Tom will spring a strident yellow, lovely sunflower, or maybe a moon-daisy disked like a cooling sun. She died a maimed death; he lived a maimed life; but why? Because his school aimed at breeding a multitude to toil and spin i' th' frost and sun to meet tomorrow's needs with the paring thrift of the day before. He learned to juggle figures to count a boss's money, and keep the figures rising; dots on a map gave him a city's vision; a line wavering a mighty river's flow; a wavy smudge, the everlasting hills; and there he saw the world. The catechism to keep him off from God; the boy stood on the burning deck to make of him a hero; and a magic-lantern slide showing hell-fire just to keep him quiet.

Nothing seemed to be able to excite the clergy. They dreaded any kind of a noise, and went about as if Jesus had never got out of the manger. Not Mr. Griffin, of course, or Harry Fletcher or his brother, Dudley. But the rest of them. He himself had shyly asked a number of them what they thought of Shelley? But all he got was a hum and a haw and some daring opinions that *The Skylark* was a good poem. Not fair, he supposed, to expect a liking for him who wrote *Queen Mab*. They had drawn away from the sensitive extension of the world. So freer men like Tom ran along a brighter road into forgetfulness of what they could become. If this kind of life was a preparation for Heaven, then Heaven could go to hell for him, for the saints would be but scurvy companions. Was it for all this poor assembly of insignificant things that the Word was made flesh, and dwelt among us? In what do we behold His glory, the glory as of the only begotten of the Father, full of grace and truth? Is it in the stunted efforts of the poor dead Tom? Did it flame from the squalor of the homes where the people lived? Is it in the roaring stampede into protective piety over the mention of shift in poor Synge's play? Or in the dismissal of Dr. O'Hickey from Maynooth for hailing compulsory Irish in the New University? Did it abide in all the gentle and furious fairy tales of the bible? D'ye call this religion? No, no. D'ye call that religion? No, no. D'ye call this religion? No, no! Midas carries the cross.

He knocked at the Rector's door, and Jennie, his eldest daughter, opened the door. A lovely lassie she was, with her trim figure, her fair face lit up by large grey-green eyes, and a sweeping flow of rich red-

brown hair falling to her waist; and a bright thrill went through his
body as she shook his hand and bade him to come in. She had often
made his heart go fast when he saw her in church, or when she walked
some of the way home by his side when the service was over; but he
had diligently driven all thought of her away from him by the calm
appeal of his books, and the whirl of his work for Ireland.

—You want to see father, John? she asked, giving a graceful toss to
her heavy wave of hair that sent dancing beams of light through the
hall in which they stood.

—Yes, he said, if it isn't too inconvenient for him to see me.

—He's very busy, always is now, John, since he became a rural dean.
Is what you want to say very important?

—It seems so to me, Miss Jennie, and maybe more so to
another.

—Stay there a moment, and I'll see; and she went into the study,
returning quick to say that her father said John was to come straight
in to him.

There he was, sitting at his desk, rather close to a good fire, surrounded by many papers, well within the protection of a copy of da
Vinci's *Last Supper*; not a hair astray in hair or in beard; a finely-cut
alpaca coat over his suit of solemn black, the slender gold watch-
chain shyly streaking across his waistcoat like a delicate sunbeam
hurrying across a sombre sky: an elegant, learned, kindly, sensitive,
handsome, broad-minded man.

—Come in, come, my dear John, pressing Sean's hand with a
firmness surprising in a hand so slender and so white; though no
wonder to Sean when he remembered the Rector had groomed his
own horse in the country, and when married, with little to go on, had
made a wash-tub for his wife by sawing a barrel in two, and he had
done other things by hand and muscle of which he was laughingly
proud. A man afraid of very little.

—Sit beside me while I finish this letter he said. John will join me
when you bring me my tea, Jennie, he added to his daughter. Off you
go, he said to Sean, when the tea was brought in; don't mind my one
biscuit; there's cake and bread and jam for you, for you look cold,
and a little tired. Take it up with your fingers, John, he said laughingly,
when he saw Sean's clumsy assay to lift lump sugar in a tongs; one
would want to be a qualified engineer to use those tongs comfortably,
so take what you want with your fingers.

After tea had been taken, he gave a steady ear to all that Sean had
to say about his brother Tom.

—Come, John, he said, when Sean was silent, we'll go now, and may God go with us.

With a warm coat over him, a dark-green scarf round his neck, his walking-stick in his right hand, the Rector marched down the street with a fine brisk step. At the Aldborough Barracks he hailed a cab, and the two of them sat silent while the mare went as leisurely as she could to where the dying man lay in his tiny room, Sean thinking of the barracks left behind where he had sometimes got a piece of liver or a kidney for the price of a pint from an Army Service Corps butcher when he was hacking up the meat for the Dublin Garrison, and when he happened to be in the giving vein.

—We could almost walk as quick, said the Rector impatiently; and that remark fell softly into the silence that had gone before it.

Silently they came to the door; almost silently knocked; and the door was opened softly by the eldest boy, for Agatha wasn't eager to come into touch with the protestant minister; and silently they mounted the boxed-in stairs to Tom's bedroom, where he lay on his back, mixed up, murmuring phrases trickling out over his twitching lips.

—Curious dying activity in a curious room, thought Sean. In a corner the wash-stand, basin and ewer, white, with a broad blue band around both; the press with drawers to hold clothes against the wall; a cane-bottomed chair beyond the head of the bed, with Tom's clothes in a tidy heap on the seat; the window half open and half hidden by yellow lace curtains; the double bed where Tom lay stretched bonily taut and motionless, save for the twitching of the mouth; on the wall above the side of the bed where Agatha usually lay, a crudely-coloured picture of the Sacred Heart; over the head of the bed, a coloured apoplectic picture of his old general, Sir Redvers Buller, looking as he might have looked after his vain attempt to push across the Tugela river; a strip of red, white, and green oilcloth running by the bedside; a slightly-swaying twig of a sycamore-tree moving gently up, gently down again, just outside a window-pane; and Mr. Griffin with a stole, instead of the dark-green muffler, round his neck, looking pensively down on Tom — one of Synge's khaki cut-throats leaving the world's villainy behind him for ever.

There he was, battling for the last few minutes of life, while poor Dr. O'Hickey, tired and near heart-broken, paced the streets of Rome, sent from Cardinal Billy to Cardinal Jack, from this holy office to that, talking Latin to the clerics, and finding none able or willing to reply; dying, though he didn't know it then, battling for the life of

Ireland and Essential Irish in the New University, his funds near gone, and poverty asking him how he was feeling.

The Rector is bending over till his handsome face is almost touching the ear of Tom, praying that here, in this poor room, another miracle of grace might be worked for a soul's safe flight from the world, the flesh, and the devil.

—My poor, dear man, he said softly, do you hear me? I am your Rector, your minister, your friend, come to mention the name of Jesus, the Saviour of sinners, in your closing ear. Do you hear me, my son?

Then a dead silence fell round the dying man for a few moments, distracted only by the faint sound of the little sycamore twig moving gently up, gently down, just outside the window-pane.

—Say, Lord have mercy on me, Christ have mercy on me, Jesus have mercy on me, encouraged the Rector, and his white, delicate hand softly stroked away a tawny bunch of hair from Tom's green-tinted, dewy forehead.

Silence for a little while, and then a tiny whisper from Tom of Christ have mercy on me, Jesus have mercy on me.

—Again, dear man, Jesus have mercy on me, and once more a tired and fainter whisper, like an echo of the last, of Jesus have mercy on me, came to our straining ears.

—O Saviour of the world, prayed the Rector, who by Thy Cross and Precious Blood hast redeemed mankind, save our dear brother, we beseech Thee. O Almighty God, we humbly commend the soul of this our dear brother, into Thy hands, as into the hands of a faithful Creator, beseeching Thee that it may be now precious in Thy sight. Wash it in the blood of the immaculate Lamb that was slain to take away the sins of the world. Then the Rector stood up and extended a protecting hand over Tom, holding one of Tom's in the other, a hand that was now waxy with the dignified bloom of death, saying softly as before, Unto God's gracious mercy, we commit thee, Tom. The Lord be with thee in this thy last fleeting moment on this our fleeting world. The Lord make His face to appear unto thee full of pardon and promise, and give unto thee salvation and eternal peace. Amen.

He drew Sean out to the little lobby at the head of the stairs and quietly closed the door.

—You should send for his mother, he said, for he'll last but for a few moments more, John, and his wife should be with him. Does she realise how bad he is?

—I warned her before I came for you, sir.

—Warn her again, Sean, like a good man. And will there be enough to stand expenses?

—Oh, yessir. He's insured, and, besides, he gets his full pay since he fell sick. And it won't cost a lot to bury him in our father's grave. And, anyway, he hasn't any claim on your kindness.

—He has a claim on the kindness of our Lord, John, and so much more a claim on mine. No, don't come down; stay with Tom. I'll call in to your mother's and get her to join you. And remember, if you meet with any difficulty, come to me at once, not formally as your Rector, but warmly as your friend. My deep sympathy, John. Goodbye.

Sean went back to the silent room, sat down on the cane-bottomed chair, furtively watching the hand of death quenching the last dim light glimmering in Tom's handsome face; turning now and again to glance at the little sycamore twig moving gently up, gently down, just outside the window-pane. It was Agatha's duty rather than his to be here with the dying man. He crept out to the lobby, stretched over the banisters, and called softly, Agatha, are you there? Agatha! But there was no answer, and he crept back to the support of the little chair. A strange surmise was snakily creeping into his mind: he was seeing Tom for the last time; no light shone through the darkness of departure; poor emptiness lay behind the brilliancy of the stars. Dimly he saw the clumsy bulk of Agatha come into the room, glance at Tom, and go over to lounge at the window and fiddle with the yellow lace curtains. Whisht! Tom was trying to say something. He bent down, and held his breath to hear.

—Jack there? Jack there? Must peel the spuds for the chiselurs' dinner.

—Here, Tom, oul' son; Jack's here beside you, and he laid a hand gently down on the tawny head.

—Doing me — best — Jack — to — keep — a-live.

Then Sean saw the thin legs do a strenuous stretch, and the arms outside the bedclothes go rigid; and his ears caught a sound like unto the sudden snapping of a sensitive cord strained too tight, so he knew that Tom's heart-strings had given way, and that he was now to lie still for ever. He was still staring down at the oddly silent form when the door opened and his mother, followed by Ella, came panting into the room.

—He's gone, he said; you're too late.

Mrs. Casside stared at the stiff form lying prone in the bed, effectively out-braving the brazen world now. She seemed not to be able to recognise what was stretched out there, her bright dark eyes blinking rapidly to impede the tears that were pushing a way out of them, her brave humorous mouth aquiver like summer lightning in a violet sky.

—My poor dead son, she said, suddenly running over and kissing the mouth she hadn't kissed since it was the fresh dewy mouth of a boy. Ah! My poor dead Tom, my poor dear son is dead! And Sean was hard set now to keep his face from twitching and his tears from falling, for he knew full well that out of all who knew Tom, she alone it was who suffered the dearly-sorrowful agony of his going.

—I hope yous are satisfied now, said the voice of Agatha behind them; yous are all satisfied now, so yous are; and Sean noticed that her clumsily-made mouth was puckering about in strange shapes, showing she shared in the emotion that the stilly-silent, rigid favour of death evoked in man, feeling that some day each one there would be stolen away into the same silence.

—Now he's where yous won't envy him any more, so yous won't, she went on, whimpering. Bid him your luscious goodbyes as quick as yous can, for, if yous want to know, I'd liefer have your room than your company. So now yous know; for I don't want his home to be a clusther of the ragged Casside army, for the one that's just gone was the only decent specimen among yous, so he was, an' all who knew him, knows that. Me husband, me poor husband, you come of a dirty lot!

Sean silenced Ella's wrathful answer with a look. He went over to his mother, and taking her arm, said gently, Looka, mother, you'd best go home with Ella, and leave me to do what has to be done. The Rector was here before he died. He's to read the Service at the grave-side, so Tom'll have an orderly burial, and you needn't worry.

—He's marble cold already, said Ella, touching Tom's forehead, as cold as cold can be.

Mrs. Casside kissed her boy again and again, ran her fingers through his tawny hair, stood up from the bed, tears trickling down a set, firm face, took Ella by the arm, and led her out of the room, forced to leave the dead Fusilier behind to make the best of it.

—So well yous may pop off when the damage is done, an' leave me here on me own to face it all! shouted Agatha after them.

Where would Tom be now in a few moments, and what would he be doing? questioned the thoughts of Sean. Shadow-hurling with the Gaels of Mooncoin, or swaggering along an empty way with the Rakes of Mallow? Strolling, maybe, through invisible groves of

Blarney with Kitty of Coleraine. Watching Canon Sheehan brooding o'er the graves of Kilmorna, or sauntering, deep in thought, beneath the cedars and the stars. Listening, mayhap, to the old march-past of the Old Toughs, the Dublin Fusiliers, and shouting out the song himself, *Hurrah, hurrah for Ireland, and th' Dublin fu-u-sa-leers!* Poor Tom, he will be remembered for ever, for the hearts in dear oul' Ireland are the hearts that don't forget.

What a doughty fellow he was, all the same! No attendance in bed for Tom: doing all for himself, by himself, and with himself, till his life left him nothing but a thought or two and a wildly beating heart. A Stoic, by God! An old tough with a vengeance. Marching to attention, gun on shoulder, to his death. Saluting death, the dark companion, as an officer and a gentleman: By your leave, sir, a pass for a few hours longer. Not in a ghostly white habit should this man be buried; but in his crimson coat, ammunition pouches full, busby firm on the tawny head, with the flaming grenade ashine in the centre. Often drunk, but never quarrelsome; whenever in a row, the tipsy Tom was ever in the centre of danger, parting the fighters. And the drunker he got the straighter he grew; his walk was a parade march when he was full to the chin. He would have made a rare Dalcassian. Though he hadn't conquered, he had died like a man. God had thought too little of him, and the active world had given him ne'er a chance. Sean was no warrior. A harper, maybe, playing others into battle; but no warrior himself. Why, even to this day he remembered with a shudder the knocking of the helmeted policeman from his horse the day of the charge in Parliament Street.

But supposing, only supposing, the rose and crown conception of Heaven be true, Tom would find it a bit awkward at first. He certainly wouldn't run to be among the catholic confraternities or the protestant associations making a round of the sights of Sion, however grand the glories before or behind them; unless, manacled hand and foot, he was frog-marched by the angels to take part in the diversion. Perhaps God would conjure up in a distant corner a radiant mirage of a cosy pub where Tom and his Fusilier butties could for ever drink without drinking, fight for ever without fighting, and die for their Queen and country without dying at all, and gather a harvest of glittering medals on their chests to show themselves off to the wondering saints. Or, as Cortez stout and all his men, standing on a peak in Darien, silent, saw another ocean, so may Tom and his comrades see a newer ocean of another life, and set sail thereon in a white-winged bark, while we go stumbling on over the flinty earth, steeling ourselves in the effort to fight and faint not, often tired, always uncertain, many of us consigned to a kind of life lived by the lesser rats.

—Of all th' things I hate above all others, broke in the voice of his sister-in-law behind him, it's hypocrites. Lettin' on to pray for him when yous wouldn't know a prayer from a pigsty!

—Now, Mrs. Agatha Casside, he said, wheeling round to her, I wish to do things, and talk as little as possible. Let's see what has to be done: first, you get a certificate of the cause of death, and report to the Dispensary Registrar — understand?

—I'll take no insthructions from you, she replied surlily.

—All right, then; where do you intend to bury Tom?

—That's my business.

—Look here, Agatha, you can't help being ignorant, but for Christ's sake try to be less stupid! Bury him where you like! I don't care, and he can't. If it be Glasnevin, it'll cost you a lot more. Now d'ye want me to give you a hand — yes or no?

The clumsy, ill-grained face twisted about for a few moments in resentment at having to give in to secure the help she needed.

—It would be a poor brother that 'ud refuse the last act of charity, she muttered; but remember, I'll keep the money in me own hands. And his Post Office friends are makin' a collection, an' Mr. Arthur says it'll come to over two hundred pounds, so it will, see now, so that'll show yous somethin'.

—I go now, Sean said, letting all she said go by, to get Mrs. Conel to come and lay him out — give her a few shillings and a lot of tea; and I'll send the barber to shave him; then I'll go to Nicholl's and arrange for coffin and hearse — there's no reason to do things too expensively.

—You'll do things th' way I want! she said loudly, and he'll get th' best funeral money can buy, so he will, see now. I want all th' best coffin goin' with all th' brass that'll fit on it, an' a four-horse hearse, mournin' coach, an' two carriages, so I do. I'm not goin' to let his people give him the funeral of a ragamuffin!

—Look, Agatha, he said. The living children need this money more than the dead father. I'd go canny with it if I were you.

—Well, you're not me, see? Mighty particular y' are, now, about the children, aren't you? An' none o' th' carriages 'ill be for any of yous either, undherstand that, now.

He gripped her angrily by the shoulder, putting his face close to hers to say venomously, Go in a carriage with you, is it? Why, you yellow-skinned Jezebel, if I could I'd put a wide sea between us both, and never bathe in it if I thought you were anyway near its margin! And listen! If I hear another word from your dark tongue, Tom or no Tom, charity or no charity, I'll leave everything for you to do, though I know you can't even sign your own name! And he turned and left her alone with her dead husband, and with the little sycamore twig moving gently up, gently down, just outside the window-pane.

HOUSE OF THE DEAD

SEAN leaned on his long-handled shovel and straightened his back. It was grand to be out in the country and close to the sea. He could enjoy it now, for he had grown into a lusty fellow of twelve stone ten, and he could feel the muscle of arm and leg go in harmony with every movement of his body, the song of the body electric. He could lift an anvil, gripping it by back and horn, as high as his breast, holding it there while another counted ten slowly. He had won a shilling from a permanent-way inspector who declared it couldn't be done, but Sean had shown him. Only one other fellow, a tall, raw-boned Tipperary man who drove the steam-roller, could throw a great weight from the shoulder, or between legs, farther than he. Now every workman respected him, not only for what his hands and shoulders could do, but also for the ready and eloquent way he could show the activity of his mind. Because of his enthusiasm for the Gaelic League and for his never-ending efforts to get all whom he worked with, and all whom he met, to join the movement, he was known along the line, from Dublin to Drogheda, as Irish Jack. He had three names: to his mother he was Johnny; his Gaelic friends knew him as Sean; to his workmates he was Jack, and when they wished to distinguish him from another Jack, they added the title of Irish, so Irish Jack he became to signalmen, engine-drivers, firemen, porters, shunters, and all others who worked along the permanent way. He was becoming famous, and he was proud of it. He wiped the bitter teeming sweat from his face. Satisfied with himself, and half-satisfied with the world, he leaned on his shovel to have a cool look around him, to more sensibly enjoy the rarer sights he so very seldom saw.

It was the first time he had laid eyes on a field of growing corn, living and rippling before him, jaunty and elegant in its way of bending from one side to the other; gently turbulent when stronger breezes blew, but always returning to its dignified sway, thoroughly at home, bowing a golden greeting to all that looked upon it with favour.

Leaving aside the glory of Constable's *Cornfield*, he had seen pictures of ripe corn on calendars, or standing stiff in pictures printed quick to teach a lesson from some bible story. He had heard of it too in some of the hymns sung by Christian people — Fair waved the golden corn in Canaan's pleasant land; and a tenor in the quoir chanting, The valleys stand so thick with corn that even they are singing; or the Rector, padding with sighs the reading of the parable of the wheat and the tares. Now he was face to face with it, lovelier than any picture, fairer than any words could tell. He could fancy Ruth standing there in that field, up to her middle in the corn, a creamy face, rosy cheeks, and big brown goo-goo eyes staring at poor Boaz, the kinsman of Naomi, all meant to furnish some lesson no-one ever learned. Or was it the lesson of a great conversion? Where thou goest, I will go; thy people shall be my people, and thy god, my god. By God! she knew who she was after, for Boaz had more than one acre and a cow. The first gold-digger! But a widow for your life, though it was ordained and predestined from the first that Boaz should marry Ruth, for from Ruth came Obed, from him came Jesse, and from Jesse, David, the royal line ending in Jesus, king of kings, lord of lords, and only ruler of princes. Luke was set on making Him out a gentleman, so as to fit Him in with kings, rulers, and princes, who soon rolled Him out to rule themselves in over life.

But it was from a field of barley Ruth displayed herself to Boaz, and this was a field of wheat. Was it wheat now? He couldn't tell; didn't know the difference between wheat and barley, so he'd call it corn. One could easily imagine Jesus Himself strolling softly through such a field as this one on some peaceful Sabbath morning, His sensitive hand calmly plucking the ears of corn as He went along, and popping them into His mouth, chewing them slowly as He thought out some delicate parable on what He saw around Him, so that He might make remembrance safer in the minds of His disciples. So wrapt in Himself, He might well put no pass on the turbaned Scribes and the phylacteried Pharisees, peeping over the hedges, on the watch, hardly able to believe their eyes at the cool way He was infringing the ritual rest of the Sabbath; hearing nothing of their whining cries of, Eh, there, eh, what do you think you're doing? Sharp and shrill they shouted then, their conscience-cry hiding the pleasant humming of the bees, thick round the scented heads of the white and crimson clover carpeting the nearby pasture fields. On He'd go, dreamily, glancing at the corncockle growing here and there among the corn, like high-born, satin-skinned ladies airing themselves among a commoner crowd. Now and again He'd touch the blooms tenderly, setting dark-rose velvety petals carefully aside so as not to soil them, their rosy petals stained with darker lines, as if they, too, had things to think of; while careless scarlet poppies like rasher ladies, flushed with wine, flaunted around the edges, the crimson of some of them fading from excess of life, puced and shrivelled now, but dying gamely in the centre of their flaming ostentation. Coloured peace was here; a gay peace; a merry stillness, undisturbed but for the ratchet-like call of the corncrake. Oh, blessed peace!

A strange smell full of sharp sweetness came to him, making him wonder, for he had never sensed such a smell before. New-mown hay, he murmured; ah! that's what it is, must be — new-mown hay. On the uplands, in the distance, he had seen the fringe of a calm sea, but from where he stood in a dip it was hidden; though when he faced towards where it was, the scent of the new-mown hay was imprisoned in the salty smell of the sea coming in the breeze that fluttered on to his sweaty, heated face. So he could take his choice: stand as he stood, and get the taste of the sea; turn, and he could get the spicy feminine scent of the hay — a golden languorous scent from the hay, or a lusty blue-scented taste from the placid fret of the incoming tide. If poor Up Griffith, unhappy in that he could never be what he thought he was, if he only could be here, sprawled in the pasture, or asquat in the shade of a rock on the velvet strand, he'd forget his love for the golden-haired Niamh, his hate for the rival black-haired poet, his ambition to lead where he could but follow, in the happy, reluctant unison of the sea-breeze mixing itself with the fragrant presence of the new-mown hay.

Christ! that was a horrible cry!

—Aw, Jack, said the grumbling voice of his mason behind him, are yeh dhreamin' again? The mortar-board's been empty now for ages, an' I'm idle for stuff.

—What, what was that?

—Wha' was what?

—Didn't you hear it, man? It came from somewhere over by the sea, and he felt the sweat on his face turn cold. A cry of lost laughter throwing itself into an icy wail that's taken the scent from the hay, the savour from the sea, and has thrust out peace from its tenancy of the sky. There it is again — good God!

It was an insensible burst of jagged laughter, turning into a savage yell, that gradually declined into a long-drawn, weary, piercing wail making him cold and making him shiver.

—Aw, that? That's only from the Partrane madhouse yeh saw from the hill yestherday, y'know, beside the round tower; biggest one in the land. Livin' here a little, yeh'd get used to yells. Look alive with the mortar.

So behind this fair, sparkling, laughing curtain that Nature let down before him many dark and evil things were lurking, or hung entangled in the bright colours and satisfying scents like decaying flies in the iridescent and lovely-patterned web of the spider. Forgotten for the moment, he had already seen these things with his own eyes, and his hands had handled them.

Out there, now, right in the centre of the corn, just where Jesus had passed by a few moments before, floated the face of Ella, a white face, a face of settled fear, tightened with a stony smile that had a seed of wild weeping in it. He went back to his work of tempering the mortar and of carrying his hod of bricks to the mason; but whenever he turned his eyes to the growing corn, there was that damned white face, stony with fear, a swaying stem of corncockle at times empurpling an eye, or the scarlet shadow of a poppy giving it a bloodily splashed mouth, watching him work; watching, watching him work. She had married a man who had destroyed every struggling gift she had had when her heart was young and her careless mind was blooming. He had given her, with God's help, a child for every year, or less, that they had been together. Five living, and one, born unsound, had gone the way of the young and good, after being kept alive for three years, till it grew tired of the dreadful care given it, leaving her to weep long over a thing unworthy a tear or a thought. Her home was a fanciful bastion of rags, bones, and bottles; the family hereditaments, a few chairs, a table so rickety that it seemed anxious to dissolve itself out of the life it tried to live; one large iron bedstead, rusty with shame at the beggarly clothes that tried to cover it. They drank their tea from jam-jars, and raked out the fire with a lath broken from the bedstead. Four of the children went to school, and learned a lot about kings, queens, and knights; of battles strong and flaming; of statesmen drowned in glory or a butt of wine; of all a cow gave to man; how to add, subtract, and multiply thousands of pounds without wasting much time; and all the important information necessary about Heaven, Hell, death, and the judgment; and through it all Ella helped them to master sums, to find places on a map, and understand God; helped them with a dimming eye, a dying mind, and decaying heart. Ah! faded into the forgotten past were the recitation of bits from Racine's *Andromaque* and *Iphigénie*, or from Scott's *Lady of the Lake*; the confident playing of waltz, schottische, polka, and gavotte on a piano in a friend's house; or the rich treble singing of *Come unto these Yellow Sands, Cherry Ripe,* or *She is Far from the Land* when the fire burned bright, the curtains were drawn, and father and mother listened to one of the sweetest voices heard by the dull ear of man. All gone now; gone into the gloom of a night hiding gifts abandoned; gone, save in the restless memory of Sean's own mind. Oh, Ella, Ella! Oh, Jesus, have pity on us! If not in harmony with Thee, let the glow of something good be in a fragment of our life!

Now she went about everything like a near-drowned fly in a jar full of water. She entertained life under a canopy of rags and tatters; a blouse warning all of its end, a skirt slit to the thigh, shattered boots, and footless stockings; and her breath of life moved faintly in the midst of it all, while her children moved round her, half perishing too, like weak and puzzled planteens hovering uncertainly around a fast-dying sun. Her mother had helped her all she could, washing, ironing, and mending things till it became dangerous to the life of the things to wash, iron, or mend any longer. She had striven to startle Ella towards resistance to decay, but Ella murmured, My husband, it is my duty, God ordained it all; so failure was in the heart of any effort before it could begin. Her mind had fashioned a weakness too great to let her strive to save herself, and life became a maze of rotting things from which there was no escape till she lay down for the last time to crumble into dust in the midst of her crumbling property and gifts. Coughs and colds, aches and pains, came her way, but she coughed and staggered along a narrow way between them on her feet, conducting a ragged and wasting retreat from the Kingdom of Heaven.

One day a younger one had come racing to him, calling Quick, Uncle Jack, me da's murdherin' me ma! He med a run at her, an' we rushed outa the house, but we heard her squealin'!

Ay, and your ma would like to change the procedure by seeing your da make a run at me, he thought, as he went along with the youngster, not too quick, either, for he knew he was no hero, and at the moment his conscience was stirring against interfering between a man and his wife. Women who lived near Ella, when they saw him coming, ran to meet him, saying breathlessly, He's morguein' her, he's morguein' her, an' for God's sake hurry, or a short time'll have another sorrowful sight in front of us all! And when they saw he did not make haste, they caught his arm to hasten his going, though he held back as decently as he could, remembering that these two had come together for better or for worse, till death did them part, and who was he to question the grandeur of God's own ordinance? Besides, he knew his mother several times had got a shock from a push or a blow meant for Ella when she had thrust her body in between Ella and the flying angry fists of her husband; and often his mother had hurried away when a row began, too full of shameful wonder to stay and share in the violence that he was now hurrying to meet.

Coming to the wide-open door of the house, and hesitating to go in, he heard the voice of Ella whimpering, Don't hit me any more. I've done all I could. For the children's sake, don't hit me any more.

This was the price of her not doing what she was told. How he had warned Ella of her husband's odd behaviour, trying to go through walls where there was no door; leaving bed to put on his red-banded cap in the middle of the night to hurry off to work in his shirt. He had complained of his eyes at times tumbling things before him, forcing him to see men as trees, and trees as men, making for him out of a red mist. At the Eye Hospital where Sean had brought him, after examination, Mr. Storey had said, Oh! drumming his fingers on the glossy table covered with silver surgical instruments, looking at Benson curiously, then glancing at Sean to say, Bring the man home; nothing here can do him any good. And when Sean had murmured, What about spectacles? Storey had pointed his grey-tinted red beard to the ceiling, craning his narrow neck to give vent to a slow sibilant laugh as he answered shortly, A pair of old boots would do as well; and he hurried away to lave his hands in a gleaming white basin between the two tall wide-spreading windows.

What the hell's wrong, Sean asked himself, leading out the silent, passive Benson, and what's this poor devil to do? And what's his wife and children to do? How the hell do I know? he answered himself. One thing was clear — he wasn't going to spend his life hawking round this poor bewildhered eejut. A thought and a fear came over him, and he tightened his grip on Benson's arm, hurrying him to Dr. Wood's surgery to hear the verdict one way or another for half a crown. Visiting his mother once, Dr. Wood had paused to look at, and handle, Sean's books, had smiled graciously, and had shaken Sean's hand when he was leaving; so he was a friend, and, as well, was loved by the poor, though the poor man's own state of health forced him to nearly live on drugs. When he had examined Benson, Dr. Wood brought Sean into another room, standing silent for some time when they had got there.

—Do you know what's happening to this man of yours? he asked at last. He's quietly going mad; but when he reaches a certain stage, he won't be quiet any longer. Your man is developing a disease known as general paralysis of the insane. There is but one thing to do now, other than to leave him in God's hands. Has he a wife? Well, then, she must certify him so that he may be brought where he can do no harm; for any time he may become dangerous; dangerous, mind you, dangerous!

But Ella had dumbly refused to sign the form, content that her husband's creeping madness should go on bringing her in a few shillings a week, for they put a brush in his hand to keep the front steps of the railway station clean, where he'd stand for hours leaning on his brush, and gazing ahead at all he couldn't see.

And now Sean was being hurried on his way to where, in the elation of misery and want, a lunatic (after fulfilling his job of multiplying and replenishing the earth) was having his share of fun with the four last things of Heaven, Hell, death, and the judgment.

Oh, Lord, oh, my Lord! Oh, my good Lord, keep me from sinkin' down, sinkin' down; oh, my Lord, keep me from sinkin' down!

With his muscles tensed, ready for a bullish charge, which he prayed wouldn't come, he swung suddenly into the room, the neighbours clinging to the doorway; he met the glaring, red-balled eyes of Benson staring at him, his body twitching, his hands tugging to pull out a loosening chair-leg so that a solid victory might at last be won over the ragged woman cowering in a corner, whimpering softly, her stony white face, empurpled eye, and bloodily splashed mouth appealing for a tempered mercy to the madman.

Not knowing what he was at, or what to do, or how to do it, Sean drew an arm back and swung a frenzied fist under the ear of the madman, putting him into a sprawl on the floor. Then he gripped the chair-leg the madman was trying to get, and, with an agonised twist and wrench, tore it from its socket, poised it over the lunatic's head, shouting, Bloody villain, you pig's offal you, I'll give your guts to the crows, you red-coated rottenness! And he brought down the chair-leg hard on the big skull below, dulling the glare in the eye, sending a shake through the twitching body that went limp now, and crept into a corner of the room, turning to stare stupidly at Sean, moaning hoarsely as an alto to the whimpering of his wife in the corner opposite. Sean knew by the dismal stare and the pitiful moan that present danger was past, and knew too that he must get the man behind stone walls before ever the frenzy would come on him again. Leaving Ella to the care of the neighbours, after he had seen her put her name to the form that would bury Benson alive, he took the lunatic home with him, keeping a firm grip on the chair-leg under his coat, sat up all night while Benson slept, waiting for the clutchers to come with the plain black cab in the morning.

It came towards the evening, a sunny one, with many sparrows frantically fluttering their wings on the road to clean themselves in the dust of the street, not one of them falling to the ground outside of God's attention; better for Benson he'd been born a sparrow than a man. It came slowly along up to the house, the black cab, and, when the driver stopped the horse, two neatly-clad keepers stepped from the cab, asked Sean if the patient was likely to go quiet, went in, and came out with a grinning Benson between them. One of them, noticing the bump on his head, asked Who done that to yeh?

—I did, said Sean.

—Be God, yeh hot him with somethin' heavier than a feather! Misbehavin' himself, was he? If it was us done that now, there'd be uproar in the pulpit an' press. But you'll see how nicely he'll conduct himself with us — won't yeh, Benjamin? See how he smiles at me. Oh, he'll be a good little boy.

—He bloody well betther, growled the other one.

Between the keepers, with Sean opposite to see him safe home, Benson, grinning helplessly, was driven to the house of strident shadows, to dress in the rough grey tweed of the loony pauper, to wear the red woollen neckerchief so tied that when one became restless, a keeper could seize it, pull, and choke all movement, quench all fire out of the gurgling, foam-lipped madman; to where he would be dust to dust and ashes to ashes before he was dead, withered grass that hadn't yet been cast into the oven, to Grangegorman. Wide gates of heavy, dull, heartless lead opened to let them in, and the black cab rolled silently along the drive, drawn by a horse with a sly and regular trot as if he felt and feared anything else might entitle him for companionship with the dread life of the still-twitching dead. Dotted here and there in the grounds were the dismal brothers of disorders grey, their red mufflers making them look as if their tormented heads had been cut off, and pushed crookedly back on to their necks again. The cab stopped slowly before the building, wide and long, built like a bully that had suddenly died shrugging his shoulders. Long rows of lifeless windows mirrored long rows of lifeless faces, their silence hymning a fading resurrection of Velazquez's idiots, a whole stonily-grinning gallery of God's images turned to dull grey clay, the emptiness of a future age in every face. Now and again, some of them would vent a laugh that rippled a shudder along the walls of the asylum. The grass everywhere grew brown and long, and fell to dust whenever it was touched; the trees twisted their branches like limbs in pain, and grew grey leaves that never seemed to move, a cold immortal grey, as if under the blight of the fig-tree Christ had cursed. Flowers that tried to grow beneath the windows were slimy stalks, crawling along the grey ground like slugs tantalising the rim of a festering lily, lost amid the quiet storm of lunacy distilling a sour air everywhere. In a corner a chestnut-tree dropped worm-worn fruit like leaden balls, and riven church bells rang out a raucous angelus three times a day, carolling rakishly mid the mindless chatter and the rasping laugh. Only ghosts of things and men were here; nor in the sky above was any balm of blue, or fleecy solace of a drifting cloud; nothing but vacancy reaching to where God had gone from. No gay bird sang, no blazoned butterfly flew through the frozen sunlight, no gentle scent of gentler flower found refuge in any pocket of the sour air here. No jocund dawn danced into sight over the hills of the morning, no night came dreaming out of the slumbering sea; no big wind ever tossed the still trees, no tremor teased the earth, no fire blinked in the dead eyes waiting, and no still small voice stole upon ears forgetting the sound of their own words, maimed and bewildered, vainly uttered.

And out of the grey light and the noisy silence strutted a stout-bellied, loud-voiced, ruddy-faced man clad in loud-looking plus-fours, puffing stormily at a big pipe. A pair of small glittering dark eyes were trying to climb out over the puffy lids that half buried them; and a gay smile on his face went about endorsing everything done by the sacred apes of God.

—Aha! he said, when he saw Benson stumbling from the cab, here's another bright lodger for initiation into the brotherhood of Bedlamites. Well, turning towards the keepers, what's this novice's *tour de force*?

—Bad case of G.P.I., doctor.

—Aha! Whores-de-combat, what? Well, lug him in, and register his name in the pigskin-covered book of the lie of the living. And you, he said to Sean, a relative, eh? Ah! brother-in-law. Well, come along and have a look around.

—I've seen as much as I desire to see, thank you.

—Frightened, eh? Nonsense, man. Those outside are more dangerous than they who are here. The delusions, hopes, beliefs of those outside — unobtainable, man. Here every man has all he wants. Outside a man lives in worlds created by others; here he lives in a world of his own. All's accomplished here, so it ceases to interest.

Come with me to a land just over the border where those who live there know nothing of their nearness — the Purple Land full of Druid moons, sleepy boughs, and voices in a fire; where all are half awake, half silent, and half a world away from life.

A commonplace-looking man, with a bullet head, bulgy eyes, and straggly grey moustache, went whirling by, head over heels, head over heels, chanting breathless as he tumbled on,

Here we go hurryin' home to Heav'n,
Home to Heav'n, home to Heav'n,
Here we go hurryin' home to Heav'n,
Leavin' Hell behind us!

—That's the holy whirligig, said the doctor, hell-bent for Heaven. He's been given three thousand years to do the journey, and he has tightened steel hoops round his belly to keep him up to it. Whisht! There's our signature tune — we've two of them. That's *Awake and Lie Dreaming No More*; the other's *Won't You Come Home, Bill Bailey?* Here we are at the entrance of the Purple Land. Stoop! Here the higher-minded muck about, a kind of limbo where they know neither pain nor joy, nor can be ever at heartsease, for all here are heart-tight and head-heavy with brooding; though all assume in company a jaunty mysticism of life's connection. Stoop! Mostly poets of a sort here, and fellows of lure and learning. Place of Masques. We've a long way to go yet.

Bending low, they entered through a darting screen of grasshoppers whistling in harmony, *Has Anybody Here Seen Kelly? K, ee, double ell, why,* and came slowly into a long, long trail of never-ending twilight.

—In this place, whispered the man in the plus-fours, is all that never was — the Cover of the Sea over the Great Secret of the Tuatha de Danaan; Foam from the Horses of Emain; the Washing-place of the Horses of Dea; the Remnants of the Great Feast; the More-than-Mystifying Breath of the Dagda; and the Four Corners of the World: so silence on your hollow head; silence on your dark body; silence on your dark brow. Make the sign of the seven-stringed harp of Aengus — it's in the air!

The colour of the place ranged from dim violet to purple that was near to jet. The trunks of the trees were dark purple, their branches a lighter purple, and their leaves a dimmer purple still. Far away in the distance, by straining the eyes, one could see the place was ringed round by dark shapes like mountains, like giant guardians watching that nothing went too far from where nothing was.

—Them dark things out there, said the doctor, are the bright spirits of the hills, where the Mountains of Dublin sweep down to the sea.

—You mean the Mountains of Mourne, don't you? questioned Sean.

—No, I don't, snapped the doctor. Nothing out of time or tune with the place is allowed to enter here. Evil things sometimes dart in to torment and disturb the brooders with such things as *Flannigan to Finnigan, Miss O'Hara and Her Emerald Tiara*, or even *I Want to Go to Idaho*; but they drive these evil things forth from the garden by a sacred berry tied to a sacred string attached to a sacred hazel wand.

Though they went a long, long way, they never stirred, the wide wings of numerous death's-head moths striking their cheeks and touching their eyelashes, frilling the violet air with tiny hovering skulls, squeaking out a tittering chant,

> Come in the evening or come in the morning,
> Come when you're looked for or come without warning,
> Thought that is sky-high you'll find here before you,
> And the longer you stay, sure, the more we'll explore you.

—This garden, or place of repose, or sanctuary of souls, or land of the ever old, said the doctor, stretches from where you are to the uttermost inns and outs of the earth; to where Jason, the mason, pinched the golden fleece of Colchis; to where Thor cools his hot backside resting on the Aurora Borealis; to the dark forest where Siegfried sings to keep his courage up; and down to wherever Lugh the Long-handed may be hiding. It is hedged in only where man and his mind ceases to exist. The twilight here is like no other twilight the world over.

—What, is it the Keltic Twilight? questioned Sean, in a whisper.

—Hush! Be simple, reverent, and understanding; and above all, be silent. The slightest touch or twinge of a question here provokes disturbance in the ensurance of calm and contemplation. Here has to be solved the mystery of the Pelican, the Green Dragon, the Black Eagle, Salt, Mercury, St. Patrick's Purgatory, the Round Towers, Cardinal Logue's Learning, and Who Killed Cock Robin? That golden owl flying by watches over the poets; that green one in the ivy, over those who love their country; the yellow-headed one, over the thinkers; and the white owl, over those who say where there is nothing there is God. Look! Here's one of the brothers, sons of Mac Eolais, Mac Emer's son. Be silent; listen; don't question him; stand still; take it all in; you'll meet an amazing experience. There are three, though there be but one; one soul with three persons, notwithstanding — a painter, a poet, a seer.

A burly, heavily-bearded man, head bent low towards the ground, came mooching towards them, his thick, red-lipped mouth rolling out sonorous, indistinct syllables of wisdom.

—He has a puce soul, whispered the doctor, and hence he thinks life is found only where everything is perpetually purple; and he indites hymns about mystical purple dew dripping from purple mystical trees, dim in a purple twilight that ends in a purple dawn. He gives the name of Dana, Donah, Dinah to the busy earth, and believes that his place in eternity is a faery seat among a thousand purple stars. There, see! He's picking up a tiny stone and holding it high above his head. Listen to his shout.

—A Star! shouted the bearded one — I call upon the names of those Illustrious Ones who were not before I am; oh! tell me, masters, how to woo ye. Teach my bosom to reveal all its sorrows sweet unto thee, all the love my heart can feel. Oh! Layo-Tsetze, Spangler Sbungler, Confusian, Cant, and Emer's Son, the pure-souled One, Spunooza, my sons, my sons, come back to your father once more and show him something exciting.

—Listen, whispered the doctor; when I call hail, he'll shout the absolute absolutum symbol of the universal wisdom; and cupping his big mouth with his thick red hands, the doctor shouted, Hail!

The big bearded fellow stopped suddenly, raised his eyes to the vacancy above, and called out to the full of his voice: Transmagnificandanbanturality!

—I heard that at a pantomime, said Sean, when I was a kid.

—Well, don't let on you did. Wait till I tell you; when I call hail again, he'll sing his symbol hymn to his mother earth; and cupping his mouth with his hands again, he called, Hail!

Opening his large mouth the bearded one sang loud and bitter and better,

Con, con, with a con, *stanti*, stanti with a constanti, *no*, no, with a no with a constantino, *ple*, Constantino*ple*!

—Sure, I heard that too, at a pantomime, when I was a kid.

—I know, I know; but listen, can't you, to his chanting?

Ancesthral Self, both near and far, come close and hear my song,
It's only eighty verses, and it won't detain ye long;
A heart-song from the mountains where the faeries dwell in glee,
And pipe their mauvey melodies through lordly Tandraggee;
Led by the starry soul concealed in drunken Mick Magee.
For he is thee, and thou are he, and you and he are sparks of me!
Ha-ha, hee-he, he's Dana's son you see;

And if anyone knows a thing or two, it's me me me and Mick Magee.
But how we'll end, sure no-one knows; but when we dee,
We'll cock our toes in sweet repose where the lordly river Shannon
    flows.

—See, said the doctor, he's going off now, for he feels his brother, the great painter, coming. Look, the spit of the fellow who's gone! He'll steal away too, whenever he feels the third brother, the poet, coming. The three of them's Ancesthral Beings, and the only ones casting a shadow who can hear the planets sing. The dree in one. Hush, here he is! That's why he's such a great painter — the greatest ever. The first you saw was the philosopher *excelso superbum*, but he's also something of a painter and a poet; this fellow coming is a painter *supersissimum*, but also something of a poet and philosopher; and the third one, that you may see later, is a poet *miracula harmonium*, and also something of a painter and philosopher. They soar above all others in thought, see only through other eyes of dream that pierce straight through the veil of blank. Now you'll look upon the greatest painter here or hereafter.

—What, greater than Constable, Turner, da Vinci, Rembrandt, or Titian?

—Far greater, man, far greater. He hasn't an equal anywhere. Stacks and stacks and stacks of pictures he has piled up against the walls in his little grey home in the south — three hundred and sixty-five thousand of them he has, one for every day of the souler year.

—D'ye tell me that, now?

—On canvas, he has filled our vision with the micky-dazzling forms of the Shining Ones.

—What Shining Ones?

—The Noble Ones, the Beings Who Never Say Die, the Ancesthral Sylphs, the Hidden Hautboys, the Higher Hierarchies — them — you know. Here he is. Stoop. Hello, Aimi Admirabilis Aminadur!

The bearded man stopped and looked with gentle fierceness straight into our faces. The doctor waved a hand towards Sean, saying, A friend of mine, O master of mysteries. The bearded one came close to Sean, staring unseeingly into his face, his own so near that Sean felt the rapid breath of the gazer flooding over his face, making him step back as he heard the bearded man murmuring, Blue aureole, stained with red streaks: intellectual plane, but soiled with some sensuality. Godship and kingship, hidden in him, are far away from him still. How long, O Lord, how long!

—I was just telling him, sir, said the doctor, what a gorgeous painter you are, so you are, tremendous, hilla-balloo holy one.

—I paint great mysteries, he said. I bring infinity to the dotted line. I paint the twilight's dream; the star-soul of the earth, and the earth-soul of the star. Yes, I paint great mysteries, revealed to me in sleep. The gods so help me, too, coming down derry down to sit on the rail of my bed to show themselves off, so that I can see to paint them in their thrue colours, pink and light blue and dove grey; with wings sprouting from their foreheads, whence rises the Well of Indra, and plumes of coloured fire, spouting from the spinal cord, by way of the pineal gland.

—What gods, sir? asked Sean.

—O Dana, duna, Krishnavoorneen, Ding Dong Dedero, Agha-doedo, Aeonius Pure Bolonius, and Kelly from the Isle of Mananan. Oh! be wary of will-doing, for none but the demi-gods can see around a corner. Goodbyee all. May the candle of candles plant a light of thought on your brows. And sinking his massive head on his massive chest, he faded away into the twilight of amethyst, a beauty among beautiful things.

—There y'are, said the doctor, now, what d'ye think of that, eh? Makes you feel a better man, doesn't it? Ruskin's in the ha'penny place with him. You can hear the planets chiming when he's talking. He's the spit of Socrates — humble, modest, retiring, and full of himself. A flaming aego. A second Socrates that drank water bubbling up from the well of the holy hazels, and lived on locusts and wild honey.

—No, no, said Sean swiftly; you're thinking now of John the Baptist.

—Socrates, Socrates, I'm saying, said the doctor loudly, his red face growing redder till it was all a purple glow. Haven't I made a special study of these questions?

—Maybe he did, then, said Sean, taken aback by his angry vehemence. You may be right.

—There's no maybe about it, he shouted; I am right!

—I beg your pardon, murmured Sean.

—Well, be more careful. If you want to benefit by a visit here, you'll have to carry on co-operation. As I was saying, after living for ages on locusts and crowds of wild olives, for saying the world moves, he was roasted to death slowly on a gridiron.

—That was St. Lawrence, wasn't it?

—What, that said first the world moves?

—No; who was roasted on a gridiron.

—I'm saying Socrates was put to death for saying that the world moves.

—I always heard it was Galileo who first said that, murmured Sean.

—Ever hear anyone here saying it?

—Oh, no; not here.

—Well, then, be silent. Socrates, or Aristotle, or someone it was who said it, standing on a peak in Darien when he was driving the reptiles out of Ireland.

—Who drove them out? asked Sean, bewildered.

—Tim Healy did it, with the Pope's connivance.

—But you are contradicting yourself, said Sean.

—Am I now? What if I am, aself? Very well, then — I contradict myself. And who has a better right to do it? And d'ye know why? Because I contain multitudes. That's why. Fix your eyes on the back of your head, straight on the top point of the pineal gland, for a week or more, and you'd soon know that many contraries are balancing each other in the psyche, up down, here there, you see, they saw, see saw, see? The top of the psyche may lust after the spirit, the bottom after the delights of the body, while the centre, intellectual, may be sceptic — see? saw? Got me? Understand? Savvy? Now quiet.

—I savvy, said Sean. Now let us arise and go farther into the recession lost receding.

The suggestion half stunned the doctor. He stood gaping at Sean for a long time, breathing rapidly as if his heart was startled. Good God, man, he murmured, you don't know what you're asking. Things in there are unimaginable to me or you. Did you feel the earth shake? That was a shudder fleeing from the breast of Dana, the earth-mother. This is as far as primal clay dare go. This place isn't either the Coombe or Sackville Street. You have to watch your steps here. Farther in's the rendezvous of the very nobbiest of the universe — princes of stars, solar kings, and pashas of constellations and galaxies, Stoop! Here's the third advancing, you see, head down, mind up, the poet one. Bless yourself — *Trio Juncta in lacunae, per amica violentio lunee.*

Before he came within range of our hearing, we heard the third bearded man singing, his red lips wagging as he sang calmly, but with fierce distinction:

O swallow, swallow, swallow, follow, follow, follow,
Follow me up to Carlow, and come home with me to Clare.
There I'll show you sights and wonders,
Till the trembling psyche sunders;
Then I'll show you all the blunders

> Made by him who knew no meaning for the whence and why
>   and where;
> Who spent a lifetime deaving
> Candles, queens, and swans with grieving,
> Broidered cloths for women weaving,
> Climbing up the winding stair.

He stopped facing us, though he still watched the ground. With a mystic wave of the little finger, he said as if to himself, but actually to us, A dream, a dream; I met a dream in th' forest of the great city, a Dream of the Chiselurs. It flooded into me as I was going down Sackville Street. Here it is for you, and for the whole world, born and unborn:

> The chiselurs, looking for berries, went into the heart of a hill,
> Saw the Shining Folk dancing like good ones, for they found it
>   damn hard to stay still.
> Their eyes burned like opals majestic, tiaras shone rich on their
>   brows,
> And flames of gigantic proportions shot up from their backs of
>   brown knowes.
> Smilin' thru the wild flame of their glory, They laughed at the kids,
>   and said, Do
> What we've done for thousands of ages, an' th' same glory'll fasten
>   on you!
> But we'll show you for just a split second what each and what all of
>   yous are;
> An' They blew with a blowin' tremendous, till each kid that was
>   there was a star.
> The kids became Spirits Ancesthral, an' towered up for miles in the
>   air,
> Enjoying with rapture uproarious all the magical funne of the Faer.
> When the scintillant vision was fading, and each infant eye nour-
>   ished a blink,
> A far-away Voice was heard saying, you can grow up like that if you
>   dhrink!

Then the red-cheeked doctor bowed low, chanting as he stayed the way he was;

> Sir, show me the way to go home,
> My heart just longs to be there, to be there, to be there,
> Where Zeus deals out the drinks from the air, and a star is an
>   sadenease chair.
> O Friend of the Primal Fire, beneath this coloured dome,
> Let loose thy power and show us a sign and show us the way to go
>   home!

The bearded, slow, majestical dree in one paused, turned round, shook himself, and waved a little finger in the eager air. Then with a musical rumble, the distant violet sky parted like a curtain, and there, in a golden haze, a scarlet unicorn and a white lion were dancing a jig like mad to the tune of a Hungarian Rapture, while Eire's King, Lords, and Commons, all in morning-dress, bowler hats on their heads, tightly-rolled umbrellas under their arms, sat around on wool-gathering galleries of clouds, clapping applause, and singing, as they clapped, *A Nation Once Again*, guided in pitch, time, and tone by the dignified little impresario, Art Up Griffith, dawn eyes, sun eyes, moon eyes, and star eyes watching the proceedings anxiously, the Royal Irish Constabulary being strictly confined to barracks owing to insufficient mental comprehension of what was afoot. Behind all these, in a vast pit, rallied in vagueness all that flourished before, and the minor men of the present, Niall of the Nine Hostages arm in arm with Conn of the Hundred Bottles; Queen Tailte telling Queen Maeve that it was a marvellous show, and Balor of the Evil Eye replying that it was only a flash in the pan; Red Branch Knights mingling with the Irish National Foresters; and the Fenians chatting to wee Joe Devlin's Ancient Order of Hibernians; while in a far corner crouched Jamie Thompson of Portadown Loyal Orange Lodge muttering darkly, I dunno, I dunno; it dusna luk dacent to me. Over all, in a sweeping arch, hung a mighty rainbow of tears and smiles from Erin's eye, colouring themselves in gorgeous stripes of green, white, and yellow, on which Aengus Og, the god of love, was busy embroidering in letters of burnished gold Clan Vic Aengus's inspiring and magnificent slogan of Guinness Is Good For You!

And Sean turned and fled away from the happy scene; back the way he had come, through the purple twilight into the violet gloom, through the darting grasshoppers, murmuring as he ran, Oh, Lord, oh, my Lord! Oh, my good Lord, keep me from risin' up, risin' up; oh, my good Lord, keep me from risin' up!

And as he ran towards the leaden gateway, he beheld a grey circle of forms going round and round a black stake driven strongly into the darker ground. On the top of the stake sat a dazzlingly white skull, and black ribbons, tied to the stake, encircled the necks of the forms moving round it so that it looked like a maypole dance in a garden of death; and one of the grey forms was Benson grinning greyly as he plodded crookedly after the grey form in front of him.

BEHOLD, MY FAMILY IS POOR

SEAN hoped no-one who knew him would come along this way, especially any Gaelic League friend or a Republican brother. Not that he cared a lot, of course, but it was just as well to keep a few things hidden from the sneaking world. And didn't he remember well good-natured Peadar O'Nuallain catching his arm one day, and drawing him aside to whisper — what d'ye think now? — nothing less than Why don't you wear a collar and tie, Sean, and not come to the Branch with a muffler round your neck? Of course, that remark ringed his neck with a muffler for the rest of his days, for he wasn't the one to germinate into unaccustomed grandeur of clothing so that Gaelic snobs of School teachers, Civil servants, and Customs officers shouldn't shiver with shame when he was near them. When I was dry with rage, and extreme toil, breathless and faint, leaning upon my sword, came there a certain lord, neat and trimly dressed, and perfumed like a milliner. Ay, indeed, there's a lot of fretful popinjays lisping Irish wrongly. Fight for Irish — no, fight for collars and ties, and it's these boyos that have handed Michael O'Hickey to humiliation, limping lonely through the streets of Rome.

Here he was, up every morning at five, bar Sunday, home again at six in the evening, after a hard day's work with hack, shovel, sledge-hammer, or hod; out again at seven to work even harder for the Gaelic League or Republican Brotherhood till he heard the bells chime at midnight; and, in between, after much agony, fear, and heart-searching, he had pulled out the jewelled pins of thought keeping together the coloured and golden Gospel-pictures of prophet, saint, apostle, martyr, and virgin singing laughingly hand in hand with the sons of the morning, so that they came all asunder, and fell into the dust and rain and cold appraisal of a waxing world, their colours dimmed, the glittering figures forced into fading, the gold between them losing its reverence, and turning an ashen grey in the red glow of all life's problems; and all this, and more, they tell me should be respectably circled by a collar and a tie!

He was leaning against a railing outside a tenement house in Summerhill on a damp November day, a cold core in the moist air that looked dark under the leaden sky that panelled the heavens. His sister, with her five youngsters, had been hunted from their home for non-payment of rent, her worldly goods had been carried out and deposited in the street just beyond the side-walk, to do with as she would, but to take them somewhere soon, as a policeman had told her, because she couldn't be let leave an obstruction in the street to impede the passage of law-abiding citizens.

His sister's husband had died in the asylum, and a sight he was when he was placed in the coffin. Practising on him they were, said Mick. One could see the marks round his head where, said Mick, the skull had been lifted, and the brain removed, so that it could be watched for developments later on in the day. Sean had pressed his hand over the poor body, and was shocked to find nothing there but flat bone. And the knee of one leg was embedded deep in the breast just under the chin. They tried, said Mick, with a block and tackle, to get it to lie down decently, but it wouldn't budge. Sean was very glad when the pitying earth covered it kindly up for ever. His sister and her young were sheltering with him and his mother for the time being, and he had taken a day off to take care of the Benson property now collected before him in the street. He was tired and sleepy, having worked for forty-eight hours without a break as a member of a gang repairing a bridge that had shown signs of wanting to sit down and have a rest itself. Poor as the things were, they couldn't afford to let any be pinched, for they were all the Bensons had, and so he was waiting for a one-eyed friend to come with an ass and car to take them to the shelter and safety of his own home.

He glanced over them again to tick them off, for he had dozed several times in spite of a continuous effort to keep awake: a kitchen table — the one whole thing among the little heap of goods; three chairs, with slats of rough wood nailed across where the seats used to be; a sofa, with a few rags of false leather still cleaving to it, and bunches of hairy fibre oozing through holes in the sacking that vainly tried to keep it under cover; a wash-hand stand with a tin basin on the top of it; the frame and laths of a wide iron bedstead; a broken, rusty iron fender; an old dresser, with two drawers that held two knives, one fork, and three spoons; two metal saucepans and a kettle; the tin bowl of a one-wicked lamp; an iron lath to do the work of a poker whenever they had a fire; a sweeping-brush that was almost bald; a butter-box with the seat painted red, two sides white, and the other sides blue; a frying-pan with a patch on its bottom; a rug, tawny now with dirt and stains, once a brilliant thing of red, white, and blue wool, with a Union Jack in its centre, that Drummer Benson had made on a frame for Ella before they were married — and two others, of blue and red cloth, made of strips torn from old soldiers' trousers, and the red stripes that streaked each leg of them. The bedclothes, the few precious pieces of crockery, had been borne to Sean's home by Ella and the kids, to keep them safe from damp and danger, with the framed strip of purple velvet — now fading to brown — holding the crossed gold guns won by Benson when he had been best shot in his regiment, all surrounded by a spray of crewel-worked flowers embroidered by Ella out of admiration and pride — the sheen of the fading guns, the grandeur of the purple cloth, the only things left her to get a glimpse, now and again, of a perished golden sky; and a framed photograph of the statue of Luther standing in the public square of Magdeburg — treasures that couldn't be left to the chance of the wind or the rain.

—Curse o' Jasus on all landlords! Sean said to himself; and especially on this one who put me into this predicament! A boyo, too, who's all-in-all with the Gaelic League, and out for a free Ireland! If even he could only go far enough away so as to seem unconnected with this shame, aself; but the kids knocking around here would steal a cross from an ass's back, and he couldn't keep too close an eye on Ella's property. A group of them were even now standing to stare at the unhappy little heap of scrap in the kennel, then over at Sean leaning against the railings of the rotting houses; for this sort of thing was to them a song, the tapping of a tambourine, or the beating of a drum in their lives. Someone in trouble, someone in sorrow, a fight between neighbours, a coffin carried from a house, were things that coloured their lives and shook down fiery blossoms where they walked.

A young woman, hatless, a jagged skirt just reaching to her knees, showing a pair of hardy, well-shaped legs, with feet thrust deeply into a man's pair of rusty rough-leather Blucher boots came unsteadily down the street. A dark-green shawl dangled from her shoulders, and a scaly basket, holding one stale fish, was hooked over her left arm. She sat down on the stone steps leading to the doorway from which Ella's furniture had been carried.

It's Mild Millie, thought Sean, and fairly sober for once in her life. He stole a glance at her, and could plainly see, by her torn and half-open blouse, that the line from her chin to her throat was fine, and went curving grandly into a bosom that was rich and firm and white. She had hips, too, that would have made a Hebe happier. Her hair, ruffled with neglect and dulled with the dust of the street, grew in thick clusters, and was as black as a raven's wing. And all these feminine assertions were jewelled with large black eyes, the sparkle of the pupils undimmed, though the delicate whites of the iris were now finally stained with thin wavy streaks of scarlet bloodshot. A handsome lass, thought Sean, and well-dressed would make many a fine man long to dance attendance on her.

—You look dead tired, son, she said to him. Here, sit down on the steps beside me, and she spread her shawl over them; sit down, an' take it aysey, for, depend on it, God'll look afther th' world when the both of us are gone.

There opposite was Hutton's, the coachbuilding firm founded, men said, when the English were still savages, to keep in order, and build, the delicate chariots of all the grand personages alive, alive O, in the country. Hutton's that wouldn't look at the cab of a commoner, cushioning the seats, making the slender wheels, the well-balanced bodies, limning on the polished panels of the doors the coloured, quartered armorial bearings of this lord and that lady, argent, or, gules, azure, vert, or sable, fessed, fracted, flanched, barry-nebuly and barry-pily; burdured and bend-sinistered; animals combatant, courant, rampant, rampant gardant, rampant regardant passant, salient, and couchant; dormant, debruised, and displayed; gemels, gores, and gyrons; ermine, vair, pean, and potens; counter-vair and counter-potens: all running about in a show of elegantissimo, for the poor people to see and make them wonder.

—Here, lean again' me, said Mild Millie, and get a wink or two, for you're hard set to keep your eyes open. Your head might easy find a worse bosom for a pillow.

Drowsy and half asleep he lay, his mind drooping into a quiet darkness shot through at times with the gorgeous colours that used to flit in and out through the rags and tatters and dust of the neighbourhood. Coachmen, grooms, footmen, linkboys, and pages, as fine, and much more forward than their masters, strutted in and out of Hutton's to leave orders about their masters' phaetons, vis-à-vis, broughams, and barouches, their wigged heads monstrously high in the air, sniffing at the lesser folk eyeing them all, and envying. Lord Wellington, in his sober frock-coat and his plain kind of a cocked-hat, strolled often down this street, and there is the Earl of Tyrone, Governor of the City of Waterford, having various little jobs in the Revenue, and now asking to be made a marquis, not a speck on his snowy satin trousers, arm in arm with the Earl of Shannon, owner of eighteen boroughs, well away now with a pension of three thousand a year for thirty-one years; with one friend made a Commissioner of Revenue, another a Prime Sargeant, another in Patentee Employment, another made the Surveyor of Courtmacsherry, while he himself picks up the additional little job of Muster Master General at a thousand and eight hundred a year, so we all know what way he faces.

—Aw, Jasus! said Mild Millie, will yous looka who's trottin' past now in his vis-à-vis? Oul' Lord Lifford, no less, who voted our country away from us for a five hundred pound livin' for his hairy oul' chaplain, an ensigncy in the 42nd Foot for a friend, a cornetcy for his son, and a thousand more in his own salary to make the weight good. Aw, Mother o' God, will you look at what's creepin' outa th' sedan-chair, in purple trews an' scarlet cape, but oul' Craddock himself, who, for his vote, was lifted outa Kilmore to be Archbishop of Dublin, with five thousand pounds a year to keep th' poor man from starvin'; an' there's Donegall's carriage goin' in to be repainted, now that he's been made the Constable of Carrickfergus, followed be Belvedere, Hillsborough, an' Clanwilliam, all havin' comfortably settled their accounts with the Castle, leavin' to a more favourable time any reckonin' they may have to make with God; with the upright Bishop of Meath, alone in his study, wondherin' why the protestant bible was ever written at all; an' wondherin', too, what final *pro bonus republico* would be his punishment for bein' th' one an' only mitred man who stood be his counthry, and braved fear an' favour to vote agin' th' government.

—And there's old Rowe the whiskey man's carriage swinging in now, said Sean, whose gold made Christ's Church safe from the bend-sinister of the weather, his coat of arms, on a field gules, three swallows guardant, or, with the motto of Just a Wee Deoch an Dhorish underneath; and, look, there's a Guinness's vis-à-vis coming out, the one who made St. Pathrick's fit for Christians to pray in; his coat of arms, on a field sable, a barrel rampant, argent; in chief, azure, a small harp decossé proper, with the motto of Roll Out the Barrel underneath.

—Eh, wake up there! Where d'ye think y'are? This isn't a night shelther, me man! And Sean opened his eyes to see a burly sergeant and a burlier constable looking down at him. I spoke to you more'n an hour ago about gettin' these things outa th' way, continued the heavily-coated constable, an' it's here still y'are, are yeh?

—Ay, it's here I am still, so I am, and bearing it patiently, said the sleepy Sean.

—Well, you'd betther stir yourself an' get them things outa th' sight of decent persons engaged in their lawful avocations.

—The hereditaments — that's the legal term, constable — will be removed as soon as the pantechnicon arrives to take them where they have to go.

—Hereditaments or no hereditaments, all I have to know, an' all

you have to know, is that you're legally responsible for th' removal
of them goods to a proper place, for it's again' th' law to leave private
property in the public thoroughfare.

—Is it telling me that it's the owner's responsibility to have them
shifted, or what?

—Isn't that what I'm afther sayin' in plain words that would fall
safely into anny ears but your own?

—Well, I'm not the owner, and, consequently, as by law provided,
have no responsibility for their removal; so you can go your way with
a quiet mind.

The two policemen whispered together for a moment, the sergeant
evidently showing the constable the course of his duty in these
problematical circumstances.

—Looka here, said the constable, again standing over Sean, me
bucko, I reprehended you before, an' I warn you again that the law
doesn't allow an obsthruction of the thoroughfare be a collection there
of sundhry an' various goods an' commodities, concerned generally
with residintial activity of a dwelling-house, cottage, or common
room, to the possible disturbance an' inconvenience of law-abidin'
citizens engaged peacefully in their usual everyday movements,
necessitated be the proper carryin'-on of their legitimate business;
and be your nearness, or proximity to the collected goods an' chattels,
you present to every reasonable person the appearance of ownership,
thereby constitutin' yourself responsible for the removal of th' same.

—If he isn't the owner, ask him who is, nudged the sergeant, after a
silence of some moments.

—If you aren't th' proprietor of them utensils scatthered on th'
highway, then who is? demanded the constable.

—Go and ask my Irish arse! rejoined Sean savagely.

—A saucy, fine, penethratin' phrase, said the voice of Millie,
stirring on the step, a fine phrase to sink deep into their two thick an'
lonely heads, an' give them a dim idea of th' way th' world's movin'.

—Take no notice of her, sergeant, said the constable, fearfully and
warningly; it's Mild Millie — a terrible female, powerful woman,
takin' ten men to lug her to the station when she goes wild with red
biddy; take no notice, for God's sake. A fearful female would have
the pair of us on the broad of our backs in th' mud of the sthreets
while you'd be winkin'!

—We're sorry for you, me man, said the sergeant to Sean, but thry
like a good fellow to get them outa sight as quick as you can, will you?
We don't want to be too officious.

—Push off, th' pair of yous, warned Millie, hitching a porter bottle
from a back pocket of her skirt, and lowering a slug out of it; push off
to where there's genuine throuble, before this red biddy takes effect,
or yous'll have something harder than a few scraps of furniture to
shift to the station. It's you, you ignorant yucks, that breed th'
throuble; g'on now, she shouted after them, for they had turned and
walked away as if they hadn laid an eye on her or heard a word she
said, for a gentleman acts like a gentleman, th' way a swan acts like
a swan, because it's th' bird's nature; but it's th' ignorant yucks
that brew th' throuble be persecutin' decent, honest, knowledgeable,
upright, innocent, an' most respectable people. If it hadn't been, she
added, turning to Sean and sitting down on the damp steps again,
that the red biddy wasn't stirrin' in me bowels, it's afther wipin' th'
dirty sthreets clean I'd ha' been with th' pair o' them!

—You're very young, aren't you, Millie? he asked, admiring the
firmly-formed, handsome, dirty face.

—I'm well over twenty-two. Me mother kicked th' bucket when I
was a yearling, an' me father had to drag me up as well as he could till
he hurt his spine on the quays tryin' to move a weight it 'ud take a
gang to shift, for he was over six foot, powerful, an' a spendthrift of
his energy. So for five years or more he dwindled away on th' one bed
we had, for we pledged all we had to keep things goin'; for he got no
recompense for his hurt, bein' told it was again' th' rules to do what
he done.

—And didn't St. Vincent de Paul's help you a little?

—Them, is it? and she cocked her nose scornfully. You'd want to be
a crawler, an' deny yourself th' right to live, to get anything outa
them. But wait till I tell you: I got a job at seven shillin's a week, and
minded him when I came home o' nights; but one night, an' me asleep,
some bright angel or another stole in an' took him, leavin' me to face
th' world an' loneliness.

The one shall be taken, and the other left, he thought; then, aloud,
he asked, And was it the loneliness that led you to the use of the
methylated spirits?

—No, not jus' that way. Th' oul' Da, you see, was fond of a dhrop
before bed, to brace him afther th' cold grip of the quays; but when
he took to th' bed, we hadn't th' means to give him what his soul
sought, an' he pined, though he kept th' cravin' silent. One fine day a
neighbour gave me a dhrop of the methylated spirit, showed me how
to spread it out, cold, or make a kinda punch of it, an' from that out,
a few dhrinks changed a long an' surly night into a short an' gallant

hour of thoughts, an' put a merry loveliness into all around us. And again she put the bottle to her lips and took a radiant, gurgling slug out of it.

—But you've to pay for that too, haven't you?

—I did, till th' money vanished, then I got it be force. I'd wreck th' shop if they didn't give it to me. I get me grub th' same way. I got one or two flighty refusals at first, but they were sorry afterwards. But I never impose on them, askin' barely what I need, and they give gladly.

—But, Millie, is this a sensible way of life for one so fairly gifted as yourself?

—Show me a betther one, you, will you? Who owns the poor stuff you're guardin'?

—My sister.

—Married?

—Yes, but husband dead.

—Children?

—Five of them.

—An' why was she hunted out of th' room she had?

—She couldn't afford the rent.

—There y'are, you see. Is she any betther off than mild-mannered Millie? You daren't say she is. I wouldn't bend me back to carry away what I see in front of me. I don't pay any rent for my room, but th' landlord knows betther than to hunt me out of it.

—Millie, murmured Sean softly, did you never think of getting married?

—Well, God be good to us, what a question! An' where's th' man in Dublin would be tantamount to Millie? She bent down to look closely into his face, and he tightened his lips to stand the whiff of spirit that flowed reeking from her mouth; barrin' yourself, for you've a fine shape on you, a sthrange atthraction clingin' to you, an' a melody in your voice, there's ne'er a man in Dublin would warrant me openin' a single button to let him come a little closer; and she took another slug of the bottle. An' who'd have me now? But wait till I tell you, and she poked his side with the neck of the bottle, and giggled foolishly; before me oul' fella died, I was a child of Mary — a child of Mary, mind you, an' look at me now! Hardly credit it.

—Never fear, he said quietly, when her derisive laughter had ceased, you're a child of Mary still, in spite of polis and the red poteen. Righteousness isn't a badge on the breast, but a living glow in the heart, like the core of flame in a smoking fire. The lives we have to live are bound to stain the skin with pitch that defileth; but one smile from

God, Millie, and we are again as Naaman was when he had washed in the waters of Jordan.

—Don't be talkin' rot! she said sharply. I know betther. I have me times of fear an' darkness till I'm lit up with th' spirit, an' then I live where few can rise to; an' when I'm hoarse singin', I lie down in th' corner of some darks threet, far from th' walled-in woe of a room; an' tell me who has a betther bedspread than the uncomplainin' sky holdin' on to crowds of drunken stars dancin' mad for my diversion as long as I elect to keep me eyes wide open.

He stared thoughtfully at the sweeping concave entrance to the great Dublin coach-building factory of Hutton's, with its great oaken gateway, and its grey-brown lion and unicorn — a little the worse of the weather now — over the entrance. In his long goings and comings through the streets he had never seen this austere gateway open. Never heard a sound of hammer falling on a nail. Never saw the flame from a forge fire. In some way they hid all sounds away from the common people. Always there was an ecclesiastical quietness about the place. Even now, in its shabbiness, it showed a fading gentility.

—Hutton's is passing away, he murmured, half to himself. What a change in factory and in street since the Union led us into the shadows.

—Th' same Union has desthroyed us all! said Millie, sitting up, and staring in front of her. Didn' Grattan know well what would happen, crawling from a sick bed to put on his black satin trousers and coat, with his black silk stocking creasing on his poor thin legs, to hurry off to sing Ireland's swan-song, sayin' as he was present at freedom's cradle, so he was present at freedom's grave. Ay, she went on, rising to her feet excitedly, an' when we got a chance to cut adrift undher Parnell, didn' th' piety-painted toughs of Ireland down him, th' envious curs, barkin' out paternosters, an' they tearin' at his white throat. Not that I'm one to say well done to a man goin' with a married woman, or with a single one for that matther, for I'm a decent woman that way, but Parnell was different; he wasn't beholden to us, but we were beholden to him — how much we know now, splashing about in lies, slandher, malice, an' spite, givin' Victoria, her gay son, and her son's son, with Princess May Victoria of Teck, the grand chance to put their fingers into Ireland's eye. Oh, me white blossom of Ireland's spring, cut down as you were openin' to th' sun! I'm tellin' Dublin that me own Da bruised an' bled anyone murmurin' again' him! If he'd ha' only laid hands on Dillon or Healy, he'd ha' made squeakin' ghosts of them. But what are Tim Healy and Johnny Dillon now but two shits fadin' away on a shamrock sod! Oh, me dear young Emmet an' me wise an' brave Wolfe Tone, wherever y'are, you're with Parnell today. Me uncrowned king, if you were here today it's Millie would go down on her knees an' kiss your strong, white, holy hand, an' daze your enemies with her thrue devotion! She lifted her voice into a scream: May Kilkenny, that threw lime in his bright eyes, go crawlin' down to Hell!

—Ay, said Sean, we've had our fill of woe with the whole of them, Balfour, Salisbury, Gladstone, Disraeli, who shook a shower of imperial holy water over us to drive the Irish spirit away, and save us from becoming the lost sheep of the house of Disraeli. Look at me, he says, in spotless linen and satinised suits and silken socks, an' ye in rags and weak with hunger and tired with toil; but, one day or another, our rags will glow like a burning bush, set alight by God Himself.

—To hell with him, an' his Primrose League an' all, said Millie.

—It's an ampler day we want, Millie, and not any primrose path, though it was Randolph Churchill, and not Disraeli, who founded the Primrose League.

—Another prime boyo for you! With his Ulsther will fight, an' his Ulsther will be right, an' a moustache like a tidal wave sweeping over a yellow beach; makin' more speeches than God made men.

—We'll have our own again, Millie — one day.

—Ay, but when? It's bellied out with braggin' we all are, an' that's what has us so low. There's nothin' for it but hard dhrinkin', and she raised the bottle again and lowered a lot of it. Then she rocked herself to and fro on the step, singing,

> By Killarney's lakes an' fells,
> Emerald isles and winding bays.

Isn't th' whole land an Eden of the west? she shouted, suddenly rising to her feet and extending her hands to the heavens. I'm askin' th' question, an' let oul' Disraeli, Balfour, or Randolph Churchill stand out there in front of me to deny it, if any of them is men, an' darin' enough to face a poor, delicate, and defenceless woman!

She's getting beside herself with the drink, thought Sean; and looked long and anxiously up and down the road for the ass and car and its one-eyed driver.

The sky grew greyer over their heads, and a misty rain, rather than falling, soaked the street with its chilly penetration, and the people hurrying by; soaked cold and anxious Sean and the spirit-warmed Millie, who had slumped down on the damp steps again, while the twilight began to darken into a sulky night. Over on the opposite side of the street, a little lower down, moving slowly along the gutters, came a short-legged, long-headed, oldish man, dolorously playing on a fife, whose brown skin had lost all its dandy gloss,

> The harp that once thro' Tara's halls
> Th' soul of music shed,
> Now hangs as mute on Tara's walls
> As if that soul were fled.

The old man accompanied the slow and mournful notes with a slow and solemn swing of his body, keeping to the time, pausing while he played a bar or two, facing the pathway, moving forward again, slow step after slow step, to play another bar or two, pausing again to face the pathway and play another snatch of the air. When he came nearer, Sean saw that tears were trickling down his cheeks, slowly too, as if in harmony with the slow sad air.

We all feel it, thought Sean, feel it in the deep heart's core, however poor and wretched we may be: they feel the hatred due to that which has turned Ireland's glory into a half-forgotten fable; from Hyde himself down to this poor devil tumbling patiently in misery and want.

Suddenly Millie thrust him fiercely away from her, shouting, Go an' sit on your own steps, you! It's a wet nurse you want, so go where you'll be more likely to find one! She rose to her feet, staring at the coming of the ragged bard, and Sean knew by the dangerous glitter in her dark eyes that the spirit of red biddy had taken full possession of her. Whirling the now empty bottle around her head, she sent it flying so that it broke to pieces against the lion and unicorn guarding Hutton's pompous gateway; and as the shattered glass jingled over the pavement, the one-eyed driver came up with his little ass and car.

—Hey, you, there! Millie shouted towards the ragged fifer, play up something less like the wind blowin' through the boneyard, an' show th' English lion an' unicorn that Ireland isn't even half-way outa step with life!

When he saw the strength of her body, and sensed the glitter in her eyes, the old fifer changed quick from the solemn tune to the lively reel of *The Grain of Wheat*, sending the notes out to scatter themselves gaily on the heavy air. Millie rushed headlong across the road and faced the massive lion and unicorn frowning down from Hutton's lordly gate. She commenced to dance, slowly at first, till she thought she had caught the time of the tune, then, with a sharp yell, her legs and body began to fasten fiercely in to the swift time of the reel. She moved sideways to the left, then sideways to the right, gesturing her body in a way she imagined added style to the gay music; advancing and retreating with her head held high, her hands bunching up her skirts so that her firm, white legs were out of them up to her thighs. She sent a venomous spit as high as she could up towards the British arms, twirling round with frantic shakes of her head, letting a yell out of her every few moments as a condiment to the swirling notes of *The Grain of Wheat*. Sean, eager to go, hurried the few damp pieces of furniture into the little car, unhelped by the one-eyed driver, who stood grinning, hands deep in his pockets, watching the dancing Millie, seconding every yell of ecstasy she gave with a piercing yell of his own.

—Come on, for Christ's sake! appealed Sean, gripping his arm, and let's get these things home before the rain dissolves them all before our eyes.

—Aw, wait a second, can't you? he replied impatiently, turning his empty eye towards Sean. It's not every day a fella sees such a gorgeous urge in a well-made woman, an' him on business bent. Looka th' way her skirts are up about her thighs! A little higher ups a daisy, an' th' world is mine!

No heaviness in her clumsy boots kept her from whirling round at the end of each bar of music like a humming-top when it had passed from the speed of a sleep to that showing its speed plain, its hum louder and more menacing; so she spun, stopping occasionally to face the lion and unicorn, to bring a foot down with a wild stamp to the ground, and send another spit flying up at the British arms. The crowd had grown bigger, and the fifer, old as he was, danced jerkily now, and a number of men and women in the crowd were doing spasmodic steps, sending spit after spit on to the wall over which strutted the symbolic animals of England's greatness, the rest of the crowd cheering whenever any of the moisture was carried to the wall anyway near them; pressing nearer to the gesticulating, dancing, demented woman, and filling the woman who owned the little sweet and vegetable shop at the other corner of Hutton's Lane with anxiety lest the excited movements of the crowd should demolish the flimsy pile of boxes that served for stands to show off her wares on the pathway below the window.

Sean, leaning against the edge of the car, saw some of the crowd edging back nearer to the boxes than the pressure of the people impelled them, and soon, following a wild yell and a wilder leap from prancing Millie, a wave of figures surged against the rickety stand, and all the oranges, cabbages, carrots, and spuds were sent rolling about the pathway and the street, where ferrety women and agile youngsters stretched out swift hands to gather in the harvest, taking whatever came their way through an act of God.

—Oh! isn't it a nice thing to see me little property scattered and mangled and bruised and batthered and stolen right undher me eyes, moaned the owner, by misbegotten savages takin' advantage of a poor woman, lit up with a little dhrink, thryin' to show her love for Ireland in an innocent an' unnatural way! An' ne'er a polisman within bugle-call of the place to even puzzle them in their pilferin'!

A dark dusk fell over the street. A lamplighter came jogging along, lighting lamp after lamp standing like sentinels at regular periods of the pavement, looking as if they had stood there for centuries; waiting, waiting, with not a stir out of them, for ever hopeful that the gorgeous crimson, yellow, black, green, or blue carriages, gently holding their stately owners, would come trooping up and down the street again, pulled by sleekly-polished animals.

—What's goin' on over there? asked the lamplighter of the one-eyed driver, as he paused in the lighting of the lamp beside them.

—Some dhrunken bitch or other thryin' to get us to fight for Ireland.

—Eh? Fight what, fight who, where, when?

—Here, now, th' British, I suppose.

—Maybe it's fightin' she wants! Fightin' a feed would be more'n her line, and he thrust his long rod, topped with the tiny bulb of light, through the hinged flap of the lamphead, touching the point of the burner till the gas grew into a yellow flame. Then he hurried off at a gentle trot, zig-zagging from one side of the street to the other, leaving little dots of light behind him, staring faintly like near-sighted people peering into the gathering gloom.

—She's bet, said the one-eyed driver, coming close to the car, bet to th' world. The glitther of her eyes is glazed, and she's sunk down there — see that dark blob on th' ground again' th' wall to th' left of th' gate? That's her. What a chance for a fella if she hadn' lay down in such a public place!

Sean went over near to where she lay, and looked down on her: a huddled mass of torn clothes and mud. There, too, though, was the mass of dark hair, the white legs still showing under the tattered skirt, the firm, full breasts now rising and falling all too swiftly, the shapely hips hidden in the hunched-up skirts, the rich, black eyes, wide open, seeing nothing — or, maybe, seeing all things — and the drink-stained breath coming in painful pants from the scarlet mouth.

She loves Cathleen ni Houlihan, he thought, in her own reckless way. In a way, she is Cathleen ni Houlihan — a Cathleen with the flame out of her eyes turned downwards. The feet of this Cathleen, the daughter of Houlihan, are quiet now, but none have bent low and low to kiss them.

Her courage breaks like an old tree in a black wind, and dies.

The pure tall candle that may have stood before the Holy Rood, was sadly huddled now, and melting down into the mire of the street, beneath the British lion and unicorn.

He turned away, and mounting the car, bade his one-eyed friend drive off with his sister's salvaged goods.

HOME OF THE LIVING

EVERY morning, now, at five-fifteen, when his drowsy ears heard his mother's call, just after the ringing yell of the alarm clock had died down, Sean knew there was something on his mind, something he had to remember. What? Oh, yes! He must go carefully when he got out of bed, for living things were sleeping on the floor. Three of Ella's children slept in his room; the other two, with Ella herself, in his mother's. Lying there with all the old clothes that could be scraped together over them, some spared from his bed, some from his mother's, with a few old blankets lent by a kindly neighbour living below. Ella and her kids had been stopping with them for some months, were there still, and couldn't go till Ella found a room, and got a job of some kind to pay the rent of the room, and food of a sort for the children. They were watching a room a few turns away where idleness had prevented the payment of rent, and the family had got notice to quit. Ella was ashamed to apply for poor-law outdoor relief, for had she done so, her mother would never have lifted her head again, and he, too, would have sent his sister packing had she sought it. (What would it have been, anyhow, but a loaf or two, a few grains of tea, and a pound of sugar or so?) However poor they were, they didn't want that hell of humiliation. So they struggled on, his mother always aiming at sparing as much as she could from her own dish as she dared, and paring a little from his own share of bread to faintly feed Ella and her kids; and she went on darning night and day to prevent their rags from floating off their backs. It wasn't a pleasant job for him to be eating a dinner with a little army of hungry eyes watching him, so, working near or far, he took his dinner with him. Taking his breakfast wasn't so bad, for they were all still asleep, though it wasn't easy always to arrange table and chair so that the legs didn't pinch their prostrate bodies; and the smell of the room from the breaths of the sleeping bodies made the air of the room thick and sluggish, even though he kept the window open, especially to him, in from a first quarter's work in the fresh and frosty air. At times, a surge of hatred swept through him against those scarecrow figures asleep at his feet, for they were in his way, and hampered all he strove to do, and a venomous dislike of Ella charged his heart when he realised that for the romance of a crimson coat, a mean strip of gold braid, and corded tassels of blue, yellow, and green, she had brought him, herself, and all of them down to this repulsive and confused condition. Sometimes his rage felt a hard desire to whip away the rags that covered them, wake them all up with a shout, and drive them with swift kicks from the house so that terror would send them flying far out of his sight; but his fury always ended in a sigh, for he knew his mother's gnarled hand would hold them there till another shelter could be found for them. Ella at last had, thank God, got a few odd jobs, scrubbing floors that would bring her in ten shillings, if she was lucky to work a full week; the room he was watching was two shillings a week, so that she'd have eight shillings to keep herself and the kids going.

He was waiting impatiently for the bailiffs to come, to send packing the people whose room he wanted for Ella. If he could, if he could, mind you, he'd give Ella sixpence a week towards the rent, though that would mean the loss of a book, or part of a book, to him. The system in the Public Library wasn't any good to him. An indicator, high as the Himalayas, with countless rows of little oblong slits of tin, coloured red on one side, shown when the book was In, and blue on the other, shown when the book was Out. After raising his eyes to the fifth or sixth row of figures, Sean found that they failed to distinguish the numbers, so the indicator was useless to him, and he couldn't well go on asking the assistant whether such-and-such a book were in or out. However, recently, he had bought Emerson's *Essays*; Zola's *La Débâcle*; Whitman's *Leaves of Grass*, a book in which the whole world danced, even on its way to the grave; and a cheap edition of Eithne Carbery's *Four Winds of Eireann*, which he found terribly doleful, the gay, grey sob of sorrow through it all; whether she sang of love or of war, she shivered in the cauld blast:

> A chill wind blows about my hair
> Where'er I go;
> A weeping voice is in my ear —
> A voice I know;

and to Sean the voice was the voice of Eithne Carbery making her moan, though the Irish Irelanders loved her, and gave her twenty thousand welcomes; so a generous drop of sleety moisture from a leaden sky lingered on every Irish Ireland cheek, just like a tear at this moment shed, turning Eire into a woman of immemorial moaning, so that a fellow turned aside and longed for a tale of bawdry.

Now he'd have to think of Ella as well as his books. There seemed to be ne'er an end to this damned self-denial. But when they were gone, and his eyes weren't within range of Ella's misery and want, he wouldn't feel it so necessary to be generous. Anyway, self-preservation was nature's first law, and he'd have to put the other law of the survival of the fittest into practice. Why did he promise Ella and his mother, in a foolish moment, that he'd give sixpence a week towards the rent? To help get rid of them — divil a ha'p'orth else, and, if he were honest, he'd say so. Besides, weren't they all wearing out his mother? Look at the way she had to ferret out the strip of wire netting she had clumsily, but firmly, fixed round her precious fuchsia, geranium, and musk, to fend them from the chiselurs' meddling mitts. But was he really concerned about his mother? Well, yes, for it was bound to be a trouble to him, if anything happened to her. Anyhow, he had a right to think of himself. How could he read right, study things, and write, the way things were? How was he to write articles for the Gaelic League Manuscript Journals in the midst of this ragged, hunger-agitated commotion? How was he to think out fine things to say at meetings in the heart of this lowly caravan carrying the lees of life? The poor, he was told, were beloved by God. He didn't see any sign of His love here. *He saveth the poor from the hand of the mighty. The needy shall not always be forgotten; the expectation of the poor shall not perish for ever. The poor man cried, and the Lord heard him, and saved him out of all his trouble* — all his trouble, mind you! *I will satisfy the poor with bread. The rich and the poor shall meet together; the Lord is the maker of them all.* Oh, words, words, words! I wonder was Solomon really thinking when he said things like these, or just about to play double or quits in bed with a woman; or was he flushed with the redness of the wine? There go David, Job, and Solomon feeding you with happy phrases. Well, maybe these under my feet aren't worth saving, though no qualification is made in the declarations. The phrases say, all. Then the poor have the gospel preached unto them. They have that, right enough — God has kept His word that way. For fear one way wouldn't be enough, we have fifty different sects bellowing the gospel into our bewildered ears. Perhaps the poor were always so many; their clamours for help so loud; their need so great; their breath so bad, that God got tired, and gave the thing up as a bad job. Well, some way or another, we'd have to tackle the job ourselves. Here he was, a ripe young man, and had never yet seen the poor satisfied with bread, nor had he ever seen the purple stain of a grape on a cracking lip. Never a flower on their table, save some autumn berries he himself had sometimes brought home at the request of his mother; never more than a faded newspaper to make the bare table look a richer thing; never a safer place to lie when sickness tossed us down; never a place to bathe away the dust and sweat mottling our uneasy bodies when the hard day's work was done; by the living God! these damaging lies of life would have to go! and he tightened his teeth, and clenched his hands till the knuckles shone white. And now this added heap of misery was sleeping heavily under his feet, while by a light from a shaded, guttering candle, he tried to read, and reading, remember all the startling things in Darwin's *Descent of Man.*

Sometimes he wished Darwin had never come into the house. He had upset everything. Everything was different from what they were before he rambled in to drag him down from the thoughts of sun-tinted clouds airily sailing the blue sky, a rug under God's feet, and force him to take an open-eyed survey of frogs and toads splashing about in the sedgy wharfage of a pond or the speary bulrushes of a marsh. Brekekekesh, koash, koash! For Sean, life was to begin all over again, if he decided to think on, and who wouldn't do that? Life that had appeared, just a day ago, as simple as the soft chanting of a coloured nursery rhyme, was now a streaming, headlong rush of shrill fifing point-counter-point, banked up by thundering or gun-blasts of millions of years of life. He had been deceived by babblers ready to live, to love, and to die in the irised lure of a pretty fairy tale. When he had ventured to ask a question or two of them who said they knew, they had stared, turned aside, and gone away from him. One, when asked if he really believed the yarn of Jonah and the whale, had looked at him in amused astonishment, had pressed a finger-tip to Sean's breast, saying, See here, boy, if the bible asked me to believe that Jonah swallowed the whale, I'd believe it; but the blessed book doesn't ask me to believe anything so nonsensical, but only that it was the whale who swallowed Jonah.

—And quite enough, too, murmured Sean. Even dear Mr. Griffin, when challenged by Sean, had sighed and said, I know, dear John, I know; the Higher Criticism has disturbed us sadly. The robe of truth has been pulled awry, and badly torn, John; but the truth is untouched. Here we see as in a glass, darkly, but one day we shall know all, and I am content to wait.

The bible? How he had fondly thought it had been handed down from Heaven, straight from the hand of God! A day ago, here was all the knowledge, all the fear, all the hope the world wanted. Life was fashioned so that all was ordered, stately, trim, triumphant, cut out and braided as deliciously as the sacerdotal garments of the High Priest about to enter the holy of holies, down to the last little bell and pomegranate nestling among the fringes. And poor Archbishop Ussher insisting that the universe was but a child of four thousand years of age, and Dr. Lightwood, going farther, light-headed with the discovery, added that it was all created on the 23rd of October, at nine o'clock in the morning. Oh, Michael Angelo, it took more than the pointing of a Divine finger to make a man! A million of years it took to mould him into what he is today, and the job is barely halfway over. It took more than a whistle to bring a world into being. Man has tried to make things all too easy for God to do. Not the first man, but the first question the man asked, brought what the clergy call sin into the world, and all our woe. Better sin and better woe than woeful fear and bitter ignorance. Ignorance found a god everywhere and in everything, and ordered life according to its imagined whims. Knowledge had been hunting the earth and scouring the heavens for but one God, but has found none. If I ascend up to Heaven, He is not there; if I make my bed in Hell, there is no sign of Him; if I take the wings of the morning, and dwell in the uttermost parts of the sea, even there shall no eye behold Him; neither shall any hand shoot up to shade a startled eye from a sudden light. The darkness and the light are both alike in emptiness. The god Cosmogony has quietly seated himself in the vacant throne of Jehovah. Farewell, a long farewell to all His greatness. Farewell to the Garden of Eden, with all its animals, all its lovely plants, and every sweet-smelling herb of its fields, with the soft, streaming rivers to water them all. Farewell to the man himself, and his wife, clinging together between the tree of life and tree of death, the twining serpent, burnished with many glittering colours, anxious for company, insinuating itself with its roguish smile and twittering chat of knowing good and evil: they are all now as the high-painted wooden animals and green-papered garden and stiff-jointed man and woman in a little child's playroom. All the magicjestic growth of man's fall, his happy redemption, and his courtly life in Thy kingdom come have faded as a Christmas-tree that had stood in a dark corner, its fairy lights and glittering gems a blaze of delight and stimulation, suddenly thrust out into the light of a fine, full, summer day to wither into a mockery, its grandeur dead, and all its jewels rayless.

He wished he had a hold of the book Donal Mac Rury had let him look over while he waited for Donal to finish grinding items in the brains of students bent on entering the Civil Service. He had read what he could of it at top speed while Donal was busy, and had begged Donal for a loan of it, even for but one night and half a day; but Donal couldn't give it, for the friend who lent it was coming that very night to get it back, for the friend's friend wouldn't let it stay any longer out of his sight. Sean had asked for it at the Library, but the assistant had never heard of it. He appealed to the head librarian to try to get it for the readers, explaining what he remembered of its scope and vision, and the head librarian had snorted viciously, saying curtly as he moved away, If it's anything like what you make it out to be, it's neither a safe nor a proper book to have knocking about here! But now Sean had something else to think of besides *The Golden Bough.*

He went along cautiously, and peeped round the edge of the house at the corner of the street, looking down the little lane with its double row of little tottering houses. Dtch, dtch, they were there still. There was the old woman, as large as death, sitting on one of her chairs beside her tiny heap of stuff on the roadside, opposite the house holding the room he had taken for Ella. She must have been there all night, and he couldn't run over to ask her when she'd be going. Neither could he let Ella go into the tenancy while the other's furniture was staring at the house out of which it had been carried by the bailiffs. Oh, here was the married daughter coming up to the oul' one now. Whishst, she's taking a chair away. Well, that's a start in the right direction. That's what they're doing — carrying it away, bit by bit. No money to pay anyone to shift it for them. Another night'll be gone before they've finished. Better late than too late.

Suddenly he saw the old woman rising from the chair — throwing her arms into the air, shaking her grey head so that her grey hair fell about her shoulders, to shout up at the sky, Jasus, help the poor! Here

I am, at th' end o' me days, bound for the poorhouse. I can't live on me daughter, can I? I can't tear down food outa th' black sky, th' blue sky, or th' grey sky, can I? I've lived nigh on seventy years with my own, an' now me few last lone days is to be spent suppin' sorra with strangers. I'll eat me skilly head bent in me belly for thankfulness, and wrestle for sleep in an odd bed with no interest in th' rest I want to take. Why don't they kill us decent an' be done with it!

Passers-by took no notice of her lamentation, keeping steadily on their way, gaping in front of them as if no voice had spoken, for to them she was already dead.

That very night, Sean, with the help of Georgie Middleton, hurried the scraps of furniture into the room, a dark room, quarter-buried beneath the pathway outside, a small iron-barred window letting a dusky light in on to the scarred walls soiled by a thousand previous tenants; and the splintery floor, showing signs of steady damp decay, exerted itself to come away from the skirting. It was a house in the lane where Massy, Ecret, and Middleton had had their battle royal, as swampy as ever, and here Ella and her clan would live a bad part of their lives in this damp gloom; but thousands were doing the same, and why should she demand any better? For the price, it was the best he could get for them, and, even so, it would cost him six golden pennies a week.

Ella said no word when she came to the room, but just went on, with glazed eyes and thoughtless face, making up the old bed on its rickety iron frame, and the other bed on the floor. Sean advised her to make that one, too, on the frame for the time being, for it would be less dangerous than the damp floor, even though they all would be a little crowded. She agreed by putting all the clothes on the iron bed without a word, and so she slept at the head, with the two girls and Shawn, the youngest, while the two older boys slept at the foot — six in all in the one room, and six in the same bed. Are ye not more precious than very many sparrows? About the same value, my Lord, about the same. It was a bitter sight for Sean when he saw them tucked up for the night, but he could do no more. He had to keep himself and his mother, give a little to Ella, take an interest in pictures, books, and the National struggle, so how could he do more? His mother gave them a chair from her meagre stock, a bowl, two cups and a saucer, an old saucepan, an ounce of tea, three and a half of sugar, and a loaf, so that they might have a housewarming on the first day of their tenancy. He gave Ella fourpence, and tacked up on the wall a church calendar having a text for every day of the year, a coloured picture of the King in the middle, wearing the uniform of a Field Marshal, and a portrait of Lord Wolseley, Lord Beresford, Lord Roberts, and Sir Evelyn Wood, in full military and naval uniforms, one in each of the corners. The scarlet and blue of their clothes, and the glitter of their orders and medals, gave a touch of glory to the ravelling oul' walls. Hold on a second! What's the text for today? Friday, the thirteenth of November, Feast of St. Lauderdamnuss: Keep right on to the end of the road, keep right on to the end.

They had been settled in, and Sean felt that he was now done with them for good. Working from six in the morning to half-five in the evening then out to Gaelic League and National work till twelve or one o'clock, he saw little of them, and never enough to give him a worrying thought. He gave his sixpence regularly, for his mother always reminded him when he desired to forget it. He missed a jug from the dresser, and guessed that it now stood on Ella's; and fingering his mother's doss on the sofa, he saw that some of her old blanketing was gone. Doesn't give a damn how she robs herself for others, he thought with annoyance.

So Sean went on with his daily work for bread, and his nightly work for the lily, labouring to bring new things to Ireland, and safely shutting himself from Ella's poverty and her children's silent shame, misery drying up their young hearts, and leading them on to an imperfect end. They went to school in their tired and timorous clothing, filling themselves, at any rate, with the knowledge of this world, and on Sundays they went to Sunday school and church, filling themselves up with the knowledge of the next one.

Oh, God! thought Sean, looking at them kneeling in their pew at the back of the church, what in the name of Christ is the good of it all! He lingered when the service was over so that they might be gone before he left, for they filled him with rage; but Ella often lingered longer to beg a few pence from him towards the children's breakfast in the morning.

The frisky spring had developed into the more sensible summer, seeking a place in which to sit and drowse and think after her racing dance with the daffodils; and Sean was at home in bed one morning for the first time for many years, nursing three badly-bruised toes, hurt by a lump of machinery falling on his right foot while he was helping to dismantle it more than a week ago. When it had happened, like a fool, he had gone on working in agony, afraid, if he took the boot off, he wouldn't get it on again; certain, if he stuck it out, he'd be all right the next morning. When he got home and took off his boot to bathe it in hot water, his mother found his sock soaked in blood, and he saw what a state his toes were in. There wasn't a walking-stick in the neighbourhood, so he had to limp as best he could to Dr. Stoker of Rutland Square to be smartly rebuked for not coming in a cab while the toes were being dressed, and a tiny splint put on one of the toes that had been broken. He was ordered to give the foot complete rest and to come again in a week's time. Not a word, though, about taking a cab home, or another about where the fare was to come from, thinking, I suppose, that it would fall down from Heaven if one waited long enough, or prayed hard enough; but Dr. Stoker wouldn't let him wait or pray in the surgery, and the police would deem it rather queer should he stay to pray all night in the open street. Delayed action on the part of Heaven would make him look ridiculous, and cast suspicion on him as one who was curiously going out of his mind.

So here he was on the broad of his back, waiting for his mother to bring him his breakfast, and reading the Everyman issue of Prescott's *Conquest of Peru*, which he bought after reading Keats's lovely lines on the eagle eyes of Cortez staring at the Pacific Ocean, staring with his awestruck men, all silent on a peak of Darien (though it wasn't Cortez who first clapped eyes on this new world of waters). He had looked for the *Conquest of Mexico* all over the second-hand barrow, but had to be content with the story of Pizarro's fast and fiery bestowal of the peace that belongs not to this world on the Incas and their people. It was odd how the symbol of the Prince of Peace appeared so often in the midst of fire and smoke and death and desolation! How often it brought to black, red, or yellow peoples, not the gentle grace of God, but the sword plunging through their bellies, and the madly-rushing bullet searing through their throats. The cross was everywhere, on almost every flag of every nation, and England had three on hers to show she was holier than the others; each cross representing a saint, one a Jew, the second a Cappadocian, and the third a Frenchman, and ne'er a one of them an Englishman. Millions made the sign in the air, or on their breasts, millions of times a day. The very hilt of their sword is a cross too. Ah, that's the real cross for the hand of a plunderer, and here it is, firmly held in the hard hand of the murdering conquistadores. The Incas' first taste of Christ was a bitter one: myrrh, myrrh, vinegar, and gall for them, with their frankincense and gold carried off, even to the scrapings from their temple doors. Had the Incas been able to moisten the air with cries of Domino woebescums, had they been able to darken the sky with clouds of Query eileisons, it would have profiteth them nothing, for the Christians were out on the make.

All the labour, the building of the ship, the coaxing together of a crew, the long tumbling trek over a salty sea, tossing them up and down for a lark, slashing its jeering billows over the rim of the deck, making the hardy seamen cough, and shake the stinging spume from their staring eyes, forcing them to hold with an icy grip any beam or rope that came their way so that they wouldn't go to Heaven too suddenly. After, the landing of figures wan, shaken, and doubtful; then the dragging of tired and thinning legs through knee-deep swampy slime like the primary ooze of Hell's first flooring; then through jungles, their blistered necks and lacerated arms entangling in the looping, twisting, red-blossomed creepers, and tearing at the climbing vines weaving themselves in and out of their legs; of the panting warriors, now content to be woe-mounted men, trying to save themselves with sweep of sword and hewing of axe and push of shoulders, thrusting out in pain from hollowed backs, halting to catch their breath in snaky woody webs, dropping their sweat into the luscious cups of curling lilies; halting among swarms of humming insects, blue, yellow, crimson, or purple, darting streaks of light, prodding deep stings into the frightened flesh of the sweltering Spaniards, hot curses dropping from the blackened lips of the warriors that they had ever put a foot outside the plains of Saragossa, or wandered from the sight of the mountains of Navarre. And all for gold and the love of God! For pomp and power, for riotous living, with the cross on their banners and the glory of God behind them.

Even here, in the midst of torn flesh, minds jagged with fear and anxiety, beset with hunger and thirst, the long, rough, gaunt hands of these struggling Christians were stretched out to grasp the cord that was to choke the life out of the son of the sun. Poor Atahualpa who, to save himself from becoming a sour-smelling burnt-offering at the stake, elected to be baptised in the name of Juan, for it was the Feast of John the Baptist, was received into the Church, and so holy cords pulled by holy hands choked the life out of him, as being a much more merciful death than burning. The Inca's Temple of the Sun is quite bare now; all that was worth while in it, or on it, lies safe in the bottom of the Christian sack.

They're all the same, thought Sean. Those who conquer others to use them woefully for their own poor benefit performance are all the same, whatever god they worship, whatever flag they fly. Today, the cross to the heathen is as ominous as it was to the Aztecs and the Incas in the days of the Spanish glory. The native of that day felt the love of God coming to him when the feathered shaft tore through his breast, today the fire and smoke of the belching guns sing out the same evangel. He turned on to his side from the delicious comfort of lying on his back, to shout towards the other room, Eh, out there — is that breakfast of mine ever going to come to me!

His mother brought his breakfast in to him — a cup of tea and some slices of toast. Nine o'clock in the morning, and all's well! It was grand to lie here, alone, except for the mother; to read and think and see visions. Better still, to realise that while other poor mugs were at it hard, he lay here like a bee in a lotus blossom. What's this it was oul' Tennyson said? Ay:

> Let us swear an oath, and keep it with an equal mind,
> In the hollow Lotus-land to live and lie reclined
> On the hills like Gods together, careless of mankind.

Like that he'd lie, careless of mankind; well, for a week or so longer, though his mother had hinted that ould Murphy's bill for provisions was mounting higher, for he got but half-pay now, and ould Murphy was always hoping that Mr. Casside's foot would soon be better. He sipped the tea and bit the toast, finding them both good, idly watching, through the open door, his mother fluttering her brown and wrinkled, but delicate, fingers through the fuchsia, the geranium, and the musk, fiddling them into further bloom.

She wouldn't give her three peculiar plants for a Christian sack of gold, he thought; she'd risk her life to rescue them from a fire; she'll miss them and mourn for them when she gets to Heaven. He heard someone coming into the room outside, and then the voice of Ella's eldest girl mumbling and crying, his mother standing stock-still to stare at her. The next minute his mother and the girl were standing in the doorway of his room.

—Ella's dead, mumbled his mother, so Sara says; she says she's gone; suddenly she went, in th' quiet of the night, so Sara says.

—Me Ma's dead, whimpered Sara; died in her bed in the night in the midst of us without lettin' us know.

—How without letting you know? What are you talking about? he asked.

—Before dawn, Sara mumbled, I felt her gettin' curious an' cold, an' I called her, but she made no answer; so I felt queer, an' I lit a candle, an' when I looked, I saw she was dead.

—Get up, Jack, pleaded Mrs. Casside; get up like a good boy, and don't leave us alone with this thing to face. You can't go on lying on one bed while your poor sister lies dead on another. Doesn't seem right she should be taken before me. Oh, what are we goin' to do, an' her out of insurance benefit for so long! Her face twitched, and she staggered so that he thought she was going to fall, but she gripped the rail of the bed and recovered a little. Get up, she went on, an' come over, for I'm not feelin' too good myself.

—Pull yourself together, can't you? he said roughly. Her shaking frightened him a little. You go over first, and see what has really happened. What happened to her? he asked, irritably, of Sara. Once or twice I met her with part of an old shawl wound round her head. What was wrong with your mother?

—I dunno, right, she said. She went several times to the Dispensary doctor, an' he said it was only erysipelas, or something; she wouldn't listen to anyone tellin' her to take care of herself.

—Divil a much care you took of her! said Sean bitterly, or the damned doctor either. Go on, the pair of you, he added, an' I'll be over as soon as I've dressed myself. He watched them go, and felt disturbed at the uncertain way his mother walked out of the room. She's shaken, he thought, and I'll have to keep a closer eye on her. He guessed she gave Ella a lot of her old-age pension, and he often had to make her share some of what he ate himself, for he knew she went without proper food to give some to Ella and her kids.

He got out of bed lazily, lingering over the putting-on of his clothes as long as he could, so that whatever had to be done, might be done before he arrived. His face crinkled with pain as he drew on his toeless boot over his injured foot. When he had dressed, he sauntered over to the window and looked aimlessly out over the golden-headed musk, the purple-belled fuchsia, looking like a prelate hearing the confession of a golden-haired Niamh, to the railway lines beyond running down to the quays, at the long rake of wagons filled with lowing cattle and bleating sheep on their way to the boats for England, with the thick, bully-like spire of St. Damnamman strutting over them like a stout jobber, wide-faced, satisfied, and silent, watching the last march-past of his treasures.

The one lovely thing about the whole place, thought Sean, is the sky. A purest blue. In it was some of the darkest blue, and all of the gentle blue of the lightest blue forming a luminous and radiant blue of its own. No fleck or frill of cloud disturbed the freshness that must have adorned it when the sky first came into being. It was as if God, in a giving vein, had draped the sky in a birthday cloak. A simple slip of it would make a rare mantle for the Queen of Sheba's shoulders; a gay shift to deck the charms of Helen of Troy; or a tempting dress for St. Bridget herself to do a dance in, before her grudging hand had marred the seductive loveliness of her face.

He brought the tea from his bedroom, poured out another cup, sat down before the fire (for his mother did her best to have a fire, winter or summer) to drink it quiet, and go on reading the goings-on of the pagan-saving Spaniards in the *Conquest of Peru*. Somebody coming up the stairs now. Looking for him, he guessed. Ne'er a minute's peace, or a chance to read his fill for once! Come in! he called to a knock at the door.

Katie Kenna stood at the door, a look of reproach on her young face already getting wizened by some sort of heart disease.

—If I were you, Jack, she said, I'd leave your book and hurry over to where your sister's sthretched out dead, for I don't like th' look of your poor mother either.

He hurried on his coat, and jumping down the stairs two at a time, ran through the street, round to the back lane to his sister's shanty. There was a little crowd of kids round the door, and a few women near by talking together who shoved the kids aside when they saw him coming. He went into the room, smelling always of damp and mustiness, now mixed with the added scent of death. He failed to see anything in the dark place at first, except the dimming blue of a sky no longer over him, and away in front of him the frightened gleam of a candle stuck into the neck of a ginger-beer bottle standing on the cracked mantelpiece. Silence, too, save for timid, whimpering sounds that came from the sides of the room. Then the blue of the sky departed from him, and he saw his sister. In the midst of the whimpering, there she was, starkly stretched out on the family bed, the clothes still disordered, part of her breast showing over the edge of a coarse shift made out of a flour sack. The remnants of the old shawl were still wrapped round her head, forming a rowdy cowl from which his sister's waxy face stared like that of a nun of the higher order of destitution salvaged from it for ever at last. He recognised in the dead face his sister of the long ago, for a swift bloom of a dead youth had come back to mock at the whimpering, squalid things arrayed around it. There were the cleverly-chiselled, features, tensed by death, the delicate nose and fine brow, the firm oval cheeks, the white throat curving into the breast as gracefully as a swan's neck, and the neatly-moulded hands, worn away now, resting confidently by her side. Here lay all that remained of her piano-playing, her reading in French of

Iphigenia, and of her first-class way in freehand drawing. All that had to be done now was to get rid of her quick as he could, and a tough job it was going to be for him. The blue sky was a mistake: a useless waste of loveliness; a work of supererogation on the part of God. Only here, in this dark room, skulked reality, a filthy divinity that shaped our ends.

The children had pushed themselves away from the silence on the bed, and were standing with their backs pressed to the walls, the two older boys quiet and staring, the youngest and the two girls weeping in a bewildered harmony together. And there was his mother, standing against the bottom rail of the bed, staring down into Ella's insensitive face. There she stood, whimpering too, and shaking with the ceaseless delicate shivering of an aspen-tree. When he looked more closely, he saw that she was breaking, that she was shivering herself into an acknowledged old age at last, while Wolseley, Beresford, the King, Evelyn Wood, and Lord Roberts, in their gay garments, watched from the wall this whining tattoo honouring the poor's natural anointing. Oh, why the hell should he torment himself with the thought of a blue robe for the Queen of Sheba, a mantle for the pert, beautiful shoulders of the charmer of Troy, or a gown of mystical blue for Bridget to dance a night away, before her ruthless hand mauled her lovely face to prevent it becoming a desirable occasion for sin!

He took his mother by the arm and led her out to bring her home, for he could see she would be useless now. He tried to think of what was to be done now, but all the images his mind could form were a medley of his sister's calmly stretched-out body seeming to say silently, Here I am, now, and the world can do what it likes with me, and whatever you like with whatever once was mine; of the steadily crying children standing like a drab and dreary guard of dishonour around the dead woman; of the coloured-paper soldiers watching from the wall; and of his mother whining and shivering in the midst of a brilliant blue sky. It was one comfort, at least, to reach home, to hand over his mother to the care of kind Katie Kenna, who set her down by the fire and planked a kettle on the fire to make her a cup of tea.

—Look, Jack, she said, as he was about to go back to Ella's, if the chiselurs haven't had breakfast, send them over, an' I'll give them somethin' hot.

—Who's to lay her out? he asked Katie. The girls are too young, and they're not much good anyhow.

—Any of the women'll do it for you. Aren't they waitin' there to be asked? They may well have begun already.

—But I've nothing to offer them for doing it, he objected.

—That doesn't signify, said Katie; someone'll have to tidy her up to meet her Maker.

He went away without thanking her, for he was full of the ordeal he had to face, and all alone, now, for his mother had come to the end of her valour. Jasus! It was terrible! A hell's pentecost to all the genteel thieves who batten on the poor! May a flame on every head eat into every brain of them, to be a soft and simple baptism of the fuller flaming life to come!

When he reached Ella's, he saw the children standing against the wall outside, and he sent them to Katie Kenna's to get a cup of tea. A woman came along with a white towel and a jug of steaming hot water, who stopped to say, You can't go in, now, for we're laying the poor creature out; and Mrs. Brady's giving us the usual sheets with the brass candlesticks an' candles to put a shape on things, so she'll look decent, neat, an' ready for all she may have to meet.

—Won't she want a shroud of some sort?

—That's got; someone got it; I dunno who.

—Ask him about th' cross, Jinny, said a woman's head, thrusting itself out through a slightly opened door.

—Oh, yes, said Jinny, beaming at Sean, I near forgot. Mrs. Brady always sends a cross with the sheets, to be laid on th' breast of the dead; but you an' her bein' a protestant an' all, we were wondherin' whether it would be sensible to leave it out, or rest it on her?

—Oh, give her the fullest measure you can, said Sean; there's no reason to hide from her the sign of suffering and the badge of shame.

—Ah, then, said the head through the doorway, if e'er a one deserved it be hard work an' hunger, it's her who ought to have th' comfort of the cross; though, to even matters, we'll lay it lightly on her breast, an' not have her claspin' it in her hands.

He left the women at it, and strolled over to the wall bordering the railway, leaning on it to try to think of what he was going to do. Where in the name of Christ was he going to get the money to bury her, even in the slinking way destitution buries its out-of-benefit dead? And to only think that she had paid enough in premiums to bury herself and her family a dozen times over! Oh, these thieving, rascally, money-conjuring Insurance Societies! Asps on the breasts of the poor! Without the slightest garnishing, plain hearse, plain horse, plain coffin, plus the burial fee, it would come to four or five pounds, and he hadn't five pence in his pocket! And on half-pay too. Then there were other things — the fares and the tips to the gravediggers. Let the parish bury her? The common deal coffin and cart, the hurried trot to the poor-ground in the early dawn, so that it would not disturb the genteel burials that came later, with flowers, nodding plumes, and top-hatted drivers? Well, beggars couldn't be choosers. Could he get up a collection? How could he ask catholics to subscribe to bury a protestant in a protestant cemetery? Anyway, they hadn't anything to give, save what they stood up in. Though a burden to him, death had been a kind favour to Ella, though it meant but carrying her from one tomb to another. No hyacinth will grow from that once lovely head, damaged by the fire of erysipelas, and turned to dry dust by the brunt of pain and the worry of want. Perhaps a burdock holding up a rusty red torch will do her some faint honour in some autumn-mirrored wasteland. The railway embankments and waste land around them were crowded with the flaring yellow of buttercups and tall, pretentious dandelions, and the demure whiteness of the dog-daisy. The Dublin lilies of the field, flaunting the papal colours. Idle creatures doing better than those who toiled and spun. He fingered the coins in his trousers pocket: tuppence ha'penny — the price of a pint or a package of Woodbines, though he wanted neither. He must shut everything from his mind but a vision of money. A gold coin had eclipsed the sun. Nothing he had, nothing in the house would raise a penny. His books? Ten shillings; no — seven, at the most, and what would they do? And then he would be destitute indeed! Even if he had now the fifteen shillings he gave to swell the fund to help poor Dr. O'Hickey to fight his case in Rome. No, no; not those. Bury her, bury himself, bury even his mother anywhere, anyhow, rather than wish the withdrawal of anything from a heartfelt fight.

He felt a tap on his shoulder, and, turning round, saw George Middleton staring awkwardly at him as he held out an envelope towards him.

—From the Rector, he said. Told me to tell you to bring it to Nicholl's, the undertaker. Says it'll make things a little easier. He scraped a foot along the pathway, stooping down to hide a reddening face. Th' envelope's open, he went on; have a look at what's inside, if I were you, before givin' it to oul' Nicholl's. Sorry, Jack, for your trouble; hope you'll be able to manage. S'long! And he hurried off without letting Sean get in the edge of a word. Sean took the letter from the envelope, and read that Mr. Griffin requested Nicholl's to furnish all things necessary so that Mr. John Casside's sister could be decently, but not extravagantly, buried. Pinned to it was a note asking Sean to let the Rector know day and hour of burial so that he might officiate at the graveside. There was also in the envelope a crumpled piece of white paper wrapped round what Sean felt to be a coin. He took it out carefully, and found it to be a half-sovereign. A few words were scribbled in pencil on the paper, and looking closely Sean read, Just a loan. Can easily spare it. Georgie.

—Cheeky boyo, he muttered, to think I wanted help from him! But Middleton was too far away now to throw it after him, so Sean carefully put the piece of gold in his trouser pocket. When he found out from Katie Kenna that his mother was sleeping quietly, he climbed the railway wall and sat down on a tussock of grass, among the yellow dandelions and white dog-daisies, under a sky again courageous with its blue banner, so as to calm a mind confused at receiving relief so suddenly. However he might change, wherever he might be, whatever he might do, he could never forget the man, the Reverend E. M. Griffin. A faultless man. No, not faultless, for sometimes he showed he had a hasty temper, and he couldn't suffer fools gladly, both qualities endearing him all the more to Sean, who himself had a hasty temper and hated fools fiercely. He had, too, a puritanical detestation of even accidental indulgence in the claims of sex, other than those allowed by law and regulation of the Church, and a real sensitiveness that couldn't allow him long to look at the effects of poverty. He had told Sean, one time, that to do so would break him in pieces. He had, too, a curious childlike readiness to accept almost anything said by one who, he thought, loved and served the Church which, to him, sprang from the love and devotion of saints Patrick, Columkille, Bridget, and Aidaun. Once in an argument around the causes of poverty, the Rector, laying an affectionate touch of his hand on Sean's arm, said, Remember, John, I have been young, and now am old; yet have I not seen the righteous forsaken, nor His seed begging bread. And once, speaking, John, to Marcus Tertius Moses, on this very verse, he claimed that, in his own experience, he could confirm it in every respect. Sean so loved the Rector that he had fallen silent rather than hurt his feelings by pointing out that a Trustee of the Church Funds and a Bank Director could hardly risk saying anything else, and that no man, banker or broker, had any authority to say that this or that man deserved to be begging bread from stranger or friend.

But what of the children when Ella had been planted? Ay, there's the rub! It looked as if his sixpence a week would have to be doubled or trebled in the future. The elder boy and the eldest girls would have to find some work to do; the rest live, or perish. Beyond what he could spare, he could do no more. Injured foot or no, he'd have to start work again the day after the funeral. He could coddle himself no longer. But he'd have to be hard. He'd have to view the kids in the calm, undisturbed way a mother robin gazed on her fledgling lying on a sturdy leaf five inches below, just having been flung out of the nest by the pirate cuckoo. There she'd sit, warming the intruder, an indifferent eye on the young of her body, helpless and alone, motionless the livelong day, save for a rare twitch of the tiny head, dozing towards death, slinking silently to its end.

He hurried off to get the death certificate, hurried to show it to the Registrar, and then hurried down to Nicholl's, the undertaker, where his tired clothes were eyed by a long, thin man, a tuft of hair on his head nicely balanced by another on his chin. He showed him the certificate, and gave him Mr. Griffin's letter which he read, looked sadly at Sean, and said shortly, That'll be all right, all right; that'll do.

—Do it all as cheap as you can, said Sean, for I don't want our Rector to be asked to pay a lot.

—All right; never fear; we won't send her a coffin of copper with a silver plate.

Not much profit for him here, thought Sean, so he isn't very interested. Out loud he said, Haven't you got to measure her?

—We'll let her have a box that'll fit her, never fear, young fellow. That'll do, now; there are other dead people in the world needing attention. So good-evening.

It was the poorest funeral the neighbourhood ever saw or ever heard of: a rough deal coffin, patchily smeared with oak stain, Ella's name, age, and year of death scrawled clumsily with black paint on the lid; and a small black box hearse, drawn by a scraggy mare bare of a plume. No neighbours gathered round the door, but stayed near their houses, looking from their windows or peeping out by their doors, for they attached the shabbiness of Ella's funeral to their own shamed inability to provide her with a better farewell.

On the morning of the funeral he sent one of the boys for two cabs, for one would be so crowded he was afraid some careless boot might stamp on his broken toes. Soon the cabs came jauntily along, but when they reached the place, the drivers remained in their seats, staring at the rough-hewn hearse and the meagre mare. The leading driver was a small wiry man with as many wrinkles in his face as an orange had, though its colour and texture resembled a mummified apple. He was wearing a heavy coat much too big for him, and a high-crowned, faded bowler hat. The other was stouter, taller, grey-haired, and tobacco juice oozed from a very wide mouth. He was wearing a claw-hammer coat, trilby hat, and a dirty white muffler powdered with big blue spots was wound round his neck.

—Eh, asked the man in the bowler hat, who was it here sent for us! And when a youngster silently pointed a finger at Sean, he shouted down from his seat, Eh, there, what are yous after leadin' us into?

— How leading you into — into what?

—What a gaum y'are, he said sarcastically, his hand stretched out to point the whip at the hearse. What d'ye call that, eh? And as Sean remained silent, he went on, D'ye call that a decent thing for any decent Christian to folla?

—A fair question, murmured his friend, ay, is it; no-one could ask a fairer.

—I'm askin' yous again, he went on, is it fair or is it honest to exact on any decent dhriver of any decent vehicle to promenade afther an unconcealable object like that?

—A fair question, I'd say, repeated the other, inserting a finger to scratch something under the muffler; ne'er a fairer. An' he too only afther gettin' his vehicle newly painted.

—It's the best we could do, said Sean tersely, getting the youngsters into the first cab, while George Middleton prepared to climb into the other one.

—I hope th' pair of you'll have as good yourselves when you're carried out feet first, Georgie shouted at them. It's not a newly-painted cab, but a puck or two in the snout yous want to makes yous decent!

—It's all very well, grumbled the driver, somewhat afraid of the fiery look on the pug-face of Middleton, but we have our prestige to mind.

—Ay, have we, added his friend, a long an' ancient one be now, an' valued. What'll Glasnevin people think when they see this arrange-ment arrivin'?

—It's not to Glasnevin, but to Mount Jerome we go, said Sean.

—Worse again, be Christ! ejaculated the first driver: a more elegant an' particular place still! He jumped from his seat and ran over to Sean, saying as he ran, I'll not keep close, I'll not do it, so I won't, not for Joe! I'll let a couple o' sthreets get between us an' that mockin' shame in front of us!

—Put the world between, if you like, said Sean, jumping into the second cab, so long as you get us there in time; and stretching from the window, he gave the hearse the signal to go.

He was silent in the cab, but thoughts swift followed one another fast so that all he saw, all he heard, all he did, appeared slantily in the mirror of a blue sky like the pageant passing through the mirror of Shalott, hurrying in and hurrying out in a continuous reel of sliding shapes, all of them headed crazily by the staggering onward of the one-horse hearse, to lay Ella on top of her husband's bones, who lay on top of Tom's, who lay on the top of his father's.

> In rags, she pray'd aloud to God,
> Who gave no answer, made no nod;
> No blossom bloom'd on Aaron's rod,
> As she went to and fro.
> No angel, flying far too high,
> Came down a perch to hear her sigh,
> Or paus'd when she stretch'd out to die,
> The lady of sorroh!

Yet in the leering blue sky he could, at least, see the elegant black sleeve of the Rector's coat outstretched, and, at the end of it, the delicate, sensitive hand extended to grasp his own in the bond of friendly sympathy, as the two cabs, far ahead of the one-horse hearse, hurried on to Mount Jerome.

DRUMS UNDER THE WINDOWS

IRELAND'S life of the golden, scarlet, and sable past came creeping out into the sun from many hidden corners; from Daingean, Bally-vourney, Vinegar Hill, Ballinamuck, Dunseveric, and the Islands a powerful hand had tipped out into the sea over the coasts. The hidden Ireland began to show herself to the astonished, astounded, and puzzled people of Belfast, Dublin, Cork, Galway, and Skibbereen, disturbing those engaged in the exciting job of buying cheap and selling dear, especially those who had the Royal Arms sprinkled on the lintels of their doorways; the younger King Coles of the nation, with their pipes and bowls, their fiddlers three, their jugglers three, and their drummers three, who were planted here by God and a few policemen to show the Irish how to live, and do things in the upright way, from shearing sheep, growing corn, rearing cattle, feeding pigs, telling the truth, acting orderly, and buttoning their flies properly.

Astonished, too, were those who worked in docks, factories, and workshops, wearing bowler hats on Sundays and on St. Patrick's Day. Ireland was giving birth to an army with banners — not the old-fashioned fancy-free ones of green cotton made in Manchester, with yellow shamrocks, wolf-dogs, round towers, harps, and sun-bursts on their fields, carried usually by solid men of the Muldoon clan, Rakes from Mallow, Rattlin' Boys from Paddy's Land, Brave Sons of Hibernia, and Paddy Haggerty, in his leather breeches, from his cottage with the roses round the door; but cunning flags made from tabinet or poplin fresh from a Dublin loom, red, green, violet, yellow, and blue banners, garnished bright with speckled designs filtered finely from the *Book of Kells*, *Book of the Old Dun Cow*, *Book of Ballymote*, and illuminated headlines from the missal of Rob Roy MacGregor O; lovely scrolls of interlaced ornament were displayed on them, and spiralled decorations of many hues, taken from the sacred psaltery of Cahirciveen, and copied into crewel work by the fair, white, modest hands of the Lily of Killarney, Maire of Ballyhaunis, the Pride of Petravore, the Flower of Finea, Nora Creena, and the Girl from the County Clare, bespeaking a new hope and a high-strung resolution to flaunt before friend and foe things that had been deep-hidden in our history.

Ikons of the old-time leaders were snatched from the walls and flung into the first fire handy: Tay Pay O'Connor, in his muttley, criss-crossed with the figuration of the Union Jack; Tim Healy, a clever bearded oul' scut whose skin stretched tight over a portly bag of rowdy venom, who was now cursing in a corner; William O'Brien, in the centre of his All for Ireland League, like a kernel in a nut, shouting south and shouting north, but ne'er a one in an Irish class, or well away in an Irish dance, cocked an ear to catch a word; Johnny Dillon, the melancholy humbug, now no more to the people than a bleating sheep with the staggers, going about with a neat green ribbon tied round its thinning neck; and though John Redmond kept his hand held up to show the people where to go, it shook so much that it pointed everywhere at once. A busy, united Ireland was quietly weaving an ample shroud of silence for them all; and these men who had gone up and down the land, led by brass bands, under an archway of banners, through a salvo of cheering, were soon to be creeping and skulking back to hidden places in the dense loneliness of forgotten times, to sit by faint firesides, reading the yellowing records of their own long speeches, never again to notice the green liveliness of another spring; never to feel again the kiss of another lusty summer; never again to lie snug in the golden leafy lap of another autumn; never again to laugh, and run breathless with the gay earth clad in the shining armour of another winter's frost; waiting, worn out, for dapper death to carry them off, and deposit them where they'd be safe from sight and sound of men, leaving behind no damp eye to honour them, or any song for their singing.

Ireland's living symbol now was a big-headed, dark, big-mouthed man, loud-voiced, with a weighty moustache that gave a bend to his shoulders, and curtained off the big mouth completely; a man who was hilarious with everyone that seemed to matter, who was ever shouting out, with his right arm lifted so that its shadow seemed to stretch from one end of the land to the other; shouting in a strange tongue, Come, and follow me, for behind me marches the only Ireland worth knowing; in me is all that went to make the valour and wisdom and woe of Clan Hugh and Clan Owen, Clan of Conn and of Oscar, of Fergus and Finn, of Dermot and Cormac, of Caoilte and Kevin, and of Brian Boy Magee; the crooning, sad and impudent, of piper Torlogh MacSweeny; of Sarsfield, Wolfe Tone, Michael Dwyer, O'Donovan Rossa, and the Manchester Martyrs; of Power's whiskey, Limerick lace, Belfast linen, Foxford wool, Dublin tabinet, and Guinness's stout.

So History, in gay-coloured pageants, followed this black-haired, big-mouthed man through the streets of Dublin; and from moving lorries, drawn by ribboned horses, Dubliners saw, in costume-clad figures, Cuchullain fighting Ferdiah at the Ford, two lifelong friends slicing up each other; St. Patrick, dear saint of our Isle, episcopally majestic, calmly showing all the snakes in Ireland the nearest way to the sea; white-bearded Brian Boru, the brave, at prayer in his tent at Clontarf, with the beaten, bloody Brodar and his men lifting its flap, about to enter and turn him into a dream of Gerontius; Tone, Simms, and Russell on the top of Cave hill, outside of Belfast, taking the oath of the United Irishmen; Private Patrick Sheehan, gone blind serving England in the trenches before Sebastopol, and when he found that he was blind, the tears began to flow, and he longed for even a pauper's grave in the Glen of Aherlow; Reynardine, an outlawed man in a land forlorn, who scorned to turn and fly, keeping the cause of freedom safe on the mountains of Pomeroy; seven-foot Kelly of Killann, leading his shelmaliers and Bargy men to take New Ross at the point of the pike; the dark-eyed, brown-skinned, barefooted West awaking to remember again how swift before the Connaught clan, the Normans' flight through Ardrahan; the Poor Old Woman high on the cliffs of Moher watching the sails of the French fleet drawing nigh to the port of Killala; Sean O'Farrell throwing his pike to his shoulder at the rising of the moon; Geoffrey Keating writing his history of Ireland in a cave deep in a Tipperary glen, the redcoats searching for him all round about it; Lord Ardilaun presenting to the Dublin Corporation the title-deeds of St. Stephen's Green for the use and recreation of the citizens and their heirs for ever; and Dark Rosaleen high on her golden throne, with a flask of wine from the royal Pope in her right hand, and a jug of Spanish ale in her left one.

And following hard after these gallant shows, marching forward through a sea of drums, a never-ending, never-ending fading into faintness, then slowly growing again, till the thunder rolled through every street, shaking life into all looking out of every window, came Guinness lorries and Cantrell & Cochrane lorries packed with all kinds of genuine things made of Irish materials by Irish labour, whole and undefiled: a jar of Bewley & Draper's ink as high and as big as an upright tower of Pisa; all manner of wedding frocks, mantles, morning gowns, evening wraps, négligés and disabilities, including holy vestments, the whole of them forming a sparkling rainbow of Dublin poplin and tabinet; a full-rigged ship, the sails of glistening Lisburn and Belfast linen, their whiteness sprinkled with the bright blue of the flax blossom; an altar candle, big as Nelson's Pillar; brooms and brushes from Varian's, each big enough to sweep the Dublin tide out; a lorry shaped to represent a Viking boat, the shields hanging by its side made of Bakecob's biscuits; a papier-mâché boot, big as a house, shining like a nugget, beside a jar of blacking big enough to hide the forty thieves, advertised Erin Go Bragh boot polish; a mountain of prayer- and hymn-books, carefully calculated so as to keep the Irish people going for ages, made by Jack & Jills; a cigarette, large as a liner's funnel, beside a placard saying, Smoke Irish Tobacco, and Die Dreaming No More; a pyramid of jars filled with aromatic boiled sweets from Lemon's of Suckville Street; a lorry decorated with galleries of spiders' webs, all mathematically made from thousands of rosary beads strung together to make aheenagons, dohagons, three-agons, caharagons, coogagons, shayagons, shoctagons, ochtagons, neeagons, and dyehagons, each set made by Irish hands from the primest horn from the heads of the purest cattle of Tara, Mt. Slemish, and the Isle of the Blest; enough to make accord of prayer from that day to the one when Gabriel would blow his blast to lift us all up to strict attention, eyes right, and salute your superior officer.

Tableau after tableau showed Ireland relying on herself alone, but

Sean felt as he looked at the display that the show lacked a model of a cow giving a ceaseless stream of milk, a pig manacled in its own sausages, a sheep hidden in its own wool, and a fat hen solving perpetual motion in the endless laying of eggs. Lemons and oranges were in heaps outside of many shops, griddle bread in the windows, slabs of Chester cake were in every kid's hand, and a stick of striped rock sugarstick in every kid's pocket, for the street sides, the windows, the pillars, monuments, eaves, and roof ridges were packed with people watching all the stir and gay commotion flowing by them, and their ears were full of the roll from a thousand drums, as the contingents marched to the place of assembly.

In front went two horsemen bearing a long banner stretching from one pathway to the other, wording a warning in red and green letters that the Irish were to Burn Everything Except English Coal. Before the warning marched a rank of drummers giving a roll every fifty yards they walked, and behind these marched a rank of trumpeters armed with barr booeys, war horns of the Fenians, who blew a flourish on them every other hundred yards, a blast that turned the call of the bucina into a squeak from a tin whistle, for their blast blew in every window, and shot in every door that hadn't been already opened. Other major and minor slogans were shouted by sections of the marching host, one crying, Ireland Divided, Ireland Down; another, Righteous Men Must Fake Our Land a Nation Once Again; another, Banish Every Whore Out of the Isle of Saints and Scholars; another — a temperance section called the Holy Thirst — Guinness Is BAD for You; the Gaelic League carried, A Country Without a Language, A Country Without a Soul. A sturdy fellow in green shawl and saffron kilt shouted, The war-cries and the slogans are here: the gun peals will follow. O'Donnell rides again in the glens; O'Driscoll rises from the waves of Cleena; Sean O'Farrell is sharpening his pike; Parnell walks the city's streets, and waits; the deer are coming back to Ireland — a stag, a doe, and a fawn; the horned stag with his head high!

And so, in the midst of the shouting, the call of the barr booeys, the insistent roll of the drums, they marched on, they stepped out together; stepped out and stepped on, as if, at last, they stepped on England, every head high, every foot firm; fixed in front was every glance, moving in a wide advance, like the deer on mountain heather, thronging men and thronging women stepped along and stepped together.

Here on the Dublin streets, in this gay and resolute procession, mingled the flowing of many streams of old, unhappy, far-off things and battles long ago — Kilmainham Treaty, Home Rule Bill, Coercion Acts, one after another, No Rent Movement, Reform Association, Land League, Cattle Driving Movement, Sarsfield's Ride, Treaty Stone, the Wild Geese, Penal Days, with minor echoes of the spirit shown at Crécy, Torres Vedras, Lucknow, the Crimea, Spion Kop, the plains of Flanders, and the battle of the Diamond; and, if one listened carefully, one could hear the yell of the Connaught Rangers, the Faug A ballagh Boys, and the wild shout of the old toughs, the Dublin Fusiliers: all that had jostled each other, fighting for the first place, mingled, and flowed into one broad stream pouring through the streets of the town of the ford of the hurdles.

Gorgeous and stimulating were the costumes of the pipe bands, some with saffron kilts and green mantles, others with green kilts and saffron shawls; Armagh's beating Banagher for colour, for no one of them was dressed alike, and they took, by general consent, the head of the procession: one wore red kilt and blue shawl, another blue kilt and red shawl; one wore green kilt and white shawl, another white kilt and green shawl; one wore yellow kilt and black shawl, while his mate wore a yellow shawl and black kilt; for Francis Joseph Biggar had impressed on the mind of Ireland that that was the way the Gael usually dressed in the days of long ago, beyond the misty space of twice a thousand years, when in Erin old there dwelt a mighty race, taller than Roman spears, conclusively proving, if proof were needed, that we were on the right track, and doing nobly.

But there was a fly in the amber; a Jonah in the midst of the good men marching; one who had sinned against the consolidated spirit of the hour. D. P. Moran, editor of *The Leader*, had, in his weekly journal, argued against leaving the cult of the King to the Unionists, calling his campaign, Collar the King; and because all the young men of Irish Ireland had bitterly opposed this singular advice, which had the silent approval of the bishops and a crowd of clergy, D. P. Moran, in a bitter article, shouted that the tin-pike men, and hillmen, and give-me-a-rifle-and-let-me-away men, and all who even gave them a pinch of salt to put on an odd potato, should be clapped into jail, to keep them out of mischief.

Another, Jay Jay Farrell, an alderman, who owned two cinema houses in the one street in Dublin, had voted, in the heart of Irish hospitality — some said he was trying to hook a title — for an official welcome to an English king; and he, too, was under the sibilant and salty hatred of the physical force party. He had received a warning telling him this act was his finale, and he would be wise to keep a safe distance between himself and the marching Gaels. But the alderman said in the papers that he defied the fretful Fenians, and that he would go, would go, and fix himself in the midst of the marchers.

So Sean felt a little uneasy as he moved about Stephen's Green, the place of assembly, helping to get the contingents into their rightful positions, his heart aglow with the colour and the life and the beating of victorious drums. Stewards, on foot and on bicycles, were rushing hither and thither, receiving instructions from Sean T. O'Kelly, a curious, quiet little figure with a calmly querulous voice, provoking embarrassment in Sean to see him among the old and new fluttering symbols of an awakened people, and he tricked out in a glossy black frock-coat, striped trousers, with a glittering top-hat on his head, the new Irish round and top of sovereignty.

Curious, isn't it, thought Sean, to see the broad blue arm-band, with Ard Mhaoir, high steward, in gold lettering on the dark sleeve of a frock-coat? Didn't seem right. At first he thought he was dreaming; but sorra a dream it was. He noticed, too, that those already marshalled didn't like their eyes to fall on the frock-coated figure, and when they accidentally did, they turned them away at once, full of embarrassment, bewilderment, and wonder. But Shawn Tee went about his business as head steward as if God had created him in a frock-coat, in top-hat created He him.

—Eh, Sean, whispered the tram-conductor, holding Sean by the skirt of his coat, looka that fella doin' the big with the top-hat an' frock-coat! Where did he break out from?

—Shush! said Sean. That's Shawn Tee O'Kelly, Chairman of the Gaelic League Dublin Committee and High Steward of today's gathering.

—It's queer, said the conductor, an' it gives me a pang to see th' like of that on a day like this. I see a glint of a thing here I don't like. It isn't natural. It's a dictum that's dangerous. It doesn't augur well for th' future, Sean, me son. Jasus! Looka what's comin' now!

Out of Dawson Street, into the gathering procession, surrounded by constables, came an open carriage, slowly, holding one man only, a man with raven-black hair and moustache decorating a ghastly, handsome white face, twitching convulsively with the fever of nervousness and wounded pride.

The frock-coat nodded the top-hat to the trumpeter of the day, the call sounded, and the procession was on the move. Some of the contingents had passed, when the police surged forward, breaking

through the marchers, holding those behind in check till the movement of the front contingents allowed enough space for the carriage
to swing into the procession, the ghastly white face of the alderman
just visible through the crowd of surrounding helmets of the foot
police who had mounted men prancing at each side of them, all of
whom kept their eyes partly turned towards the ground, for they felt
a loss of dignity by being forced to march in a procession unsanctified
by Dublin Castle.

—Good God! ejaculated the conductor to Sean, is it going along
we are in dumb denouncement with this Castle hack and his Castle
cossacks! Didn't I tell you I didn't like the omen of the frock-coat and
the top-hat? Are we goin' to let our solemn pageant of the past to be
inlaid with the insult, an' drag it through a maze of sthreets to th'
sound of pipe, drum, trumpet, an' clarinet, in th' midst of banners,
plumes, badges, an' all manner of variegated testimonies of our
hero-crowded histhory?

There was a curious hush all along those parts of the procession
following, and going before, the alderman's landau and the constables. There wasn't a murmur from those in the procession or from
those gathered along the side-walk as the marchers moved by, only
the tramp-tramp-tramp of feet, from which came a vision of many
helmets, and now and again a glimpse of the dead-white face of the
man sitting tense and bolt-upright in the carriage.

At the upper end of Grafton Street, close by the stone laid down
years ago that some day was to blossom into a Wolfe Tone memorial,
the uneasy landau suddenly halted; the crowds on the side-walks fell
back, for a thick column of hurlers were standing before the carriage,
halting it, and those in the procession behind it, right before the great
banner saying

Start not, Irish-born man, if you're to Ireland true,
We heed not creed nor class nor clan, we've hearts and hands for
you,

while the advanced part of the procession moved on some way to
give the hurlers room to act. It was plain to all that Alderman J. J.
Farrell wouldn't be let go farther on the way with advancing Ireland.
It was plain, too, that the police were feeling uncomfortable. Hurleys
were dangerous weapons: a quick upward jab of the boss would
smash in the hardiest face; a low swing would shatter a leg bone; and
a downward swing would scatter the brains out of the fort of the
sturdiest skull going — so the police were very uneasy. Those hurlers
were tough guys, though some of them were civil servants, grocers,

curates, school teachers, customs officers, solicitors' clerks, and a good many tougher ones from the farms, the railways, and the docks.

A police superintendent, dressing his face in a jocular smile, went up to the leader of the hurlers, and with a faint salute from a hand, elegantly gloved, said, We find ourselves, sir, in a very unfortunate and delicate situation, which, as you are aware, is none of our seeking. We are simply charged with the protection of a Dublin citizen who fancies himself threatened, and who insists on being allowed to participate in the public procession of a purely non-political organisation; and who wishes, he says, by participation, to testify his approval of those sentiments embodied in the published aims and objects of the organisation now quite legitimately and legally employed in their promotion in a most commendable manner, if you will allow me to say so; and it is very regrettable that circumstances have forced this unfortunate *contretemps* upon us both, though to you as a sensible man, and, evidently, groomed into responsibility of leading men, it must be apparent that I and my men are here but to carry out our duty; that no aggressive or provocative reason can be implied regarding our presence, and that we are here only to anticipate, and so prevent, a possible breach of the peace — ahem!

The hurlers' leader, with his stick on his shoulder, stood like a stock till the officer had ended his passionless speech, looking him fairly in the eyes; then he answered him never a word, but stepped past him through the police cordon to stand close to the open landau, where he stretched forth his right arm towards a side street, opposite to the direction the procession was taking, and said in a deadly and very clear voice to the quivering man in the carriage, That is your way, that way is your way; Ireland casts you out of her sight; Ireland casts you out of her possessions; that way is your way — go!

There was a silent few moments in which could be heard the panting heart of the frightened man, paler than ever now, with a look of timid hatred glaring in his black eyes; then the driver of the landau bent backwards from his seat, his face, too, getting haggard with anxiety, to whisper to the lonely shaking soul, tense on the blue-cushioned seat, Ara, take th' advice of a thrue man, sir, and slip out of all this savage hilarity, an' show be your ready an' dignified departure that you refuse to cock them up with your civilised attendance. Give a cheery back of your hand to them, man, or it's a tangled mesh of blood an' bone we'll all be before th' day ripens into another hour!

Again the hurlers' leader stretched his arm in the direction of the side street, and said quietly and in a clear voice, That is your way, and the way of your Dublin Castle consorts!

In the shimmer of the sunlight the darkly-uniformed police stood motionless, listening to nothing, but hearing all, their eyes watching their superintendent; his eyes watching the hurler; all calm, looking unconcerned, but constantly taking the measure of the hurling men, and wondering how sinewy the arms were hidden under the coloured jerseys; and, occasionally, Sean saw a furtive hand go up to press a helmet deeper down over a vulnerable and anxious skull; while the superintendent stood there, silent, watching, an uneasy smile on his rather handsome face, a daintly-gloved hand flicking another glove against the palm of a bare one.

The driver stretched himself further back from his high seat in front, getting his top-hatted head as close as he could to the twitching face of the alderman, to say, I don't want to push me words into your federated understandin', sir, but, looka, sir, you're only riskin' your life an' limb without rhyme or reason. What is it but only an as I roved out of a show, adultered cleverly with a few drum-beats an' a canopy o' coloured banners! Say th' word, an' be turnin' th' horse's head you can escape into a sensible an' sober world. Say th' word, sir, an' we'll be off outa this panicky pomp; a nod, now, an' we'll baffle them outa th' row they're seekin'. That's th' ticket, sir, he added joyously as the alderman gave a faint nod towards the side street, as he tightened his grasp of the reins. Get outa th' way, there, you! he bawled at the hurler, turning his horse in a curvetting semicircle; with the police dodging their big feet from the crunching wheels, he slid the landau into the side street and went away at a quarter-gallop, the constables trotting alongside, with the superintendent hurrying after on the side-walk in as dignified a way as the speed allowed him. At a command from their leader, the hurlers swung into the side street too, facing after the disappearing carriage. The leader raised a hand; with a roll of drums, a band broke into the swing of *Clare's Dragoons*, and the procession of Ireland's history and resolution moved forward again, having purged itself of a murky, stinging stain.

Here come the carriages holding the neatly-clad forms, trim beards, set faces, sober-hatted, silently-jubilant, respectomissima members of the Gaelic League's Central Executive, the Coiste Gnotha, their whole demeanour making all men aware of their non-political, non-sectarian natures, each bluffed out with a pride of his own, for the money the crowd was giving was rattling into the collecting-boxes, the chink-chink of the falling coins loud above the methodical medley of the rolling drums.

In a leading carriage rode Dr. Douglas De Hyde, with a pleasant little branch of bells in his hand, and a barr buadh a thousand times the size of a bucina on his lap, and he looking, in his innocent happiness, like a bigger Boy Blew. By his side sat a mauve-soutaned, crimson-girdled Domestic Prelate of the Vatican, who laughed, and slapped the Doctor affectionately on the back all the way along, calling him a jolly good fellow, and appealing for confirmation from a tinker and a flapper fairy who sat on the opposite seat. Beside them, on a prancing white horse, went Oona Ni Merrily, with rings on her fingers and bells on her toes, followed by Mary Ni Hayadawn, in a pony and trap, her tender voice ever calling on the Irish people to come to these yellow, white, and green sands, catch hands, and sing, The cuckoolin is icumen in in Gaedhilge. Next came the biggest carriage Dublin could supply. In it were two men, the sweat rolling off them, counting the money the collectors were pouring in on to the floor of the vehicle, with Stiffun Barrett, the official treasurer, holding an umbrella over them to keep the sun off their heads so that they could count calmly an tawn bo cooly. Then came Eoin Mac Neill aswing in a sedan-chair, carried by an Ulster man, Connaught man, Leinster man, and a Munster man, one at each corner. The grille in front of the chair was closed to keep the sun out, the panels were decorated with a profusion of higheroglyphical reports from the annals of the four musters, and a placard on each door-panel warned all whom it would concern to open the door softly. The next carriage held Edward Martyn, and a great banner went before it having on it, in mighty letters, the Martyn motto of I am in My Sleep, and Don't Waken Me. Trudging along in a wide space by himself came Padruig Mac Pirais, head down, dreaming a reborn glory for Ireland in every street-stone his foot touched; followed by vis-à-vis, landau, brougham, and victoria, containing the rest of the Central Executive, sleek and sleepy-looking, crooning quietly to themselves, We are all nodding, nod, nod, nodding; we are all nodding, so Irish and so fey!

Oh! here we are now! Here he comes; here's the boyo, the greatest champion Ireland's language has, who hardly knows a word of it himself: make way there, yous, keep back, keep back, give him space there, the one who said tin-pike men and hillmen should be clapped into jail to keep them out of mischief; who says that the influence of England's majesty shouldn't be left to protestant sourfaces, and that the catholics must collar the King; an eminent man, a sure sage, with almost all the priests applaudin', make way, there — silence!

Here he comes, D. P. Moran, editor of *The Leader*, in a vis-à-vis, the name of the paper on a big poster pasted round the tall hat of the driver. Here's the champion of the Catholic Association, formed to link up in a commercial and industrial Sacred Heart Sodality for all the middle-class catholics who had been blessed by God with the responsibility of a cheque-book so that they might do down the commercial and industrial giving-glory-to-God-in-the-highest pro-testants who, too, had been blessed with the responsibility of other cheque-books. Sir Gaelahad Moran had gone forth to the battle with his lance of L S Defender of the Faith, with his shield of four beautiful green fields, with the coins of the realm, proper, superimposed on a roman cross, gules, under the motto of *In hoc signum pinchit*. But Moran was worsted in the fight, and had to flee from the field, leaving the protestants to give thanks to God in a special doxology for their deliverance.

D. P. Moran, proud on his seat in the vis-à-vis, wore a sober suit of Irish tweed, his head was nicely crowned in a bowler hat, and a poplin tie of a dark green gave a gayer note to his sensible austerity that went well with the look of determined wisdom on his plumpish face. On the seat opposite sat a man, crowned, too, with a bowler hat, who was nursing a Brian Boru harp on his knee, along which his agile fingers twinkled up and down the silver strings, Moran trying to appear as if he were listening to the one and only harp that once through Tara's hall was heard, now evoking again the pride of former days, that glory's thrill was felt once more, and hearts again beat high with hope, and felt that pulse encore. Fine he looked, sunk deep down into the blue cushions of the carriage, and all was sunny and all was sure, and all was happy and all was pure.

Suddenly, from the faery Land of Erewhon, appeared the damned hurlers again, who, at a sign from their leader, caught the bridle of the carriage's horse, and took it with such a sweep from the moving procession that no hesitating halt of a moment was made by the marchers, hardly half a hundred of them knowing that D. P. Moran had been juggled from their midst out of the pomp and all the glory, and but a few saw the bowler hats sticking up from the bowl of the carriage fading away down a side street, surrounded by the silent hurling men, a faint ting-a-ling-a-ling-ting of *Brian Boru's March* stealing faintly back to them as they went marching along.

So the drums rolled, the bugles blew, the banners waved as Ireland's history and Ireland's hope went along College Green, defiantly passing Trinity College with the head up and a battling swing of the shoulders; the rolling drums shaking the doors and rattling the windows of big banks, brokers' premises, insurance offices, business houses, high-class drapery, shoe, and jewellery shops, and court photographers, all shuttered tight, and silently contemptuous of all the stir and tremble parading before them all today; opulently careless of the power germinal that thrilled the sunny air with drum-beat and bugle-call.

In that same hour, or maybe an hour or two after, the city was draped again in the colours of excitement and bristling fervour, for Dr. Douglas Hyde was off to the United States to tell the great news to Texas, Arizona, Washington, D.C., the two Carolinas, Virginia, Pennsylvania, New York, Salt Lake City, and, especially, that great community, happy and prosperous, who lived in a wide district called Tuxedos, the place of the elegant evening coats, where the Doctor was to tell of Ireland's honour, nobility, and undying devotion to her ancient language; but, above all, to rake in the needful, argent and or, at all costs. The hurlers of Sean's club were chosen to be the body-guard around the coach bearing him to Kingsbridge Station, *en route* for Cove in Cork, and thence across the Atlantic to the broad bosom of the sea-divided Gael. And so Sean, in full dress of the club's jersey, of hooped bands of alternate dark blue and dark green, walked beside the protestant Chief of the Gael, in the midst of thousands of flaming torches carried before and behind the carriage, followed by all the hurling and football clubs of the city and its suburbs. Horsemen headed the cavalcade, carrying the Stars and Stripes, the French Tricolour, and the green banner of popular Ireland; for then the green, white, and orange symbol was known only to the members of the Irish Republican Brotherhood and their few friends. Everywhere the drums beat again their lusty rolls, making the bright stars in the sky quiver, and bands blew Ireland's past into every ear, and called forth her history of the future.

—A great man an' a fine soul he is, be God! said a hurler next to Sean. He could have papered the walls of Castle Hyde with the addhresses he got at th' Gresham Hotel before he left. Were you listening to what he said? The Gaelic League, says he, is a strictly non-political organisation, and so it is the strongest political party in Ireland! Did the world ever hear a grander sayin'? I'm tellin' you, it's himself that'll make the stir for Eireann in the New Island! An Hideach abu!

On we all went slow along the mean-looking flanks of Anna Livia Plurabelle singing songs of Eireby by the dozen that would rouse up even the stone outside Dan Murphy's door. But when we came to the station, lo and behold, there was a crowd of police barring the way in to the station platform. Were we down-hearted? No! So, with a roar of, Shoulder to shoulder, Gaels! the hurlers and footballers, forming a phalanx, rushed forward, swept the horde of constables off their feet, and after a few breathless moments Sean, standing beside Donal Mac Rory O'Murachadha, was beside the edge of the platform in front of a great cheering crowd.

There was the big beaming face of Hyde, topped by the globular skull, with the bushy moustache like an abandoned bird's nest, filling up a carriage window, nodding, nodding to the excited crowd, while a band outside played *When shall the day break in Eirinn* with extreme dignity and unction.

—A bit of an oul' cod, the same Hyde, whispered Donal, nudging Sean to take notice. Look at him: oh, wouldn't he like to number on the Coiste Gnotha a few dukes, earls, viscounts, barons, and a host of right honourables! For the people, maybe; with the people, maybe; but not of the people. The Fenian Brotherhood waste their time trying to trick him into being a revolutionary even for an hour. Jasus! Listen to his Deunta in Eirinn Irish! Harsh as the crow of a worn-out old cock. Listen to Father O'Leary, and then listen to him. It doesn't come natural to the poor man, and I'm afraid it never will. He couldn't be an O'Rahaille, a Donnchadh Ruadh Macnamara, or even a Colm Wallis if he lived to a hundred. Look at him, with his arm nearly round Father O'Franticain's neck! Isn't he the one that's at home with the clergy!

—But, Donal, isn't he the one who pulled the Irish language out of the gutter and set it in the sky — a star again?

—He pinned it to the wall of a New University — or rather Hickey did — so that it could blink through the windows of Trinity College; but to set it in the sky, Sean, it's not in him to do it. That can be done only by the power and will of a free people, and your grand, gusty-mannered Hyde will always prefer having a shot at a snipe than having a shot at a Saxon.

Sean was shocked that any Gael should speak this drab way about such a man as Hyde. He couldn't understand it.

—Oh, be fair, Donal, he said. At least remember what Hyde has done as a poet in the creation of an Irish literature.

—He has created nothing in Irish literature, said Donal tersely, and he isn't, and never was, a poet. As an editor of what others greater than he has done, I'll grant you he's a pleasant and encouraging echo; then he cleans the dust of indifference from many a star; but when he signs himself, he coaxes no music into his song. Look, there! He's waving a last farewell!

The guard's green flag was waving, the engine gave a few steamy snorts, strained at the carriages, and began to slide out of the station through a storm of cheers. Hyde was high on Ireland's shoulders, and his carriage window framed the big head, the bunchy moustache, the staring eyes, draining down the last drop of the mighty farewell and godspeed, till distance hid the crowd, and stilled the stormy, sweltering roar of the gathered Gaels.

SONG OF A SHIFT

IRELAND had become again the Woeman of the Piercing Wail. Every wall in Dublin was a wall of weeping. Cork ran a high fever of hatred, and Galway was foaming at the mouth; Limerick was just lying down prostrate. It was awful, for the piercing wail sent flying the wild duck from the marsh, the wild goose from the bog, and the wild swan from the lake; away frantic the lot of them flew, far to the banks of the Nile, the rushes of the Euphrates, and the snows of the North Pole. It was awful, for the virgin statues in every niche lifted their blue or crimson alabaster petticoats over their heads to hide their shame, to cover their ears, while they wept no end. It was an outrage on their innocence, their quietude, and their breathless adoration. Statues of the Holy Fathers, Martyred Bishops and Martyred Matrons, and all the golden crowd of blessed saints, strained at their clay stands, trying to lep off to Rome for a bull of excommunication against those who had stained their sense of decorum with a wild defilement. Regular Orders and Simple Ones in the Order of St. Peter ran this way and that, and Father Malone lost his new Sunday hat, calling on all the fightful — and they were many, only a little less than the sands of the sea for number — to denounce and dismember, disjoint and distender, this sable-faced, lying offender, fresh, pagan-souled culture, decay in its heart, mocking all the eternities at home with our people. The streets were a thunder of boots running swiftly in and out again, vast brotherhoods, and sisterhoods too, from the east to the west, from the north to the south; Ulster men, Connaught men, Leinster men, Munster men, true-hearted Irishmen, Irishmen all, rallied round the standard of purity, led by the Vigilance Committee, led by Father Malone, led by Monsignor Malone, led by the right reverend John, Bishop Malone, hurried in haste to assemble and deny and assert and condemn and support the things said by Father Malone and Monsignor Malone and the Bishop Malone about this grievous and insulting thing that had hopped in among them silently, and without warning, or a second's preparation, threatening to do in an hour, or at most in a day and a half, what the British Government had failed to do in the last seven hundred years and a half, since Easter was a week old.

Hearing the alarums, the sound of the sennets, the mighty tramp of human feet in the distance, wondering a lot and frightened a little, the Viceroy poked his head out of a top window of the Vice-regal Lodge and looked down on the stout police sergeant standing on the lawn below, his ear cocked towards where the noise came from.

—What's happening? who's making all that noise — d'ye hear me, you down there?

—Divil a know, sir, I know, sir.

—Well, y'ought to know. What are you fed for? No, don't stir. Stay put. Keep your baton nice and loose. Something serious is happening.

—Be th' sound of it, I'd say, sir, the same, sir. More in it than maybe we know, sir.

—We don't know anything, man, said the Viceroy peevishly. Are all the rest of the boys on the key veev?

The answer of yessir was almost lost in the distant rumble of running feet, rising to the sound of surly thunder, and the shouting grew into a storm of anger like a forest of wild beasts growling together.

—What is it they are shouting? said the Viceroy, his face whitening. Don't you know? can't you hear, man?

—Seems like something like sing, sir.

—Like what? sing who; sing what; sing where? Be a little more explicit, sergeant.

Yeats!

—What's that now? Didn't you hear? Weren't you listening? Don't you realise this may mean the calling-out of the military? Sounds as if they were having another fight, doesn't it?

—I wouldn't like to say yes, sir, an' daren't venture to say no, sir.

—They're not coming in this direction, are they, d'ye think, sergeant?

—I daren't venture to say no, sir, and I wouldn't care to say yes, sir.

—Well, you gobeen, venture down to the bend of the road and find out what it's all about — quick!

The Viceroy stretched from the window to watch the stout sergeant running hard and stiff down the road, through the sad and soaking grass, by the bare beech-trees, till he was lost beyond the bend of the road; then his wondering eyes turned to where the shouting came from, and where a cloud of dust showed the anger of it. And here was the big thick of a policeman back again, puffing as if his last breath was leaving him.

—Well, he asked, is it peace or war, or what?

—I dunno right, sir, for all I met wouldn't wait to tell; but one of them said that if only his fist ever comes within reach of some Yeats's bake, he'd give him a homer, an' all I could get out of th' others was a shout of sing and a shout of shift, or something.

—Shift? Shift what? shift who? shift where? Is it making fun of me you are, man, or what?

—Wait a minute, sir; can't you listen, sir? Wait till I tell you — a woman said he was a kind of poet.

—Who did she say was a kind of poet?

—Shift or sing or someone, sir; I dunno which; and they said they'd hang him on a sour apple-three, sir.

—Hang who? hang what, man?

—Shift or sing or someone — I dunno right, sir.

—What nonsense are you talking? You dunno! Why would they want to hang a shift on a sour apple-tree?

—Ara, how th' hell do I know? Aren't they up to any divilment when they're in the mood!

—Is there a constable behind every bush, sergeant, as per the orders of the day? asked the Viceroy briskly.

—Oh, be God, ay, sir; behind every respectably-sized bush there's a constable concealed an' crouchin'.

—Yes, yes, said the Viceroy testily; but are they awake, on the alert, and lively?

—Ready to dive on disordher, sir, th' way a dhrone would dive on a queen bee.

—Keep them so, sergeant. I'm going to bed now, and don't call me if anything happens; and he closed the window with a bang and shot the socket home, for one couldn't be too careful.

Sean found himself in the midst of bawling clergy, professors and students of Cork, Dublin, and Galway colleges, thousands of sacred confraternities, wide-minded boyos of the Catholic Young Men's Association, the boys of Kilkenny and the boys of Wexford, side-car drivers and cabmen of the Anti-taxi Association, brimming with zeal for Ireland's holy reputation.

Puzzled and bewildered, he was pushed here and pushed there by Muldoon the Solid Man, the men of the West, Ireland's gallant hurling men, and Gaelic Leaguers foaming at the mouth, all shouting
Shift!

Jostled he was by Mary of Argyle, Mother mo Chree, Willie Reilly and his colleen bawn, several fine old English gentlemen with hearts of oak, a soldier and a man, the little Alabama coon, Uncle Jefferson with his gal, a high-born lady, Dolly Gray and Sweet Marie, all yelling
Shift!

Shoved hither and thither he was by Shamus O'Brien, Kelly and Burke and Shea, Clare's dragoons, Lesbia with her beaming eye, the Exile of Erin, the Lily of Killarney, Slattery's mounted fut, Father O'Flynn, the Rose of Tralee, the Athlone landlady, Eileen Allanna with Eileen Aroon, the man who struck O'Hara, Nell Flaherty's drake, Daisy Bell arm in arm with Thora, the man who broke the bank at Monte Carlo, Kitty of Coleraine with the two little girls in blue, their hearts bowed down with weight of woe, but still keeping their tails up, all of them shrieking
Shift!

Sean sturdily elbowed his way from the crowd to where The Poor Old Woman was standing by the kerb. He gripped her gently by the thin old arm, asking, What's it all about, mother?

—What's what all about, me son? she asked wonderingly, after letting a yell out of her that sent a quiver down Sean's spine.

—All this coarse shouting in the heart of the city's streets; all this running about of many hot and hasty feet?

—Aw, sorra know I know, son, what it's about. It's no new thing to see them runnin' round an' yellin' for they know not what.

—But you're running round and yelling with the rest of them yourself.

—An' if I am aself, what signifies? D'ye want me to be th' one odd outa th' many? It's a bit o' fun anyhow. She caught her poor thin skirt up in her poor thin hands, and caracoled along, shouting, The dirty-minded minsthrels! Belchin' out in th' sthricken faces of our year in an' year out innocence things no decent-minded individual would whisper even into his own ear! Why don't they tell us of the beautiful things we all love so well, th' dirty, dirty dastards!

Leaving her mouthing, Sean hurried to catch up with Muldoon the Solid Man, and taking him by the plump arm, asked, Who are those there in fine array on the top of Nelson's Pillar, and who is he with the domy brow, clad in the coloured gown and black cap of some ancient and learned university, whose voice is pealing out over the green hills of holy old Ireland?

Muldoon the Solid Man looked up, looked long, caught Sean's arm, and dragged him from the crowded shouting thoroughfare into a quieter side street.

—Didn't you know who that was? He bent down and brought his fat whiskered face close to Sean's, and went on, hoarsely, That's the greatest mind Ireland has today; though goin' back to Mount Sinai, fresh as a daisy still. Defender Fido Finnigan. Whisht, he's speakin'. Hush, silence there, th' whole o' yous, an' listen to his tale of woe! Ah, me sweet Mcgennis, a herald angel in a cap an' gown! Are yous all afther hearin' what he's afther sayin'? Help o' sinners! No sittin' on a stile for him. Up on one o' th' seven pillars o' wisdom, sayin', proclaimin', *Declanda est syngestoria et defendi senserationem Hibernicombactoerin.* Ah, me sweet yourself! Th' *vox Magennicensorensis* is a *vox pupuli.* Him an' his disciples'll sweep the counthry clean. There they are backin' him up: Coffey, with his old coat and the light of other days around him; Fearon, wrapped in the ould plaid shawl, sitting in mother's old armchair; Camac and Williams with letters afther their names; and Conn the Shaughraun, Arra-na-pogue, the minsthrel boy home from the wars, Joxer Daly, Maisie Madigan, impudent Barney O'Hea, the village blacksmith in his Sunday best, Roddy the Rover, Louis J. Walsh, the Brehon, with the eloquent L. C. Dempsey, Mick McQuaid and Kit Kulkin, rowled in the seven howly ordhers, Miles-na-Copaleen, Edward Martyn, and the Pope's brass band, all set to uproot with agitated, holy fingers every *harum maculatum* that tried to grow in the country. Ah, me pet, me choice, me soul-man, me sweet Mcgennis, Ireland's Saturday night's saviour, sure Hell shivers with cold when it hears you speakin'! And Muldoon the Solid Man fell on his knees to offer up prayer on prayer for the repose of the souls of those poor Irish who had passed away before Mcgennis came.

So, unable to get more out of him, Sean hurried off to his branch of the Gaelic League where he was secretary, teacher, and charwoman, coming early on class nights to clean the place up, light the fire, get out the books, and arrange the blackboard. He would find out there the cause of this great cry of Shift, and why the city was aflame with the thoughts of holy reprobation. When he got there, there was a great crowd waiting for him to open the door, all tense and talkative with indignation. There was his friend, the tram conductor, fretting, and forcing words of wrath on all who listened.

—Some blasted little theatre or other has put on a play by a fellow named Singe or Sinje or something, a terrible play, helped by another boyo named Yeats or Bates or something, said to be a kind of a poet or something, of things no-one can understand, an' he was to blame for it all, assisted be some oul' one or another named Beggory or something, who was behind the scene eggin' them on in their foul infamity. A terrible play, terrible! There was ructions in the theatre when th' poor people staggered into the knowledge of what was bein' said! What was th' play about? Amn't I afther tellin' you it was a terrible thing; a woeful, wanton play; bittherin', bittherin', th'n, th'n th' bittherest thing th' bittherest enemy of Ireland could say agin' her!

—Ordher! shouted Sean, thumping his fist on the table. Sit down, and let one at a time speak. Now what did this man say in his play to soil and censure Ireland?

—Listen, Sean, said the conductor hotly, I don't know what he said in th' play, an' I don't care; but anyone'll tell you he made a go at every decent consignment left living in th' counthry. With purpling face, he lifted his voice to shout, I tell you th' Abbey Theatre'll have to be torn down stone be stone, if it's built of that, an' brick be brick, if it's made o' that, without warnin', before one of us snatches another second's sleep!

—Ordher, ordher! shouted Sean, till we get this thing clear and straight for a fair judgment. Now where is this theatre you are yelling about?

—Didn't I tell you before I didn't know where it was, except it's somewhere near th' Liffey. For myself, I never clapped eyes on it, thank God, an' never heard of it till this outrage was flung into the face of modesty-honourin' Ireland. Where is it, is it? Stuck in some peculiar place, I'll go bail.

—Well, who is this Singe or Sinje, or whatever his name may be, and where does he come from?

—There'll be desperate work done if they don't stop this thing, shouted a member standing beside the door, if they don't banish this black thing from before our smilin' Irish eyes for ever! We don't know who this Sinje is; some foreigner paid to say th' things he said.

—And what did he say exactly? asked Sean.

—It's not a matther of what he said, but of what everybody says he said, growled a voice from the right corner of the room.

—Let's get this discussion goin' in ordher, said a tall bearded man

whose left leg had been crippled by an attack of Skyatica, an' pass our
opinions with decorum. I propose that Aloysius McConkey, P.L.G.,
take the chair, as this is an occasion at which the virtue of Ireland is at
question; no fitter man could be head of the meeting, for he is specially
endowed to warn us, advise us, and invoke our antagonism to our
pitiless enemies, having every year, in wind, rain, frost, snow, thunder
and lightning, climbed, bareheaded and barefooted, up the rough,
flinty ways of Croagh Pathrick, Ireland's holy mountain, with but a
bite of coarse bread in a hip-pocket to keep life from leavin' him;
sayin' paternosters an' ave marias in thousands, head bent down, or
head held up; takin' off his trousers when he got within a mile of the
top, th' wind blowin' through his thin cotton shirt, devastating all th'
parts that modesty keeps covered, so that when he got to where th'
real devotion started, he was only fit to think of th' three last things,
death, judgment, an' Hell, open for sinners, shiverin' away from all
thought of earthly things, fires, hot soups, balls o' malt, mulled
porther, or th' hot presence of a desire for a woman, so that his groans
could be heard all over the fields of sweet Mayo, shaking the little
houses in Connemara, and waking up the deep sleepers in the houses
of the square of Galway with his singing of Oh day of mourning, see
fulfilled the prophets' warning, Heaven an' earth to cash is burning.
Who then could be better adopted to enunciate the way we are to
think in this great world crisis, and tell how to overcome this threat
to all near and dear and clear to us, by these vultures, these waggas
sagas, who scent out and feed gluttonously on corruption of mind and
morals; these waggas sagas who rave in a row and jabber in a chorus
about freedom of self-expression and art for art's sake: so says the
Irish Rosary, a magazine pregnant with the grace of God, with knowledge, and with good feeling to all men. I call on Aloysius McConkey,
our learned and beloved poor-law guardian, to tell us how to comport
ourselves in the fight against this Synge or Sinje, about whom, thank
God, we know next to nothing.

A little old man, oh, so old, a hundred and more if all was told, was
carried up to the head of the hall and gently set down into the chair.
His face was the colour of a shrivelled and well-faded lemon. His little
eyes saw no more than the shadows of men, and his ears heard little
more than a misty memory droning a last lullaby. He rapped his bony
knuckles on the table, and his squeaky voice mumbled, Now boys an'
girls, be quiet till I tell yous, for I'm really here as a delicate delegate
of the Young Men's Catholic Christian Cross Association————
  —Who kept his bloody public-house open on St. Pathrick's

Day? shouted a voice from the hall's centre.

—Ordher, ordher, there! shouted the bearded man. No politics, no politics!

—Never mind, went on the poor old man, bouseys will be bouseys. Well, as I was sayin' — what was I sayin'? Aw, yes: I was asked to speak to this Rich and Rare Branch of the League to put before yous the exthreme case of necessity of doin' something, all we can, what we must, if we're to be loyal to the principles of faith, hope, an' charity, here and now, without hesitation, not countin' the cost, takin' the blame, full-hearted, steady-willed, and clear-minded men, firmly resolved to counter with all our energy, force, an' world-renowned Irish courage, famous from Dunkirk to Belgrade; an' always an' ever prepared to face fearlessly the enemies at home and abroad, who sedulously, seditiously, and seductively endeavour, be night an' be day, to asperse, slandher, and generally defame that honour and fair pride and sweet modesty, thriple stars of effulgent illuminants shining from the forehead of Cathleen ni Houlihan; so, having said so much in explanation of the why, the wherefore, and the wherewithal for which we have come together, as thrue Gaels should, and do, and must, proceed to banish from our virgin verdant shores the anglis in herba that have crawled from the Keltic Twilight, when no-one was lookin', to spit from the air their venom into our enchanted eyes intent on gazin' up to where Gabriel, no, no, Michael, slew, no, no, overthrew th' dragon, the father of lies, enemy implacable of Eve's poor children, lost so long, asthray so often, an' flung them, no, no, him, into the outer darkness from which there is no returning, and no hope; so now that you all understand the thrue position, and are primed with the knowledge of what is, and of what is to be, I declare this meeting open————

—Who kept his bloody public-house open on St. Patrick's Day? shouted a voice from the back of the hall.

—Their myrmidians are even here, the old man went on, but we'll shift — I refuse to say shift, for we are here to shift the word shift from lips and ears of decent people — we'll remove them as we'll remove the others. Now I call on a member to voice in a resolution the irrevocable determination of all assembled to condemn, from first to last, the terrible things said be, be, what's-his-name, though it doesn't matter much, not at all, in the face of the desperate audacity of what has been done to knock about our world-admitted sanctity, exemplified in the one fact that an hour ago today I and my donah celebrated our diamond wedding in the church of the twelve pathrons, so that me and my wife, Jemima Mary Jane, being the proud parents of twenty-five children, two hundred and eleven grandchildren, and one hundred and twenty-nine great-grandchildren, making a great grand-total of three hundred and sixty-five souls, having body, shape, substance, and feeling, movement, density, and opacity, mingling with time, and measured in space, enjoying, without any speed limit, a gay and delectable journey towards ethernity, declare that we shall end for ever this feast of horror, indecency, blasphemy, and smut.

The bearded man lepped up on his sound leg and shouted, Let's get this thing goin' without any more waste o' words, for God's sake! I propose the followin' resolution, that this Rich an' Rare Branch of the Gaelic League——

—Who dhraws the rents from th' houses of the whores of Montgomery Street? shouted a voice at the window.

—For pity's sake, whimpered the wizened old man, let's have unity in the face of a common enemy. Can't we remember, he added imploringly, how Father Guffney reminded us that we are a noble people in a noble movement, and mustn't let any low, sordid, or unsavoury thoughts into our elevated minds.

—Besides, it's a libel on the Irish Race, said a young man from Rathmines, and I protest, he went on roaring, I protest against this tirade of sulfurious infamity, for the fact is there isn't a single what-you-may-call-them from one end of holy Ireland to th' other!

—And whenever he draws his monthly salary, whispered Donal O'Murachadha, a boy from Tourmakeady, he makes straight to where the ladies are.

—Remember, will yous, what Mcgennis says about the ten commandments! whined out the old man in the chair. Will you move your resolution, an' be done with it, man, he said to the bearded one.

—I propose the following resolution, again went on the bearded man, that we, unitedly, of this Rich and Rare Branch, in ordhered assembly, do hereby, without any further posthurin' of words, or any additional *sine qua non*, declare, assert, assume, avow that this day forward we shall allow no maiden to wed, leave every harvest unreaped, every eye unshut, every mouth unopened, every ear cocked, till this vile thing is driven from the Abbey stage, from our dear city, from our verdant shore for ever, immediately, and as quick as circumstances will allow; acting according to, and always within, the canons, rules, and counsels of the astute and solicitudinising bishops of the Church, so that those refusin' to keep step with the pilgrims on the march to Heaven may be set aside, so that we may go forward, like

Christian soldiers, canons to the right of us, canons to the left of us, volleyin' an' thunderin' out th' thruth, led be Roddy the Prover surrounded by a steel-clod cohort of Holy Romans that came, in the long ago, in a ship that sailed too soon, singing his Romewards song, chirping away though pushed about by the Irish Press; seeking the hidden Ireland, even at the canon's mouth, ready to defend the faith of our fathers in rant and rhyme, against the culture taking delight in obscene literature or stage blastphemy; the relics of oul' dacency under his arm in a silver box made to the pattern of St. Patrick's bell, and he smoking a cigar presented by Professor Tim, an' leaning on a walking-stick made from the wood of a tree from Mr. Tchehkov's cherry orchard that he had cut down because it was poisoning the fresher fruits of Ireland; Nell Flaherty's drake as sign on his shield — a guyde to us all, he marches, and we march with him, *in signia sommnia, dimnia, domnia,* amen; and he sat down, exhausted.

—I beg to second that sound resolution, sir chairman, said a pretty girl on a front bench, and to regesther me own personal abhorrence of these people's poisonous approach to the dauntlessly chaste womanhood of Ireland; for the world knows, and I speak here hyperbolically of course, that wings grow from the shoulders of every thrue Irish lady.

—All in favour say ay, said the chairman sleepily, an' hurry up, for I've got to go to bed.

—Before we move to denial, said Sean, let's know what the man has said.

—I don't think a thrue Irishman should ask such a question, said the bearded man hotly, seeing what's bound to be imbedded in th' answer given. There are pure-minded, innocent girls at this meeting.

—As a writer, and as the Lad from Largymore, said a wild-looking young man with long black hair trickling into his eyes, a flowing black bow, and a wide-brimmed black hat on his head — One o' th' ones who copy Yeats, whispered O'Murachadha — I move we move that ye move the resolution without further delay. Isn't it enough that our priests have said the thing is to be condemned holus-bolus, *in toto,* without reservation, and aren't they supported by Up Griffith, Up Thomas Davis and the valiant D. P. Moran, editor of *The Leader.* We condemn Synge and all the works and vanities of his Abbey Theatre.

—Wait a second, fiercely spoke up the O'Murachadha, his tawny moustache flapping like a banner. We are Gaelic Leaguers, and as such owe no silent reception to what the priests or the politicians say. Let's hear, and then judge for ourselves.

A few stalwart members pulled the old man to his feet, and for a time he swayed about, pale with the terror of what he had to say; but gripping the table as strongly as he could with his bony hands, he opened his pallid lips to say, as a delicate delegate from the Young Men's Catholic Association of the Cross, I burn with shame at the job I have to do. In this play of Synge's, about the middle of it, before everyone, mind you, without puttin' cap or cloak on it, the principal character shouts out the word Shift!

—He said worse than that, if worse there could be, went on the oh so old man; for he made out, I'm told — for mind you, I wouldn't go near the place for love or money — he made out that the blessed saints sthrained their necks to get an unholy glimpse of the wanton Helen o' Throy, an' her sauntherin' round Heaven with a nosegay in her golden shawl!

Within the frightened murmuring of the Miserere by most of the members, the Lad from Largymore jumped to his feet, foaming at the mouth, shouting, What more do we want to hear! We'll make them feel the sacred animosity of Catholic Ireland, feel it sharp an' sudden an' always! This pagan-minded, anti-Irish ravisher of decency, Yeats and his crony Synge; ay, an' that oul' hen behind them, Gregory, with her pro-British breedin' oozin' out of everything she says an' does, must be taught a lesson! This fella Yeats, in particular, with his ribboned eye-glasses, his big-brimmed hat, his flowin' tie, this so-called poet who isn't a poet at all, must be made to feel the force of our Catholic indignation!

The young man from Tourmakeady sprang to his feet, the red glow of anger on his face, pouring out burning sentences in Irish that no-one, bar Sean, understood, then into a fierce flow of English with, You stutterers in the life of Irish Ireland, what do ye know about th' joys and perils of poetry! He who denies to Yeats the name of a poet is a liar in his ignorance. You all shouted another way when you listened to his Cathleen ni Houlihan. No-one has sung a finer song about Cathleen ni Houlihan than Yeats; no-one has fashioned her into a holier symbol:

> The yellow pool has overflowed high up on Clooth-na-Bare,
> For the wet winds are blowing out of the clinging air;
> Like heavy flooded waters our bodies and our blood;
> But purer than a tall candle before the Holy Rood
> Is Cathleen, the daughter of Houlihan.

Let any of you do as good as that, and you can be licensed to yell that not this man, but another, shall fill his place and guide us where we want to go! Yeats is a flame in the sword of light, a radiant wing on the shoulder of Aengus, a flash from the spear of Lugh of the Long Hand, a banner of song in the midst of the people!

—This is a Catholic counthry! shouted the bearded man, an' we want no Pagan symbols here.

—Didn't this same boyo write a play not long ago about an Irish queen who bartered her soul for gold? queried the Lad from Largymore, and didn't the great Cardinal Logue condemn the thing without even havin' to read it by a snap of his ecclesiastical finger an' thumb that sounded in a catholic ear clear like a clap o' thundher?

—Come on, Sean, exclaimed the young man from Tourmakeady, and let's get out of the crowd, for Christ's sake! When they got to the door, he wheeled about to shout savagely, Cardinal Logue! A big, stout, stupid, lumbering mind, more at home with a dish of bacon and cabbage than with a book or a play. But in a question of this kind, no cardinal, no, nor even the Pope himself, with his counts, knights, chevaliers, and monsignors fifing and drumming behind him, will make me draw back from a play they say should be banned, or a book they say should be burned. To hell with yous that would burn a crimson rose that had a spot of honest dust on it! And, followed by Sean, he turned on his heel and hurried away. They hadn't gone far when they heard the clatter of heavy boots running towards them, and soon the tram conductor was panting by their side.

—What yous two think, I think, he said, in the main; not altogether, mind you, but in th' main. The clergy were always in th' sthream of things goin' against Ireland. They fought men of Forty-eight, the Fenians, and then Parnell. I'm with yous right enough.

They journeyed down to where the Abbey Theatre was standing, surrounded by a multitude of people forcing themselves to hiss, blast, and boo the building. A tiny building for a theatre, thought Sean, two-storied, a circular-topped window on each side of a circular-topped door, and three narrow, oblong windows on the upper story: a glass-roofed awning jutting from the main entrance over the pathway, and, between the stories, THE ABBEY THEATRE in bold letters on a panel stretching from one end of the building to the other. The three of them went into a pub opposite and furnished themselves with a bottle of stout apiece.

—There'll be ructions here before the night is out, said the conductor.

—Let them rave, said O'Murachadha contemptuously; let them shake their throats into hoarseness till their raucous shouts smite the ears of the saints with a protective deafness.

But supposing, said Sean, a little ill at ease, that what this man said in his play was a deep and bitter insult to Ireland?

—Yeats will never let a thing be said that will be either a bad or bitther reproach to Ireland. He is one of Ireland's incantations, the Irish logos of the day, a singer of rare songs to Ireland's honour — Tara's harp is mute no longer, but the people are throwing dust on its golden sthrings.

—But, insisted Sean, it's said that this man is proud and pompous, ever standing stiff before an opinion other than his own, telling, like those cries that are as the clash of cymbals, that the voice of Yeats is the voice of God, and not that of the people.

—The voice of the people, Sean, is the voice of God when it shouts against oppression; it is the voice of ignorance when it shouts against a song. Yeats is proud, sometimes pompous; and his words at times are like sounding cymbals, but the cymbals are always silver, and his sensitive hands bring them together with great cunning. Listen! he went on loudly, turning to those who were in the place, no shouting will frighten Yeats. Holding his glass of stout high in the air he recited vehemently,

> He who trembles before the flame and the flood,
> And th' wind that blows through the starry ways,
> Let the starry winds and the flame and the flood
> Cover over, and hide, for he has no part
> With th' lonely, majestical multitude.

Listen! he cried, listen all of you — a toast to W. B. Yeats, Ireland's greatest poet; a man, too. Fit to keep company with the Shining Ones, Aengus, or Lugh of the Long Hand; fit to kiss the cheek of Cathleen, the daughter of Houlihan: I dhrink to the poet and the man! He drank till the glass was empty, and then he flung it to the floor, smashing it into foamy fragments, and no-one murmured. Then they went out, and stood watching the crowd swaying to the left and right, its spearhead swaying towards the theatre entrance. All those seen before were there again, flooded now with those who had hurried from Lanigan's Ball and Finnigan's Wake, all kinds, civil servants, clerks of all kinds, school teachers, a few workmen of all trades, and many women, haggard and soiled, long shawls covering their jaded skirts and blouses.

—Aha, said O'Murachadha, there's throuble inside too, for from the entrance a young man, struggling in the arms of two big policemen, was carried out, shoved headlong into the crowd with a parting slap on the jaw from one of them, the two policemen remaining at the entrance, grinning provokingly at the crowd.

—There he is! cried the man from Tourmakeady suddenly, pointing to a stately-looking man with long black hair, a lock of it half covering an eye, who had come to the entrance, and, in the light of a street lamp, stood looking dreamily at the agitated crowd.

—That's Yeats, Yeats the poet, the best poet Ireland has, went on O'Murachadha in his impulsive Tourmakeady way. Oh, me choice man chucked into an unharboured life of ignorance, and a piety that makes a tabernacle of a till! Jasus, will you listen to that! as a great cloud of booing gathered stormily round the head of the wondering poet. There's th' voice of Ireland for you — hoarse, hollow, and hasty, from the mouth of gobeens, sure anything they can't understand is smothered in the smoke of Hell!

—Oh, you're there, are you? screamed a fish-hawker when she saw Yeats by the theatre door. An' proud yeh look, yeh long-haired throubler of decent people, fleerin' in ecstasy at everythin' we hold to be holy, or that's sanctified be th' testimony of well-robed scholars, in writin' on scrolls no ordinary man can scan, held in awe be all th' scarlet-clad cardinals, walkin' wisely in th' sthreets of Rome. Pipe late, pipe early; pipe sad, pipe gay, you'll not pipe tauntin' tunes in th' holy city of ours. Learn to chant a tune we all understand, or you won't chant at all. Let me get a grip o' you till I sthrangle you with the ends of your own tie! Come out here an' I'll gut you th' way I'd gut a Liffey gurnet!

A policeman, pushing his way through the crowd, touched her on the shoulder and motioned her to go away. With a shrill, nervous laugh she jigged a way through the people, who made a wide path for her, singing as she danced a bawdy song to an air very like that of Whiskey Johnny.

The police manœuvred the rest of the gathering away, and Sean and O'Murachadha wandered to the quayside to lean over the parapet of Butt Bridge, and gaze up the river, going swiftly now to the sea, for the dark tide was ebbing. Sean wished he had seen Yeats's *Cathleen ni Houlihan*, so that he might know more about the man; but a shilling was too much for him to spare for a play. He wished he could see this play by Singe or Sinje, so that he might know more about him too. He lifted his eyes and saw in the distance the naked tremble of a leafless tree set dogged on the pavement, waiting for the spring. A gleaming star, low down in the sky, seemed to be entangled in its delicate higher branches: like Yeats and Ireland, thought Sean;

Ireland, naked and quivering, waiting for the spring, and the glittering poet caught in its branches.

—I'd dearly like to have a quiet talk with Yeats, murmured O'Murachadha, the young man from Tourmakeady.

LOST LEADER

SEAN with a group of comrades, all naked to the waist, was wiping the sweat off his steaming body after a rough and racy hurling match, each hurler criticising the play of another, and grumbling that but for this or that hesitation the match would have been won, and, at the end of the Hurling League, a gold medal would hang from the watch-chain of any hurler having a watch, when they caught sight of a comrade cycling furiously over the sward towards them.

—Dhress yourselves! he shouted, while he was still pedalling; dhress yourselves, an' quit arguin'. He flung himself from his bicycle to run into their midst: Ireland calls again!

—She's always at it, grumbled a back, forcing a damp body into his shirt; what th' hell's she want now?

—The Standing Committee of the Hierarchy in Maynooth has declared against Irish as an essential subject in the New University; and we're all wanted for a meeting at once.

—The bishops again! growled a lusty forward. I guessed as much, for they were always in Ireland's way when she went forward. But let them look to themselves this time, for we are not now what we once were; and raising his hurley over his head, he shouted, Who's with Dr. O'Hickey? Irish in the University — or else . . .!

All their hurleys flew into the air, and all shouted together, Irish in the University — or else . . .!

—There's more to come, said the cyclist excitedly. Wait till I tell yous: Dr. O'Hickey was summoned before the Committee, ordhered to resign, and when he refused, was dismissed from his Professorship of Irish in Maynooth College.

—They've gone a little too far this time, said the full-back vehemently, raising his hurley again into the air; we fight till Dr. O'Hickey, deafened by Ireland's cheering, marches through a lane of bowin' bishops, back to his Chair of Irish in Maynooth College in the County of Kildare!

They all raised their hurleys together and shouted with one voice,

Irish in the University — or else . . .! O'Hickey abu! Then they all
hurried into their clothes, those who had bicycles pedalling away,
those who hadn't formed fours, and marched down the Park road in
quick-step time, to get the tram at the gate and hurry to where they
had been called.

Dr. Douglas Hyde was going round and round, beseeching the
consent of the University's Senate to Irish becoming an essential
subject, Cardinal Lug, with a nod at O'Hickey, commending to others
the coy manner of Hyde's advocacy of the language, worthy of a
gentleman; while Eoin Mac Neill went another way, lullabying his
language so that a new-born lamb wouldn't hesitate to nudge his
knees. All this time the bishops were hitching up their chasubulleros
bullen a laws to make short shrift of them, helped by their clerical
coadjutants among the many curates looking to be parish priests,
parish priests longing to be vicar-generals, many of these aiming at
being bishops, and many a bishop believing the world well lost for a
cardinal's hat. Short shrift they would have made of these tame talkers
had it not been for the energy and valorous scorn of Dr. O'Hickey
who raised up a storm among the plain people for the proper recogni-
tion of Irish by the Senate of the New University. The breath of his
mouth became a big wind blowing off biretta and mitre, and sending
their chasubulleros bullen a laws flying over every Dublin chimney-
pot, while cheers for O'Hickey went rippling from one end of Ireland
to the other. O'Hickey made no fancy, polished pattern of words,
telling the University Senate, including the Archbishop of Tuam and
Monsignor Mannix, President of Maynooth College (who afterwards
blossomed out into a full-bosomed patriot), that if they voted against
the Irish National Cause, they would resolve themselves into recreant
Nationalists whose act of treachery would ever be remembered by the
Irish people.

Forced by the roar of the plain people (most of whom knew nothing,
and cared less, about the language) to make Irish an essential subject
in the University, the official clergy were furious. Realising they
couldn't hit the people, they determined to strike hard at O'Hickey, so
a College Mandamus was shoved under O'Hickey's door, ordering
him to appear before his betters to answer a charge of want of respect
to the holy, high and mighty bishops of Ireland. Without any demand
for an apology, without a chance to defend himself or to take counsel
from an advocate, or even from a friend, there was just a charge
levelled, a plea of not guilty by O'Hickey, and then the sentence:
Resign, or be dismissed. As he refused to resign, he was dismissed.

Armagh got him by the scruff of the neck, Tuam caught one arm, Cashel the other, the rest of the episcopate pushed at the back, and he was shunted out through the gates, which were shut, locked, bolted, barred, and chained against him for evermore: banished from the good cheer, sacred associations, from chapel, refectory, infirmarium, lecture-room, and Chair of the College, and from all paths therefrom and thereto, garden, playing-fields, cloisters, theological continuities, in compliance with, and in consequence of, a *nullo tremulato antea profundi craniumalis omnibusiboss episcopalitis.*

So that was what Dr. O'Hickey got for criticising the bishops, though he hadn't done so; only a possible action of criticism of the members of the Senate of the National University, some of whom happened to be bishops, but whose position as Senators had nothing whatever to do with any office in Maynooth College. But it was determined to show O'Hickey that the mitre would prove to be the Cap of Death for him. Sean was filled with a great bitterness, and he resolved to do what in him lay to fight this sanctified coercion, this mitred tyranny, this malicious resentment; so he ran around asking questions, and wondering what the Gaelic Leaguers would do now. So he rushed round asking all whom he met, Coo Ulla, cocky Sean Tea O'Kelly, Birch Aar, Finnan Hadde MacColum, Nora Greeno, Paddy Daly, and all the boys and girls of far away and long ago, but all vouchsafed the whisper of, It's up to Dr. O'Hickey himself, now.

—Don't yous realise, he kept shouting, that on this question of essential Irish, were it not for Dr. O'Hickey, Hyde and Mac Neill would have been left sitting on their backsides, some more kindly bishop, when he knew they'd got cool enough, giving them a hand to their feet again? Can't yous see it was he frightened the Senate into compliance? He led the fight, he fought the fight, and he won it for us; and are we going to leave him to fight his fight alone? But all the answer he got was a whisper of, If we once get the bishops against us, we're done.

So he ran round again, asking questions of Cunnin Mwail, Micky Free, Harry Lorrequer, Louis J. Walsh of Killeebook, the Vicar of Bray, Charles O'Malley, Luke Delmege and his New Curate, a Lad of the O'Friels, and found them a centre of silence. Accidentally coming across Edward Myrrhtyn, looking longingly in at the windows of Kildare Street Club, he put the question to him; but Edward set off at a gallop from Dublin to Galway, never stopping till he staggered through the doorway of Tillyra Castle, flung himself into bed, singing for all to hear, *I'm asleep, and don't waken me.*

He journeyed to Republican places, asking this Fenian and that, taking in Arthur Griffith, what were we going to do to help O'Hickey in his fight.

—What do you expect us to do over a question that is plainly one for ecclesiastical juridicity? asked a Sinn Feiner who had plussed himself into a Republican, while the massive-minded Griffith robed himself in the stillness of the strong, silent man.

—Was compulsory Irish an ecclesiastical question? countered Sean; and as they stayed silent, went on, Well, then, that's what he fought for; that is why he has been damned: he defeated the proud bishops, and that defeat was gall and wormwood to their voluptuous souls. They say he has been sacked because he treated the bishops with improper respect, and thereby broke the sacred Statutes of Maynooth College. Well, hasn't it been demonstrated that it was the Trustees of the College who pushed him out, so it seems the act of dismissal wasn't an exercise of ecclesiastical jurisdiction, or connected with ecclesiastical authority of any kind. And why? Because the body known as the Trustees of St. Patrick's College isn't an ecclesiastical corporation in any sense of the word. These Trustees were incorporated by an Act of Parliament of Great Britain and Ireland; so it seems they have stamped the cross of Patrick over the Lion and Unicorn (bringing the British symbol up to date), and have thrust out O'Hickey for daring to say that Irish should be an essential subject in the New University; adding a memo to the effect that this professor and fellow-priest had said boo to a few bishops who happened to be members of a secular Senate of a secular University.

—I have to go now, said Griffith to his fellow Sinn Feiner, for I have important things to think about; and off he went.

—As for the famous Statutes, continued Sean, isn't it true that the College has been ransacked from roof to cellar without a copy being found? Nor, it seems, does anyone know anything about them. So O'Hickey ups and writes to a Cardinal Log for one, who writes to say that he had read the paragraph on the Duty of Professors from the College Statutes, and that O'Hickey could read it himself in any of the printed copies; O'Hickey replying that he never had a copy, and couldn't get one. The Cardinal made reply that that surprised him, now, so it did; but anyhow he had written to Monsignor Mannix (who subsequently became an Irish patriot of purest ray segrene) to send O'Hickey a copy at once. But as none came, O'Hickey wrote again to point out how necessary it was for him to have a copy of the Statutes he had infringed.

The Cardinal then wrote to say that Mannix had promised to send O'Hickey a copy, and the Cardinal was sure Mannix would send it still, adding that the Cardinal thought the Cardinal himself had one, but found that what he had were but extracts for the students in English. Aha, me boy, aha: so Cardinal Log condemned O'Hickey for infringing a rule he had read out of a book he hadn't got! This was the enlightened boyo who put an end to W. P. O'Ryan's art-and-industry community in the Boyne valley; this was he who bawled shame towards Synge, and who condemned Yeats's *Countess Cathleen* without bothering his red-hatted head to read the book of the play. The hetman of the Catholic Church in Ireland imposing his will on far better men than himself. The Christian way of life!

When the famous Statutes were at last bored out of Mannix, it was found that they were ten years old, and had expired long before Dr. O'Hickey had been dismissed. After that, the Cardinal sent to Dr. O'Hickey a pamphlet, printed by Browne and Nolan (good references given in *Finnegan's Wake*), entitled *Statutes of St. Patrick's College, Maynooth, 1897*, whereas the reference in *Official Record of Facts* was to Statutes published in 1907; and this pamphlet bore on its cover the half-erased word of Draft, while the reference made no mention of the chapter so that it was not possible to know with certainty where Section VIII. 1. 4 was to be found (under the Cardinal's hat, maybe). So Dr. O'Hickey had been condemned by the Cardinal and his sub-equals from a bunch of Statutes of which no-one in the College had any knowledge; which, as far as could be made out, had never been promulgated; and of which the President of the College, Monsignor Mannix, couldn't ferret out a copy save one poor specimen labelled Draft.

—What does Sean O'Casside suggest we should or might do? the Republican Sinn Feiner asked, a patient smile curling his lips.

—Fight for him as he fought for us, said Sean excitedly; march into the grounds of Maynooth College with drum and colours to tell the authorities there, under their very windows, that Ireland wants Professor O'Hickey back in his Chair of Irish.

—Mob law! said the Sinn Feiner.

—It is no more of mob law to demonstrate against the bishops on an Irish National question than it is to demonstrate against the Castle gang for the same reason.

—And what do you imagine the police would be doing? asked the Sinn Finn Republican.

—We have faced the police before, we can face them again.

—We can't afford to have the bishops against us, said the Sinn Fein Republican, and, besides, Dr. O'Hickey himself would never give permission for such an action.

—Oh, no-one suggests he should be asked, retorted Sean impatiently; and as for the bishops — shall we, who have nothing to lose, run away from them, while O'Hickey, who has everything to lose, be left to face them alone?

—We're with him in spirit, said the Republican unctuously. Now I have work to do for the Sinn Fein Bank, and I must be off, so slán leat, he said, speaking the only Irish words he knew.

—So long, said Sean; go behind the curtain to work hard for your nation of bishops and bobbies! I can see now that there won't be even a stick rattled along the railings of Maynooth College.

On the advice of a friend, Dr. McDonald, D.D., a Professor of Theology at Maynooth, Dr. O'Hickey decided to take his case to Rome, and to put something of a faint flush on their white cowardice the Gaelic Leaguers started a fund to help defray his expenses, Sean handing over ten shillings that he had saved towards a new coat, and, in addition, a shilling a week till he had given fifteen shillings altogether; so that a tint was added to O'Hickey's childlike hope of finding a soft spot in the petrified piety of Rome. So this blameless priest, fine professor, everything he did done from a keen sense of patriotic and religious duty, set off for the City of the Boccaneros, Don Vigilios, Monsignor Nanis, the red-hatted Sarnos, the Abbé Trouberts, amethyst rings, pop-eyed papal counts, Swiss guards, and noble memories of Raphael and Angelo — an *athanasius contra junta episcopolician hibernica*. His fellow professors — all but those near the orbit of the President, Mannix — admitted the harsh injustice of the punishment, though not a soul of them, bar McDonald, lifted a hand to help him. Selfishness and fear dominating the teachers of the Irish Catholic world! Safety first for them: eat, drink, and be cautious, for tomorrow we live.

So with a pamphlet of thirty pages, composed into fine Latin by his friend Dr. McDonald, Dr. O'Hickey found himself in that city which some say is the front door to the gates of Heaven, the keys hanging from a nail over the Pope's bed. They got going in June of 1910, and the Sacred Rota summoned the Trustees of the College to answer for themselves; but did they come? No. O'Hickey's advocate wrote for the copy of the resolution appointing him to the professorship, and the minutes of the meetings that were held to deal with the case; but autumn came, all the leaves fell, but none came. The Promoter of

Justice attached to the Court said they were necessary, and off went an order demanding them within forty days, but after these had fled, the papers still lay, warm and snug, under some bishop's blissful pillow. Then what was called a peremptory order was sent, but sorra care the bishops cared — letter post, pigeon post, telegraph, cable, courier, or morse code couldn't coax the letters from under the bishop's pillow. They refused deliberately to comply with, or even to take any notice of, the order of the Court. Instead, after another peremptory order, Cardinal Log sent the decree of removal, adding that he had no other documents to deliver. His Eminence, apparently acting as the mouth-piece of the bishops, refused to send on the minutes of the proceedings demanded repeatedly and peremptorily by the Court. They were in existence, but the bishops, each of whom was something more than a pope in his own diocese, refused to deliver them, alleging that there were no documents to send, other than the decree of dismissal — they sent that post-haste. A year and five months after the start of the case — the ecclesiastical law's little delay — the President of the Court said that provision had been made for the delivery of the documents, and then Cardinal Log landed in Rome to complain about the slow way the case was going. It wasn't till February 1912 that three of the documents were handed in, which gave the Cardinal and the bishops a fairway of time to get things going their own sour way. In the docu-ment giving an account of the Trustees' meeting only the vote was given, and no word of what had taken place at a previous meeting of the whole episcopal bench. And when the harassed O'Hickey de-manded this, it was said that he wanted to keep the case going till Tibb's Eve, with, in the view of their lordships, a malicious intent to weary them out.

The reinforcements were sent, and more of the Irish bishops began to trickle into Rome; and while O'Hickey was pressing for documents bearing on his case, rumours began to be sent round that O'Hickey was incompetent as a professor, that he had been insubordinate, arrogant, ill-tempered, disloyal; that in fine he was, as the Trustees represented him afterwards, an anti-clerical wholly dependent for support on anti-clericals too. Is it likely he would have been hustled out of a Chair in Maynooth if they didn't know something about him which they couldn't publish without causing a scandal? They hunted in tame places and in populated quarters seeking anything they could to murmur against him. So his advocate hurried to him, saying, Get someone to write that you were a good priest; and poor O'Hickey had to say he couldn't, except some who were on the white list, and their testimony would do him more harm than good. Before going to Rome, he had asked a testimonial of the Bishop of Waterford, but that fine fellow contented himself with saying that O'Hickey was an exemplary priest when he knew him, but didn't know anything since O'Hickey went to Maynooth; and the greater Walsh, Archbishop of Dublin, who had been in close touch with him on the question of getting Irish into the common schools, satisfied himself with the remark that, as far as he knew, Dr. O'Hickey was free from censure and irregularity. Maynooth's Staff was sounded, but only two were ready to come to the fore, and, when they had heard that no-one else would, they hid themselves in silence. Is there no just man here to speak a word for another just man? None: most of them were in the hunt for a purple or a scarlet biretta.

Then the advocate decided to have evidence taken in Ireland. Then began the cooking of the questions to be asked of the witnesses — put in a form, says a brother professor of Maynooth, notably different from that in which they had been previously handed to O'Hickey; distorted in substance, and formulated in wretched and almost unintelligible Latin; while, as regards his having or not having given occasion for reprehension and admonition, the added clause — *in any grave matter* — was whipped away.

One of the Auditors of the Rota, Monsignor Prior, an Englishman, was appointed to be President of the Body for taking down the evidence, but as such men rarely act in person, someone had to be selected as a substitute. The names of three Irish clergymen working in England ,all of them Domestic Prelates of the Pope, were suggested by Dr. O'Hickey and Professor McDonald; but out of a sweet tenderness for the Irish Bishops' feelings, Monsignor Prior, who had business in England, said he would come over to Ireland and take the evidence personally. But the Bishops knew a thing or two about setting up a court in holy Ireland, for if Monsignor Prior came to Ireland he'd ask for the journal of the Trustees, and then the minutes, so long hidden nicely away in the darkness of their bottom drawer. However it may have been manœuvred, O'Hickey got word from his advocate that the bishops had protested against the appointment of an outsider, and so the bould Monsignor Prior had nominated as Judge Instructor Delegate no less a genius than the boulder Cardinal Log himself. No opposition on the part of O'Hickey could alter this, for Prior couldn't do otherwise in face of the protest that had come from all the bishops; and it was even said that the protest had flown in through the Pope's window, so that he, in the interests of justice and fair play, had interfered in the right way when tackled by the Irish bishops, equally athirst for justice and fair play for all; and O'Hickey lost his case, leaving this to be said by Dr. McDonald, Professor of Theology at Maynooth for forty years: I regret to have to say I regard the Auditors of the Rota as having judged, or not having judged, this case on prejudice, and not on evidence, and that they have, by the decrees they issued in connection with it, confirmed what those who distrusted the Holy See had often told us — that it is but a fool who would take any action in a Roman court against the body of bishops of any country. I did not, and would not believe it of the Roman Rota; now I am convinced of my simplicity.

And no cry of shame came from any Irish Seneschal, Taoiseach, or Tánaiste standing angry at the gates of Maynooth College, beside the dismantled castle of the Geraldines.

They took his living from him, says Dr. McDonald, and prevented him from getting justice, nay, a hearing in Rome; but he hasn't been injured with the Irish people, except, indeed, with those who think any man a fool who sacrifices his own interest for anything on earth, or, almost, in Heaven. It is a class that has become more numerous, especially among the clergy, many of whom — those who either have got preferment or are on the look-out for it — regard Dr. O'Hickey as a fool. Only the other day, the Bishop of Waterford wrote to him urging him to give up the struggle in Rome, and saying, There is not and there never has been any imputation on your priestly character. It's a pity, adds Dr. McDonald, that the Bishop didn't summon up the little manliness that was needed to tell this truth when asked by Dr. O'Hickey for a testimonial to his character as a priest.

Later on, Dr. O'Hickey sent a memorial to the Pope asking permission to take the case to the secular courts, and, to Dr. O'Hickey's surprise, received a note telling him the Pope was sending the case again to the Rota — a favour O'Hickey had in vain begged before. O'Hickey, because of the great expense involved, decided to refuse the favour; but before he could find the pen and ink, he was told the Holy Father had withdrawn the case from the Rota, at, it is said, the insistence of Cardinal Vanutelli (welcomed with thunders of cheers at a Gaelic League gathering with Edward Martyn and Hyde hurrying to touch his hand), primed by Cardinal Log. What a host against O'Hickey!

So he came home, and when he had managed to get a better suit of clothes, he called on his bishop, who asked him what he intended to do and what were his intentions. O'Hickey said he had none, save to serve on the Mission in any office to which he might be sent, living in the meantime with his brother in the town of Carrick-on-Suir. No offer of any kind ever came to him, and at last he died, his friends believed from a broken heart. Not the first heart the Irish bishops have broken. And some say that at times a mitred will-o-the-wisp flickers over his grave in Carrick Beg whispering in the sigh of the wind the honoured name of Mannix.

What a loneliness there was in the silent burial of Dr. O'Hickey on that cold, damp day in Carrick Beg! A few faithful friends were there to honour a death that had a sting, and a grave that won a victory. How lonely compared to the stir and vivacity around the burial of a Father O'Growney a few short years before. What a flutter there was when *his* body was brought all the way from California to be buried in Maynooth College. Hyde and Mac Neill left their beds at five in the morning, clapping their hands and blowing their cold fingers, hurrying into their flannels when the alarm clock crew, to be down in Cove in time to honour the homecoming of the dead man. All the Gaelic Chiefs from Cork and Kerry were there, with Oona Fearally and Edward Martyn, freshly toninsured, broadly belted with holy beads, his little boxed-up soul safe for the time being in the midst of the clerical cargo present on the cold quay. Out they went in the jumpy tender to watch the coffin being lowered from the great *Campania*, a rich affair — as Hyde tells us himself — costing a couple of hundred pounds or thereabouts. Carried to Cork, in goes the costly coffin to the Cathedral; me Lord Archbishop taking Hyde and his friends out to dinner, and back to the Cathedral again, where a rousing sermon was given eulogising the quiet-minded, harmless dead man for compiling five wee books of cuckoo Irish for beginners which all too frequently made them enders too. When they were done in Cork, off they hurried to Dublin where anna lividia plurahelle Irish was spoken on all sides, and into the other Cathedral with them, where they said the Rosary, and left Father O'Growney there by himself till the morning. Then at the crack of dawn, off they went in stately procession through the principal streets of Dublin, Dr. Hyde and Major Donovan in front standing out from the rest of them, Donovan to the right of the hearse and Hyde to the left of it, the mass bands playing the *Marsellaise* to a funeral step,

> An' we're all trottin', trot-trot-trottin',
> An' we're all trottin', so happy an' so gay!

to Broadstone Station.

It was a gorgeous procession, as Hyde tells us himself, taking fully fifty minutes to pass a given pint; and seven packed trains, running side by side, and one after another, carried the quick and the dead to Maynooth, there to meet a splendid coach, drawn by four great handsome black horses, with Dr. Hyde walking bareheaded by its side; followed by six hundred, the noble six hundred, students in their brightest robes, led on by Bishop O'Dea and Monsignor Mannix, President of the College. When the coffin had been laid down on the green sward, a Father O'Reilly ran out to give a roaring, rushing sermon in praise of the dead man, giving the College the devil and all for their indifference to Irish, adding that Father O'Growney, the did man, was wiser than they all; ending up with them all singing, *And so say of all of us, and so say all of us*; after which, as was quite natural, they had dinner in the College, Hyde sitting between Monsignor Mannix and Bishop O'Dawn O'Day, while a tenor of a student sang, standing on a high stool, *An Irishman's glory shines brighter than gold* while they were having their whack of good things. That night, Dr. Hyde slept in a room presented to him by Dr. O'Hickey.

But they weren't done yet; oh no, for when the first sign of the morning came, they hurried into their glows again, hurried into the church again where Requiem High Mass was said, after which the cortège wandered its way around the grounds, Dr. Hyde, barefaced and bareheaded, marched again by the erse side of the hearse, tears in his eyes, clenching his fists while he recited his own Irish Prayacawn Dove Donah to the calm and keen edification of Monsignor Mannix, O'Day, and the swarm of justickilogical, rustickological, buyological, and sellological students that followed trenchantly behind. At last the costly coffin was laid to rest in the chapel. Hyde gave it a last chaste kiss, as did many of them, for the glory of God and the honour of a poor dud man.

None of these things for Dr. O'Hickey, who fought for Ireland in a far, far firmer and finer way than the timid, gentle O'Growney. Ay, and died for her too, as many had done before him, done to death by a far cuter foe. When he was put under the sod, there was no Hyde, Mac Neill, Oona Fearally, Edward Martyn, in freshly-made suits of mourning marching down to Carrick Beg to murmur a last farewell to one of Ireland's greater dead. They stayed at home. No mitred Dawn O'Day there to see the last of him: that they saw in Rome when an iron heel, shaped like a cross, stamped down on him. No Drum Taps beaten, no Last Post sounded; only the caw-caw of many a crow flapping a dark wing through a grey sky. No sermon; no band of students chanting sad melodies; no banner of Waken up your

Courage, O Ireland, for banner, staff, and spear-point had been cast with O'Hickey into the grave; nothing here but a tiny band of friends, shivering in the centre of a cold, damp day, a little in from a lonely road alongside the noisy sullen Suir, led by the courageous Dr. McDonald, to see their comrade safely sheltered in his last home.

O'Hickey's name is never mentioned now. In the fight for the Ireland of his vision he collided with the bishops and got his death-wound. The hounds of Banba had hunted again, and had brought down their quarry. So he is never mentioned now. In a well-known Catholic Annual there appeared, under the title of *Taoisigh Gaedheal*, the pictures of those who had served Ireland well, clerical and lay, soldier and politician, and there in the gallery is the long, retiring, rather sheepish face of Father O'Growney; but none, no, not even a silhouette of Father O'Hickey.

Here is one who remembers you, O'Hickey. Here is one who, when you died, had but a flitter of a coat on his back, who walked on the uppers of his boots, who hadn't the penny to buy the paper telling of your death; here is one left to say you were a ray in Ireland's Sword of Light — a ray then, and a ray still, and no episcopal pall can hide its flaming. Though there be none to speak out your name, here is one to utter it in the same breath, with the same pride as those who speak out the names of Ireland's fair and finest sons; for you are one with her they call Cathleen, the daughter of Houlihan, though you have not been remembered for ever; one with her as is yellow-haired Donough who's dead; who had a hempen rope for a neckcloth, and a white cloth on his head.

GAELSTROEM

SEAN stood on the borders of doubt again. He was a bit bewildered about the essences in the freedom they were struggling to gain. Was this freedom within the circle of the fight they were making, or was it merely a vision floating about the rim? Strange things had happened that put an ugly look on the face of the freedom they thought so beautiful. Look at what had happened to Parnell when he was breathless with extreme toil, and leaning on his sword before having another bout with the wily foe. Stricken down he was by those he led so well within the circle of what they all aimed at achieving. Hadn't Dr.

O'Hickey been dismissed from his job, and disgraced by a covey of screeching bishops for saying a few edged words in Maynooth College on a National question? Ay, had he. Could such a thing have happened at Trinity in Ireland, or in Oxford or Cambridge in England? No, it couldn't. Then there was the case of the Rory O'Moore branch of the Gaelic League at Portarlington, whose officers had been hushed, banned, blackguarded, and some of them beggared because they had insisted, against the obey-or-be-damned orders of the local clergy, on holding mixed classes for the teaching of Irish. The clergy had disowned them, and all of them withered away. The fig-tree had been cursed for bringing forth fruit. He saw this odd thing himself in Moycally where he had gone on Sundays to teach Irish with a comrade, the two of them giving up their whole day of leisure to hasten the day of Ireland's deliverance. There the girls were forced to sit in the lower room of the local school, the men in the upper one, a local priest always present to see that this canonical rule was flagrantly obeyed, assisted by a Mr. Caocaun, steward of the Eire Gobrath estate, a stout, tall man, built up by nature to resemble a lusty pig gradually assuming the shape of a man, all dressed in a Sunday suit of rich black broadcloth, lightened by a gold watch-chain flowing across the wide, bulging belly, like a streak of summer lightning astray in a black and sullen wintry night. There he stood, pretending to listen to all Sean said, but with a keen ear cocked for any stir below that might suggest the girls were leaving; for among them was his daughter, Julia, a dashing and very handsome lass, the fear of his life in that such a sweet girl aflower in the fortunate circumstance of having a well-off father might, if his eye closed for a moment, make a fool of herself for the sake of some of the hardier and handsomer men of Kildare. When the lessons were over, they all hurried away, girls in front with quick step, the boys behind, with slower pace, pretending indifference, but sending long, searching glances after them, the priest between with a walking-stick, looking like a drover keeping one herd of cattle from mingling with another.

The branch secretary, full of fire for Ireland, strolled with Sean, the hectic skin on his face almost cut through by the sharpness of bone in nose and jowl; wasted by consumption he was, and his tense eagerness seemed to be born of a need to do all he could before he was pulled out of the play. He led them to where they would get their dinner, talking of Ireland, Ireland leading the world when she gained her freedom, turning his face away at intervals to cough into a handkerchief that Sean saw was bright with tiny spangles of brilliant blood. When they came to the cottage where they were to eat, he held out a hand to say goodbye.

—Come in and have a share, invited Sean.

He glanced around, hesitated, and coughed again. I'd like to, he said, but can't. We have to keep guard on ourselves here. The eyes of our soggarth aroons are everywhere, and they don't like us to be long with the Dublin Sinn Feiners. There's either an eye or an ear behind every bush around us, for all words here, save paternoster and ave maria alone, are secular and dangerous; and with a Gaelic farewell he left them at the door.

Then there was the row over Tennyson's *Voyage of Maeldune*, done into Gaelic by Torna, which was to be sung by the Gaelic League Choir at the annual gathering of the Gaels in Dublin. The choir had rehearsed it long and ardently, and were ready to sing it in great style, when up jumps the Reverend Father Francis Joseph Ignatius Polycarp Dominicjerome Sebastian O'Callaghan, to shout that this poem slandered Ireland of the Virgins; and away goes the Gaelic League Executive in a panic to beg the choir to give the poem up, which they did, but not before there was a split that ruined the choir completely.

Then there was W. P. O'Ryan, with his Boyne Valley enterprise in his arms, along with his journal *The Irish Peasant*, forced by a pope-eyed cardinal to work and sing no more by the beautiful banks of the Boyne, to bury his paper, and to leave Ireland a lot lonelier by leaving it himself. Look at the gush of pious venom that was splashed over poor Synge, Gaelic Leaguers firing stones through the stream — save only that queer fellow Pearse, who ventured a trenchant word or two on behalf of the playwright. And don't forget what that thick of a Cardinal said about Yeats's *Countess Cathleen*. And didn't the clergy fall flat with the weight of the denunciation they heaped on the proposal to send a caravan of artists round Ireland playing Irish plays in towns and villages, fearful of what would happen when the sun had set, and the artists were all asleep under the cedars and the stars. Hadn't he himself organised, in all innocency, Sunday evening summer gatherings between St. Margaret's and the Drumcondra branches of the League, each body marching halfway from their Club-room to meet at a pleasant cross-roads, there to sing and dance an hour or two away to the sound of fiddle and fife; and on the second evening of the gathering, didn't the St. Margaret's curate come tearing on his bicycle, sent as courier from the parish priest, a red light on the top of his biretta, to tell them that these strange ways of men with maids wasn't, and never would be, recognised in Ireland; that it was an occasion of sin; that their conduct would embarrass the Irish saints above; and that they were showing a froward example to the Royal Irish Constabulary, the Royal Irish Academy, Trinity College, the Dublin Fire Brigade, the Grand Loyal Orange Lodge of Dublin, the Anti-taxi Association, and all those who constantly thought of the four lust things. So the fiddle was locked in its case, the fife thrust into a deep pocket, and all trotted home without a word, like sheep that hadn't gone astray, leaving Sean staring at the curate, and the curate staring at Sean. Soon he departed, and Sean sat down on a grassy slope to think it over. Even the Drumcondra members, all city folk, hadn't murmured a word. Had it been the Lord Lieutenant, they would have hooted and hissed, would have gone only when pushed away by a serried rank of police. But a few words from this insignificant man had sent them slinking home. St. Patrick had sent a hot wire to the parish priest to stop this tickling jock. And a number of the men who had withered before a word were Irish Republican Brothers. Sean hadn't believed it before, but now he had seen it with his own eyes. It was a stingy republicanism that wouldn't fight for the right to dance with a girl in the open light of day.

Again, didn't the bishops every Easter, in their epistolals, denounce the Fenians, insisting that it was a mortal sin to belong to them; and the Irish Republican Brotherhood had been losing so many members who had been infected with religious scruples by this insistent and effective attack, that the Supreme Council was forced to hold a meeting of the Circles in the Clontarf Town Hall, whose caretaker, Mick McGinn, was an old Fenian. The meeting was pictured as a lecture on Brian Boru. A number of young priests were on the platform, and these, one after the other, told their audience that love of country was a paramount Christian virtue; that no Irishman loved his country better, or as well, as a Fenian; that it was no sin to be one, and that they mustn't mention it in confession; for if any man confessed that he belonged to a secret society, the confession revealed a scruple, and the father confessor could only order him to leave it immediately. But to be a Fenian, far from being a sin, was a Christian honour, and so no matter whatsoever for confession to a priest. Cheers and the roll of drums ended the meeting. Everyone was satisfied except Sean: he felt there was a twist in it somewhere, though as a non-catholic who paid no guarded or unguarded honour to the clergy's yea or nay in politics, it was no business of his. So the leakage was caulked for the time being, though there must have been an ecclesiastical spy present, for shortly afterwards the young priests were packed off to a distant mission where there was neither room nor need for a Fenian. Christ only knows how many other instances there were in which things were hushed or throttled silently, without a sigh escaping to whisper the tale into a listening ear. These were enough to make Sean pause amid the riches of Sackville Street, or the squalor of the Coombe, to ponder them in his heart, and to make him wonder why the leaders of the Irish Movement kept their Irish mouths so tightly shut about them all.

They could move when they wanted to, like the damned nonsense of the League Executive forcing a group of protestant enthusiasts, Seumas Deacon, Ernest Blythe, George Irvine, himself, and others, to abandon their special efforts to get the protestants interested in the League's work, because, the fools said, it was bringing insectarianism into the Movement; though all it sought to do was to bring the League into touch with those who opposed, or were suspicious of, it, by sending to protestant parishes enthusiasts of their own persuasion to put the objects of the Irish Ireland Movement plainly before the protestant people. Some of them had spoken in parish halls where Ireland was emblified by a Union Jack, those honouring it forgetful that the flag bore the cross of St. Patrick as well as those of St. Andrew and St. George.

Dean Bernard was asked if he'd give St. Patrick's for a service in Irish on the saint's festival. After the Dean had recovered out of a bud swoon by swallowing a big dollop of warmed whiskey, he asked, Is there anything else you'd like? of the deputation that went to see him. Then he burst out laughing, shook his hide, and frowned with kind malignity, saying, Erse? What! have a service in Erse, and in St. Patrick's? Not in Erse, surely? Yes? No, no, gentlemen, it can't be did. It couldn't happen here. We don't want our church to be filled with Conn the Shaughrauns, like a Wicklow wedding. Besides, Heaven is used by now to the English language, and it would be a nuisance for them to have to become bilingual, so that they could make some sense of what a few might say. St. Patrick spoke Erse? So he did; but it was we forced him to it. It's his one great handicap to this day. Let me tell you, gentlemen — privately, mind you — that infra-information from above has kindly let me know that the poor gentleman sits in holy isolation there because he knows no English. Wah? Tristan and Isolde spoke Erse too? I didn't know that before this. Well, we don't speak it here. We can't afford to be Isoldationists any longer. God, gentlemen, has become a thorough old English patriot, and we're not going to let a few frantic Gaels disturb Him now with their teareasonable aspirinations. With all your persuasiveness, it's no go, for such a thing isn't up our street. Be jabers! gentlemen, yous ought to have more since! Erse! Sorry I can't *noblesse oblige* you, so so-long, gentlemen all; and a footman beadle pushed them far out into the night to tell Sean, who was waiting in the garden under a yew-tree, not being suitably clad to be fit to appear before a dean.

Off they went to see the Reverend Phineas Hunt, Rector of St. Kevin's, George Irvine and Seumas Deacon taking the Rector, and Sean holding fast to his lady, a pillar of fire in her desire to evangelise the Irish. Sean testified to his belief that if the Irish would only flee the Pope, and throw themselves into the arms of Sankey and Moody or Silas K. Shocking, all would be well; and to make it sure, the two of them sang softly together a verse of a hilarious hymn:

> Sankey's as high as the Pope in heaven —
> Higher in fact if the truth were known —
> For the Pope's at the gate, a mere mean porter,
> While Sankey's well away on his own;
> And weighted with wings, like a big cyclone,
> Flies round and round and round the throne!

When the murmured song had ended, Mrs. Hunt hurried to her husband to convince him of the truth, to turn his hesitation into hasty agreement, so that for the first time in many years a service in Irish, according to the rubric of the Church of Ireland, was held in the house of the Lord and of Phineas Hunt; and once again the deers' cry went up to Heaven on behalf of Gael and Gall-Gael, making Patrick cock his ear and wonder what was happening.

In an effort to keep the good work going, Sean went himself to Gaelic Headquarters where the Central Executive was in session. He opened the door softly, and went in to where the mighty ones were sitting round a round table, discussing whether the organisers should wear the kilt or stick to the trousers. The secretary, waking out of a doze, rushed at Sean, gripped him by the hair, asked him what he wanted, adding that this was a private meeting that wasn't to be disturbed. When Sean told him what he wanted, the secretary gave a frightened squeal, rushed Sean out of the room, down the winding stairs, shoved him into the road, closed, locked, and chained up the heavy hall door to make things safe. Then Sean tried to persuade his comrade protestants to damn and defy the League Executive, but the timidity of their leaders had so nullified and dullified them that they slunk away from a fight and allowed the whole thing to dissolve into a forgotten memory.

What a difference here from the stand of his own Rector, who had joyfully promoted a debate on the Irish language between Sean and the schoolmaster. Later, the Rector wanted Sean to let him cancel the discussion, for Sean had spoken badly and brokenly at a previous meeting in the part of appointed speaker; and the kindly Rector was afraid Sean would make a show of himself in the debate, a thought troubling him more than it troubled Sean. Determined to go on with what he had set himself to do, Sean refused to back out; and to this day he could see the delight on the Rector's handsome, spiritual face after he had spoken eloquently for three-quarters of an hour; he could see the white graceful hands applauding vigorously when he sat down to give place to the schoolmaster who had been upset by the fire and vigour of Sean's talk, and his few hesitant objections were passionately disposed of in a reply, amid the smiling appreciation of the Rector. To this day he had the Irish Testament the Rector gave him in honour of his fine fight, a book that carried the escutcheon of the Rector's satisfaction in its inscription of To John Casside, with all good wishes. E. M. Griffin. 1905.

All the time, the indomitable Dr. Hyde splashed and spluttered a way through the foaming, swift-flowing, swirling Gaelstroem, saying again and again the things he had said again and again before; striving to make the Gaelic League a force to be proud of, and fiercely respectable, keeping the vision before him of the wonders in the old Irish Hierarchaeological Society of 1842, in whose bosom were embedded a duke, an earl, a viscount, and a baron, while flowering in the Society itself were three dukes, five marquises, fourteen earls, ten viscounts, seven barons, one archbishop, eight bishops, a big fistful of baronets, and an uncountable crowd of right honourables. Though the Society that followed, to Hyde's sorrow, had no gigantic people to guide it, wasn't Standish O'Grady the uncle of a lord, and wasn't his father an admiral? So Hyde went about, gathering into the League what he could, including a host of civil servants whom the law prevented from touching politics.

—Looka Birch aar, said Hyde, Paddy O'Shea, Shaun O'Cahan — customs officers all who wouldn't have had an earthly, but for the League, to toil for Ireland; but might have spent their lives weaving daisy-chains in a summer field, amusing themselves with green thoughts in a greener shade. Yes, shouted Hyde, everywhere we have brought into friendly comopinionship people who before wouldn't walk on the same side of the street!

—No, shouted a priest into Hyde's ear, not till the day of judgment will it be known how much the Gaelic League has done to bring the quarrelling Irish into the way of a sweet unity, and a refresher peace among the Gaels!

All this, and more, the undaunted Hyde said in a long letter to the editor of the American *Irish World*, who, in leading articles, was accusing the Gaelic League of butting its head against the Irish Parliamentary Party. Reams long, the letter was, and so remarkable that Dr. Hyde kept a copy of it; but one night, when he was in a deeper sleep, the little mice crept in and ate up every scrap of it. The three blind mice, maybe. Hyde, by keeping out of politics, drew all the Irish together into the bonds of an uncommon love. But, blast it, it didn't last! Over came Father Yorke of San Francisco, to give a lecture before the Central Branch of the Gaelic League; but as Hyde had no personal acquaintance with this gentleman, and couldn't tell beforehand what he'd be likely to say, he kept at home — enemies saying in a locked room, made safely dark with all the blinds drawn. Well it was he didn't go, for when Father Yorke came, he saw the way things were, and a right anger seized him. He put a point on his tongue, lashing out at members of Parliament, the press, priests, nuns, managers and teachers of schools, fathers and mothers, not sparing anyone, so that Dublin shook, saying things, says Hyde, that badly needed saying, that he himself would like to have said, were he not afraid that it might make matters worse. There were ructions the following morning, the *Freeman's Journal* letting roar after roar of anger out of it, for Father Yorke had plunged a knife up to the haft in its hiphurrahypocrisy; and Hyde, naturally, was delighted that the paper couldn't say he had aught to do with it; for had it been otherwise, they would have lost its help, and an attack on Hyde would have damaged the cause. Some defended the *Freeman's Journal*, and Yorke answered with a letter that shoved the knife still farther into the bowels of the poor quivering journal.

After that, came a shot from that bounder D. P. Moran, editor of *The Leader*, who wrote a leading article entitled *We Want a Man*, causing another rent in Hyde's temple veil of unity, and another roar to break the quietness, for many ran hither and thither, shouting, This is meant for Hyde; the article clearly implying that there wasn't enough of the man in Hyde to fit him to be head of the League. Hyde didn't believe it himself, for he had always been great with Moran, and sometimes wrote for his paper, so that the article was best forgot. But, damn it, there was Arthur Griffith screeching in his paper that there was a plot to oust Hyde and all gallant Gaels from the League, and hand over control to the King's men, desirous that the Pursuivants Sorroy and Norroy should be the chief officers of the Gaelic League; but, Griffith went on, if these people persisted in their evil work to disrupt the unity of the Gaels, they'd be cast out, stricken down, knocked silly, and burst to bits, so that the joy of unity might be held in the bond of peace.

While that thunder was still grumbling, Dr. Hyde and Norma Borthwick, an official of the League, culled out a holiday and put on their best attire and set out for Donegal to help in the unveiling of a new cathedral, built by the Bishop O'Donnell; and who d'ye think they ran into on the white steps of the new church but the bould John Dillon, and he dressed up to the nines for the great occasion! And what d'ye think, without by your leave, or a ha'p'orth, but Farella from Dublin must rush up to him, clutch a hold of his coat-tail, haul him back a bit, and shout in his left ear, Eh, you, about this question of the Irish Movement — if you're going to give it a miss, and refuse to reckon with it, it'll reckon with you, me boyo! We've a man in Ballyvourney, and we've only got to say the word and he'll be elected!

—Do you mean, said the Dillonock, nonplussed for a moment, you'll put a man up against the member who has fought in the House of Commons for Ireland, without thought for years of his own needs and necessary emolument?

—That's exactly what I mean, said Farella.

—In that case, if yous do, retorted the Dillonock, jabbing a dint in the steps with the point of his umbrella, and pulling his coat-tail out of Farella's grip, I'll fight yous while I've a leg to stand on!

—Now boys, boys, boys, murmured Hyde, the pikeman of peace; no quarrelling in the shade of the cathedral.

—Shade of a cathedral or shade of the old apple-tree! shouted Farella, it's all one to me — we're going to keep leatherin' away with the wattle O!

—What bottle O? asked the Dillonock, puzzled. Leather away with what bottle O, man?

—Not what bottle O, man, answered Farella derisively; wattle O, not bottle O, man. Aren't you even acquainted with the order given by Ireland herself, and she in the form of a beautiful young lady steppin' stately through the streets of Dublin, or the green plains of

County Mayo, your own homeland? Listen, man alive! and he caught the Dillonock again by the tail of his coat:

> Last night I strolled on a hillside bare,
> And sat me down to hear the birds;
> A wonder came to me unaware,
> For their singing changed to mighty words.
>
> A lovely damsel, tall and fair,
> With clusterin' hair that shone like gold,
> An' a tiny mouth like a cupid's bow,
> That open'd wide to shout out bold,
> Leather away with the wattle O!
>
> We'll rout the English bucks, says she,
> With showers o' shot, an' our harbours free,
> If yous only listen right to me,
> An' leather away with the wattle O!

What sort of a survival are you — giving a tug to the coat-tail — of your glorious ancestor, General Dillon, who fought an' died for Ireland on th' field o' Fontenoy?

—You're becoming quite personal now, said the Dillonock, so we'll part: I'm not accustomed to such aspersions.

—Aren't you now? Well, you soon will be, for th' threes of Kilcash are growin' again!

—Here, now, me good men, stand aside an' make room, said a constabulary man, shoving them to the side of the mighty flight of steps; are yous all blind that yous can't see the clergy comin'?

—Leggo me coat, leggo, leggo! snarled the Dillonock, twisting the tail of it from Farella's grasp; and then the golden wrangle was lost in the jangle, mangle, and tangle of the bell-ringing, as the clergy, led by the bishop, carrying his closure, led by the cross-bearer, came slowly up dem golden stairs, chanting *Deo dubilinladdi*, followed by canons major and minor, priests secular and regular, and the renowned Orders of Laurestinians, Holy Hards of Eireann, Vigilantians of the Clean Mind, Sacred Sodality of Ruddy Roverians, Standardarians, Universalists, Catholic Timerians, Bellopatricians, Crossoconglians, Monasterboiceans, Holsomlitituriurians, the Most Primitive Order of Ancient Hibeernians, led by Weejodavlin; Catholic Heralangelists, Greenflaggregorians, Knights and Squires of Honestogodians, the 1872 Company of Griffithians, Cullenites, Macabians, Breenboruvians, Tirnalogians, Banabanians; the Black and White Assembly of

Censorians, Sleevenamonites, the Knights of Columnbannus with
their blazon, on a field sable, a dove with a money order in its beak, all
proper; the sacred choir of Micuirmick, chanting the palacestraina of
Rome Sweet Rome; the united Confraternities of Bancorians, Investo-
rians, and Brokerians, their banner of white, holding three gold balls,
with holy emblazoned on each of them; the poor Sodalities of the
Guild of Matthewisons of Talbuttamia, all clad in holy rags, roses of
Sharon mingled with their hair, and tight bands of rusty steel round
their pinched bellies, and they chanting, Religion is the only d'hope
of the workers; stalwart members of the Architects of the Treasurrec-
tion, heavily cowled, all earnest students of the things written round
the angelic life of A. Job; then in slow and solemn step came the
Gulled of Dreamy Jerontius, chanting in slow time, *Oh for the wings
of Above*; while the procession was closed in by the spirited Confraternity of True Maltaterians, displaying their great banner, the
colour of liquid gold, having in chief three swallows perching on a red
cross, a silver star in each bird's beak, increated with a dancing baby
bottle of Aqua vita, inscribed with the gullant knights' inspiring
motto of Neamh na Neul — the Heaven of the Clouds.

Donal Mac Rory O'Murachadha was grumbling about it all to
Sean, the pair of them standing, hands in pockets, under the Grecian
portico of the Post Office, staring at a sharp slash of rain pelting off
the tops of the trams assembled at Nelson's Pillar.

—Hyde's always blathering about the League being non-political,
he said, but forgets it's sectarian too, hurrying off to every catholic
gathering where he hopes to meet a bishop.

—Parnell went after the clergy too, Donal.

—No fear, he didn't: the clergy went after him. They didn't like it,
so they sat silent, blinking on their benches like horned owls, waiting
their chance; and when it came, out they flew, hooting, to help the
wolves in the rending of Ireland's grandest son. They'll never do that
to Hyde, for he has a bend in his back, looking at episcopal rings.

Poor old Hyde, thought Sean, out of one dilemma into another!
There's the Tory *Daily Express* for ever aiming venom at him; and
look at Father Barry of Oldcastle, a Royal Meath townland of a
handful of frightened and scattered people, look at the malicious
lunge he made at Hyde, writing in a Meath paper of the filthy insolence
of Hyde, mixing the poor man up with the careless, conceited covey
responsible for the quarterly called *Dana* (which Sean longed to have,
but couldn't afford), the name of a kind of prehistorical, mythological
Mother MoChree to the older Irish gods, though Hyde never read a

line of the journal, never spent a ha'penny on it, and had nothing whatever to do with it, so he said. The same courtly priest came down on Hyde for mixing the clever Munster poem called *The Illbred Child and His Mother* among his Connacht sacred songs and soulos. Then the Kilkenny branch of the League staged Hyde's little Nativity play, several priests joining in it, and delighted at the bare idea; but the Church waxed indignant that she hadn't been told about it, and down comes the bishop with a train of clergy to put the kybosh on the venture, and to teach the Gaelic League of Kilkenny something more than manners. Dr. Hyde, of course, made haste to make it clear he had had no knowledge of the idea, neither had he any acquaintance with a single person active in putting it into practice.

The passion to be all things to all men is too strong in him to allow a leadership bringing the people into the promised land, thought Sean, sauntering along Sackville Street, passing Chancellor's, optical instrument makers and Court photographer, with its three-faced clock swung out before its façade, and a gilded bell on the top of it. Something like this bell Hyde was; Ireland's heavily-gilded tin bell, chiming the hours sweetly away, but never hardening into a tocsin to call the people to a battle. Sean went over the road to lean on the river parapet, looking over at Butler's, seller of everything musical, with its window festooned with oboe, clarinet, drum, and trumpet, with a gorgeous model of a uniform, dazzling in its blue-and-crimson facings, its gold-and-green collar, shoulder-strap, and epaulette, ready-made for any Dawn of Freedom or Erin's Hope band and Irish town might think of forming. Hyde played the accordion in Ireland's Brass band, keeping the turmoil in tune.

Hyde had a hard furrow to plough. There were rocks everywhere threatening to knock the share to bits. After all, the Movement was strictly non-political and non-sectarian, though Donal had asked why a special invitation to be at a gathering should be sent to a catholic cardinal, when no similar one was sent to the protestant primate of Armagh. It was plain that Hyde had to be cautious, though that wasn't a hard thing for him. He was no fool. He had had a narrow escape, though, when he went as prime speaker to a dinner in Sligo given by the Association of National School Teachers, where he sat next to the local member of Parliament whose statue, one of Connacht's wonders, stands in a public place to this very day. Hyde's bum hadn't warmed to the seat when he noticed that something was wrong, for numbers were standing up, sitting down, standing up, sitting down again, as if an invisible force was tugging them two ways at once. One of them slid from his chair, crept under the table, pulled Hyde's trousers, and thrust up the menu card to the tip of his nose, and there on the back of it, in letters of purest gold, was The Toast to the King.

—What are you goin' to do? queried the man from under the table.

—What am I going to do? Eat my dinner, what else, said Hyde. And eat it he did like a man, till he was full up, and the time of the toasts appeared in the land. Then he thrust a hand into his bosom, groped round for a moment, and drew it out again empty.

—My soul to glory! he exclaimed, if I haven't left my cigars behind me! Excuse me, leaning over towards the chairman, till I rush back to my hotel and get them. Then off he went with the speed of Master McGrath after the hare, dawdling about till he felt the coast was clear; came slowly back to find that the toast was a thing of the past in time and space, and all serene, and danger over, and hope renewed, and freed from blame. Ah, me sweet yourself, me cunning gayboy, me witty now-you-see-me-and-now-you-don't conundrum, me cameo cumonora nah erreann, one of the faithful, one of the phew!

Look at the row there was, too, over the proposed International Exhibition, held, some said, to ruin the few hen-picked industries in Ireland. So the true-hearted Gaels were all for a National Exhibition, where only the home products and native manufactures would be helled up to honour; and at a meeting held to uphold the International Idea, Mac Neill, Alderman Cole, Edward Martyn, and some of the descendants of Brian Boru spoke so trenchantly against it that the audience lost its head, and led by the solid men of the Muldoon clan, the three hundred men and three men, the Boys of Wexford, Erin's hope and pride, the young men, and the men of eighty too, some of the noblest peasantry on God's earth, and the boatman of Kinsale, helped by the wind that shakes the barley, broke up the meeting, and everyone said that gall was over. But the people behind the International Idea, nothing daunted, went their way, got Pembroke Park, and in two twinklings the Exhibition was there in substance and in fact. But wait till I tell you: no sooner was its flags flying than, before one could say Jack Robinson, Danny Boy, Kelly of Killann, arm in arm with Kelly from the Isle of Man, Peg o' Me Heart, with her bonny bunch of roses O, the peeler and the goat, Brian O'Linn were flocking in to it; and at their heels a crowd of Gaels, blocking up the entrances, keeping each other out by trying to get each other in, striving to be the first to see the sights, to purchase bargains, and to get a tasty lunch at a reasonable price, served by the prettiest girls from Clare; Flowers of Finea and Roses of Tralee, with many Shan van Vochts, were there too, among others who, on bended knees, had sworn they'd never set a foot inside; indeed, some said but two persons refrained from having anything to do with it — Sean O'Casside who hadn't the money to pay to get in; and Dr. Hyde himself, though the story went round that he was often seen there as large as life, running around, eating and drinking his fill, though he says himself he never never even as much as looked over the wall.

—Listen, said a member of the Keating branch, as he, Sean, and Donal were walking out to view the shamrock plains of Finglas, listen till I tell yous how Hyde made a cod o' poor Johnny Redmond — yous'll die laughin'. Afther Redmond made his speech in favour of Irish and again' th' Education Board, didn't Hyde discover that him an' he were stayin' at th' same hotel, an' on th' way home he let out that he was to speak at a dinner in Oxford in honour of St. Patrick, a few days before the festival, an' nothin' would do Johnny Redmond but to make Hyde promise to be at the great dinner of the Irish Party on the night of the festival itself. An' then it flashed on Hyde that, if he went, his tour of America might be mixed with a roar of derision from start to finish. In a nice fix, wasn't he?

—It takes Hyde to pull out of a fix, growled Donal.

—Sure, I know. He done it all right; but wait till I tell yous. He wrote out his speech for the Party dinner, an' sent it to the *Freeman's Journal*; then what did he do in th' evenin' but rang up the paper, tellin' them to hold back th' printin' of the speech, for he was ill in Oxford and couldn't go to the Party dinner! He told his Oxford host he wasn't well, an' poured himself into bed, an' indeed th' poor man had a pain in the head brought about by the breakfast and lunch he had had that day; an' in bed he stayed till St. Patrick's Day had dwindled away to the morning after, when he went back to London, and that night sallied off with Lord Monteagle's daughter to an Irish concert in the Queen's Hall; an' where d'ye think did he sit but plump between Johnny Redmond an' his wife — Tow-row-row, Paddy, will yeh now sit beside me, silent, silent, I'm all right!

—That's th' sort he is, said Donal.

—Redmond believed him, said the Keating member, for after some singing, when he was givin' a gorgeous speech, Hyde gave his throat an odd squeeze to bring about a whoarse-son wheezing so as to give Johnny Redmond the benefit of a doubt. Clever, wasn't he?

—I'd say he was mean, said Donal. He wouldn't do it to a bishop. Look at the way he glows telling us how an archbishop put a grand, costly dinner before him, with the company of twenty guests around the arrogant table, who, he tells us, must have been together worth upwards of fifty million dollars. Ireland's chief and a follower of the lowly Jesus find everything bright, generous, and lively in the midst of wealth, with lashins to eat and drink to make it all livelier still.

—Be fair, Donal, said Sean, and don't forget that a letter written in Irish, by Mary Spring Rice, Monteagle's daughter, converted important persons by showing them that the Gaelic Movement had the support of elegant and most respectable people.

It's far more important that Irish should be written by Mick McGilligan's daughter Maryanne, responded Donal fiercely. If all the Mary Spring Rices, daughters of all the Monteagles, spoke the Irish, and none of the Maryannes, daughters of the Mick McGilligans, spoke it, then the Irish would be dead. Hyde's arm's round everyone's neck. All things to all men. A volgayno smothering Ireland in a smoke of empty words. A king with a cushion for a crown! Keep cool, says Hyde, Keep cool, says Arthur Griffith, and cool keeps Eoin Mac Neill. To ask Ireland to keep out of politics is asking her to keep out of life; and the only politics for Ireland today is animosity to England, shown by word of mouth and blow from fist!

And keep cool, whispers St. Patrick, through his successors, to them all; you Knights of St. Patrick especially, for a lot depends on you, and cool you must keep if you're to hang on to those fifty million dollars. They weren't in this Club for the sake of fame or honour, or for the sake of their money, nor for their own personal gain, but only and alone for the good of the country at large, said the chairman; and Hear hear, says the saint, we know that well; and don't forget the boy in the biretta when yous are jottin' down your wills. So give all yous can, for yous are all sons of the Church, an' good sons too, though it's I who say it who shouldn't. Your outlook is a natural one, says Hyde, and you do well to keep out of trouble.

—Be God, he's after takin' th' words out of me mouth, remarked St. Patrick to St. Bronach and she chanting the *Star of the County Down* to herself. A nice little group, these Friendly Sons o' St. Patrick, he went on musingly; all rich men and good catholics, th' one an' only organisation the Irish rich would touch, for they found that in the others there were too much deceit, disunity, and quarrelling; or, to use betther-known phraseology, too much envy, hatred, an' malice, an' as these had all the contrary virtues, it was very wise not to go where they would be condamninated; so here, in moneyastic serenity, they could eat lunch and dinner without any untoward thoughts disturbing their contemplation of divine things. He leaned over and stretched out, hanging on by his toes to a twinkling star, so that he was near enough to ding advice into Hyde's ear: Keep your head, he said, and go warily, but not warrily; don't let them go off the rails, for that means I'm up all night sendin' therms to the bishops to get them spruced an' spined to birch it into any elementary idiot who, to make himself poplar, leads people to where their barks may be beeched, to the treemendous loss of their souls, leavin' them in the larch, tremblin', like aspens, when they find themselves with a horn beamin' from their bums, an oakasion yew never want to view. I know it's not easy keepin' them in bounds, for give them an inch an' they want a hell. You made a slip when you sung about young men with the pikes on shoulders, an' I had a time explainin' it was an innocent way you had; for well we remember the tense time we had when that free-thinker Tone an' his French fleet in Banthry Bay was only a few yards off from our holy isle, the sweat pourin' off us, an our hearts burstin' raisin' th' wind to blow him an' his back to France. An' whisper, listen, will you tell them not to be givin' so much space-time to a St. Ignatius here, a St. Aloysius Gonzaga there, an' a St. Pether of Alcantara yonder; with St. Anthony of Podua worn out attendin' them, an' his poor eyes dim with the glare of the candles lighted to him, when we have enough an' to spare of our own, like meself, Columbus, Bridget, Kieran of Kilkenny, Finbarr of Cork, Codalot of Queery Isle, Damawluvus of Sinisagoner, Tatther Jacwelsh, patron of hoboes, Corruckther, patron of dancers, with his sacred companion and martyr, Kayleegoer, Feckimgumoy, patron of seelots, Janethainayrin, patron of factories, Sheemsa, patron of marrymakers, Sullisanlay, patron of slums, Hillolureus and Ardalaunus, brother patrons of free-drinkers, Willogod, patron of workers, Ellesdeea, patron of employers, and money more who are a credit to our native land.

There the Saint stood, all alone in his glory, surrounded by a wide frame, thickly gilded, over the broad fireplace of the Jolly Topers, the happy pub in Finglas for bona-fides; there he stood in his grand green chasuble, quivering with embroidered shamrocks, harps, and round towers, a golden mitre covering half of his flowing white hair, a crozier in his left hand, his right stretched out, pointing a way to the sea, for the information of the swarm of green and yellow snakes who were, in a frenzy of fear, gliding swiftly by the crimson slippers of the saint, eager to hide themselves under the waves lest a worse fate befall them.

—Ay, said Donal, taking a swig from his frothy-headed glass of stout, there he is — a man who for centuries has done our country more harm than good.

—Ah, I wouldn't say that, now, murmured the member of the Keating branch.

—Frightened us all into a fear of thought, went on Donal, and Hyde is one of his forth-rate agitant-generals. Well, he exclaimed suddenly, here's to all the unfriendly sons of St. Patrick, the best sons Ireland ever had, and he raised his glass high over his head.

—I join you, said Sean, clinking his glass to Donal's.

—Ah, I wouldn't say that now, said the member of the Keating branch; no, I wouldn't go as far as that now; and he watched them emptying their glasses at a gulp.

HORA NOVISSIMA

SEAN was growing tired. He saw how few had gathered around Eire. His eyes, too, were aching, and forget them how he might, he'd the feeling that they weren't as strong as they had been. Dry bones everywhere. Owen Mac Neill brooding over the Brehon Laws and wondering when he'd lead the people back like a shepherd, green-ribboned crook in hand, to the Arcadian Gaelic State. The Irish Republican Brotherhood thinking always of tomorrow when the rebels would be on the hills, red coats and black coats flying before them. James Connolly for ever assuring himself that his Irish Socialist Republican ten commandments, beginning with the nationalisation of railways, canals, banks, and braes, would be observed by the common people, too busy keeping themselves in good standing with saints, angels, and parish priests, by a gallop every Sunday morning to the entrance of the Pro-Cathedral, to stand, bareheaded and silent, for short twelve Mass, so as to show they were to the fore when needed; to show God that they wouldn't be behindhand when the bell tolled, when the world was gone with the wind, and nothing was there to do, save sing the song of Bernadette while the stars looked down.

Who would be the first to make an army out of these active and diligent dry bones? Who the first to breathe into them a breath from the flame of endeavour and strife and defiance? Whose lips would first be touched by a red coal from God's altar? Who would be daring enough to snatch a flame from the burning bush and light the land with it? Not Arthur Griffith, for all his words were cold and common;

not any of the Republican leaders, for though brave and terribly
sincere, none could show a light brighter than a dark lantern; neither
Hyde nor Mac Neill, for though the one whispered while the other
bellowed, no one of the common people caught a flake of flame from
anything they said. Certainly not Bulmer Hobson, protestant secretary of the I.R.B., editor of *Irish Freedom*, and head bottle-washer of
all National activities, with his moony face, bulbous nose, long hair
half covered by a mutton-pie hat, a wrapped look on his face, moving
about mysterious, surrounded by the ghostly guns of Dungannon:
   Ireland awoke when Hobson spoke — with fear was England shaken.

   Once, leaning over the counter in the little tobacconist's shop to
speak to Tom Clarke sitting in the corner, Sean had said, Why don't
you get an editor for *Irish Freedom*, a betther and brighter man than
Bulmer Hobson? You ought to know, Mr. Clarke, that our members
read the paper, now, not for guidance or for inspiration, but merely
in a sense of duty. Hobson's articles are nothing more than hundreds
of dead thoughts on thousands of cold, leaden slabs of words; and
Tom Clarke, who had been nodding in a doze, sprang to his feet
excitedly, fire flashing from his remarkable eagle-like eyes, and said
hotly, Get out of my shop if you came to talk against Bulmer! D'ye
hear, I'll listen to nothing against him. I love Bulmer Hobson as I love
my own son!

   For a joke, some seraph must have touched the lips of De Valera
with a chilled coal from God's altar, to laugh henceforth at the sturdy
mouth's efforts to blow it into flame, to turn it into a song of derring-do
for everyone to whistle o'er the lave of it. Though Sean knew not even
of De Valera's existence, there he was walking beneath the gentle
clouds caressing Dublin's streets: a young man full of the seven
deadly virtues, punctual, zealous, studious, pious, and patriotic,
cautiously pushing a way through crowds of queerternions, stopping
occasionally to put them through their paces, numbering them off,
making minus double exes of them, forming them into plus fours, and
sending them forth in a hurray of feshelons so that one day they might
make Ireland a nation of restraints and scollars. In love with a clever
and beautiful lady he was, too, who yearned deeply to make her isle a
nation free and grand. So De Valera hurried about — for such as he
never sauntered, or strolled, or took their ayse in a walk — unknown
to all but those to whom an Irish word unheard before was another
rung in the Gaelic ladder up to Heaven.

   Yeats, the poet, wandered, lonely as a cloud, through the streets,
singing his lovely songs into his own ear, wailing at times to his own

Psyche, *Romantic Ireland's dead and gone, It's with O'Leary in the grave*; the wind for ever rustling the reeds around his feet; wild, white swans for ever flying in a blue sky over his head; and a black-and-gold theatre curtain for ever rising or falling before his eyes. No; he would not kindle a flame in the eyes of the common people, though he had kindled one in the eyes of Cathleen, the daughter of Houlihan; though in a strange, deep way he loved the common people more than Griffith, Mac Neill, or De Valera did, or ever could. Hard at his heels followed the stout, lumbering George Russell, watching figures, featured with fire issuing out of their petuitary glands, streaming from every chimney-top and every smoker's pipe; jumping hilariously, when on a holiday, from peak to peak of the Wicklow Mountains, the planets for ever chiming the advent of an avatar who would lead Eire back to her old gods; believing that the world was buried in a purple glow; staring fixedly at every person newly presented to him, so that he might see if a red, a blue, or a golden aura bathed the body, telling him on what plane of spiritual achievement the newly-presented person stood. Then there was Patrick Pearse, unknown but to a few, sitting at a desk editing the Gaelic League's *Sword of Light*; a dreamer pulled separate ways by two attractions, for one hand held on to St. Patrick's robe, and the other stretched out to grasp the Spear of Danger held out to him by the singing, laughing, battling boy, Cuchullain. None of these would do. The people still waited for a Prometheus to bring down a brand of the divine fire and set the leaden hearts of the poor aflame from one end of Ireland to the other.

Sean knew them all. He had served in the secret I.R.B. and the open Wolfe Tone Memorial Committee. He was their press steward, and was in charge of all publicity for concert, anniversary, and procession. He was ever at them to put more colour into their activities. He had persuaded them to fix the Republican green, white, and orange flag at a saluting-point just before the grave of Wolfe Tone was reached, so that the marching contingents could give eyes right to the flag and to the dead leader when they assembled to honour his memory. Then he had gone to Mr. Jamieson, proprietor of the Rotunda picture house, and had induced him to promise to make a film of the march past the flag, if the Memorial Committee agreed. Sean had long arguments with the members, for they were afraid that so much publicity would give too much information to the police, though Sean knew full well that what the police didn't know then, wasn't worth knowing. The delegates of the Wolfe Tone clubs voted for it; the film was made; and for many nights the Rotunda was crowded out by the members of the

I.R.B. flocking to it to see themselves taking part in the Bodenstown procession. But the Committee or the Centres wouldn't hear of route marches with meetings at different places, when the march ended, to get recruits. It was a secret organisation, they said, and so it must remain. He couldn't get them to see that such activities wouldn't allow the police to break into any inner secret that mattered. He couldn't get them to see that their fight would be tougher than a rough-and-tumble with the police, and that they weren't preparing for this fact. At Centre meetings he tried to put before them some of the problems they would have to face: digging sudden shelters; a slow come-together, a quick get-away, or the opposite; the use of signalling; the problem of provisions; and the care of the wounded. But the meetings of the Centres solely engaged themselves with the collection of this and that levy, or the sale of tickets for one thing or another. It was maddening to him. No important matter was ever discussed unless he himself thrust it under their nose. Few of those whom Sean knew could handle a pick or shovel, tie a knot, do a bandage round a serious wound, slash a gut-way in a hedge, light a fire and cook a simple meal in a wet field with a keen wind blowing. About these things they knew next to nothing.

Once in an effort to be mysterious, to keep him quiet, and to show how wide-awake they really were, a prominent Centre had handed him a British red-covered *Manual of Military Drill*, full of trivialities, useless and out of date, such as the way to slope, port, and shoulder arms, dig shallow trenches, and skirmishing; the guards and thrusts of an infantryman facing a mounted soldier, one, two, three, how to shield a head from a sabre-cut, how to drive a retaliative thrust, how to pin down the cavalryman when he fell from his horse, how to make it a sure thing by a twist to the bayonet as the thrust was made, and a contrary twist when pulling the bayonet back — old stuff, and useless; so he flung it back at them, saying that he'd gone through all this with a broom handle when he was ten, from an identical book given to him by his Dublin Fusilier brother.

They were all lost and dreaming in the romantic ecstasy of Thomas Davis's:

Oh, for a steed, a rushing steed, on the Curragh of Kildare,
And Irish Squadrons skilled to do what they are ready to dare —
A hundred yards, and England's guards
Drawn up to engage me there!

They were immersed in the sweet illusion of fluttering banners, of natty uniforms, bugle-blow marches, with row on row of dead and

dying foemen strewn over the Macgillicuddy's Reeks, the Hills of
Dublin, and the bonny blue Mountains of Mourne, with the *Soldier's
Song* aroaring at the dawning of the day. All guns and drums, but no
wounds. Not a thought, seemingly, about the toil, the rotten sweat,
the craving for sleep, the sagging belly asking silently for food; the
face disfigured, one eye wondering where the other had gone; an arm
twisted into a circle or a figure of eight; the surprised lung, bullet-
holed, gasping for breath; or the dangling leg, never to feel firm on the
earth again. All these thoughts he forced before them, asking them to
think of ways now by which they might be made less terrible. All your
singing is but glittering tinsel, coloured balls, and green ribbon. A
song is a fine thing so long as the arms in your hands are as good, or
almost so, as those in the hands of the other fellow. Our methods won't
be dashing cavalry charges, or daring and irresistible charges by
massed infantry. It will be a modified example of the Boer way of
fighting; not those even of Cronje, Joubert, or Prinsloo; but rather of
Botha, Delarey, and De Wet. Sean had always had a bent for criticism,
now it had been sharpened by Shaw, and those who heard it resented
the disturbance of their dreams.

However, he had persuaded them into selecting a committee from
the Supreme Council and the Centres to see how the I.R.B. could be
brought into closer touch with the militant Labour Movement. They
met in Seamus O'Connor's house in Clonliffe Road, and he and Sean
Mac Dermott were chosen to visit Jim Larkin, to get the *Irish Worker*
to record their activities. They found a hearty welcome, and a direct
promise that the paper would do all it could, which couldn't be much
more than it was doing at the moment in support of the National
Movement, which Sean knew to be true; and a firm request that *Irish
Freedom* might, in return, pay a little attention to the cause of the
workers. This, said Sean, will surely be done. The next meeting of the
Committee was to be held in the *Irish Freedom* office, so that what had
happened might be recorded, and when Sean got there on the tick, he
found Tom Clarke sitting on the counter, waiting for the others to
come. None of the rest, S. O'Connor, S. Deakin, Bulmer Hobson,
Peader Cearney, author of the *Soldier's Song*, came. Nor did any send
a reason for their absence. They just ignored the whole thing. Both
Sean and Tom Clarke waited for some time. Then Clarke slid from
the counter saying, They can't be coming. I must get back to the shop.
So in silence Sean saw him lock the office door, slip the key in his
pocket, heard him say, Well, so long, Sean, and saw him go without
breaking his silence by a single word.

Clarke knew they wouldn't come, thought Sean as he walked homewards through the once aristocratic Gloucester Street, past St. Thomas's Church where his sister's children had been baptised, standing sentinel at the top of the street, keeping back the poor from pressing into the richer part of the city. So they have decided against bringing the rough energy and virile splendour of the workers to the definite aid of the National Movement. Well, to hell with them then! Why should he give up all his energy and the little money he had to spare to a movement that left almost all the people out of it? They didn't seem to know even what they would have to face. Any shelter they might need, they would have to build it with their own hands, hands that wouldn't know how to do it. A shelter, strong, but to last through the time of danger only. Any permanent sit-down in any place wouldn't do; it would be surrounded, and dissipated in smoke and flame. Their vantage points would have to be the deep ditch, the bramble hedge tangled with the dog-rose, or the street corner leading from a maze of turnings. They couldn't hope to stand upright in the battle: they would have to come crouching, and, crouching, get away again swift and foxy. And there would be no green flag for a wounded man to wrap around him; he would be lucky to have a bandage to stay the flow from his leaking body.

Few of the Republicans were of his kinship. Here, in these houses in the purple of poverty and decay, dwelt his genuine brethren. Why shouldn't he fight for them against the frauds that kept them prisoners there? Sean had seen and felt the force of the corrupting hand stretched out for profit, sometimes from the sleeve of Christ's coat itself. A foreman where he had once worked, a highly respected churchwarden, and a good fellow in a lot of ways, had a club from which the workers had to buy what they rarely wanted, costing four times the market price. All earned by overtime went to pay what they owed. Sean refused to join, gathered the men together against it, and the club was dissolved; but from that day he had been a marked man, and found peace only when he returned to idleness and hunger.

In another job a number of arches to carry a big building had to be constructed by a Dublin firm of Jim and Jerry Dilish, and Sean was selected to watch that the job was done according to contract. He had been told smilingly that the Dilishes were a reliable firm, and that he needn't put himself out watching: immediately, Sean felt suspicious. Like Sir Boyle Roche, he said to himself, I smell a rat; I see him forming in the air and darkening the sky; but I'll nip him in the bud. When he got to the job, the foreman, a carpenter, ran to him, shook

his hand, said how glad he was a Gael had come to him; that he had
heard Sean speak splendidly at Gaelic League and Sinn Fein meetings;
said he was a good Gael too, and that they were bound to get on well
together; and asked Sean out for a drink. The rat was growing bigger.
When he saw Sean poring over the specifications, the saucy grin on
his face weakened, and he came close to whisper, This may mean a
fiver for you; and it's well to know that the firm's friendly with the
engineer, wines and dines with him.

It was a hard fight for Sean. What good would any opposition be
from him? The loss of another job would be God's own reward for
honesty: that was the hard fact, coupled with the soft one that a fiver
would be the reward for a closed eye, a shut mouth. He had never seen
a fiver, much more owned one. For one of them he could buy ten fine
second-hand books he needed. And by putting himself in the way of
getting them, he linked himself up with a new pair of trousers, and a
new skirt for his mother that she badly needed. By accommodation,
too, he linked himself with greater men, the contractor, the engineer,
and the foreman. Who was to pay for the job? A crowd of share-
holders who'd never know anything about it, so that, as the Church
would say, there was no individual soul against which to sin. Neither
would there be a betrayal of trust, for those connected with the job
were all rogues, bar the workmen, who were honest because they
hadn't the chance to be anything else. So what or whom would he
betray by taking the fiver? He'd suffer a sense of shame for a short
time, that was all; though he couldn't stop the thought that never
again would he be the same man he had been before he took the
money. To hell with them! he thought: God or no God, I'll be as
straight as I can. So the contractor's foreman paled with anger, and
cursed when Sean held him to the bond.

—Dilish's a boxer, he remarked one day, and I shouldn't like to be
you if you upset him.

—I can do a bit of rough-and-tumble myself, replied Sean, and
tell him that from me.

One day, high up on the plank of a scaffolding, along came a tall
partner of the firm, trim in a fine navy-blue lounge suit, cream
embroidered waistcoat, soft hat, and natty tie, till they touched the
rough garments of Sean, and the stalwart figure bent down to whisper
in his ear, though he looked straight in front, as if not noticing Sean,
I understand you're giving a lot of trouble here, interfering, holding
the work back, and making yourself a nuisance.

—I? whispered Sean back at him, staring frontways too. Oh, no, not at all; I'm an amiable fellow really.

—The likes of you make me sick! said the blue lounge suit venomously; for one pin, you conceited, third-class ape, I'd knock you off the scaffold!

—Oh, you would, would you? whispered Sean, tensing his muscles, still standing side by side with the lounge suit, his cheeks flaming; then you'll come flying with me, and if there's any kind of a God at all, you'll be the underdog when we hit the ground!

But the lounge suit turned away, leaving a bitter curse stinging Sean's ear, walked across the plank, slid down the ladder, snapped at the foreman when he got to the bottom, and stalked away from the job.

It was all useless: it made Dilish surly with the foreman; the foreman surly with the men; and the job a worse one. They began to work overtime, and when Sean told his own foreman this, he was told sharply that he needn't bother to stay; that a good job would be done; and that the engineer had full confidence in Dilish. So what they couldn't do in daylight, they did at night, rushing the poor men to make up for lost time. When the arches had been built, one of them began to sink on bad foundations, and when the big building began to be piled on them, it sank quicker; it began to crack, in spite of all the frenzied patches applied; and, to this day, a wide crack from floor to ceiling can be seen, testifying to the foolishness of Sean. He might as well have taken the fiver; a better job would have been done if he had; and many times afterwards, whenever he put a hand in a pocket, he flamed with regret that he didn't feel the rustle of a five-pound note there. The angels in de heabn gwinter write my name, write my name, write my name, yes, write my name with a golden pen. Sean laughed silently at the poor fancy. To fight well, there must be a crowd beside and behind you to fight with you. Dilish would be blessed by bishop and priest. They didn't know; why the hell didn't they know? The workers must be rallied to the fight.

It would be a hard job to drag them from their rag-warmed stupor. Middle Gardiner Street and Lower Dorset Street on their knees before the rich and lordly Jesuit church of X Xavier's; Cumberland Street, Marlboro' Street, Nelson's Lane, and Gloucester Street, with its Diamond, lurching and rotten, leaning for succour on the precious Pro-Cathedral; Dominick Street and Upper Dorset Street bowing their rags before the St. Saviour's Church of the fair-robed Dominicans. Jesus! the poor were everywhere, crowding the value of their Christ out of existence; their real *lux mundi* the glitter of mirror and bottle and glass in the nearest beckoning drink-shop, where all their gods dissemble. There they were safe and snug for the nonce. There they could crawl and climb away from their dung and destitution to a more exalted state of joyous misery. There they could play wild games and sing many a wild song with a mad Beethoven and many a crazy Shakespeare. Jesu, mercy! Bind up their wounds! Let Tennyson sing outside to soothe them; or David quiet them with the tinkling of his golden harp: Psalm, boys and girls, calm. John the Baptist dances, and Salome's on her knees in prayer. Hush; let her alone — she isn't the worst. Strip tease, and take the consequences. Juggle me into jeopardy.

As far as countries go, Ireland's no worse now than she was before she was as bad as she is now. Whatever happens, the colour round the throne of the Man above is an emerald green, let the orange Ulster idiot yell as he will that it's orange and blue. We had God's sky over us, and St. Joseph's Free Night Shelter for homeless women, so that the few who could be crowded into it couldn't forget that kind hearts were more than coronets. And if it went to that, there were Ulster's own grain-carriers, on their own orange quays, each of them carrying two hundred tons of grain on his own back from the hatch to the ship's rail as a fair day's work, and no shinnannican, so as to keep the other fellows in the suffocating hold from the sin of idleness, bare-footed, half-naked, coughing the dust out of their lungs, and keeping pace with the protestant tubs swinging down on them, or going up, making the men's muscles creak with the strain of keeping them full. Then there were the women and children in their protestant mills, fined for laughing, or stooping to smoothe down their hair; and the little children fined when sick twice as much as they could earn in the same time, using the quickest speed their little hands could know. Christ Himself would find it pretty hard to do this kind of work. Carrying two hundred tons of grain on a back each day, without a hope in their bowels or a thought in their minds of any ease in the future, was a heavy cross for any back to carry. And not a one of these girls, like the sprightly Pippa, the silk weaver, would spring out of her bed when the whole sunrise, not to be suppressed, rose, reddened, and its seething breast flickered in bounds, grew gold, then overflowed the world. Not a one of them would spring from her bed to rush into a Lurgan or a Belfast linen mill, murmuring, God's presence fills our earth, each only as God wills can work. Stretch and stretch, it would be, sigh and sigh, dole and dree, oh, sour and bitter first hour of the morning!

Work? Ay, work's all right; but is this work? No; it's the ripe robbery of life from the very young and the little older. Browning, Browning, you make too much of almost everything you say. Your Pippa never passed through Lurgan or Belfast, nor did she ever see a bobbin spinning on a spindle there. Enjoying the grace of only one holiday in the year, Pippa had to turn the few hours into a dance and a song, a sweet song; one of sure faith and reasonable hope enduring. May God forgive her.

> The year's at the winter, the days are still-born;
> The workers are restless, while others, bepearled,
> Sing God's made us the one wonder-light of the world!
> The workers sweat dumbly, while others are dancing,
> Their meekness forsworn, bewitched and begirled,
> Singing God's in His Heaven — all's right with the world!

If Pippa couldn't, it was Browning's yearning that she might, that she should, touch the conscience of the selfish and the slothful; make the heart of the young to see strength and fair promise in darkling things; fire the heart of the wealthy young man to strike for human freedom and a just survey of man; and stir the pulse even of a Monsignor to lift himself out of his own fear into the courage and love free and firm in the singing heart of a maiden. It is a fairy Pippa who passes, a fairy who would like, for an hour or two, to walk the way of all flesh. She is Browning forgiving and excusing his own certainty and comfort by dreaming a little mill-girl into singing a song of God's good management of man. A noble fellow, loud-voiced in his lusty loneliness. The surge of a trombone's song through the still sad music of humanity. A clever singing simpleton straying through an un-inspected isle. A red moonbeam streeling through a dark sky. With all his gay talk, his hilarious, comfortable clothing, he wore an eagle's feather in his hair. And when the day comes, Browning will see our joy, and hear our laughter.

But it is well that Pippa has passed by for ever, singing her song of forgiveness to us all. The Pippas now need a new song and a new hope; the women, side by side with their men, assaulting the castle, the big house, the board-room, till the walls are breached, the doors down, and the song of life is heard in their halls. And in the song will be the unfolding of the final word from the evolving words of the ages, the word of the modern, the word En-Masse.

GREEN FIRE ON THE HEARTH

A STRANGE fellow in every way he was, and his name was Kevin O'Loughlin. Relatively to the rest of the members of the O'Toole Gaelic Club, he was rich, for he filled out a good job in the civil service. He was very thin, except for the shoulders which seemed to be trying to climb to have a look over his head, so that the eager, alert face appeared to look out on life from the upper part of his shrunken chest rather than from the top of a neck. This slight deformity, added to a royal flush on the tips of his high bony cheeks, indicated that he had been ordained to end his days in a gale of coughing. Rather large, sloppy ears stood out from his head, and he could flap them at will like the way a fowl flaps her wings; and the muscles under his scalp were so strong that by a quick quiver of them he could throw a book from the top of his head some distance away on to the ground. He had a fine high forehead, a long, thin, aristocratic nose, and large, critical, luminous, beautiful brown eyes. Indeed, had he been of a very small stature, he would have looked like a rather handsome gnome. His lungs weren't able for a hearty laugh, and any he tried to give, and he tried to give many, for he had a caustic sense of humour, ended in an eerie sound like a moistened hiss. He was sharply intelligent, and highly respected, and a little feared, by the other members of the Club. He had the history of the Gaelic Athletic Association — at that time the finest in the world — on the tip of his tongue, and he was something of an authority on the tactics of every Gaelic game. He was a pious fellow, critical of the practice but not of the theory of his Church, a weekly communicant, broad-minded, and a sincere member of the Third Order of St. Francis. He dreaded smutty stories, and liked Sean because he hated them too, unless they were salted with wit or illumined and purified with humour. Kevin had two passions, the one something of a vice, the other something of a virtue — he loved betting, and however ill he'd be, he never liked to miss the Grand National; and he worshipped the writings of Bernard Shaw. Whenever a Shaw play or preface appeared in print, he wasn't to be seen that night at the Club, however important the business happened to be; and for nights afterwards the laugh like a moistened hiss was loud in the land.

—Shaw, Shaw! Sean would say petulantly; you're for ever shouting that fellow's name in our ears. Who is he, anyway?

—The cleverest Irishman the world knows, Sean. A wit of wonder.

A godsend to men who try to think, who's creating a new world out of new thought. Read *John Bull's Other Island*, and the Ireland you think you know and love will vanish before your eyes.

—Well, that's a damn fine recommendation! I don't wish the Ireland I know and love to vanish before my eyes, thank you and Mr. Shaw. So talk sense, Kevin, and tell what this Shaw is doing, or has done, for Ireland.

—The best thing possible by helping to make Ireland plain to her own people.

—He hasn't done that, for any Gaelic Leaguer I've asked up to now says, Shaw? Is it that fella? Him? A dangerous gazebo, hot-foot after English money, that's what he is, making game of his own people — that's your Shaw.

—Don't mind them, Sean; they've never read the man. You can get a paper-covered copy for sixpence.

—Paper-covered copy of what?

—*John Bull's Other Island*. It'll make a new man of you — I'll get you a copy if you promise to read it.

—Thanks, said Sean; but I'll buy a copy for myself if I want one; but I don't, and before he could say goodbye, Kevin had to race for the last tram for Rathmines, leaving the Pillar, and, through the lighted window, Sean could see him panting as he sank heavily down on his seat.

He failed to get that green paper-covered book out of his head; so one week, when pay-day came, instead of hurrying home to change out of his dungarees and go to the Gaelic League, he went straight to Jason's, where the decorous, trimly-dressed assistant stared at him when he asked for the sixpenny edition of the play, handing it out and taking the sixpence as if she were sure Sean was making a mistake. At tea he began to read the green-covered book, the play first, then the preface; the clock ticked, the time passed; the Gaelic League forgotten, he read on till dawn was near, and had but a chance for a few hours' sleep before he rose to begin another day's work.

From that day, for quite a while, Sean seemed to see Shaw everywhere; his tall figure, in his Irish homespuns, marched in front, and whenever he looked behind him, there was Shaw following quick to overtake him. He replaced Nelson on Dublin's Pillar, standing there with a questioning smile on his roguish face, looking cynically and sadly over all the Dublin streets, slum-poisoned and square-pampered. Sean saw him peeping from behind the fluted columns of the Bank of Ireland, whispering to Sean that lots thought the building the Temple of the Holy Ghost, but that this was all bankum, and that it was a mighty den of highly respectable, and greatly honoured, thieves. The figure of St. Laurence O'Toole towering over the top of the Pro-Cathedral had changed the head of the holy man for the head of the smiling sage. Sometimes, when Sean was swinging his pick, the red beard came close to his ear and the musical voice said — Take it easy, man; don't kill yourself for any employing exploiter. Wait till I tell you, and the voice whispered, Blackguard, bully, drunkard, liar, foulmouth, flatterer, beggar, backbiter, corrupt judge, envious friend, vindictive enemy, political traitor: all these an Irishman may easily be, just as he may be a gentleman (a species extinct in England, and no-one a penny the worse); but he is never quite the hysterical, non-sense-crammed, fact-proof, truth-terrified, unballasted sport of all the bogy panics and all the silly enthusiasms that now calls itself God's Englishman. England cannot do without its Irish and its Scots today, because it cannot do without at least a little sanity.—Then the musical voice went into a laugh, and added, Idolatrous Englishman and fact-facing Irishman are proved today, for though I shock you, you are fearlessly facing me, aren't you? Of course you are; and a lot the better for it — eh? But don't be too cocky, young fellow, for though the Irishman refuses to be a subject of England's, he is proud to be one to the Vatican. Oh, yes, I know you're not; but all the rest of you are. And though Sean had heard that Shaw was a strict teetotaller, in every pub Sean was in, he seemed to see someone very like him there, arguing with bar-tender and customers, and lowering pint after pint with the worst of them. Up on the tip-top of Tara's hill, there he was, looking for all the world like the statue of St. Patrick, his gay green cope tucked around his knees, poking his crozier about the ground to turn up the elements of ancient Gaelic culture and shouting at the bottom of his voice to all the villages lying around, I don't see any signs of glory knocking about here. If the Gaels would search the slums as diligently as they searched Tara, they would be doing wiser work.

—A man without a soul, said the Gaelic Leaguers; nothing is sacred to him — not even the slums!

Shaw showed an Ireland very different from the lady Yeats made her out to be, peasants dancing round her to the sound of tabor and drum, their homespun shirts buttoned up with stars. Shaw's was rather grimy, almost naked, save for the green flag draped round her middle. She was grey with the dustiness of flour mixed with the dung of pigs, and her fair hands were horny with the hard work of turning stony ground into a state of fertility. The look on her fine face was one of unholy resignation, like one once in agony, now at ease in the thick torpor of murphia. Inconsequence stared from her eyes, and leaving her at ease at home telling her beads, or telling small coins till they mingled and became one, throwing some of both to jingle on a street in Heaven in the way of a priesthood for one of her boys so as to endorse a claim to a rookery nook in a respectable part of Paradise. No fool, she was sure of her place in this world, and surer of one in the next. So she stood in front of what was the most powerful part of England, Broadbent, in the shape of a breezy mountain of bombast, dressed in a motor-coat, goggles, and gauntlet gloves, a fat purse dripping largesse, golf-sticks on his back; full of pompenduring confidence, ready to take away even the green flag round Ireland's middle and turn it into a gilt-edged security. There the jovial fellow stood, surrounded by some of Ireland's sons, the butcher, baker, and candlestick-maker, headed by a practical priest with an eye fixed on the bulging purse; a priest who was as ignorant as the Englishman of Ireland's close kinship with nobility; ignorant even of the piety that had sanctified every sod so that God Himself could walk out anywhere without soiling His holy feet. Near naked, Ireland stood, with the one jewel of Keegan's Dream occasionally seen sparkling in her tousled hair, attaching poverty to pride; a shameful figure, but noble still, though her story was hidden and her songs unsung. Hewing wood and drawing water ceaselessly with the thoughts amurmur on her cracked lips,

> Waste no time on paltry things,
> Life would have us queens and kings.

Two elements fought each other here, back to back: a dream without efficiency, and efficiency without a dream; but with this tense difference: that from the dream efficiency could grow, but from the efficiency no dream could ever come.

And now in every Roscullen throughout the land, still with the green flag for a hope and a battle-eye, the long, long brooding was at last becoming pregnant. The dreadful dreaming was being hitched to a power and a will to face the facts. And this Irishman, Shaw, was helping us to do it; this strange Irishman, no stranger to his kin, warm-hearted, and arrogantly protestant, who had had an orangeman for a great-grandfather, whose sister had been an abbess, and whose uncle had been hanged for a rebel: these few details giving us the queer *status quo*, the life, the soul, the dream; the unending change, the temerity, the eternal jubilate that are known as Ireland, Eire, Banba,

The Poor Old Woman, Sheila Nee Gyra: Orangeman, Abbess, Rebel — three in one and one in three, and there is Ireland.

One of the reasons, says Bernard Shaw, why the Abbey didn't do my play was because it wasn't congenial to the whole spirit of the neo-Keltic Movement, bent on making a new Ireland out of its own ideal, while my play was an uncompromising presentment of the real old Ireland.—No, no; not quite. No more uncongenial than was W. P. O'Ryan's Boyne Valley Enterprise, both of which left behind them a deep and unquenchable growth towards reality in the minds and hearts of many Irish people. And part of the Gaelic Movement, coloured and glossy though it was with many poetical and political symbols, was a trend towards realism in thought and act; a proving of most things, and a holding-fast of some that were good. The Irish were beginning to look into their own lives, not through the distorting mirrors of Westminster; nor yet through the flattering ones in the Old Parliament House of College Green; but through the reflections given from city and town, from farm and dairy, from field, factory, and workshop, from church and state, though the movement, maybe, too often draped its realism in coloured shawls and kilts and fluttering flags, and flavoured it with the music of pipe, trumpet, and drum. Neither did the play show the real old Ireland, for that went farther back than the coarse, quick, and common mind of Doran; the harassing anxiety of Haffigan over his five-acre meadow; the sober and settled acceptance by Corny and Judy Doyle of things as they were and ever will be; the forty-pounds-a-year magnificence of Nora O'Reilly; nor was it the common honouring of holy things by Father Dempsey, whose vision from Mount Carmel was the surety of a plump chicken for dinner and a plenitude of candles for his church; nor was an Ireland farther back, a Patsy Farrell, meagre and barefooted, harnessing himself in a humour of silliness against persecution, and trying to ease his misfortune and misery by giving an occasional cheer for poor ould Ireland. The Ireland farther back was more like Fadher Keegan, banished from the altar, hinging himself more closely to his breviary than ever, torturing himself delightfully with the vision of a country where the state is the church and the church the people; three in one, and one in three; where work is play, and play is life; where the priest is the worshipper, and the worshipper the worshipped; three in one, and one in three; carrying the vision around with him to pour it into the loneliness of a round tower: the dream of a madman, but the dream of an Irishman too.

Sean was now in bad company constantly. Not a week passed but he was found hobnobbing with Shaw, Darwin, Frazer, and France, and the volubility and loudness of their positive talk were having a dangerous effect upon him. One day, having honoured, in Bodenstown, the memory of Wolfe Tone, as he was coming home on a lovely late summer evening through misery-crowded Marlborough Street, he saw a crowd of Barney Dorans, Matt Haffigans, Corny Doyles, and Patsy Farrells gathered round the Church of the Immaculate Conception, known to all Dubliners as the Pro-Cathedral, staring up at the figure of St. Laurence O'Toole gesticulating with his crozier, standing tiptoe like a ballet dancer on his pedestal, and sometimes leaning down towards the street so that you were in fear he'd come tumbling down any minute. Shouting away the saint was, to the crowd below, and Sean, when he had pushed his way forward, found it was a tirade against Shaw, while Professor Mcgennis in his acodemnical gown held on to the saint's skirt to keep him from falling.

—I'm tellin' yous, shouted the saint, that Shaw said there wasn't a single creditable established religion in the world. An' they say a sayin' man said it. He's mad, an' unashamed of it! An' he follows this up with the asseveration that we've only to read the folk-tale of John Barleycorn to get a clear idea of what put redemption by the sacrifice of a Saviour into the mind of man. That's what he said here when he clambered up after I had climbed down to run and get a quick one in the D.W.D. to thry to quench the drouth destroyin' me. An' Pathrick over there on th' opposite corner never lifted a finger to stop him. So busy colloguin' with scribes and Pharisees to put Armagh to the forefront at the expense of Dublin that was thrivin' before Armagh was thought of. I tell Patrick to his face, here an' now, that he was what he wasn't, an' is what he shouldn't have been, possessin' enough ignorance of letters that ought to have kept him from being anything above a rural-tooral dean, a dimestic prelate, or a vicarago-general. He pooh-poohdled the danger of Darwin, tellin' me it was all a stunt, sayin' that man was too sensible to let himself be associated with a monkey; and so that bounder, Hoaxley, spread the good news all over England, an' a hint of it came over here, to be made into an elegant and humorous story by this Shaw fella in preface an' play. He comes along to upset things just when we've got yous into the tee-totalarian order of being happy in misery, and safe in your poverty; th' glow of hell-fire dazzlin' your eyes so that yous would, without a murmur, toil up th' slopes of our highest holy hill, with joints crackin' and feet bleedin', never thinkin' of singin' the song of *Take a little bit off the top for me, for me*; content that the hill might get higher an' higher so as you'd be climbin' an' climbin' till the praties were dug, the frost was all over, and the sumer was icumen in.

Wasn't I glad to see in *The Universe*, the other day, a reply to a query asking what was Adam's and Eve's surnames, and when did the rite of marriage begin, tellin' the inquirer that there weren't surnames then, and that marriage began with them, an' that the book which questioned it was both silly and dangerous. Now, went on the saint, stretching farther down over the parapet, so that Mcgennis found it hard to hold him, I'm tellin' yous that Shaw's books are both silly an' dangerous too. Th' Garden of Eden's as far as yous can go. There yous stop. An' don't thry to look over th' wall, either. Yous must all ask questions that can easily be answered, see? What is it to you, or to anyone, if one of the apostles tells of the flight into Egypt, and the others don't? Or that one apostle said the birth of a Saviour was told to Joseph, and another that Mary heard about it first? Things like these are neither here nor there to yous. Or that the crowding of Mary out of the inn, an' th' sudden filling of the sky with angels bursting their lungs with a rhapsody in the blue for the benefit of ignorant shepherds, was Luke's story, and his alone, the others seeming not to have heard a word about it. There's such a thing as wanting to know too much. Hasn't Luke a perfect right to be romantic if he wanted to? You just keep tight to the dogmas of your faith an' yous'll never know a poor day.

Suddenly Sean saw, at the back fringe of the crowd, the tall, lithe figure of Shaw standing, and he looking up with a smile at the raging saint. Raising a hand and his hat, he caught the eye of the saint, and said in a quiet, steady, harmonious voice, My dear man, Christ harped, not on creeds or catechisms, or sacraments, but on conduct; harped on conduct, fifed and drummed on conduct, and, were He here today, He'd saxophone on it too.

—Away with you! bellowed O'Toole. You're like the witch of the rock of the candles whose smallest glimmer when seen brought death to all who saw it; so your wizard rashlight of knowledge will bring spiritual darkness to any heyeball that catches a glampse of its gloom; but with the help of SSSSSSS, Barra, Beccan, Coman, Dima, Dalua, Flann, and Garvan, we'll down you, an' shut your sayin's out of every free library livin' in th' land.

—Still him, spill him, kill him for his bad books! roared the crowd, raising handsome sticks into the air, sthrike him down for malingerin' us! But Fadher Dempsey held them back, saying, Patience, patience, boys; not just yet. Leave him to the saint for a few minutes longer.

—You go about everywhere, Shaw, mutterin' that miracles are poor things to depend on; but what d'ye say to the saint, who in a brown study of the gospels, never felt a pair o' birds buildin' a nest in his outsthretched hand, which, when, what the dear saint saw, sat without a stir so's not to disturb them till they had mated, the eggs hatched out, and the young birds able to wing it for themselves. Was that miracle a poor dependage for the bards who have sung of it often? No, Shaw, it won't do. Many brave hearts are a-yell down in Hell; so beware, beware!

—Let him think, shouted Mcgennis, peeping from behind the saint's cope, let him think of

> The ghost of John, James, Christopher, Benjamin Binns,
> Who was cut down right in the midst of his sins;
> Now his home is down below;
> Though he gets out for an hour or so,
> When the cock begins to crow,
> It's farewell, Benjamin Binns!

—Aha, yelled a man, full-dressed in green coat, white breeches, polished top-boots, and plumed hat of the Irish National Foresters; aha, wiping the creamy froth of a newly-lowered pint from a flowing moustache, now maybe he knows what's in store for him before long if he doesn't mend his way o' thinkin'. If he wants to understand things above our poor fumin' minds, let him go an' ask poor Benjamin Binns about them.

—Shut up, and go home, you! the saint rebuked, shouting down at the plumed hat. Go home, an' look in the glass to see if you're there at all; and if y'are, keep it a dead secret. And let the rest of yous all remember, includin' the man under th' sin of conceited knowledge, that St. Uiskebaha has taught that the penny Cathechism is th' casket in which is all the knowledge necessary to be known to man; anything outside of it is either silly or dangerous. In it is a full, free, and what-you-fancy explanation of the natural and supernatural worlds, from th' fall of man to the miracle of the five thousand barley loaves and two small fishes, showing us all, including our friend on the fringe of the crowd, that no man can be made good by an Act of Parliament.

—Here, here, said the voice under the plumed hat, that only stands to reason, an' it's my opinion, an' I don't care who knows it, that th' Garden of Eden was somewhere among the lakes an' fells of Killarney.

And Sean went away with his secret that he dared to tell to no-one there, for he would have been laughed at or brained for telling that he had been in the Garden of Eden; had climbed the wall with much labour and heart-panting; had slid down with a bump on the other side, and had found the place far different from the yarns in newspaper, magazine, and religious manuals which spread the news that through the luscious venery south winds blew so soft that they barely stirred the golden hair of Neve; they filled the spaces with delectable trees languishing lovingly in the silvery mist that went up every morning to water the garden, and so save Adam from having to bend a back. They garlanded every fine tree with delicious fruits, gay in colour and rich in juice, bending so low that Adam on the broad of his back could nibble them without stirring a finger. Gentle animals padded about among the trees, and purred with pleasure, and played tig together, and bent the knees whenever Adam passed by, for he was lord over all that were there. Birds of every hue and cry, fluttering and fluting about everywhere; and neither sign nor sound of death was anywhere near in this sweet garden of rest; perpetual summer, where the nights were naked as the happy couple were, showing all their beauty so that naked night and naked couple mixed and laughed together, peace dropping from the skies, and evening full of the angels' wings.

That's how the mistory went; but Sean found it, when he got there, to be different and disturbed. It was shaking with the roaaoaring, yelelling, squeealing, and growowling of fierce, huge, and unnatural beasts, so that Sean trembled for his life and sought to get back over the wall, but found that it was as hard to get out as it was easy to get in; so the one thing to do now was to keep going on, and dodge the danger. Climbing a little way up a tall horsetail, he looked around and saw that the Paradise was a vast expanse of slime and swamp, with great masses of horsetails, huge calamitic *Mishelaymassmores* towering sky-high, stout-stemmed *Eiraillas* twining round thick clumps of *Sporangia belfusstica*, each striving to destroy the other and reign alone in the Garden of Eden; and everywhere as far as eye could reach or thought could go, there were sprinkled in and out through it all, funguses, brown, grey, black, red, white, and blue, taller than the stately elm, all topped with widely-domed roofs, like great domes of churches, roosting-places for the numerous flocks of the long-baked, snaky-necked, leathery-winged pterodactyls, who often came between Adam and Eve and a sweet sleep by their rousing way of song, which in sound was something between the trumpeting of a mastodon and the crowing of a mighty fowl, and who were, as we all know, the linnets, larks, and sparrows of that age. All the colours of the land before him were gloomy browns, sad greens, and fading purples, while overhead a leaden, scowling sky kept the heart low and terrified.

Hearing voices ahead, Sean roughly set aside the sharp, tall, green flags thrusting up from the virgin soil and clinging round his legs, and pushed on to the fringe of the rushes. Setting them aside with caution, he looked out over a wind-swept marsh, exactly like the one behind him. Over to the right, near to the mouth of a big, deep, dark dugout, squatted a hairy man and a hairy woman, and Sean knew at once that they must be Adam and Eve, for they had their arms round each other. Before them a thin, short man, sitting on his hunkers, had a flint sheet on his bare knees, and a flint pen was scratching along it, so Sean knew he was busy interviewing them. Beside the man about to take notes, stood a great big fat fellow, with a tremendous grin on his wide-open space, his tangled hair falling into his eyes, his hands keeping a tangle of porifera safely strung around his mighty loins, one of its stems held in the right hand of a little nervous-looking, dull, dumpling-faced manikin with a blue-stone cross hanging on his breast, an umbrella of palm in his left hand, a roman collar round his neck, all embellished by a look of conceited silliness on his moony face that he and his fat friend took to be thought. Sean crept nearer to hear what they had to say.

—I'm Jeecaysee, the fat man said, the mild knight of the little man, the schnapper-up of God's tremendous trifles; past, present, and to come, grand chief arranger of the greybards at play; awethor of the misuses of divorsety; and this, indicating the little man by his side, is Daabruin, suborned into life to make right what's wrong with the world, and to lead the fiat of heretics to the end of the roaman road; and this gentleman, pointing to the one with the slate tablet and the flinty pen, is a newsman from the city of cod in the land that is over the hills and far away, who has come to get from the first father and mother of men the true facts of how you vaulted into life, and the impressions that struck you when you woke to the beauty and peace of your God-given garden.

—That's it! said the newsman; I want to get at the bottom, and then at the top, of the rumours everywhere about how the first boy met the first girl, see? Everyone has a different slant on the occurrence. F'rinstance, Singasonga of Nota Chagpur says he made the first man and woman out of clay with the help of a spade; the Shillishalliucks of the White Nile say their god, Jokes, made white men from black clay, red men from green clay, black men from white clay, and brown men from blue clay, which sounds a bit far-stretched for me; and the Taaraaraarowa of Tatatiti, chief god of the world, says emphatically that he made the first man from red clay, and when he was asleep, made a female figure from the clay, sawed a rib-bone out of the man, shoved it into the clay figure, and before you could say Eire inverse, the figure lepped up into a lively, dancing woman, tapping a tambourine. But now I'm facing the real McCoy, the pair themselves, ready to get the real goods from boy and girl; and he laid the slate on an algae-covered rock, poised his flint pen, and waited for them to begin.

—Well, said Adam slowly, in the beginning, as you are all aware, there was nothing in existence, for nothing was, for everything was without form, and void, and darkness was on the face of the deep.

—Ah! said the newsman, there was the deep: now let us be clear — what actually was the deep?

—The deep? echoed Adam. The deep was the deep that was there out in the deep, dark days beyond recall — surely that's quite plain to everyone?

—Not to me, said the newsman, shaking his head.

—Maybe, remarked Jeecaysee, the exposition isn't quite clear: we must trust tradition. He turned to Daabruin: Now, vessel of inner-sense, do your bit!

Daabruin stood stiff, held his temples tight like a man in sudden and violent pain. Stop, stop, stop! he cried; stop talking for a moment, for I see half of what I'm going to say. Will God give me strength? Will my brain give one jump and see all? Heaven help me! I used to be fairly good at thinking. Will my head split — or will it see? I see half, I only see half! He buried his face in his hands, and stood in a sort of rigid torture of thought or prayer. Then a convulsion of revaluation swept over the moony face, and the tense lips opened to mutter, The deep was the deep that was where nothing that was was not.

—Ah! said the newsman; quite; I get you now. It's all quite clear.

—I knew it would be, said Jeecaysee.

—Well, now, about the way the two of you came out of what was once the great deep, eh?

—It was all very simple, said Adam. The Man above just pointed a finger at a tuft of moss and said, Come out of it, Adam! And out I had to come.

—And then? inquired the newsman.

—Then things went like clockwork: the lovely fish in the sea; the lovely birds in the air; the wonderful animals on the land all of which were named and addressed by me; and then, when the Man above saw I was lonely, he put me asleep, took a rib out of my side, and, pointing a thumb at Eve, made herself there.

—Oh, did he now? said Eve, suddenly sarcastic. That's a one-sided story if y'ask me! There wasn't a flash of a second of time lost between the making of us, as everyone knows. We were man and maid together or we weren't made at all; and took precedence over all other living things.

—You were an afterthought, I'm telling you! said Adam sharply. It's there in the book for anyone to see.

—Ay, said Eve hotly, slipped in with your connivance to give the excuse for making the woman subject to the man. But God spoke before you; and my version, the true version, is there in the book too, for everyone to see.

—Both of them can't be right, said the newsman conclusively. There's an error somewhere.

—Only so in the unmanageable mind's eye, said Jeecaysee. He turned to Daabruin: Do your bit, my boy!

Again the simplisissimust stiffened, clasped the head between his hands, tossed out bitter murmurs of thought or prayer, and then, casting down his head to gaze on his queer feet, he said, The things told are here to prove the tales. The one here is two, the two one; so what? There is neither first nor second, but two seconds in one first, and two firsts in one second. There is no Adam or Eve, but an Adam plus Eve, and an Eve plus Adam; so though there may be two persons, there is but one indivisible individual, therefore each is *nulla secundus*; therefore though both stories are different, both are identical, for each to the other is an *alter idem*, so all is one, and error is not where error cannot be.

—*Nulla secundus* or *dulla profundis*, Adam's making a wide mistake if he's thinking of getting on top of me, said Eve.

—Now that the question of the two-to-one stories is settled for good and all, said the newsman, let's touch something romantic — Did you fall in love with your good man the minute you clapped eyes on him, or what?

—There wasn't a chance of falling in love with anything else, man. Up to that time he was as good as they make 'em.

—But you were a little shy, weren't you, at first?

—Maybe; but Jeecaysee came along and gave us all the advice we needed. He sang for us *My love is like a red, red nose* and *My love is but a lassie yet*, said that our lives would be divinely arkadian; that in the mystic future we'd grow into two beautiful china figures, a shepherd and his shepherdess, side by side, and close as close together; idols of the happy and healthy peasant and peasantess, giving scope for many sweet songs to Virgil, Ariosto, Dante, and Shakespeare;

outliving the pagan gods of stone and brass, innocent boy meets innocent girl today as hc did in Eden, so that instead of wonders becoming facts, facts are becoming wonders.

—Glamour! shouted the newsman. Oh, boys, glamour! Here is a story fine and fragrant to be believed in, and enjoyed, by generations yet unborn.

—For ever sweethearts, murmured Jeecaysee; when her hair has turned to silver, he will love her just the same; he will only call her sweetheart, that will always be her name.

—And her hair will never turn to silver, but will for ever be golden, said Daabruin.

—Never afraid of the big bad wolf, said the newsman. For ever busy, for ever tireless, for ever good.

—That's just a little too much to bear, said Eve. A change in one's life is needed now and again. One longs for the luxury of a sigh and a sob sometimes.

—Now don't spoil the story, Eve, pleaded Adam.

—And all this, recited the newsman, writing it furiously down on the slate sheet, in the midst of a loveliness that stretches as far as eye reaches or thought can go. Oh, boys, what a story!

The sudden squealing yell that shook itself through the sodden air made Sean's hair stand stiff on his head, and he saw the group tear into the dugout as fast as legs could go. He heard a tumultuous thick splashing out in front in the centre of a rushy morass, and saw a frightful creature, fifty foot long, with a huge head, a yawning, yearning mouth, packed with long, fearful, dagger-like teeth, rending to bits the long, writhing neck of a dinnaseer, while the two of them squealed like huge whirling steel saws cutting wildly into flintstone, plunging madly about the slimy, inky swamp, and sending showers of the mire high into the air. Then from behind a great clump of carboniferous blacammites there trotted venomously out, towards the fighting fiends, a horrible beast, fully a hundred foot long, with an arched back, topped by a double row of huge triangular bony plates; three long belly-piercing horns on its ugly head, one over each eye, and one branching out of its snout; while a long tail, barbed with a row of fearful spikes two foot long, slashed about at everything within reach. When he got to the squealing, biting monsters, this spike-encrusted life lowered his hideous head, thrust it under the belly of what was rending the squirming neck of the other, plunged the three deadly horns into it as far as they could go, and Sean saw the frightful head disappear under a cascade of blood and tumbling guts, felt himself splashed by the greenish ooze and the purplish mire scattered into violent horrid showers by the yelling, squealing beasts rending each other, sinking lower down into the sucking slime, trying to plunge upward out of the danger to slide back to a lower depth still, screaming with dim-felt fright at what lay below them; while the great green-topped sea of rotting muck crept slowly higher, till the last Sean saw of the twisting scaly mass was the yawning, yearning mouth with its fearful daggerite teeth still tearing at the mangled writhing neck of the dying dinnaseer, hidden at last by a coil of green and purple muddy bubbles, slowly sinking down into a swaying sea of thick, unwholesome mire.

After a time, he saw Adam, Eve, and their friends come cautiously out of their cave, to stand at the mouth of it, pale and shaking. He saw that Jeecaysee kept his back turned to the bubbling muck, that Daabruin kept looking at his queer feet, and that the newsman's legs were trembling. Adam glanced nervously around him, and Eve stared sullenly at the sink and swell of the blackish-green and purple bubbles, now doing a disturbed dance of jubilation over swallowing down the horrible.

—Don't let the sobconscious disturb you, said Jeecaysee. We see the beauty only; we are privileged.

—I'm off outa this, said the newsman; thanks for the grand story. And he slunk off, sliding between fern and bracken and rock till he was out of sight.

—Do something, sing something, man, shouted Jeecaysee, catching Daabruin by his shoulder and shaking him; sing to take away the darkness; sing us into sunity, man! And in a querulous and quivering voice, Daabruin sang

>Thou art, O God, the life and light
>Of all this wondrous world we see;
>Its glow by day, its smile by night,
>Are but reflections caught from Thee.

as the two of them crept away, bent double in an effort to camoufledge themselves as animals.

—Old God's rag-and-bone men, said Eve, scornfully, after them. He who is to live for ever is afraid of dying for a day. He has all the saints worn out trying to be jolly on all occasions. He winds his way to Heaven through a maze of beer bottles, wine jars, and pewter pots. He's for ever praying to God to keep the water out of the wine.

—Shush! said Adam, shocked. He's a holy man, and a clever one too. He's a man of infinite jest and most excellent fancy. The angels think the world of him. And a clever one too. Once he said to me, D'ye know, Adam, the farther we go, the nearer we get from where we started. That's the only relatantivity that's true, says he, for it was told to me by a wild knight on a white horse of the Peppers at Notting Hill Gate, his sharp-pointed, towering spire held at the ready so as to pen Pusha Deen Inge firmly to his bethelments. By standing on its head, says he, is the only way the world will learn how to stand on its feet. When a man's the head of the house, says he, you'll find a woman at the bottom of everything. A good man to be near, said Adam, a soft and safe cushion for a parson to lean on.

—We'll go from here! said Eve suddenly. Here we shall never be more than what we are, of the earth earthy, and nurtured in slime; and she girded herself into her robe of lizard skin.

—Go from here! echoed Adam. Are you mad, woman? Go from the softness and security here to where things may be worse?

—To where things may be better, responded Eve quietly. I've a child coming, and he won't be born here. There will be others too; and in higher ground and purer air they can start to build a Paradise of their own, safer, firmer, and more lovely than anything even a God can give. So on we go, too human to be unafraid, but too human to let fear put an end to us!

And the serpent behind her, the most subtle beast of the field, reared up to his full height, expanded his plumed crest, and said gaily, Evie, allanna, now you're talking.

Immediately the firmament burst asunder and a thunderbolt shout out of it, striking the serpent a frightful blow on the nose, so that his limbs dried up and became useless, forcing him to crawl about on his belly from that day on, which can be verified to this very day by anyone taking the trouble to look at one.

—Let us be going, said Eve, fixing her cloak of skin more closely around her. By another and more dangerous way, we shall come to a finer and a firmer life. Are you afraid? she asked of Adam, seeing him hesitate, and the cold dew of fear beading his forehead; are you afraid?

—Not with you, Eve, he replied, gripping tightly his stout, horn-topped staff; not with you, my love.

And crowds of lumbering dinnaseer and dipladoci gathered to watch them go, their huge bodies drooping and their scaly eyes dim, and as the mobled mother of man and her mate went by, they raised their heads and called out submissively, Farewell, brave beginners of the human kind, hail and farewell: those who are about to die, salute you!

Under the darkened sky, in the midst of a flash of lightning, Sean saw that the low brow, the timid eye, the shivering step of Adam had changed to the alert walk, the gleaming eye, the lofty brow, and the reddish thrust-out beard of Bernard Shaw. And Sean, bending low under the Golden Bough, followed close behind him.

PROMETHEUS HIBERNICA

IT was a bitter day. Winds, cold and nipping, deeply swept up from the bay, curling crossly round into Beresford Place, trying to snarl their way through to the heat in the dense crowd packing with warm life the square that stretched out in front of the King's elegant Custom House. Here, too, had Parnell stood, defiant, speaking from the building's wide steps, like a flame-pointed spear on the people's altar, endurance and patient might in his beautiful wine-coloured eyes. The rascals, cleric and lay, out-talked thee, hissed thee, tore at Ireland to get at thee, and God remembered for many a long year, silencing their voice till He grew sorry for the work-worn people, and sent another man into their midst whose name was Larkin.

Through the streets he strode, shouting into every dark and evil-smelling hallway, The great day of a change has come; Circe's swine had a better time than you have; come from your vomit; out into the sun. Larkin is calling you all!

And many were afraid, and hid themselves in corners. Some ventured as far as the drear and dusky doorway to peer out, and to say, Mr. Larkin, please excuse us, for we have many things to do and to suffer; we must care for cancerous and tubercular sick, and we must stay to bury our dead. But he caught them by the sleeve, by the coat collar, and shouted, Come forth, and fight with the son of Amos who has come to walk among the men and women of Ireland. Let the sick look after the sick, and let the dead bury the dead. Come ye out to fight those who maketh the ephah small and the shekel great; come out that we may smite the winter house with the summer house; till the houses of ivory shall perish, and the great houses shall have an end. And Sean had joined the Union.

Following afar off for a while, Sean had come at last to hear Larkin speak, to stand under a red flag rather than the green banner. On this day the Liffey's ruffled waters were roughly lapping the granite walls of the quays; the dark-brown tide was high, and above it, the big white gulls, squealing, went circling round, tensing their wide wings whenever they went against the wind that made them turn to cut it sideways. Brown and yellow leaves, drifting from the little trees along the paths, curled restlessly along the streets, rustling against the legs of the people as if eager to find shelter and safety there from the peevish and vexing wind. A grey, sulky sky overhead was the one banner flown, but all eyes were on the brave new sign in golden letters on a green field, running along the length of the building, telling all that here was the rallying camp of *The Irish Transport and General Workers Union*, while over the massive doorway the name *Liberty Hall* gave a welcome and twenty to all who came to fight for a life something higher than the toiling oxen and the bleating sheep. Here were the sons of the Gael, men of the Pale, brought up, lugged up, in the mire of Dublin's poverty, their children slung about at school, while those a little more adventurous than the rest were carted away to the reformatories of Artane and Glencree.

Aha, here now was the unfolding of the final word from the evolving words of the ages, the word of the modern, the word En-Masse, and a mighty cheer gave it welcome. From a window in the building, leaning well forth, he talked to the workers, spoke as only Jim Larkin could speak, not for an assignation with peace, dark obedience, or placid resignation; but trumpet-tongued of resistance to wrong, discontent with leering poverty, and defiance of any power strutting out to stand in the way of their march onward. His was a handsome tense face, the forehead swept by deep black hair, the upper lip of the generous, mobile mouth hardened into fierceness by a thick moustache, the voice deep, dark, and husky, carrying to the extreme corners of the square, and reaching, Sean thought, to the uttermost ends of the earth. Here was the word En-Masse, not handed down from Heaven, but handed up from a man. In this voice was the march of Wat Tyler's men, the yells and grunts of those who took the Bastille, the sigh of the famine-stricken, the last shout from those, all bloodied over, who fell in Ninety-eight on the corn slopes of Royal Meath; here were nursery rhyme and battle song, the silvery pleasing of a lute with the trumpet-call to come out and carry their ragged banners through the gayer streets of the city, so that unskilled labour might become the vanguard, the cavaliers and cannoniers of labour's thought and purpose.

The voice of mingled gold and bronze went on picturing the men to themselves — as they were, as they ought to be; showing them that they hadn't been denied the gift of a holy fire from God; this man in the drab garments of a drink-sodden nature; that man whose key of Heaven was a racing record; yonder fellow fearing to be above a blackleg, refusing to join his comrades out on strike; and, worst of all, the unsightly scab taking the job of a comrade out in a fight for better conditions for all. The voice called for the rejection of the timid one who led them, who hid in an armchair and let their men be ruled by the strength in a policeman's baton.

—Who will stand, who will fight, for the right of men to live and die like men? he called out, the large, strong hand stretched out of the window gesturing over the head of the crowd.

—We will! came back in a serried shout that echoed along the restless river, making the gliding gulls pause, turn away, and wonder, as a cloud of chapped and gnarled and grimy hands were lifted high in the air; strong hands and daring, hands that could drive a pile, handle a plough, sail a ship, stoke a furnace, or build a city.

—Gifts of the Almighty, went on the voice, labour — a gift, not a curse —, poetry, dancing, and principles; and Sean could see that here was a man who would put a flower in a vase on a table as well as a loaf on a plate. Here, Sean thought, is the beginning of the broad and busy day, the leisurely evening, the calmer night; an evening full of poetry, dancing, and the linnet's wings; these on their way to the music of the accordion, those to that of a philharmonic orchestra; and after all, to sleep, perchance to dream; but never to be conscious of a doubt about tomorrow's bread, certain that, while the earth remaineth, summer and winter should not cease, seedtime and harvest never fail:

> The bell branch of Ireland may chime again,
> To charm away the merchant from his guile,
> And turn the farmer's memory from his cattle,
> And hush to sleep the roaring ranks of battle,
> And all grow friendly for a little while.

No; for ever. Battles of war changed for battles of peace. Labour in all its phases the supreme honour of life, broadening the smile on the world's creased face daily.

The workers of Dublin, Wexford, Cork, Galway, Waterford, Limerick, and many towns, rallied to Larkin's side. Out of jail he had come into their arms. Starting in Belfast, Larkin brought orange and green together as they had never been together before. On to Derry, city of Columkille and the brave Apprentice Boys. Down to Cork, then, where the employers marshalled their first phalanx of bitter opposition. There he was charged with a conspiracy of trying to defraud the workers of their hard-earned money by a witness who had to be sent home because he was drunk; and a Crown and Anchor solicitor who was also the solicitor to the Employers' Federation, harmonising in himself the glory of God and the honour of Ireland; though one of the two magistrates trying the case, Sir Edward Fitzgerald, had the temerity to declare that every fair-minded man in Cork had the idea in his head that if there was a conspiracy at all, it was a conspiracy of Dublin Castle and the Cork employers to prevent the working men of the city from uniting for their self-defence in the future. But, all the same, for this reason Jim got a sweet little sentence of twelve months with hard labour by the other magistrate on the bench, justifying the righteousness of the Lion and Unicorn over the magistrate's head. But the grin came off their faces when the King, after some months had passed, had the common sense and graciousness to grant a free pardon to a fine man who was dragging images of God from a condition worse than that of the beasts in the field of the poorest Irish farmer.

So Jim came out of jail, and in a room of a tenement in Townshend Street, with a candle in a bottle for a torch and a billycan of tea, with a few buns for a banquet, the Church militant here on earth of the Irish workers, called the Irish Transport and General Workers Union, was founded, a tiny speck of flame now, but soon to become a pillar of fire into which a brand was flung by Yeats, the great poet, Orpen, the painter, A. E., who saw gods in every bush and bramble, Corkery the story-teller, James Stephens, the poet and graceful satirical jester, Dudley Fletcher, the Rector of Coolbanagher, and even Patrick Pearse, wandering softly under the Hermitage elms, thinking, maybe, of Robert Emmet, the darlin' of Erin, and his low response to the executioner's *Are you ready, sir?*, of *Not yet, not yet*; even he was to lift a pensive head to the strange new shouting soon to be heard in Dublin streets, loosening the restraining hands of St. Patrick and St. Laurence O'Toole, holding his girdle, to say *No private right to property is good as against the public right of the people.*

The tramway workers, the worst slaves Ireland ever knew, grew restless, and were trying to key themselves up to make a fight of it. They had no settled job, no settled hours, no settled pay even, for every journey they made was crammed with trivial excuses for a fine that made their wages undergo a weekly shrivel, so that they deprived themselves of what they needed when they gave a penny to Jesus at

Mass on Sundays. At midnight, when the last tram had been bedded for the night, to win courage from Larkin's faith they came to Liberty Hall in trains of wagonettes, caravans of toil, playing melodeons, concertinas, mouth-organs, and singing an old Irish ballad, or a music-hall song, as the horses plodded along from the depots of Inchicore, Clontarf, and Ringsend. As the crowded cars pulled up outside Liberty Hall, they were cheered by crowds gathered there, for each arrival was hailed as a reinforcement for an army about to march to battle. The tramwaymen crowded into a hot and stuffy hall, already nearly packed to the doors, the sweat often dripping from the fore-heads of the speakers, all of them wiping it convulsively away as they went on speaking; Jim Larkin alone carelessly brushing the bigger drops aside with a sudden impatient movement of his hand, too full of fiery thought to bar the salty moisture from entering into his gleaming eyes.

The employers gathered their forces together too, to harass the workers and stamp their menace out. William Martin Murphy, their leader, who owned the Dublin tramways, Clery's huge stores, and God knows what else besides, determined to get the employers to refuse to give work to any man who was a member of Larkin's Union. Let them submit, or starve. Jacob's the biscuit-makers, Shackleton's the millers, Eason's the newspaper and magazine distributors, along with coal factors, timber merchants, and steamship owners, came along to Martin Murphy and said, We're with you, old boy. What thou doest, we will do; what thou sayest, we will say; thy profits shall be our profits; and thy god, ours too. And so it was. Catholic, Pro-testant, Quaker, and pagan employer joined hand and foot, flung their money into one bag, and with bishop and priest, viceroy and council, infantryman and cavalry trooper, and bludgeon-belted policeman, formed a square, circle, triangle, and crescent to down the workers.

A foreman came slowly to Sean, a paper stretched out in his right hand, and said, Sign this, you. It was headed by a skull and cross bones, with a tiny cross in a corner, above the motto of *Per ardua add fastra.* The document went on to say:

> Under the holy and undivided patronage of St. Ellessdee, I, M or N, do solemnly swear, without any reservation whatsoever (cross your heart, and say I hope to die), that from this day forthwith I shall cease to be a member of Larkin's Union, and will forswear his company, give him no aid, in thought, word, or deed, cross to the

other side of the street when I see him coming, inasmuch as he has persuaded me to try to bite the hand that doesn't feed me; and I further promise and undertake and expressively swear that I will faithfully serve my employers, assisted by whatsoever Union they may form, or allow me to join; and so I shall incur the beloved and much sought-after brazen benediction of the holy Saint Ellessdee, and the goodwill of bishop, priest, and deacon, till the act of God, in old age or through an accident, shoves me from the job I'm no longer fit to fill: all this I swear for the third time grinning. Aman. Inscribed with solemn derision on the twelfth day of the eighth month in the year of our Lord, William Martin Murphy.—T. GOMARAWL.

—What's all this mean? asked Sean.

—It means, said the foreman, winking an eye, that Mr. Martin Murphy knows what's good for you betther than yourself; so be a good boy an' sign.

—Tell your ignorant lout of a Murphy and his jackal, Bimberton, that I'd see him in Hell first!

—Don't be a fool, Jack, said the foreman smoothly, to do in a second what you may regret for a year. Sign, man, an' then go when the pressure gets too sthrong — there's no law again' you signin' the thing, an' breakin' it when you have to.

—Look, Bill, said Sean, a great poet once wrote,

A knight there was, and that a worthy man,
That from the time that he first bigan
To ryden out, he loved chivalrye,
Truth and honour, fredom and curteisye;

and were I to sign this thing, all these things would turn aside and walk no more with me.

—I dunno, said the foreman, and scorn touched his tongue, that e'er a one of those things ever did, or could, walk with any of us. It's only poethry talkin' big. The ten commandments are enough for a working man to go on with — too much, if y'ask me! An' more — you may be a worthy man, but you're hardly a knight.

—Well, I'd be less than a man if I signed, Bill.

—Have it your own way, Jack, but you're no betther than others who will; and raising his voice, he said, If you can't sign, get off th' premises — we want no Larkinism here! And, seeing that Sean hesitated, he added, An' if you try to cut up rough, there's police within call to come an' shuffle you out!

—I'm off, said Sean; but tell your boss, Gomarawl, and let him tell Martin Murphy that I said that they'd auction off the coat of Christ; they'd coin the stars into copper coins; make a till out of the wood of the holy cross; they'd line their hats with the silken sounds of Shakespeare's sonnets; they'd haggle with Helen of Troy about the price of a night in bed with her; and force the sons of the morning, were they hungry, to be satisfied with a penny dinner from St. Anthony's Fund: there's nothing they wouldn't do to damn themselves with God, with angels, and with men.

On a bright and sunny day, while all Dublin was harnessing itself into its best for the Horse Show, the trams suddenly stopped. Drivers and conductors left them standing wherever they happened to be at a given time in the day when the strike commenced, to be brought to their sheds by frightened inspectors and the few scabs and blacklegs who saw in Martin Murphy another God incurnate. And the employers kept on locking out all who refused to abandon their Union, mill men, men and women from the factories, from the docks, from the railways, and from the wholesale and retail warehouses of the cities and towns. They came out bravely, marching steadily towards hunger, harm, and hostility, just to give an answer for the hope that was burning in them.

The dust and mire in which the people lived and died were being sprinkled everywhere through the gallant, aristocratic streets; it drifted on to the crimson or blue gold-braided tunics of the officer; on to the sleek morning coat and glossy top-hat of the merchant and professional man; on to the sober black gown and grey-curled wig of the barrister and judge; on to the rich rochet of immaculate surplice and cocky biretta; on to the burnished silk and lacquer-like satin frocks and delicate petticoats of dame and damsel.

Those who lived where lilacs bloomed in the doorway, where the dangling beauty of laburnum draped itself over the walls, where many a lovely, youthful rose crinkled into age, and died at last in peace, where three parts of the year was a floral honeymoon — here the dust and the mire came too, and quiet minds knew ease no longer. Magic casements were opened cautiously, and handsome or dominating eyes gazed out on a newer fairyland, a Keltic twilight growing into smoky tumult, enveloping rough and ugly figures twisting about in a rigadoon of power and resolution.

Standing to arms, the soldiers were confined to barracks; town and country police began to go about in companies; and the horsemen came trotting down this street and up that one. And the clergy, if they weren't denouncing strike organisers, kept fast together in a secret silence. And at the wall of an end house in every tottering street stood groups of mingled black and blue police as if the rotting building had suddenly thrown out a frieze of dark and sinister growth. There they stood, never moving, though every eye turned slow in its socket to follow the figure of every passing man. And every passing man tried to pretend he hadn't seen them; or, if he had, that they were no concern of his, for he was on the Lord's side, out to serve the King, and loyal to William Martin Murphy. Sean, whenever he passed them, shuddered, for in his mind's eye he could see the swiftly rising arm, the snarling face, and feel the broad bone of his skull caving in on his brain, with the darkness of death beside him.

Sean wondered why the clergy didn't stand with the men for their right of choosing their own leader and their own Union. He remembered the Polish poet Mickiewicz's enthusiasm for the haughty, desperate rising of the French Communards, after he had hurried to Rome to form a legion to strike at Austria for the freedom of Italy; how mad he was at the difficulties so civilly thrust in the way of all he wanted to do by crafty, timid, crimson-clothed cardinals. Were he, Sean, able to pick the lock of the massive gate in the grounds of the Primate's palace, or climb in the dead of night over its high, cold, ashlar-moulded walls; creep through shrubbery and gaudy flower-bed, creep through window thoughtlessly left open; pass by secretary and usher, unbeknownst, right into the presence of the right reverend gentleman, reading his breviary, he would catch him by the arm, as the Polish poet caught the arm of the Pope, and say to the Primate what the poet said to the Pope, Good God, man, know that the spirit of God is under the jackets of the Dublin workers!

With six constables sitting on it, six mounted men leading, six following behind, a lorry driven by a scab came slowly down the quays. Suddenly a crowd of dockers were between the leading horsemen and the lorry; another between the lorry and the horsemen following; while a third attacked the foot police, and pulled the scab from the cart, the mounted men trying to shelter their faces and control their frightened horses in the midst of a shower of stone and jagged ends of broken bottles. Before they could recover, the scab was splashing in the river, and then, like lightning, many hands scurried the horse from the cart, dragged the lorry to the river wall, where, with a shout of All together — up! the lorry was raised and sent hurtling down into the river on top of the screaming scab.

The dust and savage creak of this bloody scuffle had no benison of feeling for Sean, so he turned away to go from the place as quick as he dared to move; for, if he met a police patrol, speed would tell them he had been doing something, and a baton might crunch in his skull. So he walked on as carelessly as he could, and oh, Christ! a staggering tatter-clad figure, clasping a jaw with both hands, caught up with him. From a side glance, Sean saw that the figure's jaw had been slashed down by a sabre-cut, and it kept calling out, A handkerchief, a handkerchief, someone! Jasus! is there ne'er a one rich enough among the millions o' Dublin's city to spare a poor bleedin' bugger a handkerchief!

Sean's one handkerchief was safe at home, thank God, and the bit of rag he was using, and always used, except on very special occasions, was too precious to be given away; for there was no way of getting another, for with them rags were as scarce as purple cloth or linen fine; so he kept walking on with the wounded man following. A jarvey driving slowly down the street stopped, jumped down, had a look, and said hastily, and with horror, Here, man alive, climb up, an' I'll dhrive yeh to Jervis Street Hospital before half of your dial is missin'; an' you, he added to Sean, jump up, an' hold him on.

Sean hadn't the courage to persist in going on his way; so he climbed on to the side-car, putting an arm round the stricken man to keep him steady, who kept muttering tensely, If I only hadda had a handkerchief, I'd ha' stayed on in the fight. Only let me get a few stitches in it, an' I'm back for the bastard who done it!

Turning into another street, they came on a police patrol, led by a sergeant, who stopped them, asked where they'd been and where they were going.

—Oh, I'm only doin' th' good Samaritan, said the jarvey jollily; jus' picked him up to bring him to Jervis Street, havin' nothin' betther to do, sergeant.

—Yous gang o' goughers! snarled the sergeant, I know yous of old. Here you, seizing the wounded man by the arm and pulling him headlong from the car, walkin's good enough for you, instead of plankin' your bum on a car in your Larkinistic idea of proper an' proverbial comfort an' calm. In this war, me bucko, th' wounded'll have to be their own sthretcher-bearers, an' carry themselves to hospital! And he gave him a woeful kick in the backside, shaking him so that he drew his hand from his face, letting the cloven cheek fall like a bloody flap over his chin, giving a howl as his hand caught it again and fingered it back to its proper place; his other hand rubbing his under backbone, as he shambled away moaning.

—And don't be so quick an' ready with your grand charity the next time, you! he said, turning on the jarvey.

—I didn't know, sergeant, murmured the jarvey. Me an' this good man here helped him, thinkin' he'd met with a purely innocent accident.

—What a pair o' gaums yous are! roared the sergeant sarcastically. Be off with you before I bring you, horse, car, an' all, to the station! An' what are you gawkin' at? he wheeled round on Sean, who was afraid to go or stay. You're another of them that want to change th' world, eh? Well, go an' change it somewhere else, yeh miserable remaindher of some mother's bad dhream! An' here's a hand to help you there; and before Sean knew enough, a heavy hand swung swiftly to his ear, sending him spinning down the street, his vision a blaze of shooting lights, his knees shaking under him as he staggered away, never waiting to give a groan till he was out of sight and sound of the savage group, glad in his heart that it had been a hand, and not a baton, that had clipt him on the head.

The meeting of the locked-out workers, arranged for the following Sunday, had been proclaimed by Dublin Castle. The night the proclamation had come to Liberty Hall, a vast crowd gathered to hear what was to be done. The meeting would be held; Jim Larkin would be there in O'Connell Street. The darkness was falling, a dim quietness was spreading over the troubled city. Even the gulls muted their complaining cries; and the great throng was silent; silent, listening to the dark voice speaking from the window. To Sean, the long arm seemed to move about in the sky, directing the courses of the stars over Dublin; then the moving hand held up the proclamation, the other sturdy hand held a lighted match to it; it suddenly flared up like a minor meteor; in a dead silence it flamed, to fall at last in flakes of dark and film ashes down upon the heads of the workers below, fluttering here and there, uncertainly, by the wind from the mighty cheer of agreed defiance that rose to the sky, and glided away to rattle the windows and shake the brazen nails and knobs on the thick doors of Dublin Castle. Resolute and firm, thought Sean; but they have no arms, they have no arms.

Oh! O'Connell Street was a sight of people on that Sunday morning! From under the clock swinging pedantically outside of the *Irish Times* offices, across the bridge over the river, to well away behind the Pillar, topped by Nelson, the wide street was black with them; all waiting for Jim to appear somewhere when the first tick of the clock tolled the hour of twelve.

In this very street, not so very long ago, the gentle Shelley had stood, handing out to the staring, passing people his Declaration of Rights. From one of the windows of the restaurant, almost facing Sean, he tossed his leaflets of hope and stormy encouragement to the gibing Dublin citizens. Shelley who sang,

What is freedom? Ye can tell that which slavery is too well,
For its very name has grown to an echo of your own.
Rise like lions after slumber. . . .
Shake your chains to earth like dew. . . . Ye are many — they are few.

Maybe he is looking down upon this very crowd now, seeing, and applauding, the change that has come to the mind of the Irish workers. Oh! If they only had arms!

—Lo, Jim is there! a voice would say, and the crowd, like a cornfield under a rough wind, would sway towards the bridge; lo, he is here! another voice would say, and the crowd swayed back towards the Pillar.

—There's a funeral to come along, said a voice at Sean's elbow, an' when th' hearse gets to the middle o' th' crowd, Jim'll pop up outa th' coffin an' say his say.

—No, no, another voice replied; as a matther of fact, he's stealin' up th' river in a boat.

—Couldn't be that way, answered still a third, for the quays are crawlin' with polis.

Sean shivered, for he was not a hero, and he felt it was unwise to have come here. He felt in his pocket: yes, the strip of rag and his one handkerchief were safe there. It was well to have something to use for a bandage, for a body never could tell where or how a sudden wound would rise. Although the police were instructed to hit the shoulders of the people, they always struck at the top or the base of the skull. He turned to look back so as to assure himself that he hadn't got too far into the crowd. No; with a quick wheel of his body, and a few swift sweeps of his arms, he'd be out of it, and a few paces only from the side streets opposite the Pillar: so far so good. Maybe the police were out just to fulfil regulations. They had to be wherever there was a crowd; it was customary, and of little significance. If they hadn't wanted the people here, they could have prevented them from gathering by cordoning the street off; and the people around looked quite at ease, and would be very peaceable. They were intent on seeing where Jim would appear, and heads were constantly twisting in every direction. A little way down, on a narrow ledge of a doorway, holding a column to keep steady, Sean saw the figure of a man whose head and face were heavily bound in bandages; and from what he saw of the cap, the coat, and the bit of the face visible, he'd swear it was the man whose cheek hung over his chin but a few days ago. A wicked thing for a man in his condition to come to a place like this, he thought.

—There he is! suddenly shouted a dozen voices near Sean. Goin' to speak from the window of the very hotel owned be Martin Murphy himself! and there right enough, framed in an upper window, was a tall man in clerical garb, and when he swept the beard from his chin, the crowd saw their own beloved leader, Jim Larkin.

A tremendous cheer shook its way through the wide street, and Sean raised his right arm, and opened his mouth to join it, but his mouth was snapped shut by a terrific surge back from the crowd in front, while another section of it, on the outskirts, surged forward to get a better view, though now the cheer had been silenced by a steady scream in the near distance, by the frantic scuffling of many feet, and loud curses from frightened men. Twelve rows or so ahead of him, Sean saw a distended face, with bulging eyes, while a gaping mouth kept shouting, The police — they're chargin'; get back, get back, there! Let me out, let me out; make a way there for a man has a bad heart! They're batonin' everyone to death — make a way out for a poor, sick man, can't yous!

Sean made a desperate try to turn, but the jam became so close that he was penned tight to his struggling neighbour. He felt himself rising, but fought savagely to keep his feet on the ground; and try as he might, he couldn't get his lifted arm down to fend off the pressure on his chest that was choking him. He could neither get his right arm down nor his left arm up to loosen the collar of his shirt, to get more air, a little more air; he could only sway back and forward as the crowd moved. The breathing of the suffocating crowd sounded like the thick, steamy breathing of a herd of frightened cattle in a cattle-boat tossed about in a storm; and over all, as he tried to struggle, he heard the voices of the police shouting, Give it to the bastards! Drive the rats home to their holes! Let them have it, the Larkin bousys!

—Jesus, Mary, an' Joseph be with us now! burst from the voice beside Sean as two sickening sounds told of two skulls crunched not very far away; and Sean closed his eyes, waiting for a blow. The ache in the pit of his belly was agonising, and the heat of the pressure against him was sending the sweat running in rivulets down his chest and spine.

—We should never ha' listened to Larkin, wailed the voice beside him. Our clergy were always warnin' us, an' we should ha' gone be them! Jesus, Mary, an' Joseph be with us in this hour o' need! If I ever get outa this, I'll light half a dozen candles to St. Nocnoc of Duenna-durban.

Sean felt he couldn't stick it much longer. Carried along by the ebbing and flowing mass of people, he saw dimly that they had gone beyond Nelson's Pillar; while, topping the crowd, he could see police helmets darting hither and thither, batoning and blustering, batoning, batoning everyone. A minute later his toe struck something soft, and a moment after his feet were trampling a body that never made a move. Now he couldn't get his feet to the ground again, and in a spasmodic effort to do it, he only managed to rise higher so that his head and shoulders looked over the struggling mass of men. He could see no women, though he had heard a woman's screaming several times. Yes, there was one, a well-dressed lass too, lying alone beside the chemist's shop at the corner of Henry Street. The part of the crowd in which he was jammed now took a half-wheel, and he saw they were battling furiously among themselves to be the first to force a way into the narrow lane that led to the Pro-Cathedral. In the pause that came while he waited to be carried to the narrow neck of safety, Sean looked ahead and saw Jim Larkin pulled, pushed, and shoved along by four constables, a crowd of others keeping guard around their comrades, their batons in hand, ready for any head that came within circling range of it. And following some distance away, there, by God! was his friend of the cleft cheek; a sleeve torn from his coat, the bandages hanging wildly round his neck, forced along by three policemen, making things worse by shouting, Up the Dublin workers! Up Jim Larkin! and making Sean shudder at the thought of what they'd make him look like when they got him to the cell and no-one was there to see.

Now with an angry surge and a pressure that cracked his ribs, Sean was borne into the narrow way that led unto life; the pressure, pressing in, eased, and his feet touched the ground. A pale paladin of the people, he stood there, his escort fleeing on ahead to crowd into the church and fill themselves with its peace and promise of security. An inward pressure pressing out assailed him now; his breathing could barely keep in time with the frantic flutter of his heart; his head ached, and the church railings seemed to move this way and that before him. He felt as if he must fall to feel safe. Each time he took a step towards the side-walk, his foot made a half-circle, and the road seemed to rise and slap the sole of it. Getting there at last, he leaned against the railing, slid down to sit on the pavement and wait for his heart to slow down and his breath to order itself into a quieter commotion. God! it had been a day and a half!

There were the two of them on the top of the building, statuters of St. Laurence O'Toole and St. Patrick, with their backs to the people, O'Toole, now a commissioner of police, bludgeoning his flock into an improper reverence for law and order. And St. Patrick was far too busy to care, with his episcopal nose stuck between the vellum leaves of one of his rarer Keltic books. What one, now, allanna? Book of Kills; the Book of O'Money; the Book of the Ripe and Edifying Thoughts in the Head of Kinsale; the Book of the Old Done Cow; the Book of the Curious Chronicles of Finnegan's Wake (That's over his head); or the Book of the Revised Version of Cathleen's Thorny Way? More than likely it's Merriman's *Mediae Noctis Consilium* he's poring over now.

God rest you merry, gentlemen, but isn't this a nice book to have burgeoned out of Ireland's bosom! murmured St. Patrick to himself. This fellow couldn't have been a true Gael. And I thinking the Gaedhilge was the sure shield of Eire's purity! Well, this book is an eye-opener anyway. Isn't it well that it's in a language that few can read. They'd lap it up if it was in plain English. There isn't half enough police in the country. This is a nice thing to be peeping over the fair hills of holy Ireland. If the English caught me reading it, I'd be ruined! The Irish have always been a worry to me and poor Laurence. He doesn't really know how to deal with Dubliners. You think you have them all nice and handy on their knees, shouting *mea culpa* the way you'd think they were cheering, when, suddenly, one of them'll lep up, roaring, To hell with it all! and, immediately, there's a pack after him, doing the same thing. What a precious, peaceful time the English saints — the few there are — have in comparison! Their sleep hardly ever broken by a row among their boyos below. But I can scarcely sit down to a quiet meal when some excited messenger must come like a whirlwind, sweeping away the little rest one gets nowadays with the wind of his wings, to whisper, You're wanted at once at the bordher, sir; they're at it again! Then to have these simpering, gone-and-forgotten English saints, not a hair astray on one of them, come up to you to admonish and advise: You're not 'arf strict enough with them, Pauddy. You allow them too many indulgences altogether. You really ought to keep them dahn with a stwrong hand. By the Ardaw Chalice, the Cwoss of Cong, and the Tahrahrah Brooch, if I were you, Pauddy, I'd be moh severe. I near lost me temper when that chit of a Saint Allsup of Shelmexham tapped me on the shoulder to say, Pauddy, the next best thing to do is to change your nationullity and settle dahn into a fine old English gentleman. Only for catching my guardian angel's eye, I'd have put his mitre asthray on his head for him!

It makes it worse that there's some truth in it all. But how, in th' name o' God, could I ever get them to confine their thoughts to dominoes and darts? Sure I know damn well if they did they wouldn't dwell so much on religion or politics. I'll be worn out if this goes on much longer. Then there's that Patricius, insistin' he was the real Patrick, a dangerous fella, goin' round, too, makin' out it was him brought four-thirds of the people into the Church, and all I done was to wangle Armagh into bein' the chief see of th' land; and that poor deluded man, Professor Rahilly, puttin' it down in black an' white, an' sayin' there may have been three Patricks altogether, so that some of the Irish are sayin' there's primae-facie reasons for believin' that St. Patrick left Ireland before he came there at all; and that though some Patrick did something somewhere, the real Patrick never existed outside of a stained-glass window, St. Patrick's Day parades, the Calendar of the Culdees, picture postcards, and the tune of St. Patrick's Day in th' Mornin'! And all this scorn of tradition in spite of what is set down in the Trippertight-tappertuttut Life of St. Patrick, sworn to as truth in the news by Roddy the Rover with his signature tune added of It could happen here for the glory of God and the honour of Eireann.

Now this Jim Larkin is tumbling my poor flock into turmoil again, snapping away from them their grand lifelong chance of working an exceeding weight of glory from their hunger, wretchedness, and want. It's all getting me down! I was lookin' at myself in a fixed star only yesterday, and I was frightened be the look of sthrain an' weariness starin' out at me. What is Bishop Eblananus of Stopaside doin'?

He seized hold of a passing blink of sun and sent it skimming down to the Bishop's Palace, to tell him to meet him immediately, if not sooner, on the top of Nelson's Pillar to see what they could do to stop the poor from running after things adamnistic and evenescent, instead of cleaving to the things not made with hands, eternal in the heavens. Then he tore a wide strip from the rainbow's end, making a lovely swung seat of it by tying the ends round the necks of two cherubs, Asseguy and Bellboomerang; and sitting himself nicely down in the swing, off the three of them went, dancing through the shining sun, waltzing, gavottering, and schottisching down to the platform of the Pillar, some hundred feet above the tumult in the streets below.

The saint made a perfect landing on the stony square of ground, and as he was passing by for the landing, he had noticed a supercilious look on the battered face of Nelson, and heard a muttered pshaw coming from between his stony lips; but he was too dignified to notice this abortive insult aimed at him by the snobbish and heretical admiral.

And there, lying flat on his broad back, was the bishop, Eblananus, feebly fanning himself with his mitre, gasping for breath; the ascent of the hundreds of winding stairs inside the cylindrical Pillar had completely blown him, for he was fairly well stricken in years.

—Pull yourself together, man, said St. Patrick, angry at seeing the bishop in a condition resembling *hors de combat*; this isn't the time for thinking of yourself.

—Take your time, man, till I get me breath; take your time, murmured the good man breathlessly. Curious spot to choose for an episcopal pow-wow.

St. Patrick leaned over the balustrade to look at the disorder below, at the little mites of men struggling with the blue-coated mites of policemen striking at the bare hands of the workers raised to shield their heads. He turned towards Eblananus, who had propped himself up against the pedestal on which Nelson stood. Nice position we'd be in, if these Dublin rowdies of yours had been armed, wouldn't we? Will you thry to tell a man what is it they want?

—Everything a man can think of, breathed the bishop: a pleasanter place be day; a warmer shelter be night; more bread for their children; and more time off for themselves.

—Be God! they're not askin' for much! ejaculated Patrick. An' what is this Larkin fella askin' for them?

—All them things too; an' an education that'll allow them, if they so will, to dip into Plato, feel the swing of the Pleiades, to climb the long reaches to the peak of song, to wonder at the rift of the dawn, and to hail with silent happiness the reddening of the rose.

—Oh! Is that all? questioned the saint bitterly. He isn't askin' a lot either. There's nothin' like hitchin' your flagon to a bar! Well, they must be taught that the penny Catechism is good enough for them. I wondher what do both of them combined want?

—I can tell you that, said Eblananus, with a tremor in his voice. They want the Oid Woman of Beare who once wore a shinin' shift, an' now wears none, to wear a shinin' shift again.

—They didn't use that actual low an' dangerous word, did they?

—They did then, an' all, holy Patrick, apostle of the pure-minded Gael.

—The fact is, Eblananus, said Patrick stormily, you're not doin' your duty be these people. You give them far too many indulgences. You'll have to learn to keep them down with a stwrong hand. If this goes on much longer, I'll change me nationullity, an' leave your little Irish colleen in her ould plaid shawl, the playboy of your Western world, the counthry dressmaker, A. E.'s great breath, the eloquent Dempsey, Professor Tim, Mother Machree, and the rest of them, to their own devices. I'll make me home in John Bull's Other island; I will, as God is me judge, if this goes on! What's preventin' them from patternin' themselves on th' English? Answer me that. No, no answer. Y'never get an answer here when y'ask a decent question. He ran to the railing around the Pillar's platform, leant over as far as he could, cautiously, and again stared down on the street below. Oh! look at them, look at them! Th' sthreet black with them, an' not a one of them with a thought in his head, or a wish in his heart, for me! Well, they're feelin' th' swing of th' Pleiades now! Sorrow mend them! He turned suddenly on Eblananus. Why th' hell, man, don't you come over here an' give them good advice?

—Oh! I've thried, an' thried, an' thried, said the bishop, petulantly, till I'm tired.

—Well, thry again! shouted the saint. Don't they know the law—that, in its blessed equality, it forbids the rich as well as the poor to resist authority coming from God, to steal bread, to sleep in the open, or to beg in the streets? Have you been teaching them anything at all, man? They must be taught to be trim, correct, and orderly like the English—d'ye hear us talkin', man?

—'Course I hear you—I'd want to be deaf if I didn't.

—Well, roared the saint, losing his temper for the first time in his life, why don't you come here an' shout it down at them?

—Shout it yourself, if you're so eager, an' see what you'll make of it! vehemently replied the patient bishop, now aroused for the second time in his life.

—Oh! said Patrick in despair, clasping his hands, and turning up his eyes to Heaven. Oh! *Hibernica salubrio, este pesta quaesta essentia terrifica tornadocum!*

—Yah! leered the figure of Nelson, leaning precariously over his pedestal, and shoving his cocked hat farther over his blind eye with his remaining hand, to get a better view; now yous know a little of what we have to contend against to keep yous in the bonds of law'n order!

—Yah, yourself! shouted Patrick, now beside himself at being jeered at be an intherloper, drummin' the platform with the butt-end of his staff; if all had their rights, me bucko, it's not you'd be stuck up there in a state of honour, but me, or that other dacent man standin' there, Eddy Eblananus, born an' reared only a stone's-throw from Lam Doyle's an' th' Three-Rock Mountain. An' who but the foolish Irish lifted you to where y'are?

—Ay, said Eblananus, now on his feet, and standing well out to fix his eyes on Nelson, with a fighting swing of his frock, an' let him be aware he'd be wantin' th' epaulettes on his shouldhers an' th' gold lace on his cocked hat, if it wasn't for the Finucanes, the Finnegans, the Fogarties, and the Flaherties at Trafalgar's Bay, and among the slimy rushes at the open mouth of th' Nile!

—Moreover, me gentleman, went on Patrick, it's not to th' English we'll look for lessons in spiritual or corporal deportment, I can tell you that!

—Let him get down here on th' platform, shouted Eblananus, an', ould an' disabled as I am with a touchy heart, I'll show him a few military manœuvres that'll stagger him!

—Control yourselves, gentlemen, murmured the stony voice of Nelson; try to control yourselves.

—Control yourself! shouted Patrick up at him. If you could, you wouldn't send your murdherous polis out to maim an' desthroy poor men lookin' for no more than a decent livin'. Gah! If me crozier could only reach up to you, I'd knock your other eye out!

Two guardian angels, afraid of a scandal, scooted down from Heaven, seized St. Patrick, hoisted him on to his rainbow seat, and hurried him back to where he'd come from; the other, Eblananus's, took the bishop's arm and led him away down the stairs for fear of further mischief.

Along a wide lane of littered bodies, amid the tinkling of busy ambulances picking them up, one by one, pushed, shoved, and kicked by constables, the man with the cleft jaw trudged to jail, the wide stitches in his wounded face showing raw against his livid skin, the torn bandages flapping round his neck; shouting, he trudged on, Up Jim Larkin! Nor baton, bayonet, nor bishop can ever down us now — the Irish workers are loose at last!

DARK KALEIDOSCOPE

SEAN staggered home from a céilidh held in Banba Hall as the banner of day was breaking out over the squalidness of Ballybough, a long, dim, grey cloth tinged with pink, and streaked with gentle yellow stripes. Force of will kept him on his tottering feet. Not a soul about to see him, gay-kilted and shawled, blundering his way homewards. Filled with new wine, they'd say if they saw him. He was a sick man: he felt it in the core of his brain. Ill; no-one to help; his mother's old-age pension to keep them both. What it did before, it could do again. From half-way down his thighs to his ankles his legs were growing numb. He'd felt it for some time, but just waited for it to go. Rain, rain, go away. It was getting worse, and now he could barely walk home.

He had done too much, and hadn't had enough food to restore the energy lost. Dry bread and tea, with an odd herring when they happened to be tuppence a dozen. His mother ate less, but she wasn't suffering for it. Too old to need much; besides, she had had a better-fed youth than he. Body and mind had done too much on too little, and he had drained himself of life. This dawn meant night to him; maybe an everlasting night too.

He got home at last, and sank down on the boards, in kilt, shawl, and feathered balmoral cap, sleeping curiously there, with pain as a dream, till his mother wakened him, anxious; helped him to bed, asking what had happened. He didn't say; he didn't know. She left a red ticket in North William Street Dispensary, requesting the attendance of Dr. Donnelly, Medical Man for the District. He came, punched Sean about, looked into his eyes, murmuring, You're in a bad way, me boy. Head like to burst, eh? Ay. Legs leaden, eh? Ay. Soles of feet feel as if you walked on cushions, eh?

—No, said Sean.

—No? Blast it, man, they must! shouted the poor-law doctor.

—Blast you, doctor, they don't! shouted Sean back at him.

—The Infirmary for this man, he said, turning to Mrs. Casside. It's the only place for him. I'll send the car tomorrow.

—Oh, there's another place, sir, she said.

—Where, me good woman?

—Here. None of us ever went there; none of us ever will, please God.

—Betther than ever you were, ma'am, went there.

—Very likely, sir; they didn't know the difference.

—Well, I've no time to argue; other poor people need my care; and he walked out of the room.

Dr. Woods of Gardiner Street came to see him. He was a five-shilling first-visit doctor, half a crown afterwards. He was loved by the poor, so gentle, painstaking; he was a wraithlike figure, said to have but a short time to live, keeping himself going with drugs. He was sent by Seumas Deakin, whom Sean had first known as a member of All Saints Church, Grangegorman, and, afterwards, as a chemist and a member of the Supreme Council of the I.R.B.

Hanging his coat up on a nail in the door, after a swift glance round the room, sighing languidly, the doctor sat down beside Sean, fingering him with quiet, sympathetic hands, sighing, sighing as he did so.

He sees the world in his own condition, and sighs for it, thought Mrs. Casside. What's th' matter with him, doctor? she asked aloud.

—I don't rightly know, he said, putting his white hands over Sean's eyes, and leaving them there for some seconds, then peering into their depths when he had suddenly whipped them away. I don't rightly know yet. He wrote a prescription. Mr. Deakin will make that up for you — a nerve and stomach tonic. Let me know how you feel, say in a fortnight, and if you're not better, Mr. Deakin will tell me to come to you; and he sighed again.

He'll come, if Deakin tells him, thought Sean; making sure of his two-and-six. His glance round the room showed him there was no money here. Even kindly, gentle Dr. Woods had to think of his wife and children.

—Porridge, Mrs. Casside, is the best thing for him; as much as he can eat; and he slid painfully into his topcoat and glided from the room.

Sean was thinking where the porridge would come from, when Deakin came, a few days later, to see him, bringing kingly presents of bundles of the *Review of Reviews, John o' London's*, Lane's *Modern Egyptians*, Washington Irving's *Mahomet*, Landor's *Imaginary Conversations*, Butler's *Way of All Flesh*, London's *White Fang*, and George Borrow's *Lavengro* — a rich load of joy, for which Sean thanks him still. When he'd gone, Mrs. Casside came to where Sean was lying, the light of Heaven in her eyes, as she held up two small glittering, golden things for Sean to see.

—On the mantelshelf, she said, two of them; sovereigns, gold sovereigns. He knew better than to offer them, so he left them quiet on the mantelshelf so's they wouldn't conflict with our pride. You'll have porridge for a few weeks now.

He looked long at the two shining coins in his hand, for he had never seen such lovely things before. A king's head on one side, St. George slaying a dragon on the other; to him they had always been deep down in the cellar of a bank. Love of money root of all evil, said Paul; not this time anyway.

All the movement he made each day was from his bed to this old sofa, his mother's bed by night. For weeks he had lain here, reading, and writing a few things for the *Irish Worker* and for *Irish Freedom*, the latter paper ignoring them; always wondering in his spare time if he would ever walk upright again. The couch was hard; the springs, thick iron, stuck up through the worn-out horse-hair, and he marvelled how his mother could sink to sleep on it. Here was a woman enduring torments quietly that would send ecstasy to a saint. The place was poorer than any saint could wish for: he glanced at the bare floor, the old cabinet, veneered mahogany, doing the work of his mother's dresser and his own bookcase; the table, the two old kitchen chairs, the fender, kept together by wire; the butter-box covered with the red cloth; the picture of Nelson, and that much-loved one of Victoria, as bright as ever, with her little crown on her grey head, her purple bodice crossed by a pale-blue sash, and the Victorian Order hanging on her bosom — gaudy guardians of a bleak room. There was the box arrangement too, carrying the musk, the fuchsia, and the geranium, doleful now, and waiting for the spring to come. Someone had given his mother another treasure, a most mysterious plant, for, she said, in winter, sift the soil as you might, you'd find no trace of anything. Yet in the spring it thrust up a rosy tip of life, and in the summer turned into a wealth of variegated leaves, garnished by thick velvety blossoms of a rich red, with a saucy blob of tasselled gold in its centre. She called it the Resurrection Plant; and years after Sean discovered that it was a begonia. It was a lonely time for him, yet his mother had spent the worst of her lifetime here, without a murmur. She and he had hunted the bugs from the rooms, but they never got rid of the fleas, and these tormented him now. How in the name of God did she sleep on such a bed! She must be getting on for eighty now. She who had been buxom, was worn away now to a wiry thinness. She was a brave woman; something of the stoic in her. Seldom he had seen her cry: once, a sudden gushing forth of tears when she saw her dead son Tom; her favourite, Sean thought, though she had never shown it by word or deed; and again, when quiet tears had flowed down her cheeks, the night of his father's funeral, when they sat together by the fireside. Beside Ella's body, she had just whimpered in fright; she had broken down for the first time. Forgot herself for a moment. Her bravery hadn't brought her much. She had certainly served God quietly and faithfully and simply in all the life through which Sean had known her; but God had been stingy in His favours to her. Such a picture as she was deserved a finer frame than this mean, cancerous room. A quiet garden would be a fitter setting, with a few flowers, pansies, mignonette, big-panelled daisies, musk, a peony or two, a clump of gorgeous sunflowers, southernwood that she loved to smell, with big tufts of tansy and michaelmas daisies; oh yes, and maybe one deep-yellow rose with a brown tinge in its rich and silky petals. A tree too — a rowan or a hawthorn, spreading its loveliness over a hard bench where she could sit, and sew, knit, or read, and mark the birds coming into the garden. What bird would suit her best — lark, linnet, thrush, sparrow, or robin? None of these: the lark was too gay; the linnet too delicate; the thrush's speckled breast a little too pompous; the sparrow too humble and commonplace; and the robin too impudent. Which then? The blackbird? Yes, the blackbird; sedate and dignified in his black dress, yet bright in his deep-yellow bill; dignified, yet quick and confident in his walk and flight; a song never boisterous, yet bold and decisive in its deep mellow notes, with a faint touch of sharpness in some of them. The blackbird would suit her best. But her bright sedateness hadn't a green canopy or a blue sky over its head. She would end her days within this dim, drab room. She would get her last look at a patch of sky through the crooked window, over the tops of the musk, the geranium, and the fuchsia — that would be her way to a further life.

Yes, she must be getting on for eighty, he thought, as he watched the gnarled hands stirring the little saucepan of porridge. Those hands could do many things yet, and she was firm on her legs, and often laughter came purling from her cracking lips. He saw she was stirring mechanically, and that her thoughts were far away. What was she thinking of? Probably of her husband, her Michael; her memory of him seemed to brighten as her body withered, for she really believed they would be together again. Well, he wouldn't hint at anything to frighten the dear delusion. She deserved her dream, coloured with the musk, the fuchsia, and geranium. Her Michael was waiting patiently for her among the asphodels; knee-deep in them now, he couldn't have long more to wait.

Ah, t'hell with it! he thought, he wouldn't stay here to dry up and die! She'd have to stick it, but he wouldn't. Her life was nearly over. She belonged to a different world, the world of submission, patience, resignation; he to that of discontent, resentment, resistance. Whenever she had been ill, he had done for her all he could — cooking, making tea and toast for her, and arrowroot when the funds allowed, lighting the fire, and washing out the damned floor when the end of the week came. But his life was away from her, and he'd have to leave her wandering in her little Garden of Eden among the musk, the fuchsia, and the crimson geranium.

He began to walk stiffly about the room, in great pain, to tip his toes hundreds of times a day, for he wasn't going to lie where he was and wait for God to call him. Though the harness he wore were strings and tatters, he'd die with it on him, resisting to the end.

Asked to be Secretary to a Committee formed to collect funds to provide clothes and boots for women and children of locked-out workers, he borrowed a stick, and hobbled down to be from ten in the morning till twelve at night in and out of Liberty Hall, helping with the Army, and, in his spare time, writing letters appealing for funds to help the women and children of the locked-out workers to cling a little longer on to life, till his heart ached for rest, and he began to set down sad thoughts in bad verses, which was his little space of geranium, fuchsia, and musk.

So here he was in Liberty Hall, seeing all the bright and excited patterns against the dark background of his illness. Always, in the throes of work, the dark grey silhouette of paralysis stared at him behind the moving picture of life. Like the changing designs of red, blue, green, white, and yellow of a kaleidoscope that never shifted from a bed of blackness. Nothing to do but to keep on, crushing out of his thought the gnawing pains in his legs from thigh to ankle; to go as far as his trembling legs would carry him, till he fell down, to wait for the fuller darkness of death.

Strange and vivid things passed in and out, figures in a candle-lighted show. Here was A. E., George Russell, looking like a teddy bear, pouring a cascade of jellied words over Jim Larkin, implying that out of them only a new heaven and earth could be built; shocked by hearing Jim say that bricks to build a new life must be hardened to a fine and fierce quality in the fire of trial.

—Well, what d'ye think of him? asked Jim, when A. E. had gone.

—Can't say, said Sean; no-one I know knows him, except the Gaelic Leaguers, and they don't like him. I've read nothing he has written, except some verses in the Christmas Number of the *Irish*

Homestead, called *The Celtic Christmas.* He has a great name in a lot of places. He looks to me like a Sanko Panko without his Don, and is a little embarrassed by the loneliness.

—Well, said Jim, most of what he's written isn't for us, except his fine letter defending us in our fight; and we must honour him for that.

A day or so after, in sails the Rev. Dudley Fletcher, Rector of Coolbanagher, a strong-looking, stocky man in fully-fledged clericals, bearded like a pard, wearing the Red Hand in the lapel of his coat, full of sympathy with the workers, shaking Jim's hand and mine, wishing us well, and honouring us with a murmured prayer that the workers might win.

He wished he had his paint-box of ten colours handy, all gone, now, but not forgotten, that he might set down in colour the figures that passed him by here. This man, Dudley Fletcher, would appear on a background of grey pain and dark anxiety, in a white robe slashed with a dimmer red cross, upside down, sobriety and sorrow commingled. A. E. would thunder slowly and heavily in under a canopy of multi-coloured fireworks, spluttering and sparkling all around him. Yeats, though he never entered, passed by, and looked up at the windows, in a trailing toga of silver and purple, a mystic rose in his hair, and a lady's golden glove at his girdle. Orpen would hop in, dressed in rusty red and bottle-green to sketch the tired and hungry faces surrounding the pale, hardy, handsome face of their leader, Jim. And Countess Markievicz, running around everywhere, would be scintillating in the suit of a harlequin, lozenged with purple, old gold, and virgin green.

In all the time he had pushed a way through a crowd of ragged women, and ragged children, bootless as well as ragged, carrying jugs, saucepans, and even kettles to collect their ration of stew, cooked in the Dagdan cauldron down in the damp and dreary basement, he had never seen the Countess doing anything anyone could call a spot of work. He often had a share of the stew, and sometimes snapped up a chance to bring home some to his mother, who welcomed it when it came, but said nothing when he came home without any; but never once did he see the Countess bearing up in the heat and burden of the day. Whenever a reporter from an English or an Irish journal strayed into the Hall and cocked an eye over the scene, there was the Countess, in spotless bib and tucker, standing in the steam, a gigantic ladle in her hand, busy as a beebeesee, so that a picture of the lady of the ladle might brighten the papers of the morrow; and, significant enough, though many mouths belled the myth of her devotion to the poor,

Orpen's sketch of the eskitchen doesn't show sign or light of the good-natured dame anywhere near. The myth, it would seem, appeared in a vision to those who wanted to see it so. Neither did the Countess understand Ireland, even when she was green-costumed in her own selective uniform of the Citizen Army. She differed from Captain White in that while she never understood the workers, and never tried to, he, though never understanding them either, failed, I imagine, by trying too ardently to do so. Gaelic Ireland she never even glimpsed; and the English-speaking Ireland she ran about in was seen as in a wonderland looking-glass, darkly; so different from Alice Milligan, who saw it clear, and was able to fondle it with both her clever hands.

Countess Markievicz lagged far behind Maud Gonne in dignity, character, and grace, and couldn't hold a candle to her as a speaker. Her passionate speeches always appeared to be strained, and rarely had any sense in them; and they always threatened to soar into a still-born scream. Ideas of order she had little, and looked rather contemptuously on any mind that had. She usually whirled into a meeting, and whirled out again, a spluttering Catherine-wheel of irresponsibility. Although he had often seen her handling a gun, he had never seen her fondling a book, and he thought that odd. In her young days she could hardly have been a Cathleen ni Houlihan, and when she grew old she had no resemblance to the Old Woman of Beare. She grew very thin and bony, and in spite of all her irritating and fantastic liveliness, there was, invariably, a querulous look on her face. No part of her melted into the cause of Ireland, nor did she ever set a foot on the threshold of Socialism. She looked at the names over the doors, and then thought she was one of the family. But the movements were no more to her than the hedges over which her horses jumped. She wanted to be in everything and to be everywhere. She rushed into Arthur Griffith's arms, near knocking the man down; she dunced into the Republicanism of the Irish Brotherhood; she stormed into the Gaelic League, but quickly slid out again, for the learning of Irish was too much like work; she bounded into the Volunteers one night, and into the Citizen Army the next. Then she pounced on Connolly, and dazzled his eyes with her flashy enthusiasm. She found it almost impossible to reason out a question, and smothered the reasonable answer of another with a squeal. She seemed never to be able to make any golden or silver thing out of the ore of experience. She tried verses, and failed; she tried painting, and couldn't do any better; and yet she never reached the rank of failure, for she hadn't the constitution to keep long enough at anything in which, at the end, she could see a success or a failure facing her. One thing she had in abundance — physical courage: with that she was clothed as with a garment. She wasn't to be blamed, for she was born that way, and her upbringing in which she received the ready Ay, ay, madame, you're right of the Sligo peasants, stiffened her belief that things just touched were things well done. So she whirled about in her scintillating harlequin suit, lozenged with the colours of purple, old gold, and virgin green, bounding in through windows and dancing out through doors, striking, as she went by, her cardboard lath of thought against things to make them change, verily believing that they did, but never waiting to see whether they did or not. Well, well, may she rest in peace at last.

Recommended in a letter from the friend of a friend, Sean went one day to see another doctor to get a final verdict about his shivering legs. This'll be the third, he thought, and remembering that the number three had often played a curious part in his life, he felt hopeful. The last two were doleful; this one should be favourable. The surgery was filled with the latest gadgets to help a sick man to feel his way about. When he had stripped, he lay down on a swung couch to be thumbed and tapped again. Nerves in knees dead, he was told; and when the doctor had stared into his eyes, he murmured a number of *mmm*'s, adding, I haven't good news for you, young man; it is serious: you have spinal disease, I'm afraid — probably congenital. He gave the dazed Sean a prescription of mingled arsenic and strychnine, to be well shaken before taken, two pleasant kinds of drinks for a warm summer's day. Saint Arsenic and Saint Strychnine between him and all harm! He had got a message as bad as saying that he should live no longer. He felt no interest in wine, woman, or song when he stepped out again into the gay hum of the street. The blue sky was a black one now, and the golden sun but a big brass nail for a coffin. Well, if he was to go, he'd go drinking aromatic tea or wholesome water, and not those other two life-punishing lotions. So he slowly tore up the doctor's kindly incantation and scattered the pieces over the stony street; but when he looked up, the sky over him was as black as ever.

So, though he stumbled, he stood among the crowd in the Custom House square, listening to the English Labour Leaders speaking encouragement to the men still fighting the employers: roaring Ben Tillett who cut Dublin into segments with his waving arms; Gosling, comically respectable, spewing out hordes of dead grey words that died dimly before they could reach the minds of the bored men;

good-natured George Lansbury, a burning core of fighting faith in his
gentle nature; all aglow with words in the midst of squealing gulls,
and the boisterous sale among the men of the *Daily Herald*, full of
good tidings of great sorrow, its daring pages distended with life and
hope, and bearing on its front as a banner a full-paged cartoon by the
doughty Will Dyson.

There was Sean, too, among the crowd on that radiant day when
the good ship *Jocelyn* sailed in, packed with food, her rigging and
lines abloom with flags, her siren shrilling, setting aside the fear of
starvation for a month to come, greeted with a cheer that shook her
masts when she hove in sight coming up the river. Then there was the
busy scene of mooring her to the quay, the opening of the hatches, the
first truckload wheeled into the store by Jim Larkin himself, crowned
with the aching jubilation of the helping men whose bellies, with those
of their wives and their children, would be filled for the first time for
weeks. But there wasn't one priestly anointed member of the Christian
faith there, from cardinal to sub-deacon, to rejoice with their flock
that had been delivered for the time being from the torture of hunger.
Here was a miracle of the feeding, not of five, but of fifty thousand
souls, and not a stoled follower of Christ there to witness it. There
wasn't one of these gentry, from one end of Ireland to the other, who
hadn't had that day a good meal, who hadn't had something over and
above his daily bread; yet not one of them seemed to sense the silent
terror a soul gets from a sagging belly.

As he watched the dockers taking the cargo from the boat, he
remembered the day when he was resting his aching legs for an
hour at home, watching the sunlight playing with the golden musk and
the purple fuchsia, a Mr. Henchy, an official — the Secretary, Sean
thought — of the Protestant Orphan Society, came suddenly to see
him. The youngest son of his dead sister, Ella, had been adopted by
the Society, and Sean had been made the guardian of the boy. The
Society gave him three shillings a week, payable quarterly, to enable
him to fulfil his duty. For some time the boy had shirked the job of
going to Sunday school, morning service, and afternoon prayers for
the young. Remembering his own experience, Sean did nothing to
force him to go, if he found the play of the streets more colourful.
So Mr. Henchy had come to make a complaint on behalf of the
Society.

—You're his guardian, you know, said Mr. Henchy, and you are
bound to see he is brought up in the nurture and fear of God.

—But don't you see, sir, you're asking me to bring him up, not in the fear of God, but rather in the fear of man? He doesn't want to go: am I to force him?

—It is an obligation, he coughed, and moved uneasy in his chair; an obligation undertaken by you, Mr. Casside, in return for what the Society gives the boy.

—That isn't a lot, sir.

—You were very glad to get it! said Mr. Henchy sharply.

Sean got up from the sofa, went over to a drawer in the old dresser, took out some receipts, and put them into Mr. Henchy's hands. Look at those, he said; they are receipts for clothes and boots bought for the boy, and if you kindly add the amounts up, you'll find that the entire quarter's gratuity, plus two shillings from Mrs. Casside, bitterly spared, was spent to get them. Should you have suspicion as to how the money was spent, these receipts will show you.

—I had no suspicions whatever, said Mr. Henchy earnestly; Mr. Griffin told me long ago the sort of man you were, and added high praise for your mother. But rules are rules, and the Society must ask you to make the boy attend his religious duties.

—The Society can ask away, said Sean shortly.

—But, my friend, if the Society takes away the grant, the child will suffer.

—Evidently he will suffer either way, sir, and we must try to select the lesser one; for me, I think it better for him to die his own way. If I make him go, he will suffer unnecessarily; if you take away the grant, he will suffer unnecessarily too. I refuse to do it. If you do — well, that is your look-out.

—Your views are odd, said Mr. Henchy, with a puzzled and rather shocked look on his face, and hardly show gratitude to those kind people who furnish the wherewithal to satisfy the needs of children in dire circumstances.

—They don't half satisfy the needs — that is my point, said Sean tersely. Look here, sir, and Sean swung his legs from the sofa, and sat so as to face Mr. Henchy; would you be content to bring up one of your children on three shillings a week?

Mr. Henchy's face flushed, his hands trembled a little, and he rose from his chair. I must be going, he said; I really shouldn't be wasting time arguing. The question is, Are you, as the boy's guardian, or are you not, going to keep the rules of the Society so that the grant may be continued?

—You haven't answered my question, Mr. Henchy.

—I don't intend to try, for there is something of an insult in it.

—You are wrong, sir. Come, you are essentially a kind man; and as Mr. Griffin has spoken of me to you, so he has spoken of you to me.

—Well, then, he said, mollified, and smiling a little, there's no analogy: you couldn't expect me to wish to bring any child of mine down to the unfortunate level of your little nephew.

—God forbid, sir; but I do wish you to expect me to try to bring my nephew (or anyone's) up to the level of your child.

—But don't you see, said Mr. Henchy, that, logically, that would mean the bringing-up of all the children of all the poor to that level too?

—Precisely, said Sean, and to a higher level than that in which your class of children presently stand.

—I confess I don't understand, said Mr. Henchy, puzzled.

—Haven't you ever read Bernard Shaw, sir?

—Shaw? Who's he, now? I imagine I've heard the name somewhere. He isn't a clergyman by any chance?

—Well, he's a priest of the theatre.

—Oh, I don't take any interest in the theatre.

—Well, sir, you've heard of Goya?

—Goya? No. A foreigner of some sort?

—Well, Raphael, Titian, Constable, Darwin, and the rest.

—Oh, I've a great respect for our National Gallery, and have gone through it, of course; but what has all this got to do with our difficulty?

He hasn't any eye for colour, thought Sean. Here are the golden trumpets of musk sounding at his very ear; a carillon of purple fuchsia bells pealing pensively, and he can hear neither; and there was the rose window of a scarlet geranium behind them, and his eyes were too clouded with worldly things to see it. This man couldn't understand that when Sean's mother reverently touched the blossoms with her gnarled finger, God Himself was admiring the loveliness He had made.

—What I am out to help to do, he said aloud, is to lift our children to the state of enjoying and understanding the visions and ideas of these great men.

—Pshaw! said Mr. Henchy impatiently, you're wasting your time. The people you mean prefer the sinful and lowering charms of the public-house. You haven't to deal alone, you know, with decent protestant children; the great bulk of them are of the roman catholic faith — hopelessly ignorant and painfully superstitious. However, we must think only of our own family of faith, so assuming that you want to give our children a better life — and a gentle, but doubtful, smile spread over his handsome face — isn't our Society trying to do that too?

—According to its lights — very dim ones — yessir; but I would do away with this protestant charity as I would the catholic one of St. Vincent de Paul: each child has a right to a full life, independent of any charity.

—Oh, that's just anarchy! exclaimed Mr. Henchy. It would mean the end of all decent things. Just what that fellow — what's his name? — Larkin tried to do, and look at the state of the poor people now! Hardly any law or order anywhere.

—Mr. Henchy, Mr. Henchy, where poverty is, there can never be law or order. Sean's arm moved in a sweep to encircle the room. D'ye think law and order could come here, could sit down, sing, and sleep in a room like this? For such as we, sir, to honour your law and order would be a blasphemy against God!

—You murmur strange things, said Mr. Henchy, strange things for a protestant. You mystify me completely. I can't understand the working of your mind.

—You've said that before, Mr. Henchy. That's your trouble — you can't understand, and you don't try.

—Maybe so. But I must be off now, Mr. Casside. Sean could see he was eager to get away. He placed a white hand on Sean's shoulder. Be reasonable, man, he said, and listen. I say this, believe me, in no bullying fashion, but in the kindliest and friendliest way I can — I am in conscience bound to report to my committee, and that committee is bound to assert the rules, if your charge doesn't keep them. Now, like a dear man, do try to — not to force — but to persuade, to persuade the boy to mind his duties.

—I'll tell him, said Sean, that Mr. Henchy came to say that if he didn't go to Sunday school and church, he'd get no more clothes or boots.

—Oh, not that way; not quite in those terms, said Mr. Henchy, a pained look on his face.

—But that is exactly what you mean, sir. I'll put it this way, then: If you don't worship God properly, then He'll put it in the hearts of kind people to give you neither boots nor clothes.

Mr. Henchy sighed. Can't you explain to him that as his earthly father loved him, so does his heavenly Father love him too, and likes to see him near?

—The boy's earthly father didn't care a damn about him, said Sean, so that way won't do. There's no way out of it except by a big change.

Let yous give the lad the whole of his due, and when he and his young friends come to worship God, let it be by song and dance and magic story, in gaily-coloured plays, flags, ribbons, and maypoles; in the music of their own bands, trumpet, cymbal, triangle, and drum; the louder and fiercer the better. Let them adore God, not in hypocritical hymn, tiresome prayer, and mind-torturing catechism, but in the fullness of skipping, a hop, step, and a lep; the rage of joy in a flying coloured ball, without a care in the world, bar their own young fears and disappointments. Then the seriousness of God's face will be broken by a smile, the very angels will sing and stagger about as if filled with old wine, and the church triumphant will shout and clap her hands, saying God has come into His own at last!

—I must go, said Mr. Henchy; goodbye. By the way, I met the boy as I came in, and I thought he didn't look too well. Maybe he'd better take things quietly for a time. Then he'll go on as usual, eh? Goodbye; and hastily shaking hands, which surprised Sean, he made off without waiting for an answer.

Sean never saw him again, but the money came every quarter from the Society, and no more questions were asked about the boy. Henchy didn't understand. Reared up in a groove, a pleasant groove in many ways, but a dangerous one to us and him. A kind man, made helpless, sometimes even cruel. He never even heard of Henchy again.

A magic shadow-show, played in a box whose candle is the sun, round which we phantom figures come and go. But Ireland was rather more of a kaleidoscope than a shadow-show: always re-shaping itself into a different pattern. Strange pattern here while they talked together: the crosses of Andrew, George, and Patrick twisting uneasy in each other's arms behind a kneeling child in front of a flame from hell, with two dim figures, mouthing methods, were halo'd by whirling crimson gerontium disks, and encompassed about with the blowing of mosque-scented trumpets of gold, and the pealing of purple con fuchsian bells.

Religion was ripening in Dublin. God was being worshipped in spirits and in drouth. Well in the background, for fear of a sudden mêlée, he watched the marchers go by, a long, deep, dark, drab mass of men roped together with scapulars, and bespangled with miraculous medals. Friends in England had opened decent homes to receive the starving children of the locked-out workers, and this holy romany ryes were out to prevent their going. Led by their clergy, the marchers, beerded nicely, and supportered by a good conscience, brandyshed sticks and cudgels, bottling their wrath with difficulty; shouting

out that everything done against the advice of the clergy was illicit
still from a malthuse to a baby powder, the red, blue, brown, black,
green, and white scapuleers, scapuliars, drinkaway boys, and sluga-
lowers marched past yodelling and godelling their war-chant,

> Faith of our fathers, we will love
> Both friend and foe in all our strife;
> And preach it too, as love knows how,
> By kindly words and virtuous life,

adding sense to it by giving a knock to the head of a father trying to
get his child out of mudesty into life, tearing skin from the face of a
friend helping the father, and the shirts from the backs of any coming
near enough to shout the slogan shame; four at the front staggering
under a banner bearing the inscription of Rear Up the Workers'
Chisulers in the Rearum Novarum Way.

The Scapular Brigade halted, and divided to let a carriage and pair
drive through, and out of it pops a venerable Knight of the Roman
Slumpire, with his portly Dame, he caparisoned with a wide and
flowing beard, yellow and white, the Papal colours, she with the order
of Eironical Virtue and Honour aflame on her bosom, both of them
walking as if they had come direct from a conference in Heaven; harm
in harm they went up the steps of Liberty Hall, down the dim corridors, straight towards the room where Jim Larkin worked, who, when
he heard they were there, said to show the lady and gentleman in, and
up, and in, they came, to be met with the question of, Well, me good
woman and good man, what can we workers do for you, do for you,
do for you, fair and virtuous lady and noble knight? Have you
come for a share from the urn holding the hashes of Irish art and
literature?

—Me an' th' missus, here, said the Knight of the Burning Apestle,
have dropped in on behalf of St. Michael an' All Angels, St. Paul, St.
Pether, and th' other apostles, an' Father O'Flynn, to place before
you their, an' our, undyin' resolution to prevent th' hawkin' of our
workers' chisulers to decent homes in England, realisin' that such
circumstances would arouse disaffection in their innocent minds with
the holy squalor endured in their own homes, assured by the remembrance that what is good enough for their guardian angels must be
good enough for them — here he shook out his white-and-yellow
beard like a banner — an' if they only looked out of the window,
they'd see that the might, virtue, honour, pride, an' holiness of Ireland
had gethered itself together to prevent this condamination of our little
ones be English unbelievers, makebelievers, an' fakebelievers, waitin'

for th' chance through gawdiness and comeforth to bounce the child away from the faith of its fathers.

Asked by Connolly if the Knight and his Dame would take five children into their own home suite home, the pair were silent; asked if they would take two, they were still silent; and turning away to go out, before they could be asked if they would take one, they were gone, surrounded by clouds of witnesses gay in medievil funcy dross, looking for all the world like pupil halbeerdears.

Another twist of the kaleidoscope, and there was the patterned scene, backed by a leaden sky like a sullen face, blotched with reddish streaks; dark clouds like hair sheltering dull, nickel-silvered madonna lilies, their pistils out and pointing; a black cloud, lower down, forming a cavern-mouth from which came pouring streams of frantic figures wearing on their drab breasts bright-coloured spots spreading out into the shape of hearts, clubs, diamonds, and spades; all of them yelling dumb *vivimus vivamus* into the delicate ears of the figurines of papal knight and papal dame, all white and gold, standing in front of these squalling deomens, like chinaware grandees who had somehow climbed from a scented cabinet and had daringly stepped down on to the deusty highway. Beyond the veil of these posturing purseline figurines, and the crowd of roaring, adoring sons of the Guile, the leaden sky with its clouds and red splotches, looking like the savage face of an angry yahoovah, English shadows of men and women were bent and bruised wiring guns, making shells, hammering ships together, burying their dead in their minds by thousands, and taking their wounded to bloody beds in tens of thousands; while queues of the very old and very young waited grouseously for food from morn till midnight, sleeping then that they might be able to begin again at daybreak; too tired to feel fear of the faint purr of a Zeppelin sailing by high overhead, their ears stirred soon by the hiss of a falling bomb, to be at once cracked with the concussion of its explosion, then stuffed with the cut-short squeal of a housemaid, on her knees washing a doorstep, as a lump of jagged metal knocked her frillied head to bits; then came the rumbling, cracking zoom as houses split asunder, their frightened walls lurching for a moment before they crashed face downwards, the uproar stabbed by the scream of a woman yelling out to Heaven, Oh, save my little one who's been buried under it all!

Sean gave the cap of the kaleidoscope a twist, and there he was, between two comrades who were carrying a round wreath to one of their Union who had been battered to death by many police batons. From Tara Street they sallied down one, to emerge into another street so poor that even the stars in the night sky seemed to be dimmed by destitution. They penetrated into a yawning hole that Sean guessed was the doorway, a comrade, the tram conductor, telling him to watch out, for the stairs weren't all there; on to a lobby lit by a dumb religious light, animated by a low murmur of many voices like the sound of many leaves chattering softly on a day of a quiet breeze. First he saw the two tall candles, topped by their flickering wisps of yellow flame; and, between them, higher up on the wall, a crucifix, a little less dim than the shadows around it, seemed to hint, As it is with you, dead man, so it was with me long ago and far away. A crowd of misty men and women, kneeling and standing, hid the dead man, so Sean and his comrades waited till the prayers were said for a chance to lay the wreath where it was to lie. On a small table, covered with vivid blue paper, stood a looking-glass, showing in its depths the candles and the crucifix among the heads of the comforters. The now slumbering fire in the grate, the kettle and saucepans on the hob, with a galvanised bath in a corner, showed Sean that here the family fed, washed, and slept; and a tiny bottle of ink with an old pen stuck in its neck, showed that the correspondence and the children's lessons were done here too. In this one room they are born, they live, they grow old, and then they die. Now he saw the widow, sitting on a chair by the head of the bed, her body bent forward so that her face couldn't be seen. What will this woman do when the shouting dies, the captains and the kings depart?

When the crowd had drawn from the bed, Sean's comrades stepped forward and laid the wreath silently on its foot, crossing themselves, murmuring something meant for a prayer.

—A marthyr — that's what he was, said the conductor; a marthyr to the workers' cause! Look, Sean, he added, turning, look at th' way th' bastards left him!

Sean went forward to have a last look at a comrade who was no more than a dumb message now. There he was, asprawl under a snowy sheet, looking like a mask on a totem-pole. One eye gone, the other askew, the nose cracked at the bridge, and bent sidewise; the forehead and one cheek a royal purple: from a distance it looked well, like a fading iris in a wide patch of driven snow. The mighty baton! Each one an Erin's rod — able at the will of the owner to bud into a purple bloom of death. A warning to Sean. Keep well away from them. That he'd do, for he wanted to live, feeling an urge of some hidden thing in him waiting its chance for an epiphany of creation.

He had had one very narrow escape, when he was dragged from one

end of O'Connell Street nearly to the other by two drunken constables. He had been in a fix: had he gone quiet for twelve steps, and
then suddenly squirmed out of their grip to make a bolt for freedom,
his legs would have let him down in a chase, and he would have given
his captors a grand excuse to pummel him to a pulp; had they got him
to the station, it would have meant manhandling with fist, foot, and
baton, and darkness. He had thought of praying, but his case was too
desperate for that; so he clenched his teeth, and was silent while they
dragged him along the road from Tom Clarke's shop to Nelson's
Pillar, with people stopping on the paths to watch. Then a helmeted
inspector had stepped out from a group standing at the Pillar, and had
said sharply to the drunken ruffians, Let him go, let him go; and Sean
had recognised the voice of Inspector Willoughby who long ago had
headed a summons against him for allowing the Pipers' Band to play
past a protestant church while service was going on — the very
church where his father and mother had married, and all of them had
been baptized. This was the Inspector's return to Sean for the courteous way he had been received at Sean's home when he came to see
him about the summons. The Inspector had saved his life, for Sean
had been in no state then to compromise with a beating. When he was
released, he had stood staring at the bit of face showing from beneath
the peak of the helmet, while the constables stood, grumbling, near.
He recovered his surprise, said thank-you to the lips smiling under the
helmet, bowed, he thought, with grace, and walked slowly away till he
got into a side turning; then he had gone hell for leather far to a quiet
spot to think it all out.

Still shaken, he stood in O'Connell Street among the crowd watching the funeral of the battered man go past; well hid in the crowd, lest
some hearty comrade should pull him, passing, into the procession,
for he determined to take no more risks. Here it came, the *Dead March
in Saul*, flooding the street, and flowing into the windows of the
street's rich buildings, followed by the bannered Labour Unions, the
colours sobered by cordons of crêpe, a host of hodden grey following
a murdered comrade.

Ay, you, he thought, dotting the upper rich-curtained windows
with firmly brushed heads, who have lived far from the life lived by the
dead man, or from his own life too. Light-years away from both. Eh,
you, up there, lean out a little more, and look a little closer. He can't
hurt you now, and his body is quite clean. He has been prepared to
meet his God with soap and hot water, for, as you know, cleanliness
is next to godliness. He is clad now in clean white linen for the first

time in his life; and his battered head lies for the first time on a snowy pillow. Look over, look closer, ladies and gentlemen — there he goes, feet first, stretched out to his fullest; and if the lid was only up, you'd see his face: a big and purple, dead and dreadful blossom, safe now, snug in a calix of lily-white linen.

Twist the cap of the kaleidoscope, and see what it's like: a thick, black sky full of the pale dead faces of workers, life but faintly sketched in each of them, like white, wan moons looking down on a broken purple star falling phut-long out of their own presunctified horrorizon.

UNDER THE PLOUGH AND THE STARS

HARDLY had he finished with the committee to aid the women and children of the workers than, tired and weary, he was called upon to take the Irish Citizen Army in hand, now moving vaguely from this place to that, and to put an orderly and adaptable shape on it — a thing he couldn't do to himself; for he was still wondering how long more he'd be able to stir, and in idle moments Despair came to sup with him.

—What's wrong with the Army? he had asked, when called upon to help.

—Oh, man alive, said the conductor, what's right with it would be an easier question to answer — nothing.

—But they looked fine a few weeks ago, said Sean, when I saw them marching in Croydon Park, Connolly leading, and the police trying to look unconcerned.

—That's it — they look fine for an hour; but if they go on in this undisciplined way, the police'll lose that look and we'll be batoned again!

—But what's Connolly, Captain White, the secretary, and the committee doing? How can I butt in on their authority?

—There's no secretary, committee, rules, or regulations; Connolly can't give much time to it, so soon there'll be no men.

He got a room, drafted a few sentences, and made out a few rules, short, simple, direct, and wise; sentences that would easily fit into the simplest mind as no sentences in a catechism could; sentences that would sing the workers' song for a fuller life in a few words: *The Land and Air and Sea of Ireland for the People of Ireland — that is the gospel the heavens and earth are proclaiming; and that is the gospel every Irish heart is secretly burning to embrace.* Well, that was John Mitchel praying, and here was O'Casside to say amen. *The first and last principle of the Irish Citizen Army is the avowal that the ownership of Ireland, moral and material, is vested of right in the People of Ireland.* Well, that was Fintan Lalor praying, and here was O'Casside to say amen. The Army stood for the absolute unity of nationhood, and the rights and liberties of the world's democracies. No scab or blackleg could be one of them, and every member, whenever possible, had to be a member of a trade union, recognised by the Trades Union Congress.

These things were heartily agreed to at a general meeting in Liberty Hall, packed with eager men, and the committee was elected from those present. Strange that out of twenty officials chosen, four were, or had been, of the protestant way of thinking about Heaven — everybody talkin' 'bout heab'n, an' goin' where? One of those elected, veiled under the name of Richard Brannigan, had been a knight of the Grand Black Chapter of the Orange Order; had served time in a Northern jail for inciting to a breach of the peace in the matter of a Catholic procession; had been presented with a purse packed with sovereigns by the Orange Brethren when he came out; had joined the Gaelic League, as the Roaring O'Kane had done before him; and had now stalked defiantly, in his Belfast way, on to the Citizen Army Committee. A right, good, sensible, energetic man he was, big and burly, with a typical heavy-jowled Belfast face, dour-looking, yet with an exquisitely dry, sly, and spry sense of humour that often sent a twinkle into his serious, questioning grey eyes. Sean often laughed at the dour look of offended agony that swelled his big face when some Army man was blathering without any idea of what he was saying, or when he would stop.

Catching light from the flame of the Irish Citizen Army, the much more respectable sons of Cathleen ni Houlihan, headed by Eoin Mac Neill, at a packed meeting in the Rotunda, founded the Irish Volunteers, into which poured many who had fought Larkin and Connolly, so that it was streaked with employers who had openly tried to starve the women and children of the workers, followed meekly by scabs and blacklegs from the lower elements among the workers themselves, and many of them saw in this agitation a plumrose path to good jobs, now held in Ireland by the younger sons of the English well-to-do. Now there were two Cathleen ni Houlihans running round Dublin: one, like the traditional, in green dress, shamrocks in her hair, a little brian-boru harp under her oxster, chanting her share of song, For the rights and liberties common to all Irishmen; they who fight for me shall be rulers in the land; they shall be settled for ever, in good jobs shall they be, for ever, for ever; the other Cathleen coarsely dressed, hair a little tousled, caught roughly together by a pin, barefooted, sometimes with a whiff of whiskey off her breath; brave and brawny; at ease in the smell of sweat and the sound of bad language, vital, and asurge with immortality. Those who had any tinge of gentility in them left the Citizen Army for the refeenianed Volunteers.

And now began an intensive campaign by both sides for the in-gathering of arms. The Ulster Volunteers had landed guns in the North, one day when England's eyes went suddenly blind, and rich men covered the cost grandly. Mac Neill's army was much poorer, and the Citizen Army much poorer still. But already they had got stocks of belts, haversacks, French and Italian bayonets, long, lithe, dangerous-looking weapons, a number of revolvers, and about a dozen rifles. Even these had had an effect, for the grace of civility and bubbling good-humour had flooded the hearts and minds of the police at all meetings. The Citizen Army began to sing on the march, and Sean began to lose the fear of a broken head, though he kept wary.

Neither the Army nor the Volunteers was satisfied with arming: they wanted uniforms. In the weekly paper of the Volunteers, article after article appeared about the uniform worn by the Volunteers of 1782; and many wanted to be seen going about the narrow streets of their own homeland, clad in green trousers, yellow coat, red busby with a blue plume; or black cutaway coat faced with purple, white pantaloons, top-boots, and brass helmet with a crimson hackle curv-ing over all. Bravery was to be twin brother to bravura. The Citizen Army, more wisely, wanted to be so that they could be a movement, they said, within the meaning of International Law. In the meantime, till money was flusher, citizen soldiers were to wear an armlet that was termed a brassard, of St. Patrick's blue, the old Irish colour, according to Madame Markievicz, and each officer was to wear a red one. These, it was said, would safely classify them as belligerents, and so entitle them to the privileges of International Law when in battle, or as prisoners of war. So argued the chiefs and lawyers of the Volun-teers. The words brassard, the Hague, belligerent, took wings, flew about everywhere, settling on everyone's shoulder, cooing a soft sense of security into every mind except Sean's. He argued incessantly and insistently that neither uniforms nor brassards would be of use to them in securing treatment of belligerents when waging war against the

British. You will simply be, he said, no more to them than decorated rebels. On the contrary, they will be a greater danger in so far as they would unmistakably reveal the presence of a foe. They would be far safer in their ordinary clothes, for, if caught, they could pretend they were there by accident; whereas the uniform or gaudy brassard would show they were there by intention. He put Shaw's comparison before them of Ireland's fight with England as a perambulator up against a Pickford van; and tried to point out that their military art must be that of strike and dodge; dodge and strike.

—Shaw's no authority on military affairs, the voice of Captain White interjected. We can't shape our course from what that man says; and a loud chorus of hear-hears came from a crowd the most of whom had heard the name for the first time.

—I say, went on Sean, that the question of belligerency doesn't exist for us. We will be rebels; worse — we will be traitors, even terrorists to England, and she will strike without stop or mercy. It is for us, as far as we can, to force her by dodgery to strike oftenest at the air. If we flaunt signs about of what we are, and what we do, we'll get it on the head and round the neck. As for a uniform — that would be worst of all. We couldn't hope to hide ourselves anywhere clad in green and gold, or even green without the gold. Caught in a dangerous corner, there would be a chance in your workaday clothes. You could slip among the throng, carelessly, with few the wiser. In uniform, the crowd would shrink aside to show you, and the enemy will pounce. In your everyday rags you could, if the worst came, hang your rifle on a lamp-post and go your way. But you couldn't take your uniform off, for, even if you did, a man walking about in his shirt would look as suspicious as one going about in a uniform — that is, if any of you has a shirt.

—We've all got one, said a voice reproachfully; we're decent men.

—It's not a matter of decency, retorted Sean, but of money — I haven't one.

—This is wasting time! said Captain White testily. Without some kind of uniform, the men will look slovenly, and feel it. They'll have no respect for the ideals of the army, and won't have an incentive to keep together.

Just before this, Jim Larkin had come in, and had listened to what had been said. Now he stood up, and the husky voice agreed with Captain White. Uniforms will give the men a sound sense of *esprit de corps*, and one of homogeneous unity, encourage the practice of discipline, and instil a pride into the men they couldn't possibly feel in their everyday clothing; and a wild chorus of hear-hears from the men showed they agreed with Jim too.

—This discussion, anyhow, is too late, said the Captain, suddenly rising to his feet, a happy smile on his face, for I've already gone guarantor for fifty pounds, the price of fifty uniforms, and Arnott's have already measured the picked men who have been chosen as the first to wear them.

Captain White had fine qualities, and a good many lovable ones, but he had a bad habit of impulsive action without consulting the committee. This matter of the uniforms had been settled in his own way, after having had a talk about it with Countess Markievicz and Connolly. Here was a commitment of fifty pounds for clothes, and it was left to three or four to get the money somewhere. Three of the committee, Sean Shelly, an amiable, self-educated fellow, an Aran Islander, Michael Mullen, a prodigious worker, and Sean himself, spent night after night sticking up bills in suitable places announcing an event in Croydon Park, organised to get the money guaranteed by Captain White, dabbing the few clothes they had with paste, and often staggering home at three or four in the morning.

While this work was a-swing, the men met to arrange for the yearly demonstration to Bodenstown in honour of Wolfe Tone. It was odd to Sean that Tone was thought of merely as a Nationalist, out for the rights of Ireland only. All seemed to be unaware that he was also out for the rights of man; that, had he won, Ireland would have stood against control by monarch and prelate; that Paine's *Rights of Man* was more to him than papal bull, encyclical, or decree; that hardships on the clergy wouldn't have made him turn a hair: a democrat away in advance of his time, and well ahead still of the right, left, and step together sons of St. Patrick.

But here the Army men were, burnishing button and buckle, and patting out the uniforms into a proper shape to honour the memory of an Internationalist and agnostic, while at a table sat Sean and the ex-knight of the Black Chapter recording the names of those taking tickets, and entering down the money they gave in exchange; when, lo and behold, into the hall came Captain White, quickly, his face flushed and angry, followed by the Countess more slowly, who was followed by Connolly more slowly still. The Captain, standing in front of the table, launched into a violent attack on Sean for not having the money by this time to pay Arnott's, who, he said, were pressing for payment; and but for this slovenly secretary the Army had, he wouldn't be in the fix of having to pay for the uniforms; all the while, the Countess standing behind him, grinning, Connolly behind her, the old stolid look on his curiously ball-like face. When the Captain's blaze of anger had exhausted itself, Sean stood up to remind everyone that the uniforms had been ordered without the knowledge of the committee, that he had opposed the getting of them from the very first, as they all knew; but the Captain turned away contemptuously and swept from the room, the Countess trotting after him, while Connolly, more dignified, waddled his slow way out after. Just as the Captain gained the door, the Belfast treasurer roared after him, in his finest northern brogue, Dinna wurry — ye'll get your money bawk! Sean guessed that the Captain had been egged on to this attack by the Countess; for the Captain, unfortunately for himself, didn't think enough about the giving of gifts, and gave to many who deserved kicking instead of ha'pence, even roughly rejecting Sean's advice when he ventured to give it him. But the Festival brought in much more than the cost of the uniforms; and the slovenly secretary had the joy of seeing the treasurer write out a cheque for what was due to Arnott's, realising that his hard work made payment possible, though he felt bitter over it all, intensified when he remembered that the Countess and Captain never raised a finger to help them. Give orders, give orders, and let others carry them out.

Then the flag came — the Plough and the Stars. A blanket was spread over a wall, and the flag spread over the blanket so that it couldn't be defiled by the grimy evil of the wall. All pressed back to have a good look at it, and a murmur of reverent approval gave the flag a grave salute — all except the Countess, who returned to the oiling of her automatic with the remark that the flag bears no republican message to anyone. There it was — the most beautiful flag among the flags of the world's nations: a rich, deep poplin field of blue; across its whole length and breadth stretched the formalised shape of a plough, a golden-brown colour, seamed with a rusty red, while through all glittered the gorgeous group of stars enriching and ennobling the northern skies.

Jim Larkin it was who first said that the Citizen Army should have a banner all on its own, its pattern and sign away from the painted commonplace ones of other national and labour bodies, its symbols showing labour's near and higher ideals. The one who actually designed it is disputed; some saying A. E., but Sean, later on, asked him, and he denied the honour. A Galway Art teacher sketched a realistic pattern, and from this Dun Emer Guild wove the lovely thing now hanging on the soiled wall. It was queer that such a lovely thing should spread itself so proudly in such a lowly place, before a crowd of hardy, rough-handed, dusty-skinned, ignorant men, tempting them to look at it, and seeming to say, Be worthy, men, of following such a banner, for this is your flag of the future. Whatever may happen to me; though I should mingle with the dust, or fall to ashes in a flame, the plough will always remain to furrow the earth, the stars will always be there to unveil the beauty of the night, and a newer people, living a newer life, will sing like the sons of the morning.

But it was hard going. Every possible obstacle was thrust into the way of the Citizen Army. The officers of the Volunteers did all they could to check its growth. They would lend them no hall in which to drill; and no place for an inside meeting could be got from one end of the land to the other. Once they managed by a ruse to get the Town Hall, Kingstown; but this was discovered, and the hall taken away from them, so that the great meeting had to be held outside of it. The Volunteers would give them no help to gather weapons, would give no support to anything the Army did to collect money to pay for what they got. Returning good for evil, the Union and the Army did all they could to help any Irish-Ireland activity; but great bitterness tinged the distant relations between the two of them. The Wolfe Tone Committee were hesitant about letting the Army travel down to Bodenstown, and when Sean went to their meeting to get the tickets, there was a discussion as to whether it would be wise to give them.

—They don't like us Volunteers, said Con Colbert, and they're a tough lot, aren't they?

—I'm afraid they are, said Bulmer Hobson.

—They are a tough lot, said Sean, and that is part of their glory, for in that they resemble the Boys of Ormond Market whom Wolfe Tone sighed to have beside him when he went into battle for Ireland. But, on a vote, only one hand was raised to invite them to come.

Then Tom Clarke came in, and took the chair. His bright eyes gleamed when he was told all that had happened. Of course they'll come, he said, and welcome. They are Irishmen, and damned good ones too. Special carriages would be there for them, and he and O'Casside would make them as comfortable as possible. And he proposed that as the Irish Citizen Army were the first body in Nationalist Ireland to become armed, they should receive the honour of marching at the head of the procession. But Clarke's intervention didn't hide from Sean that the workers wouldn't get much from this crowd if ever they came into power. These aren't internationalists; they aren't even republicans. They aren't able to see over the head of

England out to the world beyond. They would be lost among Des-
moulins, Danton, Couthon, St. Just, and Robespierre, and Marat
would frighten the life out of them. Their eyes can see no further soil
than their feet can cover. A frail few would stand at ease under the
workers' banner. They would be the heralds of the new power, having
time but to sound the reveille, and then sink suddenly down into sleep
themselves.

Never mind: to plough is to pray, to plant is to prophesy. Again, as
in an age gone by, the plough will with a wreath be crowned, and wise
men will twine the garland; and the stars will last, and those who have
loved them fondly will never be fearful of the night.

IN THIS TENT, THE REBUBBLICANS

SEAN CASSIDE had left the I.R.B. long ago, though he still swung
forward to help them in anything that came his way. His criticisms
had given offence, and he had been summoned to visit one of the
Supreme Council to be warned; summoned to meet the man who had
been so kind to him in his illness, and who now told him that he had
been selected to tell Sean in all friendliness that they were very dis-
pleased with him; that his criticisms did no good to the movement;
and that they must cease: and Sean knew now that he would have to
cease troubling Deakin for a renewal of his prescription.

—Who has done more for the I.R.B. in relation to his condition and
chances than I? he asked. Isn't it because the criticisms are justified
that they want them stopped? he asked again. Quite a few have got
jobs through its influence: have I? Bar ill-health, pain, and poverty, I
have got nothing. Nor do I want anything; but I am determined to
hold on to what is mine own; my way of thinking, and freedom to give
it utterance. Otherwise the little life I have would cease to be life at all.
Here's a question: do you, or do you not, think Bulmer Hobson the
best editor we can get for *Irish Freedom*? But Deakin mumbled that he
hadn't been empowered to argue about the literary gifts of Bulmer
Hobson.

—We can't argue on what doesn't exist, said Sean. What I want to
know is if you think his editorials inspire our members?

—That isn't the point, said Deakin. What I want to know is if you
are prepared to obey us, and stop your criticism?

—No, I'm not, said Sean. I've criticised their inner policy only in the Circles; their public policy and tactics set out in the Press, I'll criticise whenever I think they need it.

—Is that your final answer? he asked sharply. Am I to say you refuse to obey orders?

—You can put it that way if you like; and as far as ceasing to say what I think is concerned, you can tell them all to go to hell for me!

—There's no more to be said, said Deakin; good-night; and he turned to propounding a prescription. Sean took the hint, rose up, left the shop, and neither saw nor heard of Deakin for years. He knew, of course, if he asked, or even if he left the bottle, he'd get his prescription renewed readily; but he knew he would never neither ask nor go. Anyway, he thought to soothe himself, the feast of porridge was long ago over, and what good would the potion be without the porridge?

They were a queer lot, as queer as himself, and Sean was sorry to leave them; but the one precious thing he had, he'd hold. It seemed to him though, that, for democrats, they were damned intolerant. Yet most of them were, if not actual, at least potential agnostics, and all of them anti-clericals. He knew few of them who could be called practising catholics, though he had had one experience how the Faith lay crystallised in the inner corner of their minds. He got the monthly *Irish Protestant* from a friend, and in one issue was astounded to see the leading article praised the Men of '98, and with the article went the verses telling of *The Wake of William Orr*, one of the leaders executed as a rebel. The article had been written by Lindsay Crawford, who, in some way or another, had been attracted by the new Irish movement. Sean hurried down to Tom Clarke's shop with the journal.

—Look, he said, shaking Tom out of a doze which he was enjoying in a corner behind the counter, look and read — you'll find something to stir you there!

As soon as Clarke's brilliant eyes saw the title of the paper, he flung it back at Sean, saying excitedly, and with no little venom, Take it away — I don't read such slanderous rubbish! Take away that anti-catholic rag!

—I don't want to make a protestant of you, man! Sean said, savagely, surprised to see that the fear of a bigot lingered even in the bold heart of Tom Clarke. Here was a most intelligent man, ready to face a firing squad, afraid to face a protestant paper, and a rather stupid one at that. If anything, I'd but try to make an atheist of a catholic, said Sean, and then only in an argument of the catholic's own making, prepared, as a man, to give an answer for the hopelessness that is in me. This issue of the paper praises the Irish who died for

Ireland, and says that the protestants should be the vanguard in Ireland's fight for freedom.

Tom Clarke seized the paper, skimmed it with his gleaming eyes, turned, and said with rapture, Here, Sean, quick, get three dozen of them; go where you think they are, and get them — this is the best I've read for years!

Every aspect of this man showed weariness and age. His fifteen years of distorted life in jail, added to fifteen years of silent defensive fighting for mind and body, had fretted away the outward semblance of strength and virility. The full and happier growth of his life had been sucked away into uselessness and pain. Almost all his loyalties to the colours and enjoyments of life had been burned away, leaving but a slender, intense flame of hatred to what he knew to be England. Free himself, now, he plucked impatiently at those who wanted to let bad enough alone. Watch him locking up his tiny shop, slipping the key in his pocket, then giving a swift turn to where a Committee waited for him; a warm, rough, tweed overcoat belted firmly at his slender waist, a broad-brimmed hat set firm on his greying head, the frail figure went straight on, taking short, rapid steps with a tiny spice of jauntiness in them; straight on, looking neither right nor left, to where a drooping Committee sprang to interested alertness when he came among them, and bent low over the task of moulding the bullets that would tear rough and roguish gaps open in some of their own breasts.

The prominent ones of Dublin never, on the whole, tuned themselves in to the hum of a prayer-book. The rifle brown and sabre bright were what they stretched romantic hands to, rather than to the more romantic cross; the shout of a battle rather than to the chanting of a hymn. The cowl, the Roman collar, the swing-high-swing-low of the church bells and bulls didn't bother them much; and the *pro bonem* clericallous but brought to their minds the purrannual squeal of the bishops in their Easter posturels against whoring, gambling, stock-raising without a marriage licence, and the threat of a hot welcome to hell for anyone who became a fenian.

Pity, though, few of them cared a thraneen about art, literature, or science. In this respect, even, they weren't international. A few of them, one of the Plunkets, MacDonagh, and McEntee, paddled in the summertime in the dull waters of poor verse; but gave hardly any sign that they had ever plunged into the waters that keep the world green. No mention of art, science, or music appeared in *Sinn Fein* or *Irish Freedom*. To them, no book existed save ones like *The Resurrection of Hungary* or the *Sinn Fein Year Book*. None of them ever seemed to go to a play, bar one that made them crow in pain and anger. A great many of them were ignorant of the finer things of the mind, as the onslaught on Synge showed. Even Mangan was beyond them. All of them knew his Dark Rosaleen by heart; sang it so often that one got tired of her sighing and weeping, longing to hear her roar out vulgar words with the vigour of a Pegeen Mike. But Mangan's splendid Ode to The Maguire was known to hardly any of them, or, if known, never mentioned. In all the years of his sojourn in Irish Ireland, he never once heard it mentioned. Thomas Davis was their pattern and their pride. He sang for them every hour of the day, and, if he happened to tire, his poor imitator, William Rooney, Griffith's great butty, sang instead. In a literary sense, they could have chosen a king in Mitchel; instead they put a heavy gilded crown on the pauper Davis. Almost all of them feared the singing of Yeats, and many were openly hostile to him; though few of them could quote a line from a poem of his. All they treasured of him was the dream which fashioned the little play about Cathleen ni Houlihan, a tiny bubble, iridescent with a green tinge. Their plays in Irish and English were frightening. Sean saw a play called *Seabhac na Ceithre Caoile — the Hawk of the Slender Quarters* — produced in the Rotunda as a prime piece of imagination; and he sorrowed for a month afterwards for the hard-earned shilling he had given to see it. Apart from Pearse, Seumas Deakin, and Tom Clarke, few of the others showed any liking for book, play, poem, or picture.

Patrick Pearse, while filled with the vision of a romantic Ireland, was also fairly full of an Ireland sensitive, knowledgeable, and graceful; a doer of things noble, and a lover of things beautiful; and through his remarkable school of St. Enda, showed he was eager to coax others to come out of the dim thicket of convention into a clearer light, and the finer conception beginning to creep into the more modern Irish thought. The word, said he, for education in Irish is the same as that for fosterage; the teacher was a fosterer, the pupil a foster-child. To foster was not, primarily, to lead up, to conduct through a course of studies, and still less to indoctrinate, to inform, to prepare for exams; but primarily to foster the elements of character already there. Pearse told of a famous Irish king (so we see Irish kings thought of things besides war) who gathered about him numbers of boys, children of friends and kinsmen, giving them a constitution, and allowing them to make their own laws and elect their own leaders. The king provided the most skilled to teach them art, the bravest to teach them chivalry, and the wisest to teach them philosophy. He devoted one-third of the time he saved from state affairs to teaching them, or watching them at play. And if any stranger came to the Dun at that time, even though he were a king's envoy, demanding audience, there was but one answer for him: the king is with his foster-children.

We should rise up against the system, went on Pearse, that tolerates as teachers the rejected of all other professions, rather than demanding for so priestlike an office the highest souls and the highest intellects of the race. I think the little child-republics I have described, with their own laws, and their own leaders, their life face to face with nature, their care for the body as well as the mind, their fostering of individualities, yet never at the expense of the commonwealth, ought to be taken as models for our own modern schools.

This was the man whom Sean selected as the head and front of them all, and, in his limited circumstances, he did all he could to help him. When Pearse organised a pageant round the story of *The Cattle Raid of Cooley*, to raise money for his school, the funds allowed but a hundred handbills to be printed to tell the world of the venture. Sean ran to Jim Larkin, who got his own printer, West of Stafford Street, to do five thousand more, and these Sean handed out, day after day, in the busiest streets, ignoring his hunger, his aches, his grey-minded anxiety about his legs; in heavy rain he stood, without an overcoat, and with his boots starred with holes. This wasn't due to deliberate bravery, but to a dreamy and unrealistic ignorance of what would happen when he could walk no more. He was too much afraid to think about it long. Jim Larkin supplied the turf, and the paraffin in which to soak it, to make the camp-fires round which the Men of Eireann sat on their way up to attack the north.

The pageant was held in Jones's Road Park, and the opening night was one of torrential rain, so that all who came crowded into the large hall of the grand-stand, to crouch there, saturated, gloomy, and low in heart as man could be. Pearse sat, the nadir of dejection, his grieving figure telling us that once more the damned weather had betrayed the Gael; while Douglas Hyde, who came to open it, roared out eulogy and boomed out windy joy, all the time the wind shook the sodden wooden walls, and the rain slashed down on the roof above them.

Wind and water, thought Sean; we want only the fire now.

That came on the last day of the great event. The Boy Scouts had been careless with the oil, and had let a lot of it swim about the floor; then some hasty hand had flung a glow-match into a pool of oil, and in a moment the grand-stand and the dressing-rooms were crackling.

Such a scene! All the performers dressed for the pageant thought of their everyday clothes, and the money and watches hidden in the pockets, and ran from their places to save their goods. Pearse, still brooding on Cuchullain, was knocked over, and a great cry went up from the crowd to put the fire out, someone! From the balcony above the Boy Scouts flung down the clothes in heaps, and there was a terrible din of sorting, while red-shirted, brass-helmeted firemen shoved them aside and sent jets of water on to the flames. After a while, poor Pearse, with a few gaily-clad performers, wandered over to a smoke-stained, sweating fireman standing half-way up the blazing stairs, plying water on the flames, his hardy, sooty hands shaking with the quivering of the jerking hose.

— Do you think, Mr. Fireman, murmured Pearse, mounting a few of the steps, carefully to one side, to prevent his polished boots from being stained by a stream of blackened water flowing down the other one, Do you think you'll quench the fire soon enough to let us go on with the pageant?

—I'm not thinkin' whether we will or no, said the fireman gruffly; that's your pigeon.

—Quite, said Pearse; but you should know, and we'd be grateful for a guess.

—The pageant's all about the great Cuchullain, you know, said a Gael from a bottom step up to the fireman.

—That so? he asked sarcastically. Begod, we must do our best for that fella! Aw, get outa me way! he said suddenly, thrusting Pearse aside, an' give a man room to spit!

—Poor Ireland! murmured the Gael on the bottom step; the rough language of him; poor old Ireland!

But the fire was quelled, the firemen went away, the pageant went on, and Sean saw again the Boy Corps of Emain Macha playing hurley, to be stopped by a messenger telling them that Connacht was marching on Ulster, and that Ulster's chumpians were in the punishment of a trance-stupor for great unkindness to a pregnant woman, that Cuchullain, having fought Maeve's army for many days, was now in a deep sleep, and that they would have to take his place, which they did, all dying in defence of the black north. And in the whirl Sean thought he saw the Men of Eircann, clad in all the colours of the rainbow, marching, their chiefs dashing about in chariots of brass, bronze, and buckskin, shaking spears that entangled the clouds, and waving swords long as a summer's day, silver-handled, with knobs on; Sean saw the fight on the ford, all fair and even between Cuchullain and Ferdiah who wore the same old-school tie, and were sworn friends, so that Cuchullain didn't like to polish his friend off, but had to, though he knew poor Ferdiah was sure he'd kill him, and lie on top of the beautiful daughter of Queen Maeve for half a naked night as a gift of honour to him for killing a comrade; and hard it might have gone with Cuchullain but for the staggering pain his wounds gave him, and for the mocking of his charioteer standing by who told him he was getting soft; so Cuchullain took his hero's hurroo-leap upwards, and, coming down, shot the gae bolg, or magic spear, right through Ferdiah's buddy, who fled into eternal darkness murmuring

> Oh! the bitterness of leaving all that richly went before;
> Finding in the older darkness nothing new, and nothing more.

And deep Sean sighed with him at the loss of a night's unrest with the fair Findobhair, for Sean had felt that way several times here. In a corner of the grounds a Fancy Fair had set itself down, the rent it paid covering some of the pageant's cost, and while the Gaels strutted where Ferdiah and Cuchullain were fated to fight it out, the gulls flocked to where gay red, green, yellow, blue, and black pennons showed the way to the roundabout, the wheel of fortune, the aunt sallies, the crown, anchor, and club conveyance promising a three-to-one reward, but rarely giving it, and to the other jollities, regardless of the fact that their country's harp slumbered, and lay in oblivion near Tara's old hall, with ne'er a kind hand to enliven its numbers, and strike a rude dirge to the sons of Fingal. Divil a much better he was himself, for when he could snatch a few minutes of idle time before the performance, he'd hurry to the roundabout to watch the girls swinging round on the horses; for often, when in full career, the swift breeze would get entangled in their skirts, twirling them away from where they ought to be, giving his excited eyes a flash of a coloured garter embracing a rounded leg. Once he saw a fair one's dress roughly caressed by the wind; her skirt went wide, showing a trim leg with a taste of white thigh over the rim of her stocking; and as she whirled round, he saw that she saw what the wind showed him, and she smiled, lifting one leg over the other so that the skirt hid less, and she became fairer than the evening air clad in the beauty of a thousand stars; but the grey, cloudy curtain of his wretched condition came slowly down between, and shut her out of his sight.

It was funny to see the agony on the faces of the Gaels when the roundabout organ blared out loud, grinding out Tara-ra-boom-de-ay with brazen impudence, aided by the mechanical roll from a grim drum, forcing those in the pageant to raise their voices, and those of the audience, nearer the Fair, to cup their hands to their ears to catch the sound of what was said. Pearse, dreamy and colourful in his pageant raiment, with a comrade Gael strode to the booth where the proprietor of the Fair sat, watching wares and workers; and the Gael requested, rather pompously, that the steam-organ should be silenced while the pageant ran its course.

—'Deed an' I won't, she said indignantly, and it's cool customers yez are t'ask it! Th' music gives a thrill to th' gallop of th' horses, an' it's part o' what th' people pay for. I paid a good rent to get in here, an' it'll take more encouragement than I'm gettin' to see me safe outa th' hasty bargain. Stop your own show, an' let th' poor people, lettin' on they like it, come here to join in a heartier amusement. Yez can go back, gentlemen, for me organ's not goin' to be lullabyed be any other opposite money-makin' manœuvre.

—Listen, my good woman, said the Gael persuasively, we request its silence only while the pageant is in progress. You know the pageant deals with the life and deeds of the great Cuchullain during the Tawn Bo Cooley; the deeds of him who was the comeliest among the men of Eireann. Surely you'll do that much for Ireland's greatest hero who had the ninety-and-nine gifts, who was famous for the lightness of his lep, the weight of his wisdom, the melody of his voice, and the fine form of his face? You'll surely silence the organ to let us do honour and show due reverence to this great man, Cuchullain?

—He musta been th' divil an' all from what yez say; but I've never seen or heard tell of him in any circus or show I met, an' I'm gettin' on for sixty years now. Where'd he live? Was he one o' th' boys who stood be th' great O'Connell for Emancipation?

—Oh, no, no, ma'am! said the Gael testily, glancing with pity at Pearse, who stood with head bent, listening; Cuchullain had nothing whatever to do with O'Connell. Cuchullain lived his short and glorious life thousands of years ago — long before St. Patrick thought of coming near us.

—Oh! That musta been in old God's time, mister. Anyway, here's a lady doesn't want to be versed in the doin's of them who haunted Ireland before th' time o' blessed St. Patrick, an' I'd advise yez to think similar. What Cookullin was or wasn't doesn't throuble me. An', anyway, even if I hadda heard of him, no Cockullin 'ud make me give over doin' what was me due to do; so like good an' decent men, Coocoolin yourselves outa th' way, an' leave a body in peace to knock out a livin'!

—Poor old Ireland! said the Gael, shaking his head sadly as he and Pearse returned to do the best they could through the boisterous blare of the steam-organ.

And there it was on the green sward before him — *The Cattle Raid of Cooley*, with its mimic figures, coloured gaily in the floodlight, growing mighty through the mind's misty thought of what happened far away and long ago. The Boy Corps of Armagh playing hurley, veiled in blues, greens, reds, browns, and purple; the stopping of the game by the Messenger, Pearse himself, to tell them that Cuchullain, weary with the battles of many days, was asleep, and the Boy Corps would have to defend Ulster from the Men of Eireann till Cuchullain could stand to fight again, for the rest of the Ulster champions were in a trance-stupor as a punishment for great unkindness shown to a pregnant woman. And the boys stood and fought Maeve's great army till they died, but held on till Cuchullain grew strong again to fill the gap. And here were the Men of Eireann in battle array, all because of a quarrel between Oillol of Cruachan and Queen Maeve, his wife, over which of them possessed the greatest wealth in raiment, jewel, and cattle on the hills; measuring and valuing all they had, but finding that each was equal to the other, day by day, for in that day, nor bishop nor archbishop nor cardinal was there to have more than either. But Maeve knew that the White Bull of Cruachan would lick anything among her own kine, so she gathered her powers together to seize the Brown Bull of Cooley, reported on all sides, and vouched for by Roddy the Drover to be the *capax imperii* among jovine bulls, so that she'd be one up on poor old Oilleeololo. And here was the bould Cuchullain challenging Maeve to send her champions out, with a Come on the whole of you, one by one, to meet your doom, and when I'm done with you, a lot of you'll be like little green leaves in a bible; and won't your Maeve be glad when she's at home with her feet on the fender, while the old kitchen kettle keeps singing a song, and Oillol, if he can get away, to smoke another pipeful in the shade of the old apple-tree.

The last came Ferdiah to fight with the hero, and Cuchullain's heart near failed him, for Ferdiah wore the same old school gorget that he wore himself; but there was no way out, so they fought by day, and rested by night for a lunar month, till Cuchullain, full of wounds and mad with anger, could stick it no longer and killed Ferdiah without any hindrance; then came the caoining skirl of the pipes, and the sad rolling of the drum, mingling with the hues of red, brown, green, and purple kilts and shawls, ending a scene of a song that in colour, form, dignity of movement, and vigour of speech made the loveliest thing that had ever patterned the green sward of the playing-field of Jones's Road, or any other field the world over; fairer than anything the bowler-hatted Gael could think of now, much more do.

A pity death pulled Pearse away from his school, for he was a pioneer in what has now become the common sense of education. He hated the system that kept colour and life far from the child, content to stuff a delicate mind with a mass of fact and information. Ay, indeed, said Pearse, I knew one boy who passed through several schools a dunce and a laughing-stock. The National Board and Intermediate Board of Education damned him as a fool before men and angels. Yet it was discovered that he had a wondrous sympathy for nature. He loved and understood the ways of plants, and he had a strange subtlety of observation — in short he was a boy who was likely to become an accomplished botanist. A father of another boy said to me: He's no good at books, no good at work; he's good for nothing but playing a tin whistle. What am I to do with him? And the distressed father was shocked by Pearse saying: Buy a tin whistle for him.

No timid cloak of a Papal Count hung from this man's shoulders; no Order of Knight Commendatore of St. Gregory or St. Silvester sparkled on his breast: the scarlet or white cloak of Cuchullain was good enough for him, and, in his soldier's cap, a jaunty sprig from the holy oak of Derry Columcille whispering in his ear the words of the saint himself: *If I die, it shall be from the excessive love I bear the Gael.* Not for Pearse the glory that was Greece nor the grandeur that was Rome; nor even the sacred grove, olive grove, or mountain of Judea: he fixed his thoughts on the vivid and pathetic greatness of Ardee, Emain Macha, Derry, Beann Edair, Tailltin, Cruachan, Tara, and Usneach, grander than Greece or Rome; and holier to him the lonely grave of Bodenstown, where Wolfe Tone's valour has changed to dust, than the place where St. Patrick is said to be pinned down to an everlasting slumber. Pearse was the one prominent Gael among the leaders of the militant movement who fought the battle of Ireland from the midst of the Faith, well in the stream, not of Gonzaga or De Sales or Loyola, but of Columcille, Aidan, Finbarr, Enda, Kevin, Columbanus, and Brigid. Such as he couldn't be near the swashbuckling canakin-clink catholicity of Chesterton, who put up a tavern sign on the gate of Heaven and made it into a Jolly Abode.

Ah! Patrick Pearse, you were a man, a poet, with a mind simple as a daisy, brilliant as a daffodil; and like these, you came before the swallow dared, and took the Irish minds of March with beauty. A catholic with whom the roughest unbeliever could be safely silent, not from shame, but out of respect for your gallant and urging soul; a catholic who almost made one see that Ireland's blue sky was Brigid's poplin shawl; that the moon and stars were under Mary's feet, the Virgin-born on her breast, stretching out little leal hands that were to guide to a Father's home the long-banished children of Eve. Beside Pearse, men might listen to the jangling bells, and think them musical; might watch men bend sleek, slick knees, and think they honoured humility; might see men fast, and still think it sensible; might drink insipid water, and taste the wine; for your austerity was ever bright, your snowy mantle of rigid conduct was ever girdled by a coloured scarf, and golden buttons closed it over you; nay, on the very head of grinning Death itself you stuck a smiling star.

Ah! Patrick Pearse, when over the hard, cold flags of a barrack square you took your last stroll and wandered to where the rifles pointed to your breast, you never even paused, for that was what you guessed you'd come to; you came close to them; the stupid bullets tore a way through your quiet breast, and your fall forward to death was but a bow to your enemies. Peace be with you, and with your comrades too.

All the colour and song of Pearse was shadowed by the level dullness of the Sinn Fein campaign, led by Marthur Gruffith, who was busy scraping all the leisure time he could from his pullitical work to damn poor Synge and slight Yeats, damning him for his good verses. Perhaps his nerves were aching after the hysterical tornado of activity to give birth to a *Daily Sinn Fein*, when the short neck of Gruffith stretched out as far as it could go, demanding help from every loyal Gael to bring forth this new thing that would establish unity in Ireland for ever; down the British Empire; and carry Ireland up to the top of delectable mountains. At last it was born with the loudest cry Ireland had heard so far, a sullen face on it, dull and futile, no more a living daily than an out-of-date Salvation-Army *War Cry*. It gasped out a kind of a curious life for a short while, then went to its bony, mean, and silent death, forming itself into a cold monument to Gruffith's consequential conceit at having been able to bring it out at all. During its spare days of wailing life, the paper gave one rowdy, gaudy, ranting gesture when some poor fool, uninformed and daring, came to some fancy-dress gathering wearing a long golden-haired wig, and dressed in a long white robe having a brilliant red heart in the centre of its breast, entering among the dancers with a boisterously-dressed girl hanging on each arm. Gruffith at once saw his chance of getting into touch with the people, not through his politics, but through his piety, so an article denouncing the foolishness as blasphemy and sacrilege splashed the paper from side to side; though some of his Sinn Fein friends, a few years before, had sent greeting to Viviani, who had told the world that that very evening he was going to put out the lights of Heaven; but, afterwards, found that he wasn't quite tall enough. The howls for the expulsion of the blasphemer from job, house, and home, helped by *Sinn Fein*, deafened Dublin, and soon the Confraternities added their hyena yelling, till the city was a howl from one end to the other, driving the thoughtless fool from his job, then his home, till finally, by night, a cargo-boat took him to where God wasn't so well known; but the griffithian St. George, though he slew his dragon, didn't get any farther with the people; and the valiant paper, after its great fight for the good character of God, soon took to its bed and died there, another instance of the high rate of infant immortality in Ireland. But like a Boy Scout, Griffith had done his good deed for the day, for God, and Cathleen Mavourneen.

Under the sulky green tent that Dublin called the sky, these odd figures moved about and about, the huge, sable, wide-winged Morrigu, Ireland's bottle-crow, watching from the tent-pole top. There goes Bulmer Hobson with a gigantic volume of Mazzini's sermons strapped between his shoulders like a nobsack; and Yeats, trying through a loose seam in the tent's roof to catch a glimpse of the round green eyes and the long wavering bodies of the dark leopards of the moon, as he murmured longingly, I will arise, and go to Inisfree; and George Russell rushing round, booming, *Come, acushla, with me to the mountains old, There the bright ones call us waving to and fro — Come, my children, with me to the ancient go.* There stood the full-bearded Plunket, in his Papal Count's cuniform, patting the head of a young man, De Valuera, who was putting a poser to the old gentleman about the equality of *abc* to *xyz*; and there by the door of the tent was Griffith neglecting his practice of a Hungarian funtasia on a fuddle to prevent Jim Connolly from attaching a red tassel to the flap of the tent. And there was the old lady in black, Gregory by name, planked up against Nelson's Pillar, watching, and deciding that no Rebubblican name was wordy to cut away any of de bark on her topper beech; though those of Pearse and Clarke would have done well enough. And there, in his go-cart, threading through one street into another, goes the toy catholic Viceroy, chanting the Irish ballad of *Is truagh gan mise i Sasana*; the go-cart having to stop here to let the Volunteers come down this street, having to stop there to let the Irish

Citizen Army go up that one; while from the window of a snug, Tim Healy, having a slow one, looks out on the world, to murmur as the Viceroy passes, *The time's not far distant when them that are up will be down, and them that are down will be up, and your grand Viceregal Lodge will be no more than an Uncle Tim's cabin.* There goes Padruig Pearse hurrying through the centre of the city, saying swift to any who tries to check his stride, *Stay me not: I have a rendezvous with Death*; and Erskine Childers following hot-foot after him, calling out to him to wait a minute, and he'd be there too; and after Childers, Mellows and Rory O'Connor, with a string of vague forms following behind, hurrying, hurrying to make the Isle a nation, free and grand; while the great crowd of the plain people jostled and pushed them, regardless of their dustiny; for, concerned with finer things, each of the plain people clutched a key-of-heaven prayerbook in one hand and a buff British ring-paper in the other — preservers of the Irish soul and body; and all the time, unknown to most, in the core of the tumult, the timber-merchant labourer, Mutt Talbot, iron hoops and steel chain tight round his body, boring into his belly and wearing a way into his spine, a gonner on God, at the crack of dawn, squirmed about atop the steps of the Pro-Cathedral, waiting for the door to open, creeping in towards the altar when it did, hiding and chiding himself in a cloud of *mea na meala culpas.* A hero of Irish holiness! Proved, too, by the fact that when, one day, Mutt Talbot suddenly fell dead, as soon as his clothes were removed it was found, rumour definitely stated, that the iron and steel round the poor body had blossomed into hardy laurel leaves and scented honeysuckle. Over all, atop of the tent-pole, the huge sable Morrigu clapped her wide wings in glee, croaking joyously, *Thou art not conquered yet, dear land; thou art not conquered yet*; and Sean sat on a pediment of a column keeping up the façade of the Post Office, reading, reading the new catechism of the *Communist Manifesto* with its great commandment of Workers of all lands, unite! And in all the shouting and the tumult and the misery around, he heard the roll of new drums, the blowing of new bugles, and the sound of millions of men marching.

ST. VINCENT PROVIDES A BED

ANOTHER irritating trouble began to further bruise Sean's confidence and hope: a tubercular swelling began to rise up on the right side of his neck. He had had them when he was young, and he remembered (he was always remembering these things, possibly because he had so few blessings to count. Count your blessings one by one — well, he wouldn't have to work overtime) hours of swirling pain from one of them, when his mother, acting on neighbourly advice, had painted it three times a day for weeks with iodine. He thought he had got rid of them for ever, and it was maddening to feel one of them thrusting itself out again. Jesu! what is the pleasure of life, asked an Elizabethan, but the good hours of an ague! Jim Larkin, noticing it one day, sent him up, with Councillor Partridge — one of Labour's finest souls — to the Charles Street Tubercular Clinic; and there he was rudely handled by a rough-shouting doctor, who apologised, after Partridge had whispered something in his ear. The doctor muttered that he was tired after a long day, and Sean, standing up to walk out, said he was tired too, and had more cause to feel uneasy. Partridge, amiable and holy, smoothed Sean's anger, and the doctor gave him the only aid he could — a note saying he had examined the patient, and hereby certified that he needed surgical attention.

Larkin said he must go to Vincent's where the Union had several beds; but Sean decided to try the protestant Adelaide first. So off he tramped, where the house-surgeon took the note, and listened patiently to Sean. Then he said, tersely, there was no bed, and there wouldn't be one for a year. Just as Sean was fixing on his hat to go, a senior surgeon, Dr. Thompson, came out and stopped a minute to listen, and looked at Sean's swelling. Some little time before, he had lost an only son in the war, and in a burst of pity said to his comrade doctor, Oh, make out a bed for him, and give the poor devil a chance! When he'd gone, the house-surgeon, indignant, turned to Sean, saying, He knows damn all about it! If I do as he says, I'll have to pitch some other poor devil out to let you in, and what good would that do? Why the hell didn't he go in and make a bed for you himself?

So, armed with a request from the Union, he became No. 23 in the St. Laurence O'Toole ward of St. Vincent's under a sister named Gonzaga, a delightful woman, most popular with the patients; never lax, always lenient; always cheerful, with a gay greeting for everyone. Afterwards, he discovered that some of the other nuns seemed to be jealous of her popularity. But now, he innocently passed in by the heavy, wide, double-folding door, glancing at the great bronze gong in the vestibule — looking like the languishing shield of Oscar, now dedicated to God — giving different numbers of strokes for the different sisters, with a long, solemn one for the Reverend Mother. He turned left down the long tiled corridor, with high french windows along its way, on one side, giving on to a lawn on which, in brief moments of leisure, sisters paraded determinedly up and down, decidedly reading some pious manual, so that not a moment should be allotted to the unthinking world. He passed by the gaudy image of St. Michael shoving a tough spear throughout the twisting body of a a spitting dragon; perhaps a white-coated surgeon flitted by, giving importance to a quick walk or a decorous trot, on his way to, or coming from, doing damage to some poor body. Silent nuns, on duty, soft-slippered, glided to and fro, went in, came out, eyes half closed, lips faintly forming the soft names of Jesus, Mary, and Joseph. Any words ventured there were modulated into the sad smile of silence, as if speech itself was bandaged; then up a few steps at the corridor's end, if he remembered right, to St. Laurence's ward, the saint himself, frocked, cowled, and tonsured, at the entrance, standing deep in stony meditation, as if he had vaulted into upper thoughts so as to muffle his hearing from the half-repressed sighs of anxiety and fear that dignified the rough bosoms of those who lay stretched out on the beds within. The ward was a big one, long and lofty, with rows of beds on each side. At the far end was a huge fireplace with a bright fire blazing, for though it was a warm day, the hot-water system had gone agley, and big black kettles simmered on the hob ready with healing or cleansing heat, should a patient need it. Over the fireplace, filling the breast of the chimney with sorrowful significance, stretched a great black cross on which hung the yellowish-white figure of Him who is, and was, and is to come, silently manifesting forth the curious, majestic mystery of pain. Sean glanced at it very often, and wondered that the patients seemed in no way disturbed by it. Indeed, they seemed not to notice it, and when he had been a few days there himself, it ceased to trouble him with more than a casual thought. The patients passed by as indifferently as those who did the same on the day of the first crucifixion. The symbol was never mentioned — yes it was, once: when a bright young man, convalescent and about to leave, cast a longing eye on a pretty maid who was sweeping the floor, and murmured longing, lustful words about her fine and charming figure. One of some who were listening moved away, saying afterwards to Sean, Did you hear him? Right under our Lord on the cross, too! I was mortally ashamed. Yes, at times it came before them, and this genuine man was shocked again when Sean said, I'm afraid your Lord on the cross is getting used to far worse things than those hot words from the heart of a young man eager to endorse life in the arms of a maid.

Because of the defect in the water system, Sean was given a bed-bath by three nurses; and, for two of them were pretty, his mind rambled into some unholy thoughts, to be silenced by a nun dropping on her knees in the middle of the ward to honour the Angelus, the nurses flopping down too, so that when the hot water cooled, Sean's damp body got cold, and he shivered. One of the nurses, feeling the tremor, said, You'll get your death, and tried to sling a blanket over him with a sudden movement, but it covered his feet only, and Sean coughed to prevent a laugh at his ridiculous outlook in the middle of the Hail Mary, fearful they'd imagine he was laughing at the Invocation, though he felt that the Blessed Virgin Herself, if She did exist, would have laughed along with him. He didn't catch his death, for they put hot-water bottles in with him, and a soothing glow soon overspread his body, and gave him an open mind for thought to enter.

The war was singeing England badly, he thought, as he stretched gloriously into the heat of the bed, and the English stood now with their backs to the wall. The black, white, and red banner of the Germans was cocking a snoot even at the naval forces of her foe, and Gott Mit Uns looked forward to being the enforced motto of the world. England's ancient bustians of Eton and Harrow were filing her reputation. The well-mortared manners, the sleek minds, and tidy thoughts, born of Eton and Harrow, and reared into meanhood by Balliol, Brasenose, Corpus Christi, Patterhouse and Emmanuel, Trinity and Magdalen, were of little effect in a rough world, even when they were helped by the Abdominal Council. They were old-fashioned, stiff-jointed, and still swooned delusively among drawbridge and barbican. England had been warned to put her house in disorder some time before, during the inilligant row in the Commons over the curtalement of the power moneyfisted in the *viva veto vita* of the House of Lords. Yet England never despaired, and still took her ministers out of silk-lined bandboxes, sedately-coated, neatly-trousered, delicately-gloved, and technically top-hatted, repeating everything their fore-fellows had already said so well and so often, stepping out, and passing on, like a solemn file of geese and gander — Salisbury, Balfour, Bonar Law, Bannerman, and now Asquith, ponderous with a pile of classical knullidge, who calmly went on convulsing England's life into elegant argument; and scotching Ireland's life into a vellumised declaration of Home Rule curled up on a purple cushion, ready for the Irish to rede and hang up in the front parlour as a period piece between the picture of Robert Emmet in an Ireland surrounded by silence and gloom, and that of St. Patrick in an Ireland full of the light that never was on sea or land.

But when the Lords were attacked, all the decency and debonair in manners became frayed into a gorgeous orgy of vulgarity, stupidity, and ruffianism (English authority quoted); for when the *rara avis*, Asquith, got up to move the motion emending the power of miniver and muskwaw, he was jowled over with the curses, blasphemies, squeals, jeers and shouts of the Opposition, so indecorous that the marble saints in Westminster Abbey opposite had to clap their hands over their ears and chant Hallelujah, I'm a bomb! in unison, to keep their minds free from cant.

Afar off, sitting on the very end of the Thames Embankment, her eyes fixed on the revolving light of Eddystone, focussing memories of Drake and Frobisher into her mind, Britannia heard the whooproar, and jumping down from her stony seat, she flung her shield over her back, tucked up her skirts, and flew to where her sons were sitting. Bursting in on the bawling men, she hurried to the Speaker's chair, she hammered her trydent on her shield to gain silence, but A.M. went on bawling to keep P.M. from speaking.

—Eh, eh, she yelled, yez lot of Babbylon baboons, are yez not goin' to show any regard whatever for the mother who bore yez? What'll th' world say to all this hollerin', I ask yez? — and seeing Asquith blush for her common speech, she at once showed her learning by shouting, This lingua longia Horridens blasphemodicum, setting a parlous example to the Irish over the sayway; college-bred chaps yez are too, all, from the banks of the cher, boys, cher, and the cam of the good companions!

Encouraged by this, the Speaker spoke; thumping the dusk in front of him, he cupped his hands over his mouth, stretched as far as his forwardness could go, and shouted, Eh, there, eh! D'yez not hear the lady talkin' to yez? That's enough, boys! Have yez forgotten all about Ghengist an' Hoarsa, an' holy Edward, called the confusser? Steady, boys, steady! We'll fight an' we'll canker again! Looka, the Welsh are laughin'. Criccieth, boys, play criccieth! An' the Irish are enjoyin' it all, too. Erin'll remember these days of scold again' us. For th' honour of th' auld hoose, boys! What th' hell's th' Silver Rod doin'?

And all the time, calm, pale, silent, dignified, Asquith stood, quoting quietly, How can men die better than facing fearful cods for the cashes of his fathers and the temples of his goods! High up in the Speaker's Gullery, frilled ladies from Mayfair, Grosvenor Square, Mile End, and Canning Town, shouted and squealed, standing up on their cheers (English authority quoted), and the P.M.'s lady was horridly scribbling a nota-bene to the bony-faced Grey, appealing to him to be a little more bellicose, and chime in with help for the poor P.M. against the great I A.M.'s, which he did with some fine strokes that rung the hearts of many there.

But nothing could stop the clangour, though the Silver Rod ran here and there like a man who was bats in the belfry, beseeching them to remember their better natures, all in fine vain; and once, passing by the front bench, Britannia, mistaking him for a disturber, gave him a vicious prod in the behind with her trydent, causing the man great pain, and forcing him to turn to say, more in sorrow than in anger, that no genuine lady would do that to a gentleman, upsetting her so much that she fell into a comma, bringing the row to a full stop while an usher of the house made a dash to help her, getting her carried off to Guy's Hospital before any more damage was done. The Speaker, realising it wasn't possible to restore the campus mentis, took his chance to postpone proceedings, ordering the Silver Rod to shut the windows, lock the doors, and put out the lights on all that happened there that day.

Strange how placid it seemed to be in an hospital! Stones, bricks, and a few sheets of glass, helped by pain and suffering, hid the busy world away. All was dimmer and quieter now that the night had fallen, with but one nurse left in the ward to guard against the needs of the quieter hours. There she was, all but her head hidden in a deep arm-chair by a blazing fire, her head resting on its back, her hands folded over an abandoned book, her senses sinking into a vigilant sleep; while the fire made more vivid parts of the lamentable crucifix over-head, throwing other parts into an uneasy purple shadow.

Hail Mary, the Lord is with Thee — there it goes, the night-mustering mutter of the rosary, the words, only half formed, falling rapidly from the mouths of those whose heads Sean could dimly see by the humble light given by two small, crimson-coloured bulbs, one at each end of the ward. Haimary th' Loriswithee blessearthouamonwomn, it circled the ward lazily, rose to the ceiling, and died away in the sad sleep of the patients; and Sean recognised the voice of the leader as that of Den Daffy, in for urethral stricture, due for an operation soon, and dreading it: a big, burly, bald-headed docker, own brother to Sylvester Daffy who had been tried for the alleged killing of a scab by cleaving his head open with a navvy's shovel, during the big lock-out; but he had been released without a stain on his character when it was discovered that the blood on his shirt came, not from a human body,

but from the bodies of fleas, crushed when he found leisure to kill
them; own brother, too, to Cock Daffy, one of the best football backs
Dublin had ever known.

—Jesus! came a sharp scream from a centre bed. I can stick it no
longer, I'm tellin' yous! And the scream from the man with cancer in
the tongue went skirling about the ward, bringing to a keener wakefulness the drowsy murmur of Holmarmotherogo prayfrusmisrable-
sinnrs nowana thourofhoudeath. The head of the night nurse left its
haven, and stiffened to listen, and turned to where the cry came from;
then turned back, and sank slow to rest again when the murmur of
prayer and moaning of pain mingled amicably together.

Again the animal-like yelp of pain circled the ward, and again the
head of the nurse left its soft nest, to turn quick, and face towards the
stricken patient.

—You'll have to stick it, Eighteen, she said, sharply; you've had
your morphia, and you'll get no more; so sink your head into the
pillow, and don't keep the other patients awake! And Sean heard
the yelping die down into a muffled moaning. Heavy breathing
showed that the patients had woven their anxiety away into sleep;
the nurse's head again lay on the back of her chair, and nothing was
left with Sean's thoughts but the two soft red lights, and the dreary
madrigal of moaning from the centre bed.

If one only knew, he thought, there's a helluva lot of moaning in
the world today; and it would grow; grow till the common people
came to themselves. Humanity's music would be as sad as ever, but it
wouldn't remain silent much longer. New thoughts were being born,
not only in a cry, but in smoke, flame, and cannon-fire. Half the
Christian world had just discovered that the other half no longer
deserved to live. The slime, the bloodied mud, the crater, and the
shell-hole had become God's Kingdom here on earth. Deep trenches
led to the delectable mountains; and a never-ending line of duck-
boards led to where they could see Him even as they themselves were
seen. Our Father which art in Heaven, Thy kingdom of communism
come! In every ravine, on every hill, through every golden cornfield
tens of thousands of Irish wriggled and twisted to death, their dimming
eyes dazzled by the flame from a scarlet poppy, their dulling ears
shocked by the lilting notes from a rising lark. The ghosts of them who
fell at Dettingen, Fontenoy, and Waterloo were clasping their colder
arms around the newer dead.

The whole city was sadly coloured now with the blue of the wounded
soldier. They were flowing into St. Vincent's as room could be made

for them. Mr. Tobin, the head surgeon, had lost an only son in Flanders, and it seemed he couldn't see enough of forms similar to what his son last looked like. Every free moment he plunged into the middle of those well enough to talk, and would stand there silent, for he was almost stone-deaf, and could hear only a shout given into a circular disk with a delicate connection to a rod stuck into his ear. Where did you get your blighty, son? he'd say to a wounded man, sticking the rod into an ear, and inclining the disk towards the soldier's mouth. When he heard the faint echo of the place's name, he'd murmur, Ah! my son spent his last moment a long way off; but yours was near enough, son; near enough. He seemed to think when he was close to them, he was closer to his son. When on the roof of the operating-theatre, a group of them sang Tipperary, Tobin was in the middle of them, trumpet in ear, his old, slender wavery hand trying to keep time: trying to conjure up the ghost of his son from the songs and stories of the wounded men. You wouldn't get a mother doing it, thought Sean. She'd feel it too deep. She'd conjure up her boy's ghost out of the coloured shadows he left behind him. Neither in noise of song nor murmur of story would she bring back the sad, sunny dust of his shape again, but in the deep and bitter loneliness of remembrance.

Sean found out that the nuns didn't seem to love each other as sisters should. The Order was celebrating a Jubilee, and great agitation and stir blossomed out in the building. Evergreens were strewed in the wards, and special meals given to all patients who could eat them. One ward, empty for renovation, was to be a theatre in which doctors and nurses were to give a home-made show. Sean was busy helping, and when Sister Gonzaga — who was the life and soul of the activity — said, Chairs, more chairs for our theatre, Sean rushed into his ward and began to whip up the chairs, one of which stood by the end of every bed. Going out, he ran into Sister Paul.

—Where are you going with those? she asked sharply.

—Sister Gonzaga asked for them, he said busily; she wants all she can get.

—Leave them back where you got them! Sister Paul said angrily; at once, please!

—But Sister Gonzaga wants them, said Sean, surprised, and sure that Sister Paul hadn't heard what he had said.

—Does she, indeed? sarcastically. Sister Gonzaga has no authority here; and Sister Paul now tells you to leave them where you got them. And for the future, never touch a thing in this ward without my permission; and Sean had gone back ashamed, for many had heard the rebuke, and he was furious that he should be humiliated for trying to help. He went down to the grounds, and took no further part in the celebration.

It was a little embarrassing now, for, since the battle of the chairs, Sister Paul passed him without a nod or a smile. But she was always scrupulously fair, and there wasn't the slightest difference shown between him and the other patients. Indeed, she was more polite to him now than to the others. To one she would say, Sixteen, give nurse a hand with the lockers. To Sean it would be, Twenty-three, would you please give nurse a hand with the beds; but the polite request was always cold, and his short bow of obedience was colder still. Several times he meant to go, but he lingered, and clung to the hope that he had furnished himself with the skill to heal his ailment. So he waited for the operation guaranteed to remove whatever danger lurked in the lump on his neck.

Sister Paul was still cold, but she was kind on the morning of the operation. Under the warm blankets on the operating-table she had stroked his arm, and smiled down reassuringly. Sean had determined to give as little trouble as possible, and when the ether was offered, he breathed the stuff in without a murmur or movement. Once when the stuff came out in a fuller flow, he had half turned his head away, and had felt the grasp of sister and nurse tighten on his arms; but he had murmured that the movement was involuntary; the scent of the ether isn't that of the honeysuckle; but that he'd move no more. One thing troubled him — that under the power of the drug he'd loose all his rich knowledge of profanity on those who were trying to help him. But when he was coming out of his sleep, he sang Alliliu na Gamhna and the Palatine's Daughter at the top of his good baritone voice, the nurses in the ward standing round to listen to him, and when the songs had ended, the theatre nurse bent over him to whisper coaxingly, Sing us another, Twenty-three, another in Irish, please do! And through the haze of the drug that still dimmed his eyes, he swung into Mary of Ballyhaunis. When he had got a little hoarse, Sister Paul came over to warn him to rest, saying, There — that's enough. Have a rest now; and stroking his forehead, added, You were a great soldier, and gave us no trouble whatever.

So he lay, thinking, his neck feeling as if he had had his head sawn off with rough and blunt-edged tools; but he went on thinking, feeling no ill effects from the ether. He heard a patient telling another that one more ward had been given over to the wounded English. The sky over

Dublin now was covered with a red cross. And on the top of Ireland's lowest mountain, on its purple cushion, reposed the Home Rule Bill. Strange how Asquith thought to cajole the Irish into love of everything but their own. The poor devil must know nothing about us. What was Connemara to him? Or the Decies? Knights of Dingle, or Earls of Desmond? Did he know anything outside the bounds of Downing Street? To Sean his job seemed to be an easy one. The England he governed was a big, gilded, angel-protected clock, and the Prime Minister was the little figure that popped out to blow a bugle and tell the hours. His lady seemed to show that her lord didn't know all he needed to know. He woefully, wilfully disregarded the wise words of his lady, a woman of great intelligence and wide perspicacity, who said, I have never understood how anyone could be proud of having either Jewish or Keltic blood in their veins. I have often been painfully reminded of the saying —A Jew is around your neck, or at your feet, but never by your side. Keltic blood is usually accompanied by excited brains and a reckless temperament, and is always an excuse for exaggeration. When not whining or wheedling, the Kelt is usually in a state of bluff, or funk, and can always wind himself up to the kind of rhetoric no housemaid can resist.

Eh! there, sister, hold on a minute! Didn't you write to Johnny Redmond, a day before, or a day after, telling him that he had the opportunity of his life in setting an unforgettable example to the Carsonites if he would go to the House of Commons, and on Monday, and in a great speech, offer all his soldiers to the Government? Did she say that now? A grand idea. Shows brains. It showed, too, that the Kelts, however excited their brains might be; however they might bluff and funk things; however they might wheedle or whine, were good enough to go forth and die so that Margot Asquith might live her old life without any hindrance. And quite a lot of Jews, too, ceasing from hanging around necks or flopping at the feet of others, went forth to die for Britain and Big Ben.

Be fair. Mrs. Ah says she has devoted friends among the Jews; one of them, Rufus Isaacs, Earl of Reading, — one of the best fellows that ever lived. But then Rufus, though by race a Jew, was — British to the core. Encore! Markoni him well. And — He has the laugh of an English schoolboy. Oh! boy. Nice little chap, must be. But listen, thought Sean, addressing an imaginary audience in the ward, listen: She likes Rufus, not because he is a Jew, but because he is British to the encore. The less a Jew, the more she likes him. I daresay if a Kelt could be English to the core, she'd like him too; or an Indian. If only these could manage to be English to the core, even to the *esprit de corps*, how much happier the world would be! Sitting on top of it, rolling along, singing a song! But can't you see the vainglory and silly impudence of such an opinion? It's right, it's proper; but it wouldn't work.

Sean was thinking how long he could manage to stay here.

The doctor had said the wound was healing remarkably well, and the beds were in great demand. St. Vincent was being pestered with petitions for help. A few days more, at the most, and he'd have to quit this clean, airy place, the pleasant bed, the fine food, and the peace and quietude surrounding the sick. He was still measuring the time of possible respite when Sister Paul sent to say she wanted to speak to him quietly in her office. It was a cell-like little place, with a narrow austere desk of polished pine, and a spare, simple, round-topped seat before it as its sole furniture. She was standing in front of the desk, scorning the seat — mortifying herself, thought Sean — in her cream-coloured working-habit, her cap, white as snow, almost hiding her passive face, a dark stream of heavy rosary beads hanging by her skirt, and a large brass crucifix agleam on her bosom. He stood silent there, beside her, while she fiddled with some papers, waiting for her to begin speaking.

Sent to tell me I've got to go, he thought; the good hours of the ague are over.

—Well, Twenty-three, she said calmly, your wound's healing splendidly, and there is little more that we can do for you here. What you want now are good food and plenty of fresh air and sun. I've just got word that you are to go for a fortnight to our Convalescent Home; but it will be two weeks or so before there's a vacancy, so you'll have to remain with us here till they're ready for you.

A month altogether given him to get into some shape to face the harder future: that was good. It was damned kind of them. He felt like cheering. Thank you, Sister Paul, he said earnestly; you have all been very kind to me.

—Now, we must think of the future, she said, as if she hadn't heard what he had murmured — after you leave the Convalescent, have you a job to go to?

—A job? No; I'm afraid not, sister.

—Oh! That's not so good! Where did you work before you came here for treatment?

—Nowhere, he said. A few odd weeks of work, here and there, are all I managed for the past year or more.

—A few weeks only! You must be a lazy fellow, she said tartly.

He was shocked into some silent moments by this remark. It was unexpected. He felt a surge of resentment sweeping through him. His rosy hope was growing grey. Oh! well, St. Vincent's wasn't an abiding city, and he'd just have to move on.

—Not lazy, sister, he said; no, no; not lazy. For many years I have worked, never missing a single quarter while a job lasted. I have worked myself into a knowledge few labourers possess. I have made the night joint labourer with the day, working for the Irish Movement, and for my own class — no, not lazy.

He was staring into her face, now turned to him fairly for the first time, and he saw her as she appeared to eyes that were good. She was of medium height, and inclined to become buxom. She had a round, rather heavy, rosy face of pleasant plainness, with rather cold blue-grey eyes like chilly corners in a warm room. She had the appearance of dignified bustling about her work, as if she was half forcing herself towards perpetual abnegation; so set on activity that she seemed nervous her thoughts might stray for a moment from what she was obliged to do: an uneasy Martha among some Marys in the house of healing.

—But why couldn't you get steady work? she went on, turning her head away to gaze down again at the ledge of the narrow austere desk. It seems curious to me.

He wondered how she'd look if he sang Hallelujah, I'm a Bum!

Why don't you men work as other men do?

How th' hell can we work when there's no work to do!

Instead, he murmured quietly, Oh, I don't know exactly. Perhaps I was a little too prominently in the lock-out, and made too much of a rendezvous of Liberty Hall.

—Ah! now we're getting nearer to it! she said acidly. Liberty Hall! Poor deluded men! You were on the side of those fellows, Larkin and Connolly, who did so much harm to our poor people, is that it?

—Yes, that's it, sister, he said gently.

—In spite of the fact, I suppose, that they were ready to hand over our dear, Dublin, Catholic children to those who would set about upsetting their faith?

—You do them something of an injustice, he said firmly; I am intimate enough with those two fellows — as you scornfully call them — to know that neither would stand for such a thing.

—Well, maybe they wouldn't, she said slowly, and a little grudgingly; but they were willing, you must admit, to thrust our dear

children into grave danger. You should know that the people who
wanted the children would be all too ready to try to pervert the faith
of our little ones.

—I don't believe it for a moment, he said vehemently; the workers'
movement isn't out to thry that sort of thing! We are wholly indifferent
to the faith held by man, woman, or child, sister.

—There you are! she said quickly. You shouldn't be indifferent to
what faith is held by your members. It is a question of our eternal
salvation, and what we have to bear in this life is as nothing to what we
may receive, through the goodness and mercy of God, in the next.
Have you actual knowledge that these English friends of yours
wouldn't want to interfere with the faith of children left in their
charge?

—As far as actual knowledge goes, sister, I am as uncertain they
wouldn't as you are certain that they would.

—Well, she said, flushing, at least you should be able to see what
this dangerous and unchristian tumult has done for you!

That's a homer, thought Sean. I take things patiently, sister, he
said; there are wounded soldiers after every war.

—And you don't hesitate to come for help, and healing for your
wounds, to those who don't in any way agree with your activities,
do you?

Another homer! thought Sean. This was a sharp and a bitter thrust,
tempting him to reply in a kindred bitterness; but he kept silent for a
few moments, for bitterness wouldn't be a meet return for the care she
had given him, or the food supplied for the past three weeks.

—I daresay I shouldn't have come, he said; that was a sad mistake.
And he stood, silent, waiting for her to dismiss him.

—You're talking nonsense now, she said; you know you did well
to come here. I hope your stay at the Convalescent will do you good
— I am sure it will. You can go, now, Twenty-three.

He went back to the ward, his breast tight with rage so that he could
breathe but rapidly. Had he any right to be angry? Maybe Sister Paul
felt aggrieved that he was where a member of her own household of
faith ought to be. That was only natural. There were many waiting to
be given a bed; many more now that the Tommies had taken up so
much room. When the Adelaide had refused, they had taken him in,
and had helped him as much as they could. Had he a right to that help?
He held he had — as much as another. But maybe Sister Paul had a
different opinion, and she was right according to her belief. She would
be but following the direction of him after whom she was called:

Let us do good unto all men, especially unto them who are of the household of faith. Especially — there was the order. He was there on sufferance, and sufferance wasn't the badge of his tribe. She might have said her say more softly; he was poor and, in a way, helpless. Not helpless — he could go.

He wrapped his razor, soap, brush, and face flannel in an old ragged handkerchief, and thrust the little bundle into a pocket; and went over to Nurse Kelly making bandages in the centre of the ward.

—I'm going, he said; you can give my bed to someone else; and he went from the ward, barely glancing at the tonsured head of the stony St. Laurence, deeper in thought than ever; down the corridor, past the armoured Michael still thrusting a spear through a twisting dragon; past the great gong just as the porter was giving it three strokes, out by the broad doorway, into the Green opposite, and over the bridge, by the pond, under the trees, he took his first few steps homewards.

PREPARE, EVERYONE WITH WEAPONS

IT was a warm and lovely day. Sean, having eaten his breakfast, had taken his stick to go out, for his legs were feeling more numb than ever, and quivered threateningly at times. He slid over the stone wall bordering the railway, and wandered to a grassy bank where demure dog-daisies were jostled by flaunting poppies, scarlet and gay, looking like gaudy whores invading the home of quaker girls. Clearing a space, he sat down with a sigh of relief, for a cup of tea and a slice of dry bread didn't fill a body with any desire for dancing. He would forget Irish republics, dark rosaleens, and red flags for the moment, and try to be at peace, for peace comes dropping slow, dropping from the veils of the morning. No, no, Ycats; there can be no peace where poverty is, and your own cry to go to Inisfree shows there is little of it in your own heart.

He leaned back against the dry trunk of a dead thorn-tree, looking like what he himself would be when this damned paralysis got a proper grip on him. But doctors weren't always right: no-one could be always right. He gathered into his hand a spray that was circling round the dry trunk, and admired its tiny blossoms, purple and yellow. Quaint flower, pliable stem, handsome leaves — an interesting plant, and poisonous! Children called it the deadly nightshade, warning younger ones against its beautiful red berries, and tearing it down whenever it crept too near to their homes. Eat them, they'd say, an' you'll die in terrible pain. Well, thousands had died in terrible pain who had never eaten of these beautiful berries. He had read that this plant was close to the tomato plant whose fruit, it was said, was very good to eat. He had often seen them, red and luscious, lying in shallow wooden boxes, fringed with purple-and-yellow tissue paper, among green cabbages in the greengrocer's shop. He wondered if he'd like them, for up to now he had never tasted one. Come to that, he had never tasted a lot of things. What now? Well, peaches, pineapple, figs, apricots, or those funny-looking things called bananas. It was some years now since he had tasted an apple, a plum, or a strawberry, or any fruit, be God, now that he thought of it! If he were a knight-errant, with an escut-cheon, he'd bear as a motto, Poverty Must Go — *Declenda est pauperium*, or whatever the hell the Latin was.

Ay, indeed, and there's the spud too, related to this poisonous plant. Same flower almost, though bigger, and possibly like that of the tomato too, though he'd never seen it growing. Well, everything had something to say for itself, and even this dangerous plant, at least, jewelled the hedges in autumn.

Il Poverino — that was St. Francis who had beatified poverty, a *mariage de convenance* between Heaven and Hell. It was indeed easy for some who had inherited wealth to achieve a rapturous poverty; not so easy for those who had inherited poverty to show it with a fine form and bright colours. There was nothing in either dire poverty or great wealth: both were undignified, both were vulgar. Of course, the personality of St. Francis made what he touched rich, and gave to everywhere he went a veil of grandeur. But what about the poor devil whose personality had neither grandeur nor richness, and in whom poverty itself destroyed the flickering personality a simple, certain life might have saved? No, St. Francis, excuse me, poverty must go.

Apricots! Must be good to eat. My oath! Go, bind up yon dangling apricots, was a warning to Richard's poor queen that all wasn't well with her man; and wasn't it apricots that seemed to have made the Duchess of Malfi feel sick when she was with child by Antonio? They came to us, too, wrapped in coloured tissue; and peaches, sheltered in greater richness, silver tissue mostly, each in a little nest of its own. A feast of vision! Well, such as he had but little to do with the kindly fruits of the earth. How often had he prayed to God that He might give and preserve to his use the kindly fruits of the earth, so as in due time he might enjoy them! The time wasn't due yet — that must be it.

He turned his head away from the blossoms beside him to glance at the wretched backyards of the poor houses jutting out into the railway waste land. All muddy, drab, and crumbling; not a single flower abloom in one of them. In almost every yard the week's washing fluttered from knotted lines — a red cotton dress, white rags of sheets, blue blouses and drawers. Three cheers for the red, white, and blue! The banners of the poor leading the battle for cleanliness.

Well, there was peace here, at least. He had no ties at the moment. He had left the Council of the Citizen Army over a difference with Madame Markievicz, moving a motion that she should either give up her connection with the Army or the Irish Volunteers. The vote had gone against him in a curious way. She had voted for herself; a strange thing, but typical, thought Sean, for her to do. Tommy Foran, President of the Union, who had never attended one meeting of the Committee, put in an appearance at this, and, of course, gave his vote of confidence in Madame. Even with Tommy's vote and her own, she had but a majority of one; and had she refrained from voting for herself, as Sean did, like a fool, the vote would have been an even one. But Madame on this result built up a demand for an apology, and Sean obliged by resigning, and leaving the Army for good. He could relax now in a kind of a way. He looked down at his boots. God help him when the winter came again. When summer's here, winter isn't far behind. He smiled grimly as he remembered Father Jimmy Breen stopping to advise him one day, and he stumbling along Seville Place: *Keep your feet warm an' dry — that's th' chief thing,* he had said in his shrill, nasal voice. One splash of rain, and his feet would be wet and cold. Oh, to hell with this sighing when the sun shone, the birds sang, and the flowers bloomed!

Some young voice shouting his name made him turn his restless head, and he saw a boy, who lived a few doors down, running across the waste, breathless and capless.

—Mr. Casside, Mr. Casside, he said, puffing, great news! Millions of Volunteers have gone marching — down to Howth, they say — an' thousands of police an' Scottish Bordherers have folleyed them, packed in thrams!

—What for? Why? Didya hear anything else?

—Somethin' 'bout guns comin' in at Howth. Everyone's talkin'!

Up he jumped, caught his stick, crossed the waste ground, slid over the wall, and hurried up Seville Place to go to Croydon Park, on the road to Howth, where he guessed some of the Citizen Army would be drilling. As he turned right from Seville Place, on to the main road, a body of Scottish Borderers were marching by, followed by a jeering crowd, throwing tin cans, stones, or any suitable thing they could lay hands on, some of them thumping hard into the backs of the men, a few hopping off the backs of their heads. Sean saw one young soldier, almost a boy, pale as death, limping along, his frightened young face screwed tight to keep the tears back, supported by the protecting arm of an old non-com., who turned while Sean looked, to glance savagely back at the crowd.

Suddenly, without a word of warning, several rear ranks wheeled right about, brought their bayoneted rifles to the charge, and, scattering over the street, came at a swift run towards the crowd, which broke, turned, and fled away in all directions. Sean found himself in danger again. He would be spitted like a fowl if he didn't run. In an instant he conjured the speed of his old hurling days into his shrivelling legs, and flew, flew faster than Master McGrath flew after the hare, into McGlade's newsagent and tobacconist shop, just before McGlade himself banged the shop door shut as the butts of several rifles hammered on it, and the gleaming point of a bayonet shot through one of the panels. He sat down on the floor to modify the beats of his heart, and wonder how speed came to animate his legs. Silence of intense listening filled the shop, while McGlade gawked cautiously from an upper window to watch till the coast was clear.

Paralysis me arse! thought Sean; no potent or potential paralysis could furnish me with the speed I got into me legs today. Fire of life is in them still. I wonder, now, is it that I'm not getting enough to eat? That may be it, coupled with the fact that I've long been trying to do too much.

McGlade came down to say the soldiers had gone on, and the coast was clear, so Sean lumbered to his feet, went out, and ran into Sean Connolly, the one who'd worked with him in Jason's, now a member of the Citizen Army. He was full of the gun-running, and was on his way, too, to Croydon Park to pick up more news of what was happening. As they went on down the Strand, along came two young men, haversack and belt showing they were Volunteers, casually, as it were, supporting a third between them who, though walking wearily, was half reclining in their arms, his head resting sideways on his left shoulder, while the look on the faces of his comrades was that of ignoring all, but seeing everyone.

—What's happened to him? asked Connolly, anxiously, turning to walk back with them, as did Sean too, not wishing to delay aid to a hurt man.

—Gun-running, said a Volunteer laconically; bayonet thrust; Howth.

—Get a cab; I'll get a cab, said Connolly excitedly; he shouldn't be walking!

—No, it's awright, said the Volunteer consoledly; doesn't want a cab; 'tisn't that ugly, an' walkin's a better advertisement.

They were now just in front of an advertisement hoarding on which was a huge poster of a vast hairy bull slanting down a tremendous shaggy head to stare at a small balloon-bellied bottle of bovril; and there the two of them stood to look after the two Volunteers bearing home their poor hurt comrade.

—Alas! my poor brother! said Sean mockingly; and, as Connolly looked sad and embarrassed, he added, Don't look so solemn, man; the three of them are thoroughly enjoying themselves.

Just as they had begun to move on again, they were startled to another stop by a distant volley of rapid rifle-fire.

—What's that? what's that? exclaimed Connolly; listen!

—The Scottish Borderers letting bang at the crowd, murmured Sean.

—Murderers, said Sean Connolly, his face pale and tense, merciless murderers! But Sean saw again the look of tired resentment on the soldiers' faces, the dust on their khaki coats, the stones hopping off their heads and backs, the young boy twisting his face to keep back tears of pain, and the grim face of the veteran with a steady arm around him, helping him along.

When they got to Croydon Park, they found about thirty of the Army in a state of dubious excitement, all of them talking, and none of them listening. When they saw Sean Connolly and Sean coming up the drive, they ran over, several saying rapidly. The Volunteers are scatherin' everywhere, an' flingin' everything away!

—An' why th' hell don't some of you go an' get some of the scattered things? asked Sean. This is a chance you may never get again. Wait a minute! he added, as all of them started off; look, go different ways, say five or six in each group, and let each group decide who is to be non-com. to lead the way. And mind, boys, no rowing with any Volunteer; if one needs help, give him all you can; only disregard those who fling anything away. Pick up guns, or anything else you can find, and bring them here — see?

—If we see a fellow timid-like, said one of the men, couldn't we whisper there was soldiers in some bushes further along so's he'd slide his gun away from him?

—A fine idea, said Sean. A number of you had better stay here to mind whatever may be brought back.

Later on they came back, jubilant, with a number of guns, belts, haversacks, and even a few bayonets, and a quantity of ammunition. The guns were heavy and clumsy-looking — mausers, some said; and they were fed with ugly, thick-bodied bullets. They were stored away in the house, the men keeping whatever else they had found as their personal property.

Later in the evening, a motor-car swept up the drive, and a cocky cuchullain Gael sprang out before it stopped, followed by a tired-looking man with a greyish moustache, cut brusquely in a military way. He wore a bowler hat, and polished brown leggings were tightly fixed on to his legs. Long afterwards, Sean heard that he was Colonel Moore.

—Hello! said the cocky Gael cheerily; we've just slipped down here, Sean, to collect the guns you've got.

—Guns? echoed Sean. What guns? We've no guns — this is a place of peace.

—We know the kind of a peaceful place it is, said the military gent.

—If you know that, then, why waste time coming here to look for guns?

—We have heard your men have taken a number of guns, mislaid by Volunteers in the excitement of a collision with the British Authorities; and we have come to claim them.

—Have you now? said Sean; that's kind of you. Let's get this thing down sensibly, for you seem to be excited yourselves: who told you we had guns?

—We didn't come here to argue with ignorant men! said the military gent testily. These weapons are the property of the Volunteers, and it is a dishonourable thing to try to keep them.

—We aren't altogether ignorant men, said Sean, and we don't wish to be impertinent; but you are turning the question now into an ethical one. You first alleged you were told that guns were here; that these guns are Volunteer property, without proving that a gun, because it is a gun, must necessarily be a Volunteer gun; and that the keeping of a gun, unproved to be a Volunteer gun, is a reprehensible thing to do. Who the hell are you, anyhow?

—All that is necessary for you to know is that we have the authority of Volunteer Headquarters to demand the surrender of whatever guns you have.

—Look here, my friend, said Sean smoothly, laying a gentle but remonstrating hand on the military gent's sleeve; but the hand was shaken roughly away, and the military gent stepped back to be farther away from Sean; Oh, well, if that's the way the wind blows, went on Sean, it's just as well to let you know that the writ of Volunteer Headquarters doesn't run here. This is part of a Union premises, and the men, not you, sir, are in control here. Look, he said, turning to the cocky Gael, the two of you had better go.

—This isn't a brotherly way for the Citizen Army to treat the Volunteers, said the cocky Gael.

—Oh, if you want to be brotherly, said Sean, then divide the guns equally between us — they'll be in good hands. How many did you get altogether?

—That's a question concerning the Volunteers alone, said the military gent tersely.

—Aw, take your chum away, said Sean to the cocky Gael; he shouldn't be let loose. He gestured towards the car; pack him back into his cushions, and bring him home — the figure is getting a little too stiff.

—If they aren't surrendered decently, said the military gent, there'll probably be more about it.

—How more about it? questioned Sean.

—The Volunteer Authorities aren't likely to allow their property to be pilfered in this unseemly and unmanly way.

—Aw, said Sean, you've got property on the brain. Do you good to read what Wolfe Tone thought about the rights of property. And, if I were you, my man, I shouldn't be drumming threats into our tough ears, for we are apt to resent them.

—Ay, are we, growled a big Citizen Army man. We've faced an' fought authorities bigger'n Volunteer ones, so it's safer for certain people to keep from chivvyin' them as wear the Red Hand in th' sides of their hats!

The cocky Gael and military gent got into their car, and off they went down the drive, without even getting a smell of a cartridge.

When Jim Larkin came back from England, a huge bank of clay, buttressed by thick planks, was built; targets were fixed on the planks, and soon the Dublin people began to hear the roaring report of the Howth guns as Citizen Army man and Volunteer shot to improve their aim by practice. Nelson from his high post stretched his neck when he heard them, and wished for the other eye so that he could see better. St. Patrick on the top of Tara shook with anxiety and foreboding, for what he heard didn't sound like bells. No one could foresee, no one knew that these ugly signals were the songs heralding the coming of Easter morn.

THE BOLD FENIAN MEN

LARKIN was gone, and Connolly was going, to the great joy of some of the labour leaders whose harts panteth after a cushy job as a deer's panteth after the water brooks. They were never at heart's ease while either of these leaders was near; but now, like wise and sensible men, they could, thank God, set about knocking fighting Unions into safe, prudential enterprises. Larkin had gone to America, and Connolly had left his Union to give all he had to the Citizen Army. He began to write patriotic verse that shivered with wretchedness. His fine eyes saw red no longer, but stared into the sky for a green dawn. A play of his called *Under Which Flag?* blundered a sentimental way over a stage in the Hall in a green limelight, shot with tinsel stars. All the old-age punchioners of commonplace outcries were poured into the pages of *The Workers' Republic* week by week; legions of words, each the same in stature and appearance, mob-capped and mock-cussined, dumbly plodded over the paper, unled by a single officer-word in sword and sash to justify the long, swing-song, dull purrade.

The world war was waxing over Europe, and Ireland was enjoying the hardships suffered by her enemy. The advanced Nationalists carried the name of Von Kluck about on the tips of their tongues. *Dark Rosaleen*, *The Men of the West*, and *Clare's Dragoons* were near forgotten by most Gaelic Leaguers, Sinn Feiners, and all I.R.B. men, whose favourite songs now were *Die Wacht am Rhein*, *Deutschland über Alles*, *Was ist des Deutschen Vaterland*, and the sky grew greener. But all the time, the stoutest men from hill, valley, and town were pressing into the British Army, and long columns of armed Irishmen, singing Ireland's latest love-song, *It's a long way to Tipperary*, went swinging by Liberty Hall down to the quays to the ships waiting to bring them to a poppy-mobbed grave in Flanders. The I.R.B. worked hard sticking up fly-by-night posters calling on Irishmen to keep out of the British Army, while the journals *Sinn Fein* and *Irish Freedom* warned them that the coming fight must be, not for Catholic Belgium, but for Catholic Ireland; but the swinging columns went on marching down to the quays to the ships that go down to the sea. H. H. Asquith,

Prime Minister, stood side by side with John Redmond at a recruiting meeting in the house of Dublin's Lord Mayor, but the forest of British guns and bayonets round the building kept his voice from travelling; and Dublin roared out her contempt for the pair of political brokers, but still the swinging columns of Kellys, Burkes, and Sheas tramped to the quays, and, singing, went forth to battle for England, little nations, and homes unfit for humans to live in; for while the sky was green for some, for many more it turned to the solid and salutary buff colour of a ring-paper.

Connolly determined to try to damn the stream of men flowing out of Ireland, and was seized with the idea that he could turn the sky green for all to see by hoisting a flag of the same colour over Liberty Hall. He had banished the Committee, and now ruled alone; so, after being thoroughly rehearsed, the Citizen Army, numbering about one hundred and seventy men, paraded outside, and Connolly, followed a pace behind by Madame Markievicz, inspected them. Connolly wore his new dark-green uniform for the first time, and didn't look too well in it, for he had a rather awkward carriage; and bow-legs, partly ensnared in rich, red-brown, leather leggings, added to the waddle in his walk. He carried an automatic gun in his left hand, the barrel resting in the crook of his arm. Madame having dressed herself in man's attire to fight for liberty, was in full green uniform too, and carried a big automatic pistol on her thin hip.

There was a dire sparkle of vanity lighting this little group of armed men: it sparkled from Connolly's waddle, from the uniformed men stiff to attention, and from the bunch of cock-feathers fluttering in the cap of the Countess. But it was a vanity that none could challenge, for it came from a group that was willing to sprinkle itself into oblivion that a change might be born in the long-settled thought of the people. There they stood — a tiny speck of green among a wide surge of muddily-garbed watchers, still and silent too, as if from their listlessness they were draining out their last drop of energy and hope into this tiny goblet-group of men so that they might go forth and make a last short fight for them. Here was the purple heart of Ireland.

Now the escort marched with the flag, carried by a young girl, and not a murmur broke from the big crowd watching, Sean, a little loose on his legs, and nursing a septic neck-wound, among those in the front rank. Not a cheer went up when Connolly declared to his men that as soon as the old Green Flag flew from the roof, the Irish soldiers passing by would swing left, assemble before the Hall, and vow that they served neither Kaiser nor King, but Ireland. The flag was borne to the roof, fixed to the traces, and as it broke out on the breeze, the men of the army presented arms, and the great crowd cheered as if the breaking of the flag meant the ending of time for England.

Not an Irish soldier passing by to the quay, led by bands playing *Garryowen* or *Let Erin Remember,* turned aside; not one of them turned a head to glance at the lonely banner flying from the roof-top, lonelier now that the crowd had gone, pathetically flapping a call no-one heard; loneliest at night waving, seemingly, among the stars, tired and drooping, but still fluttering a faint message to those tough men of Dublin City who now slept, waiting for the dawn to come to go in full marching kit down to the ships, and set their sails for Flanders. It was a childish thought for Connolly to harbour: it was a fiery-tale, a die-dream showing a false dawn that no soul saw.

But Sean knew that Connolly's men would fight, and the Irish Volunteers would stand by them; but he knew in his soul that they were going the wrong way about it. Their methods were those of the days of the red-coats, busby, and plume; salute your superior officers, fix bayonets, and charge, boys. These uniformed batches of men attacking, holding, and defending particular positions couldn't hope to measure themselves against the heavy forces that would be sent out to down them. Once they were cut off, they were as good as gone. The arrangements were too open, and the idea that the British wouldn't use cannon, vouched for by Connolly, Pearse, and others, maddened Sean. Capitalists of England won't destroy capitalist property here, said Connolly, and so said Pearse, and so say all of us. I tell you they will, shouted Sean; And I tell you they won't, shouted back those who heard him. They used artillery in the streets during the Franco-Prussian War, said Sean, and at the siege of Paris the French soldiers battered their way over the Communard barricades with cannon-fire, careless of what property the bursting shells destroyed.

He sent an article on the question to *The Volunteer,* but it was never published; he wrote to Connolly and Pearse suggesting a debate, but heard no word of reply from either. He argued that the fight would have to be mainly an underground one; that to risk a thousand men, or even half that number, in one concentric fight was foolishness. He pointed out that the Boers, a much more formidable army than any Ireland could put into the field, had to adopt the method of surprise attack, the quick arrival, the ambush, the quicker get-away. When the Boers tried to pit a big force against a far bigger, and better-armed one, in a stand-up fight, they failed badly, as Cronje did, and Prinsloo after him. It was the fighting of De Wet, Delarey, and Botha that gave them the time to win terms from the victorious British that were the beginning of a great Afrikander nation. Take off your uniforms, he advised, and keep them for the wedding, the wake, the pattern, and the fair. Put on your old duds that make you undistinguishable from your neighbours; send out detachments of fifty so that when you've got to run for it, you may lose no more than five or ten, while with an embattled thousand you'd lose the lot.

Once or twice, with the help he gave at St. Enda's Fête at Jones's Road in his mind, deluded with the thought that it was in Pearse's mind too, he tried to catch a hold of him; but he was always shunted off by staff officers with vivid yellow tabs on their buzz-fuzz buzzoms, centres, right-hand and left-hand men, and pickothninnies of the Irish Movement. Afterwards he ceased to rage at the thought of this treatment, for a ragamuffin like him, with his oozing neck, near-sighted eyes, trembling legs, tattered clothes, and broken boots must have been a shuddering sight for Gaelic gods to see. Besides, when he was excited, he had a habit of taking God's name in vain to punctuate his points; so they turned aside, giving him a look of horrified contempt as they went their way. A swearcrow he must have looked to the lot of them, defiling Ireland with his cawing of Irish into their tenderly-turned ears.

Sean was to see more nonsense still: Wally Carpenter, son of a Wicklow Englishman, caught him by the arm one day and hustled him into Liberty Hall. Wally was hardly five foot high, with tiny hands, feet, and head; sentimental to a tearful degree, but with a hard core of grit in his tinyness.

—Wait till I show you, Sean, he panted, pulling him along one of the narrow passages; you'll soon see something you'll like — make you near jump for joy! He opened a dim door that had a red cross in paper pasted on a panel, and shoved Sean into a little, dirty, dismal room. Look, he said, there's a bit of wot you fawncy!

When Sean's eyes got used to the dimness, the grimy walls, the cobwebbed windows frightening away the beggarly light that lurked in the lane outside, he saw, stretched on the dusty floor, four flimsy camp-beds, each of them covered with a glaring white sheet looking like shrouds, their whiteness over the soiled floor showing them up like lilies afloat on the top of a murky pool.

—For th' wounded in the fight, said Wally proudly; lovely, aren't they? When Connolly showed them to me, I felt as I'd like to kiss him!

—Why th' hell didn't you? asked Sean. More childishness. Good God, man! he said, turning on poor Wally, can't you see this is naked foolishness? A child's patthern of war! Look! he added, gripping the thin little arm, if anyone near you gets a bullet in him, tell him to yell for an hospital where the facts of wounds are known; where a splint's a splint and a probe's a probe, and where there are surgeons who know how to handle them!

Connolly began his madnight route marches, sometimes ending with a furiosius attack on Dublin Castle. He seemed to see the beautiful Cathleen ni Houlihan immured within, pining away, chained hand and foot with ring-papers. The capture of the Castle would mean nothing, for shortly afterwards the fighters would find that in taking the Castle they had but been taken themselves. Behind this romantic façade Connolly was shoving the Volunteers forward, quicker than they wanted to go. His men were kibing their heels. Quicker, quicker, and Volunteers crossed and recrossed Citizen Army men, route-marching, drilling, raising the wind of war. In between this criss-cross of armed Irishmen wove the sparkling, half-galloping equipage of the Viceroy, drawn by four silky-skinned animals ridden by outriders in velvet coats, white breeches, and long-peaked jockey caps; followed by red-breasted lancers, brass-helmeted dragoons, or plumed hussars trying to weave an elegant binding embroidery through the more rough-and-ready pattern with which Ireland was busy, determined to cover up for ever every sign and thread in it of coloured conquest.

The Easter vigil was nearly over. Thousands were crumbling tobacco in the palms of their hands, preparing for the first smoke in seven long Lenten weeks of abstinence; the time had passed for forcing oneself (if you were lucky) to swallow sharply-tasting potted herrings, leathery strips of salted ling, and tea without milk. Steak and onions, bacon and cabbage, with pig's cheek as a variation, would again glorify the white-scrubbed kitchen tables of the Dublin workers. Dancing for the young; the rollicking call into Eden would again swing into life to the tune of *Hoosh the Cat from under the Table* or *Lift the Roof Higher*; older ones, thinking of their children, would be getting ready for a trip to Portmarnock's Velvet Strand, or Malahide's silver one; and those who weren't would be poring over the names of horses booked to run at Fairyhouse on Easter Monday. The danger aglow in an All-Ireland Parade of the Volunteers had passed. It had been whispered, only whispered, mind you, that it had been planned by a few of remember-for-ever boys to suddenly change the parade from a quiet walk into an armed revolt. A near thing. Only for God's gillie, Eoin Mac Neill, Chief of Stuff, and Bulmer Hobson,

God's gillie's gillie, the Volunteer Sacredary, neither of whom had been told about the plan, but who caught the wisp of a whisper, the deadly dreama would have been on top of the people. But these two sent out couriers in trains, on horseback, on bicycles, in donkey-carts, and on roller-skates, running, galloping, and puffing all over the country, to countermind the whole thing, and so muted the silver trumpets that had lifted themselves up to call to the great race that was to come. So the country stretched itself before the fire, examined the form of the horses, filled its pipe, and watched the pig's cheek simmering on the fire for the morrow's dinner, thanking God that the long threatening hadn't come at last.

And on Easter Monday, off they went to the races, to their velvet strands, or got out their pretty frocks for the night dancing, all in a state of grace after the Easter devotions, full up of the blessed *joie deo feevre*; part of the country coming to the city to see the Museum, the Four Courts, the Custom House, and the Pro-Cathedral; while up one street Roger Casement, surrounded by armed detectives, was being taken to a boat chartered to land him at the nearest point to Tyburn; and down another street Bulmer Hobson, in the midst of armed I.R.B. men, was being taken to where he could do no good. All was quiet as a none breathless in madoration. Then down the centre of O'Connell Street, silent but for the tramp of their feet, came hundreds of armed Volunteers and Irish Citizen Army, led by Pearse, Connolly, and Tom Clarke, to halt, wheel, and face the General Post Office.

—There go the go-boys! muttered an old man, half to himself and half to an elderly, thin lady beside him who had stopped to help him stare at the Volunteers. Well, Mac Neill put a stop to their gallop! What th' hell are th' up to now? They seem to be bent on disturbin' th' whoremony of the sacred day. Goin' in, eh? Wha' for, I wondher? Can't be wantin' postage stamps. Can't be to get th' right time, for there's a clock in th' window. What'r they doin, ma'am? I dunno. Somethin' brewin'? Ma'am, there's always somethin' brewin'. I'm seventy, an' I've never known an hour that I didn't hear tell of somethin' brewin'. Be God, they're takin' th' clock outa th' window! That's odd, now. Looka, they're smashin' out th' windows with their rifles! There's a shower o' glass — right over th' passers-by! That's goin' beyond th' beyond. Tha's, tha's just hooliganism. We betther be gettin' outa here — th' police'll be here any minute! Didn' I tell you before, ma'am, I dunno! They're shovin' out the Post Office workers; pointin' their guns at them. We betther be gettin' outa here

while we're safe. Houl' on a second — here's someone out to read a
paper. What's he sayin'? I dunno. How th' hell can you expect a fella
to hear from here? Oh! pushin' th' people off th' streets, now. Eh?
G'on home, is it? An' who are you t'ordher me about? Takin' over th'
city? D'ye tell me that? Well, you're not goin' to take over me! I'm a
peaceful man out on a peaceful sthroll on a peaceful day, an' I stand
be me constitutional rights. Gunfire here soon? Arrah, from where?
From where, ma'am? I dunno, I'm tellin' you! He says he's speakin'
in th' name of th' Irish Republic, so now you're as wise as I am meself.
Th' police'll soon explain matthers. Don't be talkin', looka what's
comin' up O'Connell Street! A company o' throttin' lancers — full
regalia with carbines, lances, an' all! Comin' to clear th' Post Office.
Don't be pushin' me ribs in, ma'am! Hear th' jingle of them! This looks
like business. Here we see, ma'am, the Irish Republic endin' quicker'n
it began. Jasus, Mary, an' Joseph! th' fools are firin' on them! Here,
get outa th' way, ma'am, an' let a man move! Near knocked you
down? Why th' hell are you clingin' on me tail for, then? Didn' I tell
you hours ago that it was dangerous dawdlin' here? D'ye hear that
volley! Looka th' police runnin' for their lives! Here, let's get outa
this; we've dilly-dallied too long where we've no real business to be!
    —Oh, looka them breakin' into the shops! Isn't that provokin',
ma'am? After all, th' boys are out for somethin' higher. Looka this
fella comin' along with a gramophone. Eh, sonny boy, where'd you
get that? Didja hear that answer? Go an' find out! Uncivilised lot.
Looka these comin' with a piano, no less! Didja hear that? Give them
a shove! Cheek, wha'? Look, they're bringin' out hand-carts an'
prams. A sad day for Dublin's fair name. What's that fella in beard
an' knickerbockers doin'? Pastin' up bills. Willya read that — callin'
on the citizens to do nothin' to dishonour the boys. Why doesn't he
mind his own business? Sheehy-Skeffington? Never heard of him.
One o' Ireland's noblest sons? Is it on for coddin' me y'are? If he was
less noble an' less unselfish, I'd ha' heard a lot of him? Maybe; but
he's not goin' to be let dictate to me. It's none o' his business if I want
to rifle, rob, an' plundher. Looka! There he goes, now, with two
others, in a web o' soldiers! That doesn't look like he was noble.
What was that, now, went whizzin' by me? A bullet? You're jokin'!
I can tell them, if they harm me, there'll be more about it!
    The tinkle of breaking glass wandered down the whole street, and
people were pushing and pulling each other, till through broken
windows all the treasures of India, Arabia, and Samarkand were open
before them. Sean watched them as they pulled boxes down on top of

themselves, flung clothing all over the place; tried to pull new garments over their old ones; while one woman, stripped naked, was trying on camisole after camisole, ending with calm touches that smoothed out the light-blue one that satisfied her at last. All who were underdressed before, were overdressed now, and for the first time in their frosty lives the heat of good warm things encircled them.

He heard the humming zipzz of bullets flying a little way overhead, and guessed someone was firing to frighten the looters; so he dodged into the doorway of a shop to put a protection between him and them. A solidly-built man came trotting along carrying a large jar by the handle against his right thigh, while from his left hung a pair of vividly yellow boots. A sharp ping sounded, and the jar separated into halves, letting a golden stream of liquor honour the road. The man stopped, and gazed at the jagged neck of the jar left in his hand.

—Jasus! he said, not a dhrop of it left — the wasteful bastards!

Sean squirmed round an angle of the doorway to get a look into the shop. Through the great jagged hole in the window he saw the inside was a litter of tossed clothing, caps, shoes, collars, and ties on which people were trampling, and over which they were jostling each other; ignoring the value of what lay on the floor or what was spread over the counter, for the hidden value of what lay neatly folded in the still unopened boxes. One man, alone, was rooting among a heap of caps on the floor, feverishly planting one after the other on his head, and flinging to the far end of the shop those which didn't seem to fit. Another, trying by main force to pull a delicate-looking pair of tweed trousers over a pair of big thick boots, was cursing loudly when he discovered they wouldn't go, and cursing louder still when he found he couldn't get them off again. A third was holding his old coat tightly between his legs while he excitedly thrust raggedly-shirted arms through the sleeves of a bran-new one; while yet another was calling out that if anyone came across a seven-size in socks, they might let him know. And there, too, was the old man, leaning on the counter directing with his stick a younger man on a ladder, busy searching among the boxes on the higher shelves.

—What's in that one to your left? he shouted to the man on the ladder; to your left, man! Shirts? What kinda shirts? Ordinary cotton ones? Aw, don't waste time clawin' them things! They can be picked up anywhere. That box to your right — to your right! Good God, man! D'ye not know your right from your left? De Luxe written on them? Throw them down, throw them down! Where'r you pushin', ma'am? This isn't a spring sale. You'll have to keep ordher if you want to do business here. Wha'? How th' hell do I know where to direct you to the ladies' department! One, two, three, four, five, six, an' one for Sunday — they'll be about enough for the time bein'. Have a look for a box marked pyjamas — I always had a notion of wantin' to feel how they felt on a fella. Wha's that? What do they want th' ambulance for? A woman's been shot? Wha', just outside? Who done it? A sniper, or somebody? God Almighty, where's our boasted law an' ordher!

Sean watched their wonderful activity, and couldn't desecrate their disorder with dishonour. All these are they who go to Mass every Sunday and holy day of obligation; whose noses are ground down by the clergy on the grindstone of eternal destiny; who go in mortal fear of the threat of a priest, he thought; but now he was glad to see they hadn't lost their taste for things material. In spite of the clergy's fifing and drumming about venial and mortal sin, they were stretching out their hands for food, for raiment, for colour, and for life. If the lilies of the field, that neither toiled nor spun, could be lovely, how much more that these whose lives were a ceaseless labour should be lovely too? The time would come when they would no longer need to take their kingdom of heaven by violence, for they would build it themselves, and warmth, adornment, and satisfaction in the midst of fair sounds and bright colours would be their own.

When the shooting seemed to have got less, Sean slid cautiously out of his shelter and, keeping close to the walls of shop and house, made his way home. Darkness had fallen, and his near-sighted eyes could see but a few feet in front of them. Coming to the bridge across the canal at Spencer Dock, his semi-consciousness heard a calm, tired voice say somewhere, Halt! Who goes there? A few steps farther, and the voice, tired no longer, terse and threatening, said again, Who goes there! In the hesitating shock of seeing nothing, he managed to say, Friend, and a moment after, passed by the dim form of a soldier with the rifle at the ready, who passed him by with the advice of, Answer quicker, next time, friend. A narrow squeak, that! A few seconds more of hesitation and he'd have been high among the stars. Watch your steps, Sean. A little farther on, his breast almost touched a bayonet as another voice said, Who goes there? Murmuring, Friend, the bayonet was lowered, and a soldier's voice said, Pass on, friend. They were dotted along the road up to the corner of the street that held his home. Pouring in by the North Wall, and no-one here to stop them. Poor ould Ireland!

He halted at the doorway thrust through with the knowledge that it was dangerous for him to be abroad at night. His eyes were blank in the darkness. He thought of the things that had happened, and wondered how it would all end. It was a deserted city now, but for those who fought each other. The pubs had emptied, the trams had jingled back to their sheds, the shops were shut. Lansdowne Road, Rathmines, and Rathgar gathered up their fine clothes and ran home; the janitors of the Bank of Ireland came rushing out to slam-to the great iron gates with a clang, turning the thick lips of the lock with hurried hands, and the sentries rushed into the guardroom; those coming home from Fairyhouse had been stopped by British barricades, and choruses of How th' hell am I goin' to get home ascended to God and His blessed saints. And Sean, standing in the doorway of his house, gazed back towards the centre of the city and saw a great plume of flame rising high into the sky: the first passion-flower had blossomed.

The next day, early, not allowed to cross the canal, Sean took a longer back way over the railways, and got to the nearer fringe of the city where talk was furious, and wild guesses were made of what was happening.

—Th' attack on the Castle's failed, and Sean Connolly, the modest and noble, had died, murmuring that he died for Ireland. And you can't even climb through O'Connell Street, the dead are piled that high in it. An' th' Sinn Feiners have taken th' Bank of Ireland!

—What!

—Occupied it; overpowered the senthries, shot them before, shot them behind, and flung their riddled bodies at the foot of King Billy's statue.

—No? God, what'r we comin' to! With th' Bank of Ireland gone, we'll all be ruined. How'r we goin' to get our old-age pensions; an' ring-papers won't be worth a damn!

—An' — listen, man alive — an', an' th' figures of Liberty, Fortitude, an' Justice that stood on th' top of the ayste side of the Bank is sthrewn over th' wide world. Smithereens they are now; rubble; dust.

—No! An' th' others, Hibernia, Fidelity, an' somethin' — what's happened to them?

—Them? Aw, them was took down an' brought in for safety till betther times came. Just in time.

—But wait till I tell yous: a fella standin' on the Park Magazine Hill says he could see plain an army of Germans marchin' forward dead on th' horizon. No I don't mean frontier — I said horizon. Which horizon? Dtch dtch! There's only one horizon, man, an' it's th' place where th' sky an' earth meet together. You hope it's thrue? Well, I don't; it's bad enough now between our own and the English; but what would it be between the three of them? Only the lark in the clear air 'ud be safe then, an' he'd have to fly higher than usual.

Sean was behind his mother when she gawked out of the window in the back room, seeking to see something of what was happening.

—There's some soldiers in th' church tower, she said, the last word blending with a crackling roar, while the two of them staggered about the room, choked and blinded from a cloud of powdered mortar thick as a white thundercloud.

—I'm shot, Jack, she whimpered; but feeling her all over, he found she wasn't; and he hurried her into the other room where she lay down, panting, on the old horsehair sofa. He gave her a drink of water, then coaxed her down to a neighbour below who set about making a cup of tea for her. As he was going back to see what had happened, a number of soldiers, in charge of an officer and sergeant, came in and went upstairs with him, leaving two men to guard the outside door. The officer stood beside Sean, a revolver in his hand, while the sergeant searched the back room. After some time, the sergeant came out and whispered to the officer.

—Come downstairs with me, said the officer to Sean.

They placed him stiff against the wall of the house, outside, while the sergeant searched him, taking off his old boots to have a look inside, a soldier kneeling on one knee before him, butt of rifle to the knee, the bayonet but a foot away from Sean's chest. They were searching for an automatic, they told him, and he wondered how one could fit into either of his boots. A violent explosion in the waste land beyond the wall [bordering the railway sent a storm of stones, tufts of grass, and bunches of poppies skyhigh, showers of them falling around Sean and his searchers. Another, and then, a second later, a vicious ping on the wall beside him, sent Sean word that some sniper was having a shot at the soldiers around him. The officer slid down the street into a shop, and the soldiers, bending low, followed him, leaving Sean stretched out against the wall, alone, watched by neighbours who were peeping from their doorways in the houses lower down the street. He took his outstretched arms from the wall, turned in, and mounted the stairs to his home. While by the wall, he had felt that his end was near, and had had a stiff time trying to hold on to his pride and dignity. Now he was shaking, and tense with fright. Either the badly-aimed shells fired from the gunboat *Helga* or the sniper's bullet may have saved his life. For a long time he had tried to keep out

of danger, and as often had found himself in the thick of it. Three
times, at work, he had had narrow escapes: once when a bucket had
been whipped from a swinging hand by a train passing by at fifty miles
an hour; once when a scaffold had collapsed, and he had come down
with it, escaping with a bad shock and many sore bruises; and once on
a high roof, cleaning glass, a fellow-worker, in a hurry to show the
foreman how alert he was, stepped on a plank, leading over the glass,
before him; the plank had snapped, the glass had given way, and the
poor devil had fallen forty or fifty feet, to be smashed to pieces on a
concrete floor below. And today, he and his mother had had a stream
of machine-gun bullets sweeping between their two heads, making a
hash of the wall behind them. How often during the riots of drunken
policemen had he escaped a batoning? More often than he wished to
remember. He didn't like this sort of thing at all. As he grew in grace
and wisdom, he was growing less and less of a hero. Like the fine and
upright Alderman Tom Kelly, he wanted to die in bed surrounded by
medicine bottles.

Good God! looka th' mess the back room was in! The one old
palliasse they had had been ripped open with a bayonet, and the dirty
feathers had been scattered about. Their one mattress, too, had been
torn the same way, and the straw, mixed with the feathers, littered the
floor. And all this on top of his aching, trembling legs, and oozing
neck. Had he been made of less sterner stuff, he'd have sat on the edge
of the ruined bed to weep. But he must sway his thoughts away from
an inclination to tears to hard resistance, and an icy acceptance of
what was beyond his power to avoid.

He lighted some sticks, put some water into a small saucepan, and
made himself a cup of tea. In the old dresser he found a small lump of
a loaf, and cut himself a slice; no more, for the neighbours might send
back his mother any minute and she'd need her share. But he ate all
the bread there, for he wanted all he could get to modify with new
strength the energy lost through his oozing neck, his aching legs, and
troubled mind. He was sipping the tea, when in came a sergeant and
two Tommies, and his heart sank again.

—'Ere, you, said the sergeant, motioning towards the Tommies, go
with 'em; the church; 'urry! Why? never mind the why. They 'as their
orders — that's enough for you.

—Whose orders — the Lord Lieutenant's?

—Naw! Company Officer's. 'Urry!

Sean sighed, and slipped a volume of Keats into a pocket, put on his
cap, and went with them to the church. In the porch a young officer

sat by a small table, a notebook before him, pencil in hand. Name? Address? Age? Occupation? Sean saw the officer bend a searching look at him when he said, Unemployed. Another search. What's this, eh? Oh, a book! Poetry — harmless enough. Why don't you join the army? No interest in armies — not even the Salvation Army. Civil answers, my man, will serve you better. Into the church with him.

Soldiers were asleep, asprawl, in the baptistery; others snored lying on the tiles of the chancel; and an armed sentry stood at the east end and west end of the church. Piles of haversacks, belts, boots, and rifles were heaped on, and around, the Communion Table. But two other prisoners were there, each widely separated from the other. It was strange to be this way in a church where he had so often sat as a worshipper, in which he found his first genuine, educated friend — the Rector. How angry he would be if he knew the soldiers were making themselves at home in the House of God! Do This in Remembrance Of Me were words forming a semicircle above the Holy Table.

That whole evening, and throughout the night, he sat wearily on the hard bench, finding out that things even of beauty weren't joys for ever. He could but give now the faint smile like a star shining through autumn mists. It was a wry smile, but it wasn't a tear. Even here, even now, even so, perhaps he was one with those

> Who love their fellows even to the death,
> Who feel the giant agony of the world,
> And more, like slaves to poor humanity,
> Labour for mortal good.

The deadly whiteness of the lilies was here upon him; but not the deadly whiteness of the snow: not yet, though sunken from the healthy breath of morn, and far from the fiery noon and eve's one star.

He had to put every thought of anxiety about his mother away from him. Sit here; say nothing — that was all he could do. What use would he be at home, anyway? We were all helled by the enemy. The neighbours would keep her on her feet till he came back, and they took counsel together. In spite of his pride, his bowels yearned for a share of the Maconochie stew some of the soldiers were eating.

The next evening, all the lusty men of the locality were marshalled, about a hundred of them, Sean joining in, and were marched under guard (anyone trying to bolt was to be shot dead) down a desolate road to a great granary. Into the dreary building they filed, one by one; up a long flight of dark stone steps, to a narrow doorway, where each, as he came forward, was told to jump through into the darkness and take a chance of what was at the bottom. Sean dropped through, finding that he landed many feet below on a great heap of maize that sent up a cloud of fine dust, near choking him. When his eyes got accustomed to it, he saw a narrow beam of light trickling in through some badly-shuttered windows, and realised he was in a huge grain store, the maize never less than five feet deep so that it was a burden to walk from one spot to another, for each leg sank down to the thigh, and had to be dragged up before another step could be taken. It took him a long time to get to a window, and crouch there, watching the sky over the city through a crack in the shutters. A burning molten glow shone in the sky beyond, and it looked as if the whole city was blazing. One ear caught the talk of a group of men near by who were playing cards. He couldn't read Keats here, for the light was too bad for his eyes. More light, were the last words of Goethe, and it looked as if they would be his last words too.

—I dunno how it'll end, said one of the card-players; the German submarines are sweepin' up th' Liffey like salmon, an' when they let loose it's goodbye England. My thrick, there, eh!

—I heard, said another player, that th' Dublin Mountains is black with them — coal-scuttle helmets an' all — your deal, Ned.

—Th' Sinn Feiners has taken to an unknown destination that fella who ordhered the Volunteers in th' counthry to stay incognito wherever they were — what's his name? Oh, I've said it a hundhred times. What's this it is?

—Is it Father O'Flynn? asked a mocking voice in a corner.

—No mockery, Skinner Doyle; this isn't a time for jokin'. Eh, houl' on there — see th' ace o' hearts!

Then they heard them, and all the heads turned to where Sean was crouching at the window; for in the fussy brattle of ceaseless musketry fire, all now listened to the slow, dignified, deadly boom of the big guns.

—Christ help them now! said Skinner Doyle.

Next day, he heard his name called from the hole at the end of the store where the sentry stood. Wading through the corn, he was told to leap up, and leaping, was caught by a corporal who helped him to scramble to the floor above. He was to go home for a meal, accompanied by a soldier, for while the rest were permitted to disperse home for an hour, they were suspicious of him because his room was the one that received the fire from those searching out a sniper. He was covered with the dust of the corn, and though he had pulled up the collar of his coat to protect the wound in his neck, he felt the dust of the grain tearing against its rawness, and felt anxious about it. But he

had to be patient, so he trudged home, silent, by the side of the soldier.
When he sat down, and, in reply to the soldier's question, said there
was nothing in the house with which to make a meal,

—Wot, nothink? asked the soldier, shocked. Isn't there some-
wheres as you can get some grub?

—Yes, said Sean; a huckster's round the corner, but I've no money
to pay for it.

—'E'll give it, 'e'll 'ave to; you come with me, said the Tommy;
Gawd blimey, a man 'as to eat!

So round to Murphy's went the Saxon and the Gael, for food.
Murphy was a man who, by paying a hundred pounds for a dispensa-
tion, had married his dead wife's sister, so that the property might be
kept in the family; and Sean thought how much comfort and security
for a long time such a sum would bring to his mother and to him.
The soldier's sharp request to give this prisoner feller some grub got
Sean a loaf, tea and sugar, milk in a bottle, rashers, and a pound of
bully beef. On the way back, Sean got his mother, and they had a royal
meal, the soldier joining them in a cup of scald.

In the sky the flames were soaring higher, till the heavens looked
like a great ruby hanging from God's ear. It was tinging the buildings
with a scarlet glow, while the saints stretched their ears to catch the
tenour of the Irish prayers going up, for each paternoster and ave
maria mingled with the biting snarl from the Howth guns, and the
answering roar from Saxon rifle, machine-gun, and cannon, that were
weaving a closer cordon of fire round the Sinn Feiners, the fire creeping towards the group of innocents blessed with arms in their hands
for the first time. Now it was above them, licking away the roof from
over their heads, and they were too weary to go on trying to put it out.
Their haggard faces were chipped into bleeding jaggedness by splinters
flying from shattered stones and brick; the wounded were in a corner
making their moan to themselves, while a few men and women were
risking their lives to get the seriously hurt away to some hospital,
wending through falling walls, fire and brimstone, and gauntlets of
burning buildings. The grey-green Volunteer uniforms now no longer
looked neat; they were ragged, and powdered thick with the pulverised
mortar clouding from the walls. The fighters now looked like auto-
matons moving unsteadily about, encased tightly in a fog of dust and
acrid ashes. They were silent, unshaven, maybe muttering an act of
contrition for things done before they went to war; wan-eyed, they
persuaded their drooping lids to lift again, for drowsiness might mean
a sudden and silent death to them. Those handiest with a rifle kept

firing into the flames coming closer; a few, hoarse and parched, still tried to control the flames with tiny buckets of water, their leaders, before a wall of flame, standing dignified among them, already garlanded for death; gay outwardly, and satisfied, their inner wakefulness wondering how they'd fare when the world faded. They had helped God to rouse up Ireland: let the whole people answer for them now! For them, now, tired and worn, there was but a long, long sleep; a thin ribbon of flame from a line of levelled muskets, and then a long sleep. For evermore, Ireland's Easter lilies would have a crimson streak through them.

The thyme had turned to rue. And through the ring of fire and smoke, passing by the flying bullets, went the brown-robed Capuchins, bending over the wounded, unable to do much, but standing by their people and the danger. Father Aloysius, with a white apron on a broomstick, hurries to the British barricade to ask for a surgeon, but an elegant Colonel Taylor turns his back on him and leaves him there alone with the Tommies and with God; and later on an equally elegant Captain does all a man can do to help the minister with humane thoughts and a courteous address. And Cathleen ni Houlihan, in her bare feet, is singing, for her pride that had almost gone is come back again. In tattered gown, and hair uncombed, she sings, shaking the ashes from her hair, and smoothing out the bigger creases in her dress; she is

> Singing of men that in battle array,
> Ready in heart and ready in hand,
> March with banner and bugle and fife
> To the death, for their native land.

A rare time for death in Ireland; and in the battle's prologue many a common man, woman, and child had said goodbye to work and love and play; and many more in an hour or so would receive a terse message that life no longer needed them. There they are, lying so quiet — a child surprised in the doorway; an old man stretched in the street; a young man near a lamp-post which he had clutched when the bullet struck him, and down which he had slid when he died, his curiously white face containing wide eyes staring upwards, as if asking the sky why this had happened, a stiff arm still half-encircling the lamp standard; a young lassie in holiday attire, lying on her face, maybe hurrying home when she heard the uproar, but going too slow, for on the brilliant white blouse a purple patch of death was spreading over the middle of the back; an old woman on the floor of her tenement room, alone, her blood seeping through the ceiling below: all of the

goodly company of the dead who died for Ireland. Jesu, have pity!
Quiet, comrades, quiet. It was necessary that you should die for
Ireland too. You didn't want to die. I know, I know. You signed no
proclamation; you invaded no building; you pulled no trigger; I
know, I know. But Ireland needed you all the same. Many will die
like that before Ireland can go free. They must put up with it. You will
be unknown for ever; you died without a word of praise; you will be
buried without even a shadowy ceremony; no bugle will call your
name; no gunshot will let loose brave echoes over your grave; you
will not be numbered among the accepted slain. But listen, comrades,
listen: Whitman will be there to meet you; he will marshal you into the
march-past with the greater dead; on the cornet he will give you a
shrill salute. Listen — there it goes! Forward! March!

Here comes Paudrig Pearse down the silent street, two elegant
British officers waiting for him. He comes steadily, in no hurry;
unafraid, to where two elegant British officers are waiting to meet
him. His men have been beaten; the cordon of flame has burnt out
their last fading hope. *The struggle is over; our boys are defeated; and
Ireland's surrounded with silence and gloom:* the old ballad is singing
in his ears. He wears a topcoat, for the Easter sun has gone west, and
a nipping breeze blows. It is the wind of death blowing keenly on this
brave man's pure face. His eyes droop, for he hasn't slept for days.
He has lain down, but not to sleep. Soon he will sleep long and well.
He feels this is no defeat; that to stand up in an armed fight against
subjection is a victory for Ireland. So he stands silently, and listens to
the elegant British officer demanding unconditional surrender. The
fools, the fools! So he agrees, and hands over his sword; bows, and
returns to marshal his men for a general surrender. Soon Whitman
will be shaking his hand, and reciting,

Vivas to those who have failed!
And to all generals who lost engagements, and all overcome heroes!
And the numberless unknown heroes equal to the greatest heroes
    known!

The sky had gone black and the rain was falling; cold rain, with the
sting of vanishing winter in it. Along the silent, empty street small
groups of men come marching. They are tired, tattered, and sleepy,
hungry shadows of the neat, trim, and steady Volunteers who had
marched the opposite way a week ago. Crowds behind the soldiers
cheered when they saw the proud but woebegone men come marching
through the blackened lanes of smouldering buildings. They marched
silent; no whistle or lilt came from any parched lip or dry throat: the

time was past for song. The hot, bitter vapour from charred wood, leather, and cloth seared their nostrils; and cinders, smoking red in the centre, strewing the street, crunched under their passing feet. Down they came, covered with hundreds of rifles, with machine-guns trained on them, thousands of soldiers staring at them piling their poor arms in a heap; the Tommies wondering and bewildered that such a pitiable pile of metal should try to overthrow the might and power of England's armed forces.

—Larfable, I say. Th' wild Irish. Drink gores to their 'eads! Cawn't savvy 'em. Never knows w'en you 'as 'em. Don't arst me, mite. Blinkin' lot of 'em oughter be in a 'ome! Wot was bitin' 'em? Barmy, th' lot of 'em. Wot did they do it for?

A dream! To make again the white sails crowd in on Ireland, so that her harbours, the finest in the world, could hardly hold her ships; to set up the sale again of our potteries and textiles; Huguenot poplins woven since Jacquard de Lion first sang *The Palatine's Daughter*; crowded bales of supreme cloth, red, green, green-russet, and yellow to Cologne, Naples, Catalonia, Ypres, and the Rhine. To send out fine marbles, green, red, jet, and dove-grey, fine and smooth, as Spenser vouches for in his *Faerie Queen*, to Bologna, Brabant, making palaces for princes of Lithuania; to give to the civilised world again beef, lard, tallow, bacon, butter, wax, wool, tanned leather, well embroidered; hawks and horses, gold from Wicklow, and silver from Tipperary, coined and uncoined; to send the whitest linen to the Netherlands, Italy, and the city of Chester. To make the land a centre of prime books, well tooled and illuminated, like them of old, the book of Fenagh, of Monasterboice, the psalter of Cashel, and the Red Book of the Earls of Kildare.

So that St. Furze might again become the patron saint of the fierce O'Flaherties, and the Feast of Brendan on May the tenth could be safely kept again in Galway by the ancient dwellers on the quay street; that the Dublin men might be free to again become members of the Corpus Christi Guild of Coventry, and make a new path round that fair city; and to be able to send clean white boards for the church of Salisbury, and oak and elm beams to England to be made into galleys and shapely vessels of a fine length.

—Whhoorish! shouted a sergeant; is it treadin' on th' tile of me coat yez want to be now? Oirish, an' prawd of it, wot?

—Ay, and so as to again excel in carving rich and diversified designs on all churches, within and without the walls; to build round towers higher than the high ones already here; to have multitudes of great bells and lesser bells aloft in bunches in all suitable and desirable places; and to have piles of rare images, altars, gems, and hundreds of square miles of painted glass for all our church windows.

—And mike Iahland a plice fit for 'eroes to live in, Paddy, eh wot?

Ay, and our famous fairs will no longer cower away in old, un-honoured corners, but step into the open again, like the Fair of Telltown, known to all the lords and ladies of the well-mapped world; the Fair of Garmain, the Fair of Clapping of Hands, the Fair of Opening Eyes, the Fair in the Valley of Squinting Windows, the Fair of the Foggy Dew, the Fair of the Valley Lay Smiling Before Me.

—Never 'eard of 'em, Paddy; musta been in old Gord's time.

And the Fair of Fairs of the Blessed Saints, twelve in number — Cing Bully of the Boyne of Contention, Carzen of the Papes, Mishe Lemass More, a Talbot a Talbot, Lily Bullero, Shantee Ohkay, Roody the Shrover with his Pendraggin Piety, the Irish Sweep who Beat Miraculous Melody from a Drum, Elfie Byrne of Ballyblandus, Guffer Gaffney, Prayboy of the Festerin World, Billora et Labora O'Brien, and Gee Kiaora Jesterton the Laughing Diwine.

And where are these precious things now? Buried in the black ruins, hidden in heaps of rubble, scarred with the venom of fire. All our dear dreams gone: tread light, soldier, for you tread on our dreams. These Sinn Fein madmen have tossed them into insignifi-cance ; their blow at England has fallen on the head of Ireland, and all is lost as well as honour.

—I wouldn't tike it too much to heart, daddy; no use of gettin' riled wif us — we didn't start the shindy.

—Make no sport of me, soldier, for there's no Fergus of the kindly tongue now to cool a man's anger! To hell with yous, spawn of Crom-well! May none of your race survive; may God destroy yous all; each curse of the holy book of the psalms and the prophets upon yous fall!

—Easy, easy, there, daddy; have a heart!

Oh! Every cedar in the land is down; every Irish oak has fallen! There's not that much wood left would make the lintel of a door. The starry head of the Old Woman is lit now but by the death-light in the eyes of them about to die. Listen! Listen all! And a dead silence swept the land, and all the people listened. There they go — clear on the air of a misty dawn: a volley; another, and another. What Irish heart is thrilled now by the eagle's whistle? What Irish ear bothers about the notes of the cuckoo calling summer closer? What foot will move to the sound of a violin making merry with sound? What hand will light a bonfire to welcome a joy?

The listening people hear the quick, short, sharp steps of Tom Clarke over the stony square of Kilmainham. There is the squad waiting, khaki-clad, motionless, not knowing the argument. Here, in front, halt! A brown-robed friar stands aside, hurrying prayers over his rosary beads. There is no bravery here save in the thin figure with its arms bound tight; a cloth over the gleaming eyes. The guns suddenly give forth a jet of flame, the figure jerks rhythmically, slides awkwardly to the ground, twitches for a second, then lies for ever still. Ireland has scored another victory over England, for the people begin to ponder over what this man has done, and search for everything he has said, that what was spoken by the prophets might be fulfilled — he will be remembered for ever.

Then another came forth to die, with head, usually bent, now held high, for Pearse has bidden farewell to the world, though he still holds Ireland by her rough and graceful hand, loth to let it go: farewell to St. Enda's, its toil, its joy, its golden brood of boys; farewell to Emmet's Fort, to the Hermitage, the lake in the woods, the scented hayfield; farewell to the azure sky, the brown bog, the purple heather of Connemara; farewell the pageants that wheeled broad palaces into simple places and turned greyness into magic colours; farewell the jewelled quaintness in the thoughts and play of children.—Oh, farewell! The moments have grown bigger than the years.

The face of Ireland twitches when the guns again sing, but she stands steady, waiting to fasten around her white neck this jewelled string of death, for these are they who shall speak to her people for ever; the spirit that had gone from her bosom returns to it again to breathe out hope once more, and soon to sing.

Ere the tiny curl from the gun-muzzles has hid in the upper air, the flames lash out again, and Connolly, last of the lost leaders, loses his place in life, and becomes a marbled memory.

Black prison vans, packed with prisoners, cavalry with naked swords before and behind them, move swift through the streets. Crowds, silent and sullen, watch them go by at the street corners, and stare at white faces pressed against the tiny grating at the back of the van, striving for a last glimpse of Erin ere they walk the decks of the ship that will carry them to the prisons of England. And the Castle is alert and confident; files all correct, and dossiers signed and sealed for the last time. Now the Irish may be quiet, and quit their moan, for nothing is whole that could be broken. And the glasses are full of wine, and cigar-smoke incenses the satisfaction.

But Cathleen, the daughter of Houlihan, walks firm now, a flush on her haughty cheek. She hears the murmur in the people's hearts. Her lovers are gathering around her, for things are changed, changed utterly:

A terrible beauty is born.

Poor, dear, dead men; poor W. B. Yeats.

THE END